THE ROCK YEARBOOK 1982

THE ROCK YEARBOOK 1982

ST. MARTIN'S
PRESS
NEW YORK

Editor: Al Clark

Cover and book designed by: John Gordon

Design assistants: Mandy Ollis, David Vollborth, Richard Kelly

US Correspondent: Drew Moseley

Contributors: Mick Brown, Al Clark, Ian Cranna, Giovanni Dadomo,
Robin Denselow, Mark Ellen, John Fordham, Pete Frame, Simon Frith,
John Gill, Charlie Gillett, Mary Harron, David Hepworth, Colin Irwin,
Nick Kimberley, Frances Lass, Barry Lazell, Drew Moseley, Alexei Panshin,
Dafyyd Rees, Tony Russell, Jon Savage, Ross Stapleton, Phil Sutcliffe,
Steve Taylor, Bob Woffinden, Richard Wootton

Copyright © 1981 by Virgin Books Ltd

ISBN 0 312 68784 2

For information write: St. Martin's Press, 175 Fifth Avenue, New York, NY 10010

Printed in the USA

CONTENTS

— FEATURES/6 —

The Selling Of A Myth, The Cult With No Name, The Power Of The Press

— THE YEAR/17 —

A diary of events

— THE YEAR IN MUSIC/29 —

Rock, Electronic, Soul/Disco, Reggae, Folk, Jazz, Country, Blues, Rockabilly

— THE YEAR'S ALBUMS/59 —

A comparative study of critical assessments

— THE SINGLES SCENE/107 —

Both sides of the ocean at 45 rpm

— ACTS OF THE YEAR/112 —

Adam & The Ants, Pat Benatar, Elvis Costello, Sheena Easton, John Lennon, Bruce Springsteen, Stray Cats, Talking Heads

— WHERE ARE THEY NOW?/128 —

What last year's choices have and have not done

— FILM & BOOK REVIEWS/139 —

Celluloid and paper

— BEST & WORST/145 —

Album Covers Of The Year, Thanks...(Future Forecasts), ...But No Thanks (Past Agonies),
The Way It Was (Random Memories Of A Year)
The Contributors let loose

— TRANS-OCEANIC CROSS-FERTILISATION/161 —

The Copeland brothers straddle the pond

— STADIUM ROCK/164 —

The groups that simply won't go away

— THE BUSINESS YEAR/167 —

US/UK/Independents/Europe
Tears in the boardroom

— I'M NOT GOING OUT WITH YOU DRESSED LIKE THAT/177 —

A pictorial survey of today's young concertgoer

— QUOTES OF THE YEAR/189 —

An encyclopedia of overstatement

— HOW CHARTS ARE COMPILED US & UK/199 —

The story behind the computer print-outs

— THE YEAR'S CHARTS/201 —

The exhaustive chronicle

— ROCK REFERENCE/228 —

Rock Venues, Record Companies, Radio Stations, Rock Publications

THE SELLING OF A MYTH

The full-time industry of rock myth-making has enjoyed a surprise autumnal blossoming since the Sex Pistols made it a profitable activity once more. Not that Malcolm McLaren's Stalinist rewriting of history was quite as rigorous as depicted in 'The Great Rock 'n' Roll Swindle', but nevertheless the collective did appear to have expended more energy on the manufacture of a myth than of songs.

John Lydon learnt quickly from the Pistols careering melee of mutual manipulation and when he emerged from the tatters of the band with his own outfit, he pointedly titled them Public Image Limited suggesting — with a characteristic Lydon sneer — that here we had a bunch of people who made no pretence about being a group. P.I.L. were in business, so the irony ran, as an exercise in mythologising.

The sleeve of P.I.L.'s first album 'First Issue' is really the starting-point for the whole post-Pistols boom in image-making which is being prodded at in this article.

PiL'S FIRST ALBUM

Design was by an unlikely couple who have since, in very different ways, made significant tracks in the turn-of-the-decade fashionable British culture. Photographer Dennis Morris, a young black Londoner pulled into the rock business by some early and prescient shots of Bob Marley which he'd taken for an educational magazine, pictured the four members of P.I.L. in the guises of

BASEMENT 5

magazine cover stars, carefully styled in a spread of parodies from HARPERS & QUEEN to FAB 208 by a former in-house art director of VOGUE, Terry Jones.

While the latter has gone on to co-editing and producing a streetwise fashion broadsheet called i-D, Morris is now a singer and messianic front-person of a powerful reggae/rock four-piece, Basement 5. What is interesting about Morris's transition isn't the well-travelled path between servicing bands and becoming part of one. Nor is it particularly significant that he moved from being ISLAND RECORDS design head to signing a deal with the label. This only happened after considerable doubt within the company being overcome and after the usual inter-company bidding. Indeed, the band and ISLAND have since parted company.

Where Morris exposed the phenomenal importance attached to images in current rock practice was in the way he first secured the interest of ISLAND's owner, Chris Blackwell, in the group. Before the Basement 5 lineup which now included Morris had spent a minute playing together, he took some pictures.

Morris's shots showed a quartet of heavy-looking dudes wearing anonymous industrial overalls and goggles against a stark white background; unnerving, especially in the context of a company used to the presence of regulation-dress Rastas night and day.

Blackwell's reaction "Who *are* this band?" registered his intrigue at the bizarre clash of Roots and Devo-style high-tech. His response was to immediately hand over valuable demo time in ISLAND's studios. Morris dismisses it as simple pragmatism: as ISLAND's head of design, "That was my job; the company signed a band and I had to create that image."

Morris's success with a strategy of vision without sound marks a significant jumping-off point — the fission of appearance and content — a fate which has overtaken one of Britain's brightest independent labels, FACTORY RECORDS.

In an area where presentation of product was uniformly dire, dominated by ineffectual dada-punk, FACTORY swept the board by packaging in sharp ultra-cool sleeves drafted by a then unknown Manchester designer, Peter Saville. Saville's work is about pure design, an historical approach to typography and an empirical presentation of necessary information. In an important sense it exists independently from the content of the record.

With Joy Division FACTORY were lucky enough to have it both ways — a sophistication of presentation that made much of the major labels' art departments look imbecilic combined with a smouldering grassroots image as *the* label of Northern English gothic, an aesthetic which filled the requirements of a post-punk (post-Seventies post-Sixties economic boom) depression to a T.

If the suicide of Joy Division singer Ian Curtis and the subsequent huge sales of FACTORY product marked a point of maximum symmetry between image and cruel reality, the label's attempts to cope with the last eighteen months' changes in the

SLEEVES BY SAVILLE

SPANDAU BALLET

market have seen the two move uncontrollably out-of-synch. The FACTORY myth still sells units but their musical output is struggling to cut it.

FACTORY's "funk" band, A Certain Ratio, are a case in point. Dance music has a somewhat different relation to myth from that of doomy solitary bedsitter music. It's very hard to work oneself into a conceptual frenzy about a dancefloor record if the rhythm doesn't sock you in the gut.

Which is why FACTORY boss Tony Wilson's mythical aspirations for ACR don't wash; image has superceded content to the point of rupture. Wilson's prognostications about his charges riding through Hollywood in limousines are doomed. The point applies, in varying degrees, to the whole British nouveau funk contingent; such emaciated fare isn't even enough to convince British audiences any longer — judging by the critical thumbs-down delivered to ACR's album 'To Each' — let alone US ears attuned to the slick musicianship and corporate-scale studio productions of the likes of Quincy Jones.

The re-emphasis of dance music at a time of economic down-turn has stripped away many of the opportunities for myth-spinning, but the British small-label funksters are laden with too much of the baggage of self-lacerating gloom of '78 to make much headway. 'To Each' may

boast a rousing (and very Miles Davis) cover painting, all jungle foliage, naked men and a huge sassy-looking trumpet, but the contents *still* sound like Joy Division with a funk drummer grafted on. The surgery still hasn't taken.

ACR'S 'TO EACH'

Somewhere over the last two years there occurred an historical moment in the changing fads radiating out of Britain, a moment which the normally astute Wilson had been late in realising. Incompetence has gone out of fashion. The desperate need to establish working-class roots, in a long tradition of guilt-ridden Left-orientated working-class British culture, became unnecessary.

The Police, who'd been faking it in earnest with poverty-stories about the days when their melodicism earned them ostracisation from the punk establishment, disappeared to Ireland as temporary tax exiles. It turned out that during this trying period, they had

actually been in Germany recording and touring with the leader of the Munich State Opera House, Eberhart Schoener, on one of his inflated classical/rock experiments. Try imagining *worse* credentials in 1979.

By the end of the following year none of this really mattered any more. The New Romantics were an expression of this newfound freedom from embarrassment about largesse, ambition, flashiness. Trouble was that, in general, they totally lacked the taste. They were on the right lines, however, in pointing things in the direction of clubs rather than gigs, upmarket as opposed to guttersnipe style and dance, not contemplative, music.

The freedom this afforded British rock journalism was tentatively grasped. It

certainly set off a fit of literary dandyism, a flurry of quotation and a curious little phase when rock critics rushed around reviewing Tom Wolfe's new cartoon book and Peter York's collection of essays on British sociology of style, 'Style Wars'.

Just in case, as looked highly likely, the change in the wind proved shortlived writers covered themselves by the fashionable put-down that York's book was *inaccurate*. This is the journalist's version of the musicians punkier-than-thou credibility myth. York may have been there, but was he there quite as sensitively as we were?

PETER YORK

Style Wars

Includes 'The Sloane Rangers' 'Them' 'The Post Punk-Mortem' 'Mayfair Mercs'

PETER YORK'S 'STYLE WARS'

NEW MUSICAL EXPRESS prefaced their Spandau Ballet piece with a quotation from Wolfe, but shied away from putting the young blades on the cover lest the ambiguous community-base of the Glitterati proved a no-no. Instead, in a revealing choice, they plumped for a dour Northern trio from Sheffield — Cabaret Voltaire,

CABARET VOLTAIRE

purveyors of disturbing electronic mantras.

If watching the British press struggle over the Blitz kids was a hoot, watching the American counterpart think itself into an embarrassment of intellectual gaffs was a scream. Lumping in Adam Ant with the New Romantics didn't help, though it did provide Adam with a streak of primitive mythological equipment in getting a debate going as to his relationship with the American Indian. (While researching this piece, I saw a telegram pinned up in the CBS London pressroom. It began "I'd like to correct the impression in England that the Indians are hostile to Adam Ant...") Through mouthpieces of the VILLAGE VOICE and the SOHO WEEKLY NEWS, New York reacted to the well-organised Blitz assault (Spandau Ballet's manager, Steve Dagger, managed to screw no less than twenty-three transatlantic tickets out of CHRYSALIS RECORDS for the jaunt) with a mixture of anticipation and fervent social criticism, going as far as accusing the New Romantics of incipient fascism.

In Britain, where the cycles of production of rock mythology run an ever-increasing rate of turnover, we're inured to the vagaries of rapidly changing fashion. America's mythological demands are more difficult to satisfy, except in the isolated environs of the art-sodden New York music world, where the auto-destructive legacy of Warhol still holds sway. It's hard to imagine the followers of Bruce Springsteen being satisfied with fifteen minutes of fame; they want heroes that last a lifetime, even if they *do* die young.

It is in this sweeping landscape of potential myth that the British manipulators of rock taste face their hardest challenge. Hollywood established the scale, basing it on a medium where a performance and an image could appear simultaneously before millions of people over a vast continental space. Hence the repeated comparisons made between Debbie Harry and mid-century female movie leads, and the breathless anticipations of video's potential.

The Clash are the most potent, instructive example of the difficulties faced in taking on America with a thoroughly thought-out and, on a domestic scale, highly successful post-'76 self-image. By the time of The Clash's first album release in mid-1977, the lines were drawn. SOUNDS' five-star review declared that "The Clash are the essentials of street London personified".

The band had included, somewhat prematurely, on the album a song called 'I'm So Bored With The USA'. Although one early reviewer called them "a garage band that should've stayed in the garage ... and left the motor running", SOUNDS articulated a broadly-held opinion which only received confirmation from the demise of the Pistols: "If you don't like 'The Clash', you don't like rock 'n' roll. It really is as simple as that. Period."

Even as early as then it was admitted that The Clash's image as "poor white trash" had a few holes in it; even SOUNDS said that "In Joe Strummer's case, at least, nothing could be further than the truth." Strummer's father was a British diplomat.

Not that the bullshit stopped there. Later in the same year SOUNDS ran an article by Sixties figure Caroline Coon (who later became bass player Paul Simonon's girlfriend and, briefly, joined their succession of managers). 'Janie Jones', The Clash's tribute to a jailed Society vice girl, had been written by Mick Jones on the top deck of a No. 31 bus as it trundled through Notting Hill Gate — ever the band's stomping ground, rather than Brixton.

Coon, in a grammatical slip that betrayed much unconscious irony, wrote that "Her name evokes precisely those elements of establishment hypocrisy, class discrimination and double standards which are The Clash's raison d'etre." The article's by-line read "The Clash meet the woman who was locked up for being a little bit too real."

This curious channelling of The Clash's left-wing fervour didn't prevent American critics like Greil Marcus from taking the original myth at face value, almost willing new life into it. In March '79 ROLLING STONE was still saying of the band's repertoire that it consisted of "a foray of songs aimed at the bleak political realities and social

ennui of English life, making social realism — and unbridled disgust — key elements in the punk aesthetic." The Clash must have found it hard to believe their luck.

England had already begun to go cold on them. Nick Kent, in a seminal review of their second — American recorded — album 'Give 'Em Enough Rope' in the NME mulled over the song 'Guns On The Roof'; in the lyrics, in a typically spurious attempt to aggrandise their own whims, the fining of two members of the band for shooting racing pigeons had been extrapolated into a thesis on world terrorism. "The Clash are simply using incidents," observed Kent, "as fodder for songs, without really caring."

A couple of months later Strummer was telling the ROLLING STONE reporter "England's becoming too claustrophobic for us; everything we do is scrutinised. I think touring America could be a new lease of life."

The reported £100,000 which the group received on signing with CBS had become an inconvenient millstone, despite the encouraging refusal by their American record company, EPIC, to release the first album on grounds of it sounding "too crude". Over the Pond a place was already being sketched out on the huge mythological canvas of US rock. STONE

THE CLASH PHOTOGRAPHED BY PENNIE SMITH

limo doors, under deserted-looking filling-station lamps, crossing a rain-soaked Manhattan street, breakfasting in flyblown diners — evocative of a timeless America of visual myth, now The Clash's *real* stage.

Attempts to put them back into an authentic British scenario have proved hopeless, laughable even — Miles's outrageous cover story for TIME OUT which depicted the band eating fly-posting paste at one low point in their careers (the first thing Simonon did with the CBS advance was put down the deposit on a Notting Hill Gate flat). Worse of all was 'Rude Boy', with its simplistic equation of Strummer's bar-stool ruminations and setpiece scenes from British "street politics".

Where were The Clash when Brixton erupted in the Spring of '81? In New York with Ellen Foley, still trying to gain an entry into the US mainstream?

The last thing I heard before delivering this to the publishers was that The Clash had just been the object of a virtual riot in New York over doubly-sold club dates. The outcome of the incident, broached via a press conference which included the mayor, turns out to be an extension of their run of performances to twice its original length. Only last week the management of the Ritz were offering Public Image Limited big money for a re-run of an appearance which resulted in the club being trashed.

While American audiences still seem hungry for the sort of cathartic urban anarchy which they identify with punk and its offspring, we in Britain are finding the exterior social reality as tense as we would wish. Depressed experience having caught up with our morbid, guilty imaginings, we're tired of the sort of double bind which The Clash have embraced. As producer Sandy Pearlman observed back in '77: "The Clash see the merits of reaching a wider audience, but they also like the idea of grand suicidal gestures."

Perhaps that makes them natural spokesmen for Thatcherite Britain. No matter. Here we'd like a little dancing, a little light relief. The myths can look after themselves for a while.
STEVE TAYLOR

compared them to, in order of appearance, the Sex Pistols, Rolling Stones, Bruce Springsteen, Mott The Hoople, the Who and Graham Parker.

Greil Marcus, in NEW WEST, described Joe Strummer as "Built like Springsteen...with a James Dean haircut." Aaaaah! There it was — the chance of a lifetime; musically the band could be slotted into the Great Tradition of rock 'n' roll which the Sex Pistols had been bent on destroying ("This is hard rock," said Marcus of 'Complete Control', "to rank with 'Hound Dog' and 'Gimme Shelter'.")

But *visually* they could now be placed into the pantheon of brittle, handsome, fast-livin' and young-dyin' movie

heroes of the Forties and Fifties. The idea caught on in Britain with a vengeance, especially after 'Give 'Em Enough Rope' appeared in the album charts at number two, just below 'Grease'.

"Paul Simonon is the James Dean of punk," declared THE SUN in a piece about him and Coon entitled "Why a street kid fell for a society girl". "He's rebellious, moody, good-looking and plays for the world's angriest band, The Clash". "Strummer," said the DAILY MIRROR, "the vocalist who acts and talks like a Cockney Bogart."

The back-breaking work of trying to break the American market by gigging was subsequently recorded in

Pennie Smith's book of Clash photos, 'The Clash Before And After' (EEL PIE), in which half the shots taken in '79-'80 are from US roadwork.

Photographs do the job far better than words, recording how the band work hard to fit into the mythological American landscape of the movies of their childhoods, clad in the hybrid style that superceded their action-painting home-mades; Italianate haircuts, baggy black suits, flashy ties, homburgs and boaters, thrift-store evening dress — always with those incongruous clumping Doc Martens boots.

Pennie Smith catches The Clash in airport lounges, leaning over the tops of open

THE CULT WITH NO NAME

The security guard had been pestering me for a spare album for his boy; as I went out, I handed him on impulse the Scars' 'Author Author', a Very Modern album — modern in its bright, ethnic design, its painted players, its French film blur song titles, finally modern in the disparity between the fuss made about it and the sales figures. I drew his attention to the back cover, which showed four young men posing strenuously — with much slap and theatrical costume — in a primary, 'Aztec' set. Did he mind his kid being exposed to this sort of thing? He didn't bat an eyelid: "Oh, you should see the lads round our way, crazy they are. Running around with scarves on their legs, stuff in their hair, all this gear on, real wild they are." You mean like Adam? "Yes, just like Adam and The Ants, they like them they do. Whenever they see them come on the telly..."

Adam has really made it: first with the teens, then the pre-teens, now their parents. Watch him do a Tommy Steele. *That's* success, *that's* what comes of being the only new pop star — along with, perhaps, Shakin' Stevens (Rock 'n Roll Journeyman) — of the last twelve months. In the face of that, all the competition pales, particularly Spandau Ballet and Bow Wow Wow. But what the three of them have done, together, transcends (or, at least, appears to) mere hit records: what they have done, coming all from very different sources, is to create a change in climate, a shift in the mode of pop consumption and pop thought. Instead of the aggression of punk rock, and the dourness of post-punk, we now have a new, "Optimistic", style obsessed, fast-moving, "movement" of peacocks. Hear the word "fab", read the gushing, teen-mag blurbs in THE FACE and the music press, observe the frantic pace "the movement" takes in, telescoping Andy Warhol and Aleister Crowley

THE SCARS' 'AUTHOR AUTHOR'

into: "Every man and woman is a star — for five minutes". Then watch it being sold — both internally and for export — as Swinging London Mark II along with the year's *true* gimmick, the Royal Wedding.

In parallel with this pop shift, the keyword is not now "anarchy", nor "authenticity", nor "alienation", but that elusive and wonderfully vague concept, "style". By itself, this talk appears to represent a move away from the importance of music as a mode of consumption itself — a complete reversal through punk rock of the early Seventies insistence on musical "excellence" as a premium — to a complete lifestyle, returning, so it would seem, to the fanaticism, the obsessiveness (and incidentally, the metropolitan roots) of true Sixties mod. A leisure lifestyle — so the imaginary advert could read — for the newly ennobled, for those freed from 'The Right To Work'. All the clothes you could want; all the clubs you could want; music stripped down to a functional dance beat — consider the current

mode for funk, only a staff-writer's salary away from that most functional and anonymous of musics, that last true outpost of Mod (through Northern Soul) — jazz-funk. Add drugs (blues), magazines THE FACE, i-D, and for the intellectuals, ZG), technology ("The Stowaway", "Walky" or "Walkman") and cottage industries (any stall you might see), and you have the package. See Kensington Market, See the World. As ever, it's not quite that simple.

Most of the guff that's been written about the new "movement" — which has taken the honours in most magazines this last year — with a few honourable exceptions, has missed the factors that underlie shifts in style, which, like all pop stuff, is pinned on a fragile balance between expression and exploitation. This simultaneous function makes it hard for people to work out what is valuable and what is garbage, what should be discarded and what is worth keeping. Too often, they swallow and regurgitate the garbage whole, or throw the

baby out with the bathwater. The pop press concentrates on expression, the serious weeklies on exploitation: does anybody remember Paul Johnson's famous NEW STATESMAN attack on the Beatles in 1964? It's as well to remember now that very frequently, this fragile balance does tip heavily on the side of exploitation: Cash without Chaos.

Ever since teenagers were defined as a market in the Fifties — like gays in the Seventies — and were thus enfranchised, then teenage (and gay) behaviour became channelled into forms that fitted the market. A moral outrage or two — "juvenile delinquency" was the Fifties biggie — and the package was sealed. In this manner: not only are you what you buy, but you choose what you are by the options you exercise in buying — that's called "freedom of choice". Hence expression IN exploitation. Youthful energy and, for want of a better word, "expression" is channelled alongside, and eventually into consumption: hence the balance. The transcendent moments in pop history — and pop, that bastard mutant, now has a history — occur when the balance becomes tension, when the scales dip and the tension becomes an explosion. This can be said — arguably — to have happened in England five times: 1956 — Rock, 1963 — Beat, 1967 — Hippies, 1972 — Glam, 1976 — Punk Rock. The New Romantics are now being plugged as the latest in this proud line, a fully fledged pop explosion.

I don't want to spoil the party, but I don't buy it. Never mind the lack of great pop records, bar the resonant 'Antmusic', a worthy trigger to Antmania, what is wrong is the fact that the New Romantics are being sold as a unified teen package, a community. In truth, such a community is non-existent: the market "teenager" has splintered into myriad cults, sub-cults, revivals — a demented pluralism. You've only to go to a local concert, or look in the back pages of the trades: there you'll find ads which offer the full range of rave gear: BOWIE, BALLET, MOD, SKA, VOX, ANT, 2001, TEDS, ROCK 'A' BILLY, SKIN & PUNK. Which one's yours? Here you have the paradigm, the paradigm of cultural confusion and cannibalism as pop, and those who make money out of and invest time in it, cannibalises its own past as well as flitting, magpie like, among the baubles of other places and other times. Ethnic: Turkish love songs? Easy! Just slap a dub track on. Medieval plain song? A snitch. Excuse me while I work out the synth part. And so it goes on. This whole New Romantics business has turned out to be little more than glossy paper over gaping cracks — cracks in style codes, cracks in the whole idea of the market "teenager".

The important thing is that fads are still being hyped as COMMUNITIES. This is a very Sixties notion. Pop, like other media, particularly television, has never recovered from the success of the hippies, the Sixties generation. The result of the day the teen takeover happened, baby, is for all to see in Los Angeles, and it's not edifying. It is the hippy

hangover, the Sixties mentality which pervades the press and the creative side of the industry that STILL believes in pop as a YOUTH COMMUNITY, a unified market somehow, a way of life, that indeed, still believes in youth, youth, youth.

The point was neatly taken in the pages of ROLLING STONE, that hippy cottage industry apotheosised. In their end of the year round up, Dave Marsh lamented both the decline of the industry and the lack of a 'rock' consensus: the drift of his piece was that his rock 'n' roll heart was broken, but, it was too late to stop now. Marsh is, on occasions, a fine journalist and the best biographer of Bruce Springsteen — the man who has united the Sixties leftovers as the true heir to Dylan and Lennon combined, now that the first is inoperative through religion, the second through death — but this refusal to come to terms with the fact that rock 'n' roll may not stand is indicative of the ostrich mentality that prevails. I mean, I'm sorry and everything, but one has to face facts.

Pop as YOUTH COMMUNITY was a product of a different time, when the operative bits of the Western world were labouring under the delusion that things would get better, forever, a delusion fostered by lunatic politicians. These days, we're

MALCOLM McLAREN

just about coming to terms with the fact that we're labouring under a severe depression, the like of which we haven't seen since the Thirties — a time, incidentally, when there

weren't any "teenagers", when there wasn't any "pop", or "subcultures", a time when adolescents wore their fathers' clothes and their fathers' ideas: there was no bridge between childhood and adulthood, instead of the artificially prolonged adolescence we have now. "At middle-aged joint-smoking parties, balding fatties come on as Johnny Weismuller and their wives play Rita Hayworth" — (Nik Cohn: 'Today there are no Gentlemen', 1971).

Pop as YOUTH COMMUNITY was also tied into a rare spark of unanimous rebellion that occurred in the late Sixties, that started in Nanterre in 1968 and spread throughout the world, the spark that gave hippy much of its backbone and its strength, thirteen years ago. Such a consensus, in fact, quickly evaporated: to even consider it now is ludicrous, at a time when current events read and, on playback, look like the screenplay of a particularly pulp, particularly paranoid science-fiction paperback. Arms races, right wing governments, lunatic right-wing assassins at large:

'BACK PAGES OF THE TRADES'

— 11 —

it's no wonder that our collective response is to try and blot it out, to take refuge in Martin Pawley's "secondary reality — a kind of wilful deception about the nature of events which is adopted as a survival strategy at all levels of society". Now I'm blinded, I can really see.

This lunatic fragmentation and strong desire for fantasy is reflected in pop, as things usually are. What's happened is simply that the New Romantics have been singled out as "what's happening", because something has to happen to keep the machine going, because it really is happening, in a small corner, and also because of Punk Rock, that spectre that still lies behind most youth activity even now, five years on.

I know it's been said ad nauseam, but it needs repeating here: Punk Rock really shook things up. Apart from everything else, it and the operative people concerned — Malcolm McLaren, Vivienne Westwood, and the Sex Pistols — did two things of lasting interest, which still resonate.

First, they worried the

music business quite badly in late '76 and early 1977, through the EMI & A&M sackings. Suddenly, the mechanics of a turbulent, manipulable industry were exposed for all to see: directors' houses appeared in the press linked with these "foul-mouthed yobs", who "called the queen a moron". Eventually, McLaren reduced the whole exercise, with typical hindsight, into a parable: 'The Ten Lessons' — this is how you con the music industry. The only trouble was, that in re-emphasising the generation gap, McLaren sowed the seeds for the bands' destruction: very quickly, the Sex Pistols became part of the spectacle they'd appeared to rail against, and the "great days of early '77" were turned into a flop art movie.

Secondly, the Sex Pistols and the early punks, in putting together one of the few original looks of the last ten years, initially threw every youth style since the war up in the air, cut them up, and then reassembled them with safety-pins. It was this dismembering of strict style codes that annoyed the Teds so, and pushed them to attack hapless punks: not

only were the punks stepping on their blue suede shoes, but they were *mutilating* them! At first, this was wonderful, but as the strands of punk fashion and music slowly unravelled — whole careers built on a Clash chorus — then this discoding became endemic. Individual items were picked out and turned into a look: quickly, we had Mod revivals, we had Ska revivals, Ted revivals, even Heavy Rock and Rockabilly revivals, and these ran *concurrently*. Suddenly, what had existed in isolation at a point in time, became one item on a rack full of choices — the ultimate extension of the Warhol, Art Object sensibility that had lain behind much of early punk rock.

With these undercurrents, it's not surprising that others should have come along and learnt from the Sex Pistols' apparent mistakes. Punk's rapid implosion — about 18 months from start to finish — had left many surprised, with a feeling of loss and disillusionment: for a generational cycle — from formation through impact to court case — had been completed in a fifth of the time that the Sixties cycle had taken, so accelerated is our culture. So quick was it, that many kids, and the Sixties leftovers, were left high and dry — prehyped to expect a riot of their own, but none in sight. They then set about finding one.

Disillusionment, discoding, search for a "movement" — the race was on. Not only with the audience, but more with the industry and the "tastemakers": the radio disc-jockeys, various journalists — exactly those people who'd been caught by punk rock with their trousers down. 2-Tone had been a mere rehearsal: the New Romantics, "The Cult With No Name" — so shambolic is this movement that no one can agree on a name — was *it*.

McLaren's hand was involved with two of the constituent parts — Adam and Bow Wow Wow — but the real success story was Steve Dagger, Spandau Ballet's manager, who learned from McLaren's mistakes well: the only thing was, he wasn't interested in making trouble, only money. The scam was perfect: the group played select parties, took the discoding back in time to

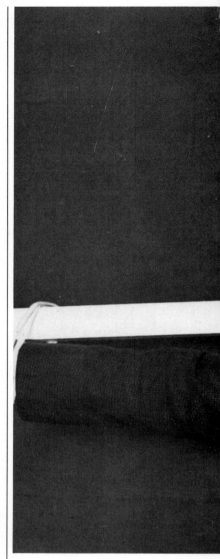

Culloden, cultivated a new pop aristocracy by word of mouth, avoided the music press (very sensibly), and finally courted TV. This, as with punk rock, was the crux event — Janet Street-Porter's excellent '20th Century Box' programme featured Spandau Ballet, Peter Powell and audience in an April 1980 programme that heavily pre-sold the whole thing. Filmed in obsessive black and white, the show made extravagant claims which were soon to be backed up by heavy record company investment — from CHRYSALIS, who'd successfully minted 2-Tone — and heavy rotation from the implicated Peter Powell. Instant exploitation! In fact, so instant that whatever was being expressed hadn't been worked out: vague mutterings about style, "looks", were eventually supplemented, through the

ANNABELLA/BOW BOW BOW

JOHNNY ROTTEN/SEX PISTOLS

osmosis that goes on when anything goes public, by McLaren's theories prepared for Bow Wow Wow: Sun, Sea, Pirac-ee — the dominance of the revolutionary Stowaway. Add Adam's predominance and his theories — brought too to prominence in the wake of his success — about tribes, sex, and the wild nobility, and you have the ingredients of the goulash that's still being picked over. For not only were the record companies and the radio jocks badly let down by punk, but so was the press.

Simply, the music press rediscovered its importance, beyond mere information, with punk rock: here was something to explain, that was worth explaining. People had to be taught to like it, and there was so much that was funny that had to be translated, interpreted. When punk collapsed, the press was left high and dry: instead of

being honest about it, most writers carried on at the same level, no doubt aided and abetted by their editors. Fads were found, written about and plugged until there was an illusion of a movement, that Sixties, even that punk ideal — except punk's demise had knocked that one on the head rather sharply. As the ripples spread to the edge of the pool, there's even less vigour, less substance there: still the press carry on, with "movements", like "Oi" and "Futurism", that have little actual basis. It's sad, or would be if it wasn't so reflexive, desperate and dangerous: I think they call it false consciousness. Creating "movements" out of thin air, artificial thought patterns, can only be dangerous at a time when our society is so fragmented that most imposed patterns can only be reactionary, or at least

simplistic — we need clear thinking, not muffled, arbitrary slogans.

Plenty of brickbats: any bouquets? There are a few to be extracted from the general confusion. Firstly, the Stowaway *is* a genuinely revolutionary piece of technology, a compact, convenient toy that demystifies and makes public, and genuinely transient, the consumption of music — instead of the unhealthy and expensive obsession with records and sound systems. At least McLaren was right on that point. Also worth mentioning is the fact that there are various people quietly going about their business of producing noise that is, on the one hand provocative — an admission of reality, and on the other humane and emotional — supportive of reality. But perhaps best is the sense that the Sixties idealisation of

youth, and youth community, indeed that the whole concept of the market "teenager" is on the rocks: there isn't much left for kids to consume except a taste of war, and, after all, everyone now knows that to be 35 is "where it's at".

Colin MacInnes got it right, in the best book ever written about being teen 'Absolute Beginners' written in 1959: "I smiled at Mr W: 'Well, take it easy son', I said, 'Because a sixteen year old sperm like you has still got a lot of teenage living to do. As for me, eighteen summers rising nineteen, I'll very soon be out there among the oldies.'

"The Wizard eyed me with his Somerset Maugham appearance. 'Me Boy', he said, 'I tell you. As things are, I won't regret it when the teenage label's torn off the arse pockets of my drip-dry sky-blue jeans'."

Will you? JON SAVAGE

THE POWER OF THE PRESS

The British rock press is by turns arrogant, imaginative, blinkered, extravagant, reactionary, zealous, ridiculed, feared, hypocritical, informed, self-righteous, provocative, outrageous, irreverent, opinionated, readable and healthy, by virtue of these seemingly incompatible elements that combine to make it arguably the best, most influential and effective rock press to be found on any continent.

But if such factors by their very existence seem a contradiction and hardly supportive of such an assertion, then consider again.

Since the mid-Sixties and the first British invasion of the US, the spiritual home of rock music, British musicians have led the world with the most exciting, inventive and lasting music around. It is therefore hardly obsequious to suggest or indeed maintain that, like uneasy sleeping partners, British rock music exists hand-in-hand with a powerful, influential rock press. The very first link in the record business chain is without doubt initial recognition by a highly competitive rock press, furiously involved in the serious business of discovery and propagation, spurred on by an understandable desire to be the first hacks on their block to eulogise the next sensation. In that regard, many UK rock writers appear motivated by personal ambitions that have less to do with altruism than the thrill of discovery or at worst, abundant megalomania. But almost despite these noteworthy excesses, they perform an incredibly important role as trail-blazing taste-makers. This is much to the credit of their publications who benignly indulge those excesses, although understandably when they are identified as serving the best interests of those publications, most notable among the four nationally distributed weekly rock papers. Those best

ADAM ANT

interests are to remain successful by continuing to feed a voracious readership, which to the credit of a succession of editors and their controlling publishers, has nurtured and nourished a generation of musically adventurous readers unique in any rock market.

Because the UK rock press is nationally based through the various rock papers and magazines — as well as a complement of Fleet Street newspapers boasting rock coverage of a varying, mostly unsatisfying degree — it immediately acquires a distinct advantage over other rock markets, particularly the United States. In America most rock publications tend to be localised. Those that aren't usually only command small circulations and therefore hardly compel the influence afforded their more

widely read British counterparts. The notable exception is the immensely successful and influential ROLLING STONE, the READER'S DIGEST of American rock journalism. Its success and influence, however, seems to grow with the depreciation of its rock origins as it becomes more of a Hollywood icon than the hip rock bible it continues to delude itself it is. ROLLING STONE'S modus operandi appears to have less to do with the serious pursuit of rock's evolving face than with hard-boiled commercial aspirations.

Even more disquieting is the neutering of critical appraisal to the point where major features in a publication like ROLLING STONE, read like a record company or Hollywood handout. Hence when ROLLING STONE somehow transgressed from its policy

of editorial "restraint", whereby two of its senior contributors wrote articles deeply critical of two of the publication's most sycophantically treated subjects, The Rolling Stones and Bob Dylan, publisher Jann Wenner felt compelled to write his personal assessments thus disowning and disassociating himself from the opinions of his writers.

The likelihood of any UK rock publisher interfering with their own writers' critical judgements has, fortunately, yet to seep across the Atlantic. But when two publishing giants, the International Publishing Corporation (IPC) and Morgan Grampian, publish all four of Britain's national rock weeklies, it says something for the relative benevolence of that monopoly that there's no appreciable confusing boardroom opinions chipping away at their writers' points of view.

So it therefore comes as no surprise to read in almost any of these papers, an album review raving about an artist, while the feature cans them unmercifully in the same issue, or vice-versa. This is an essential ingredient in making the UK rock press so competitive. However, there does seem to be an argument to suggest that, at times, any or all of these four weeklies, might deliberately "assign" a journalist to cover a subject simply because they know that person will produce a contrary view to another staffer or contributor whose view on the same subject is already known. Hedging their bets merely for the sake of it, and justifying such an approach as some sort of editorial "balance", seems just as undesirable as the most sycophantic rock publication.

If I feel that American rock music and the absorption of foreign music is horribly constrained by the absence of a meaningful domestic rock press, then it's hardly surprising that American radio should be even worse. If ROLLING STONE is viewed by the record business in the States as a trendy alternative voice in the marketplace, then it stands to reason that radio is even blander and more restrictive. Tight formats, and almost total playlist exclusion across the continent of the more progressive and left-field American and European rock of the last few years since the punk explosion, means America seems to get the kind of rock music such a mindless market deserves.

With such conservatism rampant in all branches of American rock media, is it any wonder The Police finally crack the US wide open with demonstrably their most inferior album, while major UK acts such as The Jam seem to fall on deaf ears and silent typewriters? But then you can hardly blame American kids for this failure. It's clearly a chicken-and-egg situation. While you have a media and a marketplace by and large geared to the more readily exploitative and crasser commercial instincts of the music it touts, is it surprising the hype machines that have launched and popularised a thousand turkeys from Barry Manilow to Kiss, triumph over a group like, say, Magazine, who tried while alive to crack the same market, depending purely on the excellence of the music? Under these circumstances it is not difficult to comprehend why the great American record-buying public can be somewhat misguidedly dismissed as unadventurous and devoid of a more sophisticated appreciation that can propel them beyond a market populated by The Eagles and a thousand prototypes. Although that's not to say that even the UK can pretend it doesn't patronise its own lightweight purveyors of pap'n'crap. But the gap between the two markets is still awesomely slanted towards the good sense of the typical British rock fan. As a consequence, surely it's logical to extend to America the same analogy I previously used in highlighting the strength of the UK rock market. The UK market's strength and breadth of vision goes hand-in-hand with the strength and variety of its domestic rock press. The tired and sterile contemporaneity of today's

American music just as closely mirrors the lack of balls in its rock press and electronic media.

Although this analysis is ostensibly concerned with the power and influence of the rock press, it is relevant to discuss the operation and functioning of British rock radio. By doing so I hope to substantiate a view I have long held in defending the importance of the contribution made by the rock press in the UK as well as in other markets, against the far more readily identifiable impact of radio in achieving the primary objective of the record business — a hit record. In virtually any market where rock exists, radio is the primary and most immediate influence in determining broad popular acceptance, although this undoubtedly applies far more to singles than albums. The press plays a much more significant role in the success or failure of albums, but the big success stories are nearly always reflected by hit singles rather than albums. To this end, Joy Division were a significant force after the rock press gave their debut album the rave treatment, while radio remained almost totally indifferent. But when radio could no longer ignore the band with their charting of 'Love Will Tear Us Apart' single, and the band picked up substantial airplay, their

popularity became far more widely based.

However, the record business regards the rock press as very much a secondary influence compared to radio, thus obscuring the rock press's secondary role in this process. Much of the record business either conveniently, or out of sheer blind ignorance, disregards the evolutionary process behind the majority of hits. While radio can claim the lion's share of credit in the mass appeal of the genuine phenomenon that comes along every so often — as with, say, The Police and Adam and The Ants in the UK — by the very virtue of being phenomena, they are the exception, not the rule.

If the hit is the god of rock consumerism and radio ultimately makes or breaks them, it is a fact I would dispute in only an unsubstantive minority. It is one thing to read about a record you are told you will either love or loathe, another to actually hear it. The average record buyer is far more likely to hear it via the electronic media than seek it out by the inducement of the rock press. However, all this ignores several primary steps in the process by which most artists come to have a hit in the first place. If you accept that apart from one-off hit singles — which by their nature are of extremely limited freak importance,

(apart from the indiscriminate contribution they make to record company coffers) — most hits are provided by artists with a widely differing following, which to be fair to radio, can be dictated by the very success of the hit single radio is playing. But radio play is not automatic entitlement to a hit so there are frequently other considerations, although chief amongst them is obvious listener resistance. But why, if some records get saturation airplay and by almost any criteria deserve to be hits because the music is strong, do they fail? I would suggest that in most of these instances it can be traced to a real failure to capture attention in the first place amongst the rock press.

Just as radio is responsible for hits that owe no allegiance to an initial push created within the rock press, radio can be foisted with records that become hits without initial support from radio. This can occur because there are always instances in the UK of artists capable of attracting powerful support from the rock press and thereby effectively harnessing the support of its readership, which in turn creates the demand that produces a charting record. Then radio can no longer ignore them. If you look at the evolution of one of the UK's most successful bands in recent years and one that has

THE POLICE

THE JAM

enjoyed almost universally good rock press coverage, The Jam, then it is clearly wrong to credit radio's role as central to The Jam becoming a hugely successful singles band.

While The Jam have incontestably become huge through radio's now almost slavish devotion to playing their records in the UK, earlier in their career when the band was making arguably even more potent singles, it wasn't radio that sustained The Jam's existence in relation to their importance and the following the band commanded, but the continued support and devotion of the rock press, and by extension, its readers. It wasn't BBC listeners selling out Jam gigs, it was NEW MUSICAL EXPRESS readers and the like.

By its obvious advantage over radio of being able to see and give coverage to bands at any level from literally the garage up, the rock press begins with a head start in moulding public opinion. True it can have a band like Adam and The Ants around for years and never attach more than a passing (if that) significance to their existence. Then suddenly things begin to fall into place. A change or radical overhaul in image, a new record company, a new band and new material and before the press has time to reconsider a single is released, radio picks it up, away it goes, a hit ensues and bingo, Adam and The Ants are away and running. Then even more rapidly the image captures the audience's imagination, it translates into fashion, and Adam and The

Ants go beyond being simply a hit band, and move into the stratosphere on the popularity scale that no longer bears any relevance at all as to whether the band musically amounts to much, which is usually the first commandment of any rock journalist. But here we are considering a genuine phenomenon, and no matter how much they may swim against the tide of orthodoxy that usually decrees success or failure, clearly in this instance, rules no longer exist and orthodoxy becomes meaningless. It then doesn't matter that Adam and The Ants might be a truely awful band. And it doesn't matter what the rock press might feel compelled to say if it is at all dismissive. They are for the moment simply too hot for it to make the slightest difference.

But as if to underline the power and influence of the UK rock press, even Adam and The Ants — if they suddenly found themselves on the receiving end of the sort of sustained bad press which in recent years has afflicted the likes of Rod Stewart — could find themselves in trouble. Just as journalists adopt favourite bands and then variously defend or eventually vilify them (which raises the always festering wound within the record business of journalists' fickleness, which is a subject in itself), there are times when it almost seems there is a conspiracy among a UK rock writers' mafia to see who can deliver the most savage verbal kick in the groin. Rod Stewart (with every justification I think) is the classic example of the

former mischievous likely lad much loved by the rock press, who is now seen as a jumped-up Glaswegian dandy poncing around Hollywood parties, living a totally meaningless existence far removed from his roots. But more importantly such a mockery of a talent that in his earlier solo days was a very tangible force. Sure he can still do major tours in the UK, but his star most certainly has waned. While the rock press in this instance can hardly be said to have ruined Stewart's career, it's hard to deny the backlash has seen Stewart's "charisma" decline to the extent that he's more a recipient of nasty cracks than the adulation of once adoring journalists. This has certainly reduced his record sales to that of a mere mortal in the UK, a million miles removed from his alleged superstar status. Any artist or individual in the record business who fails to take heed of the fact in any assessment of the power of the UK rock press, is sadly underestimating its ability to wreak havoc with any career over a period of time if it really takes the bit between its teeth.

Finally, bound up in the real power and influence of the rock press which the record business frequently fails to recognise, is the inevitable influence the rock press has in the wider context of the radio, television, and even popular newspaper rock "taste-makers". Since the BBC Radio One network abandoned its rotated playlist for all its programmes in 1980, thereby permitting individual producers and disc-jockeys to

formulate their own playlists, Radio One's collective approach is now much more adventurous. As the British rock press goes about its business of observing and passing judgement on the evolving rock scene, so they are actively influencing the opinions and interests of the other media "taste-makers" in arriving at their own assessments. The UK rock press IS widely read by these people, and these days with the proliferation of more specialised rock publications — such as the highly successful and commendable SMASH HITS and THE FACE — the rock press is becoming increasingly influential in dictating to the "taste-makers" developments they can no longer comfortably afford to ignore. But particularly because radio in the UK is now more adventurous, merely by association the "taste-makers" have a vested interest in keeping up with rock's evolution, and in that regard no one is better placed than the rock press to provide it. For that very reason, the rock press will continue to play an increasingly influential and powerful role and it won't simply be confined to the UK, because in most foreign rock markets developments in the British rock media (because they chronicle what is still the base of the most vital rock music in the world), are picked up and adopted. While I do hold many reservations about the nature of the UK rock press, and think it falls short of the ideal working model, you still won't find a better working model anywhere. Ross Stapleton

ROD STEWART AND BRITT EKLAND

THE YEAR

AUG.

1. Sebastian Coe wins the gold medal for Britain in the 1500 metres in the Moscow Olympics. Earlier, Steve Ovett had taken the gold in the 800 metres.

2. In the worst terrorist massacre in Italy's history, 87 die and over 100 are critically injured when a time bomb, planted by right wing extremists, explodes in Bologna railway station.

4. In a long report to the Senate committee investigating his brother's links with Libya, President Carter states that Billy had had no influence on American foreign policy and that none of the 220 thousand dollars allegedly paid to him by the Gadafy regime had come to either the President or the family peanut business.

8. Over 100 people are reported dead after Hurricane Allen, the second worst on record, sweeps across the Caribbean.

8. Three hours before their Hammersmith Odeon show was to start, the Greater London Council bans The Plasmatics' British debut on grounds of safety. "We objected to the blowing up of a car" said a spokesman.

9. On the UK album chart, Heavy Metal rules as AC/DC's 'Back in Black' displaces the Deep Purple compilation 'Deepest Purple' at number one. Gillan's 'Glory Road' also enters the chart — at number three. Meanwhile, all is lightweight on the singles front: Abba reign in Britain with 'Winner Takes It All' and Olivia Newton John's 'Magic' remains America's best seller.

11. Sixties hippie activist Jerry Rubin, now 42, is revealed to be working in Wall Street as a securities analyst. "I learned that money is power", he says. Days later, his erstwhile partner in crime Abbie Hoffman, in hiding since jumping bail on a mid-Seventies cocaine dealing charge, surrenders to authorities as his autobiography, 'Soon To Be A Major Motion Picture', is published.

12. The Home Office announces a 17% increase in registered heroin addicts — 2809 as opposed to 2402 last year. Over 20,000 are thought to be using heroin illegally.

15. George Harrison's book of autobiographical jottings, 'I Me Mine', is published in a signed, limited edition. The price per copy...a mere £148.

WENDY O WILLIAMS/THE PLASMATICS

16. A week of walk-outs sees Jah Wobble leave Public Image Ltd, Bill Ward leave

HAZEL O'CONNOR

Black Sabbath, Jools Holland leave Squeeze, and Cozy Powell leave Rainbow.

17. A firebomb kills 37 patrons of a Soho drinking club.

20. Nineteen people appear in court after the BPI's investigation into "one of the biggest counterfeiting syndicates operating in the UK". A total of 6000 cassettes, mostly K-Tel facsimiles, had been seized in raids earlier in the month.

20. 301 passengers are killed at Riyadh airport when a Saudi Arabian Tristar catches fire.

21. 'Breaking Glass', a film starring punkette Hazel O'Connor, opens in London. Meanwhile, in America, two established rock stars make their theatrical debut. David Bowie plays the Victorian monstrosity John Merrick in 'The Elephant Man' opening in Denver before transferring to Chicago and ultimately New York's Broadway and country rock pioneer Linda Ronstadt broadens her range playing the pining ingenue Mabel in Gilbert and Sullivan's operetta 'The Pirates of Penzance' in New York.

DAVID BOWIE

23. 'Ashes To Ashes' becomes David Bowie's first British number one since the reissued 'Space Oddity' in 1975.

27. The Prime Minister remains undaunted as unemployment figures exceed two million — the highest level since 1935.

SQUEEZE

1980
SEP.

1. *Poland's rebellious workers win an unprecedented concession; the right to strike. Union leader Lech Walesa demands further democratic innovations.*

1. After twelve years, Ken Hensley, founder and mainstay of Uriah Heep, quits, leaving guitarist Mick Box the sole survivor of the original group.

2. Bassist Charley Anderson and keyboard player Desmond Brown leave The Selecter during sessions for their second album. "The situation had not been right for some time" according to the rest of the band.

4. Yes, with a new line-up including former Buggles Geoff Downes and Trevor Horn, return to the boards with three nights at New York's Madison Square Garden.

6. Ginger Baker, drummer with sixties supergroup Cream, leaves the recently reconstituted Atomic Rooster to join Hawkwind — another short-lived dalliance.

10. Cheap Trick confirm that bassist Tom Petersson has left the group "by mutual agreement", to be replaced by Peter Comita.

12. *Military takeover in Turkey.*

13. Jackson Browne's 'Hold Out' album becomes his first US chart topper, but is dislodged the following week by Queen's 'The Game'.

KATE BUSH

15. Influential jazz pianist Bill Evans dies of a bleeding ulcer in New York, aged 51.

17. *Anastasio Somoza, former Nicaraguan dictator, is shot dead in Paraguay.*

18. To commemorate the tenth anniversary of his death, Jimi Hendrix fans gather for a two day tribute at Amsterdam's Paradiso Club.

19. *Johnny Owen, 24 year old Welsh bantamweight, is knocked out in the 12th round of his world title fight against Mexican Lupe Pintor in Los Angeles. Despite several operations, he remains in a coma and eventually dies 45 days later.*

19. *Twenty-two are injured and 1000 evacuated after an explosion at the Arkansas Nuclear Missile site. The accident was caused when a worker dropped a spanner into a silo, puncturing the fuel tank of a Titan II rocket equipped with a nuclear warhead.*

22. *The border conflict between Iran and Iraq erupts into full scale war as both sides bomb airbases and attack on land and sea along the 720 mile frontier.*

24. The 'Son Of Stiff' tour gets under way, introducing Joe King Carrasco, Ten Pole Tudor, the Equators, Any Trouble and Dirty Looks.

25. John Bonham, drummer with Led Zeppelin since their inception in 1968, dies on the eve of an American tour. The 32 year old was asphyxiated by his own vomit during a coma induced by some 40 measures of vodka. Led Zeppelin subsequently decide to disband.

26. *A neo-Nazi terrorist bomb explodes at the Munich Oktoberfest, killing twelve people and injuring 144.*

27. 'Scary Monsters and Super-Creeps' by David Bowie becomes the month's third album to enter the UK chart at number one this month, following Gary Numan's 'Telekon' and Kate Bush's 'Never Forever'. 'Don't Stand So Close To Me' by The Police enters the UK singles chart at number one.

GARY NUMAN

1980
OCT.

3. *Muhammad Ali loses his bid to regain the world heavyweight boxing crown when defeated by Larry Holmes in Las Vegas. The World Boxing Council subsequently advise Ali to retire for his own good and that of boxing.*

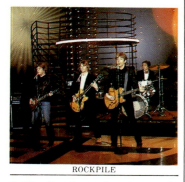

ROCKPILE

3. Finally clear of contractual hurdles, Rockpile release their debut album 'Seconds of Pleasure' — five years after their formation.

3. Following Granada TV's 'World in Action' exposé of chart hyping, implicated WEA managing director John Fruin resigns his £50,000 a year position and also surrenders his chairmanship of the British Phonographic Industry — the body supposedly alert to malpractice within the record business.

4. Ian Gillan dismisses "Deep Purple to reform" rumours as "total crap". Meanwhile, until prevented by injunction, a bogus Deep Purple fronted by original singer Rod Evans cleans up with concerts in Central and North America.

4. Stiff Records lose their appeal against a £50 fine plus £50 costs for making an "indecent exhibition" by displaying for sale a t-shirt bearing the slogan "If it ain't stiff it ain't worth a fuck".

6. Following a fracas in a Dublin bar, John Lydon is given a three month prison sentence for assault. Released on bail, he is later acquitted by an appeal court.

THE BEE GEES

6. The Bee Gees sue manager Robert Stigwood and the Polygram group for a total of 200 million dollars, charging misrepresentation, fraud and unfair enrichment at their expense.

9. John Lennon celebrates his fortieth birthday by releasing '(Just like) Starting Over' — his first single since retiring from public view in the mid-seventies. His wife, Yoko Ono, hires a skywriter to wish him happy birthday.

8. Bob Marley collapses in Central Park, New York and is hospitalised in Manhattan. Rumours of a brain tumour or similar cancer are denied and the problem attributed to "complete exhaustion". He flies to Ethiopia to recuperate but is later reported to be in a West German clinic undergoing treatment for an undisclosed illness.

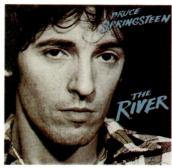

10. Bruce Springsteen hits the road for a lengthy world tour promoting his new twenty song double album, 'The River'.

10. *An estimated 20,000 people die in an earthquake in the Algerian city of El Asnam.*

THE POLICE

11. The Police's 'Zenyatta Mondatta' enters the UK album chart at number one — giving them the best-selling single and album. In US, Queen top the single and album lists with 'Another One Bites The Dust' and 'The Game'.

25. *H Block protesters go on hunger strike in the Maze Prison for political status.*

QUEEN

25. Barbra Streisand has best selling single, 'Woman In Love' in UK and US. Her 'Guilty' album heads the US chart and displaces The Police in UK a week later.

BARBRA STREISAND

26. *The Campaign for Nuclear Disarmament, which all but faded away during the early sixties, come back with renewed vigour in a march ending with a rally at Trafalgar Square. An estimated 100,000 take part.*

1980
NOV.

1. Graham Bonnet, largely responsible for Rainbow's recent rise to prominence, leaves the group to resume his solo career — following the footsteps of Cozy Powell, who had left a few weeks earlier. Replacements Joe Lynn Turner and Bob Rondinelli become the 15th and 16th musicians to play in Ritchie Blackmore's 5½ year old quintet.

4. *Former actor and Governor of California Ronald Reagan wins a landslide victory in the US Presidential election.*

DEXY'S MIDNIGHT RUNNERS

7. Dexy's Midnight Runners divide after disagreement. The three surviving originals recruit cohorts and continue under their established name, whilst the defectors subsequently re-emerge as The Bureau.

STEVE McQUEEN

7. *Film star Steve McQueen dies of a heart attack following surgery at a hospital in Juarez, Mexico. McQueen, 50, had been undergoing controversial treatment for lung cancer.*

ABBA

8. The British Phonographic Industry introduces new rules to prevent chart fixing.

8. The consistent popularity of heavy metal in Britain is reflected in top five album success by Status Quo, Motorhead and Whitesnake.

BRUCE SPRINGSTEEN

8. Springsteen fever grips America once more as his album, 'The River', rises to number one — remaining there for four weeks.

9. Bob Dylan embarks on a US tour featuring predominently "born again" material.

10. *Michael Foot is elected leader of the Parliamentary Labour Party.*

13. *Miss Germany, 18 year old student Gabriella Brum, becomes the new Miss World. Seventeen hours later she abdicates. Somewhere over the Atlantic, runner up Miss Guam, Kimberley Santos, was flying home unaware that she was now Miss World.*

17. *The Yorkshire Ripper claims his 13th and last victim, 20 year old Leeds University student Jacqueline Hill.*

21. Eagles drummer Don Henley is arrested after paramedics are called to his house to deal with a naked 16 year old girl suffering ill effects after taking drugs. Henley is subsequently given two years probation, fined 2000 dollars, and ordered to participate in a two year drug diversion programme. Meanwhile, in Britain, Motorhead and Marianne Faithfull fall prey to regular hassling by drug squads.

21. *Eighty-three people die in a 'Towering Inferno' fire at the MGM Grand Hotel in Las Vegas, the second largest casino and hotel complex in the world.*

22. Abba enter the UK album chart at number one with 'Super Trouper'. Their single displaces Blondie's 'The Tide Is High' as the nation's best-seller a week later.

DEBBIE HARRY/BLONDIE

23. *A violent earthquake, centred on Potenza, shakes Southern Italy, killing over 3000 and causing widespread injury, destruction and panic.*

25. *HM Customs and Excise reveal that during the year ended March 1980, they seized drugs with an estimated street value of £32 million.*

1980
DEC.

3. *Sir Oswald Mosley, 84, founder of the British Union of Fascists in the 1930's, dies in his chateau on the outskirts of Paris.*

8. John Lennon is murdered in the courtyard of his apartment building in Manhattan. Twenty-five year

20. 'There's No-One Quite Like Grandma' by St Winifred's School Choir and 'Stop The Cavalry' by Jona Lewie provide the year's most successful Christmas novelty hits.

20. Motorhead drummmer Phil Taylor breaks his neck when inadvertently "bounced on his head while messing around with some friends" after the group's gig in Belfast. Meanwhile, Whitesnake cancel their European tour when singer David Coverdale is confined to crutches after tearing a cartilage on stage in Hamburg.

WHITESNAKE

JOHN LENNON

MOTORHEAD

21. The Police play in a 5000 capacity tent on London's Tooting Bec Common — the first of three charity Christmas gigs.

23. *Unemployment in Britain rises to almost 2¼ millions — the highest figure since 1933.*

SPANDAU BALLET

27. The Stray Cats' British top ten hit 'Runaway Boys' spearheads a rockabilly revival whilst climbers by Visage and Spandau Ballet provoke a nationwide Futurist/New Romantics fad.

TIM HARDIN

old Mark Chapman admits firing five .38 calibre bullets into Lennon after stopping him for his autograph. The killer's lawyer says he shot the former Beatle because "I understood his words but I didn't understand his meaning".

13. MOR rules as Kenny Rogers tops both US charts and Abba continue to dominate in Britain.

18. *Alexei Kosygin, 76, dies of a heart attack two months after resigning as Soviet Prime Minister.*

19. *IRA hunger strikers take food after 53 days.*

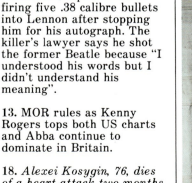

STRAY CATS

29. Tim Hardin, who rose to prominence with such songs as 'If I Were A Carpenter' and 'Reason To Believe' during the mid-sixties, is found dead in his Hollywood apartment. The 40 year old singer suffered "acute heroin-morphine intoxication due to an overdose."

1981
JAN.

PETER SUTCLIFFE

2. *Peter Sutcliffe, a 35 year old lorry driver from Bradford, is arrested in Sheffield and subsequently charged with the 13 'Yorkshire Ripper' murders. Police had been hunting him since his first attack in October 1975.*

3. 'Starting Over' and 'Double Fantasy' by John Lennon top the US singles and album charts. A week later, the re-released 'Imagine' becomes Britain's best selling single.

NEVER MIND THE BOLLOCKS HERE'S THE Sex PiSTOLs

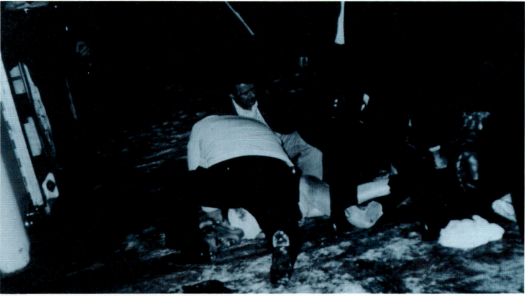

WENDY O WILLIAMS/THE PLASMATICS

9. Terry Hall and Jerry Dammers of The Specials are each fined £400 plus £133 costs after being convicted of using threatening words and behaviour during their Cambridge gig in October.

THE SPECIALS

12. 'Never Mind The Bollocks, Here's The Sex Pistols', Dylan's 'Blonde On Blonde' and 'Kiss Live' are among some 800 albums donated to the White House record library by the Recording Industry Association of America.

18. *A fierce fire kills 13 and injures 20 after an all-night West Indian party in Deptford, South London. Foul play is suspected, especially by the local black community, but after an official inquest the jury returns an open verdict.*

18. Wendy O Williams of The Plasmatics is arrested by police during a concert in Milwaukee for "simulating masturbation with a sledgehammer in front of an audience". In the scuffle, Wendy is pinned to the floor by over zealous officers and subsequently requires medical attention, including 12 stitches to a cut above the eye.

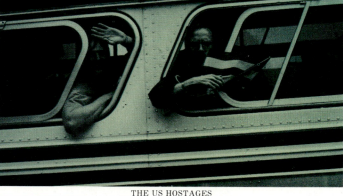

THE US HOSTAGES

ADAM ANT

19. British Phonographic Industry chairman Chris Wright predicts a cassette oriented future for the rock industry. "Record companies are still too busy thinking 12 inch records" he says.

20. *As President Reagan takes the oath of office, the 52 American hostages imprisoned in Tehran for 444 days are released.*

24. 'Kings Of The Wild Frontier' becomes Britain's best-selling album as Adam Ant establishes himself as the greatest teenybop hero since Marc Bolan.

25. *At the end of the nine week "Gang of Four" trial in Peking, Mao Tse Tung's widow Jiang Qing receives a death sentence suspended for two years to see if she shows repentence.*

27. *Recession gloom deepens in Britain as the unemployment rate breaks the 10% barrier.*

1981
FEB.

4. *A Westminster coroner's jury decides that the shooting by the Special Air Services Regiment of five of the six terrorists holding the Iranian Embassy in London is "justifiable homicide".*

7. John Lennon tops both UK charts with 'Woman' and 'Double Fantasy'.

BILL HALEY

9. Bill Haley, whose 20 million seller 'Rock Around The Clock' sounded the tocsin of the rock'n'roll revolution in 1955, dies of natural causes in Harlingen Texas, aged 56.

FRANK SINATRA

11. Frank Sinatra is granted a provisional licence to take a key job with the Caesars Palace Casino in Las Vegas. Sinatra lost a previous licence in 1963 when it was suggested that he had connections with the Mafia.

12. *The Rev. Ian Paisley is suspended from the House of Commons after displaying "gross discourtesy". A few days earlier he had led an army of 500 supporters, all wielding fire-arms certificates, in a show of strength on a remote hillside in County Antrim.*

13. Island Records appal the BPI by appearing to condone home taping with the introduction of their One Plus One series of one half pre-recorded/one half blank tapes.

14. *Forty-nine people die and 130 are injured when fire sweeps through the Starlight Club Disco in Dublin.*

YOUNG MARBLE GIANTS

THE BODYSNATCHERS

14. Two months after resurfacing with a new line-up, Generation X formally disband as singer Billy Idol moves to New York in search of solo success. Other bands to announce their dissolution in a winter of general discontent include the Young Marble Giants, Graham Parker and The Rumour, the Joe Jackson Band, The Bodysnatchers, Rockpile, The Tourists, The Soft Boys, The Only Ones, The Buzzcocks and Led Zeppelin.

PHIL COLLINS

14. Thirty-seven year old white blues guitarist Mike Bloomfield, celebrated for his work with Paul Butterfield and Bob Dylan during the mid Sixties, is found dead at the wheel of his car in San Francisco.

21. 'Face Value', the debut solo album by Genesis frontman Phil Collins, enters the UK chart at number one while REO Speedwagon's 'Hi Infidelity' displaces John Lennon after a seven week tenure as America's number one.

22. *The Reagan Administration decides to keep the issue of El Salvador at the top of its foreign policy agenda, and raises the possibility of a blockade on Cuba to stop the flow of arms to the insurgents. Four days later, Mrs Thatcher arrives in Washington for summit talks.*

23. *Two hundred civil guards led by Lt. Col. Antonio Tejero invade the Spanish parliament in Madrid in an attempted coup d'etat. King Juan Carlos successfully engineers the crushing of the revolt.*

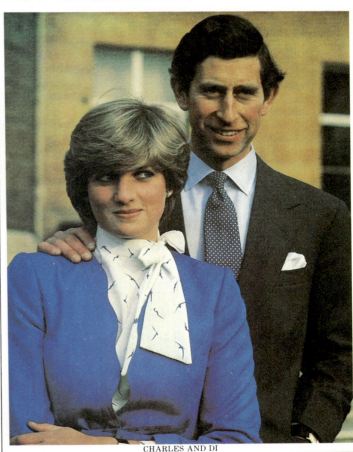
CHARLES AND DI

24. *Prince Charles announces his engagement to Lady Diana Spencer, 12 years his junior. She is the first English girl to become engaged to an heir to the throne for 300 years. "I feel positively delighted and frankly amazed that Di is prepared to take me on," says Charles.*

26. *The Home Secretary announces the legalisation of Citizens Band radio in Britain.*

1981 MAR.

2. *The "dirty protest" conducted by over 400 republicans at the Maze Prison in Belfast for the past three years is unexpectedly called off. A statement said the decision had been taken to focus public attention on the hunger strike started by Bobby Sands the day before.*

14. Roxy Music top the UK singles chart with their John Lennon tribute, 'Jealous Guy'. In the album charts, Adam and The Ants return to number one and stay there for ten weeks. Costume pop beings to prosper in their wake.

18. *Former British High Commissioner in Canada, 66 year old Sir Peter Hayman,* is linked to a child pornography scandal in a question raised in the House of Commons.

21. After slogging around America for almost ten years, REO Speedwagon find themselves topping both singles and album charts. The album remains the nation's best-seller for over three months.

22. *Mike Hailwood, 40, ten times world motor cycle racing champion and former racing car driver, suffers fatal head injuries in a road accident near his home in Warwickshire.*

24. *Great Train Robber and Sex Pistols cohort Ronald Biggs is arrested on arrival in Barbados after having been kidnapped from a restaurant in his adopted home city of Rio eight days earlier. He successfully fights British attempts to extradite him to complete his prison sentence and, 60 days later, returns jubilantly to freedom in Brazil.*

KIM WILDE

26. *Breakaway Labour MPs led by Dr David Owen form the Social Democratic Party.*

28. Blondie's 'Rapture' becomes America's best selling single, while Shakin' Stevens rides the British rockabilly revival to number one with 'This Old House'. Close behind is newcomer Kim Wilde's 'Kids In America' — written by her father Marty, who pioneered rock'n'roll in Britain during the late Fifties. The week also sees the return of The Who to the album chart with 'Face Dances'.

30. *Ronald Reagan survives an assassination attempt outside the Hilton Hotel in Washington. The 70 year old President recovers after* emergency surgery to remove from his left lung a bullet which is said to have missed his heart by only one inch. John Hinckley Jr, the 25 year old son of a Denver oil tycoon, is arrested and charged with the attempted murder.

31. *After the longest, most expensive libel action to be brought in Britain, a High Court jury decides that the Daily Mail had been justified in publishing an article accusing the Unification "Moonie" Church of breaking up families, applying communist brainwashing methods, and exploiting young recruits to finance an "evil" multinational business empire with ambitions of world domination.*

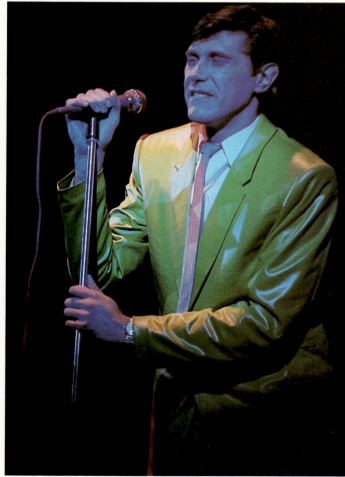

BRIAN FERRY/ROXY MUSIC

THE SHOOTING OF REAGAN

1981
APR.

1. *In the annual Academy Awards ceremony in Hollywood, Sissy Spacek wins the Best Actress Oscar for her portrayal of Loretta Lynn in 'Coalminer's Daughter'. Robert de Niro is Best Actor for his role in 'Raging Bull'. Robert Redford's 'Ordinary People' wins Oscars for Best Film and Best Director.*

4. 'Paradise Theater' by Styx becomes America's best selling album, but only displaces REO Speedwagon for four weeks.

4. Bucks Fizz win the Eurovision Song Contest for Britain with their performance of 'Making Your Mind Up', which rockets to number one only days later. The UK last won the competition in 1976 with Brotherhood of Man's entry, 'Save All Your Kisses For Me'.

BUCKS FIZZ

5. Bob "The Bear" Hite, 38, portly lead vocalist with blues band Canned Heat, dies of a heart attack in Venice California.

6. *After President Brezhnev, the Soviet leader, suggests that "anti socialist forces with outside help" were seeking to achieve a counter revolution in Poland,*

BOB HITE/CANNED HEAT

President Reagan and Mrs Thatcher write to him warning that detente would come to an abrupt end if the Russians were to invade Poland.

7. Forty-five year old former Track Records boss Kit Lambert, who guided The Who to international success in the mid Sixties, dies of head injuries sustained from a fall in his mother's London home.

8. *Britain's two largest tobacco manufacturers put 13,500 workers on short time because of the dramatic slump in the cigarette market caused by the budget, which added 14p to a packet of 20.*

10. *IRA hunger striker Bobby Sands wins the parliamentary byelection in Fermanagh, dealing a serious blow to the Government's security strategy in Northern Ireland. Sands, serving a 14 year sentence for terrorism, is unable to take his seat.*

10. *Three days of running battles between police and black youths in Brixton, South London, leave property destroyed, looted and burning. 110 policemen are hospitalised and over 100*

youths arrested in the worst race riots in Britain's history.

11. Daryl Hall and John Oates move to the top of the US singles charts with 'Kiss On My List'.

12. *Former heavyweight boxing champion Joe Louis, who held the title for 12 years, dies of a heart attack in Las Vegas, aged 66.*

12. *The 75 ton US space shuttle Columbia, the first re-usable spacecraft, lifts off from the Kennedy Space Centre in Florida. After satisfactorily completing its 54 hour mission, the craft makes a perfect landing at Edward Air Force Base in California's Mohave Desert. The Columbia, lampooned by critics as a truck in space, brings closer to reality the long held dream of a regular service into space, leading ultimately to inhabited colonies.*

18. The demise of Seventies monstergroup Yes is confirmed as drummer Alan White and bassist Chris Squire join former Led Zeppelin frontmen Robert Plant and Jimmy Page in rehearsals for a new supergroup. Meanwhile, Plant and some local mates have been playing a series of low key gigs as The Honeydrippers.

20. John Phillips, former leader of The Mamas and Papas, enters prison after pleading guilty to drug

dealing charges. All but 30 days of his eight year jail sentence are suspended and Phillips is placed on five years probation with the stipulation that he attends a drug abuse programme and performs 250 hours of community service during the next year.

DENNY LAINE

25. "We simply shan't be Wings anymore" says Paul McCartney after revealing that Denny Laine has left the band to pursue a solo career. Laine is subsequently fined £175 and banned from driving for three years after crashing his Ferrari into a fence whilst under the influence of alcohol.

27. Former Beatle Ringo Starr, now 41, marries Barbara Bach at Marylebone Register Office in Central London.

28. Gary Numan makes his "last public appearance" at London's Wembley Arena.

RINGO AND BARBARA

1981 MAY

1. *Thousands gather to support 250 setting off from Liverpool to London on The People's March For Jobs. Labour MP Tony Benn describes Liverpool as "the graveyard of British capitalism".*

SHEENA EASTON

2. Sheena Easton tops the US singles chart with 'Morning Train (9 to 5)'.

5. *Twenty-seven year old IRA hunger striker Bobby Sands dies after 66 days without food. Ulster braces itself for further serious riots as preparations are made for the funeral. Eight days later, a second hunger striker, Francis Hughes, dies after a 59 days fast and on May 22 two further strikers Patsy O'Hara and Raymond McCreesh also succumb.*

6. *The Queen expresses her distaste for "cheque book journalism" arising from the Yorkshire Ripper case, currently in court. Friends and relations of the accused had been paid to elaborate on his character and deeds in various national newspapers.*

6. *Lord Kagan, the 65 year old businessman currently serving a ten months prison sentence for fraud and theft, is stripped of his knighthood on the recommendation of Mrs Thatcher.*

9. Adam and The Ants crash into the UK singles chart at number one with 'Stand And Deliver'. In America, Kim Carnes reaches number one with 'Bette Davis Eyes'.

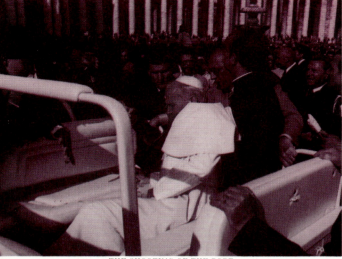
THE SHOOTING OF THE POPE

10. *Giscard d'Estaing concedes defeat in the French elections. Francois Mitterrand ends 23 years of Right rule to become the nation's first Socialist President.*

11. Thirty-six year old Jamaican folk hero and reggae champion Bob Marley dies from cancer at the Cedars of Lebanon Hospital in Miami, Florida. Two weeks earlier, his government had awarded him the Order of Merit — the country's third highest civilian award.

13. *The Pope is shot as he rides into St Peters Square in his white jeep, but a 4½ hour operation lifts the threat to his life. A note found on the would-be assassin, Mehmet Ali Agea, one of Turkey's most notorious professional killers, begins: "I have killed the Pope in order to protest against the imperialism of the Soviet Union and the United States".*

14. *After a replay, Tottenham Hotspur win the 100th FA Cup Final by defeating Manchester City 3-2. Argentinian Ricardo Villa scores two goals to become the hero of the match.*

15. Public Image Ltd are forced to flee from rioting fans after their performance at the Ritz Club in New York. They had decided to make "an artistic statement", involving their hiding behind a large video screen whilst experimenting with noise, instead of playing an orthodox gig.

15. *Princess Anne gives birth to an 8lb 1oz daughter called Zara.*

19. *A landmine kills five soldiers in Ulster. "You are fighting a war you cannot win" say the IRA, claiming responsibility for the attack.*

22. *After a trial lasting three weeks, Peter Sutcliffe, known as the Yorkshire Ripper, is found guilty of murdering 13 women and attempting to murder a further seven. The judge sentences him to 20 consecutive life terms with the recommendation that he serve at least 30 years before release is considered.*

25. *Jack Warner, alias PC Dixon, Britain's best-loved television bobby, dies in London, aged 85.*

25. Rhythm and blues pioneer Roy Brown, composer of 'Good Rockin' Tonight', dies of heart failure in Los Angeles, aged 55.

28. Renowned jazz pianist May Lou Williams, one of the originators of bebop and Kansas City jazz, dies of cancer, aged 71.

29. Bruce Springsteen plays London for the first time since November 1975.

30. *Fighting breaks out between rebel and loyalist soldiers in Chittagong after the assassination of President Ziaur Rahman of Bangladesh.*

BOB MARLEY

1 9 8 1 JUN.

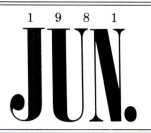

1. *The Football Association reveal that they would favour a complete ban on English supporters at overseas matches if that were the price of keeping an English team in international soccer. The statement followed criticism of fan violence at the recent world cup game in Switzerland.*

THE MOODY BLUES

2. Rock establishment recluses The Moody Blues creep out and gird up their loins for a UK tour to promote their new album 'Long Distance Voyager'.

4. *James Earl Ray, serving 99 years for murdering civil rights leader Martin Luther King, is stabbed 22 times and beaten up in prison in* Tennessee. *He is later reported to be in good condition after surgery involving 77 stitches.*

6. Magazine, formed by Howard Devoto on his departure from Manchester new wavers The Buzzcocks in 1977, announce their dissolution and punk pioneers Siouxsie and The Banshees intimate that their forthcoming summer tour will be their last. Powerpoppers The Yachts also decide to throw in the towel.

8. *Israeli jets bomb and destroy the Iraqi nuclear reactor at Daura, 15 miles fom Baghdad.*

10. *Eight leading IRA members, all being held on charges relating to terrorist offences including the possession of machine guns and murder, escape from Crumlin Road jail in Belfast.*

10. A second "supergroup" rises from the ashes of Yes ... Asia, featuring Steve Howe on guitar, former Buggle Geoff Downes on keyboards, Crimson/Roxy/Uriah Heep veteran John Wetton on bass, and ELP mainstay Carl Palmer on drums.

13. *During the Trooping Of The Colour ceremony in the Mall, a 17 year old youth, Marcus Sarjeant, is arrested and charged with treason after firing six blank shots at the Queen.*

SMOKEY ROBINSON

13. After five weeks as the nation's best selling single, 'Stand And Deliver' by Adam and The Ants is displaced by 'Being With You', Smokey Robinson's first number one since 'Tears Of A Clown' in 1970.

17. Pauline Black, their lead vocalist, plays her last gig with premier 2-tone band The Selecter. "I feel that my ideas were going in a different direction from those of the rest of the band" she says. Immediate plans involve a solo album.

18. *Prince Charles, visiting New York City, is heckled by IRA sympathisers. A small army of 1700 policemen and 300 secret service men protect him at every turn — a level of security estimated at $300,000.*

GILLAN

20. Guitarists on the move: Gerry Cott leaves The Boomtown Rats and Bernie Torme leaves Gillan.

21. Donald Fagen and Walter Becker, the only remnants of Steely Dan, admit that their 14 year old songwriting/playing partnership has been dissolved and that the group is no more.

21. *A 23 year old photographer, Wayne B Williams, is arrested and charged with criminal homicide in one of the killings of the 28 young blacks in Atlanta, Georgia.*

23. Robert Fripp reveals that his touring band will temporarily adopt the name of his turn-of-the-Seventies megagroup King Crimson — the last incarnation of which disbanded in 1974.

24. *The Humber Bridge, at 4,626 feet long the biggest single-span suspension bridge in the world, is opened to the public - four years behind schedule and many million pounds over budget.*

BOB DYLAN

26. Bob Dylan plays the first of six nights at London's Earls Court. Just as his 1965 hardcore following resented his electrification, the majority of his Seventies fans object to his "born again Christian" material.

27. 'Mistaken Identity' by Kim Carnes dislodges REO Speedwagon after their 14 week stay at the top of the American album charts. Her single 'Bette Davis Eyes' heads the singles list. In Britain 'One Day In Your Life' by Michael Jackson becomes the best-selling single while Motorhead's live monster 'No Sleep 'Til Hammersmith' bursts into the album charts at number one.

30. *Michael Bogdanov, The National Theatre director of 'The Romans In Britain', is committed for trial at the Old Bailey, charged with procuring the commission of an act of gross indecency between two actors in the play. He is being prosecuted privately by Mrs Mary Whitehouse, president of the National Viewers and Listeners Association.*

SIOUXSIE

1981 JUL.

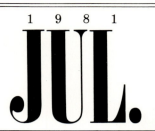

2. *The pound slumps to $1.88 — its lowest level in four years.*

3. On the tenth anniversary of Jim Morrison's death, his colleagues in The Doors — Ray Manzarek, Robbie Krieger and John Densmore — join fans from all over the world in a graveside tribute at Pere Lachaise cemetary in Paris.

3. *Race riots break out in Southall following a pub gig by skinhead band the 4 Skins. Within 24 hours the Toxteth area of Liverpool is also ablaze in the worst scenes of civil disorder ever seen in Britain. Police use CS gas to curb violent fighting and looting. Over the next few days many urban areas experience rioting as unemployment-related tension and ethnic minority problems bubble to the surface. Various official enquiries are opened to determine causes and remedies.*

4. *Turbulent "superbrat" John McEnroe, whose fines for "unsportsmanlike behaviour" during the tournament total £7500, wins the men's singles final at Wimbledon, beating five-time winner Bjorn Borg. Fellow American Chris Lloyd defeats Hana Mandlikova of Czechoslovakia in the ladies final.*

JOHN McENROE

7. *Ian Botham resigns his captaincy following two ducks in Australia's rout of the England cricket team in the second test match at Lords. Former captain Mike Brearley is subsequently recalled.*

JERRY LEE LEWIS

10. Forty-five year old rock'n'roll pioneer Jerry Lee Lewis is reported to be in an "extremely critical condition" and is given only a 50/50 chance of survival after extensive abdominal surgery at Memphis Methodist Hospital.

11. 'Ghost Town' by The Specials becomes Britain's best selling single whilst the Cliff Richard compilation 'Love Songs' moves to number one on the album chart.

13. A black teenager is stabbed to death during vicious fighting between two rival groups of pickpockets before Black Uhuru's concert at London's Rainbow Theatre.

CHRIS LLOYD

16. *In the Warrington parliamentary byelection, the newly formed Social Democrat Party comes within 1760 votes of winning. Candidate Roy Jenkins calls the narrow defeat his "greatest victory".*

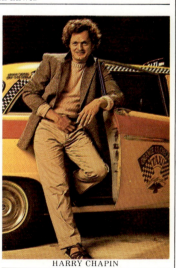

HARRY CHAPIN

16. Thirty-eight year old American singer/songwriter Harry Chapin, best known for 'WOLD' and 'Cat's In The Cradle', is killed when his car collides with a truck in Long Island, New York.

17. *At least 111 people die and 180 are injured after two concrete "sky bridges" crash down on hundreds of dancers in the lobby of the Hyatt Regency Hotel in Kansas City, Missouri.*

18. *In tempestuous street battles, police disperse 3500 demonstrators storming the British embassy in Dublin to support the demands of hunger strikers in Belfast's Maze Prison.*

19. *American Bill Rogers wins the 110th British Open golf championships.*

21. *The number of unemployed in Britain reaches a record total of 2,851,623, representing 11.8 per cent of the working population.*

21. *Former scapegoat Ian Botham and bowler Bob Willis are the heroes of England's victory over Australia in the third test match at Headingley. Not since 1894 has a test side won after being forced to follow on.*

AIR SUPPLY

25. The Moody Blues, consistent hitmakers since their chart debut 'Go Now' in 1964, displace Kim Carnes from the top of the American album chart with 'Long Distance Voyager'. 'The One That You Love' by Air Supply becomes America's best selling single.

29. *A British national holiday celebrates the royal wedding of Prince Charles and Lady Diana Spencer.*

31. Group frontwomen Debbie Harry of Blondie and Stevie Nicks of Fleetwood Mac release their first solo albums, 'Koo Koo' and 'Bella Donna' respectively.

ROCK

Early in the morning of December 9th, 1980 countless people were jerked from their slumber with the news that John Lennon had been murdered in New York City. For the next few days followers of this stuff we'd best call beat music experienced a melancholy sensation of community, a sensation as rare as it was profound.

The loss of Lennon served to dramatise the fragmentation of the music whose course he had so profoundly affected. The simple, uncontrived ardour of the Beatle records that were dusted off in tribute stood in stark contrast to the usual radio traffic. Was it rock, was it pop? Momentous or flippant? It neither presumed your full attention nor craved it. The momentum at its heart needed neither codebook nor glossary of terms. For a short space the electronic bands with their pitiless backbeat, the modern chart bands with their depressing self-importance, the heavy metal groups and their alehouse rants, all the soulless science of marketing and crossover potential and dingy specialism was perceived as so much field research. So this was how it sounded when you put it all together! Consequently December 8th is the only date that was entered in every diary. The rest of the time we attended different, exclusive parties.

Much of this huddling in tribes can be ascribed to punk's failure to forge a craft that matched its ambition. Joe Strummer has yet to make the record which could render Clash interviews superfluous and Johnny Rotten hasn't performed the trick in a fair while. Both these founding fathers spent the better part of the year sulking in their tents. The Clash ventured out long enough to confuse eclecticism with inspiration and make 'Sandinista' into one of the great follies of artistic tourism. PiL were out to

THE CLASH

destroy rock and roll but could find nobody interested in even negotiating terms. Lydon consoled himself by discrediting art-rock, but it was no substitute. Some kind of nadir was reached in May of '81 as an irate New York club audience responded to his contempt by attempting to rip him apart.

Of the first wave captains only Paul Weller and The Jam appeared to have retained any stomach for the fray, unleashing a string of singles that found the number one spot as if by predestination. But even they failed to broaden the base of either their music or their popularity and June found them holding back the release date of 'Funeral Pyre' in a vain effort to ensure that it entered at the top.

British groups have traditionally put much of their faith in the promise of pastures new abroad, particularly in America. Export Or Die is a motto that isn't lost on either The Clash or The Boomtown Rats. But for a group weaned on the immediacy of the British

scene the whole time-consuming, morale-sapping business of "breaking America" is an unattractive prospect. This campaigning is not made any less onerous by the cussedly long time it takes the American Consumer to even get on first name terms with a new act. Witness The Police and Blondie, two bands who marked 1980 by releasing their weakest albums and yet scored unprecedented paydays purely because America had finally decided they could be trusted. And once that barrier has been negotiated then it takes something terminal to sever the relationship. How else could a journeyman outfit like REO Speedwagon, a crew of such surpassing anonymity that their own mothers probably can't tell them apart, occupy a position of pre-eminence in the US charts?

Social psychologists would no doubt point to a deep craving for reassurance in the Western World. On both sides of the Atlantic the monetarist axe came down.

America's virility was affronted in Iran, Britain sluttered into the slough of economic despond, random slaughter in cities as far apart as Bradford and Atlanta became as much a part of the landscape as endemic unemployment and racial strife. In these circumstances it would have been surprising had the emphasis not swung back in classic recession style to old fashioned escapist entertainment. Ministering to this hunger for hokum came the Gold Diggers of 1981.

In the UK it had long been suspected that the major record companies were no longer capable of spotting and grooming new talent. 1980-81 saw that theory confirmed beyond reasonable doubt. On the contrary, a large proportion of the acts who flourished freely during the year had known the contempt of the record companies and the withering disdain of the music press at close quarters. The ascendancy of people like Toyah, Gillan, Hazel O'Connor, Whitesnake, Shakin' Stevens, Phil Collins, Ultravox and Motorhead underlined how out of touch both music business and music press had become.

Being hip didn't matter very much. Had it mattered then Stuart Goddard would not have been bulleted from back row of the chorus to centre stage in order to dominate the British charts with such comical ease.

More commonly known as Adam Ant, Goddard became Britain's most screamed-over teen idol since Marc Bolan. Like Bolan he'd experienced enough bad deals and false starts to make a realist out of Mary Poppins. His vanity had been extinguished, but what remained was a deal of pride and a fearsome desire to make it. And, like Bolan, he substantially reinvented himself. Following an ill-starred liason with Malcolm MacLaren he recruited a new band and came out of his corner with a new sound, new clothes, new patter and an album that was both a manifesto and a shameless bid for massive fame.

"We're gonna move real good/We're gonna dress so fine/It's dog eat dog eat dog eat dog eat dog eat dog eat dot eat dog..."

As succinct an analysis of the state of play as anyone else managed. His Burundi beat, Gary Glitter chanting, bare chest and swashbuckling schtick touched a national nerve and magnetised the affections of a bunch of kids for whom punk was something their elders endlessly muttered about. Like the born trouper he is he offered up all the old fashioned glamour, sex and escapism their hearts could hold. Admitting in interviews that he didn't have a single original thought, he nonetheless wrapped the finished package in some pretty transparent tosh, but it mattered little to the people who were dancing to the insect beat of 'Stand And Deliver' and 'Kings Of The Wild Frontier'.

Britain's insatiable desire

SPANDAU BALLET

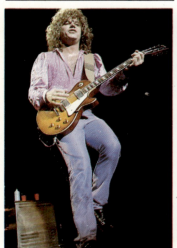

REO SPEEDWAGON

ADAM ANT

STEVE WINWOOD

for novelty, for fast turnover, is in stark contrast to the stifling conservatism of the American scene. Recent albums by old soldiers like The Who, Steve Winwood, Steely Dan and The Rolling Stones, which were quite rightly shown the door in Britain, were embraced whole-heartedly in the USA by fans who seemed oblivious to their wretched lack of inspiration. The Stones once again displayed their utter contempt for the human race by following a dire new album, 'Emotional Rescue', with 'Sucking In The Seventies', a compilation which could have been employed as a teaching aid

for anyone lecturing on the subject of their senility.

The Who's 'Face Dances' was probably even more of an embarrassment because, unlike The Stones, they were actually trying. Townshend's apparent inability to come to terms with the fact that his band tramples the meaning out of his songs is sad indeed.

Because America is a country with no real pop scene, the form of rock has for so long dictated its content that any band with designs on stardom settle for trimming their ambitions at the outset and compromise themselves into a vacant slot in the market. In the light of such weary inertia, Pat

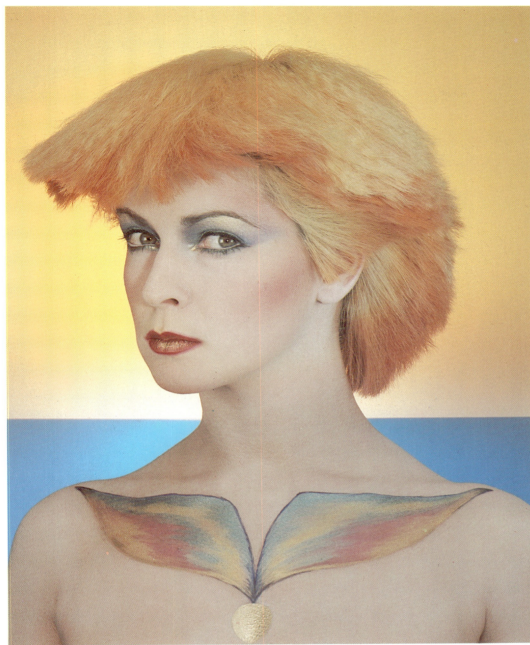

TOYAH WILLCOX

teeth of considerable competition. This five piece sprang, ready-to-serve, from a London club scene teeming with bright young things to whom self-promotion was only slightly less important than breathing. Tags were produced, but none fitted; the New Romantics, Blitz Kids, Futurists, the Cult With No Name. Everyone fought shy of the word "exhibitionist". Whether decked out as Thirties boulevardiers or gothic clergy, whether professing their undying love for teutonic art-rock or negro funk, they had one common passion and it overrode all other considerations. They were all besotted beyond reason with David Bowie.

They prated freely about individualism and style and creativity but the greater part of their waking hours were devoted to refining the same air of aesthetically pleasing ennui. Compared to Madness — who are young and sharp and not afraid of cameras — they were eminently forgettable. It must be said, however, that Spandau Ballet were capable and hardly boring at all but

MIDGE URE/ULTRAVOX

Benatar's wily exploitation of the heavy metal audience is almost a stroke of genius.

Heavy Metal is less a form of music than a cipher for a series of purchasing patterns, and sex has unaccountably dropped out of the formula. Benatar's massive success proved what many of us had suspected — that there are those who desire Debbie Harry but find her music just that worrisome bit too deep.

But even Heavy Metal could not stand aloof from the recession and, with ticket sales following record sales into decline, even those bands who most disdained the fickleness of pop were forced to look the singles market in the eye. Bands like Rainbow approached hardened tunesmiths like Russ Ballard for songs that might accommodate their blistering excess within a format that radio programmers could come to terms with. Styx and REO Speedwagon responded by evolving new and yet more emotionally neutral variations on the ballad format.

Britain remained consumed by fads and revivals masquerading as progress. CRYSALIS RECORDS followed up their success with 2-Tone by recruiting the leading lights of the next movement-shaped crop of groups when they signed Spandau Ballet in the

DAVID BOWIE

GRACE JONES

KILLING JOKE

the limitations of their emotional range were apparent to the few people who got the chance to see them. By mid '81 the coterie that had nurtured them had tired of the idea of having a band at all and were rifling enthusiastically though jazz and funk in search of new shapes to throw.

For clothes-horses of various kinds it was a time full of possibilities; for David Bowie (who notched up his first number one proper with 'Ashes To Ashes'); for Steve Strange (who inaugurated his 15 minutes of fame by featuring in the accompanying video); for Grace Jones (who assaulted a chat show host, thereby ensuring that her reputation no longer resided exclusively in her physical stature); for Toyah Willcox (who was very noisy and quite versatile but unfortunately born too late to find her real niche in the cast of 'Hair'). Their ever changing aspects were recorded in the glossy pages of THE FACE, the most significant new publication of the era, a magazine that operated on the principle that a picture is undoubtedly worth a thousand words or so.

In the train of The Exquisites came a new generation of groups who had heard Johnny Burnette's 'Rock'n'Roll Trio' album, liked it, and named themselves after different varieties of cat. The lucky ones were produced by Dave Edmunds; the rest took what they could get. Only Shakin' Stevens — yet another good and faithful servant — really prospered by dint of a string of singles which applied disco polish to rockabilly manners and were rarely bothered unduly by the problem of originality.

In the same way that Stevens' hard-bitten distance

produced music that surpassed the fumblings of the rockabilly "movement", Phil Collins artfully mined the same seam as Spandau Ballet and came up trumps with 'In The Air Tonight'. And he wasn't the only "muso" to grasp the fact that glacial sophistication was once again a marketable commodity. Spandau Ballet's records were produced by Richard Burgess, a jazz-rocker who could have been excused for thinking that a gold watch was the best he could look forward to.

The theme tune of the year

ELVIS COSTELLO

— "this means nothing to me" — was given voice by Midge Ure, another regular soldier who had tried most approaches (teenybop with Slik, hip with The Rich Kids, full gonzo with Thin Lizzy) before finally securing fame and fortune in the unlikely company of Ultravox, least fashionable but by far the most tenacious of all techno-bands. 'Vienna' announced the continued popularity of pomp rock. Less vulgar than its antecedents it may have been, but still it rated decorum above all things.

The exhibitionists and

rockabilly rebels apart, rock continued to look outward with increasing desperation. The dance underground, as much a part of British musical life as country and western fans in East Anglia, was dragged protesting into the light of day to substantiate rumours of a healthy strain of home grown disco music. At its best this meant Linx, a pair of youngish black blades, smart as whips and entirely conversant with the disciplines of pop. Other than that it amounted to little more than the sub-Crusaders doodling of Level 42 et al.

But more depressing by far was the moribund crudity of the punk rock reactionaries who loudly threatened to lock us all up in 1977 and throw away the key. Represented by the likes of Crass and Killing Joke in the UK and X and The Dead Kennedys in the USA, they restricted their means of expression to a brutish grunt in order to emphasise the fact that they had nothing to say but were going to repeat it endlessly nonetheless. All the qualities that most bands sought to suppress they proudly

flaunted and found a degree of stability by catering to the needs of those who sought solace in the ugly and enduring certainties of rocknoise.

The preponderance of all these secret societies, comprised of people who feel impelled to consume records but dislike music (sometimes deeply) chisels away at the very basis of pop music; a receptive audience that follows the advice of its ears.

You could even ascribe the commercial decline of Elvis Costello to something of the sort, although the slapdash nature of his live performances could be another factor. Certainly, in a climate less obsessed with identification, 'Trust' would have remained in the album charts longer than it did and 45s as marvellous as 'Clubland' would have hummed more frequently from daytime radios. 'Trust' achieved a rapprochement between sophistication, vigour and insight which few fifth albums can boast and it failed to sell.

So why do people buy records if not for the very qualities of an Elvis Costello? Or more to the point, it's possible to see how and why they purchase albums by Spandau Ballet or PiL or Killing Joke or Meat Loaf or Kenny Loggins but how and why do they listen to them? Where do they fit into their daily lives?

PHIL COLLINS

The crushing emphasis on the implications of liking this or that artist has resulted in a terrible suspicion of simple things like good tunes and good lyrics. People must have other, more concrete, excuses for liking things. This would be no more than bothersome did it not threaten the progress of bands like XTC and Squeeze and The Undertones, bands who have great songs and believe that great songs should be enough. All three of the above are rare examples of groups who emerged in 1977 and have steadily improved, groups who've survived the first fading novelty and emerged at the other side, possibly because real talent resides less in momentary inspiration than in the capacity to outrun decay. The same gulf that separates Neil Young and Stephen Stills is what sets Andy Partridge apart from Howard De Voto.

Similarly, few people would doubt that Ian Dury will bounce back from what has been a poor year by his standards with something new and worthwhile. 'Laughter', which fared poorly in the marketplace, proved to be his last album for STIFF. But after signing with POLYDOR he has renewed his collaboration with Chas Jankel and gone to work with Sly Dunbar and Robbie Shakespeare (without doubt the two most frequently dropped names of the year). Talent like Dury's does not evaporate in the teeth of adversity. It feeds and grows.

Collectors of well made songs are pinning a good deal on The Teardrop Explodes, a band whose leader Julian Cope is emerging as a fine singer and refreshingly eager writer — he at least sounds to be relishing his work. However he has to muster the conviction to make new records with the alacrity that he re-releases old ones. Of the new non-aligned bands it's possible that U2 have an even better shake because their instrumentation speaks to ears accustomed to hard rock.

Buzz-word of the year was "rockism", coined by Pete Wylie of Wah! Heat to denote all the ponderous rituals that stifle both expression and entertainment. And to be sure many bands sought to assure us of their contempt for rock and roll immediately prior to hurrying off and making sounds that were only too redolent of the last great age of emptiness, the early Seventies. All the heart-sinking paraphernalia of art without tears — the mixed media extravaganzas, the poetry readings, the strobes and dance troupes and alienation techniques — came out of the cupboard, most of it in more depressing shape than ever.

Cheap air travel meant that Manhattan continued to enjoy a special relationship with the UK. Just as Blondie and Talking Heads found a niche in this country long before most of their fellow countrymen had even heard of them, it seems more than likely that Kid Creole and The Coconuts will become this year's adopted sons and daughters. While the major part of New York's much vaunted second wave, The Bush Tetras and their like, traffic in the most tiresome of postpunk clichés, August Darnell and his polyglot extended family came out of a disco background, a

background they were by no means above debunking. More or less the entirety of 'Fresh Fruit In Foreign Places' had of course been done four or five years before by Van Dyke Parks but he had neither Darnell's chic nor his cheek. And at least the detachment of the products of the ZE label, as evidenced by Was (Not Was) and The Waitresses, was tempered by a congenial sense of humour and dedicated more to getting people to dance than simply demonstrating dance rhythms.

Ever since Elvis Presley first played the blues, country-style beat music has gone in for more eclecticism than is decent in a respectable art form. But the fact that it is a magpie medium doesn't make it any less a medium. The span of time at issue here was bounded at either end by a death. In May of 1980 Ian Curtis killed himself in the North of England. A year later Bob Marley succumbed to cancer in Florida. Both deaths were identifiably Rock Deaths and so they will go down in the books. But what did these two have in common? What would Curtis, the pale, haunted leader of a band whose two albums spoke of a terrible desperation, have to say to a Jamaican whose age, culture, background and religion could not have been further removed from his own? Would they have recognised each other as kin of a kind, even as fellow musicians? And if not, does rock amount to anything more than a way of selling things to the youth of The West?

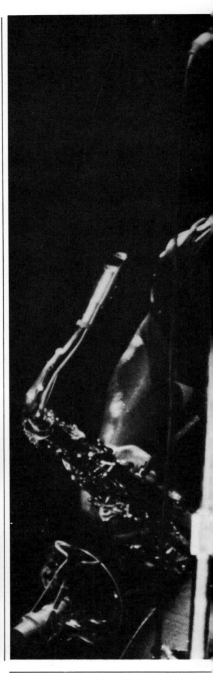

KID CREOLE AND THE COCONUTS

BRUCE SPRINGSTEEN

In a recent article Greil Marcus pointed out that rock and roll was so irreversibly splintered that it barely qualified for a definition at all, only one artist refused to recognise this fact and addressed all his work to celebrating its late spirit. Bruce Springsteen's 'The River' and the mammoth world tour that followed its long delayed release will to many people stand as The Event of the Year. Nothing else will even come close. For those who had come to regard the detachment of the Seventies as simply one of those qualities that music always had, his arrival in Britain took on the dimensions of a visit from another planet; friendly but passing strange nonetheless. At one Birmingham show he put forward the only definition of the music that made sense to him. Talking about the records he'd heard on the radio as a teenager he said, "It seemed like those singers knew about a better place — you could hear it in their voices. And it seemed like the only thing you could do was try and find that place."

Springsteen has been called a reactionary. If that is intended to point out that he swims against the tide then it's probably true. While so many have built careers on the basis of things *not* done — no solos, no guitars, no showmanship, no sentiment, no laughs, no love songs — he has shamelessly poured every last iota of his craft, enthusiasm, humour and passion into giving back to people what he himself got from the likes of The Drifters and Smokey Robinson and The Who. Which is, when you come down to it, simply a thrill.

His albums can be accused of being laboured — but trying too hard is what made him what he is — and the furniture of his songs is rarely rearranged — but then the same goes for the home we each go back to. What is plain is that nobody else either could or would have taken upon themselves the responsibility of going on stage in Philadelphia the night after John Lennon's murder and meaning every word when he said, "If it wasn't for John Lennon, a lot of us would be in some place different tonight. It's a hard world that makes you live with a lot of things that are unliveable. And it's hard to come out here and play tonight, but there's nothing else to do."

Depending on where you stand, that's either an admission of defeat or it's a declaration of faith.

DAVID HEPWORTH

ELECTRONIC

The management would like to make a little announcement. We reserve the right to refuse admission to hi-fi nuts. And SF freaks. And people who only go to the movies for the special effects. We had better establish right now that electronic music has got to pass the same tests as rock, jazz, blues, folk, classical, free, concrete, ethnic and all other musics. If you want funny noises go see 'Star Wars'. If you want atmospheric drones listen to Ligeti's 'Atmospheres' or 'Volumina' — the definitive riposte to Tangerine Dream, and written/performed without the aid of a NASA grant.

Electronic music — since we're here — should wax divine like Ellington, jump like Parker, swing like Sinatra, shock like Coleman, rock like The Stones, slice/rearrange like Beefheart or Soft Machine, evoke like The Doors or early Floyd, demand, assault and outrage like The Pistols, Joy Division, Pop Group, Material (talking of whom...).

Here, many will probably slink away to their collections of old Tangerine Dream or Tonto's Expanding Headband albums. Thank God. We've enough trouble demystifying this music without having to put up with snobs, hippies, puritans, academics and the plain emotionally under-nourished. This noise must appeal to everyone and anyone. Any Joe Blow can switch on a machine, but few can make the machine sing. We're going for the big one.

Common mythology dates the birth of electronic music as around the time when Cage started chopping up tapes, or maybe when Stockhausen started switching noise generators on. Fragments of tape unearthed recently show that it was happening — crudely — in the 1910s; specifically, in Italy. Composers and musicians like Pratella, Corra and others in the Italian Futurist movement were

YELLO

already "composing", recording and performing electronic music, employing machinery and other concrete sources. The music was, naturally, part of the Futurists' dangerously dilletante-ish glorification of the machine society — an idea which led to their espousal of and eventual destruction by Mussolini's Fascists. Disturbingly, certain aspects of the British electronic music scene have shown signs of following a parallel to the Futurists. Just how far they are prepared to go we'll return to later.

On an instrumental level, Europe can also lay claim to having produced the first electronic instrument, the Ondes Martenot, invented by Maurice Martenot in the 1920s. Depending on your point of view, it's either an overgrown tone generator or a crude monophonic synthesiser, capable of producing a wide range of tone-colours but, alas, only one note at a time. It's rarely, if ever, used these days, but can be heard in Oliver Messiaen's 'Turangalila Symphony'.

Although Europe can point to these and other facts which highlight its supremacy in the field of electronics, Europa has been resting on her laurels for a number of

years now. From the groundbreaking days of early Can, Kraftwerk, Tangerine Dream and Faust, we have reached a level where European electronics could almost be dismissed as masturbatory and indulgent.

The nigh-legendary SKY RECORDS set-up in Hamburg, home for many years of Cluster, Earthstar, Adelbert von Deyen and the solo works of Hans-Joachim Roedelius, would now seem prepared to release an album of anyone who cares to invest in a polyphonic synthesiser. Its stars still keep producing the goods, such as Cluster's recent 'Grosses Wasser' and Roedelius's 'Selbsportrait' trilogy, but these are buried in a slew of unimaginative, undistinguished albums. Having created its own market — basically, variations on Tangerine Dream and hybreds doodling somewhere between Mike Oldfield and the Systems composers like Philip Glass and Steve Reich — SKY is now bleeding it for all it's got. Like the German jazz label, ECM, which has gone in a similarly bland direction, SKY is in need of some strict quality control. There are, in fact, suggestions that SKY is losing some of its better acts to newer, stronger labels.

A definite contender for

SKY's crown is the new INNOVATIVE COMMUNICATION label, controlled by Klaus Schulze. Among its half-dozen or so initial releases are albums by Baffo Banfi, Richard Wahnfried and, notably, Popul Vuh, whose 'Sei Still, wisse ICH BIN', although poorly recorded, is a superbly evocative, dreamy album, and can stand alongside the soundtrack work they have done with film director Werner Herzog ('Heart of Glass', 'Nosferatu'). Schulze himself released 'Dig-It' a while back, generally panned by his purist fans but commendable in the way it mixes avant-garde collage techniques with the predictable synth effects.

Mention must also go to the small KUCKUCK label, home of composer Peter Michael Hamel (no relation). Approaching from a classical background, Hamel mixes classical romanticism with electronic watercolours and, unlike too many of his counterparts, manages to find something new to say about both. It would seem that many German electronic composers have a congenital urge to have their music played in lifts, and the listener is advised to enter this area with extreme caution.

It must say something about the paucity of ideas in Europe that it's the older names who are coming up with the most provocative music. Can, while the unit is in abeyance, are busier than ever on solo projects. Keyboardist Irmin Schmidt has released two albums on Can's SPOON label, the subliminal 'Filmmusik' soundtrack collection and the righteous, speedy systems album, 'Toy Planet'. Can producer and ex-bassist Holger Czukay has, of course, released 'Movies', and by the time you read this the follow-up 'Perfume', and a collaboration with ex-PiL bassist Jah Wobble (tentatively titled 'Sounds Pretty Weird to Me'!) will be out. Can, incidentally have also re-released their first six albums, from 'Monster Movie' to 'Soon Over Babaluma', on SPOON.

The biggest event of the year was, unquestionably, the re-emergence of Kraftwerk, with their European and American tours and the album, 'Computer World'. While, stylistically, 'Computer World' is no great progression from 'Man Machine', its appearance triggered off a re-appraisal of Kraftwerk, notably by such writers as the NEW MUSICAL EXPRESS's Chris Bohn. Hopefully this renaissance has put this sorely-misunderstood group's sociological conceits and squibs into their true context. Unlike their many imitators, Kraftwerk have the complexities, contradictions, achievements and failures of their culture pulsing through their far from cold blood.

There are rumours that France is cloning long-haired hippies whose first words are 'Robert Moog'. The place is bulging at the seams with acid-casualties who know how to switch on a ring modulator. Jean-Michel Jarre continues on his own sweet, dreary way, although thankfully there has been no word from brain-damaged Brit Tim Blake for quite a while. But they still keep coming. The latest prodigy to make a career out of whooping noises is Didier Bocquet ('Sequences' is his most recent). His hair reaches his backside.

France does offer us Bernard Szajner and Richard Pinhas, though. Newcomer Szajner's latest, 'Some Deaths Take Forever', is an album of awesome verve, passion and, given its chosen subject of Amnesty International's campaign against the death penalty, rage. A non-musician, Szajner has managed to come up with some of the most unsettling formal electronic music in years.

Handsome Dick Pinhas, driving force behind the late Heldon, has just formed a touring band with Heldon co-hort Patrick Gauthier and the rhythm section from Magma. Although his latest studio outing, the travelogue 'East — West', sounds a mite flash and mechanical, when caught live in Paris Pinhas's band set fire to Montparnasse and posed a serious threat to the pan-cultural funk of Talking Heads, Byrne/Eno et al.

Although hardly known for breaking new ground in electronic music, Switzerland has just come up with Europe's brightest hope — Yello. Their debut album for The Residents' RALPH label (and that about says it all), is a crazed jumble of folk, funk and fun, owing something in style to their benefactors but presented in their own off-the-wall manner.

San Francisco's finest and weirdest still show no signs of relenting, even though some may feel that technique is getting the upper hand on spirit. 'The Residents' Commercial Album', a collection of 40 one-minute-or-less pieces, is a heady distillation of styles; movie soundtracks, Indian war dances, Gamelan music, classical chamber music, the ubiquitous 'Third Man' theme and just about everything Zappa was too scared of doing. After 'Eskimo', this particular box of chocs struck many as rather too sickly, but their next douching of American culture is awaited with interest.

The Residential empire grows apace, with releases (although not strictly electronic) from Snakefinger, Tuxedo Moon, MX-80 Sound and Fred Frith. Snakefinger's rockier eccentricities work on a more humane level than his employers'; sadly, after their brilliant debut, 'Half Mute', with 'Desire' Tuxmoon seem to have slipped into gross parody (before, it was merely hinted at, not chucked at the listener); Frith is producing stronger, varied and more accessible music than at any time in his career with Henry Cow. As for MX-80 Sound, to these and many other ears, they sound like a heavy metal band with — you guessed it — funny noise.

With Wendy (nee Walter) Carlos keeping a low profile these days — she has been seen around the international music fairs and festivals — and Malcolm Cecil off with Stevie Wonder, you have to turn to America's new wave to find good electronic music. Larry Fast, he of Synergy and the excellent electronics on Peter Gabriel's third album, attained audiovisual canonisation recently, on the videotape 'Odyssey'. Perhaps predictably, the computer visuals induce eyestrain, but Fast's flaccid warblings fail to strain anything — bar, that is, your wallet.

Help is at hand, though, in the shape of young bands like San Francisco's Units and NY's Our Daughter's Wedding. The former, especially, produce a dizzying, multi-referenced dance music — akin, almost, to Britain's Human League or BEF. Their

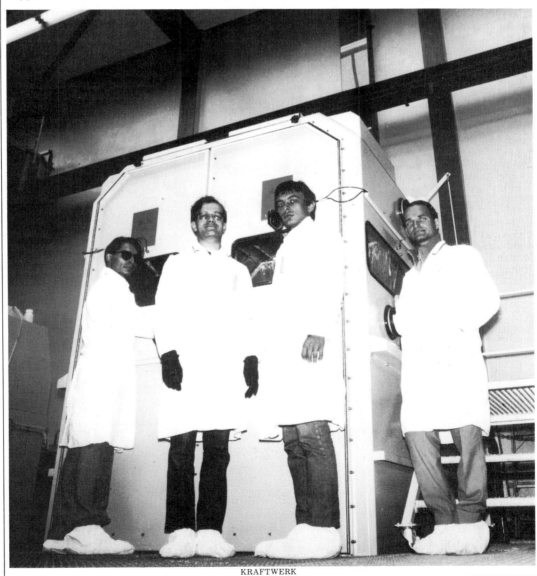

KRAFTWERK

DAVID BYRNE/BRIAN ENO

debut album, 'Digital Stimulation', takes inspiration from Africa, Bali and your average jukebox, and offers what must be America's first party-time electronic album.

Interestingly, the bands originally termed "electronic" — Pere Ubu, Devo, et al — now dismiss the term or connection, Pere Ubu vehemently so. Even Suicide, considering Alan Vega's recent r'n'b sleaze album, would seem to have left the genre. One new wave band who, while being unconnected, deserve honorary ambassadorship to the genre are NY's Material. Basically a hard-funk band, putting the punk into bebop, harsh volcanic electronics play a large part in Material's dance terrorism.

If you ever wondered what happened to the spirit of the Gong/Matching Mole et al axis of the early Seventies, look no further than RANDOM RADAR RECORDS of Maryland. Again, the bands revolving around the RADAR beacon aren't specifically electronic, but improvisational electronics contribute to the sound of Mars Everywhere,

The Muffins and the albums of Steven Feigenbaum and Tom Scott (no relation).

One brave, if demented, figure, who is still holding dear the memory of Dada, is Boyd Rice. Based in Santa Monica, and linked with the LA Free Music Group, Rice is a non-musician and actually admits some of his music is unlistenable. But his album 'Boyd Rice', is a priceless example of bravery in the face of a hostile audience. It consists of several tracks of free noise, electronics, and concrete sounds, sped up and slowed down, which, like some of La Monte Young's pieces, can be played at any speed. Depending on the speed you chose, it can either sound like a racket or inspired aleatoric experimentation.

Britain is flooded with electronic music — from the chart-topping inanities of Gary Numan, through the academic experiments of Eno, to the avant-garde outrages of Throbbing Gristle. And even that leaves out the garage-recorded tapes released almost daily by DIY musicians. Not unnaturally,

Britain/London acts as a focus for world electronics; luring bands like Germany's Deutsche Amerikanische Freundschaft away from their home country to live in London, giving support to foreign musics (such as Japan's extraordinarily large electronics scene) and, while not always being just or fair, encouraging its own electronics. British listeners and critics have also championed the likes of The Residents or Can in their earliest/darkest hours, and brought to light such rarities as the groups evolving around Tokyo's Ylem Multi-Media productions.

Yet in Britain electronic music is rife with factionalism, often involving opposition within the same tribe. Gary Numan and Ultravox are (perhaps rightly) the unacceptable face of populism. The amoebic division of The Human League into The Human League and British Electric Foundation are the acceptable side. Throbbing Gristle won't talk to either side, although Daniel (The Normal) Miller feels at home

in either camp.

Neither side is right, nor can any of them claim a patent on electronics (although they all try, and keep on trying). More than anywhere else in the world Britain has the opportunity to define the qualities of electronic music, and put it into its proper perspective. Most blow it.

There is something rather unhealthy about the Numan phenomenon; a mindless, degraded music that can't even be defended by the admittance of commercialism, and a lyrical canon which makes a spectacular mess of plagiarising Burroughs, cybernetics, future-shock and totalitarian imagery. Numan is a paradigm of the dangerous idolisation of the machine — his brief career has the unmistakeable air of spiteful misanthropy about it, and he doesn't seem to have the brains to control the confused morality of his work. Unlike his predecessors, Ultravox and Kraftwerk, who saw the parallel inevitability of this clumsy update of Futurism, Numan opened a Pandora's

THROBBING GRISTLE

box of unpleasant allusions and images for his many imitators and followers to play with.

The other half of this loveless universe is "New Romanticism" (sic), potential victims of Numan's apocalypse who respond to the threat by throwing themselves into decadence, taking as their precedents pre-war Berlin and Jay Gatsby's America. Thankfully, without exception its exponents — such as Visage, Landscape — produce music so devoid of any moment that pretty soon they'll all be picking up guitars again. The fop flagship, Spandau Ballet, have already done so, and have said they want nothing more to do with synthesisers.

Far more admirable are the humane commercialists such as The Human League and BEF — the League's 'Travalogue' and BEF's 'Music For Stowaways' are both sterling examples of progressive, responsible electronic pop, whether they're singing about dancing or world politics.

One could even extend that to the nightmares of Throbbing Gristle, whose provocative art-attacks work on the basis of "If it hurts it must be doing you some good", and confrontationists Deutsche Amerikanische Freundschaft, whose Nietzchian music and imagery is an attempt to shock the listener into some moral stand (this, incidentally, camouflaged as dance music). One this note, due recognition must be given to Manchester's The Passage, who also offer an alternative to Numan's nightmare, and do so against a backdrop of predominantly electronic music, drawing from both avant-garde and popular sources.

It may seem odd that a note of morality has crept into a music previously notorious for its lack of feeling, but a brief anecdote may point out the opposing forces at work here. One of the dozens of small British electronic outfits working at present is called Whitehouse. Masterminded by one William Bennett, it also goes under the name of Whitehouse, or sometimes the Come

Organisation. Its latest album, 'Dedicated To Peter Kurten' (ie: the murderer who inspired Fritz Lang's 'M') includes such titles as 'Pissfun', 'Pro-Sexist', 'Rapeday' and 'Ripper Territory'. Some of these tracks were originally dedicated to Peter Sutcliffe, the "Yorkshire Ripper", until Mr Bennett was advised to change the title...

On the egghead front, Eno gave us his collaboration with David Byrne, 'My Life In The Bush Of Ghosts', borrowing heavily from the work of Holger Czukay (as Eno has, apparently, admitted), and collage artist supreme, David Cunningham, finally released the second Flying Lizards album, 'Fourth Wall'. Here, too, you can spot similarities with Czukay's improvisational collage music — although Cunningham's style is purely his own, and is a lively antedote to Byrne/Eno's rather academic outing.

Unquestionably the weirdest British release of the period was the debut from Portsmouth duo, Renaldo & The Loaf, 'Songs For Swinging Larvae',

released, tellingly by RALPH. Sounding not unlike an Anglophile version of their West Coast counterparts, Renaldo & The Loaf do for British musicology what The Residents do for American musicology.

It would be impossible to enumerate every single electronic release/event around the world, known or unknown, here. But the ultimate criteria for judging electronic music must be quality, and where commended, all the above mentioned have it. In their own individual ways, they move electronics out of the twin ghettos of academe and novelty, and help electronics establish itself in the mainstream. That's not to say it's all instantly accessible — some of this requires a lot of patience from the listener — but these examples prove that electronics can lay claim to the same verities, emotions, values and qualities as all other musics. If anything, we can now say that electronics have broken free of the laboratory and moved into the lounge. Where it belongs. JOHN GILL

SOUL/DISCO

In these pages a year ago I discussed the widening gulf between the disco scenes of the American and British sides of the Atlantic, and also the even more noticeable divergence between the music of the US club scene and the mainstream of soul music which had traditionally been its staple diet. 1980/81 saw nothing happen to reverse this trend; in fact, the way things are going, 'The Rock Yearbook 1983' may well need completely separate 'Year In Music' sections for soul and disco — it could be that they will scarcely have anything in common any more.

The 79/80 trend in American discos was towards formularisation, apparently

LINX

aimed mainly at dancing hordes of gay whites who had become the backbone audience of the trendsetting clubs. Producers and DJs played games with mixes, remixes, and endless rejiggings of a basic rhythm pattern. Black dance music in its straightforward form was generally out in the cold, and the soul genre as a whole responded by ceasing to automatically pander to disco sound fashions. In Britain, the club scene was completely different, with a more adventurous attitude by both DJs and their punters, but the staple diet was not a formula disco beat, but the more flexible rhythms of jazz-funk.

To some extent, this

LANDSCAPE

SPANDAU BALLET

overview still holds true twelve months later. However, through the first six months of 1981, a new musical force has burst upon the disco scene which owes less to the original wellspring of black dance music than do either producer-generated disco or jazz-funk. Futurism, electronic dance music, the New Romantic movement, or whatever else may be this week's fashionable name for it, owes little to America at all, but is consciously European in origin and prevailing feel. It is a glamourised revitalisation of the heavily electronic and synthesised, metaphysically-inclined music which has characterised the serious end of the rock spectrum in

Continental Europe (and noticeably Germany) for around a decade now. British and American audiences have traditionally shunted the bulk of this aside under the crowded label of "Euro-Rock" or "Krautrock", reserving commercial acclaim for occasional forays by acts of the calibre of Tangerine Dream or Kraftwerk.

Seeping into the British new wave movement via highly electronic bands like The Human League, the European influence has sired the new UK breed of electronic Futurists, bands like Spandau Ballet, Duran Duran, Landscape and Classix Nouveaux. As well as oozing style and fashion, their silicon chip syncopations happened to be excellent dancefloor material; disco DJs began to feature Futurist nights as a change-of-pace from the normal jazz-funk fare, and it was not very many moons before Futurist clubs and wholly Futurist or electronic-oriented DJs appeared to satisfy the dance needs of the suddenly active of New Romantic rock fans.

Futurist rock has not yet come to the attention of the majority of America's record buyers or, presumably, its radio stations, but it is making its mark with ever-increasing rapidity in discos west of the Atlantic, where the dreaded formula is being broken up everywhere by an almost epidemic fervour for British imports — dance-orientated New Wave and Futurist music. BILLBOARD magazine's disco top 100, compiled from club and DJ returns, listed some 25 electronic New Wave Britishers among its ranks recently. This is all based on imported UK records serviced to pools of DJs by a couple of specialised disc promotion organisations; when the Futurists start to get widespread US release through the record companies, this could be the foretaste of another British musical invasion with a capital computer-printed "I".

All of which has nothing to do with soul or black-orientated music at all, and further emphasises my original point that the once interchangeable disco/soul genres have reached at least decree nisi stage in divorce proceedings. Significantly, much of the best (and most successful) black music made during the year was designed to sweeten the ears or tug the heartstrings rather than to get the feet moving, while the uptempo soul hits were often characterised by a tight, sophisticated brand of funk — as exemplified by Kool And The Gang, whose 'Celebration' was America's only double-platinum (two-million selling) single of the period under review.

Britain, in spite of the challenge of Futurism in the clubs, has actually witnessed a revolution in black-orientated music during the last twelve months, in the sudden rise to commercial success of a whole movement of home-grown soul and jazz-funk talent. In a manner characteristically British, in that it parallels the similar beginnings of punk and new-wave rock, this revolution started through small, independent grass roots labels, set up for the most part either by the acts themselves, or even more significantly by specialist black music retail outlets, whose production expertise comes largely through being steeped in their own market, recognising the kind of talent which will sell, and knowing exactly what kind of sound and material is required. This indie-scene has thrown up labels like ELITE, GROOVE, RECORD SHACK, AVES, PINK RHYTHM, ULTIMATE and EARTHSHAKER, and has introduced acts like Linx, Freeez, Surface Noise, Shakatak, The UK Players, Atmosfear and The Evasions. All of these have gone on to specialist and then national pop chart success, with many being eagerly picked up by major labels along the way. As with the first New Wave rock impetus, this rash of grassroots enterprise has acted as its own catalyst, the success of the early signings encouraging both new talent by reputation, and the labels themselves through financial reward. A new and commercially viable genre of British music has suddenly flourished here as a result, and it continues to grow. Future music historians will,

I hope, give credit where it is due, but already the major labels are aware of the value of the indie black music production houses, with EMI, for example, signing a deal with GROOVE, and ARISTA with RECORD SHACK.

To take a more detailed look at the major hit records and events in soul (or black-orientated) music through the

DIANA ROSS

period under survey by The Yearbook, we now turn to a month-by-month survey, beginning in August 1980. The two singles which were biggest both in the US and Britain were 'Upside Down' by Diana Ross, and 'Give Me The Night' by George Benson; both scored because they had appeal right across the board from soul to pop and even MOR audiences. Each was also the highlight of a chartbusting album ('Diana' and 'Give Me The Night' respectively) which was to yield in turn further hit singles. Larry Graham, formerly of Graham Central Station, had a soul chart number one and a top ten pop hit with the ballad 'One In A Million You' in America.

STEVIE WONDER

Another disc with multi-format appeal, its comparative failure in Britain is difficult to understand. We were preferring to buy hard, danceable funk at the time, as epitomised by The Gap Band's 'Oops Upside Your Head'. Released many months earlier, this funky chant gradually grew into a dancefloor anthem of such

proportions that the record finally went to number one on the disco-soul chart almost six months after first entering the listings. It also launched the hitherto specialist-appeal Gap Band into a string of UK pop successes.

Other major singles of the month included 'Backstrokin' from Fatback; Tom Browne's 'Funkin' For Jamaica', which was big in Britain some time before cracking the US: 'Dynamite' by Stacy Lattisaw; Kurtis Blow's 'The Breaks' (last major stand of the rappin' craze of some months earlier); and another ballad, 'Old Fashion Love' by The Commodores. Home-grown talent hitting the disco and pop charts in Britain included Shakatak with 'Steppin', Surface Noise and 'Dancing On A Wire', and notably Kelly Marie with the shamelessly disco-pop 'Feels Like I'm In Love', a number one hit.

September's major release was 'Masterblaster (Jammin')' by Stevie Wonder heralding his long-awaited 'Hotter Than July' album. This infectious groover was an immediate

KELLY MARIE

smash everywhere, while Stevie triumphed also in a series of British concerts at Wembley. Other big soul singles in the States were Teddy Pendergrass' 'Can't We Try'; 'Girl, Don't Let It Get You Down' by the O'Jays; and 'I've Just Begun To Love You' from Dynasty. In Britain, Randy Crawford, previously best-known here for her vocal on The Crusaders' 'Street Life', sold hugely with 'One Day I'll Fly Away'; while further big sellers were 'Big Time' from Rick James, 'Searchin' by Change, and a Euro-disco smash which had returned home with the holiday-makers from the Mediterranean discos. 'D.I.S.C.O.' by Ottawan. a new major British black act, Linx, from North London, debuted successfully with 'You're Lying'. It was first released, true to pattern, on their own AVES label, but quickly picked up by CHRYSALIS who signed the band to a deal.

A quite unexpected disco-soul smash on both sides of the Atlantic came from the unlikely source of UK glam-rock band Queen, whose 'Another One Bites The Dust' had an irresistible heavy funk rhythm and took the band to the top of both pop *and* soul charts in the US.

October was a significant month for album releases, with not only Stevie Wonder's 'Hotter Than July' finally hitting the shops, but also 'Triumph' by The Jacksons and Earth Wind And Fire's 'Faces', both of which were to sire their share of hit singles. The Wonder album was his first new studio material (excluding the soundtrack music for 'The Secret Life Of Plants') since the legendary 'Songs In The Key Of Life' nearly four years earlier. It was almost as well received critically, with items like the

FREEEZ

rolling 'Happy Birthday' (dedicated to Martin Luther King, whose birthday Stevie was attempting to have declared an American holiday) and the devastatingly simple ballad 'Lately' standing out in particular. Notable single hits at the time included Zapp with 'More Bounce To The Ounce', Michael Henderson and 'Wide Receiver' and L.T.D.'s 'Where Did We Go Wrong' in the States, while Britain bought 'Casanova' from Coffee, 'Love X Love' by George Benson, Diana Ross' 'My Old Piano'. Two more home-grown acts, Black Slate and Light Of The World, both enjoyed disco-soul top five chart placings with 'Amigo' and 'London Town' respectively; both

were released on the ENSIGN label, fast becoming a major force in UK-originated black music.

November saw the arrival of Kool And The Gang with their 'Celebrate' album and 'Celebration' single. The latter was an immediate smash in the UK, but took a few weeks to make an ascent in the US charts before

KOOL AND THE GANG

BILL WITHERS

finally becoming the band's all-time biggest seller across both the black music and pop markets. Other big stateside chartmakers were 'Love T.K.O.' from Teddy Pendergrass, The Jackson's 'Lovely One', and 'Uptown' by the controversial and overtly sexual young performer Prince. British tastes differed again, with Young and Co's 'I Like (What You're Doing To Me)', Stephanie Mills' 'Never Knew Love Like This Before' and Wilton Felder's 'Inherit The Wind' all scoring, alongside two more huge UK productions in 'Feels Like The Right Time' by Shakatak, and the chart-topping 'Do You Feel My Love' from Eddy Grant.

December's sales charts were dominated by Kool in the US and Eddy Grant in the UK, but by the arrival of the New Year competition was fierce again from both established artists and newcomers. In the former category were Aretha Franklin, who returned via ARISTA with 'United Together'; The Gap Band, who smashed on both sides of the Atlantic

with 'Burn Rubber (On Me); Heatwave and 'Gangsters Of The Groove'; and James Brown with 'Rapp Payback'. This latter cut and its parent album 'Soul Syndrome' were cut independently by Brown whilst between POLYDOR contracts. Released in the States by TK and in Britain on RCA, it was generally acclaimed to be his strongest and freshest work for years, and the single in particular lived up to this accolade with excellent soul and pop sales.

The newcomers included Yarbrough And Peoples, a boy/girl duo whose chugging and gimmicky 'Don't Stop The Music' completely took over the dancefloors and airwaves at the beginning of the year. Its impact was so strong, in fact, that it was the song rather than the act with which the public identified, and the duo have been totally lost for a comparable follow-up ever since.

Apart from Yarbrough And Peoples, February's major US soul hits included 'Fantastic Voyage' by Lakeside, 'Heartbreak Hotel' from The Jacksons (neither this nor the previous Jacksons single 'Lovely One' fared nearly as well in Britain as in the US, oddly), The Whispers' 'It's A Love Thing' and Stevie Wonder's second 'Hotter Than July' single 'I Ain't Gonna Stand For It'. Britain's significant sellers of the month were nearly all by domestic artists, most notably Freeez with 'Southern Freeez'. This London-based jazz-funk band, veterans of one minor disco hit a year previously, recorded and issued their own 'Southern Freeez' album on the indie PINK RHYTHM label, receiving such a positive feedback from the specialist market within a couple of weeks that the band were signed by BEGGARS BANQUET. The album was immediately reissued and the title track extracted as a single, to become a disco chart topper and a major pop hit following extensive airplay.

Joining Freeez in the chart came a host of other British jazz-funkers. Cloud, from Swindon, scored with the double-sided 'All Night Long'/'Take It To The Top', originally on another indie label, FLASHBACK, before being picked up by DJM's black music subsidiary CHAMPAGNE. The Inversions, on GROOVE, offered 'Mr Mack', while Light Of The World revived

'I Shot The Sheriff', and Central Line went from their own label to MERCURY with '(You Know) You Can Do It'. On ENSIGN, Light Of The World offshoot Beggar And Co debuted with '(Somebody) Help Me Out' and scored a pop crossover hit, while Spectrum with 'Takin' It To The Top' had a disco-soul top tenner for another indie label, RECORD SHACK.

New US biggies during March included 'Watching You' by Slave, 'Thighs High' from the jazz-funker trumpeter Tom Browne, and two extremely strong ballads which were to develop into two of the year's biggest pop hits a few weeks later, 'Being With You' from veteran Motown artist Smokey Robinson and 'Just The Two Of Us' by saxist Grover Washington Jr. The latter disc benefited from a guest vocal by Bill Withers, a highly regarded artist in his own right. The Whispers' 'It's A Love Thing' crossed over to Britain and shared the charts with 'Get Tough' by Kleeer; 'Can You Handle It' from Sharon Redd; The Jacksons similarly-titled 'Can You Feel It'; and Kool And The Gang's follow-up 'Jones Vs Jones'. Domestic winners included 'Tarantula Walk' from Ray Carless; The Breakfast Band with 'L.A. 14' (on another specialist indie, DISC EMPIRE); and Linx with another huge crossover winner in 'Intuition', also the title of their debut album.

April in the States belonged almost completely to Smokey Robinson and Grover Washington, with their respective albums 'Being With You' and 'Winelight' also selling hugely across the soul, pop and (in Grover's case) jazz charts. Quincy Jones arrived with a sparkling remake of a British song by Chas Jankel, 'Ai No Corrida'; Atlantic Starr reached the top three with 'When Love Calls'; white soulsters Champaign arrived with their all-formats ballad winner 'How 'Bout Us'; and A Taste Of Honey, quiet since their 1978 disco monster 'Boogie Ooogie Oogie' revived the old Kyu Sakamoto Japanese-language hit 'Sukiyaki' in a lightly funky arrangement. Stevie Wonder's 'Lately', after long anticipation, was releasd on a single in the UK and became an immediate top tenner. Stevie shared the April charts with Sugar Minott's

reggae crossover 'Good Thing Going', 'Time' by Light Of The World; UK band Level 42 and 'Love Games'; 'Hit'N'Run Lover', a traditionally styled disco record by Carol Jiani, and Eddy Grant's 'Can't Get Enough Of You'.

Smooth'n'funky soul consolidated its dominance of American black music

ODYSSEY

Whicker sound-alike intoning typical black dance music slogans with the familiar deadpan delivery — all over a killer dance track which quickly made the record one of the hottest items in British discotheques.

As 1981 approached the halfway point, Motown suddenly found itself in demand again in Britain.

through May, with the arrival of Ray Parker Jr and Raydio with 'A Woman Needs Love (Just Like You Do)'; Chaka Khan's 'Whatcha Gonna Do For Me'; 'Make That Move' from Shalamar; and The Gap Band once more with 'Yearning'. None of these had an equal impact in Britain, however, where once more home-grown acts were calling the chart shots. Freeez hit again with 'Flying High', Imagination gave the R&B label a first-try smash with 'Body Talk', Touchdown appeared on RECORD SHACK with 'Ease Your Mind', and the GROOVE label scored its biggest hit yet (and first major pop crossover) with 'Wikka Wrap', an inspired idea which featured an Alan

EDDY GRANT

After sleeping for months, Smokey Robinson's 'Being With You' finally took off like a rocket to soar to the top of both the soul and pop charts. It was closely followed by Jermaine Jackson's 'You Like Me Don't You', another early Spring release which had been sleeping both here and in the States before finally charting in the US a while before its sudden British awakening. These two were joined by Motown's current funk king Rick James, whose 'Give It To Me Baby' restored a harder sound to the upper echelons of the soul charts. Back in a ballad vein, however, Stephanie Mills dueted with Teddy Pendergrass on 'Two Hearts' to find a big seller both in the UK and America, and Motown found another surprise big seller in a six year-old track by Michael Jackson titled 'One Day In Your Life'. Upcoming mid-year US smashes also included 'Pull Up To The Bumper' from Grace Jones and the 1980 release 'Double Dutch Bus' by Frankie Smith, which had been a disco hit in Britain some months earlier

SMOKEY ROBINSON

without any US reaction. The Strikers' 'Body Language' scored healthily in both countries and made good pop chart inroads in Britain too, while undoubtedly the biggest soul record in the UK at this time was Odyssey's sizzling and celebratory 'Going Back To My Roots'. Crashing the disco-soul chart at number one a week after release, its impact was felt right across the board as it gained massive airplay and pop sales too. In a year when discos moved towards electronics and the creators of soul music *did* go back to their R&B, funk and soul ballad roots, Odyssey's success seemed refreshingly appropriate.

BARRY LAZELL

REGGAE

Any attempt to assess the reggae year stumbles when it comes to Marley's death. Reggae's view of itself has largely relied on the figure of Marley: he represented both the spiritual rebel who could give Jamaican music a place in the world and its marketplace, and the relentless critic of that world; in the end he was the only singer who really meant anything outside Jamaica. How will the music handle itself without such a vital figurehead? At the moment it's impossible to tell; there's a good chance that his absence will somehow regenerate reggae by example (*de mortuis nil nisi bonum*), and by freeing the musicians and producers from the need to emulate what The Wailers achieved. Or perhaps once the eulogies are out of the way, reggae will rumble on regardless; perhaps after all much of Marley was lost to rock music some time ago. Whichever the case, his musical legacy is enormous. The tracks he recorded for ISLAND in the Seventies are well-known; somewhat less familiar is the music he was making before that, when his mix of biblical warnings and proverbial wisdom was best served by his tunes, and by the male harmonies of Peter Tosh and Bunny Livingstone. In 1967 he made his most notable contribution to rock steady, on the short-lived WAIL 'N' SOUL

GREGORY ISAACS

BUNNY WAILER

label: 'Hypocrites', with its stunningly simple horn riff sounding like something straight from STUDIO ONE, was a catalogue of condemnation which cried out to be re-recorded. When reggae came along in 1968, Leslie Kong's BEVERLEY's label gave us 'Caution' ("...hit me from the top, you crazy mother-fucker"), and then in 1968 Marley's most fruitful period began with recordings for Lee "Upsetter" Perry and for his own TUFF GONG label. For Upsetter there was 'Duppy Conqueror', 'Small Axe' 'More Axe', while TUFF GONG presented 'Lively Up Yourself', 'Craven Choke Puppy' and perhaps the best Wailers record of all, 'Screw Face' with its arrogant boast "Not even the pestilence which crawleth by night can

do me no wrong." In the end of course it did; but as the unprecedented funeral arrangements suggested, Bob Marley won't be forgotten in a hurry.

Sugar Minott's chart success with 'Good Thing Going' (HAWKEYE) gave us all the chance to admire the gap in his front teeth on 'Top Of The Pops', and incidentally confirmed that, Marley apart, he's far and away the most popular Jamaican singer at home and abroad. Although the record had to be signed over to RCA before it got anywhere nationally, Sugar's own BLACK ROOTS label will no doubt feel the benefit eventually. It remains to be seen whether his likeable personality, level-headed ambition and sheer workrate contrive to make him a chart

regular — reggae stars are notoriously one-hit wonders. If anybody deserves better, it's Minott, but there are certain disadvantages to a career in pop; Sugar has continually made it clear that his commitment is to ghetto youth in Kingston, and that commitment won't receive delicate treatment in the chart world. Perhaps in the long run reggae's better off with the devil it knows, the reggae market with all its attendant problems and rewards. Sugar kept his standards fairly high throughout the year, although the most enjoyable record he put out was 'Ghetto-ology Dub' (BLACK ROOTS), a mere two years after the original vocal set appeared.

Reggae on stage tended to be the usual shambolic affair, although not all the problems occurred inside the hall: just in case we needed to be reminded who controlled the streets of London, the police turned out in force for Gregory Isaacs at the Rainbow, and Sugar Minott at Hammersmith Palais, and even inspected everybody's ticket at the door. Other difficulties included the familiar mismanagement, which resulted in poor Al Campbell not having time to do his top-of-the-bill spot at the Black Echoes Award Shows; short notice cancellation, which put paid to Hugh Mundell at the Rainbow; illness, which prevented Johnny Osbourne's first show at the Rainbow; and audience indifference: when Osbourne rescheduled that show, less than 300 people turned up, leaving a lot of wide open spaces in the newly-denuded auditorium. All in all it's tempting to write off live reggae, at least in large halls; I for one wouldn't be sorry to stay at home with the records.

And what about the records? After all that's what the music is really about, isn't it? There was the usual crop of oddities: Papa Tarzan apeing (sic) his namesake on 'Feeling Harty' (TOP NOTCH);

Mikey Dread's 'Master Showcase' (DREAD AT THE CONTROLS) making a mountain out of a molehill by using one rhythm throughout; Mutubaraku's 'Every Time 'A Ear De Soun' (HIGH TIMES), a strange kind of dread poetry completely unrelated to Linton Kwesi Johnson's. In the end, though, their novelty wears out and you look for more solid musical virutes to remember the year by. Lee Perry's 'Blackboard Jungle' (CLOCKTOWER reissue) has been a legend since the day Perry pressed only a few hundred copies in 1972; it was the first stereo dub album, and in 1981 its outstanding feature is its simplicity, nearly all bass-and-drum, with just a trace of echo. Like that other dub pioneer, Herman's 'Aquarius', 'Blackboard Jungle' shows us how to enjoy dub austerity, when listening to most other dub albums is like clawing your way through booby-trapped treacle. A couple of other dub LPs were just about worth the effort: Coxsone's 'African Rub A Dub' (STUDIO ONE) and Pablo's 'Rockers Meets King Tubbys In A Firehouse' (YARD), not as momentous as the previous confrontation between the two teams, but easily bearable. Pablo also produced one of the year's best vocal LPs, Te-Track's 'Let's Get Started' (MESSAGE). Other good vocal sets were Johnny Osbourne's 'Truths And Rights' (STUDIO ONE), the best of far too many Osbourne records; and, most surprisingly, 'Bunny Wailer Sings The Wailers' (ISLAND), in essence a pretty pointless exercise but somehow successful. After years of being available in a really horrible pressing, 'Studio One Presents Burning Spear' (STUDIO ONE) was at last pressed so that you could hear the music; it's the best vocal group record in reggae, so this new issue (even though it was slightly remixed à la syndrum) does no harm at all. TROJAN's best effort was 'The Upsetter Collection', side one of which featured chugalongaScratch instrumentals like 'Cold Sweat' and 'Django Shoots First', while side two mixed straightforward singing (notably 'Better Days' by The Carltons) with Upsetter's more outlandish monologues like 'Bucky Skank' and 'Cow Thief Skank'. 'The Trojan Story', a 3-LP boxed set, was reissued without having the impact it had when it first appeared in 1971; still it made a good introduction to the various phases of Jamaican music up until 1971. Black Uhuru's 'Red' (ISLAND) was pressed on red plastic, but that couldn't conceal the fact that Sly and Robbie were getting a bit predictable, not to say monotonous, in the rhythm department. Still, 'Rockstone' stood out as a convincing picture of dreads forced to make a living "Throwing rockstone upon a dumper truck...forcing jackhammers through the concrete wall".

Trying to pick out the best 45s is a thankless task; too many have faded from memory already. Barry Biggs' 'Wide Awake In A Dream' (AFRIK) was an enjoyable piece of falsetto slush while Gregory Isaacs was at his most convincing on 'What A Feeling' (TAXI), another Sly and Robbie production. Dennis Brown's 'Bloody City' (HIGH TIMES) had a lovely brass section, nicely supported by harmonica and one of Dennis' better songs, and The Heptones did a good job of updating The Gladiators' 'Roots Natty' on 'Streets Of Gold' (TOM TOM). Pride of place for the whole year, though, has to go to Cornell Campbell for his utterly dreadful version of 'Tom Dooley', called 'Banduloo' (LIVE & LOVE). While such musical atrocities are still possible, you have the feeling that even now reggae has only just begun to discover itself; can we expect to see the recorded oeuvre of the Singing Nun, for example, incorporated into the reggae canon? I certainly hope so.

In a year which saw publication of the first full-scale, if unsatisfactory, history of reggae (Sebastian Clarke: 'Jah Music': HEINEMANN), it's sad that so much of the best music made available was reissues (granted that personal preference distorts the picture somewhat). But we prophets of doom have never managed to dent reggae's self-esteem, which is all to the good of course. The flow of new music won't stop just because I get bored easily; but it's worth considering the possibility of a sort of natural life-cycle for a popular music, be it reggae, gospel, blues, cajun or whatever. The bass-and-drum sound of Sly and Robbie is barely recognisable as a development from the reggae of The Upsetters and The Dynamites, while the dub sound of 'Blackboard Jungle' might seem so rudimentary as to bear no relation to modern dub. Are we seeing reggae engaged in a struggle with itself to produce something new, or is 'Banduloo' the death croak of the music we know and love? You'll have to watch this space for latest developments in a year's time.

DENNIS BROWN

NICK KIMBERLEY

FOLK

Against the longest odds since Foinavon won the Grand National, the folk scene spent much of 1981 clawing its way back on a credible survival course.

For years the death of the club circuit has been freely predicted — not least from within the scene itself — and while the enthusiasts have fought an almost bohemian battle to preserve the folk world, with all its inherent traditions and rituals, it has steadily lost virtually all believable relevance in the eyes of the rest of contemporary music.

In the spring of 1981 it finally overcame its self-destructive lust for exclusivity and lifted a finger to help itself. Dick Gaughan, one of the most gifted and committed folk singers ever to come out of Scotland, originally suggested the idea of a national conference in a letter to ACOUSTIC MUSIC magazine the previous autumn. And it was largely due to Gaughan's reputation that the meeting ever came about and proved so exhilarating (they came and offered support from all over Britain and even parts of Europe).

The conference took place at London's Cecil Sharp House — ironically the headquarters of the English Folk Dance and Song Society, which tended to be nominated as the prime scapegoat for the scene's ills — and proved immensely entertaining if only for the relish which singers, agents, and club organisers transformed themselves into public orators. Even the floor itself was admirably raucous and uninhibited to counteract the moments of dullness.

Artists as diverse as John Martyn and the Watersons even turned out at an epic fund-raising concert during the conference, and the least that came out of it was a huge general boost in morale, seemingly through the mere evidence that so many like-minded souls actually *cared*. More practically, a national

TONY CAPSTICK

body called Perform was set up under the chairmanship of Dick Gaughan with the basic stated aims of fighting the cause of folk music wherever it can.

It's formulation has coincided with a startling upsurge in activity, from the top league to the grass roots level. Two more long-established folk acts, Fred Wedlock and Tony Capstick (both somewhat snidily regarded by the purists with the term "entertainers") suddenly found themselves projected into the strange world of Top Of The Pops and multi-figure contracts with unexpected hit singles ('Oldest Swinger In Town' and 'Capstick Comes Home' respectively). De Danann, the Irish band who made startling strides during the year with the addition of Maura McConnell, would surely have emulated them with their stirringly inventive instrumental version of 'Hey

Jude' had the single got half-decent promotion and distribution.

On the same high-powered level, there was also Steeleye Span re-forming amid a hail of cynicism that was perfectly understandable in the light of their notable failure to make much of an impact as individuals. Steeleye's reunion album, 'Sails Of Silver' was neither a triumph nor a disaster, it was merely ... *innocuous*. Much was made of their break with tradition, literally, for the album was entirely their own material; but this proved to be less of a diversion than anybody anticipated. The album scarcely nudged the best-sellers, but the band did embark on two large, relatively successful tours, in which they trotted out 'Gaudete', 'All Around My Hat' et al, and again they proved inoffensive but irrelevant.

Yet by the summer of '81,

the electric folk genre was to prove less moribund than might have been assumed. The Albion Band for a long time waved a lone flag for the music, and did it almost exclusively from the restricting confines of the National Theatre, for which Albion mainman Ashley Hutchings appeared to harbour an obsessive love. Much of the Albions' work at the National was admirable, even innovatory, marrying folk music with the theatre in an inspiring way — notably their contribution to 'The Passion' and 'Lark Rise To Candleford', which found its way on to a partially successful album released by CHARISMA at the end of 1980.

Yet their commitment to the National was a source of constant frustration to both their fans desperate to see them touring, and — one increasingly suspected — members of the band themselves. This dissatisfaction finally manifested itself publically early in '81 when all the Albion members, apart from Hutchings, quit to form their own offshoot band, which they originally titled The First Eleven, and then changed to The Home Service. Hutchings was resolute and philosophical, insisting the Albion Band had always been a flexible unit and would continue, with the comment "Where there's a will there's an Albion Band".

Any assumption, however, that The Home Service itself was merely a whim to fit in around theatre commitments, was dispelled with the news that they'd signed to the management of Jo Lustig — a signal of serious intent if ever there was one. It's still early days to gauge their chances of large-scale success, but enthusiasm at their initial gigs has been unrestrained, and the imagination and integrity of the musicians involved (including John Tams and Bill Caddick as dual front men backed by the likes of Graeme Taylor and Howard Evans) certainly

THE ALBION BAND

inspires the promise of great things. The arrival of the Home Service at the very least enlivened a dull-looking summer.

And while Albion was fragmenting so dramatically, there were even more curious goings-on in Ireland. With Planxty still consolidating the acclaim that greeted their comeback with a low-key, yet still quality album called 'The Woman I Loved So Well', rumblings of a new band emerged. Planxty members Donal Lunny and Christy Moore quietly formed a new electric band, Moving Hearts. A six-piece utilising uilleann pipes, electric guitar, drums, *and* brass, Moving Hearts were ecstatically received during their first experimental gigs in Ireland, and again expectation is massively high for them in the coming year. They insist the new band will not affect their involvement with Planxty, but you never can tell with this lot ...

There have been one or two signs, too, that the media may be wising up. Radio Two thankfully dumped the embarrassing 'Folkweave', replacing with the inestimably better 'Folk On Two' — still not ideal but wholly more current and representative. BBC television was also filming the Cambridge Folk Festival, and the combination of a (slightly) more enlightened media, the general optimism and lobbying inspired by Perform, and a rock world becoming increasingly more absurd and shallow by the second, have contributed to a greater sense of pride within the scene. The supercilious smart-ass rock press continues, of course, to despise and discredit anything remotely connected with folk music, adhering to their usual clichéd view, parading their own ignorance of the ideals and values of the scene, but still proving a large thorn in the side. The folk scene remains in crucial need of youthful innovation and vibrancy, and the mass commercial success of the likes of Fred Wedlock won't have helped any in this direction.

Perhaps, then, more relevant were the activities of one Tymon Dogg, a thin, bedraggled character with a weird wailing voice and a breathless style of playing fiddle, who's been working the folk clubs by night and playing with the Clash by day. The Clash featured him singing 'Lose This Skin' on their 'Sandinista!' album, and Ellen Foley has also recorded his material. Now *here* is a character who just may restore credibility to the folk movement.

Another renegade figure, Andrew Cronshaw also pursued a fascinating wayward path, restlessly experimental and one day surely bound to start hitting jackpots. One of his most interesting ventures was to mastermind the first solo effort by Suzie Adams of Muckram Wakes — a strange, eerie version of Kris Kristofferson's 'Casey's Last Ride'. Muckrams themselves went through a major change — shortly after releasing the gloriously titled 'Warbles, Jangles & Reeds', founder members Roger and Helen Watson quit to go their own ways, and were replaced by Keith Kendrick, from Derbyshire band Ramsbottom.

More intriguing, though, was the re-formed Kitsyke Will, who made their first official performance at the Easter festival in Poynton, Cheshire. Only Irishman Peadar Long remains from the earlier incarnation, but his vision of using traditional music as a base for merging all musics via the classically-trained Patrick Gundry-White and aggressive multi-instrumentalist Jon Burge (who broke up his longstanding partnership with Mick Ryan and membership of Crows to join) looks set to invigorate the scene to a grand degree in the year ahead.

There were various other reasons to be cheerful. The guv'nor himself, Martin Carthy, once again showed his willingness for adventure, by broadening his solo gigs and work with the Watersons to encompass yet another new band. Despite Carthy's own insistence on a low profile with the project, the occasional unit he's formed with John Kirkpatrick, again involving the use of brass, pointed another exciting way forward.

The common complaint about lack of emergent new talent was also allayed by the rise of several promising prospects. Not least were Tom McConville and Keiran Halpin, who launched themselves with a superb album, 'Port Of Call' (on Rubber) and toured the clubs to great acclaim. On some gigs they even took with them another new face, Yorkshire singer-songwriter Jon Strong, one of several artists forced to base themselves in the more lucrative market on the continent, but now beginning to be attracted back. Mike Silver, Dave Evans, and Jake Walton were others who made prodigal returns during the year.

Songwriting in general had an unexpected upsurge — possibly attributable to the brilliant work of Eric Bogle. Paul Metsers, a young singer-songwriter from New Zealand came and decided to stay, and made quite a few waves in the clubs with his clean, classy material, though his reputation had preceded him with Nic Jones' version of his classic documentary song on prospecting 'Farewell To The Gold'. The innate camaraderie of the folk scene — claimed by many to be dead — was demonstrated by the incomparable Jones himself, insisting on taking Metsers with him on his own gigs to do a set and thereby get the invaluable introduction to British audiences. It worked — Metsers is an outstanding prospect.

Initiative wasn't confined to the upstarts. Hot Vultures, who've long been shocking people with their unique approach to playing blues Farnham style, crashed through several more sacred conventions, this time also dragging along several widely respected members of the traditional fraternity. They formed an occasional group boldly titled the English Country Blues Band — merging their own Southern-blues-with-English-accents with the doyen of English rural country music, Rod Stradling. Even the extreme purists had to gulp that one down. Vultures' Ian Anderson's energy also ran to forming a new agency, absorbing many of the

clientele of the retired Jean Davenport/Jane Winder agency, and to co-editing the magnificent SOUTHERN RAG magazine, initially conceived as a shamelessly chauvinistic trumpet for the folk scene in the south of England, but which rapidly became popular all over the country, particularly in the wake of the agonising demise of the only two national folk papers, FOLK REVIEW, and ACOUSTIC MUSIC.

Stradling's own regular group, the Old Swan Band, at last saw their 'Old Swan Brand' album released on the now-mysterious FREE REED label (three years after it was recorded) and relaxed and broadened their own approach considerably, waylaying those who considered them too academic and worthy. So too did their spiritual cousins Webb's Wonders, fronted by the best singer on the planet, Peta Webb, who shook off their image as a starchy dance band and launched themselves as a club act, even claiming to be the folk scene's answer to the Monkees!

Darlington Arts Centre incongruously added a milestone in the folk revival's history, by appointing the first-ever full-time folk singer in residence. They appointed Bernie Parry to use the arts centre as a creative base for folk music, and in particular producing material benefiting and reflecting the locality. Parry took up his duties early in '81 and was quickly involved in folk operas and the like.

There were various other notable events. The sad death, in relative obscurity at the turn of the year, of Tim Hardin. He was a fringe folk artist but his songs are still widely sung around the folk clubs.

Isla St. Clair finally used

TIM HARDIN

her glamorous new connections to benefit her extensive background in folk music, with a telly series that investigated the tradition. And there was the continuing re-emergence of political awareness and commitment on the folk scene in tandem with the re-emergence of CND, who backed various folk concerts and found numerous champions, notably Steve Ashley, Ewan MacColl, Peter Bond, Leon Rosselson, and Alex Campbell, for whom 1981 represented his silver jubilee as a folk singer.

And then, there were always the festivals. It's difficult to believe the scene is in a genuine groggy state when the festivals abound so rampantly, with Cambridge again at the helm, maintaining an extraordinary record for bringing in American artists.

In August '80 the big attraction was Rambling Jack Elliott, making his first British appearance for something like 18 years, and poor Jack was seemingly overwhelmed by it all. He was so introspective he

FRED WEDLOCK

nearly disappeared into his own nervous system, forgot the words to 'Don't Think Twice It's Alright', and made youngsters in the audience wonder why he was such a legend. Cambridge also displayed their penchant for the bizarre by wheeling out Lonnie Donegan, arguably a founding father of the folk revival via his skiffle escapades in the Fifties (which ignited much of the folk club movement). Don McLean, cruising on the crest of the success of his 'Crying' single was a rather more orthodox success, while Vin Garbutt led the *real* folk singers home.

Cambridge organiser Ken Woollard showed no less imagination in 1981 with a bill that included ex-Loving Spoonful and Woodstock hero John Sebastian, Byron Berline, punk poet John Cooper Clark, the Chieftains, the Roches, and the Home Service.

And it'll be a major surprise if *they* don't figure strongly when this review comes to be done for the next year. COLIN IRWIN

JAZZ

BILL EVANS TRIO

Not so long ago, a good many younger musicians were agitatedly trying to scrape off any detectable acquaintance with jazz as if it had been something they'd accidentally stepped in on the street. In the past year, "jazz-funk" has become a respectable passport to carry around, and the New Romantics have found an appeal in earlier versions of the music that never cut much ice with hippies. Both developments look like doing jazz some good.

In the Sixties and early Seventies rock had come to symbolise not merely the sentimental frustration of shit-kicking teenagers that it had in the decade previously, but the dawning of an Indian summer in which youth and beauty would lick the system. Every sort of music wanted to sound like it. Symphony orchestras played it, ethnic musicians of all kinds played it, highbrow pundits all fell over each other to write about it. The connotations of the word "jazz" at the time — shabby, round-shouldered blokes with goatees exchanging old Lenny Bruce routines, over-technical music that made you nervous — were decidedly unhip.

But in the Eighties, quaintness is no problem, and neither is plundering the past. Just lately Landscape — a British jazz-rock band that started life at the Barry jazz school in Wales and hiked around the pubs for years — has started to clean up as an electronics and special effects outfit, and the references to traditions like Duke Ellington's are audible in the general backwash. In pop music you could always hear, though maybe years later, echoes of the sounds that gave promoters coronaries in the jazz clubs, though only recently has it been possible to deal with the identity of the music face to face. If the word "jazz" has at last acquired even a halfway contemporary meaning, then 1981 is a landmark.

But of the musicians who vanished into the billowing folds of easy listening years ago, little else has been heard. Stanley Clarke, a fine bassist who came to the fore in Chick Corea's bands and was one of the standouts of Corea's first 'Return to Forever' album for ECM, has now reduced his public performances to circus routines in which he and the pianist George Duke endlessly trade clapped-out riffs and pretend that they've only just thought of them. Herbie Hancock has handled his conversion with more flair, but he was a distinctly soul-oriented player from his early days in jazz and the transition has been almost painless. Keith Jarrett, whose voluminous over-recording has only served to demonstrate that he has more flair than vision, seems to have finally lost grip of the skill that produced the great 'Koln Concert' and produced a mystifying solo piano tribute to Gurdjieff this year, and a resoundingly awful symphonic piece called 'The Celestial Hawk' (both ECM) which seemed to subject the work of a posse of 20th century classical and pop composers to the attentions of a kind of musical liquidising machine.

Jarrett, Hancock and Corea, virtually household names by now, have performed an extraordinary Cheshire cat routine on their entire history in jazz. Having evaporated to leave only the grin, they have left behind much of that eloquence, succinctness and depth that they have all demonstrated in earlier times. They drew much of the inspiration for their best playing from the enormous contribution of Bill Evans to contemporary keyboard playing, which is why Evans' death last autumn at the age of 51 has left such a gaping hole in music.

Evans' London performances a couple of months previously made his departure all the more unexpected. A quiet, introspective man, whose bowed stance at the piano made him look as if he were staring at his reflection in a pool, Evans came to Ronnie Scott's in July 1980 with what seemed like a new lease of life. His playing, which was always more taut and sinewy than his deceptively lethargic manner usually implied, took on a bright, jubilant urgency. He even raised his head from the keyboard to cheer on the band, which was a bit like seeing a prelate at a barn-dance. The performances had all the verve and punch that you vainly sought out in the more "accessible" work of Evans' musical descendents, for whom the terror of boring the audience with what it might take to be highfalutin' notions has led to a nightmarish elevation of the cliché to the status of a popular musical vocabulary. The younger men's bank managers however, would doubtless find puzzling the proposition that such carryings-on might be a mistake.

If Bill Evans' death was the most unpleasant surprise of the year, a couple of pleasant ones came with the resurfacing of the 57 year-old bop pianist Al Haig (who Charlie Parker had described as "the best accompanist I know") and a late blossoming in the public eye for the tenorist George Coleman who is now touring again with an impact like a runaway truck.

Coleman, a Memphis hard bop player who had briefly performed with the Miles Davis band in the early Sixties, is in the Johnny Griffin mould of dazzling pyrotechnics with heart, and his music — which could have been played in much the same way virtually any time in the last 35 years — has reached an audience wider than simply the inner sanctum of jazz buffs. In fact, the reception that his band received from a crowd of Berkshire punks at the Bracknell Festival two years ago was so unexpectedly euphoric that there were even raised eyebrows on the bandstand, from a bunch of grizzled veterans who looked as if they wouldn't have

GIL EVANS

blinked if the tent was on fire. The presence of the drummer Billy Higgins in Coleman's group is a major contribution to its open, freewheeling style, and the saxophonist's repertoire of jazz evergreens never seems remotely dated because of the dazzling accompaniment of sparks that signals their journey through the forge.

This is one of the fascinating paradoxes of the music, and the reason why a hip idiom won't camouflage a lack of ideas but a style as old as the hills can sound as fresh as today's news. Coleman's record 'Big George' (AFFINITY), an octet album full of old chestnuts like 'Green Dolphin Street', bears it out. The whole thing sounds like it was born yesterday, and in a way it was.

Although jazz didn't experience any revelatory visitations during 1980/81, not everything amounted to revivalism or wall-to-wall music by any means. One of the most energetic and exciting albums of the year outside of the avant-garde was an ECM release called 'In Europe', featuring the drummer Jack deJohnette (who had worked with Miles Davis on the spacey rock excursions of the early Seventies) with John Abercrombie on guitar (a one-time Billy Cobham sideman), Lester Bowie (of the Art Ensemble of Chicago) on trumpet and Eddie Gomez on bass. Though the music advances with a loose-limbed swing, the playing of Abercrombie and Bowie (an ingenious matching, since the latter's playing is as effervescent as the former's is laconic) actually achieves a rare happy marriage of the innovations of early jazz-rock and the out-of-fame adventures of the free scene. The ECM label, though it produces more than its share of music for insomniacs, still holds an important place for its inclination to pitch together unusual combinations of players, and this set is a perfect example of it.

Black American improvised music has shown through the year that its roots in the earliest forms of jazz are not being substantially replaced by the work of European players. The latter though, continue to demonstrate a growing independence from the ideas of the Americans. A few isolated bursts of cross-

talk were heard nevertheless, notably the collaboration of the Chicago tenorist Fred Anderson with the rather severe and cerebral Austrian group Neighbours. But in general the popularity of bands like the Art Ensemble of Chicago, Old and New Dreams, and individuals like Sam Rivers, George Adams, Don Pullen, Ornette Coleman and the New York violinist Billy Bang all bore witness to a reinforcement of black traditions.

In Europe, the younger players divided more sharply into the defenders of orthodox jazz virtues (harmony, structure, strong rhythmic pulse) and the representatives of the permanent revolution. British players like John Surman, Alan Skidmore and John Taylor continued to spin out attractive variations on old shapes, and men like Harry Miller and Louis Moholo straddled the gap between straight jazz and the free scene, as did the pianist Keith Tippett. Tippett however, brought a real revelation to the London concert in which he performed opposite the Chicago trio AIR; he had clearly attacked the thorny problem of making unorthodox use of the piano's mechanism sound as interesting as the regular use of the keyboard with some success. The American Greg Goodman, who had struck up a partnership with the English free saxophonist Evan Parker on the latter's tour of the States, has come up with a lighter, more flirtatious version of the same thing.

All kinds of free music have become more readily accepted, which may at least mean that a few more creative players may be able to keep the wolf from the

MILES DAVIS

door — though it's rough luck that an easier passage for the music should have coincided with an economic slump. Free music gigs aren't the angst-ridden occasions that they used to be, in which there was more activity from members of the audience heading for the bar than there was from the stage.

Derek Paisley's 'Company', an ever-changing ensemble of improvising players drawn from America, Europe and the Far East has been an influential catalyst for change, and has done much to develop a sympathetic audience for the outer limits in Britain. The inspiration may originally have come from the public image of the music in Germany, Holland and Italy, where free playing has until recently been better financed, better promoted and better received, and where musicians who don't play blues aren't regarded as candidates for the bin. Such a configuration of improvisers from so many cultures, some more jazz-based than others, produces such fascinating results at times that you wish that bands could more frequently be formed — as Company's subgroups are — before the individuals in them have hardened their notions of what they want to play. It's not difficult to see how such unexpected developments occur when you look at the track records of some of Company's members. Jamie Muir, a percussionist who returned from a spell in a Buddhist monastery to join Bailey this year, used to work with King Crimson. Steve Lacy, the saxophonist, has appeared with Thelonius Monk and Gil Evans.

Evans, incidentally, is one of the hottest draws in the music once again, and has taken to energetically touring the globe with his band at the age of 69. Since a conspicuous slice of his repertoire includes tunes by Jimi Hendrix, and his band makes some of the most ingenious use of electric instruments to be heard in any kind of contemporary music, there's not much sign of age slowing him up. And Art Pepper, the West Coast saxophonist whose disappearance from music in the Sixties was assumed to be permanent, has kept up the stream of appearances and album releases that have accompanied a story-book return to the spotlight. The London record shop Mole

Jazz released sets by both Gil Evans and Pepper on its own label during the year, and both albums comfortably eclipsed recent recordings from the big companies. Pepper's record 'Blues For The Fisherman' (MOLE 1) was a classic example of what a contemporary idiom — in this case a kind of dapper, elegant funk — can actually add to an improvising style that was founded in much more spacious territory. Helped by terrific themes, Pepper's

ART PEPPER

slow, sensuous way of developing his solos struck an immediate chord with the punters. Some of them had probably lost track of him in the early Sixties, others had underrated his work as being just another slice of West Coast cool school music, many had never heard of him. Pepper's return to jazz, and his return in such spectacularly successful style, hitting the big-time without cheapening his playing one iota, has been one of the most heartening developments of recent times.

Over all the music hangs a huge question mark. This summer Miles Davis, who went out of circulation in 1975, promises a return to the studio and the stage and the rumours about whether he'll be able to wrench improvised music into yet another revolutionary direction or become a disco star are bouncing off the walls like squash balls. Nothing could do music more good than that this enigmatic and visionary performer, whose gifts as a trumpeter were rivalled by his genius for picking musicians with a highly-developed sense of their own time and place, should come back as an inspiration rather than a sideshow. It will be a tantalising wait.
JOHN FORDHAM

COUNTRY

Musically it has been a fairly typical year; the usual 90% that's dross — either banal, overtly sentimental, saturated in strings, or too sweet; but 10% worth an ear, including some fine new releases from established "names", and interesting recordings by bands and singers exploring the fringe areas of new country, bluegrass and western music.

For business it has been an excellent year, with the popularity of contemporary country continuing to grow while other genres have slumped. In America, sales of country albums now exceed those of pop and soul, and are second only to rock. Some record industry chiefs have even predicted that country will become the hottest music (in financial terms) of the 1980s.

It's a dramatic transition from three or four years ago, when the lawyers, accountants and business men who run the American record industry, gave country scant attention. It was the poor relation of rock; run from Nashville by experienced producers like Chet Atkins and Billy Sherrill, who could be relied upon to release a steady stream of records which would sell well, but almost exclusively to the country market of hardcore fans who lived in the predominantly rural areas of the south and central USA, and who'd been buying similar records for years.

Then came "crossover", and the company bosses in New York and Los Angeles took more notice, and started to get actively involved, pumping in extra money for promotion and recording. Artistes like Waylon Jennings, Willie Nelson and Dolly Parton had become in vogue with rock and pop fans, having "crossed over" from a genre where 50,000 sales of an album constituted a major hit, to a market where sales of half a million, or more, were possible.

Country is now the growth area of the music business. Its image has changed; there are less whining steel guitars, high-pitched nasal vocals, twanging banjos or twin fiddles. Singers and musicians have deliberately smoothed the rough edges and toned down the distinctive instrumentation. The result is much closer to rock or pop, but with a country flavour.

Record companies are confident that the boom in contemporary country will not be a short-lived fad like disco; they sight the music's long history and solid base of hardcore fans, and point to surveys which reveal Americans who buy country albums are mainly in the 25-45 age bracket, a substantial and economically

KENNY ROGERS

powerful grouping whose tastes are less fickle than teenagers'.

The boom is an exclusively American phenomenon at the moment, but it's assumed that once the music's more subtle and sophisticated image is exposed via movies, television and radio, it will be big everywhere.

Increased radio exposure has certainly boosted country sales in the US. At the last count there were 1600 stations — three times the figure ten years ago — including WKHK in New York, formerly the big jazz outlet WRVR; KHL in Los Angeles, once hugely popular for its "boss rock" format; and KSAN in San Francisco, the station where Tom Donahue pioneered progressive, free-form rock radio in the late 1960s.

A proliferation of TV shows and specials have helped make many country artistes into household names. Kenny Rogers has been particularly successful; after the runaway ratings victory of the dramatisation of his hit 'The Gambler', his work this year has included portraying a flamboyant, self-styled preacher in a telefilm inspired by the song 'Coward Of The County'.

The bearded Texan commands enormous fees for his sell-out concerts, and has continued to rack up large sales for his albums, notably the 'Greatest Hits' package (LIBERTY), which has been one of the strongest sellers in the pop, as well as country market for the

WAYLON JENNINGS

second year running.

The movie 'Urban Cowboy' wasn't a great success for the star, John Travolta, but it's done nothing but good for Mickey Gilley, who played himself in the film and is now one of the richest men in country music; making money from his records, his share of the Houston club Gilley's (now a major tourist attraction), and from his mechanical bulls — he owns the manufacturing rights, and since the film's release there has been a proliferation of country discos throughout the US, in which mechanical bucking broncs are "de rigeur".

While Nashville's Grand Ole Opry can't be challenged as the home of traditional country, Gilley's can, with some justification, claim to be the focal point in contemporary music. Willie Nelson has stopped his annual 4th July picnic at Austin, so Gilley's club has inaugurated its own, with some of the biggest names in country. Meanwhile the fully-equipped studio next to the club is used for the weekly syndicated radio show 'Live From Gilley's', and there's a growing list of artistes who want to make their albums there (Willie Nelson's chart-topping 'Somewhere Over The Rainbow' (CBS) being one of the first to prove the studio's worth).

Interest in Gilley's has brought country fans flooding into the Texas city and boosted the live music scene, which was already one of the liveliest in the US. There are more than a dozen authentic honky-tonks (and several others with plush carpets and chandeliers, for the sophisticated folks who like the music but not the fans!), including Johny Lee's, a Gilley's spin-off, and Moe and Joe's which is owned by Moe Bandy and Joe Stampley and features a mechanical armadillo.

Honky-tonk "outlaw" music is big business in Houston, and Waylon Jennings and Willie Nelson can command as much money as anyone for appearances there, but they're no longer the innovative musicians who changed the face of country back in the mid-Seventies. All sense of adventure and recklessness seems to have gone from their work.

Willie hardly writes any original material these days, and has turned to middle-of-the-road standards for his material. He still has an enormous following, and 'Somewhere Over The Rainbow' (which included a version of 'Twinkle, Twinkle Little Star') was one of the year's biggest sellers.

Waylon is still singing about cowboys and such, but now sounds tired and bored, perhaps because he's trapped with a style he no longer likes but which continues to make him money — his 'Greatest Hits' LP (RCA) has been high on the charts for nearly three years. A duet album with his wife Jessi Colter, 'Leather And Lace' was one of the most disappointing releases of the year.

The best renegade music these days comes from Hank Williams Jnr., whose career changed direction dramatically after a near fatal accident on a mountain in 1975. Instead of singing the songs made famous by his legendary father, he's developed his own progressive style; writing and singing with a disarming honesty and frankness. The album 'Rowdy' (ELEKTRA) finds him in top form displaying a varied mix of lyrical themes, from spitting venemous hatred at trendy urban cowboys, on 'Texas Women', to mourning the loss of romance on 'You Can't Find Many Kissers'.

Bobby Bare, an original outlaw from the Nashville "system", in terms of demanding and winning independence in choosing his own songs and musicians, has continued to upset many country traditionalists. 'Drunk And Crazy' (CBS) followed last year's successful 'Down And Dirty' with more irreverent songs from the pen of satirist Shel Silverstein. With titles like 'I've Never Gone To Bed With An Ugly Woman (But I've Sure Woken Up With A Few)' and 'Drinkin' And Druggin' And Watchin' TV' the album has something to upset all but the most broad-minded listener. Aware that he might have gone too far, Bare has followed those LPs up with a more conventional release, 'As Is' (CBS), a collection of songs by some of the finest new country writers including Guy Clark, Townes Van Zandt and Ian Tyson.

It's been a good year for both Johnny Cash and George Jones, two of the most respected and revered singers in the business. Cash was elected to Nashville's prestigious Country Music Hall Of Fame (a rare honour for someone who's still alive), receiving his award from Kenny Rogers who told him, "There are a lot of people who sing country music, there are only a few who are country music."

He made a strong album titled 'Rockabilly Blues' (CBS) which recalled his pioneering days at Sun Studios in Memphis 26 years ago; and was involved with the enterprising 'Jesse James' concept album (A&M), based on the life and death of the southern outlaw, which also featured Emmylou Harris, Charlie Daniels and Levon Helm, and was written by a talented young English writer and singer, Paul Kennerley.

Like Johnny Cash, George Jones's life and career has had several ups and downs

since he started making records back in the Fifties. Overcomng all manner of personal problems, he's now back at the top again, winning the CMA Best Male Vocalist of the Year award, and releasing one of his finest albums to date, 'I Am What I Am' (EPIC).

Because so many country artistes stay at the top so long there are few openings for newcomers, but two who've "broken through" this year in a big way are Terri Gibbs, a blind singer from Augusta, Georgia, whose single 'Somebody's Knockin'' (MCA) was one of the biggest crossover hits of 1981; and Razzy Bailey from Alabama, whose successful middle-of-the-road style combines a mixture of the "outlaw" sound, with the smoothness of a Kenny Rogers. He's the personification of contemporary country pop.

JOHNNY CASH

Two girls who "broke through" a couple of years ago have consolidated their positions near the top with engaging new albums; Lacy J. Dalton, whose vocal style recalls a country Janis Joplin, released the energetic 'Hard Times' (CBS), and appeared in the movie 'Take This Job And Shove It' (based on the David Allen Coe song); while Gail Davies, who has a folksy, softer style, and who's broken Nashville's traditionally sexist recording barriers by producing her own albums, scored with 'I'll Be There' (WARNER BROS).

Emmylou Harris personifies another area of country music, leading the musicians who are striving to create something different from the "Nashville sound", but are also conscious of country music's roots (which many of the "crossover" artistes have all but abandoned). Two years ago

Emmylou won awards galore for her two pure-country albums 'Blue Kentucky Girl' and 'Roses In The Snow', but anyone expecting a similar release this year were in for a shock.

'Evangeline' (WARNER BROS) ran a guantlet of styles, from the Forties pop sound of 'Mr Sandman', to the country-rock of 'Hot Burrito No. 2'. After vainly trying to get Emmylou to make more rock-orientated albums in the past, her record company were appalled when she chose this year to change style — "At a time when country music is at its most accepted, this is my least country album," she explained, "But I'm not going to make any apologies for it."

Emmylou's strong stand for "doing things her own way" has inspired and helped others, like Rosanne Cash. She's married to Rodney

GEORGE JONES

Crowell (who used to work with Emmylou), and he's produced her excellent 'Seven Year Ache' (CBS – USA, ARIOLA – Europe), a successful country album made in California with musicians who were once with Elvis Presley, then Emmylou, and are now Crowell's Cherry Bombs.

They are also featured on Bobby Bare's 'As Is' and Guy Clark's superb 'South Coast Of Texas' (WARNER BROS), again with Rodney Crowell producing. Not a big country seller, because Clark's growly vocals and unusual songs don't seem to have commercial appeal, but a rough diamond that bears repeated plays.

Guy Clark is perhaps fortunate to have the support of a major record company. Most of the imaginative, but uncommercial musicians on the fringes of country are struggling along without a contract, making their own records, or are signed to

small independent companies like SUGAR HILL, ROUNDER and FLYING FISH, three of America's most eclectic labels, who seem more concerned with making good music than money.

Deep in the heart of Texas, friends of Joe Ely have continued to release unusual home-made albums. Butch Hancock's third LP, 'Diamond Hill' (RAINLIGHT) is his most commercial and accessible offering to date, though he's still too lyrically adventurous for most major record companies to consider touching with a barge pole.

Similarly Terry Allen, the painter who enlivens his one man shows at art galleries with live performances on piano and vocals, in an eccentric honky tonkin', rock 'n' roll style. 'Smokin' The Dummy' (FATE) continues where last year's promising 'Lubbock (on everything)' left off; more songs about truck driving, waitresses and Lowell George.

Peter Rowan has been the new country cult figure of the year; a mandolin virtuoso who worked for a time with Bill Monroe's bluegrass band, spent time with Jerry Garcia and members of the Grateful Dead, and was part of a mediocre country-rock band with his brothers, The Rowans; he's now brought all the diverse music he loves together, and launched a solo career with a trio of refreshing and envigorating albums, 'Peter Rowan' and 'Medicine Trail' (FLYING FISH) and 'Texican Badman' (APPALOOSA). Rowan mixes folk, country and western, bluegrass and Mexican music, and plans to extend his repertoire still further. He's one of the most eclectic figures in any musical area, and his influence on progressive country music is likely to be enormous in the future.

Finally, the most surprising revival of the year has been inspired by a Nashville based trio called Riders In The Sky, who think it's time that country was reunited with western.

Their debut album, 'Three On The Trail' (ROUNDER) recalls the best of Roy Rogers, The Sons of the Pioneers and Gene Autry, before the singing cowboy era went stale in the early Fifties. They revive the old songs and write authentic originals, and their live show is a revelation. RICHARD WOOTTON

BLUES

An expatriate Englishman writes from Memphis with what purports to be a photograph of Robert Johnson. A Texas record dealer advertises for sale the first known copy of one of the world's rarest blues 78s, a 1931 Paramount with Skip James on one side and Son House on the other. Evidently 1981 is going to be remembered at one level of bluesmanship.

But what of the singers still active, and the records still well this side of the thousand-dollar mark?

The world of blues musicians and their audiences is one in which news travels slowly and reputations are hard won. The Chicago label ALLIGATOR has put out three more volumes (4 — 6) in its 'Living Chicago Blues' survey (available in Europe on SONET), but they are scarcely showcases of new young talent. Each of the nine bandleaders featured has served years apprenticeship, and only one of them is, and only just, under 40. That one, as it happens, is a woman, Sylvia Embry. She's one of the few women singing straight blues these days, and does it assertively and well. Many of the others lately added to this illuminating, but in this respect faintly depressing, series are men who have long played second string to better-known artists: A.C. Reed with Albert Collins, Lacy Gibson with Son Seals, Luther "Guitar Junior" Johnson with Muddy Waters. It's good that they are getting these breaks, and it confirms the continuity of Chicago blues tradition, up to a point, but where are the younger men? *Are* there younger men?

One at least we do know of, Lurrie Bell, guitarist and son of the established harp-player Carey Bell, and lauded in these pages last year. He makes an appearance in the 'Living Chicago Blues' set, though a modest one, backing pianist Lovie Lee, and British aficionados had a chance of seeing him on a blues tour

SON SEALS

recently. As encouragement this is not exactly fulsome, but it has never been easy to move up fast in Chicago.

The inching-along progress of Son Seals to something like fame illustrates what I mean — and his latest recording, 'Chicago Fire' (also ALLIGATOR/SONET) maintains it but does not enhance it. As often with albums on this label, the outstanding track is a long slow blues in a minor key — label-boss Bruce Iglauer admits to a weakness for them — and if the whole LP were like 'Leaving Home' we might be contemplating a considerable achievement.

As for Muddy Waters, he too has an album out, 'King Bee' (CBS-BLUE SKY), produced as usual by Johnny Winter, and really not much different from the last few. Proud, dominating, energetic: all of that. Muddy continues to run, and to hold together, one of the toughest bands in Chicago. But there are limitations in recycling one's own past hits, and it isn't clear that Muddy can make many more records cut from this cloth, however hard-wearing it may be.

The other vanguard artists from Chicago have been productive to less effect. Buddy Guy and Junior Wells turn out records from time to time; it's usually difficult to get very excited about them. Not long ago, for instance,

they helped a new French label, ISABEL into being. First we had Buddy Guy; then Junior Wells, featuring Buddy Guy. Taking heart from this ingenious approach, the company then rounded up a team of second-line Chicagoans on Eurotour. First they recorded pianist Johnny "Big Moose" Walker with Willie James Lyons on guitar. Then Lyons, with Walker. Then Lefty Dizz, with both of them. The same rhythm section attended throughout, and five-sixths of the three LPs were recorded on a single day. Even the notorious taskmasters of the bad old days never stretched their employees this far, for the good reason that the results would have been, as they prove to be here, uninventive and lacklustre.

An undistinguished platoon going by the name of the San Francisco Blues Festival visited Europe also, and was caught by another new French label, PARIS ALBUM. The most impressive name on the bill was that of Texas pianist Little Willie Littlefield, a sometime boogie practitioner of great charm, and a pleasant smoky singer. But his solo LP for this company was a sad travesty. Apart from one low-down blues track, 'Dirty', enormous tracts of album-time were devoted to vacuous courtesies on the theme that it's great

to be in Paris in the spring, tinkle tinkle. Very cosmopolitan, no doubt, but we've had Champion Jack Dupree over here for ages dong that sort of thing. The best compliment a visiting blues musician can pay a foreign audience, if it's music we're talking about, is to take no account of their foreignness.

Europe, however, has a habit of indulging performers' miscalculations, even encouraging them. It is interesting and alarming to see the generous response earned by the latest of the Lippman-Rau travelling blues caravans — an uneven a bunch as has ever flown under that flag, and featuring several artists of well-defined mediocrity. Lippman and Rau have also expanded from promotion into recording, by all accounts disastrously. (Or nearly so. A couple of J.B. Lenoir sessions, recorded in Europe in the Sixties have been released, and these at least would need no apology.) Risking jingoism, one would have to say that recent Continental activity has yielded one of the most artistically barren programmes of recording that has afflicted the blues in its lifetime.

Stands England as she did, flagship of the reissue armada (and a pirate no longer)? Actually, yes. Even if you believe that any fool can repackage the old stuff, while it takes real wit to produce the new, you would have to allow that there are divine fools at work amongst the indies these days. The recent rosters of CHARLY, FLYRIGHT and ACE are playgrounds for any bluesfan who's only a generation or so out of step.

CHARLY, under Cliff White, have been reanimating the corpses of a few fine old catalogues, especially Chicago's VEE JAY — whence the new compilations of Jimmy Reed, John Lee Hooker and Elmore James. There are two by each, and the Elmore James stuff is most of his finest work. Also, slightly more adventurously, they have LP'd-up a scattering of 45s and unissued items by Eddie Taylor, great Chicago sideman and, unlike many such, a damned good leader on his day. Other desirable issues: a fine T-Bone Walker set from the Forties and a curious relic of blues psychedelia, Lowell Fulson's celebrated 'In a Heavy Bag' album from 1970 (retitled 'Man of Motion'), which undeniably retains a peculiar charm. Their sleeve designer, Hamish, has done idiosyncratic and excellent work on this series, and so far as selection goes even the most stiff-necked of collectors would be forced to approve them.

As well as pushing ahead with their 20-odd-volume series of Louisiana recordings from the Jay Miller vaults, FLYRIGHT (c-in-c: Bruce Bastin) have extricated the fabulous COBRA and JOB catalogues and put out albums of J.B. Lenoir, Johnny Shines and Robert Lockwood (separately, that is — and including all that exists of the superlative Shines 'Ramblin'' session) and a harmonica anthology, 'King Cobras', leading light of which is a riveting Sonny Boy Williamson track, 'Steady Rollin' Man', made out of nothing more than voice, harmonica and string bass. JOB and COBRA were primary outlets for hard blues in the Fifties, and these compilations do them all the necessary honours.

One fleeting caveat, though, about some of this sort of records, and I am singling out no label in particular. The purpose of reissues should be to rehearse past glories: occasionally you feel that compilers are glorying in past rehearsals. Does the majority of blues listeners really welcome a prefab of false starts, multiple takes, half-comprehensible studio chatter and talkback? Some of the recent reconstructions of 25-year-old sessions have had to be noticeably stretched to make respectably timed LPs. It isn't as if we're dealing with the cumulative inspiration of a Charlie Parker take-series — more, a simple sequence of trying to get things right and taking a bit of time to do it. It all rather whips up nostalgia for those older compilations, doubtless now deleted, which could draw only upon material judged good enough to be issued commercially in the first place.

ACE (the moving spirit here seems to be Ray Topping) have now and then been guilty of resuscitating rejects, but they've also taken the self-protective step of putting a lot of them on to mid-price 10-inch LPs with charmingly tacky sleeve artwork, which disarms a good deal of criticism. The West Coast artists are particularly rewarding: Little Willie Littlefield (two volumes), Jimmy McCracklin, and, well above all, the little-known shouter Jimmy "T-99" Nelson. This unassuming record is an extraordinary shot in the arm: a sturdy singer, yes, and stout band backings, all right, but what absolutely first-rate songs! Also on ACE are decent collections of early Elmore James (prior to the CHARLY period), early John Lee Hooker (likewise) and early B.B. King. Also the Memphis oddball Rosco Gordon, a sort of crypto-New Orleansian singer/pianist and, apparently, a heady influence at the genesis of bluebeat.

The definitive catalogue of postwar West Coast blues and R&B, however, remains the Swedish ROUTE 66 label's — and now, with almost a score of releases to their name, they can fairly be said to have put the far-west blues scene as clearly on the map as Chicago's. Their latest efforts range through Charles Brown, Ivory Joe Hunter, Ruth Brown, Jimmy McCracklin, Floyd Dixon (some of these are Volume 2s), Bull Moose Jackson and Jimmy Liggins. When this

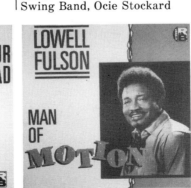

SLEEVES DESIGNED BY HAMISH

subtle idiom earns the tribute (or millstone) of copyists, as one day it must, the ROUTE 66 catalogue will be their bible, or Baedeker.

Now for a few isolated but bright beacons along the 1980-81 blues horizon. The reputation of Robert Nighthawk, a backroom maestro of slide guitar, was established for good with the release, on ROUNDER, of a blistering open-air session, recorded live in Chicago's Maxwell Street junk market in 1964. The atmosphere is credible, the playing fiery — and this is not a term you would expect to utter about this normally rather austere musician. The elegant St. Louis bluesman Henry Townsend broke a several years' silence with an album, 'Mule' (NIGHTHAWK), which if not thrilling was deeply satisfying — and rather unusual, too, for not only were many of its contents newly written blues, but many also presented Townsend as a pianist rather than a guitarist. This is a development that has been coming gradually, but all the same it's not common for a veteran to reshape his approach so.

Some bankable names were not much seen on the market. YAZOO's only contribution to the year was a double album by the Memphis Jug Band. But some hallowed names could be hallo'd again: ORIGIN, seminal country blues reissue label of the Sixties, suddenly swept back, potent and mysterious as ever, like a Garbo out of retirement. They casually dropped a Peg Howell LP — invigorating black stringband music from the Twenties — and a Lonnie Johnson. They also went, improbably, Modern, with an album from a Sixties Fred McDowell session, and, incredibly, White, with a release of a Thirties Western Swing Band, Ocie Stockard and The Wanderers (in effect Milton Brown's band *post* Milton's *mortem*).

There was not much more for the blues historian other than a couple of sets from the Dutch label AGRAM: guitarist Scrapper Blackwell and pianist James "Stump" Johnson. As hitherto, scratchy but useful.

MUDDY WATERS

Storming one of the last Bastilles of obscurity in black music, Nashville discologue Doug Seroff set to work telling the world about gospel quartet music. 'Birmingham Quartet Anthology' on the CLANKA LANKA label (you will have to get it to find out why the name) is a sumptuously presented 2-LP set of Alabama gospel groups like the Famous Blue Jays and the Heavenly Gospel Singers, ranging over 30-odd years of recording. Such quartets were the architects of the tradition that later bloomed in the great modern gospel groups — and of course they had a lot to do, too, with doo-wop and The Drifters and the secular side of all that. Some of the older material is perhaps a trifle quaint and slow-moving, but its fervour and harmonic ingenuity lithely jump the time barrier.

The pleasure of discovering something entirely new in or around the edges of your field of interest is as keen a stimulus as any in the music game. Sometimes it's looked as if the blues was not going to be too productive in that way any more, and the past year has not been one of revelations, unless you consider it surprising that live blues continues to draw healthy audiences. But there are promising stirrings here and there, both in contemporary music and — in the rediscovery of what lies behind it, in the blues itself and in allied traditions. In the fragmented and arbitrary surveying of twelve months it isn't always easy to convey this sense of things bubbling away hopefully, but anyone whose curiosity is in good working order should have some chances of exercising it over the next year.
TONY RUSSELL

ROCKABILLY

This, at last, was the year that rockabilly music shook off the spell that has held it dormant for 20 years and began to stir, to move, to bop'n'rock. To shake the window, rattle the walls, and to roll up the record charts.

For fully 20 years, ever since the turn of the Sixties — the full lifetime of many of those who have lately been listening to hot country bop and are now attempting to play it — rockabilly music has been in stasis. Unchanging. Frozen in time. Just as it was before Elvis got his hair cut, before Buddy died in the plane crash and Eddie in the car accident, before Gene became crippled and fat and Jerry Lee fell into scandal. Rockabilly has been a cult music, a private enthusiasm, the special interest of a few fanatics — mostly English and European — who have taken delight in digging up and sharing around the secret treasure of an earlier day which the world at large had largely forgotten.

In the last year, however, rockabilly has been reborn — both the same as before and different. It has begun to change and evolve, to move out into the world at large and to have effect.

More than a mere cult audience is now involved. Rockabilly is *the* teen fad in

CRAZY CAVAN AND BILLY HANCOCK

STRAY CATS

Finland, where youngsters can buy jeans embossed with the logo of ROLLIN' ROCK RECORDS, a California speciality label most Americans have, as yet, not even heard of. In Britain during the past year, a number of rockabilly singles have been general hits, and the first album by The Stray Cats, a young group that left America in 1980 to seek their fortune in England, shot up the charts to Number 3.

The music has been set on fire.

Back in the Fifties, rockabilly was country music's contribution to rock'n'roll. It was simple music played on simple instruments — guitar or piano, slap-bass and drums. It was spare and hot, as powerful and efficient and light on its wheels as a stripped-down dragster. It was the leanest, meanest, most hard-hitting rock'n'roll around. Pure ducktailed anarchy.

But first, there came the long list of tragedies and disasters. Then there were the Frankie Avalons and The Fabians shoved to the

forefront to skim off the screams of the teenage rock'n'roll audience. Altogether it seemed that rockabilly was too raw and too country to fit into the smoothness of the early Sixties.

And when the new rock music was put together around 1965 out of rock'n'roll, folk music and blues, rockabilly was one element that largely got left out of

the synthesis. Like doo-wap, it didn't lend itself to mindtrips, flower power and 40-minute instrumental solos.

Oh, a few country rockabilly performers might try to continue to do their thing, but if they persisted in this folly eventually they got shunted off into three-stool bar-rooms in Moose Jaw where the word hadn't got around that rockabilly was out, dead, done. And almost all of the little that these good ol' boys managed to get down on record during the later Sixties and into the Seventies was lame and leaden, rote walk-throughs of the handful of rockabilly tunes that the general audience they hoped to recapture might be presumed to be familiar with.

Their would-be imitators, those eager young lads in England and France and Holland and Italy who had got hold of the rockabilly spirit and didn't want to let it go, didn't fare all that much better. They tried. They did their best. But if you lack the authority, the wit, the lightness of touch that mark rockabilly at its best, you can easily look and sound... off. And if all you can do is attempt to repeat what you've heard on record note for note without adding anything from your own individuality, then you may

THE MAGNETICS

seem no better than a parrot. And that's what many British and European would-be rockabillies did come to seem during those years in the wilderness. Why listen to them when the folks they were copying weren't worth the bother of listening to?

But even so, during these years, the audience for rockabilly widened. Rockabilly speciality shops were opened. New pressings of long-lost 45s were issued — sometimes with authorisation, more often without. New rockabilly record labels were begun: ROLLIN' ROCK, RIPSAW, COWBOY CARL, MAC, ROCKHOUSE, WHITE LABEL, CHARLY.

Around 1977, about the time that Elvis Presley died, the long slow process of unearthing records, figuring out what had been good and why, and fitting it all together finally began to come to something. The French issued chronological summaries of the careers of Gene Vincent and Eddie Cochran. The Germans revived lesser-known performers: Bob Luman, Janis Martin, and Sid King and The Five Strings. The Dutch combed the American Southland and issued state-by-state compilations of rare and obscure rockabilly. The British went through the record vaults of all the major American recording companies and compiled anthologies of rockabilly for each. And they topped everyone with their six-record boxed set of Buddy Holly — a record package that is a monument of taste, research, care and love.

In the Fifties, rockabilly was largely a local and regional music, with considerable impact on the country music marketplace and a much lesser but still significant influence on the national rock 'n' roll scene. It was music of the moment, sold on single records to an audience that seized it, used it up and threw it away.

The rockabilly releases of the late Seventies summarising the original Fifties-era music were aimed at an international audience, small in scope but fanatically loyal, that might buy ten or twenty thousand copies of a record album. The music was valued for itself, for its power and purity, and not for its chances of being an immediate popular hit. The result of all this revival of long-lost and never-heard music has been that in the past few years more original-era rockabilly has been available than at any previous moment. And has been more easily available to those who might care to hear it than it was even in its own day.

And there have been those ready to listen. Rock stars like Bruce Springsteen and Tom Petty have been quoted as saying that they were listening to rockabilly. And almost anyone, Paul McCartney, Jorma Kaukonen, Ry Cooder, Led Zep or The Clash, might include a rockabilly-influenced track on an album. Most important of all, the rockabilly revival programme caught the interest of a large number of record retailers. I knew that Matchbox and Shakin' Stevens had had hit singles in England and I'd heard that The Stray Cats had taken off phenomenally. But still I wasn't prepared for this kind of coverage: stories of new groups I had never heard of signed to major labels, ads for one new record after another, lists of albums for canny record dealers to stock.

Wow! In a time when the record business as a whole has been falling off, are the corporate gamblers seeing something in rockabilly to put their money on?

I went down the road to visit my friend Little Nelson, who runs RIPSAW RECORDS with his partner The Spider and produces rockabilly singles for the cult audience, to see single, Martha Hull's 'Feelin' Right Tonight'/'Fujiyama Mama', on their own RIPSAW label. And now Little Nelson is off to France with Billy Hancock and Tex Rubinowitz to join other American, British and French rockabilly acts in a 14-city tour from Paris to Strasbourg.

Little Nelson has never seen a year like this last one. Pitfalls and opportunities everywhere.

And what is the source of the change? Is it the new audience, the new artists, the new money? Or is there some basic underlying need of the moment for the essence of rockabilly that is jerking money and people around into startling new configurations like a magnet tugging at iron filings?

THE KINGBEES

young musicians — a whole new generation — who had come to feel that rock was the property of The Rolling Stones, The Who, and all of that old lot and were looking around for something new all their own. And found that something in rockabilly.

These youngsters have been practising these last three or four years. I heard some samples of what they were up to a couple of years ago, and frankly, it wasn't all that good. But now, now these kids are finally coming of age musically.

Just recently, my friends in England sent me five large pages photocopied from an issue of RECORD BUSINESS, a trade journal for British what he would make of this. I handed him the pages from RECORD BUSINESS and waited until he had read them through. At last he looked up at me and said, "It's a whole new ballgame, isn't it?"

It is. But then, if the scale of things in the rockabilly universe has suddenly changed, Little Nelson may already be a part of the shift without having completely appreciated the fact. This has certainly been his busiest year. He and The Spider have produced a couple of albums, The Zantees 'Out For Kicks' (BOMP) and a forthcoming album by Washington, D.C. rockabilly star, Billy Hancock, on SOLID SMOKE. They put out an excellent New Rockabilly Whatever it is that is going on, the difference can already be sensed in the music being issued on record. A few observations can be made.

One is that the great days of reissuing Fifties material on long-playing records as though the amount were endless are just about over. No doubt there will be a few more anthologies here, an obscure performer brought to light there. Careers will be tidied and set in order. But there will be very few big surprises.

But the result of all this activity is that the basic rockabilly repertoire available for performers to draw upon has been vastly increased. Doing original-era material is the first step into rockabilly, and now, for the first time, there is a sufficient base that a new group need not do the same five numbers as everyone else.

Clearly, the best reissue to come out in the United States in the last year was 'The Complete Buddy Holly' (MCA), first put out in Britain two years ago, but eminently worth a re-recommendation. Buddy Holly was a genius singer. His whole career is laid out here. This boxed set includes a 64 page book with pictures and clippings and other documentation of Holly's story. This package is an essential record and a fantastic bargain.

A second observation is that if what has happened is that the inner power of rockabilly has been turned back on, surviving first-generation rockabillies have been feeling the current. They've started to get it on again. Oh, one or two tired trots through over-familiar numbers did come out. But no less than four albums were distinctly better than that — records more than able to stand comparison with the best work laid down in the Fifties.

Man mountain Sleepy LaBeef, as frequently recorded as any rockabilly in recent years, has turned out one stiff and lumbering album after another. This year, Sleepy changed record labels to the Massachusetts folk-record cooperative ROUNDER RECORDS. He went down to Nashville, picked his own material and his own musicians, and produced himself. The result was a fine album, easily his best, 'It Ain't What You Eat It's The Way How You Chew It'.

Roy "The Hound" Hall, an old sly dog who plays piano and sounds like a rockabilly Professor Longhair, has been represented on a couple of DECCA compilation albums, but never been allowed to show what he can really do. One side of 'Rock-A-Billy Lives' (BARRELHOUSE) was laid down in Memphis, the other four months later in Nashville, with two different sets of first-rate musicians. Randy old grandpas were one of the delights of Fifties rockabilly and Roy Hall comes across as the real thing.

Ray Campi and his slappin' bass are the very foundation stone of California's ROLLIN' ROCK RECORDS, but there have been times — most of the

time — when Campi has sounded a bit light, a bit thin, a bit tame. Not on his new album 'Rockabilly Music'. Campi feels the juice, too, and this time he climbs right out onto the edge of the ledge, and then takes tremendous vocal and instrumental chances. His best album.

But the real find of the year in old-line rockabilly is 'Teddy Reddell Is Back' (WHITE LABEL). Reddell's Fifties' work, most of it previously unreleased, was recently put out on another album by this Dutch record company. They must have liked what they heard. They made a trip to Arkansas, turned themselves

into record producers, and recorded Reddell. And the results were splendid. Reddell has only got better over the years. His little finger of his right hand should be dipped in gold.

In a younger generation of American country performers, there is a stirring toward rockabilly as a protest against the artificiality of so much current country music. It's a way of getting back to roots and being elemental and real again.

Joe Ely, a honky-tonker whose band comes form Lubbock, Texas, turns toward rockabilly on his latest album, 'Musta Notta Gotta Lotta' (SOUTH COAST RECORDS). The title track is a real experiment in

New Rockabilly, and is probably my choice for single cut of the year.

Billy Burnette, son of Dorsey Burnette, after two country(?) albums on POLYDOR last year, put out a sizzling rock'n'roll album titled 'Billy Burnette' on COLUMBIA. This record leaps beyond simple rockabilly — but if Buddy Holly was rockabilly, then so is this. Burnette is a super-star of the future.

It is apparent that the ante in the rockabilly game has been raised in the last year. Records that would have been "good enough" a year ago simply because they were new and were rockabilly aren't good enough any more.

THE JOE ELY BAND

The best of the new British groups to reach me so far, The Jets (EMI), three brothers named Cotton, are a marvellously tight band. They have great taste and deliver their numbers with real authority. But only two tracks are original numbers. A year ago, The Jets would have been a unique find. These days they've only got an opening hand.

By comparison, a hot young American group, The Magnetics 'Rockabilly Fools' (ROLLIN' ROCK), are just as tight, tasteful and authoritative. But they have five singers, including a girl who sings lead on half the cuts, and they have written half their material themselves, songs up

to the level of the originals they do.

I'm not yet sure that the same is true of The Kingbees, an American group whose second album, 'The Big Rock', is on RSO. I tend to like them better when they are doing oldies. But that may only mean that I haven't yet completely caught the style of their original music. They are definitely a sign that rockabilly is in for continuing change.

The new audience that brash rockabilly groups of today are aiming to reach is not at all like the one addressed by the likes of Jerry Lee Lewis and Carl Perkins 25 years ago — except in being young and frustrated. If rockabilly proves to be the new music of the Eighties, which is beginning to seem a real possibility, then it not only *will* change, it *must* change.

The real sign of rockabilly's future may perhaps be seen in The Stray Cats 'Stray 1' (ARISTA). A little more than a year ago, The Stray Cats were members of a New Wave group, The Bloodless Pharoahs. Now they are the top rockabilly band in the world.

I can't recall when I have heard a more impressive first album of any sort. Brian Setzer, writer and lead singer, is a spiffy guitarist, master of half-a-dozen styles. The band — guitar, bass and drums — is tighter than tight and makes a big sound. The Stray Cats reach back for their influences as far as the Forties and Thirties — reminding us that original-era rockabilly itself was a synthesis of earlier kinds of music. But they assimilate all this variety within the compass of the new mythology they are creating.

The Stray Cats are masterful musicians. All by themselves, they have staked out a vast new mental territory and a vast new musical territory for rockabilly music, adjacent to rock at certain points, but not the same as rock. 'Stray 1' is a pivotal record. If Album of the Year has any meaning, this record is it.

And if what The Stray Cats have accomplished on their first album is now the standard in New Rockabilly, then the stakes in the game have just been raised again. It's going to take *real* good cards to play next year.

ALEXEI PANSHIN

THE YEAR'S ALBUMS

— (WELL, MOST OF THEM) —

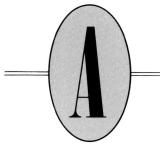

ABBA
Super Trouper *(Epic)*
Super Stupor is more like it...What's the point of being a pop millionaire, if you're stuck in a dead-end job?
NEW MUSICAL EXPRESS
Is unadulterated escapism any worse than the gloom and defeatist pessimism of, say Killing Joke? Maybe not.
MELODY MAKER
...Abba are as expendable as they are exportable. In treating pop music as a computer game, they're Sweden's answer to Space Invaders.
ROLLING STONE
The Abba formula is as institutionalised as a Mills and Boon novel. It is constant. Its idyllic creations are flaunted as an unobtainable perfection which degrades its audience's ability to enjoy their own emotions yet its perfection makes it all the more desirable.
RECORD MIRROR

ADAM AND THE ANTS
Kings Of The Wild Frontier
(CBS)
...the new Ant vision is a heady mix of technicolour images — of pirates and Red Indians and everything bold, brave and free...
NEW MUSICAL EXPRESS
The chilling starkness of the early Ants is replaced by a warm, rich Apache beat, their monochrome obscured with a vivid splash of colour.
SOUNDS
Adam seems to have abandoned his deviant sexual imagery for a more romantic approach: pirates, gangsters, cowboys and Indians are the heroes, people who don't like the Ants, the enemy.
RECORD MIRROR

If your're trying to create your own personality cult, it generally helps to have a bit of personality. Adam and The Ants don't.
MELODY MAKER
...what may be the most successfully silly musical organisation to appear since The Monkees, maybe even the Mickey Mouse Club gang!
TROUSER PRESS
...these guys are going to have to do a lot better than this if they hope to conquer America...sounds like it was recorded with two Dixie Cups and a thread.
ROLLING STONE

AFTER THE FIRE
80-F *(Epic)*
...to anyone who dismisses ATF as just the Christian rock band — forget the religious tag; these guys are good musicians and have turned out a fine zappy pop album.
MELODY MAKER
Sing-song hooks crackle out in rapid succession and bounce along with a healthy, grinning energy.
SOUNDS
...a hybrid band combining the strong beat and singalong choruses of Slade with the immaculate production and sophisticated keyboard sound of Supertramp.
RECORD MIRROR

ALTERNATIVE TV
Strange Kicks *(IRS)*
...a confused and confusing mixture of songs and ideas.
NEW MUSICAL EXPRESS
At the last minute the old group moniker has been revived in the interests of continuity and money but in truth the end product of such cynicism is about ten times better than it has any right to be...Alex 'n' Mark: Peter and Gordon for pop pulp perves!
SOUNDS

ALLMAN BROTHERS BAND
Reach For The Sky *(Arista)*
If the Americans like this stuff then they deserve a B movie actor for president. To carry the imagery of the album's title a little further

these outlaws have had their day — they should hang up their guns or prepare for a sudden death.
MELODY MAKER
Once again, the only Allman in the Allman Brothers Band is pretty near irrelevant. Dickey Betts is the dominant personality here, and he has the charisma and poetry of a parking meter.
ROLLING STONE

JON ANDERSON
Song Of Seven *(Atlantic)*
Anderson is an incurable soppy romantic in a way that makes Barbara Cartland seem downright brutal.
NEW MUSICAL EXPRESS
This album is the best thing Jon Anderson has done away from Yes, eclipsing the achievement of his collaboration with Vangelis...
MELODY MAKER
Absolutely crass, but I love it.
RECORD MIRROR

ANDROIDS OF MU
Blood Robots *(Fuck Off)*
...they seem to make music as if fired by some obscure grudge against the whole listening public...a strangely glum and sloppy record, one that virtually defies you to like it.
NEW MUSICAL EXPRESS
Psychedelic revival? Geriatric more like.
MELODY MAKER
The Androids of Mu are the lost remains of glorious punk — the principle of playing music, enjoying yourself and damn the consequences...
SOUNDS

ANGEL CITY
Darkroom *(Epic)*
...a very *pleasant* album. Note-perfect, precisely produced, decoratively performed, it's the kind of record that slides on the back of a few spins into 'easy listening' chrome-finished average standard rock...
SOUNDS
...it doesn't quite reconcile their obvious intelligence with an urge to boogie the night away.
TROUSER PRESS

Angel City come on like a five-man thrashaboogie missionary force.
RECORD MIRROR

ANGELIC UPSTARTS
2,000,000 Voices *(Zonophone)*
...represents both the band's most cohesive album achievement to date and further proof if any's needed that the The Upstarts stand for the most concious, most humanist wing of street punk.
SOUNDS
For those of you who've always ignored the Upstarts like the plague, considering them little more than a bunch of sub-Sham, flash-in-the-pan, three chord louts. '2,000,000 Voices' should serve as the proverbial short sharp shock.
MELODY MAKER

ANGELWITCH
Angelwitch *(Bronze)*
...the vinyl answer to fouling the footpath...
SOUNDS
It's an acceptable debut, no more.
MELODY MAKER

APRIL WINE
The Nature of the Beast
(Capitol)
This isn't a stunning album but is a good one, excellently played and produced for maximum impact on the chosen target area. Heads will bang.
SOUNDS
...a positive step towards rehabilitation.
RECORD MIRROR
All I can really say for April Wine is that their LP makes UFO's album sound dynamic and original in comparison. This takes some doing.
NEW MUSICAL EXPRESS

ARTFUL DODGER
Rave On *(Ariola)*
With a clean, clear production, jangling guitars and simple effective drumming, 'Rave On' puts Artful Dodger alongside Dirty Looks and The Dead Kennedys as three good reasons why I'm not so bored with the UDA
MELODY MAKER
...finds Artful Dodger still

pursuing their deep-dyed, tough-tender style of rock & roll as if The Faces were the only mentors who mattered, as if punk had never happened.
ROLLING STONE

THE ART OBJECTS
Bagpipe Music *(Heartbeat)*
It's an immediate, vibrant pulse of beauty and reason — hell, you can even dance to it! It all speaks for itself, but only if you are prepared to listen,
SOUNDS
...an odd LP, naturally flawed and imperfect and rather stilted in places, but nonetheless a worthy attempt at interdisciplinary entertainment — an overdue updating of the "jazz and poetry" and mixed-media events of the Sixties.
NEW MUSICAL EXPRESS

ASHFORD & SIMPSON
A Musical Affair *(Warner Bros)*
Ashford & Simpson's love songs accurately mirror the emotional aspirations of black Americans through the past prosperous decade-and-a-half in much the same way that Gil Scott-Heron has remained the articulator of their concerned conscience and anger.
MELODY MAKER

ASWAD
Showcase *(Aswad)*
With the added bonus dub extensions, 'Showcase' is more than a timely nudge in the ribs.
NEW MUSICAL EXPRESS
...halfway between a new album and a compilation set; an interim offering while they wait for another record deal.
MELODY MAKER
They prove that British reggae has as much virtuosity as its Jamaican counterpart.
RECORD MIRROR
...transformations, a chance to give former glories a new lease of life, to get them sounding perfect.
SOUNDS

ATLANTA RHYTHM SECTION
The Boys From Doraville *(Polydor)*
It's impossible to get excited about The Atlanta Rhythm Section; dullness hovers over their heads like halos.
MELODY MAKER

ATOMIC ROOSTER
Atomic Rooster *(EMI)*
Anyone for Blodwyn Pig?
SOUNDS

...the Rooster crow once again means happy listening...
RECORD MIRROR
...Rooster won't have much to crow about until they set aside their former reputation for showmanship and concentrate squarely on the most important matter; the songs.
MELODY MAKER

AU PAIRS
Playing With A Different Sex *(Human)*
...a well above-average example of new English rock as it is rolled in early 1981. If you want, you can dance to it, and if you like, you can think to it as well. If all else fails, simply listen and enjoy.
NEW MUSICAL EXPRESS
...a record that undoubtedly contains the seeds for future prosperity, but is too self-concious, too locked up in itself to breathe properly.
MELODY MAKER
What the Au Pairs have to say, never mind the fact, wonderful in itself, that they manage to say it successfully, strikes a magic chord of common sense.
SOUNDS
...a sustained attack of frenetic scratchy guitars that chop out the beat and the melody and hard drumming that remains imaginative throughout.
RECORD MIRROR

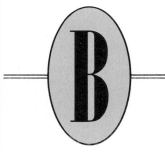

THE B-52'S
Wild Planet *(Islan)*
They are a thinking fun group: they produce songs by a witty process of elimination and illumination. They stand for the glamour of show-biz, the art of showing off, the vitality of fantasy, the glorification of Style...avante-garde Eighties pop: radical puerile, distinctive, an art-pop-art.
NEW MUSICAL EXPRESS

The B-52's still write absurd, brash, brittle, compulsively listenable trashpop which totally lacks pretension...Let's dance, gang, and leave the stick-in-the-muds out in the drive. The B-52's have *not* bombed!
SOUNDS
...the joke is wearing so thin it's close to snapping point.
SOUNDS
They're connoisseurs of trash in a world full of it. To hear them is to lose yourself in the echo of pop arcana.
ROLLING STONE
...the B-52's have done it again — sort of, just like last year's debut album — almost.
TROUSER PRESS

THE BABYS
On The Edge *(Chrysalis)*
The Babys splash around amid the veneered slush in which The Cars pitched tent so definitely on their heads debut: all guitars fuzzed and phased, and the drums sounding as though they're lined with best velvet. It's quite nauseating.
RECORD MIRROR
America can keep 'em.
MELODY MAKER

BAD MANNERS
Loonee Tunes *(Magnet)*
The album's sense of fun and humour reconfirms my high opinion of Bad Manners, who are definitely for people who have a gut full of politics and taking life seriously.
RECORD MIRROR
...not a work of wisdom, maturity, subtlety, relevance, insight or redeeming social value — yet it offers rumbustious fun and simple amusement, and I'm sure these things are good for us too, every so often.
NEW MUSICAL EXPRESS
...the same old lavatorial music-hall jokes set to the same old stupid skanking beat and leading us the same old merry, mindless dance.
MELODY MAKER
Kick out the jams, ska-boot dances and burger contests, and Bad Manners could turn into Etiquette not to mention required listening.
SOUNDS

MARTY BALIN
Balin *(EMI America)*
That voice is still there, if anything improved with age. But Balin has wasted it here on a collection of songs not even of his own making...does America, or any other country for that matter, really need an album that sounds like 'Red Octopus' outakes?
MELODY MAKER

RUSS BALLARD
Barnet Dogs *(Epic)*
...a rather dreary hard rock album which lacks scope and imagination...full of proud peacock music which struts along showing off its shiny and superficial masculinity.
RECORD MIRROR
At long last the man has made an LP full of meaty rock'n'roll and it's a helluva change from the melodic ballads of his previous releases.
MELODY MAKER

BARCLAY JAMES HARVEST
Turn Of The Tide *(Polydor)*
They're inventive, pure, honest and craftsman-like with no pretence towards pomp-rock. This is a lively, interesting LP from a band which has been quite a success story for 14 years, prophets with inadequate honour in their own land.
MELODY MAKER

THE BARRACUDAS
Drop Out With The Barracudas *(Zonophone)*
What could have been a cross-cultural game of mirrors, using The Beach Boys and surf sounds, protest and garage music, and early West Coast psychedelia, is no more than a dull, narcissistic pastiche.
NEW MUSICAL EXPRESS
The Barracudas have a level of affection, respect, freshness, excitement and an overwhelming sense of mischief to their source material that never allows them to stray over the boundaries into the pedantic.
RECORD MIRROR
...an ideal album for those who still cherish their Sixties musical memories, but whose interest waned when self-indulgence replaced adventurism.
MELODY MAKER
...there's nothing more empty than a gimmick that's been stretched to elpee proportions. The Barracudas have overreached themselves.
SOUNDS

BASEMENT 5
Basement 5 In Dub (Island)
...doesn't stand up to a lot of listening, its surface is all. It slumps forward unremarkably, softly softly, in anticipation of the official album.
NEW MUSICAL EXPRESS

BASEMENT 5
1965-1980 (Island)
Basement 5 seem to use the music as little more than a vehicle for their opinions...
NEW MUSICAL EXPRESS
...a band with a lot to say — it's just that they're still searching for the best way of saying it.
MELODY MAKER
Dennis Morris's voice grates to the point of intense irritation, it's something that you either love or hate and personally I hate it.
RECORD MIRROR
It's all very much of a muchness and you can't help feeling it could have been much sharper, better, more 'relevant' in a real sense.
SOUNDS

STIV BATORS
Disconnected (Bomp)
...an exciting album of strong sounds by anyone's standards and begs the appropriate amount of attention.
RECORD MIRROR
You won't be inspired to murder random pedestrians after hearing 'Disconnected'. At most you'll just want to slap them around a little.
ROLLING STONE
The former Dead Boy presents a palatable cartoon alternative to Iggy Pop: he sneers, threatens and poses with suitable bug-eyed intensity.
TROUSER PRESS

MIKE BATT
Waves (Epic)
The great thing about "musicians'" albums is that the rest of us need not buy them. The great thing about "producers'" albums is that even fewer need buy them.
NEW MUSICAL EXPRESS

BAUHAUS
In The Flat Field (4AD)
...trundles abysmally along antique mistakes, old frosty corridors full of cobwebbed errors that were blown away years ago...
SOUNDS
...shallowness amd uncertainty seep through after a couple of listenings.
TROUSER PRESS

THE BEAT
Wha'ppen? (Go Feet)
... a settle Beat product with a consistent sound - lazy, sunny, sinuous, sexy. And still pushy.
RECORD MIRROR
... the album sounds flat and self-limiting. Instead of a confidence-brimming, sweeping improvement on the rough genius of the first album, The Beat decide to wear the same neat tidy clobber.
SOUNDS
Memorable, stylish modern dance music, sharpened by a radical sensibility.
NEW MUSICAL EXPRESS
... a wealth of influences and invention...
MELODY MAKER
...presents a band that, far from suffocating in a dated trend, has shed its Two-Tone chrysalis for full-fledged individuality. It's a breathtakingly vital record.
TROUSER PRESS

CAPTAIN BEEFHEART AND THE MAGIC BAND
Doc At The Radar Station (Virgin)
There's a lot of depressingly moderate music about, but this shines through, thought-provoking and soulful; it's music to argue about, and that's a good thing.
RECORD MIRROR
... as much evidence as could possibly be desired that the Van Vliet muse is still as intractably stimulating as ever.
NEW MUSICAL EXPRESS
'Doc' says and tries nothing that wasn't successfully created on 'Shiny Beast'...
MELODY MAKER
... a whoop in the ear, and probably the best exposition of Don Van Vliet's free-fall poetry, right-angle saxophone toots and lycanthrophic howl since 'Trout Mast' - which 'Doc' sort of sounds like.
TROUSER PRESS
... the artist and his art go on a cultural rampage, ripping and tearing at dense, lush undergrowths of melody while hurling imprecations of the airiest, most elliptical wit.
ROLLING STONE

PAT BENATAR
Crimes of Passion (Chrysalis)
Lacking both subtlety and playfulness. Benatar delivers the brunt of 'Crimes of Passion' material - most of it leaden reworkings of hard-rock clichés...with a shrill seriousness that rarely varies.
ROLLING STONE

...lashings of show and lots of sweet nothing, all well-wrapped in twee admissions of sanitised angst...about as attractive as a crumpled Kleenex: a useless wisp of society's waste. An eminently disposable item.
NEW MUSICAL EXPRESS
Career rock you could call it...She will sing in the rock idiom until she's old enough to do cabaret in Vegas. She does it very correctly, making all the right noises and the production is pristine.
SOUNDS
... agreeable pop, attractively arranged and produced with a solid thrust...
MELODY MAKER
... raunchy pop rock, easy to listen to and easy to forget.
RECORD MIRROR

BERLIN BLONDES
Berlin Blondes (EMI)
One suspects that if Berlin Blondes spent four hours dressing up they'd still get something wrong.
MELODY MAKER
...an enterprising, if not flawless, debut which deserves an unprejudiced hearing if nothing else.
SOUNDS
... one of those bands trying to hitch a ride on the tail of Numan's comet; theirs is the usual bag of semiotic tricks, the semaphore of synthi-lore -all the attendant myths of art, science, decadence and the like...little more than posing by numbers, an album more definable in terms of fashion than music.
NEW MUSICAL EXPRESS
This lullaby collection of nine numbing synth-pop tracks is more likely to find itself on the tapes of Muzak than in the collection of a record buyer.
RECORD MIRROR

THE BIRTHDAY PARTY
Prayers On Fire (4AD)
By a million miles Australia's hippiest rock export to date...
SOUNDS
The Birthday Party will have an indelible effect on your brain.
RECORD MIRROR
... a celebratory, almost religious record, as in ritual, as in pray-ers on fire; a combustible dervish dance, and another great debut of '81.
NEW MUSICAL EXPRESS
... sound that is uniquely personal, angular, thick and fleshly. It's spat out with demonic ferocity that's enough to scare the Y-Fronts off even the most blasé of

listeners and recorded in what sounds more like an inferno than a studio.
MELODY MAKER

STEPHEN BISHOP
Red Cab To Manhattan (Warner Bros)
On 'Red Cab To Manhattan', Stephen Bishop - pop music's most endearing wimp and an unabashed acolyte of Paul Simon's and Paul McCartney -adds Steely Dan to his roster of idols in a chauffer driven excursion into the very heart of the Emerald City.
ROLLING STONE

BLACKFOOT
Marauder (ATCO)
...the Southern album to end all Southern albums.
SOUNDS

BLACK SLATE
Amigo (Ensign)
An assured debut...
RECORD MIRROR
... a fairly ordinary reggae album - pleasant enough and pretty in places but without enough substance or pace or coiled up energy to string out the listener's interest over more than half of the ten tracks.
SOUNDS

BLACK UHURU
Red (Island)
Their strongest album yet, this could be, by definition, the best so called reggae album this year. Whatever: 'Red' stands alone as a fine achievement, and a demonstration of what music can do to both body and brain.
MELODY MAKER
For the third time Black Uhuru have concocted a combination of ingredients to ease your head.
NEW MUSICAL EXPRESS
... and a combination of vocal and instrumental achievement that is a devoted blend of the unique. Whatever your conceptions of reggae are, this record will shatter them like a stone through thin ice.
SOUNDS

CARLA BLEY
Social Studies (Watt)
...a truer, more affectionate, more cutting evocation of Old Europe than anything by the likes of Ultravox.
NEW MUSICAL EXPRESS

BLONDIE
Autoamerican (Chrysalis)
'Autoamerican' is just a half-baked (cable) TV dinner, and it's full of unhealthy

preservatives and artificial sweeteners.
NEW MUSICAL EXPRESS
... a flit through a bewildering array of styles, barely getting on nodding acquaintance with them before moving on.
MELODY MAKER
... where the bright lights of Broadway blur Deb's and Professor Stein's eyeballs, where they get fed up and bored with rock and roll and start tiddling around with would-be decadent and luxurious cocktail-bar songlettes, and end up on their sweet backsides.
SOUNDS
... passes its roadtest but next years model will require a thorough overhaul.
RECORD MIRROR
... a terrible album, but its bad in such an arcane, high-toned way that listening to it is perversely fascinating.
ROLLING STONE
... the most interesting and (dare I say it?) cohesive album Blondie has made.
TROUSER PRESS

BLUE ANGEL
Blue Angel *(Polydor)*
This is the most wholly satisfying album by a young new (to me) band that I've heard in a dog's age and I'm already beginning to think about strict rationing of plays-says a cupola hunnerd a day...God knows how they'd describe their music: I've a feeling they wouldn't be ashamed of being called a rock and roll band.
NEW MUSICAL EXPRESS

THE BLUE CATS
The Blue Cats *(Charly)*
If their album hadn't been saddled with such a drab, flat production, it would have had that razors-and pomade flash on which rockabilly depends...The Blue Cats' album is rockabilly stuffed and put on a pedestal. A labour of love, but a labour.
NEW MUSICAL EXPRESS

THE BLUES BAND
Ready *(Arista)*
What gives the album (and the band) its character is a certain sense of atmosphere and drama, with effective contrasts between restraint and aggression...
MELODY MAKER
'Ready' isn't new, it isn't complicated, it's just bloody good. I'd recommend it to anyone who isn't actively adverse to getting happy.
SOUNDS
... I expected a lot more excitement on this album.

What's let them down is the choice, and the general dull standard of the songs on show here.
RECORD MIRROR

BLUE OYSTER CULT
Unknown Origin *(CBS)*
Some rubbish, a handful of gems...Not enough, really.
MELODY MAKER
The misty conspiratorial imagery, the power chords, the spiralling, quicksilver guitar lines, the cynical, sarcastic AOR tendencies. Fire Of Unknown Origins boasts of them in spades, my dear.
SOUNDS
As Fire...unequivocally shows, the lords of chaos are among the true greats of rock history.
RECORD MIRROR

BLURT
In Berlin *(Armageddon)*
As a document of a Blurt concert it's fine: it works too as an adequate introduction to Milton's bizarre imagination. The rest of us, however, already familiar with his bitter, funny assaults on conventions and expectations, hoped for something more...
NEW MUSICAL EXPRESS
Blurt could play the same song for ever and you wouldn't even worry about them ever ending. You're hooked...Recorded live in Berlin it captures brilliantly what they're all about, all the rough and tumble and tough rumble spilling gloriously out of the speakers with ten times the energy and attack of a studio album.
MELODY MAKER
Blurt exhaust your patience with this undermining cool catness, this inner surety that they are the inheritors, sniff, sniff, of the spirit and the challenge of the world-brutalized Jazz Greats. They are too clever at what they do, and they do not even do that quite right.
SOUNDS
I'm confused. Is this paranoid jazz or mutant disco?
RECORD MIRROR
Instead of leaning on language for meaning, Blurt lets the music do the talking, eliminating the middleman, or maybe the id.
TROUSER PRESS

GARY U.S. BONDS
Dedication *(EMI America)*
Gary is one of the great daddies of American rock and soul with a sound as immediately familiar as The

Drifters or Doug Sahm. He's a master of his genre, sha la la music dressed up in organ, brass and constant romance, the kind of guy who'd drive all night just to buy his baby some shoes.
RECORD MIRROR
... a fine album in its own right, and probably the nearest thing to a new Springsteen album we'll hear this year...glorious proof of rock 'n' roll, alive and kicking today. Succumb now, for the sake of your head, heart and feet!
MELODY MAKER
On 'Dedication', love and big ideas are treated — correctly — as aspects of the same problem. The results are adventurous and moving, without ever sliding into the condescension that usually ruins most superstar-meets-his-hero projects.
ROLLING STONE

THE BOOKS
Expertise *(Logo)*
The Books are the fault of one Stephen F. Betts, who writes all the songs (and actually seems proud of it!), and appears to have spent the last few years alone in a room with only the first Devo album and a bunch of Yes albums for company.
NEW MUSICAL EXPRESS
... bubbles with shocking, teasing and delightfully madcap ideas from its opening electrical surge to its final fading clap of thunder.
MELODY MAKER
... a token drum machine drags the group reluctantly into 1981, and at this rate, I doubt The Books will see '82 as the same unit.
SOUNDS
While not as esoterically elitist as many of their ilk, The Books aren't overtly commercial either, leaving them in an unsteady middleground that could see them going either way.
RECORD MIRROR

THE BOOMTOWN RATS
Mondo Bongo
(Phonogram/Columbia)
Hollow pop, quaking under a plethora of poorly integrated rip-offs, with only the glossy sheen of Tony Visconti's production to keep all the clumsy gestures balanced just so...moves from the irksome to the infuriating.
NEW MUSICAL EXPRESS

...there's a helluva lot of depth and decision and *emotion* missing from what is one of the most self-indulgent pop scenarios I've heard of late.
SOUNDS
The album proves the infuriatingly wayward nature of Geldorf and The Rats -they pour words into songs that mostly evaporate with ease.
MELODY MAKER
... an intoxicating mixture of pop and punk.
ROLLING STONE
... rock puritans will undoubtedly find 'Mondo Bongo' campy, garish, condescending and in thoroughly bad taste. Some people also don't know how to have fun...an enormously enjoyable LP, with hardly a dry patch on it.
TROUSER PRESS

DAVID BOWIE
Scary Monsters And Super Creeps *(RCA)*
... shorn of all hope, yet it represents a call to arms. It is an album which presupposes defeat, yet it is unashamedly and unequivocally confrontational...harsh, strained, inelegant, cluttered, verbose, elliptical, yet Bowie communicates with an honesty and directness that suggests that an informed pessimism can be more inspiring - in real terms - than any obtuse optimistic fantasy.
NEW MUSICAL EXPRESS
... displays Bowie back in virtually complete control of his distinctive musical destiny...on nodding terms with his past, but, as ever, more concerned with - and able to face - the unknown future.
MELODY MAKER
... an accessible, fun, pop compilation.
SOUNDS
... brilliant, innovative, visionary, articulate, eloquent, inconsistent, unpredictable, majestic, frigging genius...
RECORD MIRROR
... represents a plateau in a career made up of plateaus. Its songs are quirky, intriguing and meticulously presented...
TROUSER PRESS
... presents David Bowie riveted to life's passing parade: streamlined moderns, trendies and sycophants in 360 degrees of stark, scarifying Panavision.
ROLLING STONE

THE BOYS
Boys Only *(Safari)*
The Boys are a veritable delight. They're nice 'n' naughty. They'll demand a smile from a corpse, a dance from a paraplegic.
MELODY MAKER
... a series of dour midtempo tracks with invariable rhythms and prosaic vocals.
NEW MUSICAL EXPRESS
Imagine distilling the essences of The Kursal Flyers, Radio Stars, Ronnie Lane, The Bishops and The Cars into the lowest common denominator of all five and you've sussed The Boys. Post power pop, heavy on nostalgia and token R&B, 'forged' from extremely competent instrumentation and some fundamentally duff rock 'n' roll compositions...
SOUNDS
... songs that show The Boys' good, bad and ugly sense of humour for what it's worth.
RECORD MIRROR

PAUL BRADY
Hard Station *(WEA)*
Brady doesn't deal in half-measures. That's why we've waited three years for his 'contemporary' album. That's why the aggression is full-blooded and overwhelming. That's why the sentiment is dripping in tears. That's why this is a superb album.
MELODY MAKER

BRIAN BRAIN
Unexpected Noises *(Secret)*
Packed with gimmicks but few ideas, one wonders how or why this record ever came into being except as a means of advertising its maker's penchant for, yes, making Unexpected Noises.
MELODY MAKER
... sees him scrambling around desperately for ideas, picking up occasionally on tested ones without really grasping their meaning. Only once does he really manage to rise above the general level of mediocrity...
NEW MUSICAL EXPRESS

THE BRAINS
Electronic Eden *(Mercury)*
... it proves a smart band can rock as ferociously as a dumb one.
TROUSER PRESS

Amid the flood of American New Wave music, only The Brains seem able to bridge the gap between raw garageland punk and slick techno-pop. Because they value and employ both in honest pursuit of a middle ground the band remains appealingly genuine and dangerously tentative.
ROLLING STONE

BRITISH ELECTRIC FOUNDATION
Music For Stowaways *(Virgin cassette)*
... one of the few unselfconscious ambient/electro-pop products yet made. Its a wonderful new accessory to daily living, one that should be used on buses or trains, in the supermarket or at the launderette, as an accompaniment to household chores, for anything as long as you're not sitting still.
NEW MUSICAL EXPRESS
... the strongest, most diverse and human electronic album to come out of Europe in ages.
SOUNDS
A wealth of synthesisers are abused rather than used in creating a largely unlistenable barrage of abrasive noise that's got about as much in common with stimulation as scraping one's fingernails down a chipped window pane.
RECORD MIRROR
The image is of some brave new world in which Sony have taken the place of Aldous Huxley, everyone hedonistically plugged into their own pleasure centres, grooving along (on roller skates, natch), listening to Ian Marsh and Martyn Ware.
MELODY MAKER

HERMAN BROOD
Wait A Minute *(Ariola)*
...sounds vaguely like it's been gathering dust for a decade, knocking around the same rheumatic riffs that Rogers, Kirke and Co flogged, exhausted and ditched for dead somewhere well back in their doldrum years.
MELODY MAKER
The Stones meet Johnny Thunders meet obscure Chicago bluesers. Regulation "gospel" backup vocalists and a muscular brass section only go to prove it's easier to open a cheque book than this artist's imagination!
SOUNDS

JAMES BROWN
Live/Hot On The One *(Polydor)*
...appears mainly to be an excuse to make a few quick yen from the Japanese market.
NEW MUSICAL EXPRESS
...a legend and genuine innovator at work.
MELODY MAKER
Even if you have a very hot imagination and you can smell the atmosphere on the basis of a few crowd whoops and hollers, the overweening Brown ego must be hard to bear. His name or his initials are spoken or sung by the MC, the backing vocalist and Brown himself approx 84 times.
SOUNDS

JAMES BROWN
Nonstop *(Polydor)*
No new shapes are formed, but old ones are rearranged to startling effect. The blast and edge given to the music is as exciting as anything you'll hear all year.
NEW MUSICAL EXPRESS

JACK BRUCE
I've Always Wanted To Do This *(Epic)*
This album has its moments, but not enough of them to bring Bruce back to the centre stage which is his by right.
MELODY MAKER
The stimulating tension that so many of Bruce's albums have induced is seldom apparent here.
SOUNDS

T-BONE BURNETT
Truth Decay *(Chrysalis)*
...a work of authentic originality.
MELODY MAKER
...an album that has the mark of individuality in a field that's been churned over so many times even the weeds are getting depressed.
SOUNDS
This record makes you laugh — and gasp — at the richness of one man's passion.
ROLLING STONE
...may not be one of 1980's most inflammatory gestures but it will have few revivals to match its depth and clarity.
NEW MUSICAL EXPRESS
...an album that has the mark of individuality in a field that's been churned over so many times even the weeds are getting depressed.
SOUNDS

BILLY BURNETTE
Billy Burnette *(Columbia)*
If The Stray Cats haven't convinced you that rockabilly didn't end the day Elvis walked out of Sun Studios, then Billy Burnette will.
MELODY MAKER
By compensating for his own band's overly clean, top-of-the-beat style with his own vigorous vocals, Burnette manages to capture some of the Rock 'n' Roll Trio's barnstorming sound...Hell, this guy can even throw in a rockabilly hiccup and not seem like he's choking on history.
ROLLING STONE

BURNING SPEAR
Living Dub *(Island)*
...the strength of 'Living Dub' — from Spear's 'Social Living' album — is not so much the effects he adds on as those he leaves off. It's the space between the spaces that gets your imagination working overtime...
MELODY MAKER
...betrays its age, but it's still strong.
NEW MUSICAL EXPRESS

THE BUS BOYS
Minimum Wage Rock & Roll *(Arista)*
Because The Bus Boys' music is at once so familiar yet so distinct from any other current style, their debut album immediately sets them apart while drawing you in.
ROLLING STONE

KATE BUSH
Never For Ever *(EMI)*
When contemporary music offers an almost unrelenting diet of puerile lyrics, Bush is a jewel of fertile imagination...Any doubts that this is the best Bush album yet are firmly obliterated by the inspired unorthodoxy of the production.
MELODY MAKER
...a work of ingenuity, exquisite modern MOR of the very highest refinement and delicacy. But it's perfection in a vacuum.
NEW MUSICAL EXPRESS
...not an "instant" record but one which I imagine could grow on you if you gave it the chance.
SOUNDS
You don't have to be a neurotic, well-to-do airy-fairy dreamer to like Kate Bush but it probably helps.
RECORD MIRROR

PAUL BUTTERFIELD
North South *(Bearsville)*
Considering that 'East West' is the title of one of the best albums Paul Butterfield ever made, it's ironic that 'North South' should be the title of his worst.
ROLLING STONE

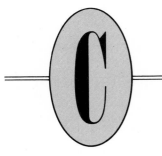

CABARET VOLTAIRE
Live At The Lyceum
(Rough Trade Cassette)
...a fabulous dense mist of taped voices, primal rhythms and guitar treatments seemingly geared to confusing and disorientating.
NEW MUSICAL EXPRESS
Their sound is a sort of telephonic miasma, with shadowy forms filtering in and out, briefly suggesting patterns, then exploding them, then shifting away to form new ones.
MELODY MAKER

CABARET VOLTAIRE
Voice of America
(Rough Trade)
Voltaire's music is of a phantom reality: no hard, obvious "social comment", no comfortable blank statements of alienation, no black and white message of politics or hope. It's trance music, technologically achieved: soul music, spiritually received.
NEW MUSICAL EXPRESS
Cabaret Voltaire's basic problem is that they have no understanding of what they are doing. They appear to have no love for their music. They definitely have no feel or instinct for it. They do like mucking about in backrooms and pretending it's Art...
MELODY MAKER
Cabaret Voltaire are terrifyingly stark, intense and friendly: they are probably the most un-hippy band in the country.
SOUNDS
...a stern and powerful achievement, unaffected by the pop world or anything else...
RECORD MIRROR

...not an album for weary or casual listeners, but it may have a lot more to do with living in the Eighties than more conventional rock ever will.
TROUSER PRESS

J.J.CALE
Shades *(Shelter)*
...*another* J.J.Cale album, and not a particularly marvellous example of the breed.
NEW MUSICAL EXPRESS
Step forward J.J. Cale, place hand on heart and swear that 'Shades' is the best you can do in 18 months.
MELODY MAKER
It's unassuming horizontal character instead gives it the perfect aura for early hours background music — chewing gum for the ears when the lights are low and the mood restful.
SOUNDS
The wash of warm guitars has been replaced by more piano orientated and orchestrated arrangements in an attempt at an updated, even "pop" sound which, for once, has not destroyed but rather positively enhanced this artist's innate charms.
RECORD MIRROR
Only someone as elegantly lazy as J.J.Cale could make kindred spirits like Eric Clapton and Dire Straits appear affected by comparison.
TROUSER PRESS

JOHN CALE
Honi Soit *(A&M)*
Dark of heart and mind and strong of song and singing, John Cale is back, his high anxieties utterly unappeased.
NEW MUSICAL EXPRESS
Cale refuses to grow old gracefully; his music remains dangerously tempestuous, often crashingly unhinged. He continues to be obsessed with the macabre: with breakdowns, extremes of emotion; the soiled half-truths of reality, the unsettling glamour of disaster....it won't leave your dreams alone.
MELODY MAKER
Of late, he's taken to surrounding himself with brutish, unimaginative rock ensembles which he bends to his own will, and that tendency is what I don't dig about 'Honi Soit'.
SOUNDS
...pulls the carpet from under your feet, proving there's plenty of life in the old leek yet.
RECORD MIRROR

CAMEL
Nude *(Decca)*
...a good album, and the finest Camel have produced for some years, simply because they are doing what they do best: a patchwork of romantic tunes and an easily followed theme... So it says nothing new, but it speaks nicely.
MELODY MAKER
...maintains their traditional depth of arrangement and melodic grace.
RECORD MIRROR

CARAVAN
The Album *(Kingdom)*
There's just too much of everything and not enough of anything. These boys need a mission in life.
MELODY MAKER

ERIC CARMEN
Tonight You're Mine *(Arista)*
Eric seems to be able to play almost any type of music he likes - what *can't* he do?
RECORD MIRROR
...a nearly wonderful Eric Carmen record...He's still lost in hearts, flowers and backseats, but he's growing up in spite of himself.
TROUSER PRESS

KIM CARNES
Mistaken Identity
(EMI America)
Kim's a sweet and wholesome all American girl, but once in a while I just wish she'd try gargling with Listerine.
RECORD MIRROR
Hollywood Studio Horrid of the most banal variety imaginable and should be avoided by those not currently in need of deep, restful slumber.
NEW MUSICAL EXPRESS
Kim Carnes used to exploit her rusty soprano for weepy pathos, but her suds were too synthetic to wash. Her new brassiness is far more convincing.
ROLLING STONE

THE CARPETTES
Fight Amongst Yourselves
(Beggars Banquet)
The Carpettes are nice boys who want to make a lot of money by copying others and removing any threat present in the originals. 'Fight Amongst Yourselves' is for neat, malleable punks who'll pogo to order next time.
NEW MUSICAL EXPRESS
Why do bands exist on £30 a week or less just to produce music as uninspiring as this? Why do they bother?
MELODY MAKER
...an album which you can not only dance and wreak havoc

to, but an album which you can actually sit down and listen to as well. Go for it...
SOUNDS
A blend of naive lyrical charm and forceful music which forms an indispensable whole despite occasional lapses in vision.
RECORD MIRROR

**JOE "KING" CARRASCO &
THE CROWNS**
**Joe "King" Carrasco & The
Crowns** *(Stiff/Hannibal)*
...clean and simple dance music, given a haunting quality by the thin piping of the Farfisa organ....
MELODY MAKER
Joe "King" Carrasco & The Crowns sound like a cheap five dollar transistor radio with the dial jammed on 1966.
NEW MUSICAL EXPRESS
Quite simply what we have here is 'Son And Daughter Of 96 Tears' times twelve.
SOUNDS
What's all the fuss about? I've heard better music in the nightclubs of Lloret de Mar at the height of the season....
RECORD MIRROR
Imagine Freddy Fender on acid. Consider the Sir Douglas Quintet on speed. Stand up and dance.
ROLLING STONE
Wear the grooves out in a week; don't worry, you won't want to listen to it after the flush of excitement has worn off. That's what pop music is all about.
TROUSER PRESS

THE JIM CARROLL BAND
Catholic Boy *(Atco)*
The Jim Carroll Band play like a well-rehearsed New York Dolls — blunt, loud and catchy, but lacking that late, great group's vehement humour and spontaneity.
ROLLING STONE
Some of his songs sound good, but others suffer from pretentious lyrics; or emotional vocals that hint at the real futility of this recording project. A poet, perhaps. A rock 'n' roller? Not really.
TROUSER PRESS
...all churning N.Y. Dolls rhythm guitars painting a backdrop of romanticised squalor across which he drapes his Lou-Reedette pout of a voice, spewing up a thousand drug references a minute.
SOUNDS
...a confident, intelligent writer with a uniquely strong and compelling delivery.
NEW MUSICAL EXPRESS

It's a harsh aggressive sound of the city, punk with panache, but lacking the killer graces to make the debut a real nugget.
MELODY MAKER

THE CARS
Panorama *(Elektra)*
This is one too many albums of the same from Rick Ocasek and his Boston blo-wavers; patience runs short. If you're one of those who's been keeping an open mind about this allegedly promising outfit, then 'Panorama' should be enough to make you close it once and for all.
NEW MUSICAL EXPRESS
As an alternative to contemporary US rock they're like Jimmy Carter as an alternative to Ronald Reagan. They make slightly different noises at time, but essentially they're pillars of the system. And boring pillars at that.
MELODY MAKER
In many respects it is a facsimile of its predecessors...It's a "good" record.
SOUNDS
'Panorama' isn't merely a joyless joyride, it's an out-and-out drag...the New Wave version of a bad William Burroughs novel...
ROLLING STONE

ROSANNE CASH
Seven Year Itch *(Columbia)*
The high points of Cash's second LP are when she forgets what a pretty voice she has and gets loose...
TROUSER PRESS
...when she's in top form, Rosanne Cash sounds better — stronger, slyer, funnier — than just about any pop singer right now.
ROLLING STONE

A CERTAIN RATIO
To Each *(Factory)*
...a complex mesh of rhythmic, patterns where any number of percussive permutations are pushed and herded by thick, grainy bass lines and harsh, spiky brass textures.
MELODY MAKER
A mental stab at our conciousness. Almost as if you were sitting watching a friend about to scream, about to cry, you will him to crack up, you want him to break down. The tension is just so strong, but the beat goes on. And on. You break down.
SOUNDS
...very good but not brilliant.
RECORD MIRROR

...throughout its nine tracks 'To Each' sounds as if it was played by people with hangovers into microphones wrapped in dusters and produced by someone with a very compressed, obsessively neat and tidy conception of sound.
NEW MUSICAL EXPRESS

CHEAP TRICK
All Shook Up *(Epic)*
What the songs are like is all the same, with only the enigmatic-goofy titles changed to protect the illusion that you are getting your album's worth...This record is guaranteed free of all known redeeming features.
NEW MUSICAL EXPRESS
...clumsy, unimaginative, repetitive, derivative...
RECORD MIRROR
...a very satisfying album.
MELODY MAKER
...ultimately it grates, jars and irritates by its lack of melody or light and shade.
SOUNDS
Cheap Trick are the latest in a long line of spiritual heirs to the Fab Four's Anglo-pop tradition, traceable back through The Move, The Electric Light Orchestra and such hard-rock tangents as The Who and The Yardbirds. And they carry that weight with humour as well as enthusiasm.
ROLLING STONE

CHELSEA
Alternative Hits *(Step Forward)*
Chelsea are the sort of band that a hardcore of fans can really cherish and have faith in. After all, unlike certain other fallen punk heroes, Chelsea haven't been corrupted by the fleshpots of commercial success. Then again, on this evidence they're never likely to get the chance.
NEW MUSICAL EXPRESS
...a barometer of punk as it developed onto its two later fragmentations, the light rock typified by the Undertones and represented here and the electronic dirge.
RECORD MIRROR

ALEX CHILTON
Bach's Bottom *(Line Records)*
One of the biggest lies in rock revolves around the old-fashioned idea that it is justifiable to be as wired up and whacked out, as generally out of your tree as possible, and that this will ultimately correspond to a leap in achievement.
MELODY MAKER

CHROME
Half Machine Lip Moves *(Beggars Banquet)*
I can find no excuse for ugliness, pretension and fraudulence of this kind.
SOUNDS

CITY BOY
Heads Are Rolling *(Vertigo)*
...one of their strongest and most commercial albums to date.
RECORD MIRROR

ERIC CLAPTON
Another Ticket *(RSO)*
...more of the same, with a slight change of emphasis and musical partners.
NEW MUSICAL EXPRESS
...a record that majestically continues the Clapton story with songs that are either freshly minted or unhackneyed; with the man in great, commanding voice; a major guitarist at the peak of his powers; and a songwriter gaining more confidence to stretch his styles and lyrical originality.
MELODY MAKER
...this is far from being one of his best albums.
SOUNDS
Consumately as tasteful AOR as only a combination of post-cure Clapton, linseed-oiled seasoned sidesmen...and funky Nassau's Compass Point Studios could possible concoct.
RECORD MIRROR
To be sure, Eric Clapton's music has the air of conviction rather than the stench of exploitation, but what it lacks is verve, momentum, anger, wit and consequence.
ROLLING STONE

GUY CLARK
The South Coast Of Texas *(Warner Brothers)*
...passable, but tediously pleasant...it's an album that leaves you only rarely stirred, never shaken.
MELODY MAKER

STANLEY CLARKE/GEORGE DUKE
The Clarke/Duke Project *(Epic)*
In which two respected jazz-funk biggies aim for the mainstream and end up condescending to an audience they don't even have...Stanley and George do little more than spend the entire length of an album demonstrating that music is far too important to be left to musicians.
NEW MUSICAL EXPRESS
Clarke and Duke have eschewed all cerebral jazz leanings and gone for accessible funk, rock and pop...about as easy to like as mother's apple pie.
MELODY MAKER

THE CLASH
Sandinista! *(CBS Epic)*
...ridiculously self-indulgent communique from internationsl Clash City headquarters...This record is strong testimony that The Clash have - temporarily at least - lost a grip on their bearings and find themselves parked in a cul-de-sac.
NEW MUSICAL EXPRESS
...a floundering, mutant of an album(s). The odd highlights are lost in a welter of reggae/dub overkill...it represents an emasculation of the raw, urgent energy of The Clash, and suggests - in its bewildering aimlessness -that the band are floundering, uncertain of their direction.
MELODY MAKER
...an adventure of diversity and wit, of struggle and freedom, of excellence and dross. When it is good it is very good. When it is bad...maybe aiming to provide us with three album's worth was aiming too high.
SOUNDS
...a Clash amalgam, powerful, and as suited still to a sound system or a battery radio. It's loose, occasionally anarchic, sometimes fun, always different: technique and experimentation that spills out rhythm and aces when you're least expecting them. A mash up and a surprise every track.
RECORD MIRROR
...an everywhere-you-turn guerilla raid of vision and virtuosity...a sprawling scattered smoke screen of styles, with an expanded range that's at once encyclopedic and supplemental...

ROLLING STONE
That The Clash can produce 36 songs, two-thirds of them generally high calibre, and then deliver them with a variety of conception and execution proves this band's collective talent runs ever onward.
TROUSER PRESS

CLASSIX NOUVEAUX
Night People *(Liberty)*
It comes packaged like a box of super-expensive chocolates full of Eastern promise but reveals little more than a re-recorded romp through the chap's chequered past - all soft centres in flash, trash wrappings.
SOUNDS
...the sense of familiarity, as manifested in trite, banal lyrics, music of agonising mediocrity and sterility, and to cap it all abysmal self-production is overwhelming.
NEW MUSICAL EXPRESS

CLOCK DVA
Thirst *(Fetish)*
...both better than might be expected, and not quite so good as it could have been...the first important debut album of 1981
NEW MUSICAL EXPRESS
You might imagine that it would be hard for a band with such an obvious debt to Captain Beefheart to sound totally bereft of life-giving forces, but Sheffield's Clock DVA manage to achieve this not inconsiderable task, cloaking every note and space with a daunting shadow of grey...an album choked with minor, irrelevant happings but no real *events*...reviewing it was a horrific chore, provoking constant tuts of exasperation.
MELODY MAKER
Clock DVA are full of fear, insecurity, shadows. But there is a smilingness, a love at the root. This constant shift comes out in the music. They favour a rich, dark and very sensuous noise that is hard and deep and most of all wide.
SOUNDS

BRUCE COCKBURN
Humans *(Millennium)*
...a quirky, passionate account of this Canadian Christian mystic's struggle to reconcile his rage about a bad relationship with the intense spirituality that's long been the focal point of his writing...probably the perfect introduction to Bruce Cockburn's music. At its best, it's feverishly lovely.
ROLLING STONE
...there are always questions that gnaw away at the mind, bringing you back to his album time and again.
MELODY MAKER

COCKNEY REJECTS
Greatest Hits Vol 2 *(Zonophone)*
...an album for people who aren't afraid to like the sound that they liked a couple of years back. It'a an album to persuade all those people who pogo in the dark that it's time to come out of the closet, have a party...
MELODY MAKER
...the spotty visage of retrogression, a dark and vaguely depressing collection of loutish drivel, facile and of little merit.

COCKNEY REJECTS
The Power And The Glory *(Zonophone)*
...a brave and encouraging step forward for the band.
MELODY MAKER
...proves the Rejects are immensely talented and even though a lot of their potential has been squandered in the past, it also proves that they can still mean a hell of a lot.
SOUNDS

COLD CHISEL
East *(WEA)*
...simply the sort of record you can play and enjoy for what it is; a collection of strong rock songs, well played and presented with a variety and confidence and a large glimmer of life.
MELODY MAKER

PHIL COLLINS
Face Value *(Virgin)*
What sinks the whole affair is the numbing flavourlessness of what's on the stall; filigree scraps of melody dandified into whole songs, lyrics a hash of old singer-songwriter blather.
NEW MUSICAL EXPRESS
... confirms Collins as something of a musical cosmopolitan; a more suburban imagination would probably have selected one style and disciplined its repertoire to fit. Collins runs riot through a variety of settings, committing himself to the disparate moods and styles with genuine zeal.
MELODY MAKER
As Genesis fans are well aware, Phil Collins wears plenty of hats. But he never tried one on that doesn't fit.
SOUNDS
Play this album until your stereo needle powders to dust.
RECORD MIRROR

THE COMSAT ANGELS
Waiting For A Miracle *(Polydor)*
XTC's inventiveness clothed in the dense, doomy textures of John Cale. A robust, adventurous pop that moves on weighty bass and booming drums, right upfront, while strange sounds hover over the edges, dabbing in melody of weirdness with consistent surprise.
NEW MUSICAL EXPRESS
... simply the most exciting debut album of the year.
MELODY MAKER
... give the album enough plays (you have to) it becomes apparent that some kind of rock 'n' roll vision is at work.
SOUNDS
... a collection of disarming ideas, dropped hints, scattered clues, unexploited melodies, flickering tempo rates, quips, examinations, shifting balance.
RECORD MIRROR
As this quartet juggles the simplistic and the self conscious, they create evocative mood pieces that resonate and insinuate long after the record stops.
TROUSER PRESS

THE CONGOS
Heart Of The Congos *(Go-Feet)*
... one of the reasons for the intense beauty of the delicate tapestry of harmonies and meditative, pathos-tinged music with which they interweave *is* inspired by The Congos' love of The Creator...
NEW MUSICAL EXPRESS
... truly remarkable...Few such essential purchases exist.
MELODY MAKER

RY COODER
Borderline *(Warner Bros)*
... so formidable an album that only a person suffering from terminal ear-cancer could twist the knife into it...
NEW MUSICAL EXPRESS
It's absurd to try and compare Cooder albums.
They're all so different and individual. Just let it be said that this is up there with the best of them.
MELODY MAKER
Unfashionable, hardly likely to inspire the barricades but deeply humane and wonderful. Perfect maybe.
SOUNDS
... this record, like every darn Cooder work, positively shines with tender loving care and on first hearing, the freshness positively screams out to be purchased.
RECORD MIRROR
... his choice of material is inspired. Oddly, though, innate good taste results in inappropriate stiffness; it's not as if this stuff were 500 years old, after all.
TROUSER PRESS

ELVIS COSTELLO
Taking Liberties *(Columbia)*
... this collection of 20 B sides, British album cuts, and outtakes is backhanded right down to its reversed negative cover photo. By ceremoniously gift-wrapping his trash, the artist treats himself (after only four LPs) with an archivist's reverence usually reserved for the dead.
ROLLING STONE
... this is prime stuff — as good as any of his preplanned albums, and certainly more consistent than Get Happy!!'s' 20 maybes.
TROUSER PRESS

ELVIS COSTELLO AND THE ATTRACTIONS
Trust *(F Beat/Columbia)*
Costello — like hardly anyone else the eye can hear — has the ability to invest fresh meanings in a hitherto trustworthy old phrase. This music respects *everybody's* intelligence — not just an intellectual clique here, an ineffectual clique there.
NEW MUSICAL EXPRESS
... arrives like a flurry of punches, pinning back your ears as it pins you to the ropes; ducking one punch, you walk into another.
MELODY MAKER
... has much of what made Costello famous and little of what endeared him to me in the first place.
SOUNDS
The Costello formula should be getting boring by now but while he still invests energy and care into his work and then sidesteps the pitfalls with agility and intelligence then he's going to put off the execution a few times more.
RECORD MIRROR

... a collection of images picked up and dropped, each verse shedding a bushel of bon mots like so many hot potatoes.
ROLLING STONE

JOHN COUGAR
Nothin' Matters And What If It Did *(Riva)*
The late Seventies saw the search for 'The New Springsteen' take on Grail-like proportions. A strong contender must be John Cougar, not because of his musical or lyrical originality, but simply by his comprehensive assimilation of Springsteen's hallmarks.
MELODY MAKER
There's hardly a track on this album that I could recommend...
RECORD MIRROR

LOL COXHILL AND MORGAN FISHER
Slow Music *(Pipe Music)*
Without ever slipping into studiousness or contrivance, they straddle the fence between modern classical and ambient "rock" music, bringing out the best in both.
SOUNDS
... it has an initial attraction, but one which soon fades due to the two musicians' seeming lack of emotional involvement.
MELODY MAKER

KEVIN COYNE
Sanity Stomp *(Virgin)*
... an album which displays both the absolute highs, and the desperate lows, of Kevin Coyne. The human strengths and weaknesses.
NEW MUSICAL EXPRESS
... the presence of The Ruts on the first two sides gives it an energy which could be allowed to protect the listener from the words he is singing, and could possibly make this his most commercial album yet.
MELODY MAKER
... full of good tunes and articulate lyrics with a pleasing variety of sounds coming from two completely different backing bands.
SOUNDS
Kevin's old edge is missing on these albums, he sounds whimsical and self-indulgent, badly in need of editing.
RECORD MIRROR

THE CRAMPS
Psychedelic Jungle *(IRS)*
Instead of authentically recreating the sound (like The Stray Cats and other slap-bass bands here), they update the music's hell-raising aesthetic to inspire the outrage now that rockabilly did 25 years ago.
TROUSER PRESS
There is nothing like this music anywhere, unless it's on other Cramps' records.
NEW MUSICAL EXPRESS
... while this does lack the impact of the first gloriously frenetic LP, further acquaintance points to more subtle delights.
MELODY MAKER

CRASS
Penis Envy *(Crass Records)*
... shows Crass developing a more sophisticated form of punk and realigning their attacks on society from close to a radical feminist standpoint.
NEW MUSICAL EXPRESS
An obvious, blatant fingernail pushed in the mute bubble of disguise and normality that bounces around Patrick McGoohan's 'Prisoner' set, frequents mainstream modern music cultures in the guise of subtlety, and patrols every avenue of 'society' like some silent, stalking Securicor dog.
SOUNDS

THE CRAVATS
In Toytown *(Small Wonder)*
... the songs — which are obviously written as *poems* rather than lyrics, and dreadful 3rd Form doggerel at that — are boring rants at easy targets like TV commercials (anyone *really* concerned about such things has far too little to think about), spiced with the occasional customary declamation that the singer is vital, alive, and an individual.
NEW MUSICAL EXPRESS
One of the year's strangest releases but also one of the best.
RECORD MIRROR

RANDY CRAWFORD
Secret Combination *(Warner Bros)*
... played and sung with sureness of touch and style.
RECORD MIRROR
... the album exudes care, class and emotion.
MELODY MAKER

CREEDENCE CLEARWATER REVIVAL
The Royal Albert Hall Concert *(Fantasy)*
Eleven years after the event, Creedence Clearwater Revival remain the essence of the rock and roll group as a motivating force.
NEW MUSICAL EXPRESS
Better than 'Live In Europe', where the three-piece Creedence sounded awfully tinny, the band perform carbon copies of their greatest hits with so little deviation that it makes the album a bad buy for anyone with 'Creedence Gold'.
MELODY MAKER
... a fitting tribute to their ability to crack the mainstream while remaining true to their southern swampland R&B roots.
RECORD MIRROR
This belated testament to John Fogerty's genius proves conclusively that burning originality and rock 'n' roll traditionalism can mix.
TROUSER PRESS

THE CRETONES
Snap! Snap! *(Planet)*
Snap! Snap! isn't as crude and ungainly as 'Thin Red Line', which is a mistake, I think. At least on The Cretones' first album, desperation oozed out of Goldenberg's whiny, half-shout singing and keyboards that stomped all over the rest of the mix.
ROLLING STONE
Perfect for summer lawn parties.
TROUSER PRESS

PETER CRISS
Out Of Control
(Mercury/Casablanca)
... and a foolish and overweight collection of nonsense, wrapped in a nasty airbrushed cover and burdened with a huge list of dedications...
MELODY MAKER
... perhaps the greatest album by an ex-member of Kiss of all time...
SOUNDS
This stuff may be aesthetically rewarding to Criss, but it's totally unambitious and uninspired.
RECORD MIRROR

THE CURE
Faith *(Fiction Records)*
It's very well played, beautifully recorded and says absolutely nothing meaningful in a fairly depressing way.
NEW MUSICAL EXPRESS
It swings like a warm summer night, its warm breezes and rarefied beat transcend everyday dance music.
SOUNDS
... hollow, shallow, pretentious, meaningless, self-important and bereft of any real heart and soul...
RECORD MIRROR

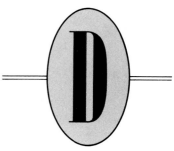

THE DAMNED
The Black Album *(Chiswick)*
Being an institution, The Damned always turn something up: they're stray nocturnal cats who return in the daytime with old rubbish or wax-work jewels.
NEW MUSICAL EXPRESS
... a brave try from a band who realised they couldn't keep on playing punk forever.
MELODY MAKER
... A humid double set of inspiration and confusion. Where 'Machine Gun Etiquette' was a reaffirmation of yobbo strength 'The Black Album' is evidence of their melodic maturity.
SOUNDS
... highlights the band's metamorphosis from speedy young yobbos to acidic adults.
RECORD MIRROR
The better parts of this disc make me hope they'll stick around.
TROUSER PRESS

THE CHARLIE DANIELS BAND
Full Moon *(Epic)*
The musicians play well and the production is crisp but the album fails to satisfy.
MELODY MAKER
... plenty of power chords and Led Zeppelin backbeats for the heavy-metal crowd, hard-luck blues for roots' sake, a ghost story, gypsy violins and Spanish guitars, a bearish breath of patriotism and even an antebellum waltz.
ROLLING STONE

JENNY DARREN
Jenny Darren *(DJM)*
Sugar-coated in pompous strings, ham-strung by puffed up riffs and drowned in bloated arrangements.
MELODY MAKER
... alternately the wrong side of 'laid-back' the wrong side of 'raunchy' and the wrong side of 'sophisticated'.
RECORD MIRROR
Darren has, in spite of her other inadequacies, a damn good voice.
SOUNDS

MILES DAVIS
The Man With The Horn
(CBS)
...shows him still alive and kicking, if a little reticent at times...Don't knock it — it's the rebirth of the cool! And whatever you do, don't miss it.
NEW MUSICAL EXPRESS

THE dB's
Stands For deciBels *(Albion)*
The dB's are refined almost to the point of weirdness and a bit too frenzied to fit on any juke-box...If there are any flags left to wave, then, The dB's deserves to be among them.
NEW MUSICAL EXPRESS
For the most part there's something too forced about the band's attempt to forge intelligent mainstream pop/rock, and it brings them dangerously close to the burial ground of that deaf old buzzard power pop.
MELODY MAKER
... marvellous though parts of 'Stands For deciBels' may be, it tires me, as if these dB's are just a touch too frantic and desperate about being so bent.
SOUNDS
This isn't the first time; but I think I'm in love. I'm in love with the notion that the dB's could be the ideal pop band...The dB's beat is wrapped up in the realms of authentic pop, crafted, textured, but uncalculating.
RECORD MIRROR
... anyone who was touched by the music of a decade and a half ago should hear this record. Anyone wondering if that music is valid today will find it alive and kicking in the form of the dB's.
TROUSER PRESS

DEDRINGER
Direct Line *(Din Disc)*
... a unit of strong identity and purpose with only the inconsistent nature of the material occasionally letting them down.
RECORD MIRROR
... falls away rather too often into the faceless rifferama that characterises so many of the bands that were signed up in '79 and '80. Dedringer do have good ideas, they just don't seem to have enough yet.
SOUNDS

KIKI DEE
Perfect Timing *(Ariola)*
After nearly two decades in the biz, Kiki Dee has finally achieved something approaching excellence.
RECORD MIRROR

DEF LEPPARD
High 'N' Dry *(Vertigo)*
...a titanium toecapped kick in the teeth for Def Leppard's British critics. My dentures are on order already.
SOUNDS

DEFUNKT
Defunkt *(Hannibal)*
Defunkt's harsh laughter might ring hollow if it weren't reinforced by such a pulverising soundtrack. As it is, Defunkt are to funk in 1981 what The Pistols were to Rock in 1977.
NEW MUSICAL EXPRESS
... for all the immediate appeal that Defunkt have, they need to move themselves off the dance floor and in a new direction. Or Defunkt will be.
SOUNDS
The band's light-handed (and lightning-quick) rhythm section navigates this album's eight cuts like young Muhammed Ali dancing around his prey.
TROUSER PRESS
Defunkt declares a credo and a challenge in their first cut, 'Make Them Dance,' but should you try to comply, the only place these frenzied funk-jazz grooves will land you is in traction.
ROLLING STONE

DEKE LEONARD
Before Your Very Eyes
(United Artists)
...gleams with the trimmings of authentic blues archaelogy. It is real music played on real instruments by real musicians.
NEW MUSICAL EXPRESS

DELTA 5
See The Whirl *(PRE)*
...almost an embarrassment of riches.
RECORD MIRROR

RICK DERRINGER
Face To Face *(Blue Sky)*
... in one ear and out the other.
RECORD MIRROR
... makes you wonder whether Mr D might not have been better off waiting till he'd written enough new material to fill a whole album rather than going into the studio with just over half of one.
SOUNDS

Clueless, clumsy and incomprehensibly cliched, it beats me how 'Face To Face' has the nerve to suggest that 'Rock 'n' Roll' will never die when it single handedly bores it to death.
MELODY MAKER

DEUTSCH AMERIKANISCHE FREUNDSCHAFT
Alles Ist Gut *(Virgin)*
... one of the few records that totally immerses itself in the world of modern disco while remaining conscious enough to see what's really going on outside. It's also the first genuinely original European disco LP since early Moroder/Summer collaborations and Kraftwerk's 'Trans Europe Express'.
NEW MUSICAL EXPRESS
Even after repeated hearings, 'Alles Ist Gut' seems to be the monochrome relative to the queer and colourful cameos of 'Der Kleinen'.
SOUNDS
Repetitious, boring and cerebral, this album is about as inspiring as a frontal lobotomy.
RECORD MIRROR
Most of the ideas here are at best half-baked, resulting in what sounds like a poor imitation of the New York electronic duo Suicide playing in the aftermath of the Dresden bombing raid.
MELODY MAKER

DEVO
Devo Live *(Virgin)*
...completely unnecessary, not to say misleading.
NEW MUSICAL EXPRESS
Since Devo's live shows emphasise the band's visual rather then musical prowess. I'll leave you to work out what a waste this really is.
RECORD MIRROR

NEIL DIAMOND
The Jazz Singer *(Capitol East)*
... some of the songs are so strong as to stand up convincingly outside the film. ...an entertainer who truly lives his personal tensions through his songs and his voice.
MELODY MAKER
Diamond proves that he isn't entirely washed up.
RECORD MIRROR

MANU DIBANGO
Ambassador *(Island)*
A vast amount of money and energy have already been wasted on this project. It is not recommended that you compound the error by investing any of yours in it.
NEW MUSICAL EXPRESS
... it's a happenings record, with so much going on, bridging so many styles, and never easy to pinpoint.
RECORD MIRROR

DILLINGER
Badder Than Them *(A&M)*
... after all these years the wacky DJ is finally heading for the fat white cat market with no apology.
NEW MUSICAL EXPRESS
Nervously neutred for mass consumption the infamous Dillinger runs through a meaningless mess of up-tempo steppers and offensive macho (so-called) love songs that no amount of flash vocal effects and sharp production techniques can save from the dumper.
MELODY MAKER

DIRE STRAITS
Making Movies *(Warner Bros/Vertigo)*
But let the lights go up and the trumpets blast. This is the big one.
RECORD MIRROR
... a winner. It has a distinct character of its own...without losing any of the quality and depth that are the band's trademarks.
MELODY MAKER
The result is richer, glossier sound that also contrives to appear more natural than that on earlier product. There's less sense of clever novices showing off their skills.
NEW MUSICAL EXPRESS
I really wish I could praise this album as some kind of brave new work — a reaffirmation of past strengths with ingenious and daring innovations. But the sad truth is this just left me feeling indecisive and generally disappointed.
SOUNDS
The combination of the star's lyrical script, his intense vocal performances and the band's cutting-edge rock and roll soundtrack is breathtaking -everything the first two albums should have been but weren't.
ROLLING STONE

... a surprising departure on a number of levels. Anyone who wrote this band off as a one-style-wonder will have to reconsider upon hearing 'Making Movies'.
TROUSER PRESS

DIXIE DREGS
Dregs Of The Earth *(Arista)*
I wish the Dixie Dregs would find a way to harness their considerable individual ability. Right now, they are just another fusion band fusing nothing at all.
MELODY MAKER

DOLLAR
The Paris Collection *(WEA)*
... uniformly lightweight pop/MOR, with an abundance of sensitive chord changes and poignant lyrics.
MELODY MAKER
I adore Dollar. There is something accidentally almost pure about their confection-making that makes them more than the throwaway delight they would settle for and places them up there with Abba and Racey.
SOUNDS

DOLL BY DOLL
Doll By Doll *(Magnet)*
A captivating and provocative album, its power to lure the listener into its extravagant world is equalled by the integrity of its content.
NEW MUSICAL EXPRESS
You could pile superlative on top of hyperbole and still fail to capture the seductive magic of this LP.
MELODY MAKER
... a fashion-free and surprisingly commercial record that sounds happy with itself, that sounds complete.
SOUNDS

DOME
Dome 2 *(Dome Records)*
Lewis and Gilbert have achieved an effective aural poetry that's a smooth and growing fusion of words and music. Like Joy Division and PiL, their unspecific sound sketches frequently offer a perspective on human isolation.
NEW MUSICAL EXPRESS
... genuinely original musically, with the modernist tools of synth, guitar, moaning and groaning as elusively used as they were on Cabaret Voltaire's 'Mix Up', a project in many ways similar.
SOUNDS

THE DOOBIE BROTHERS
One Step Closer *(Warner Bros)*
... the group's best album to date, and, furthermore, the work of a unified — at last! — band, pulling together, in one direction, for maximum effect.
MELODY MAKER
The low quality and cynical carelessness of 'One Step Closer' is actually rather shocking — at least if you think of the Doobies as professionals with artistic aspirations and a stake in pop culture.
ROLLING STONE

DR FEELGOOD
A Case Of The Shakes *(United Artists)*
It doesn't do to think too long and hard on Dr Feelgood, actually. Their own approach is straight to the point, makes a good excuse for inviting a few pals round and cleaning out the off license. I'll drink to it.
NEW MUSICAL EXPRESS
Predictable can still be pleasurable.
TROUSER PRESS
... simply the best Feelgoods album ever-and more, it achieves a commercial crossover into pop music never suggested, let alone explored, by any of the band's previous records.
MELODY MAKER
... it's just too boring.
SOUNDS
... The Feelgoods certainly sound fresher than they have for years.
RECORD MIRROR

Dr. FEELGOOD
On The Job *(Liberty)*
No sparkle, no life and no atmosphere, Dr Feelgood needs some major surgery.
RECORD MIRROR
That's the attraction, the pleasure of hearing them do it again, that persistent committed, energetic old R&B trip.
NEW MUSICAL EXPRESS

DR HOOK
Rising *(Mercury)*
... two sides of wall-to-wall pap, weak-kneed ballads dripping with simpering strings and feeble harmonies.
MELODY MAKER
'Rising' for what it's worth is an excellently recorded and produced work. Artistically, however, this is dire stuff.
RECORD MIRROR

MIKEY DREAD
World War III *(Dread At The Controls)*
Mikey Dread confronts the forthcoming conflagration in as light and upful a manner as possible : as bright and positive as his subject matter is gloomy and threatening.
NEW MUSICAL EXPRESS
... this computermix works on a more nervy, unpredictable level but at very least has the positive character and individuality lacking of ninety per cent of current reggae LPs.
SOUNDS

DURAN DURAN
Duran Duran *(EMI)*
... with this fine collection of easily-ignored, candy-flavoured muzak, they've actually performed a remarkable feat — the conceptualist's paradise — an album which it's actively better not to listen to.
MELODY MAKER
Duran World Domination starts here with a saccharine-sweet sound and, most importantly, a proper i-d.
SOUNDS
... stylish and sophisticated dance beats with just enough in the way of youthful edge and ideas to make it interesting.
RECORD MIRROR
...a sensibly-packaged, respectably safe and self-consciously worthy record that belies the promised glamour of their two earlier singles.
NEW MUSICAL EXPRESS

IAN DURY & THE BLOCKHEADS
Laughter *(Stiff/Epic)*
'Laughter' mostly pulls against itself: the Blockheads' get-down groove versus Dury's overambitious concepts. When Dury hones his wide-ranging vision, he'll make music that's compelling as well as entertaining.
TROUSER PRESS
... a cat's cradle of an album, rich and complex, demonstrating yet again Dury's extraordinary blend of Dan Leno music hall surrealism, the raunch of manic rocker Gene Vincent and his own unique self.
MELODY MAKER
'Laughter' in the face of adversity, laughter at other people's expense, laughter at ourselves and those more or less fortunate, teddyboy Ian Dury cocking a snook at the social workers, laughs all round.
NEW MUSICAL EXPRESS

Despite the unseemly rush of having to force out an album a year, quality control has not wavered. 'Laughter' is another cracker — though not of course from quite the same team that brought you 'New Boots' and 'DIY'.
SOUNDS
... grows in strength with each listening and the new simplistic but more raucous Blockheads show an honesty and commitment that is to be admired and enjoyed.
RECORD MIRROR
... he's raw, relentlessly bawdy, self-indulgent, sly — and, beneath it all, often warmly, albeit grimly, humane. Dury's albums have captured the sprawling charm of his music with increasing accuracy and fervour, and 'Laughter' is the best yet.
ROLLING STONE

THE EAGLES
Eagles Live *(Asylum)*
'Eagles Live's' only achievement is that it hits a new low in worthlessness.
NEW MUSICAL EXPRESS
...a redundant album, and I write as someone who likes both The Eagles and double live albums.
MELODY MAKER
That four years later they're still peddling the same old stuff is an indication of how they're staggering along on empty. The highlighting of this situation in barely an hour's worth of time is just bare-faced greed.
RECORD MIRROR

EARTH, WIND AND FIRE
Faces *(CBS)*
Like a cowboy's farewell to his horse, this LP will mark the last bubbles as WE&F explode into a super-vacuum.
NEW MUSICAL EXPRESS

SHEENA EASTON
Take My Time *(EMI)*
Her image is a triumph of tailored packaging around a product so average and innocuous that almost unnoticed, she's slipped into a commanding position.
NEW MUSICAL EXPRESS

Groomed and confident, talented and tuneful. Sheena Easton will confound them all, for her music is an unpretentious tonic in these dark days.
MELODY MAKER

This is one perfectly produced album, with faultless playing and spot-on singing, our Sheen coming out like Barbra Streisand and The Carpenters all rolled up into one lovely, profitable little bundle.
SOUNDS

ECHO AND THE BUNNYMEN
Heaven Up Here *(Korova)*
Liverpool's finest continue to sing the blues, continue to devote themselves to the glossy celebration of existential sadness. 'Heaven Up Here' offers an anatomy of melancholy, resplendent with the glamour of doom.
RECORD MIRROR

At their finest, The Bunnymen are continuing to play majestic, uplifting music that will shine hard through the dark days ahead of us.
MELODY MAKER

Echo And The Bunnymen have moved on yet again, and, in moving, made more moving music than they've ever done before.
NEW MUSICAL EXPRESS

The typical (anti-) rock traditionalist's second album, that rare oft-mocked *angst* we don't get these days — a big quiet form of traditionalism in these times of small loud innovations.
SOUNDS

EDDIE & THE HOT RODS
Fish 'N' Chips *(EMI)*
...full of forced bravado and bonhomie, dumb irresponsible drug references, and pathetic paeans to mindless violence.
MELODY MAKER

In their brief prime Eddie & The Hot Rods were the Paul Revere & The Raiders of the new wave — not as classy (i.e. pretentious) as the competition but easily as energetic. Now, well, the sooner the scrapheap the better.
TROUSER PRESS

DAVE EDMUNDS
Twangin' *(Swansong)*
...like a shop full of reproduction furniture. Finely crafted and well upholstered but never the real thing.
NEW MUSICAL EXPRESS

This album is bliss. There's not a wasted second on any of it.
MELODY MAKER

An album of two sides, the first classily up to form and the second a dreadful pointer to the future. 'Twangin' ' perfectly and ominously sums up the post-Rockpile-split dilemma.
SOUNDS

...a humdinger that simply blow-torches the ass off just about every other veteran's release this year.
RECORD MIRROR

Edmunds, at his best, combines reverence with vitality, but 'Twangin'...has the odour of mothballs.
TROUSER PRESS

JOE ELY
Must Notta Gotta Lotta *(MCA)*
Joe Ely's star remains in the ascendant and I hope he gets all the commercial success he deserves. The rather over-wrought hyperboles that have so far greeted this album don't do him or his fans any favours.
NEW MUSICAL EXPRESS

...Ely has everything going for him but success.
MELODY MAKER

...the album never gels completely. The live excitement Ely bases his reputation on is sadly absent from the grooves.
SOUNDS

Hard country aficionados will love it, but like previous efforts it is too patchy and narrow in perspective to appeal to a broader public.
RECORD MIRROR

...overflows with joyous, crackling rock 'n' roll that exposes most of Ely's fellow classicists as rank poseurs.
TROUSER PRESS

KEITH EMERSON
Nighthawks *(Backstreet)*
...classic Keith Emerson...it matches the film superbly.
MELODY MAKER

BRAIN ENO/DAVID BYRNE
My Life In The Bush Of Ghosts *(Sire/EG)*
If 'My Life' lacks anything in large degree, it's feeling. There's no sense of resonance here, no strangeness, wonderment or mystery, no real consideration for or understanding of, the subject matter at hand.
NEW MUSICAL EXPRESS

...somehow draws together the disparate strains into a coherent, vibrant whole which adds neither insult nor injury to its pristine catalysts.
MELODY MAKER

...skilful juxtaposition of styles, skilful exploration of resources and, some would say, skilful plagiarism too. But don't confuse it with Art with a capital A. Craft with a capital C would be far more appropriate.
SOUNDS

...for the most part...comes over as half-baked self-indulgent twaddle.
RECORD MIRROR

Maybe the message is that a bunch of iconoclastic Anglo-Americans can make us think and dance — two actions, which have never been mutually exclusive.
TROUSER PRESS

...an undeniably awesome feat of tape editing and rhythmic ingenuity. But, like most "found" art, it raises stubborn questions about context, manipulation and cultural imperialism.
ROLLING STONE

ROCKY ERICKSON AND THE ALIENS
Five Symbols *(CBS)*
...a disappointing record, and one which leaves a slight but lingering taste of cynical artifice.
NEW MUSICAL EXPRESS

...an oppressive experience...Delightful uniqueness.
SOUNDS

Erickson sings like a preacher after a few too many whiskeys, sweetness with an edge and some good old Texas soul.
TROUSER PRESS

THE EXPLOITED
Punk's Not Dead *(Secret)*
...a crude, fast playing bunch of sloganeers with a Scottish singer whose accent is as thick as a lard sandwich.
NEW MUSICAL EXPRESS

...The Exploited and the rest of the new breed stand poised to build a new, more real wave of punk, a riot of our own. And you won't shut us up. Ever.
SOUNDS

EYELESS IN GAZA
Photographs As Memories *(Cherry Red)*
...a dreary collection of castrated and wilfully contorted neu-pop songs — post amateurism at its most grubby and preciously screwy, pre-art school at its most pedantic and self-conscious.
NEW MUSICAL EXPRESS

...constantly strives for something special, very seldom fully succeeds but even its many pitfalls and

failures make for an interesting, invigorating listen.
MELODY MAKER

This is awful. Not just ordinary awful, but STINKINGLY AWFUL.
RECORD MIRROR

THE FABULOUS THUNDERBIRDS
Butt Rockin' *(Chrysalis)*
... it does manage to capture and combine that uncluttered zing of early rock 'n' roll/rockabilly with the polished power of musicianship that thankfully adds lustre to a well-trodden but still vital style of music instead of drowning it in half-assed incompetence or needless studio gimmicks and gloss... Quite simply, they're the best.
SOUNDS

If you like music that is *alive*, buy this album.
NEW MUSICAL EXPRESS

... a truly three dimensional album. The sound is deep and rich, horns and keyboards flesh out the hard driving simplicity wherever it suits...beaten out with that casual American flair that makes their European counterparts, from Rockpile to Dr Feelgood and 9 Below Zero, sound like semi-pro schoolboys.
RECORD MIRROR

... nothing fancy; just the goods delivered with vigour, humour and the musical clout of a confederate cavalry charge.
MELODY MAKER

FAD GADGET
Fireside Favourites *(Mute)*
... sounds good enough — discounting a few whining aberrations — to become just that. For once an album that's as wittily subversive as it is listenable.
NEW MUSICAL EXPRESS

I'm afraid that Fad Gadget is not my fireside favourite. Currently he's sitting in my yard inside a large metal container awaiting collection.
MELODY MAKER

Fad is making a commercially alternative music with a

perverse sense of humour and this confident album deserves a lot more than just a place in the cliquey alternative charts.
RECORD MIRROR

... quite simply the best electronic album since the release of 'Mix Up' by Cabaret Voltaire. I recommend anybody who enjoys aggressive electronic music to buy this album.
SOUNDS

THE FALL
Grotesque After The Gramme *(Rough Trade)*
The Fall remain murky and weird, a unique pop nightmare of urban wastelands, new Puritans and H.P. Lovecraft horror, brusquely spiced with Northern wit and pride.
NEW MUSICAL EXPRESS

... an uncompromising barrage of overlapping, sometimes obscure, tonal anecdotes covered by Mark Smith's hectoring vocals. It can be exhausting, stark, fascinating, unintelligible, even unlistenable, but hardly ever boring.
MELODY MAKER

... an aggressive, cohesive, strong bonded album — the most complete to date and the most diverse.
SOUNDS

... better than Blondie or Boomtown Rats but that's no argument. It doesn't have a soul, it's loveless, it doesn't do a thing for me.
RECORD MIRROR

LEE FARDON
Stories Of Pleasure *(Aura)*
Scanning fraught emotional landscapes with a brawling intensity and a fierce disregard for sentimental disguises. Lee Fardon's debut album whips off the bandages, tears at its wounds, lands bleeding on the deck; a victim of its own nightmare vision.
MELODY MAKER

WILTON FELDER
Inherit The Wind *(MCA)*
It says something about the state of "soul" music, in its broadest sense, that young British people can groove on a middle-aged, balding American saxophonist.
RECORD MIRROR

... over produced and often far too slick for its own good, a series of polished exercises in various styles that eventually leaves you begging for more and more substantial content. Felder's own, distinctive roots in tough Southern R&B push through the gauze all too rarely.
NEW MUSICAL EXPRESS

FIRE ENGINES
Lubricate Your Living Room *(Pop Aural)*
Fire Engines are crude (with a production to match) and compelling, rough stuff indeed that leaps up, down and inside out, nagging your mind with its worryingly unusual rifts for hours afterwards.
MELODY MAKER

By any conventional standards, 'Lubricate' is atrocious, but it sure achieves what the blurb claims, "providing a background for active people". I love the idea of a record being an "accessory" and this one could get life out of a tortoise!
SOUNDS

... Fire Engines' messy assault of dirty metallic guitars comes as a welcome alternative at a time when everyone else is going out of their way to sound clinically clean.
NEW MUSICAL EXPRESS

FISCHER Z
Red Skies Over Paradise *(Liberty)*
Another case of a band with a couple of promising singles to their name spreading their talents thinly over an album's worth of material.
MELODY MAKER

If this isn't the year of Fischer Z then there isn't any justice.
RECORD MIRROR

They add nothing: just another band in a mass of "just another" bands.
NEW MUSICAL EXPRESS

... the dawning of beauty, pure metallic beauty, from a band I'd never dreamed of investigating or writing about. In these few moments of vinyl, every wrist-slashing emotion, every music I'd longed for smashed through the speakers — giving me some hope I might live to love — on a new day.
SOUNDS

...one of those rare instances where a band is both worthwhile *and* commercial.
TROUSER PRESS

FIST
Turn On The Hell *(MCA)*
Fist shouldn't be dismissed but 'Turn On The Hell' shows them punching at air.
MELODY MAKER

Fist fall between too many stools, the desire for originality dwarfing the songs themselves and knocking them offbeam.
SOUNDS

...this does take a while to grow on you, but the rewards for putting in a little listening effort are well worth it...
RECORD MIRROR

FLASH IN THE PAN
Lights In The Night *(Ensign)*
It's a non-committed, shallow album. It's everything that's wrong with today's pop (using the word in the lowest sense) yet it doesn't quite dare to be pop so all the time it's laughing at itself - and at the same time it's laughing at you.
MELODY MAKER

...they sound like they had plenty of laughs making the album, and doubtless gain immense pleasure and self-satisfaction showing emergent Oz rockers how simple it is when you know how.
SOUNDS

MICK FLEETWOOD
The Visitor *(RCA)*
...a finely crafted piece of work, recorded in Ghana with back-up, collaboration and occasional composition by native musicians...They knock spots off the fake Burundi bashers, believe me.
RECORD MIRROR

FLEETWOOD MAC
Fleetwood Mac Live *(Warner Bros)*
...eminently playable, containing the best tracks from the group's last three studio records...
NEW MUSICAL EXPRESS

Fleetwood Mac let technical perfection go hang in favour of a joyous celebration of live rock... They have the self-confidence to live with the unexpected, and have no need to hold themselves up as infallible gods.
MELODY MAKER

Some parts of this album are good and others are bloody awful, it's really as simple as that.
RECORD MIRROR

...these two discs don't encourage you to go see them play.
TROUSER PRESS

Overall, Buckingham emerges as a likeable, hard-working oddball, one whose excesses are usually justified by the beauty of the finished product.
ROLLING STONE

THE FLYING LIZARDS
Fourth Wall *(Virgin)*
...positively bubbles with life, humour, aggression and fun, and has a dance beat that sounds as though it's produced for and by human beings.
SOUNDS

David Cunningham, the quirky and innovative creator and purveyor of The Flying Lizards sound offers something more compulsive than the run of the mill bleep and flash syndrome because he composes - if that's the word - with soul and just a little humour.
RECORD MIRROR

...bizarre experimentalism a patchy texture and the occasional satisfaction.
MELODY MAKER

Artistic plunderings...is one of the strongest features of the second Flying Lizards LP...which is a strange museum with a lot else in it besides.
NEW MUSICAL EXPRESS

ELLEN FOLEY
Spirit Of St Louis *(Epic)*
...a progression as brave as it is undoubtedly absurd in parts.
NEW MUSICAL EXPRESS

Ellen Foley dabbling in the mask of Man Ray and the pose of Edith Piaf... Ellen 'n' Mick are nice people, and to be scrupulously fair it's obvious this is *meant* as a slab of high rock art rather than a piece of seamless, trendy MOR.
SOUNDS

If you're up to appreciating all the shades colouring the rock 'n' roll spectrum, investigate this album.
RECORD MIRROR

...struck me as the power behind the throne being of more interest than the monarch occupying it.
MELODY MAKER

...mannered, precisely assembled and reeks of an art-students-on-holiday atmosphere that would mortify Clash headbangers if even a whiff were detected on one of their heroes' albums.
TROUSER PRESS

Though Ellen Foley's spirit may be willing, her sound is weak.
ROLLING STONE

STEVE FORBERT
Little Stevie Orbit *(Epic)*
...something of a half-and-half affair. When he grits his teeth the album bites back but when he's trying to please the album just grins dopily.
SOUNDS
...an artist capable of entertaining, but not inspiring. There is definitely a burgeoning talent which is not fully realised here.
MELODY MAKER
Since Forbert's sense of rock & roll is a good deal livelier than that of most of his singer/songwriter competition, I suppose that there's not much point in belabouring his failings. He's doing exactly what he wants to do, and his collegiate audience will more than likely lap it up.
ROLLING STONE

FOREIGNER
4 *(Atlantic)*
...whilst remaining true to those sturdy AOR values of well-heeled melody, vocal harmonies and spacious keyboards sophistication, they've acquired an AC/DC-style turbo-charged feel for aggression that's well in order.
RECORD MIRROR

4 OUT OF 5 DOCTORS
4 Out Of 5 Doctors
(Nemperor)
4 Out Of 5 Doctors' musical medicine slides down as smoothly as cheery cough syrup, but the culminative effects of a large dosage (i.e. repeated listenings) make a day's rest in bed seem, in the long run, more rewarding.
ROLLING STONE

ARETHA FRANKLIN
Aretha *(Arista)*
...exactly the sort of work she's been turning out since she dipped away from her heyday.
SOUNDS
Aretha's obviously fired with a new vitality that comes from a new deal. It comes from feeling important again, regaining confidence and tackling songs with the fire and soul of old.
RECORD MIRROR
Other singers used to be foolish in the extreme if they ever so much as dreamt of covering a song Aretha had recorded and, therefore made her own. Is this still the case?
MELODY MAKER

FRED FRITH
Gravity *(Ralph)*
Umpteen variations of European ethnic music, various ages of jazz, chamber music, rock 'n' roll all collide with Frith as he leads a New York street band in a medley of Soul and Hispanic standards. Marvy.
SOUNDS
Ostensibly an album of dance music, 'Gravity' fuses both ends of Frith's guitar spectrum (music and noise) into a free-fall zone of rhythms and textures, "found" sounds and minutely arranged compositions.
TROUSER PRESS
...a *positive* album, in all senses of the word, and has a warmth and honesty not present in most recent music - in any field you care to name.
NEW MUSICAL EXPRESS

FRED FRITH
Speechless *(Ralph Records)*
It's the sort of music that can't decide if it wants to be flamboyant and outrageous, moody and clever, or if it just wants to go on seeking the solution to intelligent popularism.
MELODY MAKER
This is furious creativity with a clear eye for the end result.
TROUSER PRESS

FREEEZ
Southern Freeez *(Beggars Banquet)*
...flowing, mostly beauty music, out to get you with its various wiles...
RECORD MIRROR
...an album of soft-shoe shuffling, laid-back jazz funk with a cocktail stick in the side and a glacé cherry on top.
SOUNDS
...their idea of jazz-funk is closer to the old-hat filmsy fusion of Herbie Hancock or Spyrogyra than the embroiled grit of American new-wavers like Defunkt.
NEW MUSICAL EXPRESS

ROBERT FRIPP
The League Of Gentlemen *(EGED)*
Most of the album is excellent and has former XTC keyboard wizard Barry Andrews, weaving vibrant bursts of organ through the manic fingerings of precise guitar maestro, Robert Fripp; both of them offering calculated and powerful presentations that never cease to amaze and appeal.
RECORD MIRROR

My unease with this album is not that Fripp's one-time uniquely inventive touch has apparently been confined to format, linear playing, but it sounds too damn smug and comfortable... This is an album that bewitched me briefly but bored me rapidly.
MELODY MAKER
...manages to provide one with an aural xerox of the group's basic musical clout, but is also impaired by Fripp's penchant for tossing in myriad shards of self-indulgent conceptualist blather.
NEW MUSICAL EXPRESS
Robert Fripp has made it a point never to separate his music from his Gurdjieff inspired theories about individualism and the impending socioeconomic apocalypse. Here, as on his previous discs, you can't buy one without the other.
ROLLING STONE

G

JOHNNY G
G-Beat *(Beggars Banquet)*
...an amalgamation of roots and influences derived from reggae, blues, rock and roll combined with a touch of whimsical and eccentric Brit humour.
SOUNDS
You've got to be tolerant of unostentatious bar music — jug band sans jug, if you will — to get excited about Johnny G, but he's got a lot to offer if you're willing and able.
TROUSER PRESS

RORY GALLAGHER
Stage Struck *(Chrysalis)*
...not an album that will make Gallagher new friends from past enemies, but it's one that will be eagerly received by the faithful. And justifiably so.
MELODY MAKER
...a consolation for those who didn't get to see him, and a souvenir for those who did.
RECORD MIRROR

GAMMA
Gamma 2 *(Elektra)*
HM freaks will want to try this antidote to Asprin. It's

just a shame that so many precious old-based grooves are wasted.
MELODY MAKER
...a damn fine album that could well see Ronnie Montrose triumphant at last.
SOUNDS
...merely a shadow of its predecessor, lacking both the incisive sharpness and refreshing synthesisers and hard-rock vehemence which characterised '1'.
RECORD MIRROR

GANG OF FOUR
Solid Gold *(EMI)*
...nothing more than a mirror — as opposed to a hammer — reflecting a dank, contradictory, noisy precinct of fevered activity where nothing is ever resolved, let alone actually achieved.
NEW MUSICAL EXPRESS
Gang Of Four have deliberately steered away from the abrasive polemics of their earlier material. They've gone instead for more of a cohesive feel.
SOUNDS
For all their drama they are too inward-looking, too competent, too encircled by a neat rationality and a tidy set of responses to reach out or successfully project their music...They should buy more singles and read more comics.
SOUNDS
...the principles are more principled than ever: few opportunities for a bit of light relief and a laugh here, although the pressure on the listener is always cleverly maintained to within a tolerable level.
RECORD MIRROR
...disappointing only in the way a second album never has the impact of a debut.
TROUSER PRESS

THE GAP BAND
The Gap Band Three *(Mercury)*
...they try to prove they are all-round variety entertainers and come over as superficial dabblers in a number of fields.
NEW MUSICAL EXPRESS
Their style of soul is indulgent but imaginative, irreverent but irresistible. It's mean and funky, that's all that matters.
RECORD MIRROR

LEIF GARRETT
Can't Explain *(Scotti)*
It depends on your mood, really. You can either take this album as a joke or a bad dream.
MELODY MAKER

I'm ecstatic over the back cover photograph showing Leif cosying up to a rather powerful-looking white stallion.
RECORD MIRROR

MARVIN GAYE
In Our Lifetime
(Motown/Tamla)
Gaye is one of the few soul stars who make whole *albums*. Only mirror fluctuations in mood enable one to draw dividing lines between songs, and most of his melodies happen to be in the same key.
NEW MUSICAL EXPRESS
Gaye here achieves an unexpectedly high standard, brilliantly resurrecting his previous glorious ability to create what can only be called a sensuround wall of music, designed to ensure the listener a world of floating sensuality.
MELODY MAKER
...it has the feel of a classic work oozing in every department the kind of finesse most "true professionals" don't even have the talent to conceive of.
SOUNDS
Many of these songs are in the old Seventies Gaye style, rolling along, creating an overall bonhomie.
RECORD MIRROR
...a dense, sometimes breathtaking montage of funk and soul grooves in which Marvin Gaye muses about art, love, karma and Armageddon.
ROLLING STONE

GLORIA GAYNOR
I Kinda Like Me (Polydor)
In short, not recommended to people who demand the marvellous on a regular basis.
NEW MUSICAL EXPRESS

GEN X
Kiss Me Deadly (Chrysalis)
Gen X, in spite of odd flashes, have never shown themselves capable of tears or rage. They're just in-betweenies, the most deadly fate rock 'n' roll can wish on anyone.
NEW MUSICAL EXPRESS
The group's now able to take elements of pop, rock and punk, light the gas under the melting pot and serve up a selection of exciting and original songs with a heavyweight clout.
MELODY MAKER

Gen (note the abbreviation) X have finally lived up to their excessive advance and monumental amount of publicity that has surrounded their career by producing a varied collection of bullshit-free rock songs.
RECORD MIRROR
For all its negativism, 'Kiss Me Deadly' is full of the melodic leaps and singsongy phrases that always set Gen(eration) X off from the rest of the pack.
TROUSER PRESS

THE GIBSON BROTHERS
On The Riviera (Island)
...shows them grasping more and more traditional and boring themes.
NEW MUSICAL EXPRESS
Merry music to do mindless things to.
MELODY MAKER

BC GLIBERT/G LEWIS
3R4 (4AD)
...satisfying, but not vital — and with no pretences in that area.
NEW MUSICAL EXPRESS
...music emanating solely from their collective heads, and on the evidence their heads haven't got too much on offer at the moment.
MELODY MAKER
...smug and lazy wallpaper music to play at blank walls and piles of bricks. Arts Council grant music.
RECORD MIRROR
...let's hope they leave ambient/drone music alone; it doesn't seem to be fertile ground for them.
TROUSER PRESS

NICK GILDER
Rock America (Casablanca)
God, this easy listening is hard work...In the absence of melodic thought or any emotions more complex than those expressed in 'Chips' or 'Fantasy Island', Gilder brings us noises. Clean, exquisitely recorded noises, each one in exactly the right place.
MELODY MAKER

GILLAN
Future Shock (Virgin)
Ian Gillan and his band have finally cracked the magic formula for heavy metal ecstasy...Vintage material.
MELODY MAKER
...simply a magnificent rock album guaranteed to rattle the foundations of blind pejudice and send the whole new-wave-of-British-heavy-metal shithouse up in flames!
SOUNDS

...moves Gillan two paces sideways which in Heavy Metal terms is ten paces forward.
RECORD MIRROR

GORDON GILTRAP
The Peacock Party (PVK)
...well played, well produced but, well, a bit devoid of emotion. It's all too perfect, all too precise and if the truth be known, it sounds as though in trying to include as many twiddly bits as possible, Gordon has actually forgotten about the *tune*.
RECORD MIRROR

GINA X PERFORMANCE
X-Traordinaire (EMI)
Far from being the feast of libido — liberating fun it might be, 'X-Traordinaire' makes pleasure seem a grim, tiring business.
NEW MUSICAL EXPRESS
...should not be easily dismissed, for beneath the disingenuous surface, there's a lot to absorb.
MELODY MAKER
These Krauts have got no idea. They love to dabble in experimental electronic music and always come out sounding arty-farty and heartless.
RECORD MIRROR

GIRLSCHOOL
Hit And Run (Bronze)
One day they're going to get bored with the one-dimensional bashing to which they're currently committed, and once they begin to broaden their sound and range they'll be a very interesting band indeed. Until then, pass with an option.
NEW MUSICAL EXPRESS
...an excellent album.
MELODY MAKER
Two songs do not an album make.
TROUSER PRESS
...a minefield of imaginative rushes with more variety than a kelloggs factory and more red hot power than the starting line of the British Grand Prix...It's not just a good HM album...
SOUNDS
Their approach now overflows with individual freshness and controlled strength...in heavy metal terms Girlschool are rapidly becoming the standard by which lesser mortals must be judged.
RECORD MIRROR

GLAXO BABIES
Put Me On The Guest List
(Heartbeat)
...a good album both as history — filling in a niche of Bristol history — and as music.
NEW MUSICAL EXPRESS
...just a collection of scrappy demo tapes that any self-respecting band wouldn't have the nerve to release, featuring yet more paper-thin guitars, the most contemptible sound in rock.
MELODY MAKER
...a collection of deceptively soothing dream sequences and flashes of forgotten nightmares, sketched by the unremitting, inauspicious bass backgrounds and the dangerously indulgent funk drumming, which is viciously and diplomatically strangled by the kinetic, liltingly discordant guitar.
SOUNDS

LOUISE GOFFIN
Louise Goffin (Asylum)
...another tasty serving of melodramatic pop. If she doesn't fall prey to the self-importance that handicaps Stevie Nicks, this bold, original performer (and songwriter) will end up one of the greats.
TROUSER PRESS

IAN GOMM
What A Blow (Albion)
The understanding of pop styles is there — and believe me, they're *all* kicking around somewhere on the album — but the mastery isn't.
SOUNDS
...a versatile demonstration in having a good time.
TROUSER PRESS
As background music it's pleasant enough, on a toe tapping hummable level, but when you listen more closely you realise what a boring record this is. It's what you'd expect from the non-famous member of Brinsley Schwartz: Nick Lowe without the panache, Rockpile without the beer: professional amateurism.
MELODY MAKER

ROBERT GORDON
Are You Gonna Be The One
(RCA)
He's no longer the rockabilly savior we once thought he was, but if "crossover" isn't a dirty word in your lexicon Robert Gordon is the brightest hope for a rock 'n' roll/pop fusion.
TROUSER PRESS

There are many vulgarist illusions and delusions, they are inescapable and indefensible, but there's richness and an authenticity to Gordon.
MELODY MAKER

GRACE
Grace *(MAC)*
Refined raunch and soft-rock melodicism...it's hard to see a market for them here. They're just too "nice", too old-fashioned. Lakers to America might be the wisest move.
NEW MUSICAL EXPRESS
...a refreshingly original debut.
SOUNDS

LARRY GRAHAM
One In A Million You
(Warner Bros)
There's so much joyful karma that I felt constrained to examine the needle after each side had played to make sure it wasn't hopelessly clogged with extract of jasmine.
MELODY MAKER

EDDY GRANT
Can't Get Enough *(Ice)*
As the Mickie Most of the reggae scene, he's got it sewn up.
SOUNDS

GRATEFUL DEAD
Reckoning *(Arista)*
...more a document of a once-memorable progressive group grown somewhat sluggish over the years than a compelling aural artifact.
ROLLING STONE

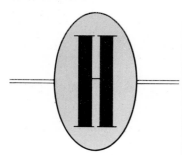

½ JAPANESE
½ Gentlemen/Not Beasts
(Armageddon)
A curious artefact built in the wasteland bordered by the TV Personalities, Sex Pistols and Captain Beefheart: a funny, annoying, bizarre mix of the rudimentary, the loud and nasty, and the idiosyncratic.
NEW MUSICAL EXPRESS
As an idea, it's a blast; a conceptualist's dream come true. Whatever they are trying to do with music (tearing down the

walls/taking the piss?), there's a force and a love of risks about it which promises a lot more than experimentation.
SOUNDS

DARYL HALL & JOHN OATES
Voices *(RCA)*
Like all Hall & Oates' records since the eponymous silver album 'Voices' is just so much ersatz, a series of AOR motions competently gone through for no discernible reason save the purely economic...A forgettable album. In fact, I've forgotten it already.
NEW MUSICAL EXPRESS
Immensely dull, tragically miscalculated. It reveals an enormously talented songwriting duo living in a far off, long-dead myth whereby the rock dream can be roughly compared to the dying remnants of Thirties Hollywood. Too many hairdryers, too much organisational know-how and not enough roughage in the r'n'r diet.
SOUNDS
It's hard to see them winning any new friends with this patchy collection.
MELODY MAKER
These aren't sacred songs, but damn good secular fun.
TROUSER PRESS

PETER HAMMILL
Sitting Targets *(Virgin)*
Along with Kevin Coyne, Richard Thompson, Pete Brown, and Roy Harper, for my money Peter Hammill is one of the *poets* of English rock songwriting.
MELODY MAKER
...his most commercial work to date, the sound clean and clear, the rhythm strong.
NEW MUSICAL EXPRESS
...a diverse, different album, standing apart from his cannon and sidestepping the direction trumpeted by 'Future Now' and 'Ph7'.
SOUNDS

BUTCH HANCOCK
Diamond Hill *(Rainlight)*
An album to rekindle a spark of enthusiasm for American music, at the end of an appalling year when so much of it has been boring, insipid and uninspired.
MELODY MAKER

HERBIE HANCOCK
Mr Hands *(CBS)*
...and a half-hearted half-cocked attempt to tie together the disparate strands of Hancock's recording career, weaving

them on the loom of his growing preoccupation with rinky dink electronics like the clavitar...
NEW MUSICAL EXPRESS
If you'd gone off Herbie Hancock because he was selling his soul to the disco devil you can come back now because he's bought it back again.
SOUNDS

PEARL HARBOUR
Don't Follow Me, I'm Lost Too
(Warners K)
As the bike girl cover warns, Pearl is out to prove that she's one of the boys.
NEW MUSICAL EXPRESS
There's nothing in the music which is going to stop you in your tracks, but a few of the verbal jokes provoke a wry grin.
MELODY MAKER
...simply one of the best rock 'n' roll albums I've heard since all of this rockabilly nostalgia dust was dragged out from under the carpet of time.
SOUNDS
...masterfully recaptures the footloose spirit of rockabilly.
TROUSER PRESS
...presents Pearl Harbour in various what's-chic-this-week guises — as spunky New Wave rockabilly singer, a spunky all-round New Wave hotshit entertainer.
ROLLING STONE

EMMYLOU HARRIS
Evangeline *(Warner Bros)*
It reminds you exactly why sensible young citizens with responsible jobs were reduced to slobbering wrecks all over the country by the exquisite delicacy of her wonderful debut album 'Pieces Of The Sky'. The lesson of 'Evangeline' is that the Harris voice can still fracture emotions with the ease of a penstroke; that her nose for the right material, perfect arrangements, and magnificent musicianship never falters; and that she has a chilling empathy with songs of desolation and loss.
MELODY MAKER

GEORGE HARRISON
Somewhere In England
(Dark Horse)
... Harrison at his most musicianly, articulate and lyrically imaginative since the spectacular 'All Things Must Pass'.
MELODY MAKER
Scarcely the most ground-breaking opus of the year, but nonetheless a collection of dignified, uncluttered tunes

whose quiet, inoffensive unpretentiousness will be welcomed by those of a likewise disposition.
RECORD MIRROR

HAWKWIND
Levitation *(Bronze)*
Whilst it's too early for this to get any "best of all time" accolade, it is nonetheless a vast improvement on the four albums recorded with Charisma and indisputable proof that they are far from being outdated hippies.
RECORD MIRROR
There's little bite on 'Levitation' and not much bark either.
TROUSER PRESS

HEART
Heart *(Epic)*
I won't waste time or space on this abomination...
RECORD MIRROR

THE HEATERS
Energy Transfer *(Columbia)*
It'd be nice to report that 'Energy Transfer' venerates not only The Heaters but the whole fiasco of Hollywood pop-rock, too. No such luck...in the end, The Heaters' praiseworthy fervor can't compensate for their prosaic, over-worked material.
ROLLING STONE
... mainstream rock, or AOR, or FM rock, or whatever euphemism they're using this week for schlock.
TROUSER PRESS

HEATWAVE
Candles *(GTO)*
... behind Heatwave lies the formidable authority of Rod Temperton. Without him they are just another bunch of cocktail-drinking dudes on the Sunset Strip.
NEW MUSICAL EXPRESS
... a soul album of completeness to rival 'Off The Wall'...
RECORD MIRROR

LEVON HELM
American Son *(MCA)*
An uneven overview of the South, the new album is terrific when it evokes simple moods...And terrible when it tries to make a full blown statement about the nation's crisis of faith.
ROLLING STONE

MICHAEL HENDERSON
Wide Receiver *(Buddah)*
... he sings like a hirsute record company executive might sing. One can smell the Terylene.
NEW MUSICAL EXPRESS

— 74 —

JIMI HENDRIX
Woke Up This Morning And Found Myself Dead
(Red Lightnin')
Of considerable interest to Hendrix collectors, inevitable Sixties kids and devotees of rock stars in their (musical) underpants.
NEW MUSICAL EXPRESS
If you want to hear (Jim) Morrison crashing off the stage advocating the wonders of his favourite sexual angle and Hendrix meandering through tired scenarios you'll take to this album.
MELODY MAKER
As with most affairs of this type, the billing is more impressive than the music...More a curio of the era than required listening.
TROUSER PRESS

RUPERT HINE
Immunity *(A&M)*
This is a very low key affair altogether, so low-key in fact that it disappears from view. It's so boring! There's nothing really wrong with it technically, but nothing excites you, revives flagging spirits, gives you hope...you know, that sort of thing.
RECORD MIRROR
The rest of Hine's work, especially his spell at the head of Quantum Jump, now seems like a long lead up to this dazzling, challenging album.
MELODY MAKER

ROBYN HITCHCOCK
Black Snake Diamond Role
(Armageddon)
Hitchcock's gift is to construct a personality, out of the past that gains relevance from his sheer commitment to discovering himself in his chosen tradition. As a result both he and the tradition come alive on this record. Lots of laughs and dark corners.
RECORD MIRROR
Robyn Hitchcock inhabits a universe he discovered all by himself. A place with beauty not greatly dissimilar from the worlds of Echo and The Bunnymen and Teardrop Explodes, cold and monumental...It's by, about and for people who don't feel "right" in the world.
SOUNDS
It's time for the real Hitchcock to stand up and cast aside the ghosts of Syd Barrett and the Soft Boys that haunt much of this work.
MELODY MAKER

THE HITMEN
Aim For The Feet *(Urgent)*
Don't let the title fool you, The Hitmen are aiming straight at your pocket...A greatest pop hits package, issued before the singles have actually made it.
NEW MUSICAL EXPRESS
It's easy enough when a record is stunningly good or crushingly awful. But The Hitmen have cunningly devised a 12-incher which goes in one ear and slides straight out of the other.
MELODY MAKER
Pop kids, fret not and clock the tunes here. A sterling debut.
RECORD MIRROR
You may never have heard them before, but if they don't mess it up themselves, you'll definitely want to hear loads more.
TROUSER PRESS

HOLLY AND THE ITALIANS
The Right To Be Italian
(Virgin)
... an album that bends so far backwards to impress that it topples onto its bloated backside and lays sprawling helplessly in the gutter like the aftermath of a Bunter and banana skin encounter.
MELODY MAKER
Heavy, screaming guitar pop with its affection for the Sixties worn on its lapel, but with a definite suggestion of tongue in somebody's cheek.
SOUNDS
... the right to be Italian on this showing is the right to be a cliche.
RECORD MIRROR
The sad fact is that Holly Vincent, in spite of everybody else's drab endeavours to prove otherwise, is a reasonably talented pop composer and a strong singer possessing a rich vibrant singing voice that projects and pitches excellently. With a decent producer this album could have been a formidable tour-de-force.
NEW MUSICAL EXPRESS

HUMAN SEXUAL RESPONSE
Figure 14 *(Don't Fall Off The Mountain/Passport)*
What this album really lacks is clarity of intention or expression or any real commercial appeal.
RECORD MIRROR
The question inevitably arises: haven't the Americans got anything better to sing about than this pseudo-crazy bullshit.
MELODY MAKER
The trouble with Human Sexual Response is that

they're too clever, but not sufficiently brilliant. These people need to get out more, find themselves hobbies and so on.
NEW MUSICAL EXPRESS
Human Sexual Response represent the best kind of art rock: you think while you listen, and then you listen while you think.
ROLLING STONE
Human Sexual Response has some good, strange ideas about song construction and coupling perfect, clean-cut harmonies with a street-punk lead voice is certainly a novel idea. But, like those kids on the cover, they don't quite seem sure of what they're sticking their fingers into.
TROUSER PRESS

HYBRID KIDS
Claws *(Cherry Red)*
A lot of care, emotion and humour went into producing the album. The result is both reverent and irreverent, wonderful and outrageous...It's experimental and entertaining in a way you'd expect from a Residents/Spector collaboration.
SOUNDS

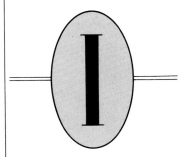

ICEHOUSE
Icehouse *(Chrysalis)*
Icehouse possess a generous dollop of commercial appeal, heavily concealed though it is.
RECORD MIRROR
Not an album that smacks you between the eyes, but a real warm grower that creeps up from behind and forms a romantic attachment with you.
SOUNDS

THE INDUSTRIALS
Industrials *(CBS)*
...a two bit heavy metal band hanging on Gary Numan's every synth setting.
RECORD MIRROR
The Industrials are a passable pop band who play boppy, synthook-rock for blissed out dancers in New York clubs. Their pretensions, all wielding masks and heavy stares, brings barely a smile to the

lips while their music is quick, clean and disposable...Slick pop for slack minds.
MELODY MAKER

THE INMATES
Shot In The Dark
(Radar/Polydor)
...a worthwhile slice of R&B documentary whose lack of originality is made up for by the amount of passion in the playing.
RECORD MIRROR
....a good R&B collector's album but not an awful lot more. I do wish they'd take some risks...
SOUNDS
...is never dead on target but the band's musical marksmanship is saved by some consistent good groupings - perfect for parties in fact.
MELODY MAKER
If The Inmates aren't exactly blazing new paths, at least they're good at what they do and know their limitations.
TROUSER PRESS
...instead of groping towards an art that's beyond them or posing as working-class avatars, they churn out chunky R&B cover versions and by-the-numbers originals with a cheeky unpretentiousness that shows they know how lucky they are.
ROLLING STONE

IRON MAIDEN
Killers *(EMI)*
The traditional iron-hard trademarks of the band are still very much in evidence vis a vis an aggressive honesty and basic hammer-drive. To these qualities have now been added a distinct layer of maturity...
RECORD MIRROR
I must admit that they've improved tremendously.
MELODY MAKER
...is this *really* the Maiden we know and love?
SOUNDS
One of the appeals of the genre...is its constancy. It is cosy, safe, unchanging, and so unable to disappoint (or stimulate) its followers overmuch.
NEW MUSICAL EXPRESS

THE ISLEY BROTHERS
Grand Slam *(Epic)*
It's a case of old men trying to relive and appeal to youth and, of course, they end up presenting a Fiorucci merchandiser's disco nightmare.
NEW MUSICAL EXPRESS
...an album of terrific funk power and every bit as good as all those other platinum albums a-hanging on the T-Neck office wall.
MELODY MAKER

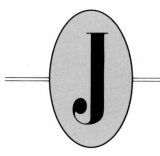

THE JOE JACKSON BAND
Beat Crazy *(A&M)*
Jackson skips deftly across shifting sonic currents to create an LP that's about the interplay between opposites: black and white, male and female, mugger and muggee. Though the singer is by no means entirely sure footed, when he connects, he's uncommonly graceful and engaging.
ROLLING STONE
It's the music that makes 'Beat Crazy' go, and if Jackson and Band can keep expanding this fruitfully they should be worthy of attention for some time to come.
TROUSER PRESS
There's no mistaking his talent in 'Beat Crazy'. It leaps out and smacks you in the face. Jackson has matured tenfold even in the space between 'I'm the Man' and this effort, his lyrics displaying a remarkable insight into everyday life and emotions.
RECORD MIRROR
A pretty lame apology for an album and absolutely nowhere as regards thinking dance music. It masquerades as a series of meaningful meta-music musings on rock'n'roll and youth culture in general, which comes down to little more than a couple of hip references/dedications to The Cramps and LKJ, respectively, and the sort of vague, purposeless social-realist songwriting we've come to expect from Jackson.
NEW MUSICAL EXPRESS
In moving more into exploration of rhythm and construction, he's left behind the engaging, eccentric little tunes that so endeared him to American disc jockeys and MOR audiences.
MELODY MAKER

JOE JACKSON
Joe Jackson's Jumpin' Jive *(A&M)*
A dozen tunes lovingly dusted down from the attic and then lovingly recreated with an ear for authenticity and arrangement that would do Ry Cooder proud.
RECORD MIRROR
...lay this on the old bakelite Noisola and jitterbug yourself into a brace of horned corns.
MELODY MAKER
...if you take your rock and roll seriously, and with one eye over your shoulder to see who else is looking don't bother.
SOUNDS
As an imperfect introduction to ridiculous delights, as a playful acknowledgement of past masters and great jesters, as a shuffling celebration of jump and tease, it's acceptable, even respectable.
NEW MUSICAL EXPRESS

THE JACKSONS
Triumph *(Epic)*
The smiling, self-confident edge of perfection is shot through this album like letters through seaside rock, and 'Triumph' becomes their strongest piece of humbug yet.
NEW MUSICAL EXPRESS
Doing everything competently, confidently and energetically, but, sad to say, standing still.
RECORD MIRROR
Doesn't have a weak track on it and the Jackson writing, producing and performing combines to make as strong, exciting and satisfying a pop record as we're likely to get before Christmas. It's title is no exaggeration.
MELODY MAKER
If 'Triumph' isn't much more than an uneasy holding pattern, it at least manages to work up a good sweat.
SOUNDS

JERMAINE JACKSON
Jermaine *(Motown)*
This album lives in a world of safe marketing, plastic mannequins and cheap roleplay. It has all the sheen of VOGUE and all the emotion of JACKIE comic strip serial. How can anyone be so spineless?
NEW MUSICAL EXPRESS
...the pervading impression is of an encouraging piece of work, that proves he wasn't a one album Wonder.
RECORD MIRROR

THE JAGS
No Tie Like A Present *(Island)*
Uninspiring is the best word with which to describe the middle-of-the-road pop starch served up by The Jags. Bland, insipid or unconvincing would do just as well. Whichever way one looks at it, they've yet to inject anything near to passion, gaiety or originality into their tidily dispensed music.
SOUNDS
Recording Cat Stevens' spiffy 'Here Comes My Baby' only emphasises the shortcomings of the band's own material.
TROUSER PRESS
Pass next side in coma, noting that it's a less interesting rerun of side one. Fall profoundly asleep and wake to darkness and the sound of a blunted stylus thudding against the dead end of the final groove. Reflect on the folly of all human endeavour and make way downstairs. Fill kettle.
NEW MUSICAL EXPRESS

THE JAM
Sound Affects *(Polydor)*
What I hear is a Jam I respect, but don't necessarily like.
MELODY MAKER
Paul Weller talks to ordinary people in an extraordinary voice but minus the usual deceit or malice or man-of-the-people big bootisms...A truly stirring record. It has a depth that appears impenetrable...Powerful, maintained orthodoxy from probably the last great English singles band. It is total music, the most outspoken and most rounded Jam LP yet.
SOUNDS
Where 'Sound Affects' is good it's great, and where it's not so good, it's still good. The Jam should go on being number one in our hearts and charts because they go on earning the right to be.
NEW MUSICAL EXPRESS
Another fine Jam set that still eschews complacency but adds a new positive softness to the established abrasion, attack, rawness and life of previous outings.
RECORD MIRROR
Examining the ironies and injustices of Britain's economic decline, the band approximates the pompous anachronism of orchestral grandeur: simple melodic invention puffed up large and loud, boldly dashing from fanfare to fanfare, eschewing the modest continuities of a danceable beat.
ROLLING STONE
An album of contrasts; pretty ballads, dance-beat tunes and traditional Jam-style rockers bounce off each other giving the record a dreamlike ambience...Transitional in many ways, as if The Jam were striving to create a new sound without losing old fans.
TROUSER PRESS

RICK JAMES
Street Songs *(Motown)*
It's nice to hear this again, but from Rick James, self-advertised "punk funk" person, you expect something more innovative and punchy.
NEW MUSICAL EXPRESS
It's a good job that the narcissistic Mr James has some talent to put behind the bragging.
RECORD MIRROR

JAPAN
Gentlemen Take Polaroids *(Virgin)*
Contrived, complex introspective romanticism for the impoverished rich.
SOUNDS
This is just a patchwork quilt of half-digested influences that will do nothing to solve the group's dilettante image problem.
RECORD MIRROR
Beware of albums which feature credits on the sleeve for "Makeup" and "Hair". Beware of bands that Derek Jewell recommends in THE SUNDAY TIMES MAGAZINE. Beware of bands in 1980 who sound like Roxy Music. Beware of Japan...This album carries a sticker "Do Not Pay More Than £3.99". It should carry a sticker which says "Do Not Pay Anything For This Album".
MELODY MAKER
They're still stronger on image than on imagination, and seem content to drift listlessly wherever the prevailing winds of fashion dictate...If only Japan's music were as eloquent as it's elegant. They don't sound cold so much as apathetic about conveying anything beyond a sort of wistful ennui. Instead, they lavish tender loving care upon the surface sound - a beautifully polished empty shell of a sound.
NEW MUSICAL EXPRESS

JEAN MICHEL JARRE
Magnetic Fields *(Polydor/Pois)*
I just found it nullifying,
stultifying...ultimately
BORING.
RECORD MIRROR
...the acceptable face of
electronics, producing the
sort of not-quite-Muzak one
might expect to hear burbling
gently in the background
around St Germain-des-Pres
drugstore, a music that is
neither as mechanistic as
Kraftwerk, as romantic as
Tangerine Dream, or as
obviously contrived as Gary
Numan.
MELODY MAKER

KEITH JARRETT
Sacred Hymns of G.I. Gurdjieff
(ECM)
...little more than drawing-
room tinkling and this
lacklustre set of
transcriptions only cements
the idea. A lot of wanly
pretty melodies receive a
suitably rapt treatment but
there's nothing to set a torch
to the soul.
NEW MUSICAL EXPRESS

JEFFERSON STARSHIP
Modern Times *(Grunt)*
If you're a hard rock fan who
fancies himself as a
sophisticate then this is for
you.
SOUNDS
The current Starship's
histrionic nonsense can easily
match the overblown fluff of
Styx and Kansas...
TROUSER PRESS

GARLAND JEFFRIES
Escape Artist *(Epic)*
More trouble seems to have
been spent on dragging star
names into the studio than
coming up with a batch of
killer songs...A child of the
ME Generation.
MELODY MAKER
Though not a faultless album,
there are some good songs
here and a team of crack
backing musicians that could
blast yer average LA
sessions squad half away
across the Pacific.
RECORD MIRROR
Your attention please.
NEW MUSICAL EXPRESS

JETHRO TULL
A *(Chrysalis)*
The precision in songwriting
and the diligence of this
record, marking a newly
injected burst of energy in
one of Britain's best bands,
make it convincing and
refreshing.
MELODY MAKER

'A' sounds not so much a new
departure as the frenzied,
sagging sound of trying to
teach an old dog new tricks.
NEW MUSICAL EXPRESS
'A' is musically and lyrically
dull. But Tull fans will find it
secure enough.
SOUNDS

THE JETS
The Jets *(EMI)*
Another example of the
slavish imitation that could
quickly crush the revolt out
of the burgeoning rockabilly
renaissance.
NEW MUSICAL EXPRESS
While the Jets' sound lacks
the aggressive flair of their
rockin' contemporaries, they
do offer further proof of an
authentic British rock'n'roll
revival.
MELODY MAKER
The Jets leave me cold and
thinking that I ought to get a
new stylus for my record
player.
RECORD MIRROR
If I was a Jet I would leave
EMI and start again. If I was
YOU, I wouldn't buy this
album.
SOUNDS
A good example of how not to
make a rockabilly record.
TROUSER PRESS

JOAN JETT
Bad Reputation *(Boardwalk)*
Of the Runaways, Joan Jett
was the true rocker,
instinctively realizing rock &
roll's opportunities for
pleasure, violence and
triumph...A determined
retelling of what sometimes
seems like the truest rock
story there is.
ROLLING STONE

ELTON JOHN
The Fox *(Rocket/Geffen)*
The result at least ends up
sounding like an Elton John
album, with all the dual joys
and irritations that entails.
Precious, finely crafted,
sentimental, catchy,
impeccably tuneful, and
grandiose...all the
characteristics that made you
weak at the knees/rush to the
lavatory in the first place.
MELODY MAKER
He proves he can still come
up with the goods. For
mainstream rock'n'roll and
wholesome ballads those
heady years of experience
just can't be beaten.
RECORD MIRROR

Melody-wise at least, Pinner's
own Reynard lost his plot
years ago. Now, not even
Quorn and Pytchley pink-
coats will find him of interest.
NEW MUSICAL EXPRESS

LINTON KWESI JOHNSON
LKJ In Dub *(Island)*
One of the most ambitious
dub projects yet.
MELODY MAKER
Whatever its audience, be
sure that it's a statement of
will and power. A most extraordinary album.
SOUNDS
A powerful, brooding, angry
sound. Unfortunately, it may
end up as mere background
music for armchair radicals
-people like the present
writer, in fact.
NEW MUSICAL EXPRESS

WILKO JOHNSON
Ice On The Motorway
(Nighthawk Fresh)
Wilko's sense of humour and
affectional musical delivery
adds a welcome to his
album...Wilko's association
with The Blockheads is
helping to bring the best out
of this eccentric R'n'B master.
RECORD MIRROR
Roughly produced by Wilko
himself in a crafty attempt to
emulate his scratchy live
sound, it could well be a
series of dicey first takes
chosen for their punch more
than detailed perfection,
resulting in a characteristically vicious package of
vintage Wilko R & B.
MELODY MAKER
Sensibly contrite; modest
ambitions fulfilled beyond
expectation. Johnson affects a
juvenile Boris Karloff-as-the-
Frankenstein-monster pose on
the cover, while innerwise
delivering a hefty batch of his
vices and virtuosity.
SOUNDS
Collects together the best of
Johnson's stuff from the past
couple of years, and his best
is very good indeed.
NEW MUSICAL EXPRESS

**JON AND THE
NIGHTRIDERS**
Surf Beat *(Vox)*
The vital pulse of classic surf
music underpins each track,
supporting the mosaic guitar
interplay determinedly. That
singular sparkling surfin' vibe
echoes faultlessly,
breathlessly, so confident and
proud, through every song.
SOUNDS
Faithfully played oddities
that sound just as archaic as
their inspirations. Small
doses of this stuff can be
delightful; an LP's worth is

the equivalent of eating a
whole bag of sour candy.
TROUSER PRESS

GRACE JONES
Nightclubbing *(Island)*
Underneath the sophisticated
exterior is as canny a
collection of songs as the lady
has ever wrapped those dark
vocal chords around...A
subtle, dominantly Latin feel,
with esoteric but effective
percussion textures and a
distinct leanness of
orchestration above the bass
line, weaves its way through
the nine longish tracks.
SOUNDS
An album with something for
everyone: reggae, electronics,
disco, blues - even a snatch of
salsa funk.
MELODY MAKER
Grace isn't gifted with a
particularly memorable voice
but her character and sense
of the surreal are the
cohesive bonds needed to
elevate just another brilliant
reggae album to a higher
plane.
RECORD MIRROR
I spent an otherwise
miserable weekend with the
sound of Grace swirling
around my little headphones,
grooving on songs effortlessly
sung but put together with a
jeweller's eye for detail.
NEW MUSICAL EXPRESS

GEORGE JONES
I Am What I Am *(Epic)*
He's learned he can live out
his miseries in song without
having to repeat them in real
life. He sings the truth and
country music needs it.
ROLLING STONE

QUNICY JONES
The Dude *(AMLK)*
It's perfect for disco fans who
want to sink a few overpriced
cocktails without really
listening to anything except a
dance beat. And with the
exception of a couple of
numbers, there's no danger of
any personality being allowed
to sneak through.
MELODY MAKER
Seeing Qunicy Jones' name
writ in large letters on a
album cover is roughly
similar to Herbert von
Karajan's top billing on an
album of Beethoven
symphonies. Neither bloke
actually plays anything, or
writes much, merely their
august presence is enough to
justify it.
NEW MUSICAL EXPRESS

JOURNEY
Captured *(CBS)*

Listening to Journey is like watching the mechanical rabbit that sets the pace at greyhound races: it's fast, but does it go anywhere?
ROLLING STONE

'Captured' offers four sides-over seventy wretched minutes of desultory, browbeating rock & roll.
ROLLING STONE

A singularly unadventurous exercise.
MELODY MAKER

The Crowd cheers and there's a lot of nonsense about this album belonging to the audience.
RECORD MIRROR

JUDAS PRIEST
Point Of Entry *(CBS)*

Nothing less than a complete disservice all round.
RECORD MIRROR

Rocks with a classic heavy metal vengeance.
ROLLING STONE

Judas Priest immerses itself so wholly in the metal aesthetic that the band come on as cynical poseurs.
TROUSER PRESS

Perhaps the most devasting Judas Priest album to date indisputably HM...It makes Raging Bull look like The Railway Children and has as many frills as Steve Strange in a shredding machine.
SOUNDS

...is more of what you hard-case long-haired community singers like, though a little softer and slower.
NEW MUSICAL EXPRESS

I can't wait to hear the shape of things that this new and stimulating direction will produce.
MELODY MAKER

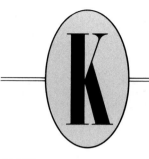

JOSEF K
The Only Fun In Town *(Postcard)*

...a laboured album that mistakes realism for reality. Kafka would be ashamed, not to say laughing.
SOUNDS

KANSAS
Audio Visions *(Kirshner)*

The overall standard's high but lacks the bite and inspiration — and perhaps most of all the freshness — that was there.
SOUNDS

The sound of Kansas is a typically American obscene blend of unvaried, early Seventies, dated rock 'n' roll played with less heart, soul, conviction and balls than practically anything else I've heard all year.
RECORD MIRROR

The musically over wrought and lyrically fatuous product of a collective hubris gone haywire... If Audio-visions represents Kansas' current state of mind, it's time to consider relocation.
ROLLING STONE

KID CREOLE AND THE COCUNUTS
Fresh Fruit In Foreign Places *(Ze/Island)*

Makes you glad you've been given ears. Thank you God.
RECORD MIRROR

Plenty of style, but l'il soul...simply disappears up its own arsehole.
SOUNDS

Urgent come-ons, squeals of mustachioed laughter from The Coconuts do not amount to a fun-fest, and all that skipping about the globe cannot conceal a mediocrity of imagination.
MELODY MAKER

KILLING JOKE
Killing Joke *(EG Records)*

Ultimately the songs lack fierce introverted intensity or harrowing lust just as much as the synth-kids...Killing Joke are parasites sucking all the goodness out of important musics. Graceless. A poor joke.
NEW MUSICAL EXPRESS

Exit one mentally bruised, highly excited reviewer.
SOUNDS

Killing Joke's irony rests on their name alone: the emphasis on Killing, the emphasis on noise, aggression, fiery flatulence. The LP, their first, is an obssessive, metallic threshing of guitar and keyboard noise -by turns thrilling and daunting and infuriating.
RECORD MIRROR

The musical attacks here are a form of self-flagellation and if you need to know why it's so enjoyable then ask a psychologist...So just throw

JOURNEY

your intellect to the wind, turn up the volume to ten and soak up the noise.
MELODY MAKER
Attention all you heavy metal fans ashamed of your arterier yearnings, and chic new wavers looking for something herady to shore up a collection of limp electronics: have a Killing Joke with your cocktail.
TROUSER PRESS

KILLING JOKE
what's THIS for... *(EGMD)*
Killing Joke wallow in their darkness, take pride in their priesthood as leaders of the doomed and damned.
RECORD MIRROR
...the walking, talking incarnation of evil, the first tangible evidence of the New Brutalism (the next big thing) which is abroad in the land. Considered in a vacuum, it's an album of incomparable verve, energy and aggression, and you might even risk a dalliance with the slumming glamour of its violence...the greatest rock music I've heard since the Pistols.
SOUNDS
On its own terms...'what's THIS for....' is an excellent record - even if those terms are the most hopeless ones to be found in rock today. It's the same wardance as before, slightly better realised.
NEW MUSICAL EXPRESS

BB KING
There Must Be A Better World Somewhere *(MCA)*
The overall feel of this record is much more deeply entrenched in BB's true blues roots, so if that's the kind of purist approach you prefer, then there's virtually nothing about these recordings to disappoint you.
SOUNDS
More than most of his recent albums, this one displays the various strands that went into the making of his style.
MELODY MAKER
Music as soulful and sophisticated as any BB King has ever made...A more than honourable addition to BB King's Collected Works, and irrefutable proof that the blues form is only as limited as the people who work within it.
NEW MUSICAL EXPRESS

BEN E KING
Street Tough *(Atlantic)*
It's neither streetsy nor particularly tough.
MELODY MAKER

KRAFTWERK
Computer World *(EMI)*
Kraftwerk can be cold but elegant, stark by poignant. Their medium is ruthlessly mechanical; their spirit is warm and glowing. They make the modern world seem empty yet beautiful...This is Kraftwerk's first pop album. Didn't you always guess that beneath those show-room dummy exteriors was a bunch of whacky Germans looking for a party. Well it looks like they found one.
MELODY MAKER
Kraftwerk are like the people at the party sitting round waiting for the orgy to start, but still always on the brink and never in the midst of the fun, keeping a barely disapproving eye on things...'Computer World' betrayed by its own colossally small title, is an album by a band trying to squeeze back into a context that's long been lost.
SOUNDS
Even slightly substandard Kraftwerk's preferable to the half-assed posturings of latter-day "Futurist" synthesists, the majority of whom won't even come close to understanding what makes Kraftwerk special.
NEW MUSICAL EXPRESS

FELA ANIKULAPO KUTI
Black President *(Arista)*
A record that cries out to be heard, both for its unique Afro-funk synthesis and for its radical regrouping of party and politics.
NEW MUSICAL EXPRESS
While anything which helps break down the prevailing ethnocentricity of Western rock audiences has to be A Good Thing, I can't help feeling just a bit cynical about the prospect of long-standing African musicians like Fela Kuti suddenly being lauded by the ever-hip rock press, only to be hurriedly dropped as soon as Adam Ant joins the likes of David Cassidy in the ranks of "dead" pop stars and Brian Eno discoveres a new continent to construct a theory about.
MELODY MAKER

LA DUSSELDORF
Individuellos *(Albion)*
...comes across like nothing so much as an old SA reunion in a noisy bierkeller.
NEW MUSICAL EXPRESS
...an album of lightweight, sugar-plum fairly unset that could be a demo for an Abba backing track of a Heidi Hi Muzak cassette for a Bavarian mountain top caff.
MELODY MAKER

THE LAMBRETTAS
Ambience *(Rocket)*
... an accurate enough reflection of the mood of much of the country — not hopeful, not despairing, just about holding on.
NEW MUSICAL EXPRESS
... a not unpromising pop band floundering in search of an identity. Nine rivetingly unoriginal tracks, and a cover of a 1966 Beatles song indicate a band bound to a false recreation of the past.
MELODY MAKER

LANDSCAPE
From The Tea-rooms of Mars...To The Hell Holes of Uranus *(RCA)*
Landscape used to be a worthy somewhat dull jazz-rock group until they discovered computers...Their sudden whole-hearted embracing of binary systems is a definite improvement on their previous directionless fusions; but though it's a step forward for them personally, it's not necessarily a giant leap for mankind.
NEW MUSICAL EXPRESS
... powerful and impressive, and it simply blitzes the oppostion.
MELODY MAKER
Landscape are no longer a bunch of old fogeys doing impersonations of Weather Report. It is now produent to see them as very much to the fore of the hi tech revolution, using synths, computer hardware and assorted electronic percussion in a way practically unrivalled elsewhere.
SOUNDS

ROBIN LANE AND THE CHARTBUSTERS
Imitation Life *(Warner Bros)*
The band bursts with power, but they, along with Robin's voice and the songs, are just constituent parts that create an irresistible whole.
MELODY MAKER
... a powerful second showing from a band of weighty integrity.
TROUSER PRESS

JENNIFER LARA
Studio One Presents Jennifer Lara *(Studio One)*
... Jennifer Lara sings original West Indies soul with an unaffected and contagiously appealing straightness of heart, a woman burning hot with passion in the aftermath of the fashion for chilling Ice Queens.
SOUNDS

NICOLETTE LARSON
Radioland *(Warner Bros)*
... aural Kleenex. Use once, then dispose.
MELODY MAKER
At her best, Nicolette Larson was never more than a second-string Linda Ronstadt or Bonnie Raitt. At her worst...she's an insecure soprano whose thinness of timbre is matched only by her inability to convey an emotion other than boredom.
ROLLING STONE

ARTHUR LEE
Arthur Lee *(Beggars Banquet/Rhino)*
...a depressing array of archaisms, mundanities and mediocrities.
NEW MUSICAL EXPRESS
...effectively shatters not only my slenderest hopes that the man's psychedelic genius might have survived over the years, but also it makes a complete mockery of my romanticised notion of Lee as some curiously gifted rock 'n' roll casualty.
MELODY MAKER
The old sod musta got better at last. Good for him, bad for us. Forever has changed for the worse.
SOUNDS

LEMON KITTENS
We Buy A Hammer For Daddy *(United Dairies)*
... Britain has not seen an album, debut or otherwise, like 'We Buy A Hammer For Daddy' in years. It has the spirit and willingness to take risks like few albums in the last decade.
SOUNDS

The feel is of mystery, with elusive lyrics matched by equally elusive sounds. The voices can be stifled chokes or droning ghosts or direct singing, however fragmented. All the usual rules of meter, tempo, and sequence are secondary.
MELODY MAKER

JOHN LENNON AND YOKO ONO
Double Fantasy *(Geffen)*
... a fantasy made for two (with a little cot at the foot of the bed). It sounds like a great life, but unfortunately it makes a lousy record...I wish Lennon had kept his big happy trap shut until he had something to say that was even vaguely relevant to those of us not married to Yoko Ono...
NEW MUSICAL EXPRESS
John and Yoko wanking off while gazing into each other's thighs...ultimately it's a record these two made for themselves, a 14 track diary.
SOUNDS
... the time spent in seclusion and semi-retirements appears to have dulled the man's sensibilities and blunted his once impeccable feel for rock 'n' roll. The whole thing positively reeks of an indulgent sterility...The man who once preached revolution has embraced the innocuous world of the bourgeois individualist.
MELODY MAKER
A master of reality luxuriating in any kind of fantasy is not what they want, John.
RECORD MIRROR
'Double Fantasy' works toward twin goals, John Lennon, rock star, wants to be taken seriously as a "normal" person — a husband and father, Yoko Ono, famous wife, wanted to be taken seriously as an intelligent artist. The two paths cross on this record.
TROUSER PRESS

DAVID LINDLEY
El Rayo-X *(Asylum)*
...as bright and out of the blue as its title — which, in David Lindley's translation, is sort of a cross between X-ray vision and the mark of Zorro.
ROLLING STONE

LINX
Intuition *(Chrysalis)*
Linx have both the outlet and the ability to make marvellous subtly subversive music. From the evidence of 'Intuition', they have chosen to stand back and make a

career out of being unremarkable.
SOUNDS
Sophisticated but not slick; danceable but never dumb.
RECORD MIRROR
I'd like to see the duo at the heart of Linx try out different schemes, teams, means — stick in the studio and produce classy, classic singles by themselves and for other people. We could certainly hear such records in better clubs than the places gigs are put on.
NEW MUSICAL EXPRESS
... the sound of two very accomplished songwriters, with a dynamite band creating the *Linx* sound. And that sound is a killer sound.
MELODY MAKER

LIPPS INC
Pucker Up *(Casablanca)*
... electronic disco music, especially styled for the Beverly Hills Night-club circuit or perhaps the fun-parlours of Florida.
MELODY MAKER
Disco played by Woodentops for Cloggies to dance to.
SOUNDS

LIVE WIRE
Changes Made *(A&M)*
Integrity isn't something one usually finds rock 'n' roll castles built on. Yet it runs through Live Wire's river of creative energy like the fluoride stripe in toothpaste.
MELODY MAKER
I always feel guilty about hating them but once again I came away with the feeling that I've been sitting in a vacuum.
RECORD MIRROR
... the band's most immediately accessible album to date, built largely around a succession of snappy 'pop' tunes full of catchy riffs, indelible hook lines and a smooth, inviting recording gloss...a perfectly understandable, if not understandably perfect album for a band in Live Wire's position to make.
SOUNDS

LOCAL HEROES
Drip Dry Zone *(Oval)*
... a promising, if overly earnest outfit that could yet develop into something with a touch of excellence.
NEW MUSICAL EXPRESS
The message is "We are intelligent — but ordinary". The music says exactly the same.
MELODY MAKER

LOCAL HEROES/KEVIN ARMSTRONG
New Opium/How The West Was Won *(Oval)*
What it basically comes down to is the thorny question about whether art forms in general and (popular) music in particular can carry truly revolutionary content.
RECORD MIRROR
These songs aren't so much political as mystical: struggle is seen in terms of incantation rather than strategy. This bias is continued on the other side of the album, a showcase for Armstrong's recent work on which he plays all the instruments.
NEW MUSICAL EXPRESS
(Local Heroes)
... pretty weird, not to say drug-induced, but forget your hippy prejudices, close your eyes and just let the music wash over you.
SOUNDS
(Kevin Armstrong)
... the result of this one-man-show is often self-indulgent and dreary.
SOUNDS

KEN LOCKIE
The Impossible *(Virgin)*
... an oddity: minimal yet meaty, layered yet loose, full of atmosphere, soul and feeling. It's most distinctive feature, Lockie's unique vocal style, binds it all together handsomely.
SOUNDS
... a meaty record, an angular thrash featuring rhino sax and a tendency to clutter itself with peculiar noises ...Lockie is too human to be a mannered, jerky puppet, too contrived to be fully human, too "clever" to be content to be poppy. As a result he never quite takes this record by the throat.
RECORD MIRROR
...for all the wit, invention and originality Lockie displays, there's barely an ounce of passion in evidence on 'The Impossible'.
NEW MUSICAL EXPRESS

ROY LONEY AND THE PHANTOM MOVERS
Contents Under Pressure *(War Bride)*
Loney's mythic, deranged pose would appear to be the result of some heavy iconography with a copy of Elvis '56...mirrored in the yelping music from the opening 'Sorry' onward.
MELODY MAKER

THE LOUNGE LIZARDS
The Lounge Lizards *(Editions EG)*
... highly evocative mini scenarios that match pop, wit and bravado against an assured virtuosity. It might be faked, but who cares? The Lizards' playfulness is the important thing.
NEW MUSICAL EXPRESS
A five piece with impeccable jazz and avant-garde credentials, The Lounge Lizards play dense, demanding music.
MELODY MAKER
The rules are adhered to, but not too much. Just about right: these are limited players, as yet, but they obviously aspire to nothing less than virtuosity.
SOUNDS
Not only do they pull off a snide imitation of a potted-palm-and-zoot-suit combo, they manage to transcend that imitation with sheer gleeful noise, mocking both the notion of hipster cool and the intellectual hauteur of the parody itself.
ROLLING STONE

THE LURKERS
Last Will and Testament...Greatest Hit *(Beggars Banquet)*
The Ramones may have turned mindlessness into an art form but The Lurkers are too far gone in pig ignorance for that, as they follow one awful riff with another.
NEW MUSICAL EXPRESS
When it comes to beano popping, loutish drivel, oi-some man-of-the-people pop-punk, and carefree cranium-crunching, this lot has it sussed.
SOUNDS

M
The Official Secrets Act *(MCA/Sire)*
Robin Scott's come up with one good single and a timely conceptual superstructure in his time; unfortunately, on 'The Official Secrets Act' there's none of the former and far too much of the latter.
NEW MUSICAL EXPRESS

This album is probably just what you'd expect from its creators — arty, over-decorative, conceptual pop. However, research has shown that it's rather good fun too.
MELODY MAKER

It's an open book — read it as much or as little as the whim takes you. It's thought-provoking or crass, but certainly tongue-in-cheek and hotly commercial.
SOUNDS

It's your worst fears confirmed, to borrow an advertising slogan. That is, your worst fears if in your heart of hearts, you were hoping for another poppy album with hit singles on the side.
RECORD MIRROR

...impressively weird and diverse novelty music with genuine undercurrents of 20th-century fear and loathing.
TROUSER PRESS

MADNESS
Absolutely *(Stiff)*
...they provide traditional English entertainment at its simplest and the nation takes them to its heart for that reason. What people like about Madness is sanity; daft lads, but a good turn. 'Safe' and 'Nice'.
NEW MUSICAL EXPRESS

...Madness are, and always have been, a pure pop group at heart with more in common with the early Kinks, Ian Dury and even The Beatles, than Prince Buster and the million obscure ska outfits usually bandied around as seminal influences.
MELODY MAKER

Whereas rock is still pretty much a male domain, Madness pop is for boys and girls. It's the perfect soundtrack for contemporary teenagers. You can bop to it, you can flirt to it and you can love to it as well as wearing it to football. This band, in my humble opinion, make music to be alive to.
SOUNDS

They're not out to say anything significant, dealing only with the thoughts and goings on of young working class kids.
RECORD MIRROR

...they're still the Blues Brothers — though it's unlikely anyone will give them $30 million to waste on a third rate movie.
ROLLING STONE

The carnival atmosphere remains intact as songs bounce along almost without letting you pause for breath.
TROUSER PRESS

MAGAZINE
Play *(Virgin/I.R.S.)*
...well-recorded, well-performed, well well well. Great value for Magazine fans.
NEW MUSICAL EXPRESS

Not an essential album if you've already got the first three, but nevertheless a set that shames most other releases.
MELODY MAKER

...a live album that breathes real life. It is not dead, nor blanched, nor greedy. It consolidates Magazine's future whilst enhancing their (neglected) past.
SOUNDS

...an impassioned dance album.
RECORD MIRROR

Here Magazine shoots from the hip instead of deliberating. Here Devoto wise-cracks once in a while. The Magazine of 'Play' has learned to relax.
TROUSER PRESS

MAGAZINE
Magic, Murder And The Weather *(Virgin/I.R.S.)*
Any more records and the tensions, the branding teases, the brooding twists, the knowing comedy, would begin to spoil. This presentation is complete. 'Magic...' is the magazine art perfected. It's all fit to burst.
NEW MUSICAL EXPRESS

...doesn't so much represent a band deliberately altering their route as one that's been blown wildly off course.
MELODY MAKER

...all the signs of greatness are there, that aura of timelessness that has characterised each Magazine LP...It is, as always, confusing, uneasy but rewarding, a painting in sound and feeling.
SOUNDS

The quality of songs, playing and production is as superb as you'd expect from Magazine, but the diversity of the material is a revelation.
RECORD MIRROR

TAJ MAHAL
Live *(Magnet)*
...the rhythmic potential of the band is awesome, but Taj and the boys settle on a mid-paced lope through the latest version of his musical geography lesson.
MELODY MAKER

I almost think this band is *too* good. Everthing slips by with such consummate artistry, such tasteful understatement, they lose the rush, the *edge*, that comes with the struggle.
NEW MUSICAL EXPRESS

MANFRED MANN'S EARTH BAND
Chance *(Bronze)*
...falls between the two deckchairs illustrated on the cover. It's not music which makes one want to free oneself...from all inhibitions and *dance*. And it's not cerebral music which strikes the listener with each consecutive hearing.
MELODY MAKER

...an album of moments rather than one of lasting memories...
RECORD MIRROR

If you've decided to pass Manfred by as an ageing hasbeen that's your problem. If you haven't you'll get a kick out of this.
SOUNDS

MANHATTAN TRANSFER
Mecca For Moderns *(Atlantic)*
...another updating progression, but within almost undefinable limits, there's none of the 10 feet sideways action that has destroyed so many other bands.
RECORD MIRROR

RITA MARLEY
Who Feels It Knows It *(Trident)*
This is sweet, poppy music, light but not throwaway: melodies that stay in your head long after your feet have finished dancing to them.
NEW MUSICAL EXPRESS

...no continuity between cuts, no single idea coming through: no glimpes into Rita Marley's soul at all.
MELODY MAKER

...a bland collection of pleasantries that, despite being penned by artistes like Bob, Rita and Bunny Wailer, give an impression of a Rasta-style Lena Martell sitting in a green field and praising the Lord.
SOUNDS

Rita's failure to discuss her own feelings and situation reduces this album to a very competent exercise in an overworked genre.
RECORD MIRROR

MARTHA AND THE MUFFINS
Trance and Dance *(Dindisc)*
They have cutesy-slick lyrics — the kind of thing you write drunk at 14 and tear up in disgust the next day...They sing songs about the suburbs, bank clerks, old actresses, primal screamers.
NEW MUSICAL EXPRESS

They flirt unconvincingly with risque subjects like unwanted pregnancy, madness and drunks with all the social commitment of Kate Bush and the authenticity of Showaddywaddy.
MELODY MAKER

...every bit as enjoyable as Part One, if not as novel.
SOUNDS

You still haven't got it right, Muffins...Go away and have a long look at yourselves.
RECORD MIRROR

MOON MARTIN
Street Fever *(Capitol)*
...he may not be any sort of innovator, but he remains one of the few performer/composers to approach "safe" rock 'n' roll as a job, a professional exercise, while yet managing to walk away with dignity and very little egg on his face.
SOUNDS

...there needs to be a slight sense of peril for him to be totally effective and get beyond being a pleasing lovable diversion.
RECORD MIRROR

JOHN MARTYN
Grace & Danger *(Island/Antilles)*
It's always been tempting to use the consistency and quiet, careful innovations of Martyn's work as a stick with which to thrash at the monstrous dumbness of so much contemporary rock 'n' pop, but to do so is to render Martyn a disservice. 'Grace & Danger' is perfectly capable of recommending itself on its own considerable merits.
NEW MUSICAL EXPRESS

...he continues to use the seductive timbre and tones of electricity with the experimental joy of the neophyte rather than the hacking compromise of the predictable professional. He is worth your time.
MELODY MAKER

Martyn is one of the few artists undeniably in a rich and fertile field of his own making, possessed with a highly inventive and beguiling controlled free-form style that defies both description and emulation...
SOUNDS

Grace and danger aptly describe the poles of John Martyn's music. His delicate jazz-tinged pop-folk is among the most elegant of its kind, while his lilting, seductively throaty vocals trace intricate vulnerabilities.
ROLLING STONE

NICK MASON
Nick Mason's Fictitious Sports *(Harvest)*
...whimsical, charming, funny in an off-the-wall way, and above all, very musical.
MELODY MAKER

The most (only?) admirable thing about this album is that reclusive millionaire Nick Mason has used his riches of Carla Bley's band and compositions...Music for an imaginary Gloria Swanson movie, music for cuckoo clocks in 9/4; the woman can't do anything without playing it for laughs.
SOUNDS

...a belly laugh of a record. The lyrics pout in teasing riddles, flirt with (non)sense; the music pokes fun at your idea of traditional rock, balloons out around the vocals...and spirals away in a bawling horn solo or hunches up into a big block-chorded extravaganza.
NEW MUSICAL EXPRESS

MATCHBOX
Midnite Dynamos *(Magnet)*
...their ability to capture the spirit of rock 'n' roll without findng it necessary to revere the original. They have harnessed their enthusiasm for a particular kind of music with the technology of the Eighties and manage to create authentic sounding rock 'n' roll.
MELODY MAKER

MATUMBI
Matumbi *(EMI)*
...reggae that has everything except the passion and power and in these times we need all the passion and power we can get.
NEW MUSICAL EXPRESS

...it reaks of uncomfortable and uneasy compromise. The most militant moments are sugar-coated with a nervous eye on chart consumption.
MELODY MAKER

...tending to stick to too many of the Jah traditions that can bog the music down.
RECORD MIRROR

CURTIS MAYFIELD
Back To The World *(Curtom)*
...a unique mixture of Mayfield's typically choppy rhythm arrangements and the most original use of string and brass arrangements in pop music since Love's 'Forever Changes'...There's a subtle sense of tradition underlying the entire album, its preachy, evangelistic tone harking back in certain ways to the manner in which blues and gospel music were used as transmitters/recorders of social and cultural events and emotions.
NEW MUSICAL EXPRESS

DELBERT McCLINTON
The Jealous Kind *(Capitol)*
...proves that Delbert is still Fort Worth's white playback to the almighty James Brown...
NEW MUSICAL EXPRESS

Every note and every nuance of rhythm is exactly right and with McClinton's abrasive voice on top this conglomerate charts the exact point where country, funk, rock 'n' roll and blues meet on an equal footing.
RECORD MIRROR

Though the song selection is unusually excellent, there's just no bar-band spontaneity to kick the LP into high-gear.
ROLLING STONE

McFADDEN AND WHITEHEAD
I Heard It In A Love Song *(Philadelphia International)*
Only the title track from the McFadden and Whitehead album sounds remotely Philly or even remotely McFadden and Whitehead. The rest of it is the same old standard soul fare; the tuneless ballads all black singers fall back on when they can't get any more real material together.
NEW MUSICAL EXPRESS

KATE AND ANNA McGARRIGLE
French Record *(Hannibal)*
...a delightful album of compositions sung in French...
ROLLING STONE

The sisters' charmingly informal singing and "quaint" accompaniment — fiddles, accordions, etc. — recall a lost (imaginary?) innocence that everyone should remember occasionally.
TROUSER PRESS

I'm intoxicated by its shambling nonchalance; I'm

seduced by its gentle, subtle nuances; and I'm in gleeful awe of its absolute, uncalculating disregard for the dictates of current style or influence.
MELODY MAKER

RANDY MEISNER
One More Song *(Epic)*
...it succeeds within its limitations with a directness and lack of coyness or guile that is in its way admirable.
MELODY MAKER

...for the most part it's old man, old memories. And boy, do they sound sad.
RECORD MIRROR

THE MEKONS
The Mekons *(Red Rhino)*
This album is not comfortable to listen to, it is jarring, difficult; but entertaining because it is still very much by the people who once wanted to come on stage on a sofa with the word "spaceship" painted on it.
NEW MUSICAL EXPRESS

War, the future, love and hate — a mixture of modern emotions fighting and tumbling against each other, rolling and screaming.
SOUNDS

Their second album finds the group playing arty disco-rock — a foursquare drum beat with vocals and other instruments rotating at their own speeds — to convey messages of social isolation, dislocation and estrangement.
TROUSER PRESS

THE MELODIANS
Sweet Sensation *(Island)*
...allows the tracks to breathe, spreading out in all their full glory: the power and simplicity of the vocal and instrumental arrangements coming through in a fine style.
NEW MUSICAL EXPRESS

...sweet melodies and perfect harmonies.
MELODY MAKER

BARRY MELTON
Level With Me *(Rag Baby)*
Listen, Barry, forget about Woodstock and chop that silly bubble-cut, curly hair off for God's sake! That'd be a start, would it not Barry? That and the beads. Oh God, the beads!
NEW MUSICAL EXPRESS

MERGER
Armageddon Time *(Emergency)*
...agreeable more than truly dynamic...well meant, but harmless.
SOUNDS

...low blood pressure music.
RECORD MIRROR

...the reggae equivalent of hip easy listening — there's an odd conceit about its meaningless "sophistication".
NEW MUSICAL EXPRESS

BETTE MIDLER
Divine Madness *(Atlantic)*
I think we need people like Bette Midler very badly, if only to show the pretensions of other "artistes".
NEW MUSICAL EXPRESS

It's sort of live. The soundtrack of a film of the show. It cuts out all the dirty East Side chat which is three parts of her charm and leaves a pretty sketchy outline of her music.
SOUNDS

MIDNIGHT FLYER
Midnight Flyer *(Swansong)*
...just what you would expect from a Bad Company clone; turgid, repetitive, and a crashing bore.
NEW MUSICAL EXPRESS

...predictably leans towards a blueish hue — up with the times but true to its heritage — and with the intonation currently in vogue. The next album, I'm sure will be a classic, this one is merely excellent.
RECORD MIRROR

JONI MITCHELL
Shadows And Light *(Asylum)*
...a translucent masterpeice that embodies both the personal freedom and the artistic majesty rock and roll continually strives for but rarely attains.
ROLLING STONE

...a trail of clues, a blaze of sights seen, an on-the-road exhibition of her favourite (?) bits and pieces. She keeps on being busy, she's pretty pithy, she's often lousy. But more like a strolling player than a rolling stone...
NEW MUSICAL EXPRESS

A good clean sound, a cross section of recent favourites, suitably enthusiastic applause; the song finishes, the record ends, and there's no change, no involvement, all part of an aloof mystique, love songs which lack tangible substance, empty in their abstraction.
MELODY MAKER

The jazzers give Mitchell a masterly rock-cool jazz backing, swinging at points but preferring, it seems, to play coffee-table music for the most part. It's left to Mitchell's distinctive vocals and guitar to steer the songs anywhere near the precise vision of the originals.
Sounds
A face cross bred between shire horse and Garbo, a voice swinging through the registers of jazz and rock 'n' roll, pen touched with genius and pretension. The facets of Joni Mitchell.
Record Mirror

MODERN ENGLISH
Mesh And Lace (4AD)
Modern English exist in the twilight zone of Joy Divison and Wire...In some respects, theirs *is* the modern, English sound, Eighties dark power stung with a certain austerity — a loss of humanity, if you like — though never quite toppling over into the Gothic vistas of say, Bauhaus, despite some similarities of tone and temperament. There's an edge of sincerity which sets Modern English apart from the new gloom merchants...
New Musical Express
...in the vanguard of the rare new breed of Modern bands. Cherish them, indulge them, but definitely enjoy them.
Sounds
...when it comes to gloomy musical psychosis this quintet knows their LSD backward and forward.
Trouser Press

MODERN EON
Fiction Tales (Dindisc)
Modern Eon: the name alone conjures up calculated confusion; a careful confrontation between momentary flash and lasting memory...their debut album fulfils that promise, instantly seducing and maturing more with time.
Melody Maker
...a bit too clever and devious, it's almost too perfect and sterile.
Sounds
...this record buzzes, hums, and pulsates its way into the listener's dream world — creating a mystical place in your subconscious...Each song is an act of love which climaxes and envelopes itself in the oblivion of ecstasy.
Record Mirror

...by turns adventurous and old-fashioned, lyrical and dull, reflecting an uneasy alliance between pomp, art rock and intellectual synthetic muzak.
New Musical Express

MODERN MAN
Concrete Scheme (MAM)
Their songs are given titles like 'Cosmetics', 'Wastelands', 'War' and 'Advance'...and the band have an indecipherable blurred photo of themselves standing in a line on the back cover. You know the kind of thing.
New Musical Express
It observes and comments, in best documentary style, it offers no solutions. It is also one of the best debut albums I have heard.
Melody Maker
Modern Man sound much more at home with the overtly commercial pop stuff than the synthesiser-oriented parts which often sound like token gestures made by Midge Ure to spice things up a bit.
Sounds
...busy turning out gently electronic pop songs which range from the punchy to the limp.
Record Mirror

THE MODERNAIRES
Way Of Living (Illuminated)
...doesn't know whether to laugh or cry, tries to do both, ends up doing neither, and is a confused and confusing record as a result.
Melody Maker

MO-DETTES
The Story So Far (Deram)
Each song is nutty Camden cameo, humourously conceived, shambolically performed, tackily recorded and delightfully mis-phrased by Ramona's gorgeous French accent.
Melody Maker
...a polished and positive pop statement, a rich and rhythmically robust recipe of intoxicating melodies and amazon grace that the band's shambolic slap-happy beginnings barely began to hint at.
Sounds
This album is one of the freshest I've heard in a long time, and also one of the most original...
Record Mirror
Harsh, brutal and immediate in both sound and content, they prove on their debut LP that straightforward playing and minimal production sometimes says it all.
Trouser Press

MOLLY HATCHET
Beatin' The Odds (Epic)
While MH are a good live band, they tend to be far too slick in the studio.
Sounds
...all the bloodcurdling guitars and bellowing in the world won't cover up the songwriting cracks in Molly Hatchet's rusty armour.
Rolling Stone
...although still primarily raw, racy, rhythmic rockers, their albums do hold back from waging full-scale sonic warfare on your ears.
Record Mirror

ZOOT MONEY
Mr Money (Magic Moon)
"None of this is the Eighties," he at last protested. "It's got nothing to do with inflation, the unemployment problem, Thatcherism, Tony Benn or oil wars".....'Precisely," grinned George Bruno Money and downed another pint.
New Musical Express
...the actual musical content is frankly the pits.
Sounds
Stylistically the record is soulful and funky which is the style Zoot has always been best at and the old standards he has chosen to record here are well served.
Record Mirror

THE MONOCHROME SET
Love Zombies (Dindisc)
The last word in arty pretence: ten pointless, dreary dribs and drabs of vaguely chic muzak, neither likeable nor unlikeable, and devoid of effect on any level...
New Musical Express
...songs with conventional structures but no inspiration, no surprises, no feeling, no love. How did a band like this ever get signed up?
Melody Maker
...a collection of hollow, empty, emotionless, passionless songs which are neither poppy or commercial, whose only partially redeeming feature is a kind of vague pleasantness bordering on the bland.
Sounds

MOODY BLUES
Long Distance Voyager (Threshold)
The 1981 Moodies are bang up to date with a collection of one-off hit singles.
Melody Maker
It reeks of contractual obligations...of bored men out of ideas and clutching at straws.
Record Mirror

MORE
Warhead (Atlantic)
...an album which fails by thrusting itself in the wrong directions and then slumbering into inertia. The image is so obviously stressed with macho photos, metallic logos and song titles like 'Road Rocket' but the reality is as threatening as a toothless alsation with palsy.
Sounds
...play with such blunt ineptitude that to say they lack thrust is akin to calling the Great Fire Of London an intimate barbeque.
Record Mirror

VAN MORRISON
Common One
(Warner Bros/Mercury)
What saves Morrison — and makes 'Common One', despite its narrowness, boring stretches and large and small retreats, impossible to dismiss — is his unwilling, embattled awareness that inner peace is every bit as demanding as emotional warfare.
Rolling Stone
...meant to be appreciated on its own merits as a spiritual testimonial, a mature pop exerciser — and, yes, an example of musical poetry.
Trouser Press
An album of spiritual and musical rejuvenation, 'Common One' is Van Morrison's most notable achievement since 'Veedon Fleece' in 1974.
Melody Maker
...a wet and woolly hour's worth of bland self-aggrandisement.
Sounds
...colossally smug and cosmically dull; an interminable, vacuous and drearily egotistical stab at spirituality...the most indulgent and irrelevant LP I've heard in months.
New Musical Express

THE MOTHMEN
Pay Attention (ON-U)
...a surprisingly accomplished and idiosyncratic debut, showing them to have a fine grasp of mixing and matching styles and approaches with a pointed sense of individuality.
New Musical Express
The Mothmen, I'm reliably informed, are something to do with Alberto Y Los Trios Paranoias. This fact alone raises considerable doubts as to the sincerity, seriousness and sanity of their intent. The record raises a few more.
Melody Maker

MOTORHEAD
Ace of Spades *(Bronze)*
...rages from start to finish and the pace never slackens. The overall sound is heavier than ever, if that's possible. The headbanging fraternity will revel in these fresh delights.
MELODY MAKER
This is not an album for the faint-hearted...the titles alone are enough to make your ears bleed and if truth be told, even with twenty packs of cotton wool balls it took a total of five attempts to actually play the twelve tracks all the way through in one senses-shattering go.
SOUNDS
...a surefire winner, although listening to it from beginning to end is an experience akin to being aurally mugged, and repeated spins are liable to leave even the sternest listener shaken and shell-shocked. It's loud, brash and greasier than a lorry driver's breakfast.
RECORD MIRROR
...proves that for sheer blood-and-guts overdrive Motorhead has few peers.
TROUSER PRESS

MOTORHEAD
No Sleep Til Hammersmith *(Bronze)*
Motorhead's frustrated soundtrack is a real haunting, a facing of facts, a searching for the past to define the present, a wasted caricature of the brutal truth. 'No Sleep Til Hammersmith' is disgusting, bleeding, gruesome magnificence and Motorhead are one of the Great Popular Groups. The LP represents the limitations, absurdity and rare glory of HM rock so comprehensively and madly it has to be considered a major work.
NEW MUSICAL EXPRESS
...'No Sleep' has set the standard for heavy metal in the Eighties. It's a yardstick by which everything else will be measured.
MELODY MAKER
...the most growling mind-garrotting metal excess ever unleashed on humankind to date, a pummelling pounding total experience.
SOUNDS
...an essential Motorhead album and a fine testimonial for their particular brand of mayhem and fun.
RECORD MIRROR

JUDY MOWATT
Black Woman *(Island)*
...it seems to owe more to soul than to reggae, Judy's strong vocals appealing, asserting, drawing out the emotion from her words.
NEW MUSICAL EXPRESS
Optimistic, warm and sincere, Mowatt comes across as the archetypal earth mother. She sings evangelical songs without giving the impression of moralising or lecturing. Instead, she allows us to share the joy she is experiencing within.
MELODY MAKER
...The cliches of reggae are avoided and the album burns with a personal intensity employed in the often mutually exclusive causes of women and rastafari.
RECORD MIRROR
Cheerful, girlish and sincere, it exudes a firm yet happy-go-lucky feeling; a little bit jazzy, a little bit ska and faithfully guided by a strong though not overbearing rhythm..
SOUNDS

PAULINE MURRAY AND THE INVISIBLE GIRLS
Pauline Murray and The Invisible Girls *(Illusive)*
This is the romantically infused easy listening epic Patti Smith never made with 'Easter'. Murray's personal touches, the quiet fire of her bewilderment and almost lullaby-like disillusionment transforming it into a great work of passion.
NEW MUSICAL EXPRESS
It's rare that a record's so clever and commercial that it makes me smile but XTC managed it with 'Black Sea'. It's also very seldom that a band can commit such passion to vinyl that it brings me out in goose-flesh but Joy Division (produced by Hannett) did it with 'Love will Tear Us Apart'. If I tell you that Pauline Murray and the Invisible Girls do both, I hope you'll get the message.
MELODY MAKER
...an album of strong lyricism, technique and locomotion.
SOUNDS
...cool, elegant music, far more subtle and polished than anything Penetration did.
TROUSER PRESS

N

NASH THE SLASH
Children Of The Night *(Dindisc)*
Despite the modern trappings — camp dressing up, electronics and a laboured emphasis on the lack of guitars — he's really just an excessive hard-to-heavy rock instrumentalist neither competent enough to earn a place in the Muppet band, nor witty enough to be a successful mimic.
NEW MUSICAL EXPRESS
...it's quite fun, but doesn't really repay too many hearings.
MELODY MAKER
Electric mandolins, violins and percussion fed through a battery of keyboards, pedals and other devices make for a distinctive noise. The problem is...once it's attained, there's not a lot to be done with it.
RECORD MIRROR
A flashy one-man band. Nash sings in a troubled shout...a broad sampling of his talents without cohering into a satisfying whole.
TROUSER PRESS

NAZARETH
The Fool Circle *(NEMS)*
..remarkable for its restraint and sensitivity...a thoughtful and colourful collection of songs...
MELODY MAKER
They deliver good old chunkalong rock 'n' roll quite a lot, the odd bar-room shouter...and one or two more surprising nice noises which may well show the benefit of former Steely Danner Skunk Baxter's knob twiddling.
SOUNDS

BILL NELSON
Quit Dreaming And Get On The Beam *(Mercury)*
In keeping with the keyboards-orientated times he's subordinated his considerable guitar skills to the electro-flow of the music, but his muggy landscapes are both lacklustre and incomplete.
NEW MUSICAL EXPRESS
Unfortunately, these particular pictures are almost two years late back from the chemist...a useful diary entry, but can't claim to be an accurate reflection of the man today.
MELODY MAKER
...as fresh and inspiring now as when it was put on ice back in June '79. Great works remain great even if the artist has moved on to pastures new.
SOUNDS
...he should concentrate on quality and not quantity — forget the technical prowess of his fingers and get closer to his soul.
RECORD MIRROR

RICK NELSON
Playing To Win *(Capitol)*
Welcome back one of the most underrated Fifties rockers and a founding father of country rock in the Sixties.
TROUSER PRESS

WILLIE NELSON
Somewhere Over The Rainbow *(Columbia)*
...may be the most audacious album thus far in the revivalist phase of Nelson's career. It's certainly the clearest expression yet of his conviction that all enduring popular music — be it Southern blues, Nashville country or Hollywood soundtrack — is equally pure.
ROLLING STONE

NEW AGE STEPPERS
New Age Steppers *(On-U)*
...music set in a twilight melancholy, free from melodrama but not without passion, gentle superfluous frolics, the closest you'll get to a new age MOR LP...
NEW MUSICAL EXPRESS
...a complete pretentious bore with the whole revoltingly hip "dread inna Ladbroke Grove" psyche crawling out of it like maggots...The whole project lacks imagination, humour, rhythm and soul.
SOUNDS
...this type of music has a wonderful way of soothing the spirit. Use The New Age Steppers instead of valium.
RECORD MIRROR

NEW MUSIK
Anywhere *(GTO Records)*
How can an album this innocuous be so annoying?...polite, neutral pop with a spacious sound constructed in a clinically clean environment.
MELODY MAKER
...couldn't have been more unerringly bland and boring if they'd tried.
SOUNDS

By comparison the likes of Ultravox, Visage or Duran Duran sound like so many dead butterflies.
RECORD MIRROR

COLIN NEWMAN
A-Z *(Beggars Banquet)*
'A-Z' would actually pass muster as an acceptable Wire album in its own right...It shows Newman continuing to utilise the technique of layered minimalism, using textural building-blocks of stark simplicity to create edifices of, at times, almost baroque ornamentation.
NEW MUSICAL EXPRESS
...the canvas is frequently more diverting than the paint...Musical force and mystery or cold, unemotional epigrams of the determinedly mundane: Newman's got both for you.
MELODY MAKER
Newman offers you few clues about himself, a feature that you'll either find enigmatic or a pose depending on which side you finally drop.
SOUNDS
A true singer with enough emotion in his voice to make everything he does sound special. A modern voice of unmatched intensity.
RECORD MIRROR
...an honestly experimental work: challenging, stimulating and all that.
TROUSER PRESS

COLIN NEWMAN
Provisionally Entitled The Singing Fish *(4AD)*
...a marvellous collection of *mood* music, to be used either as background muzak (in the true sense of the word) or more actively as a direct catalyst for mood-setting.
SOUNDS
...draws surreal dreamscapes whose icy beauty is unusually attractive.
NEW MUSICAL EXPRESS

NICO
Drama Of Exile *(Aura)*
...probably the most accessible of her romantic tales of gloom...The songs, as ever, are about a kind of tragic individual splendour, failure coupled with fame, or the romantic self-destruction of the drug-addict.
NEW MUSICAL EXPRESS
...a tiny miracle...The album sounds like it cost a million dollars, when it obviously didn't.
SOUNDS

Nico has fallen headlong into the pit of self-parody, that pseudotragic, doomladen voice decidedly unconvincing in the Eighties.
RECORD MIRROR

WILLIE NILE
Golden Down *(Arista)*
...for all his admirable assimilations of style, lacks the persuasive charisma to bring his cliches to life...imitative, second-hand entertainment.
MELODY MAKER
Nile has elected to believe the balance sheets rather than his own ears, and like that squadron over the Bermuda Triangle who didn't trust their instruments he's shot straight for the perils of oblivion.
SOUNDS
...still a thoughtful craftsman who knows the difference between sensitive and maudlin...
TROUSER PRESS

HARRY NILSSON
Flash Harry *(Mercury)*
Nilsson has said that he will quit making records after his twenty-first album — and this is his nineteenth. Time is running short.
NEW MUSICAL EXPRESS
Even for Nilsson, this is an eclectic album.
MELODY MAKER

NINE BELOW ZERO
Live At The Marquee *(A&M)*
If they are to move beyond their present image of a hard-working, good-time band, somehow a more positive, individual approach will have to be established.
MELODY MAKER
It's very good: essence of pub; dirty, true music and a reference point for the merits of just about any rock variant you could name...
SOUNDS

NINE BELOW ZERO
Don't Point Your Finger *(A&M)*
...too predictable, two-dimensional and very dull. After a couple of tracks, the tunes all sound the same, not a patch on the live feel.
NEW MUSICAL EXPRESS
...sees the band coming to terms with their abilities as songwriters and the results are at best adequate and at worst plainly pedestrian.
MELODY MAKER
...their first major tilt at big league status and asks whether a snappy cover and a 12 day recording session with ace face producer Glyn Johns

can move these muscular mods out of the clubs and into the charts...The answer could just be yes.
RECORD MIRROR

999
Concrete *(Albion)*
...a startling collection of what I can only think to call maverick bubblegum; a curious blend of the cute, the rowdy and the plain ole weird.
SOUNDS
...just a mish mash of elements begged, stolen or borrowed and not compiled in a way to make any distinctive impact.
RECORD MIRROR

TED NUGENT
Intensities In 10 Cities *(Epic)*
Ever since Ted Nugent revealed that he wears ear-plugs onstage because he's deaf in one ear, it's been difficult to take him very seriously. It was a bit like Hitler confessing that he did, after all, possess one ball.
NEW MUSICAL EXPRESS
For electric, gonzoid, guitar wrenchin' metal lunacy this man simply can't be beat...
MELODY MAKER
Great title, shame about the record.
RECORD MIRROR
...an all-live, all-new extravaganza...it sees the Nug back on the pinnacle of grossness...
SOUNDS

GARY NUMAN
Telekon *(Beggars Banquet/Atco)*
...a woefully dull and monotonous album, pompous in the extreme and exceptionally limited in its range of tempi and tonalities...
NEW MUSICAL EXPRESS
...an album of weird, instant magic that will be on my turntable for months.
MELODY MAKER
Gary Numan is a micro-chip Elvis Presley gone wrong on the marketing table. He is, in current terms, the Charlie Chester of modernism...He is dangerously insidious.
SOUNDS
...you can sleep to it.
RECORD MIRROR
Scarcely out of his adolescent years, Gary Numan is already, in terms of attitude, the Samuel Beckett of British New Wave. On 'Telekon', however, his despondent sentiments are attached to the most wistfully beautiful music he's yet created.
ROLLING STONE

The music oozes forward with the force of thick molasses, spreading a gloom that obliterates all other considerations.
TROUSER PRESS

GARY NUMAN
Living Ornaments '79
Living Ornaments '80
(Beggars Banquet)
His oafish futurism has long been known for the sham it is, and the lame, two-dimensional performances on these albums...elevate the music to that same pedestal.
SOUNDS
He came, he saw, he conquered. Then the shrewd bleeder pissed off as quick as he appeared.
RECORD MIRROR
...ideal background music for the "Space Invaders" generation.
MELODY MAKER
...all the old adjectives are summoned forth once more: the *eerie* synthesisers, the *dank, drab* metronome of a pulse-beat, your whining vocals, the empty gestures, the numbing bombast. It's unhealthy stuff, Gazza.
NEW MUSICAL EXPRESS

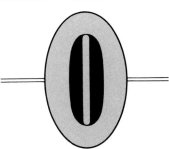

HAZEL O'CONNOR
Breaking Glass *(A&M)*
...not only are the goods on offer hopelessly out of date (consume before July 1973), but the now cliched image of a rock star possessing neo-Messianic qualities has already been enacted in finite detail by Bowie in his Ziggy Stardust role.
NEW MUSICAL EXPRESS
...the end result, however decorative, smacks of ridiculous pretensions.
SOUNDS
Hazel has a peculiar singing technique which involves gulping air in a lot and opening your mouth as wide as possible. At least it's original...I like it.
RECORD MIRROR

HAZEL O'CONNOR
Sons And Lovers *(A&M)*
The songs deal mainly with hurt, cynical accounts of failed relationships, or else

with social themes like loneliness and war, and these latter show a basic decency of outlook — it's just unfortunate I don't like the arrangements or find the voice emotive.
NEW MUSICAL EXPRESS
...a further episode in Hazel's futuristic-punk-by-numbers. If initially she seemed to have been assembled from an identikit parade, this album will only compound the growing theory that she doesn't exist at all, but is a free sample in a sophisticated range of singing robot dolls.
MELODY MAKER
...a simple, unpretentious album that shows Hazel has dismissed the hype around her. Whether her audience can do the same remains to be seen.
SOUNDS
...after a whole album's worth all that stylised tweeting and moaning gets on your tits.
RECORD MIRROR

MIKE OLDFIELD
QE2 *(Virgin)*
Titanic might have been a better title...
RECORD MIRROR
...you're already effectively finished as a questioning human being if you've even considered buying this record.
NEW MUSICAL EXPRESS
Poor Mike: lost in a twilight zone of over-dubs, and making it pretty, passive music that won't reach beyond his pre-sold cult...What a waste!
TROUSER PRESS

THE 101'ERS
Elgin Avenue Breakdown *(Andalucia)*
The 101'ers weren't exactly true precursors of punk; more of an advance raiding party on the rock establishment..Brash, untutored, they stripped rock to its essential dynamics. Like the later punk bands, they were aggressive, but unlike their successors they were never *bullying*.
MELODY MAKER
Pure pop for now people? Let's just say then music for all-time enthusiasts.
RECORD MIRROR
A slipshod compilation of unreleased stuff from Strummer's old rhythm and blues pub combo...
NEW MUSICAL EXPRESS

For the terminally rockist only, or people who visit the sites of air disasters.
SOUNDS
...a document, like a grainy 8mm home movie.
TROUSER PRESS

YOKO ONO
Season of Glass *(Geffen)*
It's a public statement yet an immensely private LP and this context makes it difficult to criticise without feeling monstrously callous...
MELODY MAKER
...a warm, understandably brittle yet triumphant album...a powerful piece of incisive poetry set to simple music.
NEW MUSICAL EXPRESS
Yoko has made a record of fragility, grief, and ultimately, of great human strength.
RECORD MIRROR
Mysterious inner thoughts and feelings, personal doubts and memories are fairly passively sung over, in most cases, tenuously tacked on music.
SOUNDS
...an intelligent blend of aesthetic experimentation and pop form, in which each genre complements and illuminates the other.
ROLLING STONE

ORCHESTRAL MANOEUVRES IN THE DARK
Organisation *(Dindisc)*
All very pleasant, but not really the sort of thing I'll be booking a return ticket for...
NEW MUSICAL EXPRESS
...not so much a collection of songs as a pervading mood, a feeling of restfulness spiked by an unsettling edge that never allows the music to descend into complacency.
MELODY MAKER
...they face the problems with an irrepressible intuitive sense that makes the best pop of any time. They are young enough to make brilliant mistakes and feel the dizzy modern confusion with an unaffected perceptiveness.
SOUNDS
...happy, sad, warm, cold, funny, sombre, fast and slow, and, most important, a joy to your ears.
RECORD MIRROR
Orchestral Manoeuvres sound like Freddie Cannon doing the Ultravox song-book...bland music; Gary Numan set houses on fire by comparison.
TROUSER PRESS

ORIGINAL MIRRORS
Heart Twango And Raw-beat *(Mercury)*
...a patronising fanfaronade of adolescence, full of Skids-ish "la-la-la" chants, and hooks from similarly "epic" teen anthems of yesteryear.
NEW MUSICAL EXPRESS
Certainly the band deserve, and will certainly gain, some recognition. I'm just not sure if 'Heart Twango And Raw-beat' is the most truthful way of gaining it.
SOUNDS
If you saw them when they first came on the circuit you would have witnessed a full-blooded fusion of new wave and disco, but this has been watered down into too many trite phrases that result in the album sounding technical and slightly cold.
RECORD MIRROR

OZZY OSBOURNE
Blizzard Of Ozz *(Jet)*
Oz has planned his latest onslaught with diligence and has almost veered into the territory of thinking man's metal.
MELODY MAKER
Ozzy's lack of anything faintly resembling taste is his saving grace.
SOUNDS
...a move away from the murky twilight world of grass-roots Sabbath and an energetic entry into the land of the living.
RECORD MIRROR

OSIBISA
Mystic Energy *(Calibre)*
Osibisa keep their African roots but tend towards jazz funk and lightness, rather than 400 years in captivity for I and I...a hub-bub of flugel horns, cabassa, marimba, bongos and bells, mixed with delicious refrains of flute and piano.
RECORD MIRROR

OTTAWAN
Ottawan *(Carrere)*
The Frogs are at it again. They've never forgiven us, of course, for thrashing them at Agincourt, Crecy and Waterloo. Now comes the final insult.
Ottawan...Personally, I think it is about time the Foreign Office was brought in on this one.
MELODY MAKER

ROBERT PALMER
Clues *(Island)*
'Clues', with a cool 50% of strong numbers, has the strength to suggest that...Robert Palmer may finally be in the right place at the right time.
NEW MUSICAL EXPRESS
...an imaginative stylist with a fine tone, always in control, an exceptional ear for the correct phrasing, and for picking and writing good songs and the musicians most suited to perform them.
MELODY MAKER
...one of the best albums of the year...an obvious attempt by Palmer to modernise his repertoire, mostly by getting wise to new wave — or at least, Gary Numan's version of it.
SOUNDS
...Palmer flavours his uptown honky jive with enough danceable synthesiser to ride the current rock-disco wave.
TROUSER PRESS

THE PARAGONS
The Paragons *(Island)*
All in all the 'The Paragons', then and now, are a pretty irresistible trio.
RECORD MIRROR

RAY PARKER JNR AND RAYDIO
A Woman Needs Love *(Arista)*
..while one cannot deny the competence and sophistication of the set, there is a certain lack of originality about it which will prevent it from becoming essential listening.
RECORD MIRROR
Raydio is a containment, a gift-wrapping of disco. Resting on the safe bedrock of synthesized bass, its sound risks nothing and transports nowhere.
NEW MUSICAL EXPRESS

PARLIAMENT
Trombipulation *(Casablanca)*
At his worst he's a black Frank Zappa, but for true words spoken in jest and rhythms that will not quit, you can do a lot worse than chuck George a few quid every so often and let him

confuse you. Funk art — let's dance.
NEW MUSICAL EXPRESS
...an often humourous and stylish album that leaves many of its contemporaries standing.
RECORD MIRROR
...when the mood is right nobody understands 'Body Language' better than George.
SOUNDS

THE ALAN PARSONS PROJECT
The Turn Of A Friendly Card *(Arista)*
...let me recommend this Alan Parsons album to people who have bought every other Alan Parsons album and for people who are fed up waiting two years for a Pink Floyd album.
MELODY MAKER
...hardly a concept at all but loosely based on the gambling theme, is as full as usual with the advanced invention and musical accomplishment that usually gets termed AOR.
RECORD MIRROR

DOLLY PARTON
9 To 5 And Odd Jobs *(RCA)*
...hear the album, see the film, learn the lessons; this Dolly mixture is both sweet and sustaining.
NEW MUSICAL EXPRESS
...an impressive comeback...sweet, but never coy or mawkish. It's nice to have Dolly Parton back from the trash bin unscathed.
ROLLING STONE

THE PASSAGE
Pindrop *(Object)*
With the disquieting 'Pindrop', The Passage can be accepted as major even by the cowardly, cautious and cynical: it's a work of disciplined intellectual aggression, frantic emotions and powerfully idiomatic musicality.
NEW MUSICAL EXPRESS
...The Passage confront love, fear, repulsion and pain and all the most negative, most vindictive emotions humans are capable of, in the same sober, relentless way Joy Division did.
SOUNDS
...twisting insanity; frightening, surreal experience; the pain of clashing relationships...their subjects are as sophisticated as their songs' structural make-up, which belies the overall impression of idealistic youthfulness.
RECORD MIRROR

...dark, spacy, disturbing and quite beautiful.
TROUSER PRESS

THE PASSAGE
For All And None *(Night And Day)*
...an experimental of quiet devastation, a sort of highly structured, complex — but never complicated — pop.
NEW MUSICAL EXPRESS
...a group with plenty of ideas chasing around in circles in search of an adequate means of expressing them.
MELODY MAKER
This wonderful, horrifying album has felt the cold touch of the *zeitgeist*. Only Peter Hammill before them evoked the touch of dead flesh and dead lives so eloquently...I haven't encountered an album of such musical and lyrical depth and substance for ages.
SOUNDS
Built around receding, pounding drum figures, swirling, muddy keyboards and flat, Mancunian vocalisings, this record collapses under its own weight.
RECORD MIRROR

TEDDY PENDERGRASS
Ready For...Teddy Pendergrass *(Philadelphia International)*
...here we have the most potent soul singer of his generation...Pendergrass is equally commanding on ballads and uptempo songs. He comes to the boil rather more slowly as befits the nature of the material. But when he gets there the passion or anguish, depending on the lyric's bias, is devastating.
MELODY MAKER

PERE UBU
The Art Of Walking *(Rough Trade)*
Those who listen to Pere Ubu without laughing, without laughing a lot and loudly, might as well not be listening to Pere Ubu...A comparison that springs to mind is Laurel & Hardy backed by later Miles Davis: its moments of banality, its extending periods of farcical agitation, its fascinating spells.
NEW MUSICAL EXPRESS
...the collective output is so generally lacklustre and low on spark that the album becomes a short-sighted attempt to out-weird the weird.
MELODY MAKER
The only way 'The Art Of Walking' isn't a record full of much excitement, fun and

compelling interest as if you don't want it to be so...Pere Ubu, far from being stilted and pompous r'n'r intelligentsia, are the music's winos and layabouts getting high on something cheap.
SOUNDS
...much of 'The Art Of Walking' is taken up by tone poems or sonic landscapes — whatever they call their aural renderings of light and dissonance.
TROUSER PRESS

PERE UBU
390 Degrees Of Simulated Stereo *(Rough Trade)*
...quite simply *fries* nearly everything currently on the conveyor, serving as a salutary pointer to the directions the Great Beast rock 'n' roll could have taken in the '80s.
NEW MUSICAL EXPRESS
If you were ever interested in Pere Ubu, this album is required listening.
MELODY MAKER
...variable sound quality apart, the songs remain powerfully effective, and in years to come should still stand witness to the unique nature of this bizarre beast.
SOUNDS

MARK PERRY
Snappy Turns *(Deptford Fun Records)*
It's fascinatingly bad, his intensely morbid vision of life complemented by music that bids to be totally unmusical. Stripped bare of almost all semblance of tune or melody, what remains is a skeleton.
MELODY MAKER
...the cold fact is the 'Snappy Turns', for all its interesting facets, is almost unlistenable, save as a record of commentary.
RECORD MIRROR

TOM PETTY AND THE HEARTBREAKERS
Hard Promises *(MCA)*
Instead of finding glory in pure assertion, 'Hard Promises' finds a dignity in acceptance.
NEW MUSICAL EXPRESS
Petty is very definitely a contender, but a little more inspiration and a little less imitation would leave the rest of America's rock romantics standing in his dust.
MELODY MAKER
...Tom Petty has two real options for his next album. Either he can remain the ageless rocker with unlimited teen dream appeal, or he can follow the direction 'You Can Still Change Your Mind'

points to which is up and out, broadening the horizon for himself and his audience.
SOUNDS
Like prime time Nick Lowe, he's a perfectionist in his field. Or simply, the best. An adolescence spent soaking up vintage Sixties mid west radio has ensured a generous fund of riffs, solos, tunes, phrases, ideas and so on to refashion for his own glorious compositions.
RECORD MIRROR
Though clearly proud of himself, Petty's secure enough to acknowledge he's one of a multitude, not a messiah.
TROUSER PRESS

PHANTOMBAND
Phantomband *(Sky)*
...Succeeds remarkably well within the modest limits it sets itself...this sort of restrained, mature musicianship is perhaps too easily overlooked these days in favour of modish ephemeralities.
NEW MUSICAL EXPRESS
Touches of free improvisation...lover's rock, stratospheric dance music and, yes, even the flash-flood lyricism of Can, are filtered through an elegant, sexy and populist production.
SOUNDS

WILSON PICKETT
Right Track *(EMI)*
The tunes are mostly deadly dull formula disco and have nothing of the required excitement.
NEW MUSICAL EXPRESS
...further evidence that this excellent and influential R&B singer has at last hit a spate of form something like the equal of that which made his exciting Sixties' sides so universally popular.
MELODY MAKER

THE PIRANHAS
The Piranhas *(Sire)*
The Piranhas cheerfully chart a course through life's petty pitfalls, gamely slipping on one social banana-skin after another while comforting themselves with the old cliche that if you don't laugh you'll cry.
NEW MUSICAL EXPRESS
...a reasonable, but flawed effort.
MELODY MAKER
...proffers a multi faceted goldmine of merriment mated to all kinds of modern pop...the Piranhas have a wit and variety that's all their own.
SOUNDS

...a smorgasbord of slightly familiar sounds — pleasurable and witty, but a bit too underdeveloped to call their own.
TROUSER PRESS

THE PIRATES
A Fistful Of Dubloons *(Edsel)*
...however narrow their chosen ground, they're masters of the little eclectic touch.
NEW MUSICAL EXPRESS

THE PLASMATICS
New Hope For The Wretched *(Stiff)*
...the Plasmatics' constant search for new depths of grotesqueness to plumb has an almost child-like innocence to it...Your mother wouldn't like them — thank God.
MELODY MAKER
...so insanely over the top that it staggers the senses into undignified capitulation. A colourful catalogue of grinding powerchord repetition that is quite hilarious and totally priceless.
SOUNDS
To say the Plasmatics are untalented would be akin to stating that Adolf Hitler had a slight personality problem. The Plasmatics make one think that one's parents and peers were right all along about this sordid, noisy degeneracy called rock. The Plasmatics, to use their own vernacular, suck a big one.
RECORD MIRROR
Theoretically, if you crossed the ninety-mile-an-hour, fuzz-busting pop of the Ramones with the heavy-metal, DC Comics corn of Kiss, you could come up with a fascinating monster. Not this time. Instead, what you get are the Plasmatics.
ROLLING STONE

THE PLASTICS
Welcome Back *(Island)*
Plastics make spirited facsimiles of UK and US original styles: pushed through the culture warp of a modern Japanese sensibility, the results are distinctive and enjoyable, and a valuable input in their own right.
NEW MUSICAL EXPRESS
This is like sin in Toyland. The backing is sugary sweet in its innocence, the top layer rancid. Chica Sato yelps her vocals like a scalded guinea pig...The Plastics are Japanese but that's hardly an excuse.
MELODY MAKER

...a sharply produced, cleverly conceived, fun loving, spunky little debut album.
SOUNDS
Funnier (as in sillier) lyrics and further development of the drum sound are in order. (Some English lessons wouldn't hurt, either.)
TROUSER PRESS

THE PLIMSOULS
The Plimsouls *(Planet)*
When you can barely tell what decade an album's recorded in, that's taking the notion of classicism to ridiculous extremes. There's no reason why timeless pop should have to be faceless too.
ROLLING STONE

POISON GIRLS
Chappaquiddick Bridge *(Crass)*
It's a dour, depressing, pleasureless experience and, what's more, it's meant to be...articulate their humourless, squalid view of the world by making humourless, squalid noises.
MELODY MAKER
...one of the most valuable impressions Poison Girls leave with me is that they are a group of people who can be trusted.
SOUNDS

THE POLECATS
Polecats Are Go *(Mercury)*
...unfailingly brilliant; a boppin', bouncin' ballroom lesson in it ain't what you do but the way that you do it.
MELODY MAKER
...a taste to refresh jaded palates. It is teen bop, sugar coated, sweet toothed re-interpretation of (outdated) rockabilly styles...Their sound is gaudy, but not brash — a shoving, clean smiling summer noise. A fun, funny romp along fantasy avenue instead of memory lane.
SOUNDS
...most of the songs have something going for them — a nice blast of sax or guitar here, a good melody or lyric there but as a collection there's something missing.
RECORD MIRROR
...knows exactly where it's going and wastes no time in getting there.
NEW MUSICAL EXPRESS

THE POLICE
Zenyatta Mondatta *(A&M)*
...the third in an unbroken line of stupid titles that attempt to clothe plain fare in mystery, like the menu in a greasy French Bayswater cafe. Too much of a mediocre thing.
NEW MUSICAL EXPRESS
Instead of the spring onion freshness that we're used to we've been dished up soup kitchen banalities. Riffs that plod without conviction. Less than ingenious playing from hearts of coal. Kindergarten lyrics to make us squirm with embarrassment.
MELODY MAKER
...not pretentious, not bombastic, not lazy. Their art and craft were fully engaged. Their only hesitation seems to have been a certain lack of adventurousness; giving it all they've got, but within already known limits.
SOUNDS
..not only great, it is of enormous cultural significance. Fifty years from now, critics may regard it, along with one or two Beatles creations, of *historical* cultural significance.
RECORD MIRROR
...offers near-perfect pop by a band that bends all the rules and sometimes makes musical mountains out of molehill-size ideas.
ROLLING STONE
...the Police can be airtight for driving rhythm or a pop feel, or loose to show off their chops. They avoid, or at least rearrange, cliches (by putting them into a new context), and they just *sound* so damned good. And that's the whole idea, isn't it?
TROUSER PRESS

POLYROCK
Polyrock *(RCA)*
...Polyrock are all thin and worried. They blast out small synthesiser splashes that smear like underwater ink gutts. The sound keeps running and running quickly, almost tripping over itself in its attempt to get — either there or away, it's not sure which.
NEW MUSICAL EXPRESS
...not so much a rock band as a dance unit programmed by computer...Until they learn to shed the cool facade and release some hard-core emotion, they are doomed to continue creating mechanical drivel.
TROUSER PRESS

IGGY POP
Party *(Arista)*
...he fires his songs...with a rock urgency that traditionally promises far more than it can deliver. But as 'Party' is pretty much about broken dreams and subsequent disillusionment, the music's empty bluster matches the mood.
NEW MUSICAL EXPRESS
...Pop is by turns the perfect pasticheur with a mind of his own and a jaded hard-rock hack who'd have difficulty writing his name, let alone a decent song. The question is, does anybody care?
MELODY MAKER
The majority of tunes on 'Party' push their themes of work, beer and stupidity quite convincingly till you almost want to join in.
SOUNDS
There's nothing new or fresh about this record; indeed the only thing that kept me listening all the way through was his voice, which is as dark and compelling as ever. Other than that it's just a rock and roll LP, and who needs another one of those?
RECORD MIRROR

POSITIVE NOISE
Heart Of Darkness *(Statik)*
...such an unrelenting rush that it's easy not to recognise its real qualities underneath the rock blur.
NEW MUSICAL EXPRESS
Their forte is, eponymously, passion, which is what this album, in its ultimate criminality, lacks. What it finally dies from.
SOUNDS
Positive Noise occupy the curious niche of a group who plunder the music of their contemporaries with skill and discernment, but haven't quite enough skill to effectively disguise what they're doing wrong.
RECORD MIRROR

PRAYING MANTIS
Time Tells No Lies *(Arista)*
Laced with a veritable armada of lush arrangements, awash with finely sculpted yet bracing harmonies and encrusted with more gems than a royal tiara. 'Time Tells No Lies' is a joyous ode to the art and form of hard rock...a real Rembrandt in a wasteland of disposable grafitti.
RECORD MIRROR

...ultimately it's the shortcomings of this album that stand out most. Without their vocal problem Mantis could have done so much better.
SOUNDS

PRETTY THINGS
Cross Talk *(Warner Bros)*
...May's the only member of this line-up whose creative talent is unarguable. His band's a 'solid working unit' alright, but lacks real distinction in nearly every department.
SOUNDS

...yet another hippy band from yesteryear who won't lie down and die.
RECORD MIRROR

...the Pretties' very unpretentiousness may be their own undoing. These guys deserve more than they'll probably ever get.
TROUSER PRESS

PRINCE
Dirty Mind *(Warner Bros)*
...this precocious 20-year-old may pose the biggest potential threat to "Born Again" WASP Amerika since Jimi Hendrix's guitar-humpin' had him dumped from the Monkees' tour in 1967.
NEW MUSICAL EXPRESS

...a slightly dusky individual with blown-dry hair, sensitive eyelashes, a thin moustache and an apparent penchant for relaxing in high-cut posing briefs and woolly stockings.
SOUNDS

...It's weak kneed disco masquerading as rock, but so limp wristed it barely reaches a twitch on most tracks.
RECORD MIRROR

...a pop record of Rabelaisian achievement: entirely, ditheringly obsessed with the body, yet full of sentiments that please and provoke the mind. It may also be the most generous album about sex ever made by a man.
ROLLING STONE

JOHN PRINE
Storm Windows *(Asylum)*
In the course of making an album of deceptively slap-happy folk-rock songs, John Prine has managed to slip in some of the most delicate, compressed wordplay of his career.
ROLLING STONE

THE PSYCHEDELIC FURS
Talk Talk Talk *(CBS)*
...a dull, disappointing album.
MELODY MAKER

...this is a really terrible album...I am practically in awe of its huge, unshapely

grotesqueness...Psychedelic Furs give being bad a bad name.
SOUNDS

...there is some fundamental re-thinking to be done and the Furs will have to find a way of writing stronger stuff than this.
RECORD MIRROR

...can easily think of ten reasons why I wouldn't have it in my home.
NEW MUSICAL EXPRESS

PSYCOTIC PINEAPPLE
Where's The Party? *(Richmond)*
Twerpy longhairs who love their moms and play brash trash, like The Dictators, destined to sell ten copies and become cult figures in Paris...They cannot sing to save themselves, but they play a guitar just like wringing a wet rag: strong, no finesse. Imagine a dishwasher on the rampage.
SOUNDS

...one of the finest and funniest albums I've ever heard.
RECORD MIRROR

When Psycotic Pineapple cuts the thirdgrade showmanship and sticks to driving albeit goofy pop, they come off as a real hot party band in the best high school bash mold.
TROUSER PRESS

PUBLIC IMAGE LIMITED
Paris au Printemps *(Virgin)*
Whatever PiL's intentions, the music here is guaranteed to affect you like no other music you've ever come across. Whether that's a good thing is up to you.
MELODY MAKER

..equivalent to paying somebody to throw the contents of the average sewer over your head...An album of blank noise would have said more about PiL, been more redeeming than this lifeless lump of rehashed vinyl.
SOUNDS

...perfectly summarises the whole PiL thing and what's expected of it. Lydon sneers and acts hateful, not helped by his boorish audience; he threatens to walk off the stage, but doesn't; he acts disinterested; he's bored.
RECORD MIRROR

Apart from marking time while PiL decides what it's doing, this is basically as purposeless as most live LPs (for musical growth if not commercial exploitation).
TROUSER PRESS

...the album on which PiL's formlessness finally became formulated — which is to say

that if they could reproduce their apparently inchoate, unpremeditated music letter-perfect live (and they could), then it wasn't really orderless or even all that experimental. Yet it is visceral.
ROLLING STONE

PUBLIC IMAGE LIMITED
The Flowers Of Romance *(Virgin/Warner Bros)*
...a laboured and lazy "ideas" LP — the sort of thing Eno might once have produced if he hadn't had a neat and tidy upbringing — interesting only if you're interested in join-the-dots behind the drawing. The perfect illustration, really, of PiL's (currently) misplaced ideals and passions.
NEW MUSICAL EXPRESS

If there's a more innovative record released during the next 12 months I'll be astonished.
MELODY MAKER

What stamps 'FoR' with greatness is its shocking honesty, elemental emotion and total lack of contrivance...an avant-garde album with the spirit of rock 'n' roll...This is the album mankind has been waiting for : Absolute Music.
SOUNDS

The overall positive, driving, optimistic drum-based sound is occasionally let down by outbursts of unlistenability but PiL-poppers never did like their poison too tasty.
RECORD MIRROR

...the sheer desolating force of the music he and Levene make — a blaring, claustrophobic, rapacious tumult of atonal piano, metallic drums and furious singing — seems to act out the passions of murder while simultaneously seeking to annihilate those passions.
ROLLING STONE

Lydon has a flair for words and private images, but until Public Image learns to play in more than one emotional key he'd better refine his talent. It's hard for one person to carry a band: just ask Johnny Rotten.
TROUSER PRESS

JIMMY PURSEY
Imagination Camouflage *(Polydor)*
...the old diatribes resurface with far more flesh on their bones, expressed in Real Songs of considerable power and variety, rather than the erstwhile riffs 'n' chants...Like John Lennon and a couple of others, Jimmy Pursey can be ridiculous and

splendid at one and the same time.
NEW MUSICAL EXPRESS

This is music that has a lot to do with experiment and atmosphere and emotion and very little to do with charts or commerciality...Pursey's still an important figure in rock 'n' roll because he's still thinking and questioning and moving on.
MELODY MAKER

...synthesisers, horn sections, rolling pianos, make-believe orchestras, girlie singers, dated guitar solos, funk, junk, (no punk), rock ordinaire, heavy metal, disco, pomp — all piled high and incongruously on top of each other like a cartoon sarnie. This man is striving for highbrow recognition in a big way.
SOUNDS

...a confusing mess of differing styles and half-hearted "experimentation", the bulk of which just doesn't work.
RECORD MIRROR

By rights, a Jimmy Pursey "solo" album shouldn't be more than a tedious rehash of Sham 69. Amazingly enough, 'Imagination Camouflage' is a damn good record.
TROUSER PRESS

PYLON
Gyrate *(Armageddon)*
...one of the year's most fundamental rock & roll celebrations.
NEW MUSICAL EXPRESS

Pylon would be a great hip disco band, the ideal sound to nudge the evening towards a fruitfully physical conclusion.
MELODY MAKER

Pylon beat out a sparse but eminently danceable rhythm so characteristic of the best of North American new wave pop (52s, Heads, Muffins et all), possessing that endearing lack of fussiness or contrivance that seems to be in such short supply here at home.
SOUNDS

...could easily become the milestone, and offer a new dimension in rock music; a whole new approach.
RECORD MIRROR

With forceful rhythms and a kooky aura, Pylon should be ideally equipped to follow the trail blazed by the B-52s.
TROUSER PRESS

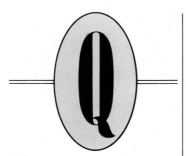

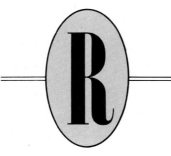

Q TIPS
Q Tips *(Chrysalis)*
...this album stinks. The cover versions lack the wit or energy to be either interesting or offensive and, without a single original note, the rest is instantly forgettable.
MELODY MAKER
...this album is living proof that you don't always have to go forward to make good music, sometimes it's sufficient just to not go backwards.
SOUNDS
...they can take an era and update it successfully.
RECORD MIRROR
Like the song says, there ain't nothing like the real thing. And this ain't nothing like the real thing.
NEW MUSICAL EXPRESS

QUARTZ
Stand Up And Fight *(MCA)*
The songs are all about women or drugs or drink or devils or fire or fighting or the end of the world...and the music either rattles along at a fair old pace or struts with carefully constructed dignity. Devotees of Quartz will love it. I find it about as thrilling as a cold bath in the middle of winter in the tundra region of Norway.
SOUNDS
...overloaded with bruising riffs couched in muscular melodies, perfectly encapsulating the best of both old-style and 'new wave' metal values.
RECORD MIRROR

QUEEN
Flash Gordon *(EMI)*
Freddie Mercury only sings twice (which some may consider a bonus), and the intervening instrumentals are thin on memorable moments.
NEW MUSICAL EXPRESS
...as a film soundtrack 'Flash Gordon' is something extraordinary.
MELODY MAKER
Serious Queen fans may be distressed by the paucity of full-fledged songs; others will merely be relieved.
TROUSER PRESS

TREVOR RABIN
Wolf *(Chrysalis)*
...a pretty boy who can write his own pretty tunes.
NEW MUSICAL EXPRESS
...the hair of the dog. It growls, spits and snaps like a rabid hound in quarantine.
SOUNDS
The grand wazir of metallica has finally broken free of his self-imposed chains. He roars into Motivation City with a strong sense of voracious vinyl virtuosity. Trevor Rabin delivers the goods with a lavish, almost opulent, magnificence.
RECORD MIRROR

RAF
RAF *(A&M)*
Nothing to do with DAF, but possibly some relation to BOF.
MELODY MAKER
...two tracks out of ten don't really make a rock album. On the other hand eight tracks out of ten do make a pop album, and RAF seem well-equipped for success in that vein.
SOUNDS
...the most commercial sound to have emerged from the whole new wave scene, Police/Jam included. Pomp-punk lives.
RECORD MIRROR

RAF
The Heat's On *(A&M)*
...Having delivered one of the finest debut albums of all time in the eponymous 'RAF', this (now) quintet have gone several stages beyond with 'THO'.
RECORD MIRROR

THE RAINCOATS
Odyshape *(Rough Trade)*
...this is a feminine album, a feminist album, bursting with both the strength and warmth innate in today's women. Sometimes the music is soft and dreamy, then fierce and demanding. This record could not have been made by men alone.
SOUNDS
...uniformly a beautiful and exceptionally refreshing work...By following their

instincts and emotions, the Raincoats have produced music that sounds so natural and organic it could have been grown in pots at Rough Trade.
MELODY MAKER
They're a serious ensemble, saved from being cerebral by the emphasis they put on emotion and feeling, in the songs and the playing.
NEW MUSICAL EXPRESS

THE RAMONES
Pleasant Dreams *(Sire)*
...that LP the Ramones have always dreamt of making. A whole album of wholly realised songs, framed with non-stop pop expertise by producer Graham Gouldman and lovingly set in a running order which not only accelerates but, in doing so, accentuates Exactly What the Ramones Got That Nobody Else has.
NEW MUSICAL EXPRESS
...states firmly that their heavy metal days are a memory — for the future, they've come of age.
SOUNDS
...another year, another shove in the right direction and another fund of good tunes.
RECORD MIRROR

RED CRAYOLA WITH ART AND LANGUAGE
Kangaroo? *(Rough Trade)*
...set in a warm, mocking music with an elastic, airy structure that leaves plenty of space for its many tangents and surprises.
NEW MUSICAL EXPRESS
...an intriguing album with overtly intellectual lyrics that tackle everything from the modern American artist Jackson Pollock to Lenin, Trotsky, Plekhanov and gestalt experiments with a sly humour that finds a mirror in the controlled madness of the music.
MELODY MAKER
I'd be very surprised if Thompson was serious about these windy Left-wing persemantics. I'm no Roland Barthes, but that inability to distinguish sums up this album's mystifying nature.
SOUNDS

RELUCTANT STEREOTYPES
The Label *(WEA)*
I think Stereotypes have a future. It's a pity this album couldn't have made the fact more apparent.
MELODY MAKER
...that rare album where the lyric sheet offers more than the record itself.
TROUSER PRESS

...an accurate summary of the band's live work...there's an easy flow about their music, live and recorded.
RECORD MIRROR

RENALDO AND THE LOAF
Songs For Swinging Larvae *(Ralph Records)*
If only you could put the sounds/noise of psychotic smurfs/vampire insects having stakes driven into their hearts, into words.
MELODY MAKER
...I'd gladly sacrifice half the frenetic lunacy on this album for a sense of soul, and some emotion behind the urgent desire to impress.
SOUNDS
...an enjoyable, and promising album.
RECORD MIRROR
Renaldo And The Loaf want to be the Residents so bad it hurts. They don't use synthesizers, but otherwise it's all there: splintered vocals, mad percussion, tape manipulation — the whole shebang.
TROUSER PRESS

REO SPEEDWAGON
Hi Infidelity *(Epic)*
Punters keep reassuring me that this is Reo's finest work to date. I tend to disagree.
SOUNDS
...one of the greatest albums I have EVER heard in the HR genre.
RECORD MIRROR
...this Illinois quintet has simply added a little more AOR gloss to the already classy fusion of pop savvy and hard-rock moxie that first drew national attention in 1978.
ROLLING STONE

THE RESIDENTS
The Residents Commercial Album *(Ralph)*
They're no longer something special, they're simply the lunatic fringe and personally I hate the theory, love the record and couldn't give a monkey's who they are.
MELODY MAKER
...the Four Interior Decorators of the Apocalypse infuse their tantalising cameos with a disturbing, almost-out-of control energy. They can tippy-toe through an intense rhythm and make it sound like something out of 'South Pacific'...an exasperating delight.
SOUNDS
...I predict it will make the band a household name along with the likes of Dollar, Abba and Rolf Harris.
RECORD MIRROR

If Frank Zappa shared some of some of Mike Oldfield's romantic orchestral tendencies, he might make an LP similar to The Residents Commercial Album, a kind of un-Lumpy Gravy that'd go down relatively easy but still leave a strange and fascinating taste in your mouth.
ROLLING STONE
...does nothing to vitiate their most experimental, exasperating qualities, but it will open their door to a whole new audience.
TROUSER PRESS

THE REVILLOS
Rev Up (Snatzo/Dindisc)
...trash of a devastating and awe-inspiring purity, an album that trugs along a tightrope strung between Fireball XL5 and The Ghost In The Invisible Bikini. Lovingly handcrafted to contain not even the faintest trace of redeeming artistic merit.
NEW MUSICAL EXPRESS
Forget about concepts like "the trash aesthetic". That belongs with "the future of rock 'n' roll", in the corner where the people live who think more about what they ought to like than what they really like. This belongs in the corner where the people sit who need cheering up.
MELODY MAKER
...a non-starter based on a virtually extinct Sixties revival and plundered for effects. It is 13 cuts of exhibitionist trivia...They are lost in a bundle of hapless memories and trapped in an image which they dare not shake away.
SOUNDS
...essentially disposable, but it's also a great deal of fun.
TROUSER PRESS

CLIFF RICHARD
I'm No Hero (EMI)
Criticising a new Cliff Richard album is like taking a hammer to a half-set jelly.
MELODY MAKER
Ageless, asexual, cute, versatile, uncontroversial and talented, too. We can add up all the parts without ever getting a tight fix on the whole.
SOUNDS
...a perfectly conceived pop album...song after song of near-perfect MOR rock that offends none and pleases many.
RECORD MIRROR

RICO
The Man Is Forward (2 Tone)
Music for sunny afternoons, for late at night, for day dreams...very classy aural backdrop.
NEW MUSICAL EXPRESS
Live, it would probably go down over a few liveners but coming out of your standard hi-fi it lacks any real pulling power, however much you crank the sound up. It's flat.
SOUNDS
This is either your sort of album or it isn't.
RECORD MIRROR

THE RINGS
The Rings (MCA)
These cool Bostonians could be the Cars in a good mood...A clever debut and a bright future.
TROUSER PRESS

MINNIE RIPERTON
Love Lives Forever (Capitol)
She has left us the memory of a truly soulful singer, sometimes too sweet, but inimitable on those incredible high jumps.
NEW MUSICAL EXPRESS
Pop music's loss of this gifted writer and singer is still obviously considerable.
MELODY MAKER

LEE RITENOUR
Rit (Electra)
...shuffles and bumps along with a pleasant but unpleasing pointlessness and the requisite number of creamy-smooth and sugar sweet solos.
NEW MUSICAL EXPRESS
Just the right amount of danceability and tantalising nuances of soul, tasteful vocals and all of it swathed in Ritenour's masterful guitar work.
RECORD MIRROR

THE RIVITS
Multiplay (Island)
Roden is certainly not the bright, bugeyed optimistic waif of yore. Rivits play tight and hard but there's a mechanical feel about the band which live work will dispel.
MELODY MAKER
The lyrics are intelligent and brashy, in touch with the Eighties, while the melodies are always understated and smoothly executed.
RECORD MIRROR

BA ROBERTSON
Bully For You (Asylum)
Purveyor of some of the wittiest pure pop music since 10cc, BA Robertson weighs in with an enjoyable second album...Fun for the frivolous and a few more.
MELODY MAKER
...only pokes feeble fun from a safe distance, and BA blusters through two sides of an album without really saying anything at all...not much more than an ingratiating minstrel who's currently giving a conservative media exactly what they want.
NEW MUSICAL EXPRESS

SMOKEY ROBINSON
Being With You (Tamla)
...renews his commitments and reminds us of his qualities... With Smokey Robinson, you still get sunshine on a cloudy day.
NEW MUSICAL EXPRESS
Smokey certainly isn't the consistently stunning writer he was in the Sixties. His bitter-sweet love songs have lost their sharpness but he's matured as a composer with considerable dignity.
MELODY MAKER
Smokey Robinson is that rare pop singer whose rhapsodic lyricism hasn't diminished with approaching middle age. Indeed time has added a metaphysical depth to his art.
ROLLING STONE

THE ROCHES
Nurds (Warner Bros)
The Roches can be very good and 'Nurds' is wittier, livelier and more adventurous than the Fripp-produced debut that last year won them a degree of cult notoriety.
NEW MUSICAL EXPRESS
...another game of skittles entirely. It has none of its predecessor's initial charm to sweeten the pill, and in this case the pill is wholly more sour.
MELODY MAKER
They look like if they went to bed with you they'd want a three-hour discussion first and then demand to go on top.
SOUNDS
Instead of relying on their own pitiful attempts, they would have been better off buying some decent songs, cutting back on the royalties, and giving us all a break.
RECORD MIRROR
As their wonderful and witty Nurds demonstrates, the Roche sisters collectively make such a perfect team because they are, individually, so distinct — both from one another and from the rest of the world.
ROLLING STONE

ROCKPILE
Seconds Of Pleasure (F-Beat)
Ironically, it's Rockpile's newly-acquired democracy that blunts the fine cutting edge one took for granted on various solo efforts...the album doesn't cut it satisfactorily as either an Edmunds or Lowe vehicle.
NEW MUSICAL EXPRESS
...won't extend your intellectual horizons. But it will remind you why you thought rock 'n' roll was such a damned good idea in the first place. 'SOP' treats your heart like a Saturday night, puts a smile as broad as a barmaid's hips on your face and sets your ankles on fire with its irresistible invitation to roll up the carpet and hoof across the floorboards.
MELODY MAKER
...simply the best firmly traditional UK rock 'n' roll band in existence, bar none save The Rolling Stones on a good night.
SOUNDS
Edmunds and Lowe have developed their craft with precision and care, and the resulting excellent albums don't pall with playing.
RECORD MIRROR
On their solo discs, Dave Edmunds and Nick Lowe ransacked rock & roll history, from blues to rockabilly to the Beatles. 'Seconds of Pleasure' continues this tradition of honorable plunder, with some new twists.
ROLLING STONE

THE ROLLING STONES
Sucking In The Seventies (Rolling Stones)
Sucking In The '70s is right. The Stones devour everything around them — and become more bloated and flatulent every year.
NEW MUSICAL EXPRESS
The album's cover, with its drab black lettering on a plain white background, reflects the paucity of its contents.
MELODY MAKER
The world is not short of Rolling Stones compilations from the Seventies.
SOUNDS

THE ROMANTICS
National Breakout (Epic)
...unless The Romantics take a look around and really try to get to grips with what's happening then I fear their only contribution to the Eighties scene will be as additions to the dole queue.
NEW MUSICAL EXPRESS

...narcissistic, plagiaristic, hackneyed and heartless...the standard Stateside obsessions with wet dreams. Wranglers and wrist jobs from yet another typically pea-brained pretty-boy powerhouse fourpiece.
MELODY MAKER
...the Romantics are doing little more than the Flamin' Groovies and the Rubinoos were up to four years ago. But without the skill and the flair.
RECORD MIRROR
...the title of the Romantics' second album is just wishful thinking.
TROUSER PRESS

ROMEO VOID
It's A Condition (415)
...adopt a stance that is specifically independent and original while still flying in the face of the new conventions. Their best shot is a fluidity that is quite at odds with the contemporary funk punk and generally its master.
NEW MUSICAL EXPRESS
...they sound like a cross between Blondie and the Doors, a peculiar, but enjoyable, combination.
MELODY MAKER
The band treads dangerously fine lines between droll wit and unconscious parody, dramatic understatement and amateur-hour bull.
TROUSER PRESS

LE ROUX
Up (Capitol)
...good clean-cut pomp and well worth chasing.
SOUNDS

THE RUMOUR
Purity Of Essence (Stiff)
They're too relaxed and comfy: no adventures take place, few sparks are struck.
NEW MUSICAL EXPRESS
With Graham Parker they have a direction, a force. On their own, it's music by committee.
MELODY MAKER
...unobtrusive pop songs which all but passively entwine you as if you were a cat playing with a ball of string.
SOUNDS
Like the four members melt into the wallpaper on the rather hideous cover of this effort, the music follows suit, and you wonder why on earth they ever bothered to record it.
RECORD MIRROR
...a collage of stick-in-your-head tunes that recall everyone from the Move to

the Flamin' Groovies with alluring accuracy.
TROUSER PRESS

THE RUNAWAYS
Flaming Schoolgirls
(Cherry Red Records)
...the girls dig deep into their West Coast heavy metal bag of tricks for some pretty, woeful songs dedicated to boozing, boogeying and boys.
RECORD MIRROR

TODD RUNDGREN
Healing (Bearsville)
...given its "spiritual" subject-matter, the album's almost totally lacking in true feeling, being as gleaming, soulless, and sumptuously sterile as a high-tech operating theatre.
NEW MUSICAL EXPRESS
...despite the grandness of the music and the passion of the sentiments, I can't see it having the lasting appeal of its classic predecessor.
SOUNDS
Rundgren's more devoted listeners may be receptive to this album's trance-like qualities, but there's little incentive on 'Healing' for the rest of us to hear him out.
TROUSER PRESS
The man is one of my top four favourite musicians on this planet and his albums either solo or with Utopia have given me a lot of pleasure over the years. But this is a turkey.
RECORD MIRROR
...a sublime, subliminally incandescent album — the music shimmers, the words pull seductively.
ROLLING STONE

RUSH
Moving Pictures (Mercury)
For pseud heavy metal they have no equal.
RECORD MIRROR
...may well be technically superb but it really doesn't generate much excitement.
MELODY MAKER
...impeccable rock; violent, frightening, exciting and fed up with the old rules of HM.
SOUNDS
...Rush's woolly concern isn't much more than the sound of bewildered innocents adrift on their insecurity. Why waste either your sympathy or money?
NEW MUSICAL EXPRESS

LEON RUSSELL AND NEW GRASS REVIVAL
The Live Album
(Paradise Records)
...completely lacking in vitality, originality, excitement or feel for country music.
MELODY MAKER

THE RUTS
Grin And Bear It (Virgin)
Given Owen's untimely death, the Ruts deserved a skilful re-write of their recorded history. But 'Grin And Bear It' just drags their best stuff down to the rather erratic level of their rest.
NEW MUSICAL EXPRESS
...patchy collection that sadly only gives the occasional glimpse of the band at their best either in the studio or live.
MELODY MAKER
...a great goodbye to stage one of one of the best bands to come out of punk, and an excellent reminder of just how superb the Ruts were.
SOUNDS
...committed modern music from a band with the talent to carry on and develop their wide-awake musical ideas.
RECORD MIRROR
...a fine presentation of the brilliance and appeal of the overlooked Ruts and the late Malcolm Owen.
TROUSER PRESS

RUTS DC
Animal Now (Virgin)
Ruts DC can grow in confidence and stature but they'll have to find within themselves an inner vitality, that sense of animal now-ness that eludes them at the moment.
NEW MUSICAL EXPRESS
If this album is a pointer to what's to come, then the troubled times really will be coming to an end for Ruts DC.
MELODY MAKER
The original heart and soul, the daring and the guts or punk is still....alive!
SOUNDS
The Ruts just seem to be dabbling in whatever musical form that whim dictates and this gives it all a rather parasitical feel.
RECORD MIRROR

THE SAINTS
The Monkey Puzzle
(New Nose)
Bolt all the windows and lock all the doors and for God's sake turn it up.
MELODY MAKER
...an unhappy mixture of the fine and the embarassing.
SOUNDS
...the only resemblance to the Saints of '77 is a free live single including a pretty horrendous version of 'Stranded'.
RECORD MIRROR

RYUICHII SAKAMOTO
B-2 Unit (Island)
...a weird concept to say the least.
RECORD MIRROR
...who says the Japanese don't have a sense of humour!
NEW MUSICAL EXPRESS

JOE SAMPLE
Voices In The Rain (MCA)
...reduces everything to a lowest common denominator. This is jazzak.
NEW MUSICAL EXPRESS

SAMSON
Shock Tactics (RCA/GEM)
...a monolithic masterpiece of musical might.
SOUNDS
...a supreme consummation of their undoubted talents. Heavy yet primitive, majestic yet savage.
RECORD MIRROR

DAVID SANBORN
Voyeur (Warner Bros)
...sounds as though it was a grinding drudge to make.
NEW MUSICAL EXPRESS

DAVID SANCIOUS
The Bridge (Arista)
Anyone who sits lonely at a piano, plays the first thing that comes into his head and releases the results either has monumental confidence in his ability or has been down the pub.
MELODY MAKER

DEVADIP CARLOS SANTANA
The Swing Of Delight (CBS)
...this shabby artefact amounts to the worst-ever advertisement for Sri

Chinmoy's purgatorial cosmic propaganda, depicting the guru's *star* disciple blissfully unaware of having had his spiritual greens well and truly strained once too often.
NEW MUSICAL EXPRESS
...beautifully displayed work from the pioneer of *infectious* laid-back music.
RECORD MIRROR

SANTANA
Zebop *(CBS)*
Some would say it is a change for the worst. Others would say that would be somewhat difficult to achieve; but then, they've probably not heard it.
NEW MUSICAL EXPRESS
Twelve inches of playing not to be left near easily ignited materials.
MELODY MAKER
...a totally ordinary bunch of songs that could have dribbled out of the coke-crippled brains of any gaggle of buck-eyed session automatons that tend to loiter around LA recording studios.
RECORD MIRROR

SAXON
Strong Arm Of The Law *(Carrere)*
The album's only virtue is that the band play fast throughout and finish their songs more quickly than HM groups used to in the early '70s. However, this is small consolation, as you just get more tracks per album.
NEW MUSICAL EXPRESS
I'm hesitant to call it their best effort yet since its predecessor was such a strong record, but rest assured it doesn't disappoint.
MELODY MAKER
a raucous celebration of the Greatest Form Of Music Known To Mankind: a vivid vinyl equivalent of an in-concert situation.
SOUNDS
...another Saxonic shot in the arm, superbly played, packed and produced.
RECORD MIRROR

LEO SAYER
Living In a Fantasy *(Chrysalis)*
...this album oozes blandness like cold blancmange.
NEW MUSICAL EXPRESS
Personally I wouldn't subject a lift to its nonsense.
MELODY MAKER
...lifeless coffee-table cop-outs.
RECORD MIRROR

THE SCARS
Author! Author! *(Pre)*
The Scars epitomise the post-punk new seriousness that has radically re-activated pop music, destroying the dichotomy between intelligence and emotion and confronting a whole range of different fears and desires. New pop that treats the transient thrill seriously.
NEW MUSICAL EXPRESS
...an album teeming with a sense of re-found faith in the pop ethic.
SOUNDS
It shows that pop music doesn't have to be characterised by blandness and fashion but that it can be crafted by simplicity and thought.
RECORD MIRROR
This wonderful record fizzes and splutters with most of the things that make records worth listening to.
MELODY MAKER

THE MICHAEL SCHENKER GROUP
The Michael Schenker Group *(Chrysalis)*
...affirms his position alongside the top axemen.
MELODY MAKER
...the most satisfying HM album I've heard in ages. Quality and energy are plentiful here, a healthy return from one of the few guitar heroes left.
SOUNDS
You vill buy and you vill enjoy.
RECORD MIRROR

IRMIN SCHMIDT
Filmmusik *(Spoon)*
...whereas most film music plays Cinderalla to the visuals, the pieces on 'Filmmusik' overflow with style, spirit and adventure, even when divorced from their film context.
SOUNDS
Schmidt's forceful melodic gifts were necessarily submerged within the larger whole that was Can, whereas here they're amply showcased.
NEW MUSICAL EXPRESS

THE SEARCHERS
Play For Today *(Sire)*
...another sharp collection of neat, melodic songs rendered with characteristic vocal harmonies and jangling guitars.
NEW MUSICAL EXPRESS
...sees them still holding onto their virtues of harmony, sound and their impeccable taste in choice of material.
RECORD MIRROR

SECRET AFFAIR
Behind Closed Doors *(I Spy/Arista)*
...flawed, certainly, but impressive enough to reassure the boys that the show isn't over yet.
MELODY MAKER
...despite my prejudices I like this album a surprising amount and I still reckon Secret Affair have got genuine mass market potential.
SOUNDS
Secret Affair have stopped worrying about getting stains on their tunics and applied themselves to producing some first rate music.
RECORD MIRROR
I'd like to think Secret Affair have a great album in 'em. This isn't it, but half the tracks show their capabilities. Someday that self-importance might be justified.
RECORD MIRROR

SECTOR 27
Sector 27 *(Fontant/IRS)*
...likeable and in many ways even admirable, but despite everybody's best efforts and intentions they're still trapped in the stodge. One wishes devoutly that it was otherwise.
NEW MUSICAL EXPRESS
...brash, heavy handed, and strives too hard and self-consciously for stridency.
MELODY MAKER
...an intellectual 'oi 'oi album, typified by the first two tracks... - which are rough and ready street anthems for those who use their heads more than their fists.
SOUNDS
Tom Robinson isn't demonstrating perfect politics but how difficult it is to be a political human being. And that makes 'Sector 27' not only a fine album but a brave one.
ROLLING STONE
...the effect is direct, the music fine, the message both personal and political, and clear: We are what we live.
TROUSER PRESS
Sector 27 entertains, Sector 27 adds spikes and jaggedness for those beyond the committed to grip onto, Sector 27 demand that you listen rather than offer their goods for those who might be interested.
RECORD MIRROR

THE SELECTER
Celebrate The Bullet *(Chrysalis)*
...a good album, boasting not one bad track and a string of potential singles.
NEW MUSICAL EXPRESS
...the immense movement of the band's music allows them to skank with a subtlety and invention that is a comfort and a surprise.
MELODY MAKER
...rather like a second debut, a *restatement* of potential without quite driving it home.
SOUNDS
Less bounce and more brains, that's the equation in operation here.
RECORD MIRROR
...the illuminatory qualities of the group's political stance is dimmed; what's left gives the impression of a self-congratulatory social conscience built around catchwords.
TROUSER PRESS

PHIL SEYMOUR
Phil Seymour *(Epic/Broadwalk)*
...an album of obvious yet powerful dynamics carried largely by the verve and enthusiasm he injects into every groove.
MELODY MAKER
That perverse and flourishing phenomenon among young American musicians, a prediction for colour-xeroxing The Beatles, gets an expert airing here.
SOUNDS
...the songs that *don't* sound like something else here don't sound like much.
ROLLING STONE
Seymour can't consistently summon up the magic that makes the difference between fun and fabulous...
TROUSER PRESS

THE SHAKIN' PYRAMIDS
Skin 'Em Up *(Cuba Libre/Virgin)*
Although The Shakin' Pyramids don't twist the '50's forms into any startling directions, they do invest them with a great deal of spontaneity and freshness...
NEW MUSICAL EXPRESS
As a debut album, 'Skin 'Em Up' is confident, fast and fun.
MELODY MAKER
With a deep-rooted love for the Everlys, the hardy ability to busk their way around the nation's bus stops and the confidence to rely on the minimum of instrumental muscle, they are *different* from the rest, in a perverse way.
SOUNDS

No cheap shots about Virgin bulk-buying Scotland, thank you very much, but one can't help noticing that they've signed a rockabilly band just when that music *happens* to be hipper than it has been for years.
RECORD MIRROR

THE SHIRTS
Inner Sleeve *(Capitol)*
At their lowest ebb, The Shirts sound muzzled. At their best, they're loud and lively.
SOUNDS
The Shirts must supply better tunes and find a producer who can bring more out of Golden's star presence. If they don't — well, I suppose they can putter around like this for another record or two before they sink from sight.
ROLLING STONE
With a bouncy pop tune to wrap her voice around, Golden is infectious, engaging and original; when she sinks to Melissa Manchester or Broadway corn, though, she's just another singer.
TROUSER PRESS

THE SHOES
Tongue Twister *(Elektra)*
Once they sounded eager and fresh, now they seem flat and more than a little stale around the edges.
MELODY MAKER
...the lack of fresh air or maybe an overdose of candy bars has sent them into a severe regression.
SOUNDS
...an exhilarating fusion of clean-cut British pop and semipunk rough-housing in the grand Midwest manner of the Raspberries and Blue Ash.
ROLLING STONE
...an album that plays down their wimpiness for a good measure of solid rock guitar and gutsy vocals.
TROUSER PRESS

SHOWADDYWADDY
Bright Lights *(Arista)*
You know what Showaddywaddy sound like and this album sounds like Showaddywaddy. I don't like it.
NEW MUSICAL EXPRESS

DAVITT SIGERSON
Davitt Sigerson *(Ze/Island)*
...plainly rock, stubbornly ordinary...
NEW MUSICAL EXPRESS
...a surprisingly mature and relevant first album.
MELODY MAKER

SIMPLE MINDS
Empires and Dance *(Zoom)*
...a weird, agitating record, unsettlingly existing as if between the world of pure imagination and the world upon which it depends.
NEW MUSICAL EXPRESS
Simple Minds won't bring you to sudden arousal but they'll crawl out of the shadows behind you and heat you up with warm touches and whispers.
MELODY MAKER
...a successful album because like any successful album these hazy crazy days it acknowledges the r'n'r inheritance it belongs to and then it goes out and develops it honestly and energetically.
SOUNDS
Blowing like a refreshing, cool breeze, Simple Minds music revitalises the tattered and invigorates the heart of any synthesiser sycophant.
RECORD MIRROR
...embarrassingly artsy aspirations fallen flat on their collective arse.
TROUSER PRESS

PAUL SIMON
One Trick Pony *(Warner Bros)*
...the same sleek, devious AOR. Graceful tunes, a little old fashioned rock 'n' roll, elusive references...
NEW MUSICAL EXPRESS
...a lush, frequently emotive album, and any lack of dynamism or spirit of adventure is tempered by the delight of having Paul Simon back again.
MELODY MAKER
It's the lyrics that make this album...the words are brilliantly sculpted into shape to nudge your reactions coolly but directly.
SOUNDS
Simon makes demanding middle of the road music which calls out for careful listening before the loosely constructed melodies finally become satisfyingly familiar.
RECORD MIRROR
Simply by raising the question of whether the rock & roll life is just for kids, Paul Simon admits that he's already on the outside looking in.
ROLLING STONE

THE SINCEROS
Pet Rock *(Epic)*
...a gently beaming, relaxed atmosphere that scrubs away the frowns, even if it doesn't race the blood.
MELODY MAKER
They might be tuneful but they certainly ain't twee.
RECORD MIRROR

SIOUXSIE AND THE BANSHEES
Ju Ju *(Polydor)*
...a gliding, comfortless delivery of self-distrust, infatuation and fetishism.
NEW MUSICAL EXPRESS
They've already composed quality nightmare soundtracks and don't need to do it again. They seem stuck in their own little world which bears little relation to ours, and like spoilt children refuse to come out and play.
MELODY MAKER
...doom is at the door, creating what is hardly the sound of the summer but what is something intriguing, intense brooding and powerfully atmospheric.
SOUNDS
Closing comment? "A must for Siouxsie fans," I suppose.
RECORD MIRROR

SIR DOUGLAS QUINTET
Border Wave *(Takoma/Chrysalis)*
A must.
TROUSER PRESS
...if last year's consistently good blues record 'A Hell Of A Spell' proved that Sir Doug was capable of ageing gracefully, the vigorous 'Border Wave' is the work of a man both reluctant and unready to begin the process..
NEW MUSICAL EXPRESS
...a genial, absolutely unforced record, with an offhand, slumming swing that's never really been duplicated.
ROLLING STONE

SISTER SLEDGE
All American Girls *(WEA/Cotillion)*
Sister Sledge emerge from the whole exercise as a lame, faceless and impoverished proposition, aspiring to grand ideals and unbelievably prissy modern-girl stereotypes.
NEW MUSICAL EXPRESS
So this is what it feels like to stand in a plummeting lift.
MELODY MAKER
Congratulations, girls: at this rate you could all soon be Real Entertainers, just like Diana Ross.
RECORD MIRROR
...a fine album that shouldn't be ignored.
ROLLING STONE

SKIDS
The Absolute Game *(Virgin)*
At its best, 'The Absolute Game' comes close to being great pop music. It always *sounds* good, though Jobson thinks it has probably got more depth than that.
NEW MUSICAL EXPRESS
...a worthy offering from Skids and certainly not one which could be overlooked.
MELODY MAKER
...a staggering achievement, a perfect progression for a band who must be numbered amongst the most innovative and refreshing in the country. It's one of the finest and most forward-looking albums you'll hear this year...
SOUNDS
As pop of the simplest, most standardised order, the third Skids album is an aural delight; as everything else, as "just another" Skids album, it's disillusioning.
RECORD MIRROR
Whether or not The Skids have anything to say, they make unique and intriguing music, and continue to develop in unexpected ways. They've got me hooked.

SKY
3 *(Ariola)*
Look, I'm a tolerant bloke, but Sky's the limit.
NEW MUSICAL EXPRESS
It's drawing room pop, pass the port and stilton, and takes no chances...The LP has a predictable air of excellence; a piece of flawed experimentation from such master players will be welcome.
MELODY MAKER
...with ever increasing success they've clearly done more to resurrect the connotation of 'respect for rock musicianship' than anyone else in the post-punk era.
RECORD MIRROR

SLADE
Slade Smashes *(Polydor)*
...the same coarse, good-humoured fun they always were.
NEW MUSICAL EXPRESS
If 1980 has given us anything worthwhile it's creating a climate where you can walk into a store and buy a Slade greatest hits album and *still* look yourself in the mirror.
MELODY MAKER
...a useful but ultimately unsatisfying reminder of the joy and exuberance of the Birmingham quartet.
RECORD MIRROR

SLADE
We'll Bring The House Down *(Cheapskate)*
Not all the songs here are vintage Slade, but they do seem to have thrown off the ennui that overcame them in the mid-70's.
NEW MUSICAL EXPRESS
They don't gush with subtlety, they make no leaps

for mankind. What they do have is an awful lot of front which they flaunt with joyous brashness and a sense of self-parody.
MELODY MAKER
...an invaluable addition to the realms of demolition rock.
SOUNDS
Slade are essentially a live act and on vinyl the vital ingredient of spilt beer is sorely missed.
RECORD MIRROR

TV SMITH'S EXPLORERS
The Last Words Of The Great Explorer *(Kaleidoscope)*
Could this be a comedy album?
NEW MUSICAL EXPRESS
Determinedly dull and criminally uninteresting, T.V. Smith has somehow contrived to fill a whole album with almost nothing.
MELODY MAKER
much of the album is wonderfully satisfying in a commercial manner.
SOUNDS
...accomplished and professional, but the overall impression is like a good movie with a weak and confused plot.
RECORD MIRROR

SNAKEFINGER
Greener Postures *(Ralph)*
Snakefinger's major problem is that, for a Ralph artiste and associate Resident, he just isn't weird enough.
TROUSER PRESS
...he's thinned out the action, opting for simply-crafted songs illuminated by his/The R's gaudy production.
SOUNDS

SNIFF AND THE TEARS
Love Action *(Chiswick)*
...just one of those albums you always have to bear with at other folks' parties and try to sneak up and change when no one is looking.
SOUNDS
Sniff 'N' The Tears play the music you might have loved five years since and that will still have a market five years hence.
RECORD MIRROR

SNIPS
La Rocca! *(EMI)*
Evidence of technical ability is there in abundance but committment isn't and it shows. Only Snips himself seems to be trying.
NEW MUSICAL EXPRESS
...a punchy album, but could be better still.
MELODY MAKER
Unless you're a keen amateur Spot The Influence player,

avoid. Teeth-gritting enough to be a danger to dental health.
SOUNDS
...measured and layered but still retains enough sharp edges to catch and scratch the imagination, scoring with space and simplicity as well as sophistication.
RECORD MIRROR

PHOEBE SNOW
Rock Away *(Mirage)*
The fact that Snow is as intuitively good at rock & roll as she was at esoteric material is further evidence of the enormity of her talent.
ROLLING STONE
She needs to rid herself of the idea that she was put on this earth to make record companies rich.
MELODY MAKER

THE SOUND
Jeopardy *(Korova)*
...one of those records that makes me want to throw all the windows open, crank it up to full volume and blast it out to the world. It clears my head of boredom, strips away the gloom, and singlehandedly restores my belief in the power of pop to make people stop, think and question.
MELODY MAKER
...an inconspicuous but real missing-link between the Modernist Jam and the vibrantly Post Mod, Joy Division.
SOUNDS
...lovingly pieced together. It's an attractive start.
RECORD MIRROR

SOUTHSIDE JOHNNY & THE ASHBURY JUKES
Reach Up And Touch The Sky *(Mercury)*
...the kind of double live album that is so alive that it isn't just the next best thing to being there.
MELODY MAKER
There's nothing new in Southside's values. They are the bedrock of American rock and roll but he delivers them with an irresistible warmth and genuine commitment.
SOUNDS
The first three sides of this album captures the spirit of the songs and the performance: atmospheric, full-bodied R & B...But the last side, oh dear!
RECORD MIRROR

SPANDAU BALLET
Journeys To Glory *(Reformation/Chrysalis)*
...an awfully ordinary record.
NEW MUSICAL EXPRESS

...nothing more than a bundle of fancy rags without a peg to hang them on. Superficial music for superficial people with superficial concerns.
MELODY MAKER
Spandau Ballet are here for those who take their enjoyment seriously. Be one of the happy people.
SOUNDS
...a more than fair debut album with some good songs and a couple of duff ones, a talented set of musicians and a singer who needs a tragic love affair or something to put a little humanity into his performance.
RECORD MIRROR
...easily one of the most undynamic dance records of the past 18 months.
TROUSER PRESS

SPARKS
Whomp That Sucker *(Why-Fi)*
Not even Russell's baby face or Ron's baleful glare can disguise the fact that their frothy concoctions have dissolved into sweet nothings.
NEW MUSICAL EXPRESS
Russ and Ron show that they've still go what it takes to bop their way into our hearts and up the charts.
MELODY MAKER
...in Sparks' venerable case, the word 'contenders' is always an understatement. 'Former champs' shall we say for now?
SOUNDS
The Mael brothers have returned and you're a sucker if you don't find out what they're about. Sparks score a knockout in the first round.
RECORD MIRROR

THE SPECIALS
More Specials *(2 Tone)*
Musically, the Specials have done a double back-flip. Fans expecting more frenetic ska re-runs will do a treble-flip when they hear the conglomerate of Zhivago-esque movie soundtracks...Their energy has become more sensual, too, less St Vitus's dance, more mellow hip-grind.
NEW MUSICAL EXPRESS
In general 'More Specials' is a massively successful gamble, wider, warmer, weirder and as good if not better in its own way than its predecessor.
SOUNDS
...to be applauded for its consistent standard of enjoyment and addictive playability.
RECORD MIRROR
The Specials make no attempt to write beyond the

obvious, to bend a cliche or find unlikely targets. It doesn't seem that these guys are capable of doing more for their principles than mouthing them.
ROLLING STONE
...a ~~pressingly~~ bitter, self-righte~~ous~~ and self-important record, with little of the understanding or compassion displayed on their extremely enjoyable debut.
TROUSER PRESS

RONNIE SPECTOR
Siren *(Red Shadow Records/Polish)*
...an unfortunate reminder of better days past.
MELODY MAKER
...makes an unanswerable case for its nomination as 1980's most miserable rock album.
NEW MUSICAL EXPRESS
...totally uninspired.
RECORD MIRROR
...Spector's characteristic, wavery tones battling it out with laboured submetal arrangements and *the* most tortuous lead guitar breaks this side of early Amboy Dukes records...
SOUNDS

SPIRIT
Potatoland *(Beggars Banquet)*
The secret must be to interest a few more people than the converted though and the album's nifty artwork and silly comic just do that. Incidentally, the music inside is mostly liquid gold.
NEW MUSICAL EXPRESS
... a typical mix of invigorating wisdom and infuriating whimsy.
MELODY MAKER
... one legend that stands up to close scrutiny well.
RECORD MIRROR
... in between the flimsy story-line is possibly the finest music that Spirit have ever recorded.
SOUNDS

THE SPIZZLES
Spikey Dream Flowers *(A&M)*
Spizz's songwriting just can't keep up the pace — a pace which has worn away the irrational, defiant clown in him, leaving behind a sadly conformed, tragically lost, little man grasping for the intuitively great pop he was once capable of.
NEW MUSICAL EXPRESS

... is the album on which Spizz and the gang attempt to sever any clinging Rough Trade, independent cult connections, make a brave bid for a wider, Top Of The Pops audience and nearly get it right.
MELODY MAKER

The Spizzles have made the name snappier, the image smoother, the music sharper...Here is the new, improved melodic and thoughtful Spizzles.
SOUNDS

... while each song shows potential sparkle, it fails to mature into a little gem.
RECORD MIRROR

SPLIT ENZ
Waiata *(A&M)*
... sees them shedding their old skin with a certain reluctance, as if they're concerned with the loss of credibility that might ensue from a wholehearted commercial plunge.
NEW MUSICAL EXPRESS

... another collection of instant, energetic pop songs, familiar as soon as you've heard them, unforgetable after two listens.
MELODY MAKER

... the finest album Split Enz have produced to date, which qualifies as an essential buy for the countless pure-pop-noise enthusiasts.
SOUNDS

More flippant than political. 'Waiata' will nevertheless enhance Split Enz's considerable reputation.
RECORD MIRROR

Behind that appealing exterior, they're as crafty as ever. Enjoy the magic.
TROUSER PRESS

SPLODGNESSABOUNDS
Splodgnessabounds *(Deram)*
Ten pints of lager and no crisps would probably help you get the jokes.
NEW MUSICAL EXPRESS

... act as a running (nose) commentary on the trash TV culture of Britain today, court jesters to the King's new clothes.
MELODY MAKER

Noisy, nasty, brainless, boorish, guaranteed to offend Tory councillors, witless liberals, NME writers and other bores, Splodge — The Album is complete undiluted rubbish, and I love every minute of it.
SOUNDS

It neither inspires nor outrages, it just lies there in a pitiful sniggering heap.
RECORD MIRROR

SPORTS
Suddenly *(Arista)*
Pop doesn't mean dumb. Obtuseness doesn't mean smart, either.
TROUSER PRESS

... evenly good, no true highs and no lows.
NEW MUSICAL EXPRESS

BRUCE SPRINGSTEEN
The River *(CBS)*
This is great music for people who've wasted their youth to sit around drinking beer and wasting the rest of their lives to.
NEW MUSICAL EXPRESS

I emerge from a weekend with this record feeling as my parents did when they survived the blitz. Tattered and frayed round the edges and yet with a glow for man and womankind which might lead to dangerous excursions like embracing someone I've never met before.
SOUNDS

I hadn't realised I was thirsty until I tasted this album. Four sides of pure magic; the current running strong and true throughout.
RECORD MIRROR

Unable or unwilling to cast off the cliches of his past records, 'The River's' attempt to Make a Statement is buried in an avalanche of repetition and evident lack of inspiration.
TROUSER PRESS

... a contemporary, New Jersey version of 'The Grapes of Wrath', with the Tom Joad/Henry Fonda figure — nowadays no longer able to draw upon the solidarity of family — driving a stolen car through a neon Dust Bowl...
ROLLING STONE

SQUEEZE
East Side Story *(A&M)*
... a new pop album excellence. It succeeds on all the levels that a great pop record is bound to realise and it dictates its own pace.
NEW MUSICAL EXPRESS

... the most accomplished and versatile display of pop songwriting since Costello's wildly undervalued 'Get Happy!' In plain English: it's a masterpiece.
MELODY MAKER

BRUCE SPRINGSTEEN

Industrious always, gifted and exciting only some of the time, Squeeze are the quintessential mainstream pop band.
SOUNDS

Chris Difford confirms that he's amongst the most adroit of lyricists with an eye for details that grows beadier by the hour. Sailors, waitresses, housewives and lovers all come under his keen compositional gaze which proves there's no substitute for touring when it comes to broadening the mind.
RECORD MIRROR

If Squeeze didn't set such high standards for itself, the band could get away with mediocrity; instead they too often settle for cleverness.
TROUSER PRESS

VIV STANSHALL
Teddy Boys Don't Knit
(Charisma)
Yes, we're very much in the gothic rickety English country house, and the incumbent is pissed.
NEW MUSICAL EXPRESS

HOLLY STANTON
Temptation *(War Bride)*
If rock isn't smart enough to accept her, she's got enough grit to sing lowdown country.
TROUSER PRESS

First thing that strikes you about this girl Holly Stanton is that she sounds like our own very lovely Kim Wilde. The second is that there is no second thing: nothing else of note at all.
NEW MUSICAL EXPRESS

... may help War Bride pay the office rental. It's all there, down to the country-girl warble and the grinding guitars.
SOUNDS

STATUS QUO
Just Supposin' *(Vertigo)*
The old boys still contrive that distinctive eunuch-style harmonising but they no longer quite sound like the Everly Brothers trapped in a heavy metal discotheque.
NEW MUSICAL EXPRESS

Okay, so Quo can "boogie" and "rock out" with the best of them. But what they've come to mean is as threatening and provocative as the Eagles or ELO.
MELODY MAKER

Nuthin' Fancy. Same ol, solid logo; plain talkin' label; no posh wordsheet; simple sleeve design. Just a miniscule nod to topicality —
SOUNDS

Gasp as Quo became the Abba of heavy metal.
RECORD MIRROR

STATUS QUO
Never Too Late *(Vertigo)*
Quo can walk away, guiltless, from anything; after all, they are licensed to bore.
NEW MUSICAL EXPRESS

If this album proves anything, it proves that Status Quo are strongest when they're treading familiar paths.
MELODY MAKER

CRASH! Head's gone through the glass front door. WHAM! There goes the partition wall.
RECORD MIRROR

They already have overtaken the ability of any reviewer to enhance a reader's enjoyment of their music by fresh and illuminating observation. Hallmarked 22-carat gold is just that, any which way you look at it. If boogie is what you value, they deliver.
SOUNDS

STEELEYE SPAN
Sails Of Silver *(Chrysalis)*
...the album that Steeleye Span should have made instead of breaking up.
MELODY MAKER

STEELY DAN
Gaucho *(MCA)*
...the music is a session-man's idea of perfection, an ultimately sterile enterprise. But there's an irony here, because that kind of mentality is the one either celebrated or satirised on several of the tracks on 'Gaucho': are Becker and Fagen playing the smartass again, and if so just *who* is the joke on?
NEW MUSICAL EXPRESS

...it's full of more contradictions than a chinese puzzle. One minute sublime, the next inexplicably banal: evidence, perhaps, that occasionally even creative genius gets sidetracked along the way.
MELODY MAKER

Steely Dan have sadly slipped from being purveyors of some of the most powerful and thought provoking pop on this earth to become manufacturers of nothing more than sophisticated wallpaper music — the thinking man's cabaret band.
SOUNDS

JIM STEINMAN
Bad For Good *(Epic)*
No wonder that Meat Loaf didn't do the vocals; he was probably struck dumb when his writer delivered the songs.
MELODY MAKER

...the one you've waited nearly four years for.
SOUNDS

...while Meat Loaf's presence and delivery equalled Steinman's overweight imagination and endowed it with a lightening dose of tongue in cheek humour, Steinman himself is too literate and literal for comfort.
RECORD MIRROR

SHAKIN' STEVENS
This Ole House *(Epic)*
...a cleanly-produced, perfectly executed rock 'n' roll album.
NEW MUSICAL EXPRESS

...on the top of the pile as Britain's best rock 'n' roll singer.
RECORD MIRROR

AL STEWART
24 Carrots *(RCA/Arista)*
Despite its silly title, this is an important album, better than either "Cat" or its successor.
MELODY MAKER

...Stewart...presents himself as a jack-of-all-trades and, suprisingly, makes it work.
ROLLING STONE

An honestly quaint, masterly album, as forgivably coy as anything that's likely to come out this year.
RECORD MIRROR

ROD STEWART
Foolish Behaviour
(Riva/Warner Bros)
Stewart hasn't been content to just daub himself with rouge and mascara. It's all over the music too.
NEW MUSICAL EXPRESS

The only reason I even care about this forty-five minutes of purgatory is that a long time ago Rod Stewart made a couple of good albums.
SOUNDS

With a predictability that underlines with dulling thoroughness how calculated the big league rock biz has to be, the machine starts, produces, stops and an album appears right on calculated time.
MELODY MAKER

It's just another Rod Stewart album, it rocks and rolls with the punches. More than that I can't say.
RECORD MIRROR

...no return of the glory days of 'Every Picture Tells A Story', but it's hugely preferable to the smirk-and-spandex of his last few recordings.
ROLLING STONE

Keeping up with Rod and his pals no longer seems worthwhile. Stewart's a competent cartoon now, and not much of a laugh either.
TROUSER PRESS

STIFF LITTLE FINGERS
Hanx *(Chrysalis)*
'Hanx' is released as a thank you to the fans for three years faithful support. It's more a limp slap in the face.
NEW MUSICAL EXPRESS

There's nothing like the real thing: being there. And that's why I'd rather listen to a studio set than a second-hand, doctored live album.
MELODY MAKER

SLF are still potentially one of the strongest exponents of eighties punk...For Christ sake pull your stiff little fingers out and knuckle down. We've still got a world to win.
SOUNDS

STIFF LITTLE FINGERS
Go For It *(Chrysalis)*
At least, SLF have proved you can build on crude political punk without banging your head against a brick wall of static sound and stances.
NEW MUSICAL EXPRESS

Welcome to the continuing transition from furious teenage rebellion and political protest to energetic yet provocative rock music.
SOUNDS

They don't change, they just get more professional at what they do. It's unfair that getting better doesn't necessarily improve a punk band.
RECORD MIRROR

NICK STRAKER BAND
A Walk In The Park *(CBS)*
The title track was maybe the worst single of '80. The rest of the album is indistinguishable from the single.
NEW MUSICAL EXPRESS

RICHARD STRANGE
The Live Rise Of Richard Strange *(PVC/ZE)*
If I remain sceptical of Strange's claim to current political relevance — and I do suspect his tendency to romantic *gestures*, his lapses into a cosy humanistic overview that *devalues* people by ignoring their

specific political context — I also remain curious.
NEW MUSICAL EXPRESS
Strange has proved he has the guts and energy to go out and do something dramatically different, even if the musical vehicle he's riding could have been more streamlined.
SOUNDS
A sturdy album, then, that serves as an appetiser for the complete studio concept.
RECORD MIRROR
Whatever his authenticity, the relentlessly drab tone makes for a powerful deterrent.
TROUSER PRESS

RICHARD STRANGE
The Phenomenal Rise Of Richard Strange *(Virgin)*
As a political tract, an expression of Richard Strange's innermost thoughts and theories, 'The Phenomenal Rise' makes a fine soap opera.
NEW MUSICAL EXPRESS
An overall, if not unqualified, success...
RECORD MIRROR
...sung in an affected voice which falls half-way between Steve Harley and a third-rate David Bowie impersonator.
MELODY MAKER
...wins in the end by sweeping you off your feet by a million switches of musical direction, by its wit, by above all its sheer nerve...
SOUNDS

STRAY CATS
Stray Cats *(Arista/Pin-UP)*
Cats of caricatures? There's more on the line than just another hit single.
NEW MUSICAL EXPRESS
...a confident debut, but you get the feeling that the Stray Cats will have been glad to get it over and out...Perhaps they'll realise now that they have nothing to live up to and start living it up.
MELODY MAKER
...this band possess a fiery spark of imagination both original and exciting.
SOUNDS
Men, It can be done!! Forget the hype and the inevitability of yet another revival and get stuck into this. The Stray Cats have come up with the most auspicious debut since 'The Clash'.
RECORD MIRROR

THE STRANGLERS
The Gospel According To The Meninblack *(Liberty)*
It could've been disastrously grandiose, but The Stranglers' archetypal,

awesome steam-rolling rhythms keep the whole thing from floating away into the stratosphere.
NEW MUSICAL EXPRESS
...a prima facie example of the "I've suffered for my art and now it's your turn" school of thought.
MELODY MAKER
...a proudly psychedelic album, easily the most psychedelic yet from a band whose roots were always closer to the Doors and Love than to Iggy Pop or the New York Dolls.
RECORD MIRROR
...far and away the Stranglers' worst album. It sees them tired and songless.
SOUNDS

BARBRA STREISAND
Guilty *(CBS/Columbia)*
The mark of a true second-rate talent is that it always tries to move with the times.
NEW MUSICAL EXPRESS
...music which wallpapers your imagination, plugging every critical orifice with its bland professionalism.
MELODY MAKER
...a romantic entertainment with no ambitions beyond making billions of hearts flutter and earning millions of dollars, it's also as beautifully crafted a piece of ear candy as I've heard in years.
ROLLING STONE

POLY STYRENE
Translucence *(UA)*
...all that Poly Styrene shares now with her co-punk pioneers is a common failing — a dissipation of energy, a loss of focus. It's as if they've thrown away a great victory by not knowing what to do with it.
NEW MUSICAL EXPRESS
Goodbye Polystyrene. Hello Marion Elliot. I never thought I'd live to see the day the world turned wallpaper.
MELODY MAKER
...without a doubt, one of the most satisfying and one of the bravest albums to slide stealthily from the recesses of '77 into the coldly calculating cynicism that is approaching '81.
SOUNDS
It's summer folk, all bongo drums and flutes with a shrill prettiness that recalls the wet waterfall world of Sally Oldfield.
RECORD MIRROR
One hopes that repetition and refinement will strengthen Poly Styrene's message, because if her music were any more lightweight it

would float away — and her potential with it.
TROUSER PRESS

STYX
Paradise Theater *(A&M)*
A&M are now conducting a publicity blitz on radio and elsewhere to push Styx products in Britain. This clearly must be resisted.
NEW MUSICAL EXPRESS
...one cannot find fault in either the musicianship or the production, but simply in their sense of direction.
MELODY MAKER
...a near-perfect album, chock full of soaring melodious songs, benefitting from crisp, immaculate production and undoubtedly one of Styx's finest.
SOUNDS
...pretty close to perfection.
RECORD MIRROR

DONNA SUMMER
The Wanderer *(Geffen Records)*
...the whole Born Again routine really ties in with the insistent lack of guts about this album. It's so white, so anything goes, so slack and rock and weak.
NEW MUSICAL EXPRESS
With the exception of the wholly charming title whimsy, *no* threat to Dion, this is one for the cultural dumper, folks.
SOUNDS
By placing her firmly within a rock & roll context in which she thrives, The Wanderer clearly proves that she's an artist as well as a star. The result is music that exudes both strength and delight.
ROLLING STONE

SUPERTRAMP
Paris *(A&M)*
...when rock cuts the cord that connects it to the time and circumstance of its creation, it becomes the most pointless, self-important form of escapism, unable to recognise even its own decay.
NEW MUSICAL EXPRESS
Even if you're a die-hard Supertramp fan, you're getting a bum deal.
MELODY MAKER
For all the technical faultlessness...there's a dearth of real feeling.
RECORD MIRROR

SURF PUNKS
My Beach *(Epic)*
...the surf 'n' sand myth already enjoys stale joke status, so there's nowhere to go but sillier and dumber.
TROUSER PRESS

The Surf Punks are a one-joke act that barely musters up a moment's mirth throughout the seventeen excuses for songs on 'My Beach'.
ROLLING STONE

SWELL MAPS
Swell Maps in 'Jane From Occupied Europe *(Rather/Rough Trade)*
...less playful, more purposeful and less happy/accidental than its predecessor. Still awkward, brave and the more desirable side of unique.
NEW MUSICAL EXPRESS
...they stayed on the right side of rough enthusiasm, with schoolboy "Biggles" type of humour and most important of all, remained true to their ideals. The Kings of DIY are dead. Long may their spirit live on.
MELODY MAKER
A bumper album, consistently excellent, a huge, lovable adventure playground to forget the bad times in and still emerge with full integrity.
SOUNDS
...the album title is irrelevant, the music a clunking, clanking mush of gorgeous irony; awful and enthralling, pointless and necessary, flawed and perfect.
RECORD MIRROR
...always seemed on the verge of making an important statement. Their demise shows them still on the precipice.
TROUSER PRESS

T

TALKING HEADS
Remain in Light *(Sire)*
Given time to lower preconceptions and heighten senses I found myself overtaken by an album of brave inventions and haunting textures.
NEW MUSICAL EXPRESS
...no rock album since 'Station To Station' has sounded so radical without deserting the mainstream it has to occupy if it's to be heard.
MELODY MAKER

No-one else in the rock strata does these things. You have to look to jazz...to find someone using traditions in new ways, *thinking* about the present with a *feeling* for the past. Talking Heads are telling us news. Not history.
SOUNDS
Side one is great music, side two is for the most part, good music. The choice is their's and they've made it.
RECORD MIRROR
...yields scary funny music to which you can dance and think, think and dance, dance and think, ad infinitum.
ROLLING STONE
This album taps a primeval vein in the subconscious: You'll tap your toes but you won't be able to shut out what these songs mean. Like the inverted A's in its name on the cover, Talking Heads has stood the dance concept on its head.
TROUSER PRESS

TANGERINE DREAM
Thief *(Virgin)*
...quite simply, the best Tangerine Dream album in a long, long time.
MELODY MAKER
...bloody awful...The last time I saw Edgar Froese he looked dead. After hearing 'Thief' I think I should have taken his temperature to make sure he wasn't.
SOUNDS
...two sides of quality background music.
RECORD MIRROR

JAMES TAYLOR
Dad Loves His Work
(Columbia)
...the sonic polish that coats 'Dad Loves His Work', while making it easy and pleasant to listen to, also seals off an interestingly turbulent world of emotion, keeping half-hidden the impulses that made the songs worth writing in the first place.
ROLLING STONE

ROGER TAYLOR
Fun In Space *(EMI)*
Forced fun in empty space. Lacking feeling, lyrically vague, a novelty, the novelty wanes, the android moves on.
MELODY MAKER
'Fun In Space' does very little that the entire catalogue of Queen albums hasn't already accomplished.
SOUNDS
...the most fun you'll have apart from playing a game of Space Invaders.
RECORD MIRROR
It's not quite so much the music, even though it's

pretentious, insipid and quite frankly, bloody old-fashioned. It's the sheer smirking ignorance of the man that makes me see red.
NEW MUSICAL EXPRESS

BRAM TCHAIKOVSKY
Funland *(Arista)*
...a patchy set that undeniably has its high spots, but would have fared better with a bit more vigour and consistency.
MELODY MAKER
Not a classic perhaps but one that went a long way towards living up to its name.
RECORD MIRROR

THE TEARDROP EXPLODES
Kilimanjaro *(Mercury)*
...an up and down LP. The songs deal with the ups and downs of festering fate and fortune, the lyrics suggest emotional highs and lows, the music jumps up and down. I can feel up and down about its merits.
NEW MUSICAL EXPRESS
...it's in the promising but flawed catergory; but it's a beginning, not an end in itself. Too many trappings can drown talent. Too much ambition can stunt the growth.
MELODY MAKER
...the only worthwhile thing I can say is that the first Teardrop album is a record that falls between two stools neither of which have enough legs to stand-up.
SOUNDS
...ultimately it's a record entangled in both business and directional uncertainty; it's gorgeous pop but with all exits blocked.
RECORD MIRROR
...they dress up their psychedelic heritage in pithy pop arrangements and refined hooks. The results can best be described as avant-bubblegum: a cross between the kaleidoscopic chaos of early Pink Floyd and The Soft Parade-era Doors.
ROLLING STONE
...The music is eclectic and thoughtful, not experimental or visionary.
TROUSER PRESS

TELEVISION PERSONALITIES
And Don't The Kids Just Love It *(Rough Trade)*
...their songwriting has at times a natural, unforced beauty impossible to fake.
NEW MUSICAL EXPRESS

On first hearing it all sounds simplistic and superficial. Shame, cause they do have something to say.
SOUNDS
...the sound of true unfettered talent...and the longer it's allowed to stay that way the better.
RECORD MIRROR

TENPOLE TUDOR
Eddie Old Bob Dick And Gary *(Stiff)*
...a slapdash boisterous, good-humoured sort of affair.
NEW MUSICAL EXPRESS
It's the most tuneful barrage of raucousness this side of Slade, and it's all gloriously, unequivocally, wonderful.
MELODY MAKER
As a straight rock outfit, Tenpole Tudor is above average, but not ready for mass adulation yet, there isn't enough drunken lunacy here to catch anyone's attention.
TROUSER PRESS
...Tenpole Tudor could provide the perfect sound track to the summer of 1981.
RECORD MIRROR
Not the definitive oeuvre yet, but certainly a darn fine first instalment.
SOUNDS

THEATRE OF HATE
He Who Dares Wins *(SSSS)*
...a headstrong, hard-edged record; a rash record and a rush. In a world of reactionary "futurism", conservative "anti-rockism", and bloodless white "funk", Theatre Of Hate thrash about like bulls in a china shop.
NEW MUSICAL EXPRESS
Some independent label had utter *cheek* to put out this sickbag of a sound and expect people to *pay* for it!..
MELODY MAKER
This is progressive rock. Meaning, no songs, ephemere over-structured like Wishbone Ash...TOH really are hippies!
SOUNDS
...London's most primal punk cult combo combining drum-fired rhythms with unclear politics.
RECORD MIRROR

THIN LIZZY
Chinatown *(Vertigo/Warner Brothers)*
...leaden platitudes, expert but empty guitar solos, laboured and tired myth-making and cliches of all description...quite simply the pits.
NEW MUSICAL EXPRESS
...quite a listenable effort.
TROUSER PRESS

...unquestionably Thin Lizzy's finest studio offering.
MELODY MAKER
...set firmly in the mould of the previous vinyl incarnations.
SOUNDS
Technically this is the best thing they have ever done...Lizzy can justifiably feel very proud of themselves after this effort.
RECORD MIRROR

THIRD WORLD
Rock The World *(CBS)*
With a bright, bouncy production, technical expertise second to none, and ten joyful songs no doubt destined for sensational live development, there's not a dull or depressing moment.
MELODY MAKER
...this will no doubt appeal to everyone across the world they're rocking over, but few will find it satisfying.
RECORD MIRROR
Third World take the Western rock influences they want and plant them in their own garden, not vice-versa.
SOUNDS

THOMPSON TWINS
A Product Of...*(T-Records)*
...stuffed full of fun and interest.
NEW MUSICAL EXPRESS
The net result of all this ethnic dabbling is that the album sounds too much like a compilation of abstruse sources.
MELODY MAKER
The spirit is willing, the songs are fine but, without the visual stimulation that's so intrinsic to the band's appeal, the result is ever-so-slightly out-of-place.
SOUNDS
...only a rattling where it might be a storm, a shower instead of a tornado.
RECORD MIRROR

LINCOLN THOMPSON AND THE RASSES
Natural Wild *(UAG)*
...sees him exploring the problems of space travel, mechanisation and human rights with no less a personage than Joe Jackson and band along for some of the ride. A mistake.
MELODY MAKER
Musically, this is a long way the most entertaining 'white reggae' I've ever enjoyed, played with some sort of respect and liking for the mood, instead of going flat out to kill all the subtlety and rhythmic feeling.
SOUNDS

GEORGE THOROGOOD AND THE DESTROYERS
More George Thorogood and The Destroyers
(Sonet/Rounder)
...a disappointment for purists and popsters alike.
MELODY MAKER
...his career on record only suggests that being able to play the blues perfectly is the next thing to not being able to play them at all.
ROLLING STONE
It's fast and it's white but if you're bored with playing your Dr Feelgood albums then this is just as good to get drunk to.
SOUNDS

TOOTS AND THE MAYTALS
Toots Live *(Island)*
...dance music of the highest order.
NEW MUSICAL EXPRESS
...The sound of happy, party reggae.
RECORD MIRROR

PETER TOSH
Wanted Dread And Alive *(Rolling Stones)*
...he's stepped into a creative void which is made worse by his inability to come up with the kind of potent songs that set him up in the first place.
SOUNDS

TOTO
Turn Back *(CBS/Columbia)*
Superficial, smug and souless, they throw countless musical balls in the air, and conspicuously fail to catch any of them.
MELODY MAKER
...this collection of tired retreads and borrowed riffs should have been left to gather dust.
RECORD MIRROR
...the band sound terminally depressed and dying for a holiday.
SOUNDS
Every bit as bland as its name, Toto neither excites nor offends. In rock & roll, that's definitely the dreariest sin.
ROLLING STONE

THE TOURISTS
Luminous Basement *(RCA/Epic)*
...has unwelcome reminders of rock-operas, folk rock, overblown "concepts", gratuitous instrumental extravagance and airy theorising all raising their unwelcome heads from a base of shallow pop.
NEW MUSICAL EXPRESS
I hope they get through this stage quickly, ditch the unstructured and messy

guitar breaks, shake off the blues and get on with the bright, clever music they've done so well before.
RECORD MIRROR
...an experience as deep as wading through a puddle.
MELODY MAKER
Innovative it ain't, but the band shines on.
TROUSER PRESS
When I first saw them grinding away at the Hope And Anchor I had no doubts at all, but practically everything they've subsequently done fills me with dismay.
SOUNDS

TOY PLANET
Toy Planet *(Spoon)*
...succeeds on every count. I doubt we'll hear as good an album in this field until Schmidt and Spoerri make another like it.
NEW MUSICAL EXPRESS
...bombs cultural roadblocks with a devastating, arrogant elegance.
SOUNDS

TOYAH
Toyah! Toyah! Toyah! *(Safari)*
...it's a means of keeping up the steady flow of Toyah product even when she's too busy to make proper records.
NEW MUSICAL EXPRESS
...uniformly cold and brittle.
MELODY MAKER
Toyah is a fake. You can spot her a mile off from the way her would-be Siouxsie's squeal contrasts with a Surbiton actress high note, right down to the self-conscious, would-be cockney banter low bits, wherein she displays that ugly nauseating lisp.
SOUNDS
...truly excellent.
RECORD MIRROR

TOYAH
Anthem *(Safari)*
A muddled, self-consciously lush celebration of instinct, mystery, the dark, a semi-hysterical rejection of the surface of me, an unsophisticated representation of an obsession with decadence and occultism.
NEW MUSICAL EXPRESS
...a collection of varied, powerful and moody songs; rich in scene setting and as much about places and atmospheres as thoughts and people.
MELODY MAKER
...at least it is listenable. And the fact that she's utterly untrendy and has very little style probably means she's

well on the way to becoming womankind's answer to Gary Numan.
SOUNDS
...an overtly musical work, much needed these days as a refreshing alternative well deserving of your attention.
RECORD MIRROR

TRANSMITTERS
And We Calls This Leisure Time *(Heartbeat/Cherry Red)*
...seriously, unbegrudgingly, almost innocently bleak and industrial; they give that fabled tag credence through their smug amateurishness and most of all a diabolical lack of commitment.
SOUNDS

PAT TRAVERS
Radio Active *(Polydor)*
...certainly the man's most inspiring effort to date.
MELODY MAKER
Travers picks up the torch from Robin Trower, peppering his moody music with hot guitar that would probably make Hendrix smile.
TROUSER PRESS

THE TREMBLERS
Twice Nightly *(Epic/Johnston)*
Rather implausibly, most of the songs adopt the guise of feisty adolescents out for sex, rebellion and kicks. It's a sort of exercise in nostalgic self-delusion.
NEW MUSICAL EXPRESS
...a laudable attempt by Peter Noone to try and regain some of his former popular glory, while striking out firmly for the notorious "artistic credibility".
MELODY MAKER
...this album is what you want, or what you *ought* to want, if you really can't wait for the next Tom Petty album.
SOUNDS
...sharp, post-punk pop music with a strong American feel.
RECORD MIRROR

TROGGS
Live At Max's Kansas City *(Max's Kansas City Records)*
...adds nothing and doesn't even mark time. But funnily enough, I'm still glad it's around.
NEW MUSICAL EXPRESS

ROBIN TROWER
B.L.T. *(Chrysalis)*
Lordan and Bruce hardly get a look in on this experimental studio album, the most democratic aspect of which is the title and front cover.
MELODY MAKER

The three talents seem almost to be merely going through the motions.
RECORD MIRROR
...contains exactly what you'd expect, neither more nor less.
TROUSER PRESS

TRUST
Repression *(CBS)*
Strange how it takes a band from the musical wasteland of France to teach bands like Tygers of Pan Tang and Iron Maiden how to make good, relevant and original heavy metal.
RECORD MIRROR
Trust combines the sharp edge of English punk consciousness with the stereotyped heavy metal sound of AC/DC.
NEW MUSICAL EXPRESS
Quite unlike anyone's idea of the hard rock archetype, Trust songs are anything but clogged up to the bowels with the tarty old images, lyrical devices and generally unimaginative blur of a goodly proportion of their less credible contemporaries.
SOUNDS

THE TUBES
The Completion Backward Principle *(Capitol)*
...its principle of completion is certainly backward.
NEW MUSICAL EXPRESS
...why does about a third of this album sound like a toothless Dachsund?
MELODY MAKER
...All exceptionally glossy but ultimately rather too much of a bland-out.
SOUNDS
It is of no more interest than the works of, for example, Reo Speedwagon or Styx.
RECORD MIRROR

TUXEDOMOON
Desire *(Pre/Ralph)*
...one of the most stimulating and acutely contemporary works to be released this year...its joys go on for ever.
MELODY MAKER
Tuxedomoon stick pretty firmly to their predominant atmospheres of despair and desolation, producing musical images of strangely stark, flowing beauty occasionally hurtling right over the top into climes of bleak melodrama.
NEW MUSICAL EXPRESS
Their outlandish, take-it-to-the-hilt style just sends this album sashaying into ultimate somewhere elseness.
SOUNDS
...a good medium between yesterday and tomorrow.
TROUSER PRESS

THE TWINKLE BROTHERS
Countrymen *(Virgin)*
The vibration remains positive throughout both sides, without a weak track showcased. The Twinkle Brothers are one of the only groups from the mid '70s reggae focus to fulfil their early promise.
NEW MUSICAL EXPRESS
...an album of mixed moods.
MELODY MAKER
Amazingly for any reggae album, all the music is original in lyrics and melody, songs thought through into a well constructed collection.
SOUNDS

THE TWINKLE BROTHERS
Me No You, You No Me
(Twinkle/Rough Trade)
...the loving harmonies never cloy.
NEW MUSICAL EXPRESS
...will both satisfy the long standing Twinkle Brothers admirer and send the newcomer to their music on a hunt for their back catalogue of work.
SOUNDS

TYGERS OF PAN TANG
Wild Cat *(MCA)*
Could the Tygers really be those lovable, late-lamented, heads-down-no-nonsense Albertos in disguise? If this is a joke, it's the worst since Derek and Clive...MELODY MAKER
...as a debut 'Wild Cat' is impressive to say the least.
RECORD MIRROR

TYGERS OF PAN TANG
Spellbound *(MCA)*
At last! An NWOBHM band who've actually managed to sustain some agression and move along the lines of progression.
SOUNDS

SEAN TYLA
Just Popped Out *(Zilch)*
...this album sounds desperate, drab and distinctly American. Maybe he should emigrate.
MELODY MAKER
...once again Sean throws down the gauntlet on which is emblazoned his brusque: love me or leave me.
SOUNDS

JUDIE TZUKE
I Am The Phoenix *(Rocket Train)*
As a songwriter, she is strangely attractive, as a singer utterly unique.
MELODY MAKER
I've never been embarrassed by my love of hard rock *and* Judie Tzuke, but it would be rather nice if you'd care to join me.
SOUNDS
...isn't quite the rebirth the lurid cover would have you believe but it's more a logical growth of the talents within the band.
RECORD MIRROR

U

UB40
Signing Off *(Graduate)*
The music might be mellow, but the hard-backed sentiments are hardly those of the nice reggae band you may have pigeonholed the UBs as. With that strength of character and committment, their future should be interesting.
NEW MUSICAL EXPRESS
At last a positive album to feel about.
MELODY MAKER
UB40 are important. Their subtle dance music is opening up a lot of ears to the pleasures of British reggae.
RECORD MIRROR
'Signing Off's songs are just too ponderous and quiet. UB40 should stay away from 33rpm.
TROUSER PRESS
It's rare to find a debut album so detailed, so excellently played...and so packed with bite — I sometimes think it really hasn't happened since The Clash.
SOUNDS

UB40
Present Arms *(DEP)*
Unwilling rather than unable to take enough chances and steps forward they've clung to formulae and shrouded their instinctive humanity with an anonymous blandness. It's not a totally disastrous LP but it is one helluva disappointment.
NEW MUSICAL EXPRESS
...a record to put on after a hard night's working/posing/drinking to unwind to the lazy dreamy sound...It's good but not great...
SOUNDS

...succeeds effortlessly in highlighting their skill for creating the most uplifting of reggae based rhythms.
RECORD MIRROR

UFO
The Wild, The Willing And The Innocent *(Chrysalis)*
...the best thing about headbanging is it's so pleasant when you stop.
NEW MUSICAL EXPRESS
The overall impression is of a band refreshed and rejuvenated, cocky and confident and still proudly scaling the heights of hard rock achievement.
SOUNDS
A satisfying platter.
MELODY MAKER
...will leave you with mud in your palm and grit in your eye.
RECORD MIRROR

UK SUBS
Crash Course — Live *(Gem)*
Live, they appeal not to the head or the heart but to the very basic, primitive instincts. Now and again. I can find time for that.
MELODY MAKER
...a mighty confirmation of all we stand for. For as long as our youth feel a compelling need to jump up and down and bellow incomprehensibly then our battle against head-music and hippydom will not be in vain.
SOUNDS

UK SUBS
Diminished Responsibility *(Gem)*
The heritage of punk — musical and ethical — has swollen like a scab of rancid pus into a new patriotism. It is a thoughtless creed, regaled and stoically preserved by numbskills...The UK Subs are a reactionary cess-pit.
NEW MUSICAL EXPRESS
...a small step forward for the observer, and a brave one for the band. It won't lose them any fans. And it might gain a few.
MELODY MAKER
Charlie and the chaps ahve now notched up a slick studio hat-trick of explosive high energy goodies with the ease of Eric Bristow hitting a dartboard from three feet.
SOUNDS
There's something about their power and aggression that holds a spell over me. It's the same sort of animal magnetism that compelled me to see the first 'White Riot' and 'Anarchy' tours.
RECORD MIRROR

JAMES BLOOD ULMER
Are You Glad To Be In America? *(Rough Trade)*
...a splendid statement of intent...honest emotional and invigorating.
NEW MUSICAL EXPRESS
...an invitation to change, primarily, jazz and funk structures and then, almost accidentally, to re-evaluate what goes on in the hugely disappointed world of contemporary rock music...a truly subversive record.
SOUNDS
We have been here before, and — since it's a cul-de-sac — back.
MELODY MAKER
...drenched, dense and very hard.
RECORD MIRROR

UNITS
Digital Stimulation *(415)*
...the debut from San Francisco's Units is possibly the colony's first ever partytime electronic album, and frequently achieves the exquisite pop vertigo of our own Human League.
SOUNDS
Though they've developed quite a few interesting tricks, the band seems unsure about its identity. Finding it could turn the Units into one of America's most important groups.
TROUSER PRESS
...one moment, smooth provocative harmonies and the next a scandalous mad-cap shriek. They're weird.
RECORD MIRROR

THE UNDERTONES
Positive Touch *(EMI/Ardeck)*
...although flawed, it affirms their position as superior pop realists and originators...like a *Coronation Street* for the record deck: well crafted, very accessible and highly entertaining.
NEW MUSICAL EXPRESS
...a pretty intriguing album and you've got to respect the lads for breaking away from the sledgehammer dynamics of hardline rock.
RECORD MIRROR
...a company album. A company joke. A limp, self-doubtful attempt at continuing a career in show business. I vaguely hate its would-be-boys-together youthfulness (when it is very old). I detest its unconscious total lethargy.
SOUNDS
...sits easy alongside 'Revolver', 'Forever Changes',

and any other well-proven goodie you care to mention as one of the truly classic pop albums of all time.
MELODY MAKER

UTOPIA
Deface The Music *(Bearsville)*
When I played it backwards I thought I thought I heard someone say, "Danger; men jerking off", but it was just the people downstairs.
NEW MUSICAL EXPRESS
Utopia mangle together elements of Beatle songs from "Please Please Me" to "I Am The Walrus", in what seems to be half affectionate tribute, half parody and a kind of smugness creeps in, as though the group are saying "look, you see how easy it is".
MELODY MAKER
It's all great fun and clever without being *clever-clever*...the icing on the cake is that somebody's finally revived something *worth* reviving.
SOUNDS
...characteristically well crafted but redundant attempt to make the lost Pleasers album.
RECORD MIRROR
...the ingenious, engaging way they go about it here is a tribute to the spirit of fun that marked the originals. That kind of imitation is the sincerest of flattery.
ROLLING STONE
Without laughing at the old days or being swallowed up by them, Utopia takes a good-natured romp through the music of their youth.
TROUSER PRESS

U2
Boy *(Island)*
...touching, precocious, full of archaic flourishes and modernist conviction, genuinely strange.
NEW MUSICAL EXPRESS
Like all great rock, you feel you *must* have heard these songs somewhere else — and yet they're unlike any other that you can think of.
MELODY MAKER
...an overall feeling of loving care and energy intertwined with simplistic and direct hooks and chords.
SOUNDS
...a record to place a bit of faith in: a record to lean on and learn from. Next to Echo & The Bunnymen's 'Crocodiles' it's one of the year's most significant releases; a restrained masterpiece.
RECORD MIRROR

US is talented, charming and potentially exceptional. But as a new Next Big Thing, they're only the next best thing to something *really* new.
ROLLING STONE
...a startlingly good but flawed debut LP.
TROUSER PRESS

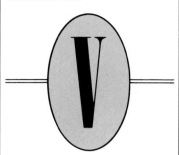

VANGELIS
See You Later *(Polydor)*
Anyone who dismisses people like Floyd for relying too much on effects for their own sakes should listen to this album, because really there is little more than the effects to latch on to.
MELODY MAKER

VANGELIS
Chariots Of Fire *(Polydor)*
Really quite impressive, actually; pomp with a purpose.
NEW MUSICAL EXPRESS

VAN HALEN
Fair Warning *(WEA)*
...one of the few HM bands who through their particular style come close to broaching the unspeakable but logical HM question of whether men's interests and women's interests might not be actually opposed rather than merely different.
NEW MUSICAL EXPRESS
...one helluva record.
MELODY MAKER
...the HM equivalent to a McDonalds hamburger restaurant. It's tacky, gar(n)ish, big mouthed, Big Mac'd, flabby, disposable, fast-food trash metal.
SOUNDS
Van Halen had the potential to become a classic fun HM combo, maybe even bridging the gap between Kiss and Motorhead. 'Fair Warning' never gets close to living up to its name.
RECORD MIRROR

THE VAPORS
Magnets *(Liberty)*
The Vapors need a rest, a think and a resurrection.
NEW MUSICAL EXPRESS
A pleasant enough album, an enjoyable enough album

comes nowhere as near as 'New Clear Days' to establishing a rapport between listener and disc.
SOUNDS
...the Vapors have the opportunity and ability to corner their market.
RECORD MIRROR
The more you listen, the more you want to hear. You could get addicted to this perverse little record.
TROUSER PRESS

VARDIS
100 mph *(Logo)*
...captured in their element and what you get is 40 minutes of guitar-dominated thrashaboogie like a Motorhead version of Love Sculpture's 'Sabre Dance' on a continuous tape loop.
SOUNDS
...but the deck spitting sonic shrapnel in all directions.
RECORD MIRROR

VARDIS
The World's Insane *(Logo)*
At times, it rocks like a boat on the high seas, rolls like a bitch on heat, but its scope, its emphasis, its lack of histrionics, clear it of any imagined metal connection.
MELODY MAKER
The world's insane? The sleeve's too plain, the songs are all lame, the music's too tame...message ends...
SOUNDS
Vardis eh? Well it rhymes with Tardis, I suppose. Goodnight.
RECORD MIRROR

VARIOUS ARTISTS
Babylon *(Chrysalis)*
...a movie soundtrack that makes you proud to be British.
NEW MUSICAL EXPRESS

VARIOUS ARTISTS
Dance Craze
(2-Tone/Chrysalis)
...an accurate reflection of one of the rare times in rock when people, place and social climate collide to transcend the limitations of mass entertainment and provide a deeper insight into public concerns.
NEW MUSICAL EXPRESS
...already about memories. But that's no excuse to get nostalgic. Youth ain't about yesterday, it's about tomorrow.
SOUNDS
It is a truly joyful thing that such groups as these are actively breaking barriers of race, age, gender and musical style. More power to them.
RECORD MIRROR

The performances here could be a little hotter, and the crowded grooves force down the sound level, but the rotating line-up downplays the bands' weaknesses so evident on their own albums.
TROUSER PRESS

VARIOUS ARTISTS
The Legend Of Jesse James *(A&M)*
...a praiseworthy sample of its genre.
NEW MUSICAL EXPRESS
Paul Kennerley comes close to achieving the impossible: a concept album which hangs together thematically, and from which individual songs stand on their own merits outside the context.
MELODY MAKER

VARIOUS ARTISTS
Marty Thau Presents 2x5 *(Criminal)*
...that rare record, the harmonious compilation.
NEW MUSICAL EXPRESS
Five bands Marty Thau thinks you and I should be listening to right now.
SOUNDS
It's the beat, more than blazing originality, which links the New York area bands showcased on 2x5.
TROUSER PRESS

VARIOUS ARTISTS
Minatures *(Pipe Records)*
...this sampler from the twilight zone will entertain and startle you on every play.
SOUNDS
...the vinyl equivalent of a vaudeville show...That's entertainment!
TROUSER PRESS

VARIOUS ARTISTS
Mutant Disco: A subtle dislocation of the Norm *(Ze/Island)*
Ze understand that what works in hard times is good times so while others get into silly political preening, physical poncing and apocalypse there's a party in NYC, and everybody is invited.
NEW MUSICAL EXPRESS
The secret is just to try to mystify its simple charms.
SOUNDS
...a collection of six discomix-length funk delights from the stable that will turn passing fanciers into rapid disciples.
RECORD MIRROR

VARIOUS ARTISTS
Oi! The Album *(EMI)*
...really is the utter pits of rock 'n' roll...celebrates the empty-headedness and grubbiness of it.
NEW MUSICAL EXPRESS
...the finest twelve inches of white produced plastic to sping on the office hi-fi in a good two years.

VARIOUS ARTISTS
Oi! The Album *(EMI)*
...really is the utter pits of rock 'n' roll...celebrates the empty-headedness and grubbiness of it.
NEW MUSICAL EXPRESS
...the finest twelve inches of white produced plastic to sping on the office hi-fi in a good two years.
SOUNDS
...a project invested with loving care, brainless noise, non-terminal chaos and a bloody good laugh.
RECORD MIRROR
...routine headbanging rubbish, with a couple of nonsense items thrown in for comic relief.
TROUSER PRESS

VARIOUS ARTISTS
Popeye *(Boardwalk)*
Written and produced by Harry Nilsson and arranged and orchestrated by that mad genius Van Dyke Parks, the music has a whimsical intimacy and make-believe magic that's missing from Robert Altman's stilted, earthbound film.
ROLLING STONE

VARIOUS ARTISTS
Rock Against Rascism's Greatest Hits *(RAR Records)*
...too little, too late. It fails, crucially at being exciting music.
NEW MUSICAL EXPRESS
...will be seen by many as purely nostalgic — a representation of those "good old days" when it was proved that militancy and fun weren't opposing concepts.
MELODY MAKER
Beautiful nostalgia but straight out of a sadly mourned history book.
SOUNDS

VARIOUS ARTISTS
Strength Thru Oi! *(Skin)*
...from the fascist connotations of the title inwards, is all bully and boy bravado, boots and braces, rucking on the terraces, blood on the streets...Oi! is about standing still — or at the most falling over drunk. Some fun.
NEW MUSICAL EXPRESS

1981 Punk/Oi is a more desperate street scream — a constricted raw rage at Being Alive Now!
SOUNDS

VARIOUS ARTISTS
Sly And Robbie Present Taxi *(Taxi/Island)*
Everyone in Jamaica has played with these two — at this rate they'll have been produced by them as well.
RECORD MIRROR
...thoughtful and highly entertaining compilation, brought slap bang up to date to present the finest selection of the dynamic duo's choicest cuts featuring a host of top reggae talent.
SOUNDS
If you want to know what's been happening in the past year or so, there's no better album than this one to keep you up to date.
MELODY MAKER

VARIOUS ARTISTS
Times Square *(RSO)*
Mostly well-known stuff, good bad and indifferent; a mish-mash of contemporary background noise and static diversions.
NEW MUSICAL EXPRESS
The only track of any real interest is XTC's 'Take This Town' written especially for the film, a typically singalong jaunt with a whistled chorus and dreamy ascending mid-section.
MELODY MAKER
...a curious hotch-potch that succeeds by dint of some surprisingly sharp 'underground' choices among the kind of fodder you'd normally expect to grace a Stigwood movie.
SOUNDS
The good stuff more than atones for the bad.
TROUSER PRESS
...a commercially viable New Wave sampler. Not a great one, certainly, but better than Warner Bros. *Troublemakers.*
ROLLING STONE

VARIOUS ARTISTS
Wanna Buy A Bridge? *(Rough Trade)*
Is there a 'Rough Trade sound'? Probably. If so, it's any or all of the following; jarring, jolting, disquieting; brash, or subtle; emotional, or intellectual; abandoned, or restrained; the tunes may go wild but the rhythms spring back like elastic.
NEW MUSICAL EXPRESS

Much as I love to hate Rough Trade and their modernistic hippy ideals, you can't deny that they've got a pretty unbeatable black catalogue.
MELODY MAKER
A neat and exhaustive run-through of the Rough Trade Theory, singles-wise at any rate.
SOUNDS

ALAN VEGA
Alan Vega *(PVC/Ze)*
Alan Vega and The Cramps are really all anyone needs to know about rockabilly in the '80s. Accept no substitute!
NEW MUSICAL EXPRESS
...either a cunningly crafted piece of contemporary musical parody that inspires detached appreciation rather than emotional participation, or it's a typically dilettant venture that's grabbed all the right ingredients but plumb forgot how to dance.
MELODY MAKER
...one of the most genuinely exciting releases in recent memory.
TROUSER PRESS

THE VILLAGE PEOPLE
Renaissance *(Mercury)*
Although they may seem to have lost their marbles, let me tell you that the music is as good, even better than before. Mellower, but with a new-found edge.
RECORD MIRROR

GENE VINCENT
The Gene Vincent Singles Album *(Capitol)*
All too often the passing years show up previous idols for their feet of clay, but this man was no empty legend — his blue suede shoes still haven't got a scuff on them.
SOUNDS

VISAGE
Visage *(Polydor)*
...a bunch of fairly talented people pissing about in no apparent direction; this is what happens to extreme Roxy Music casualties when they grow up.
NEW MUSICAL EXPRESS
As a record this isn't bad, but as a soundtrack for the bright young things it's not quite appropriate. It's neither dance music or a statement...It's unpretentious — strangely ordinary, like the 'movement' without its clothes.
MELODY MAKER
...the best context for it to be judged in is at full volume on a full dance floor.
SOUNDS

...a highly listenable album of quality background music and the fruit of a useful collaboration amongst talented like-minded musicians.
RECORD MIRROR
...well-crafted entertainment, eminently danceable and catchy.
TROUSER PRESS

THE VT'S
The VT'S *(Criminal Records)*
Effectively Kiki Dee's old backing band, the VT's have created an album of competent, lush, West Coast funk that reeks of sterile professionalism.
MELODY MAKER

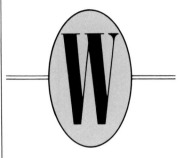

WAH!
Nah Poo: The Art Of Bluff *(Eternal)*
Wah's first LP is no disappointment. If the Heat's dropped off their name, it certainly hasn't gone out of their music.
NEW MUSICAL EXPRESS
A brilliant 'rock' LP...music as it should be. It is exciting, it is inspiring. Buy it!
SOUNDS
Wah! are great at justifying themselves, at succeeding on their own terms but they don't always head out anywhere.
RECORD MIRROR

BUNNY WAILER
Bunny Wailer sings The Wailers *(Mango/Island)*
...so polished and controlled that it's easily absorbed as background music. When you *listen* you realise its remarkable quotient of heart.
NEW MUSICAL EXPRESS
...one reggae artist whose time has definitely arrived.
MELODY MAKER
...for the discerning *occasional* reggae freak — who would normally be waiting for the next Burning Spear or Marley waxings — this long-player is as indispensable as they come.
SOUNDS
...the authentic unhurried ska feel is lent a swaying reggae shading that almost makes it

sound like a new genre rather than an adroit renovation.
ROLLING STONE

TOM WAITS
Heartattack & Vine *(Asylum)*
But in a time when hipness is often equated with selfishness, Waits' woozy, far-out optimism has never seemed fresher...a unique and lovable minor talent.
ROLLING STONE
Waits' voice no longer sounds like it's simply been *lived* in — more like it's been squatted in by 13 separate Puerto Rican junkie families with tubercular in-laws...This man's so great he can even give a hangover a sense of dignity.
NEW MUSICAL EXPRESS
Part with the folding, soldier.
MELODY MAKER
...you can forget all that lightweight stuff you get from those amateur street hustlers like Springsteen, Parker and Dylan...I get my kicks strictly from The Man.
SOUNDS

RICK WAKEMAN
1984 *(Charisma)*
If the medieval air of sweepy fluted strings and twiddley electronic bits is what you're into, then you'll love the rest too.
RECORD MIRROR
...the familiar Wakeman casserole of overcooked fiddly lines, churchy organ chords and plodding bass notes.
NEW MUSICAL EXPRESS

JOE WALSH
There Goes The Neighbourhood *(Asylum)*
A restful, pleasant album, honest and totally professional.
NEW MUSICAL EXPRESS
Urgency is what it's bereft of, but I damn well know it'd sound *perfect* in a big black limo sliding effortlessly along the LA freeways at 5pm.
SOUNDS
Smile you old bore for Christ's sake.
RECORD MIRROR

THE WANDERERS
Only Lovers Left Alive *(Polydor)*
There's nothing here which will cause barricades to be erected in Whitehall nor even trigger a new wave of hairstyles in the land.
MELODY MAKER
...the Wanderers question the viability of a future for the youth of today, and also happen to rock like rabid bitches on heat.
SOUNDS

...a curious mixture of over dressing and understatement.
RECORD MIRROR

JOHNNY WARMAN
Walking Into Mirrors *(Rocket)*
...one of the finest albums to hit the streets this year.
RECORD MIRROR

DIONNE WARWICK
No Night So Long *(Arista)*
Good manners and genuine sparkle is at a premium.
MELODY MAKER

WAS (NOT WAS)
Was (Not Was) *(Ze/Island)*
...totally absorbing, technically luxuriant, idiotically silly but crackingly danceable.
SOUNDS
...a small-time, easy, evacuated equivalent of Carla Bley's moody, mighty, misplacing 'Escalator Over The Hill.'
NEW MUSICAL EXPRESS
...as fine an album as you'll hear this year. Promise.
MELODY MAKER
What's operating here is two cool intelligences more than hip, to all kinds of musical and political information who've not got steady bouncing feet and a crazy sense of humour.
RECORD MIRROR

GINO WASHINGTON AND THE RAM JAM BAND
Hand Clappin' — Foot Stompin' — Funky Butt Live *(Pye)*
...conveys the feeling of a fanzine on vinyl and, as an engineering feat, is a quite brilliant blend of music and constant, crazy crowd response.
SOUNDS

WEATHER REPORT
Night Passage *(CBS)*
...this music has nothing to do with narrow musical genres, 'jazz-rock' or otherwise. It simply utilises the jazz tradition as a base for stepping out into unexplored areas. Just unwax your ears and plug in.
MELODY MAKER
Enjoying the music of Weather Report is rather like being able to speak a foreign language. It takes some effort but if you've mastered it, you get that much more pleasure out of it.
RECORD MIRROR
Weather Report have rarely been a more going or growing concern. Their complete creative renaissance is unbelievably welcome.
NEW MUSICAL EXPRESS

STAN WEBB'S CHICKEN SHACK
Roadies Concerto *(RCA)*
What is amazing, though, is that after so many years of "the same old 12-bars", Stan Webb can still play with so much fire.
MELODY MAKER
One to hide away with your secret Blues Band album while you wait for the Beat Boom revival.
SOUNDS

MIKE WESTBROOK
Bright As Fire *(Original)*
...intensely committed, humanistic, caring music, which looks in the face of ugliness and death and sees the rose beneath the stone. It is Westbrook's finest work to date.
MELODY MAKER

JOHN WETTON
Caught In The Crossfire *(EG Records)*
This is where Wetton finds himself today, caught in the crossfire of a generation possessed of fresh inspiration and his own flagging, uncertain drives.
NEW MUSICAL EXPRESS
...boosted by enough elegant touches to make the package ideal for a US market bored with the synthetic, clinical approach of bands like Boston.
MELODY MAKER

THE WHISPERS
Imagination *(Solar)*
...I long for less sophistication and more imagination.
NEW MUSICAL EXPRESS
...they've continued to build and 'Imagination' neatly repeats the trick from last time.
RECORD MIRROR

JAMES WHITE AND THE CONTORTIONS
Second Chance *(PVC/Ze)*
James Chance turns the discordancy of self-loathing into an ultra-chic dance product...Listen one time, be sick, contort yourself.
NEW MUSICAL EXPRESS
...a retrospective second chance to ignore nine tracks haphazardly culled from the 'Off White', 'Buy' albums.
MELODY MAKER

WHITE NOISE
Re-Entry *(Pulse)*
...the definitive statement of what can be achieved electronically at this point in time.
MELODY MAKER

...a lively, diverse and (at times literally) ear-startling work...Vorhaus is outside of the electronic mainstream, but frequently manages to beat the roborockers at their own game.
SOUNDS

WHITESNAKE
Live In The Heart Of The City *(Liberty)*
...offers little that hasn't already been perfected and repeated a thousand times before.
MELODY MAKER
...it bustles with purposeful character.
SOUNDS
...one of the best live albums I've ever heard.
RECORD MIRROR

WHITESNAKE
Come An' Get It *(Liberty)*
Superb musicianship, compact songs that should strike a chord in everyone who's honest, and, above all that indefinable sound of confidence from a band that has been gaining stature for two years.
MELODY MAKER
...warm and beguiling, mightily and excellently performed.
SOUNDS
...solid timeless entertainment.
RECORD MIRROR

WHITE SPIRIT
White Spirit *(MCA)*
White Spirit will probably survive, not because they're particularly good but simply because they're different.
MELODY MAKER
...a classic first offering that surely has placed the North Eastern quintet firmly among HM's future immortals.
RECORD MIRROR
Much as I enjoy this album, there's scarcely a note, riff or vocal phrase that hasn't been borrowed from elsewhere.
SOUNDS

THE WHO
My Generation *(Virgin)*
...the sound of youth, anger and frustration wrapped round some of the best pop songs ever written.
MELODY MAKER
By their later standards much of it sounds pretty dull, but as a documentary period piece there's much of interest.
RECORD MIRROR

THE WHO
Face Dances *(Polydor)*
The Who are trapped in a bubble of sound that is like a

heavily sedated Gang Of Four. They are slaves not creators...For Pete's sake, how much longer are we going to have to endure your irrelevant fantasies?
NEW MUSICAL EXPRESS
Where once they were a guiding, potent force they now seem a sluggish, stubborn creature...'Face Dances' lacks courage. It's merely indifferent. It's ordinary, in fact, and from the Who that's the worst kind of sell out.
MELODY MAKER
...his lyrics...are acutely perceptive and he's still setting standards for young punks to emulate.
SOUNDS
The Who are still retching out great sounds, new styles of songs and bursting with a passion tragically lacking in today's pretenders to the throne.
RECORD MIRROR
Episode 442 in the band's continuing story. On its own, it's winsomely slight at best, bafflingly circumlocutory at worst.
ROLLING STONE
...proffers no wisdom or insights — either on life or the men who make the music. Once upon a time, a Who album was an important event; now it's just another batch of radio tunes.
TROUSER PRESS

WILD HORSES
Stand Your Ground (EMI)
If for their next album Wild Horses can combine the outstanding achievements of their first two albums into one splendid melting pot of Celtic pop/rock, the group will then begin to truly fulfil their real potential as possibly one of the greatest, most lasting British rock experiences of the early 80's.
SOUNDS
Wild Horses really should be put out to grass. This album is one hell of a shameful mess.
RECORD MIRROR

KIM WILDE
Kim Wilde (RAK)
...a true masterpiece of fake ranting, stunning guitar tiffing, suggestive trembling and pop flashin' and that. It is the classic emptiness of pop presented with serious style and not much shame.
NEW MUSICAL EXPRESS
...a good pop album from a girl who doesn't try to over-reach herself and who is nothing if not unpretentious.
RECORD MIRROR

CARL WILSON
Carl Wilson (Caribou)
...ought to fit like a well-worn pair of jeans, but it feels as if someone's tried to sew in a fancy designer's label. Too much class, not enough sass.
ROLLING STONE
...It's lightweight, it's even rather dated, but it's not unpleasant.
NEW MUSICAL EXPRESS
...very likeable, listenable rock album.
MELODY MAKER

JESS WINCHESTER
Talk Memphis (Bearsville Records)
...all talk and very little action.
MELODY MAKER

WINDOWS
Uppers On Downers (Skeleton Records)
"Made Loud To Play Loud" it says on the sleeve, but for me it works best turned down to a discreet murmur.
MELODY MAKER

STEVE WINWOOD
Arc Of A Driver (Island)
Rare in these strange days of vain revolt and regimented gesture and style is the album that has no pretensions to be anything more or less than a collection of songs sweet and (not always quite so) simple.
NEW MUSICAL EXPRESS
...the sound of a man treading water and though his style may be effortless it's all far too safe. Next time he should jump in at the deep end and leave the water-wings behind.
MELODY MAKER
This album's biggest problem is that it's too classy for 1981.
SOUNDS
...his finest work since Traffic's 'John Barleycorn Must Die' (1970)
ROLLING STONE

WIRE
Document And Eye (Rough Trade)
As an insight into the Wire approach to 'entertainment' it is a fascinating, intriguing collection of live performance intercut with related dialogue.
SOUNDS

WISHBONE ASH
Number The Brave (MCA)
...this album demonstrates that the band who have been pissed upon more times than they care to remember, are still fighting.
RECORD MIRROR

WITCHFYNDE
Stagefright (Rondelet)
...a good band who deserve praise for their independent bravura, but their determination to steer away from the biggies is rapidly causing artistic atrophy.
RECORD MIRROR

JAH WOBBLE
V.I.E.P. (Virgin)
Given a year or two, Wobble could well be making records of real and lasting worth; meanwhile, he's very lucky that his celebrity can buy him the possibility of pleasant indulgences like 'V.I.E.P.'
NEW MUSICAL EXPRESS
His lyrics, are at best schoolboyish, when they're not being sarcastic, and it's not difficult to realise how much 'true' effort went into the whole affair.
MELODY MAKER
The slapdash approach to musicmaking on his two albums could indicate Wobble's contempt for his audience or for himself. In the tawdry tradition of B-movie producers, he is grinding them out to fill a void.
TROUSER PRESS

STEVIE WONDER
Hotter Than July (Motown)
...a collection of good songs performed in a familiar way and all the better for it.
NEW MUSICAL EXPRESS
...carries an exhilarating air of positive spirit and certainty about it.
MELODY MAKER
...after 'The Secret Life Of Plants' it's a blessed relief and warmly to be welcomed.
SOUNDS
If you'd thought about writing this man off, forget it.
RECORD MIRROR
...the artist's blend of pop hooks and African chants, his synthesised expressions of pipe-and-drum tribal dreams and his powerful vocal mixture of baby talk, galloping gospel singing and flowery melismata all add up to a unique style.
ROLLING STONE

BETTY WRIGHT
Betty Wright (EPIC)
It's as if the ease with which she is able to cross a variety of styles has meant that she never presented the market place with an integrated pre-packed persona.
NEW MUSICAL EXPRESS

The quality of her work has stuttered and staggered in the last three or four years and her first album for Epic doesn't dispel one's lingering doubts.
MELODY MAKER

BILL WYMAN
Green Ice (Polydor)
If Wyman ever retires from the Stones, on the evidence of this album he has a reasonably rosy future ahead writing film scores.
NEW MUSICAL EXPRESS
...there must be some connection between Emeralds and music for bull rings, which is how a lot of 'Green Ice' pans out.
MELODY MAKER

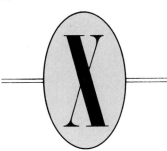

X
Wild Gift (Slash)
...the most exciting album released so far this year. Its music is thunderous, raw, complicated. Its songs are brutally truthful, honest in a way that is uncommon in pop or any other form of communication.
NEW MUSICAL EXPRESS
...contains plenty of likeable songs, but X plainly feel they'll be more "credible" if they can pass themselves off as sub-culture subversives from the New Babylon. They're stunting their own growth.
MELODY MAKER
X keep the promise of punk, use the devices of pop and exploit the inexhaustible legacy of the Fifties and Sixties to frame their soup kitchen romances and accelerated sleepwalks through a battlezone of teenage confusion.
SOUNDS

XDREAMYSTS
Xdreamysts (Polydor)
...Xdreamysts simply plunder and emasculate their source music. Lip-service is a feeble pastime especially when it's practised five years too late.
NEW MUSICAL EXPRESS
...a minor gem full of pure, uncontaminated pop-songs.
RECORD MIRROR

XTC
Black Sea *(Virgin/RSO)*
...awash with confidence and crawls with a brimming rock bravado that makes full satisfaction a complete certainty.
MELODY MAKER

...a perfectly inconsequential and hugely diverting combo who have never once threatened to produce great art.
NEW MUSICAL EXPRESS

This is a Very Important Album not only because it's a joy to listen to, but also because it's likely to be influencing a whole lot of other bands in the near future.
SOUNDS

...the band's youthfully aggressive, revved-up white-noisy style has settled like dust around an industrious sculptor, leaving a finished product that combines streamlined originality with Beatles-type buoyancy.
ROLLING STONE

File under refreshment for the ears, body and spirit.
RECORD MIRROR

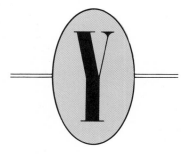

YACHTS
Yachts Without Radar *(Polydor)*
Even if the Yachts' lyrics sometimes get the best of them...it's hard to fault a pop group that deftly manages to mock its own insignificance.
ROLLING STONE

...rocks more noticeably than the Yachts' debut LP. 'S.O.S.' Gone is that album's slightly obnoxious over-achiever cockiness, replaced by better-adjusted cleverness.
TROUSER PRESS

YELLOW MAGIC ORCHESTRA
Multiples *(A&M)*
The YMO beat is rarely dull, the multi-layered production never flat. They strive for and attain a brisk and colourful balance of asphyxiating rhythmic twists and an unparalleled melodic strength.
NEW MUSICAL EXPRESS

At their best they play brilliantly conceived electropop that parks its luggage and invites itself to stay in your brain a while...At their worst the Magics are intensely irritating.
MELODY MAKER

...this album leaves me still waiting for something fresh and exciting from the Land of the Rising Sun.
SOUNDS

I don't know what to make of this album. At the beginning you set out with one opinion and by the end you don't have any.
RECORD MIRROR

YELLOW MAGIC ORCHESTRA
BGM *(A&M)*
They bring the same over-dressed and over-important approach to their music as the Spandaus and the Ultravoxes of our brave new, modern and slightly farcical world.
NEW MUSICAL EXPRESS

...reveals a change of tsunami strength; a moody, mature and devastating collection of keyboard pieces far from the previous oriental bob to rock.
MELODY MAKER

YMO have successfully opened up their warmer, deeper side whilst still retaining every inch of their unique oriental charm.
SOUNDS

...a bland, neurotic, boring and above all, pointless exercise in synthesised garbage.
RECORD MIRROR

YES
Drama *(Atlantic)*
...an anachronistic turkey of monstrous proportions, an all-too-obviously desperate attempt to recapture former Yes fans who've drifted in the general direction of Styx and Kansas.
NEW MUSICAL EXPRESS

One would have thought (hoped!) that after Anderson's departure, the band might have come lyrically down to earth, particularly with the Buggles' penchant for concise, witty pop lyrics. Not this time around.
MELODY MAKER

Downes and Horn have been faithful to the pomp and splendour of Yes, but somehow they've made the band looser and more accessible.
RECORD MIRROR

They've condensed their sprawling artistry into a dense-yet-diverse album that hangs perfectly together.
SOUNDS

YES
Yesshows *(Atlantic)*
It's a better album than 'Drama' on the whole, but less significant of the band's future development.
MELODY MAKER

At their best they can produce timeless music which actively defies categorisation.
SOUNDS

...the last live legacies of Anderson and Wakeman...Recommended for nostalgic memories.
RECORD MIRROR

...not only pointless but cowardly and dishonest.
ROLLING STONE

NEIL YOUNG
Hawks And Doves *(Reprise)*
Neil Young 1980 is a compromised man, the personal demon that drove his past now exorcised to a state of confused equilibrium.
MELODY MAKER

In such depressing times, maybe this is the best Neil Young can do.
SOUNDS

The old whino might warble on about young mariners heading for war working for the queen and so on, but generally he's continuing in his own sweet way, moving at as sharp a tangent as ever from the r'n'r mainstream.
RECORD MIRROR

...goes down smoothly, like a tasty drink doctored with an undetectable knockout potion.
TROUSER PRESS

...if 'Hawks & Doves' is a major statement, it's also an understatement. Another throwaway masterpiece, dashed off like most of his LPs — like a letter, letting you know what he's thinking, for the moment.
ROLLING STONE

JOHNNY VAN ZANT BAND
No More Dirty Deals *(Polydor)*
If you liked Lynyrd Skynyrd and don't have any principles, buy this and make this good

old southern boy a star. I wouldn't.
RECORD MIRROR

FRANK ZAPPA
Tinseltown Rebellion *(CBS)*
...a double album of tedious, cliched music, mean-spirited and exploitative sexual fetishism and furious hatred of anybody less narrow-minded and screwed up than Zappa himself.
NEW MUSICAL EXPRESS

There's some strong and inventive music on 'Tinseltown Rebellion' and there's also a lot of crap.
MELODY MAKER

If you're still with him, shell out.
SOUNDS

Recorded in eight different locations on both sides of the Atlantic and crediting nearly three years worth of changing personnel, it sounds suspiciously like it was thrown together to satisfy some contractual commitment or other.
RECORD MIRROR

WARREN ZEVON
Stand In The Fire *(Asylum)*
Hats off to him for taking a big chance and surprising everyone, probably even himself.
TROUSER PRESS

...learn to treat the geezer simply as a fun character with a throaty roar for a voice, a loopy imagination, and a sharp sense of the absurd, then you won't be sorry you made his acquaintance.
MELODY MAKER

If you hear this unique, kinky, left-field cross between a Frederick Forsyth character and a rock Raymond Chandler howling around your kitchen door, I think you better let him in, soonest.
SOUNDS

If there remains an acceptable face of Californian AOR, it belongs to Warren Zevon.
RECORD MIRROR

...one of those rare and remarkable in-concert LPs that's not just the souvenir of a successful tour or a low-cost resume of former glories and recent hits.
ROLLING STONE

THE SINGLES SCENE

In Britain 1981 meant new pop, new romantics, new tribes; the decline of "disco" and a flurry of new dance floor adventures. The ubiquitous sound was funk and in the USA 1981 was the worst year for pop ever.

Blame it on the radio. There are good stations scattered round the States (though the most adventurous programming comes from non-commercial, campus DJs), but singles only matter when they are everywhere and it is formula radio that still provides the national sound of everyday life.

These days Britain and the USA sound quite different. The British year belonged to Adam Ant — his double-drummed chants driving us through the recession, his striped face grinning cheerily out of a hundred magazines. The star of the year in the USA was Christopher Cross — elderly, hesitant, bald; his slight, neutral songs diffused through every shopping mall. British musicians are still determined, one way or another, to have fun. American musicians are concerned only to give no offence, and American pop is now subordinated to a style of radio programming that resembles a production line for musak.

There are good material reasons for the continuing decline of American radio. An increasing proportion of the

CHRISTOPHER CROSS

stations' commercial space is being bought by national advertisers advised by national market researchers, by precise measures of which show on which station has which percentage of which audience. Radio stations are less and less able to build their own markets, more and more pressured to reflect the national average. And so the playlists get smaller, the range of sounds narrower (there is less black music on American pop radio now — AM and FM — than at any time since 1953). So the essential pop sense of change and novelty and *presence* is sapped — the US has far fewer hits than the UK these days; Kim Carnes' 'Bette Davis Eyes' took *months* to get from number 30 to number 1 and back to number 30 again. All American pop is beginning to sound like the songs at the end of Hollywood family films — vaguely cheerful ditties to hum as you leave the cinema and forget thereafter (and,

indeed, Hollywood family film music, like Neil Diamond's songs from 'The Jazz Singer', now has its guaranteed US chart place).

Whatever happened to American youth? American pop has returned to its pre-rock'n'roll, pre-teenage condition: bland, middle-aged performers; records that appeal simply as songs, as accessible melodies; a pervasive lightweight 4:4 beat; clean textures, intimate harmonies, the singer as a good friend; love songs unchanged in romantic cliché since the early Fifties; music made by MOR professionals, the Perry Comos of our time. Even the newer names (Gino Vanelli, John Cougar, Pat Benatar) are old troupers and the biggest US chart group of the year, REO Speedwagon ('Keep On Loving You' and 'Take It On The Run') distills (like the similar sounding Styx) years of rock touring into no-risk music, smooth songs which hint at hard rock but take refuge in well-

modulated choruses.

No one is engaged by this music (not even its performers): it is heard, but never listened to. The premium is on familiar voices — hence the continued success of Neil Diamond, Steve Winwood, Barbra Streisand — and "strong" songs — hence the continued success of country performers: Ronnie Milsap, Eddie Rabbitt, Delbert McClinton, Juice Newton and, above all, Kenny Rogers, whose biggest hit, 'Lady', was put together by Lionel Richie of The Commodores — proof that old pros from all genres can work together in the middle of this easy listening road.

American pop, Radio Two music, no longer makes much of a mark on Britain. There are fewer and fewer shared US/UK pop hits and these are mostly UK hits that happen to follow US radio rules rather than US hits which pull in British listeners too. (The exceptions this year were the records which charted after John Lennon's death — his own, moving 'Woman', George Harrison's banal 'All Those Years Ago'; the best post-Lennon single, Yoko Ono's hypnotic 'Walking On Thin Ice' was, of course, not a US pop hit — too weird.)

The biggest UK names on the US charts in 1981 were familiar: Queen continued to

KIM CARNES

FREDDIE MERCURY/QUEEN

STRAY CATS

develop their skill with pop pastiche ('Another One Bites The Dust', 'Flash'); The Police consolidated their position as a multi-national ('De Do Do Do De Da Da Da'). Phil Collins found the classy pop audience (ie Genesis and Supertramp fans) everywhere ('In The Air Tonight'). But Europe's MOR sounds also now get US radio time. And so Cliff Richard (and Abba) have, belatedly, got their regular notch in the US Top 20. And so Sheena Easton, a routine club singer, packaged for television and the British idea of light entertainment, given a "modern" sex appeal derived from the fantasy world of the temp. ads, made a US number 1, 'Morning Train (9 to 5)'.

In this context there can be no doubt that Kim Carnes' 'Bette Davis Eyes' was the American pop single of the year — it was about the only US white hit to sell in Britain too! An old pro record in one sense (it was co-written by Jackie DeShannon, and Kim Carnes uses every trick in the Rod Stewart rock book to equate huskiness and sexiness), it was also crisp (most American pop is limp) and compelling — a sexual song that hints not at hard rock or pop cliché but at something harder to hold: a lesbian aesthetic.

Britain has its own MOR

DEPARTMENT S

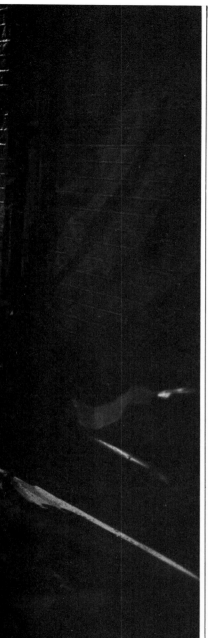

groups (Bucks Fizz and the admirable Nolans) and novelty hits (Joe Dolce's 'Shaddup Your Face') but they no longer dominate the charts. British singles nowadays feed on specific audiences and specific experiences; British pop retains a sense of life — it expects a response (in the US, only Bruce Springsteen's 'Hungry Heart' had any sense of audience at all). American pop is socially vacuous. The sign of its conservatism is the absence of any reference to the real world at all — who would know from the hit parade that Reagan was elected, that the moral majority rules?

The most successful British pop groups, by contrast, are directly puzzling out the condition of England. The Jam's 'That's Entertainment' and 'Funeral Pyre' fused the brooding, flickering sounds and images of street violence to the desperate escapism that is, for Paul Weller, the fuel of rock'n'roll. The Undertones are still working

on teenage pop ('It's Going To Happen!', 'Julie Ocean') as if the sounds themselves can make sense of growing up. The Specials 'Ghost Town', an apparently eccentric mixture of party sounds and a chilled response to Britain as an industrial wasteground, reached number 1 as the sound of the summer of youth riots.

British pop groups remain rooted in the punk assumption that music is youth culture, records are a way of shaping lives. 'Grey Day' situated Madness's music hall "nuttiness" in an acute account of boredom, and even the most old fashioned pop singers (Toyah

THE PASSIONS

and Hazel O'Connor, Kim Wilde and Kirsty MacColl) take for granted their audience as "us" — their pop task is to feed (and feed off) this sense of youth community.

The biggest pop movements in Britain in 1981 had even more precise audience appeal. There was, to begin with, the teenybop revival. Adam and The Ants shifted as many posters and magazines as records; their "tribal" music, derivative and messy to outside ears (and cheekily parodied in these terms by Tenpole Tudor's 'Swords Of A Thousand Men') was, in fact, the sound of children's play-time fantasies — 'Kings Of The Wild Frontier', 'Stand And Deliver'. And even Ant music wasn't simply child's play. Bow Wow Wow, featuring the ex-Ants and developing with Adam the sounds of tribal youth, made 'W.O.R.K.', an expression of manager Malcolm McLaren's continued flirtation with anarchism and art, and the Ant sound was

SHAKIN' STEVENS

only one strand of new romanticism, as the Blitz kids and Bowie boys emerged from their dance floors to find that they too had teenybop appeal. Spandau Ballet's and Visage's sense of style, their well designed combinations of new fashions and the electronic bop suddenly meant teen appeal too for old musos like Ultravox and Landscape, for new pin-ups like Duran Duran and Depeche Mode.

1981 was a year of tribes — Ant people, the new romantic mix of teenyboppers and stylists, heavy metallers (the sharpest single of the year was Motorhead and Girlschool's joint version of

KIM WILDE

'Please Don't Touch'), rockabillies (a great year for Shakin' Stevens and The Stray Cats). And intellectuals.

1981 was a good year for British singles, a year when the possibilities of the popform (ephemeral, gimmicky, fun) were restated. Some restatements came from mellowing punk intellectuals like Siouxsie and The Banshees — 'Spellbound', confident female verve, Budgie's hard percussion, tight anti-pretty music — but the year's most interesting records were made by younger, newer bands, pushing further the post-punk pop (anti-American pop) principles : beat is more important than melody in structuring a song; repeated riffs add tension (traditional pop choruses dissolve it); words are about mood and nuance; singers make just another sound; musical signs must be exaggerated, declaimed, not effaced; the pleasure of pop is its artifice (not its "naturalness").

The year's best singles explored these possibilities : The Passage's 'Devils And Angels', repeated echoing phrases, Wah!'s heavy, throaty, clanging 'Seven Minutes To Midnight', Girls At Our Best's deliberate unpolished anthem, 'Go For Gold', Fire Engine's 'Candyskin', an impassive, cluttered chant, Department S's insistent Sixtiesh 'Is Vic There?' and 'Going Left Right', The Passions' laid-back fade, 'I'm In Love With A German Film Star', B Movie's driving mood piece, 'Remembrance Day', The Teardrop Explodes' fanfare, 'Reward', and The Associates' 'Tell Me Easter's On Friday', rhetoric over a tape-loop, the singer, as on many of these songs, picking his way through language as if it were a minefield.

This sort of music risks

GRACE JONES

AUGUST DARNELL

(and often reaches) self-indulgence, pretentiousness, introversion. Most of these groups are one-offs : they make one or two good singles and a run of dull albums (which is why the singles form still matters). But their short term sales success reflects a significant intellectual pop audience — the hip sixth formers and students serviced now by the major record companies as well as the small labels (the distinction no longer means anything in musical terms), by the BBC's evening radio shows, by the music press. 'I'm In Love With The Girl On The Manchester Virgin Megastore Check-Out Desk', sang The Freshies, and 'I Can't Get Bouncing Babies' by Teardrop Explodes — dull records but a sharp sense of the new pop and its institutions — institutions lacking on a national scale in the USA and therefore without pop effect there, whatever the importance of the new pop scenes in particular centres like LA and New York.

British pop of all sorts is music made (unlike white American pop) around a beat, around a commitment to *dance*. British pop audiences, of all sorts, are shaped not by radio but in clubs and discos, in the spaces where the cults divide. It is on the dance floor that musical boundaries are drawn, tastes formed, definitions made, the decisions taken, cult by cult, about what sound goes with what. One effect of this in 1981 was the prising apart of "disco" as Grace Jones, for example, applied her account of the gay club aesthetic to the more supple reggae rhythms of Sly Dunbar and Robbie Shakespeare, as Robert Palmer applied his account of rock to a snappier beat, a more neurotic sensibility, to make a structuralist epic, 'Looking For Clues'.

The only American music that still sounds through Britain, still dominates the British charts, is dance music, and the only way interesting or unusual or challenging music can get into the American charts is through disco clubs, disco radio, disco sales. This was the success route, for example, of Blondie's 'Tide Is High' and Devo's 'Whip It', and is the only way Americans can hear experiments — Pig Bag's

'Papa's Got A Brand New Pig Bag', superb anarcho-funk, Heaven 17's 'We Don't Need This Fascist Groove Thang', passionate electronic funk, ESG's 'You're No Good', eager sparse-funk.

There are ironies in this. For years rock fans have despised disco for its tight formulas, its rhythmic restraints, its "mindless" calls to dance floor action. For years, in fact, disco music has been more imaginative, more open, more intelligent than anything produced in the rock mainstream. There are disco formulas — this year's trick was to string together old hits over a disco pulse — but in day to day practice "disco" refers to a far wider range of pleasures than "rock".

Even in the black pop mainstream, 1981 meant Stevie Wonder's 'Master Blaster (Jamming)', reggae solidarity, as well as Diana Ross's 'I'm Coming Out', Chic play Vegas. It meant joyous synthesiser music (Kleer's 'License To Dream', Quincy Jones' 'Ai No Corrida'), James Brown's hard line 'Rap Payback' and Odyssey's traditionally soulful 'Back To My Roots'. It meant closing time disco schmaltz (Smokey Robinson's 'Being With You', Champaign's 'How 'Bout Us') and mid-evening seamless jazz funk (Alphonse Mouzon's 'By All Means'). It meant Linx, a sophisticated British dance band, writing, performing, producing songs ('Intuition', 'Throw Away The Key,' 'You're Lying') for the smart teenage weekend.

Disco cults are disorganised and different favourites reflect different DJs, different clubs, different contacts; *my* favourite routine rhythms were Carol Jiani's 'Hit'n'Run Lover' and

THE FRESHIES

Taana Gardner's 'Heartbeat' — music to be hypnotised by. But the British cult sound of the 1981 was "mutant disco", the New York music of ZE RECORDS — images and sounds of Big Apple night life through the ages : August Darnell's spicy reworking of the Latin tinge for Kid Creole and Coati Mundi; Was (Not Was)'s mixture of early Seventies funk rock and contemporary intimacies — the public beat of private nervousness, 'Wheel Me Out', 'Out Come The Freaks'; Material's 'Bustin' Out', modern jazz-disco-rock — it turned out that rock's most experimental music only made sense on an old-fashioned disco floor.

Alongside the rap. 1981 meant pop raps, spoofs, uneasy white exercises in a secret black style — Blondie's 'Rapture', Tom Tom Club's 'Wordy Rappinghood', cruder jokes like The Evasions' 'Wikka Wrap'. And as every performer in every genre began to throw rap in (even reggae DJs — rap came full circle back to talk-over in General Saint and Clint Eastwood's 'Another One Bites The Dust') the rap masterpieces — Grandmaster Flash's 'Adventures On The Wheels Of Steel' and 'Birthday Party', Funky Four Plus One's 'That's The Joint', Disco 4's 'Move To The Groove' — remained almost impossible for straight white pop fans to find.

Rap matters not for its form (quickly wearing) but its content : it is the only American music up-picking and un-picking words and voices from outside the studio. Rap reflects a more general movement — black punk, do-it-yourself funk, music made by local bands about local streets. The

STEVE STRANGE/VISAGE

history of rock is the history of young blacks and whites and their relationship in the USA is presently as bad as it has ever been — it was The Clash's New York audiences which drove the supporting black rappers off stage. (And even in Britain, despite 2 Tone, despite the continued success of UB40 and The Beat, reggae remains outside the popular music mainstream, picking up airplay and sales only occasionally — this year's hit was Sugar Minott's 'Good Thing Going'. In Britain, too, black and white audiences, black and white musicians, remain obviously separate, meet only to dance.)

The new black sounds may filter into the US mainstream (Prince's black and white blend of funk'n'punk has already made a sales mark) but, meanwhile, it's American

SUGAR MINOTT

youth now that has no music of its own (US chart artists are, on average, at least ten years older than UK chart artists) and so the best news of 1981 was an outbreak of American Ant-fever — radio stations, it seemed, were playing Adam's records "spontaneously", under pressure from suddenly mobilised teenyboppers. True or CBS hype? Neither Adam's records nor any other new romantic sound has yet turned up in the US Top 20, but I'd like to think something is in the air. British pop was transformed by the punk manouevres of 1976-7 — punk died but at least the new music-making routines are fun, can still surprise. American pop singles in 1981 were no fun, offered no surprises at all. SIMON FRITH

ADAM & THE ANTS

In August 1980 the NME was still referring to Adam Ant as "the man who snatched defeat from the jaws of victory". But in the end that honour belongs to Malcolm McLaren, who reinvented Adam, dismissed him, and then saw him win the mass audience McLaren had intended for Bow Wow Wow. By October 'Dog Eat Dog' was in the Top Ten and the phenomenon — a combination of the right look, a great album and some mysterious convulsion of the adolescent collective unconscious — that was to make Adam into 1980s one proper teen idol was underway.

In October when Adam and the Ants played the Lyceum the audience was boiling. It looked like the theatre had been hit by a typhoon: waves of punks were tossed to and fro, as teams of bouncers charged into the audience to carry off struggling fans. Most of the fans belonged to Adam's original constituency. They were punk loyalists, in their ripped leather jackets and bondage trousers; they blocked the stage at a thousand concerts, pogoing and knocking the drink out of your hand. They loved Adam because he had slogged for three years in his old offensive punk style, earning nothing but derision and never giving up.

In November an interviewer from SOUNDS mentioned that a lot of Ants' fans were also fans of Crass and Adam replied, "I think they're pitiful. Very sordid and very dirty, and not much to do with anarchy. I really don't want to know about it." This reads strangely from a man who has consistently stated how much he loves his fans, how loyal he feels towards them. Adam probably no longer thought of those old supporters as *his* people — because the truth was that Adam as punk underdog and Adam as a success could not have the same fans.

The mystery lies in trying to connect the old Adam with the new. In the same interview he said "I identified a lot more with what McLaren was doing with Sex than with all that 'What have we got — fuck all' rubbish." He was attracted by the shock horror side of punk, and in those songs that got him branded as fascist he was simply playing with the thrill of words and images. And because he was clumsy and humourless the critics couldn't see, at the time, that he was presenting a lurid cartoon.

It is quite possible that Adam didn't quite realise it either. Never one of the great minds of our time, Adam can be quite intelligent when dealing with specifics — his career, making music, sex — but with theories he turns to mush. He deserved criticism for writing a line like "war is the world's only hygiene" in the song 'Animals And Men', and it is not enough to say he was simply reproducing part of the Futurist manifesto. He wrote it just because he thought it sounded cool. People like Adam just shouldn't operate at a serious time.

But 1980 unlike 1977 was not a serious time for rock. Adam blossomed, became almost lovable, as soon as he moved away from the (supposedly) realistic, significant context of punk into perfect, shallow fantasy pop. Adam did it by going teenage, for teenage is what he always was in his naive celebration of blasphemy and S&M.

At the end of 1979 Adam met McLaren and paid him £1000 to re-model his act. They sat down for two hours as Malcolm went through every word of his songs, grilling him over what they meant. "You have to be on the ball with a guy like that because he'd just murder you. And a lot of them weren't obvious enough, weren't clear enough for the market. They were a bit *esoteric*."

Out of that association came the Burundi tribal rhythms, the glitter rock for the 1980s: gold and pirates and hedonism, Red Indians and war paint. The story, the answer as to who created what, is shrouded in a mist of "no comment", but one can trace the different influences. The vision is obviously Malcolm McLaren, as Adam has no gift for conceptual thinking and had never in his career shown any clairvoyance. The talk about an alternative to the recession, that teenagers should reject the work ethic, the tribalism, the ethnic influence is probably all McLaren's.

The dumb sincerity, the spaghetti Western romanticism in the lyrics must be Adam's:

He who writes in blood
Doesn't want to be read
He must be learned by heart.
(*The Magnificent Five*')

In interview Adam would repeat endlessly his theories about the warrior ideal, their integrity and independence, pride and self-sufficiency. But rather like Steve Strange trying to convince us that putting on makeup was some kind of awakening of youth consciousness, Adam was simply suffering from the punk hangover. Ideology had been important for so long, it was hard to start a new fashion without one.

But Adam did bring something of his own, something really valuable, to McLaren's theories. His list of personal favourites printed in RECORD MIRROR shows his top two songs to be 'School's Out' by Alice Cooper and Gary Glitter's 'Hello! Hello!' Adam may not have had the saving irony of these two masters of rock show business excess. But he did bring to the Ants a real glam-rock heritage. Marco Pirroni was probably responsible for the form, but we can credit Adam with giving them that football terrace surge — those whoops and cries, that sense of exuberant participation. The Ants new songs were wonderful pop epics; they carried you forward in a way that Bow Wow Wow — although wittier, defter, better on stage — have never quite managed to do.

The album 'Kings Of The Wild Frontier' appeared at around the same time as Talking Heads' 'Remain In Light', when there was much talk of David Byrne's and Brian Eno's excursions into primitive territory. Adam was less reverent and yet less exploitative: you couldn't accuse him of ripping off ethnic culture because what he was really doing was ripping off old Hollywood movies and, in the process, turning his influences into something new.

And curiously enough, for all his talk about a new race of peacock people and pride and independence through dressing up, Adam and the Ants didn't catch as a street fashion. The idea was good — as he described it, "It's like you're some marauder who's broken into a place, grabbed as much as you can, pinned it all over yourself and run out the other side. It's slightly flamencoish, Red Indian, there's also a very romantic swashbuckling element in it." But the High Streets of Britain were never crowded with kids in warpaint and his look had far less impact than the rather frumpish Spandau Ballet were later to have.

Adam Ant was not a model to imitate, he was a few great pop songs and a face to pin on your bedroom wall. The way that face has changed is perhaps the most interesting aspect of his progress. The cover of the single of 'Kings Of The Wild Frontier' shows him in one of his old punk Grand Guignol poses; he seems to have a rivet stuck in his neck. On the LP the image had blurred into a new fantasy, the swashbuckler, but there was still the hammy, eye-popping pose.

Gradually the makeup softened, the hair began to curl like a 1930s movie dream. The cover of THE FACE shows him without makeup, looking naked, sweet and vulnerable, trustingly grasping a single red rose. And your heart could melt. Do not speak of corniness with respect to a performer whose most endearing statement to date is that he wouldn't mind being Liberace.

Much of Adam's success, finally, is due to his conviction. Not that he hasn't abandoned his original followers, traded (and believed) in spurious theories. But like Gary Glitter, what is charming about Adam is that he is blissfully at home in showbusiness, loving the stage, the crowd — any crowd — loving the camera. 1981 may not be the year of Adam Ant, but in 1980, for a few months he glowed with fame.

MARY HARRON

PAT BENATAR

Pat Benatar is filing for separation from her image. Her name should no longer conjure up pictures of tight black spandex and form fitting leopard skin tops. Although she is the first to admit that she helped to foster that image, she claims she didn't realise how far it would go towards making her into a rock and roll version of Farrah Fawcett. These days she's more interested in making people listen to her than having them look at her. "To me," Benatar murmured to Steve Pond in a ROLLING STONE interview, "the point is to be strong but to still be a woman, not to be tough. I'm not a little flower, but I'm not somebody's sexual fantasy of a cold, hard bitch either. There are some women who want me to be like that, to stick it to the men.

"I try to tell people that they're missing the point. I'm not gonna be masculine, and I'm not gonna be a frilly girl who gets what she wants because she's frilly. There's a middle ground, and that's where I want to go. I get a lot of shit for going down the middle, but I'm hanging in there."

So far, however, the middle ground seems to be eluding her. The hits from both of her albums, 'In The Heat Of The Night' and 'Crimes Of Passion', have been tough songs like 'Heartbreaker' and 'Hit Me With Your Best Shot'. Benatar has got a lot more mileage out of her fantasy potential than she has from being a down-to-earth, confident woman. Her act implies that she can give as good as she gets, but the compassion and understanding that go along with strength are missing.

To be fair, Pat has tried to tackle issues beyond anger at rejection. She co-wrote the track 'Hell Is For Children', a song condemning child abuse on her second album, but the song was never released as a single in America. Before Benatar can project the image of her choice, she may have to give up the image that brought her success.

Pat Benatar grew up on Long Island, the child of a labourer in a sheet metal factory and a former New York City Opera singer. Her childhood was normal, middle class and straight, featuring a Catholic upbringing, a stint as a cheerleader and beach parties. In fact, the only thing that really bothered the young Pat Andrezejewski was the fact that her teachers insisted on enrolling her in special voice classes instead of physical education, which she preferred.

In 1970, at the age of 17, she began her vocal training in earnest in preparation for operatic studies at the Juilliard School of Music. But she never made it that far. Disgusted by the rigorous training procedures, which included the use of a harness, Pat dropped out and married her high school sweetheart, Dennis Benatar. When he entered the army shortly after the wedding, she made the move to Virginia to be with him.

"I was a bank teller for two and a half years down there," she sighs. "I had always been able to do whatever I wanted, and suddenly I had to face the reality of marriage and a lot of bills. I sat in that teller's cage every day, looked at the money and thought, 'I know there's a way for me to have this without going to jail...' " The two things Pat had going for her at that time were a brief fling at studying health education and her voice, so she took a job as a singing waitress at the Roaring 20s club in Hopewell, Virginia. There she was allowed to sing Top 40 and show tunes in a fake leopard skin outfit with food stains all down the front.

It was clear that she was getting nowhere fast. She quit the singing waitress circuit and tried the local bar band scene, but found that she was still dissatisfied. She and Dennis packed up all of their belongings and moved back to New York, where she auditioned for and won a spot at Rick Nielson's Catch A Rising Star.

"I was broke, and I mean *broke*," she says. "Rice and beans and stuff like that. It makes you mad to be hungry, and it makes you mad to want to sing rock and roll and have people tell you, 'Janice Joplin died, give it up.' I learned more in New York between 1975 and 1978 than at any other time in my life, because I was so mad!"

That three year period also gave Benatar a chance to shake some of her operatic training and learn to scream. Slowly she transformed herself from the self-conscious, five foot tall girl with the voice that seemed too big for her into a snarling temptress daring to challenge men on their own terms.

"When my voice started coming, so did the confidence, and pretty soon the person who wore leopard skin dresses in Richmond started to emerge. It happened gradually, but by the time CHRYSALIS came down to see me, I was in tights and boots, almost where I am now."

It was during this period, too, that the Benatars' marriage started to fall apart, although it lasted through the release of Pat's debut album, 'In The Heat Of The Night'. Pat began to find herself in rock and roll, and Gidget from Long Island disappeared.

"I really want to have a family and stuff," she muses, "maybe live in the country and wear flat shoes and flannel shirts. Real normal stuff. I'm not cut out to be a star — I'm not really secure enough to be a star. It's like not being able to admit that I like a record until I see that everybody else likes it. I hate being vulnerable."

Benatar once claimed that the first thing on her list of goals was getting a Top 10 record, and with the now platinum success of 'Crimes Of Passion', she's achieved her dream. 'Crimes' held the number two spot on the US charts for weeks, edged away from number one by the phenomenal success of John Lennon's 'Double Fantasy' LP. It seems safe to say that Pat Benatar will remain a musical force in the '80s, in spite of her apparent reluctance.

It remains to be seen whether or not Benatar will find a way to the middle ground she claims to long for, but everyone's favourite fantasy has the cushion of success to lean on while she plans her strategy.

DREW MOSELEY

ELVIS COSTELLO

Unlike the others in this section — whose inclusion has been justified by varying measures of skilful strategy, unyielding professionalism, artistic soundness and commercial acceptance — Elvis Costello has only his boundless excellence to recommend him.

Not that it has been a *bad* year for him. He has little difficulty in filling a medium-sized concert hall with voluble supporters; his albums enter the charts as a matter of course, although they don't tend to stay for very long; and, by disregarding the attentions of the press for as long as he has, he is still considered the Penny Black of interviewees. Characteristically, he has restricted his appearances in British periodicals in the past year to an OBSERVER magazine spread about the minutiae of life on his tour bus and a RECORD MIRROR interview he wasn't even aware he was doing with a journalist who, when discovered, enjoyed a frank and colourful exchange of views with his voluble manager. Other than that, his perverseness has been equalled only by his sense of television prime-time. He appeared on the children's programme 'Jim'll Fix It' in response to a miniature viewer's request, and on 'This Is Your Life', the Mount Rushmore of British television, when they chronicled the back pages of Joe Loss, in whose band Costello's father Ross McManus once played. There was not much more in the US where his televised exchange with Tom Snyder was reported in the music press with an awe customarily reserved for Old Testament miracles. He walks, he talks, he is capable of civil conversation with non-partisans!

In other words, he's done alright even if his record sales appear to diminish in direct proportion to his growth as a songwriter, in which field he is second to none. Of all the people who came to prominence during the long-overdue Spring-cleaning of 1977, he is the least trend-conscious, the most tenaciously individualistic, the one most in touch with the evasive heart of popular music. To achieve the latter at least, you have to be a real *fan*, which is what Costello is. His recording career has been littered with odd B-sides, bonus singles, covers, different versions and discrepancies between British and American releases. For anyone less prolific, or less zealous in applying quality control to his output, this might have been viewed as opportunistic desperation. In Costello's case, it was simply a question of having an enthusiast's appetite for producing material of all kinds and being buggered if record industry protocol was going to interfere.

It was hardly surprising, therefore, that last October should have seen the release of a 20-track collection of curios called, depending on which side of the Atlantic it was purchased, 'Taking Liberties' (an American LP) or '10 Bloody Marys and 10 How's Your Fathers' (a British cassette). Providing a timely reminder of how Costello's also-rans are more substantial than most people's front-runners, both editions include the sublime miniaturised perfection of 'Hoover Factory' and 'Tiny Steps'. More significantly,

both include a version of Rodgers and Hart's 'My Funny Valentine'. A choice of material which most of the self-important stooges who masquerade as arbiters of taste would dismiss as maudlin for fear of losing some illusory status, Costello's stark reading — just voice and guitar — simply reminds you of what a marvellous song it is.

Like all superior interpreters, Costello sings somebody else's song so that you never hear it quite the same way again. At one of his London concerts in March, he performed Randy Crawford's 'One Day I'll Fly Away' with such ingenuous clarity and conviction that anyone who thought he might have been joking was thrown out of gear and spellbound into a lay-by within six bars. Both his voice and his manner had changed subtly but tellingly. He was congenial to his audience, who responded with unselfconscious eagerness, and he finally appeared to have worked out the difference between idiosyncrasy, of which he has in abundance, and mere mannerism, which occasionally deflates the very effect he intends. He had obviously been listening more to Frank Sinatra than to Bruce Springsteen, and his exquisite choice of material — punctuated, of course, by the customary ebullience just in case anybody thought he was a crooner — reflected his newly-located vocal confidence.

It is this quality which is most apparent on 'Trust', so far the most potent album of a confused, anything-goes decade which has so far amounted to some grisly mating of a clothes horse and a computer that guzzles cocktails. On 'Trust' Costello goes straight to the heart of the matter and, apart from the occasional relief-deviation, stays there. Monopolised even more by its terrific songs than by Costello's considerable presence, 'Trust' is abrasive, ambiguous, thrilling even, with a particular highlight in 'Shot With His Own Gun', a moment which, with a mixture of skill and judgement, treads the tightrope between perilous melodrama and nailing the listener to the floor. Accompanied only by piano — as he was on the high-octane live version of 'Accidents Will Happen' —

Costello glides over the notes, soaring on the choruses, with the benefit of the crispest, most resonant production available.

The fact that 'Trust' failed to change the shape of the universe is understandable. It is, after all, only a record. Its lack of success, however, is genuinely bewildering. Costello appears to have offended numerous people in America, where his picturesque altercation with Bonnie Bramlett and Stephen Stills — out of which he somehow emerged a sinister bigot rather than a playful provocative sod who'd had a few — is still related as if it had occurred the week before. As a result of it, or at least of the way it was reported, he became no stranger to the occasional death threat, although he did his best to eliminate the spectre with a sizeable (and successful) US tour.

In Britain the only national pop station, Radio One, is controlled by a new breed of concerned young disc-jockeys with nice haircuts and aspirations who probably consider Costello to be slightly old hat. They are quite happy to play "oldies" — oldies, after all, have acquired a picturesque dignity with which one can't go wrong because they are no threat to the present — but Costello is neither old enough to be safe nor new enough to appeal to career builders.

It might even have been the traditional case of choosing the wrong single. Between the two countries, the three tracks chosen were 'Clubland' (probably his best ever, but too complicated), 'Watch Your Step' (too downbeat, difficult to programme) and 'From A Whisper To A Scream' (too loud, doesn't know its place). In retrospect, 'New Lace Sleeves' now seems like the perfect choice: poignant,

memorable, it positively defies the listener not to be riveted.

The next Elvis Costello LP was recorded in Nashville with Billy Sherrill producing and The Attractions augmented by local players. It featured nothing but country standards and brings to a suitable apotheosis Costello's fascination with the world of shit kicking, revealed in his own compositions like 'Stranger In The House' and confirmed by his mateyness with George Jones. It'll be great but it'll be confining.

After that, he should do a cover version of Nat King Cole's 'Nature Boy'. Then he should concentrate on being the best songwriter in the world. Sinatra, one day, if he has enough of them left, will record 'Big Sister's Clothes'. He won't understand a word of it. But then, that never mattered to Linda Ronstadt.
AL CLARK

SHEENA EASTON

This Sheena is most decidedly *not* a punk rocker. Searching for parallels with the 22 year-old Scot whose rise and rise has been one of the year's most spectacular success stories, one lights instead on such super-safe commodities as Doris Day, Lulu and, most appropriately — both in terms of instant wholesomeness and similarities of appearance too remarkable to be ignored — Julie Andrews.

British pop's new Mary Poppins owes a considerable amount of her current status to her nationwide exposure on a documentary TV show name of 'The Big Time', hosted by that nauseatingly helpful pundit Esther Rantzen. It was the programme's transmission during the summer of 1980 which sent Easton's second EMI '45, '9 To 5' ('Morning Train' in the US) rocketing up the British pop charts, where it peaked at third place for two weeks in mid-August. Sheena Easton's debut single, 'Modern Girl' had been released at the end of February and reached number 56 in the charts, in itself no minor achievement for a first single by an unknown artist (although radio play was made easier no doubt by the presence of hit producer Chris Neil — Dollar, Gerard Kenny — at the controls). The success of '9 To 5' revived interest in its predecessor, and 'Modern Girl' spent four more months in the UK Top 100, peaking at eighth position in the second week of September. '9 To 5' was just on its way down, and the two records crossed each other's paths in the Top Ten in the first week of September, making Easton only the second girl singer to have two records in the Top Ten simultaneously — previous title-holder, Ruby Murray in 1956. '9 To 5' was the ninth best-selling single of 1980, 'Modern Girl' a more modest 47th.

Such statistics (Easton was also the first British female singer to have both her first two singles make the Top Twenty) obviously carry some weight on the international market: '9 To 5' went on to be a smash in Japan and Australia and, Easton's most astonishing feat to date, Number One in the US. Following a national tour alongside production company stablemates Dennis Waterman, the TV tough-guy turned not-so-tough pop star, Gerard Kenny, and Leeson and Vale, authors of her third hit 'One Man Woman' (seven weeks in the Top 100, peaking at 14 in early November), Easton was asked to appear before The Queen Mother in the annual Royal Variety Show, a role ideally suited to what was by now an established archetypal pretty-girl-with-pretty-voice MOR personality.

In nine short months Sheena Easton had gone from being a complete unknown to what's known in the business as a hot property.

And a safe investment. In April of 1981 the trade magazine BILLBOARD carried the news that the Japanese segment of EMI, TOSHIBA-EMI, were about to sink a hefty $200,000 on a three month promo campaign. This followed hot on the heels of a weekly 15-minute radio spot which, said BILLBOARD, "has been instrumental in pushing sales of her single, 'Modern Girl', up to 50,000 copies". By June, Easton's commercial respectability was further enhanced by her recording of the theme song for the latest James Bond film, 'For Your Eyes Only'. Considering her current track record and, more importantly, the vast amounts now invested in her as a commodity, it seems very unlikely that Easton's career will cease to blossom for some time yet. More disappointingly, considering the likeable enough zip which characterised her first three singles, it seems equally unlikely that she will veer away from an increasingly obvious trend towards traditional showbiz standards. Or the mediocrity that this implies.

But the most regular criticisms levelled in Easton's direction rarely have anything to do with her music. Rather, she's accused of being little more than a puppet in the hands of the seasoned old pros who surround her: Deke Arlon, her manager, a self-made showbiz mogul now in his forties who'd started life in a pop group in the late Fifties, toughened up as a pub and fairground bouncer, worked in TV as an actor and, teaming up with a 'Crossroads' co-star both in marriage and business, quickly proceeded to make a fast buck in music publishing, production and management, most notably in collaboration with Ned Sherrin and his various 'Side By Side By ...' confections for the stage and television. Producer Chris Neil has had hits with the aforementioned Dollar and Gerard Kenny and had, in fact, recorded Bugatti and Musker's 'Modern Girl' as an A-side of his own some eighteen months prior to the Easton version. Arlon and Kenny had, between the two of them, claimed the more simple-minded press cynics, constructed Easton to their own design, the one telling her what to wear and how to move onstage, the other telling her what to sing and how to sing it.

To some extent this is bound to be true; that's what managers and producers are for, after all, and it's a role that's been energetically taken up by everyone from, say, Giorgio Moroder (Donna Summer), to Bernie Rhodes (The Clash, early Specials, Dexy's Midnight Runners etc.).

And particularly by Sex Pistols/Bow Wow Wow mentor Malcolm McLaren. How out of character then, to find the self-styled Fagin sniping in Easton's direction

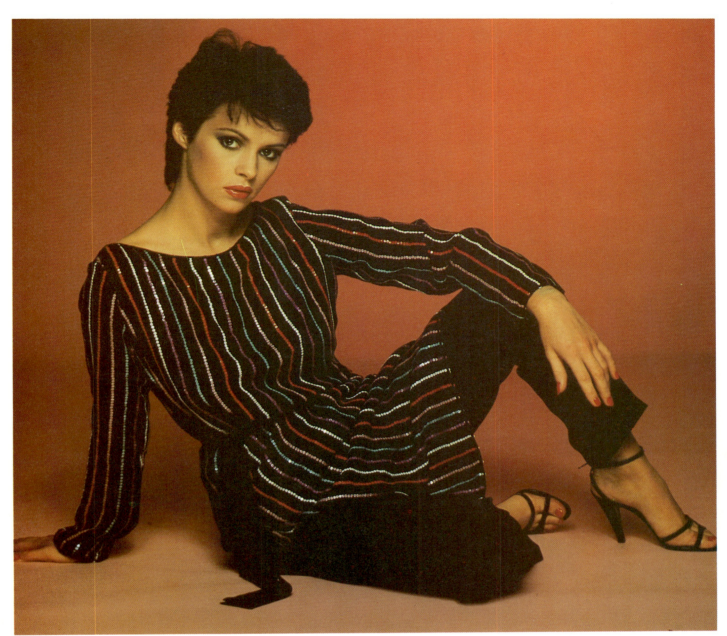

via a SUNDAY TIMES magazine spread. "Music today is much more manufactured than it was," McLaren told the TIMES' Gordon Burn. He went on to suggest that Sheena Easton "was given to EMI by the BBC. With an hour-long documentary in the offing, the company couldn't afford *not* to take her on. Three minutes on 'Top Of The Pops' does after all, virtually guarantee any record a place in the chart".

Easton's EMI audition had been part of the making-of-a-star format of the TV show. But in the same feature, then EMI A&R head Brian Shepherd insists he'd gone to the audition intending to pass, but was overcome by Easton's talent, nothing more. Easton herself is more than used to accusations of a conspiracy. Her invariable reply is to point out that at the time of the audition she didn't even have a manager.

One of six children who were left fatherless when she was ten, Easton's background if nothing if not courageous. Despite coming from a traditionally depressed area, her high academic standards in both 'O' and 'A' level G.C.E's (or Scottish equivalent thereof) earned her a place at the Scottish Royal Academy of Music and Drama, a course which she completed successfully while the 'Big Time' TV show was still being filmed, and she's now a qualified teacher of speech and drama. While at college, she was already supplementing her grant money by singing with a group four nights a week, and from the outset she was nothing if not ambitious. She had, she says, no serious ambitions as an actress, but thought the college training would help in her intended career as a singer. However, she's always been honest about the fact that she had no specific role in mind for herself, that all she really wanted was to be a successful entertainer, and that she'd follow the line of least resistance whether that lead towards pop, rock, Streisand-style balladeering, or even opera!

She is young, attractive, and just enough of a tease to be an accurate translation of Mary Poppins into contemporary terms. Her voice is adequate without being astonishing, and her material is inoffensive at worst. She is most palpably not a feminist, happily reinforcing stereotypes both via her material ('9 To 5') and her regular photo-spreads in the popular tabloid press.

Sheena Easton was perhaps best summed up, if inadvertently so, by Kenji Ogino, the A&R manager for EMI and sister company CAPITOL at TOSHIBA-EMI, upon announcing his company's $200,000 investment in the Scottish cupcake's future. "We believe that Easton will be the star this year," said Ogino, "following Cheryl Ladd last year".

And that's all you need to know about Sheena Easton.
GIOVANNI DADOMO

JOHN LENNON

The conversation had turned to the subject of assassination in general — which nowadays it seems to do more often than feels comfortable — and the murder of Lennon in particular. "Of course", someone said, "he was killed by the CIA. Because he had the ear of the world."

It was a tempting notion at first...But I did not believe it then, and I do not believe it now. Was Lennon *really* that influential, that powerful, a figure — at least in the way they — whomever *they* may be — understand influence and power? Could *they* really be that paranoid? Fantastic enough that the idea should even arise at all. Killed by the CIA...As an idea, perhaps it helps to make sense of what was otherwise the most senseless and horrifying act of violence. One has to blame someone, *something*, after all, for how could anyone truly blame Chapman the assassin; he was, after all, only barmy, bananas, a kook — superfan.

Still, it is a measure of Lennon's standing in the eyes of the world that he is probably the only figure in rock whose death could possibly have prompted that line of speculation. "Most people", Lennon once said, "live their lives vicariously", and he more than anyone was fuel for their fantasies — in death as he had been in life. People have taken from Lennon's murder what they wanted: the belief that they were mourning a prophet or a saint, or a victim of political machinations and power conspiracies. I am pretty sure myself that his death was not, as some have suggested, the death of an era of hope, or the dawn of a era of hopelessness. But it was, perhaps, for a lot of people, the symbol of the death of a part of their own youth, and with it something of their idealism, for it was Lennon more than any other performer who had seemed to keep that idealism alive. Lennon's death provided the opportunity to exorcise ghosts, relive one's own past, dwell in nostalgia, buy a record or a poster or a book (no shortage of any of those), and for those who had actually

always thought him a bit *strange* — not quite as loveable as a Beatle was supposed to be, a bit bolshie — a chance to forgive him his trespasses, his be-ins, bag-ins, bed-ins and all the other things that at the time had raised only a laugh. "Everybody loves you when you're six feet in the ground" wrote Lennon on 'Nobody Loves You' from the 'Walls And Bridges' album. And they did.

Lennon wrote that song during his separation from Yoko Ono, at what was probably one of the lowest ebbs of his life. Following 'Some Time In New York' in 1972, he had experienced a fall from grace with the critics and the record-buying public. Songs about Attica, Ireland, feminism had brought only accusations of political naivety and cause-mongering; and, a constant bone of contention, some people thought there was "too much" Yoko on the record. 'Mind Games', released in 1973, was to only partly rectify his standing. Lennon was living in Los Angeles, drinking more than was good for him — on one occasion becoming involved in a notorious incident where he insulted a waitress while, for reasons which are no longer clear, if they ever were, wearing a tampon on his head. 'Walls And Bridges' came out of that period of solitude and confusion; one of Lennon's most under-rated albums because, possibly more than any other work, it reveals his vulnerability, and his willingness to expose it, as he exposed all things, to public gaze. It was this that made him as endearing as his idealism and strength made him admirable.

Perhaps Lennon was so honest because he was too lazy to think through the consequences of that honesty and therefore censor it. Perhaps he didn't care either way. Certainly he could be tactless, brutal, even vindictive: 'How Do You Sleep' must have wounded McCartney more than he could ever admit. But Lennon, of all the Beatles, gave the impression of caring least what people thought of him, and behaving accordingly. This had not been

the case at the height of Beatlemania when Lennon, it would subsequently emerge, believed himself to be living in a state of almost constant compromise by helping to perpetuate the entire Beatle circus. Certainly, from then on he would never allow himself to become a prisoner of anyone else's expectations. When he wanted to quit the Beatles, he quit. And when he decided, in 1975, that he wanted to retire from music — for all anyone knew, for good, — he retired. It was his prerogative as a human being, no matter what others may have thought were his "responsibilities" as a performer.

What apparently offended so many people so much about Lennon's retirement was it's implication that he was turning his back on "rock and roll" at a time when the music needed him most. The truth of the matter was, however, that Lennon realised even if others didn't, that there were more important things in life than rock and roll, and that peace of mind and the well-being of his family were two of them. That one of the most influential and important figures rock music has produced should, temporarily at least, have attained greater satisfaction from breeding livestock and being what he described as "a househusband" is a salutary blow to the mythology of rock and roll which those who seek salvation in the music would do well to heed.

Ironically, it was those who chastised Lennon for desertion who were to express the most disappointment in the album which signalled his return, 'Double Fantasy'. Those who had loved Lennon at his most vitriolic, accusing or didactic, found the record too inward-looking, tranquil and content. Lennon had emerged from five years of domestic bliss singing about...domestic bliss: the joys of family life, his all-consuming love for Yoko and hers for him; the amenability of role reversal — all with an almost embarrassing candour.

Some appeared to see all this as some sort of abdication of Lennon's responsiblities

to the world at large — whatever they may have been. But what the album rings with is a sense of completeness, of a man who had found himself and laid his torments to rest. In his marriage to Yoko, Lennon had clearly found what every song from 'Help' onwards had yearned for, no matter how obliquely, and 'Double Fantasy' is John and Yoko's declaration of the fact. The key song here is 'Woman', a song, inevitably, about and to Yoko which in its honesty, humility and affection radiates a sense of love and tranquillity which is ultimately more powerful and affecting than the confusion and bitterness of say, 'Working Class Hero'. One is Lennon's pain; the other is what vanquished that pain. It's "political" message, if that is what anyone was in search of, is clear. Lennon's idealism had not been "co-opted" by domesticity; that domesticity was all the ideals in practice, for how else do you start to give peace a chance if not in the trust and love between two people? This is not a message which reduces easily to slogans, or that appears to shift the world perceptibly on its axis, but it is ultimately the most revolutionary of all because all goodness can proceed from it.

What is so cruel, so incomprehensible, is that John Lennon was struck down at a time when he had everything to live for — as an artist, a husband, a father and a man. In the days before the shooting he and Yoko were supposedly in an exhilarated frame of mind. 'Double Fantasy' was selling well. They had been writing and recording prolifically, and there was even talk of live performances. John Lennon was content. Once he had wanted to shake the world — and he had succeeded. But his dreams had become more modest with time. Asked on one occasion to picture he and Yoko at 64 he saw them as "a nice old couple, living off the coast of Ireland or something — looking at our scrapbook of madness". But the madness was to catch up with him long before then.

MICK BROWN

BRUCE SPRINGSTEEN

If 1981 was The Year Of Bruce Springsteen, it was also the year of maintaining perspectives. In a musical climate so drastically fragmented, one figurehead couldn't be expected to unite so diverse a spectrum. At the very least, though, he could serve as a focus for a shared belief in its essential values.

In England, more than anywhere else, Bruce Springsteen's re-emergence was to be felt all the more acutely. At a time when the more over-zealous sectors of the Press were blinded by "mutant dance" and the ridiculous conceits and introspection of The New Romantic Movement, he proved, with the minimum of fanfare, to be the largest concert draw in the entire world. It took many by surprise that a man whose obsessive adherence to beat music's most traditional elements could have won many more hearts than did the frontiers attempting to undermine them. Nostalgic, perhaps; but equally progressive and optimistic.

The statistics spoke for themselves. Springsteen and his E Street Band had left Shea's Buffalo Theatre on May 23 1978 and concluded 109 shows before a total 1,000,000 audience — with only a month off — by January 1 1979. Undaunted by the trials of recording his long-awaited fifth LP, 'The River', Springsteen was back onstage on October 3 1980 at Ann Arbor, Michigan, before it had even been released. Thus began yet another in a series of exhausting treks around the US, the physical strain of his now legendary four-hour sets eventually resulting in a collapse that delayed British and European dates by a required three months.

Despite never having had a hit single in the UK, nor recent promotion through the usual channels (TV/Radio), 300,000 people applied for the available 105,000 seats. Almost simultaneously, an East Coast radio

announcement concerning a concert to inaugurate the new 20,000 seater stadium in New Jersey, coupled with a few bars of 'Born To Run', the State national anthem, drew a staggering half million ticket requests in only two days. Springsteen's name had never even been mentioned.

As the tour drew to a close, the E Street Band had played to a further 1,000,000 people, subsidised by CBS to the tune of $1 million, apparently without condition. Sales of 'The River' had doubled in England alone in the few weeks Bruce had been in the country.

'The River' had, in typical Springsteen tradition, defied the established rock business "process". The yawning gap of over three years since his last album, 'Darkness On The Edge Of Town', had threatened to be disastrous in the eyes of an industry attuned to an increasingly rapid turnover of style and product. Still in the shadow of various litigations — against agency, management and the persistent bootlegging of his unrecorded material — Springsteen had defied all expectations and come up with a truly epic double album. It was a

development in every way: he'd compounded the sparkling romantic vision with its vantage point of the back alleys of night-time New Jersey; he'd repointed the production to a clarity that managed to combine both the music's drive and complexity in a way that sounded both simple and spontaneous; and, more importantly, he'd built upon the essence of the E Street Sound. Already spanning two normally separate sectors of the market — in Steve Van Zandt's observation of black Sixties soul and Bruce's own sinuous white rock'n'roll roots — the new styles embraced were simply stunning. 'The River' material sounded the primal depths of his country's heritage — beat, C&W, dustbowl, rockabilly. Enhanced onstage by Woody Guthrie's 'This Land Is Your Land', and by the usual string of hard rock'n'roll encores, it wouldn't be an overstatement to suggest that Springsteen '81 represented nearly four decades of American tradition — delivered with the most awesomely powerful live performance rock music can ever really hope to perfect. Even those who'd grudgingly entered the out-dated

spaciousness of the 8,000-seater Wembley Pool were stunned by the man's intimacy and the warmth and projective strength of his sound.

What little that could be unearthed by the Press revealed Bruce to be a deal more cautious than on his last UK visit nearly six years ago. He refused to entertain any formal interviews, and had his obvious reasons; the various legal debacles and the twin-cover "hype" assault of TIME and NEWSWEEK back in 1975 had certainly left their scars on a man determined to maintain control of his own destiny. (Strange, though, that he talked to selected journalists for over an hour and yet refused to be tape-recorded, thus laying himself open to misquotation.)

There were inevitable attempts to demean his talents, and they seemed to take effect. It was widely assumed that two shots by the NME to discredit the personality behind the lyrics — and, with it, the supposedly outmoded Great American Dream — had made his Wembley debut a conspicuously wary one. The British liked his music, 'The River's' sales confirmed it. He was less confident as to whether they liked its presentation too. Only mid-way through his UK dates did he revert to his celebrated onstage monologues.

The last, and not least, factor in establishing Springsteen this time around has to be the Dave Marsh biography. Inevitably titled 'Born To Run', it was scheduled — as was the 'No Nukes' movie — to coincide with his British visit, and the timing was crucially exact. This exhaustive and touchingly enthusiastic chronicle was about as near as anyone could hope to get to the man Marsh post-scripts as "the last of rock's great innocents", adding: "There can never be another quite like him".

No-one who saw him would beg to differ. MARK ELLEN

STRAY CATS

The Stray Cats' success was as dramatic as a rather corny movie script. They arrived in London in the summer of 1980, unknown and broke, after wisely deciding that the British music scene held better prospects for them than in their native New York. They found friends and help, started playing around the clubs, and quickly attracted a devoted following for their updated brand of rockabilly. The record companies jostled to sign them, and they landed themselves an old-fashioned, highly profitable deal. They then notched up hits with their first three singles and first album — despite the fact that they were even better live than on record.

Within a year of leaving New York they had not just found fame and (even more difficult) rock respectability, but they had gathered some very distinguished patrons. Several of the Rolling Stones publically enthused about The Cats, and by mid-summer it was revealed that the Stones were considering asking the Stray Cats to join them as support band for their long-delayed return to perform in the States, and maybe Britain, if the tour actually went ahead.

Bill Wyman, the Stones' bass player, became particularly friendly with the trio, as he made clear during an interview in which he was supposed to be promoting his soundtrack for the film 'Green Ice'. For him, the Stray Cats were in many ways the Eighties version of the Rolling Stones. "There are lots of similarities in the way they started and the way the Stones started. They've come out on their own, playing a completely different music to what's been in the charts. Then they've got a different line-up (guitar, stand-up bass, minimal drums) just as we had in the early days when we had maraccas, harmonica and tambourine. Then they look different — they've got tattoos, distinctive hairstyles,

and a different image, like we did. It's the sort of image that — well, you wouldn't want your sister to marry one of them. It's the same old thing — we were very raw when we played live, and they are as well, but tough."

And of course there are similarities in the way both bands had updated classic early rock styles. "We were steeped in Fifties Rhythm and Blues, and they are into that Gene Vincent, Eddie Cochran early echo guitar rock'n'roll stuff. Then there are more similarities — they are taking off far bigger live than they are on record, they are a great live band just as we were a great live band. And they are enormous in France where we were much bigger than the Beatles..."

You can't argue with that. But then perhaps it wasn't

surprising that of all the new bands around, a blues and early rock enthusiast like Wyman should like the Stray Cats most. For of all the new musical styles of the early Eighties — futurism, electronics, pop pirates, or the still developing ska and reggae scenes — the Cats had their music the most rooted in the past, even if it's dressed up with contemporary lyrics and presentation. It's significant that guitarist Brian Setzer sites his favourite music as the songs of Gene Vincent and Eddie Cochran, along with Amos Milburn and Etta James, and his favourite guitarists as bluesman John Lee Hooker, jazzer Charlie Christian, and rocker Cliff Gallup from the Gene Vincent band. In other words, rockabilly and early rock, but

with a touch of swing and jazz thrown in there as well.

Rockabilly enjoyed a remarkable revival during 1981, largely because of the success of the Stray Cats. Various other types of rocking mog also appeared in the British clubs — bands like The Pole Cats or The Blue Cats. For mass audiences, the "rockabilly revival" might have appeared to be something new, but in fact a strong rockabilly cult had been building up in Britain, and in Europe, during the Sixties and Seventies. The music itself was, of course, an all-American style, a danceable, cheerful, jumped-up form of country music (with a little boogie, R&B and Western swing added in) that had flourished from 1954 to 1959. Those light but vital glorious tracks that Presley first recorded for SUN are an example of rockabilly at its best. In the Sixties and Seventies, the style faded from popularity in America (though good-time bar-room bands like Commander Cody were likely to keep a little rockabilly in their repertoire). But in Britain and Europe, rockabilly fans sought out the old records, and even sought out the old artists like Charlie Feathers, who were brought over to tour.

In retrospect, then, it makes perfect sense that the Stray Cats should have brought their music over to Britain and done so well here (particularly as the power and simplicity of rockabilly also fitted well into the post-new wave British club scene). But what that doesn't explain is why three kids from Long Island, New York, should have been so steeped in rockabilly in the first place.

Guitarist Brian Setzer, bassist Lee Rocker and drummer Slim Jim Phantom had all played in a variety of different bands around Long Island or Manhattan before they got together and turned to rockabilly. Setzer had played in one set of bands, while Lee and Slim had played together in another,

performing in bars, at parties, and "wherever they could". Setzer, the son of a construction worker, had in fact acquired something of a local reputation even before the Stray Cats got going. He sites his early musical influences as Presley, the first Beatles album, and Hank Williams, because those were the records his parents had around the house when he was growing up. But the band with which he first made his reputation in New York was apparently more influenced by early Roxy and Eno.

The Bloodless Pharaohs certainly had very little in common with the Stray Cats, at least judging from the two tracks of theirs that have been released over here, on the Marty Thau compilation of new New York bands. '2 x 5' (released here on CRIMINAL RECORDS. Both the Pharaohs' tracks on the album were co-written by Setzer, according to the credits, and neither is particularly inspired. Both Bloodless Pharaoh and Nowhere Fast are cool, controlled, pounding, and ultimately rather ponderous. The first song is an over-long work-out around a predictable, repeated chord sequence, with a little fancy keyboard work over the top. Bloodless Pharaohs was the band that took Setzer in to Manhattan, to play at Hurrah's, Max's or the Mudd Club. All very impressive, except for the fact that Setzer didn't like the music. So he joined Lee and Slim to start a new rockabilly band.

In an interview back in the summer of 1980, he described the attraction of rockabilly like this. "There's something so cool about it — the clothes, the hairstyles. The spareseness of the music is so exciting. It had the same thing that attracted me to punk — the rebellion and the sense of style." The new Stray Cats apparently eased gently into their wild form of updated rockabilly, and after building a following on Long Island they moved in on the Manhattan clubs. The initial reaction was apparently cool, but after playing around Manhattan for almost a year they began to develop a following. Then they decided they were fed up with the place and set out for London.

Their success in Britain was due in part to the fact that they were playing the right new music at the right place at the right time, and in part to the fact that they were lucky enough to meet up with some of the more helpful people on the British scene. They were introduced to Claudine Martinet-Riley, then working for Keith Altham, publicist for The Who and the Rolling Stones. Claudine started trying to get them gigs, while Keith (who had been impressed by a tape they'd played him) started putting the word around about the band, and let them stay in his office. The band had only $1,000 between them, and when not at Keith's they crashed out at such romantic haunts as the Scala all-night cinema.

Then they started to play, and they made the corny movie script story come true. When I first saw them — down at the Half Moon pub in Herne Hill, south London — it wasn't the hairstyles or tattoos that seemed so remarkable, but rather the instrumental line-up. It was odd enough that a bunch of young toughs should be playing with a stand-up bass and a tiny drum kit, but quite remarkable that they should produce such a sound from such equipment.

The Stray Cats, I suspect, will remain more of a live band than a recording band, but their recording debut was certainly no disgrace. They kicked off with a truly inspired single, 'Runaway Boys', that managed to encapsulate their image of contemporary teenage rebellion and updated rockabilly with a mood that's both sleazy and romantic. Dave Edmunds produced, adding echo and a live drum sound to Lee's stomping, descending bass line. The next single, 'Rock This Town', was almost as good, though more in the conventional rock 'n' roll format, while the third, 'Stray Cat Strut', was a slinky, rhythmic croon that showed off the more controlled side of Setzer's voice. All three were taken from the band's first album, 'Stray Cats', that was at its best (which means very good indeed) on those tracks produced by Edmunds. Elsewhere, songs like 'Fishnet Stockings' sounded more like rockabilly revival than anything new, while the stomping 'Storm The Embassy' was a display of American political macho thinking at its most naive. But then in a corny movie script success story like this you can't have everything.

ROBIN DENSELOW

TALKING HEADS

"We're not the same as we were" understated rock's favourite twitchy presence, David Byrne, before proving it to the valiant 5000 assembled in New York's Central Park in September 1980.

Indeed, a zap through this last turn of the zodiac has shown Talking Heads are nothing at all like they were. From being the cerebral end of the new wave to being the celebrated spearhead of the afro-punk polyrhythmic party; from numbering four to numbering nine; from being cult darlings to commercial dynamite. This was the year Talking Heads finally became famous.

A glance over Byrne's shoulder is in order to see just how far the winds have changed (to mix metaphors). A member of Rhode Island School of Design (conceptual art major, naturally!), Byrne met up with Chris Frantz and Tina Weymouth in the early Seventies and formed a dance band known as The Artistics which got transmuted to

Autistics by some bright but dyslexic spark.

Expelled from art school for compiling questionnaires ("People reacted strongly because it wasn't 'art related'. They thought I was just some nut infiltrating the art community" he told Roy Trakin of BOULEVARD). Byrne moved to New York where, in early 1975, he formed Talking Heads with Frantz and Weymouth and took up residence in that punk mecca, CBGBs. They were later joined by Jerry Harrison, who had recently left The Modern Lovers.

A year and a half after that, Seymour Stein signed them to SIRE and released the album 'Talking Heads '77'. The rest, as common parlance has it, is history.

The summer of 1980, however, saw the Heads at a major crossroads. 'Fear Of Music' nutshelled the crisis. Looking both forward and backward, the album was seen as the zenith of the Heads' previously successful format.

Embodied in songs such as 'Life During Wartime', 'Air', 'Cities', were the quintessential characteristics of the familiar Head style — fingernail-regarding lyrics, the manic detail contrasting with the block-hard rhythm sections overlaid on disjointed shards of melodies. The presence of the opening track 'I Zimbra' in the midst of all this familiar stuff was weird to say the least. The result of the collaboration between Byrne and Eno and their twin interest in the mystical quality attached to African chant music, 'I Zimbra' was much the most arresting of all the tracks on the album.

In July, the record company released 'Cities' as a single and it fell flatter than a learner's soufflé. The daytime d.j.'s were still not ready for the band whose "difficult" status had stuck to them like flypaper.

Stories had started circulating about a possible rift between the Weymouth/Frantz

partnership and the Byrne headship. Whilst Byrne was holed up in the West Coast reading books about African tribal rhythms with Eno turning the pages, Frantz and Weymouth went to Jamaica to hang out with the likes of Lee Perry, and Sly and Robbie, no doubt debating who exactly was the finest rhythm section in the world. Meanwhile, Jerry Harrison amused himself with producing bands like The Escalators in New York and a French band who had supported the Heads in Lyon. "They're actually quite good," he told Paul Rambali. "They write songs about fucking in elevators..."

The two knob-twiddling kids had their experiment in filtering Afro-tribal kineticism through the Western technology ready and waiting to be released. 'My Life In The Bush Of Ghosts' inspired by 'African Rhythm And African Sensibility' by John Miller Chernoff, was not to see the light of day for a while. The evangelist shouter used on one of the tracks had upped and died, leaving the family less than happy about granting the go-ahead for the album. The project was put on hold until after the release of 'Remain In Light'.

But, as usual, the quality of a band is made up by the sum of its parts and if those parts go off and pursue other interests it can only be an advantage when those parts get back together again.

When Talking Heads played in Central Park that day last September, the culmination of all their extra-mural interests was evident in a nine-piece skin-tight funk outfit. "This ain't no party, this ain't no disco, this ain't no foolin' around," said Byrne. He wasn't kidding. Double the personnel, double the attack, and twice the fun(k). The Heads had undergone something of a sea-change.

Eschewing the awkward, spotlight-avoiding persona of yore, Byrne jerked and

danced and spasmed all over the stage, playing it up to the hilt. The extra guitarist was Adrian Belew, he of the hysterically passionate squeezed guitar style which so heightened Bowie's last albums. Keyboardist was Bernie Worrell — Parliament/Funkadelic star. The percussionist was Steve Seales: bassist was Busta "Cherry" Jones; and Dolette McDonald sang and rattled anything that needed rattling. The Talking Heads funk wagon had started to roll.

In November, the Heads released their fourth album, 'Remain In Light', produced by Eno, featuring the now nine-headed Heads and a recommended reading list for the critics from Byrne who could never resist the temptation to conduct seminars.

The album was greeted with suspicious applause. It was good, but it wasn't Talking Heads. There were even fears for Byrne's sanity — had he finally plumped for normality, they wondered. As always, Talking Heads had proved themselves to be a band who kept pushing back the frontiers of possibilities;

they had given the complacent cult acceptability that surrounded them a good kicking which had produced ripples of applause that spread ever increasingly outwards.

Gone were the self-obsessed, disaffected lyrics about Middle American middle-class mediocrity to be replaced by a series of chain-effect chants and exchanges, a triple-tiered construction of replies and answers that dealt with the breakdown of society rather than that of the individual.

The swirling polyrhythmic forces at work in all the songs were part of the dervish dance that made them so attractive. At once, horribly complicated in construction and yet simply commercial, it was the irony of the songs that their instant appeal almost negated the Byrne/Eno theoretical treatment.

In December, the T-Funk wagon rolled up to the twin Hammersmith venues in London — the seated Odeon and the dancing Palais. Reviews were mixed since the band neither gelled properly on the key songs nor

could they handle the demanding chorus interchanges. But Talking Heads continued to be respected because they refused to stagnate or to operate within circles they have already proven work.

In March, this acceptability found a concrete expression. 'Once In A Lifetime', one of the best tracks off 'Remain In Light', finally got on the TV programme, 'Top of the Pops' in recognition of its Top 14 position in the charts. The video which accompanied it — Byrne's impersonation of a man trying to learn to swim on dry land — was a highlight of the programme and an extraordinary sight.

'My Life In The Bush Of Ghosts' was finally released to the sighs of Eno/Byrne fans alike and proved to be everything we had expected. Researching even further the textures and soundweavings of the East, 'My Life' utilised all manner of percussive instruments for its effects — including spare car bits.

Meanwhile, the component parts of Talking Heads went about their own business — a characteristic of which has served to keep the freshness

of the band alive. Weymouth and Frantz retired to their home in the Bahamas and formed the Tom Tom Club with Monte Brown, T-Connection's guitarist and Jamaican producer Steve Stanley on keyboards. In June they released 'Wordy Rappinghood' on ISLAND, a neat piece of exotica. An album is promised for the summer months.

Headmaster Byrne is satisfying his work ethic by producing the B52's — an inspired piece of coupling. Meanwhile, the Heads are expected to return to the studio in September to record their fifth album.

So, the end of term report reads like the Headboy forged it. Three gold stars for achieving the seemingly impossible: to have taken the cult status awarded them for their new wave art school beginnings and broadened it out to include a kind of campus acceptability and commerciality being won without the loss of either the original driving impetus of the unique funk-filtered band, or a stagnation or compromise in their music.
FRANCES LASS

WHERE ARE THEY NOW?

Last year's favourites pursued and their activities (or lack of them) revealed by Ian Cranna

PRETENDERS

The Pretenders did the next best thing for their reputation short of retiring — tantalising the public by withdrawing from the scene while their interest remained high. In this case, however, it was more by necessity than by design. November 1980 saw the band in a Paris studio to start on the follow-up to their acclaimed debut album but lack of material — a legacy of the constant touring of the year before — meant that only five or six songs were recorded. The hit single 'Message Of Love' was one of these.

The band then took a break to write some new material. Ignoring the pressures for new product from the US — where public demand had sent the five-track twelve-inch 'Extended Play' EP soaring up the Top 100 album chart — wisely concentrating on quality, enhancing their standing still further by not releasing second rate material.

Following a further period of absence from the public

eye for rehearsals, The Pretenders slipped quietly back into a London studio to complete the second album. They emerged at the end of June with the announcement that, whatever the subsequent critical opinion, they themselves considered it better than their first and then braced themselves for a further round of touring.

In a quiet period for the group which saw almost as many private as public engagements — drummer Martin Chambers and

guitarist James Honeyman Scott both got married in the Spring (though not to each other) — it was the affable Chambers who emphasised The Pretenders' commitment to quality not quantity.

"We're willing to risk a time lapse," he said. "We're willing to risk losing a few fans. We want to make really good records — that's the main thing."

If the rest of the music industry thought the same way, it would have considerably fewer problems.

— 128 —

After a year of doing more granting than taking, 1981 was the year that 2 TONE became taken for granted. Having been left to carry the banner alone by the departing Selecter, The Specials virtually became 2 TONE. The Swinging Cats' 'Away' and Rico's 'Sea Cruise' and 'That Man Is Forward' album provided them with their first non-hits and the honeymoon with the public was over. The Swinging Cats went through more line-up changes in a few weeks than most football teams manage in a season and together with the opportunist Bodysnatchers (some of whom regrouped in The Belle Stars and signed to STIFF) soon passed away, leaving few mourners.

The Specials themselves however reminded everybody that they were in a different league with an unbroken succession of Top 10 hits —

which also served as a reminder of the band's collective writing strength — and a brilliantly adventurous album in 'Mor(e) Specials' which deservedly enjoyed considerable critical and public acclaim. In The United States both albums went Top 100 but none of the singles took off.

In Autumn 1980 The Specials embarked on an ill-fated British tour, taking with them a brass section of Rico and Dick Cuthell plus former Swinging Cat Paul Hesketh on sax. After unpleasant mini-riots at Cardiff and Newcastle, a full scale fracas erupted in Cambridge during which Terry Hall and Jerry Dammers were arrested for "using threatening words and behaviour". In fact they had been trying to stop the fighting, for which they were fined £200 each plus costs in January in a blatant

miscarriage of justice.

Around this time the 'Dance Craze' film was also being put together from live footage of The Specials, Madness, The Selecter, The Beat and The Bodysnatchers plus Bad Manners, together with old cinema newsreels of old dance crazes. (It was eventually released as a sort of documentary without commentary in March to mixed reviews.)

For all these Specials activities Jerry Dammers had assumed full responsibility in order to get it right as he saw it. Instead it now looked as if he might crack under the pressure so a break and a radical re-think was undertaken.

In future, it was decided, there would be no more general touring, just one-off gigs for specific purposes — like fund raising for local racial harmony organisations — so that everyone would

know why they were there. Secondly they would only release records as and when they felt it necessary.

The Specials then took a holiday from being The Specials to indulge in various solo projects. Brad formed RACE RECORDS and put out releases by Team 23, Night Doctor and The People. Neville co-founded SHACK RECORDS with his girlfriend Stella of The Belle Stars and released singles by 21 Guns (who included two Specials roadies), Lieutenant Pigeon and Eddie Peters. Roddy formed a sideline band called The Tearjerkers while Dammers himself worked on a single 'The Boiler' with Rhoda Bodysnatcher.

Whether all these activities mean that The Specials will lose their impetus or that they will return with renewed energy remains to be seen. Personally I'd put a lot of money on the latter.

THE SPECIALS

SELECTER

The sound of splitting was the dominant theme of the past year in the turbulent history of The Selecter. The band's departure from 2 TONE was accompanied by claims that their ideas were being hampered but The Selecter didn't exactly flourish in their new found freedom with CHRYSALIS.

As the euphoria of 2 TONE evaporated, increasing friction among the different styles of an essentially ad hoc lineup led to rows that were public knowledge and eventually scuppered their stated ideal of sticking together. First to leave was keyboards player Desmond Brown, to be followed shortly after by dreadlocked bassist Charley Anderson who was asked to leave. Both subsequently ended up with original Specials drummer Silverton in a band called The People who signed to Brad of The Specials' RACE RECORDS.

Replacements were recruited in the form of James Mackie (horns and keyboards) and Adam Williams (bass) from Lancashire band The Pharoahs. The band then took their management into their own hands, toured hard and released a second LP 'Celebrate The Bullet' to politely encouraging but hardly enthusiastic reviews. Public acclaim for the album and singles was similarly muted.

A Spring tour of the UK was followed by yet another split, with charismatic lead singer Pauline Black leaving to follow a solo career. Leader Neol Davies then appointed a male replacement but despite his optimism for the future, it seems that with the band's failure to capture their live excitement on vinyl or indeed to pen truly memorable melodies, a large question mark hangs over the future of The Selecter.

THE BEAT

In many ways The Beat proved to be the surprise package at the 2 TONE party. Another ad hoc line-up, The Beat grew together where The Bodysnatchers fell apart. They also went for an altogether gentler approach, opting for a girl instead of a man as a logo and adopting the smoother rhythms of reggae instead of the aggro-inclined, skinhead-dominated primitive jerk of ska.

The Beat also contributed something of worth to the music scene, a rare combination of beauty and brains who jogged the nation's conscience by singing about things that mattered, like racial unity and nuclear threats. And they didn't just sing, they acted as well — donating a cool £15,000 worth of royalties from the 'Best Friend'/'Stand Down Margaret' single to the Anti-Nuclear Campaign last Christmas. All this while rejecting the whole star trip and remaining thoroughly nice, approachable people. Above all The Beat were a band you could trust, and seldom has a band been so worthy of that trust.

The Beat's ability to write good songs also meant that they had hits and lots of them, while their second album 'Wha'ppen', a subtler development of the pop tunes of their first, also sold well. The band's American development was hampered by their label SIRE being swallowed up by the giant WEA company but they were kindly received on live dates with The Pretenders and Talking Heads.

The Beat also used the powers of their own GO-FEET label to put out records by other people, including the reissue of a classic reggae album 'The Heart Of The Congos' at a cheap price and a single by local Birmingham band The Mood Elevators. The two Davids, Steele and Wakeling, also contrived to appear as actors in photo-strip stories for the romance magazine PHOTO LOVE!

In between all this activity, The Beat found time to tour, doing charity gigs with The Specials in Ireland, dates and festivals in Britain, Europe, Scandinavia and Ireland as well as returning to The United States and Canada.

The future for The Beat looks healthy enough, as indeed it should. We could do with a few more like them.

THE CLASH

After the impact of and the impetus given to their career by the successful 'London Calling' double album, the following twelve months was a disappointing period for The Clash.

The closing months of 1980 had seen the band in a London studio adding yet more to the marathon session that had begun months earlier in New York and which was finally to emerge in December as the ungainly and uneven triple album 'Sandinista!' (Oh well, quality control in the idea department was never The Clash's strong suit.)

Ill focussed and sloppily executed, 'Sandinista!' duly received a welcome from critics and public that might diplomatically be called lukewarm. Some writers were even unkind enough to suggest that some of it should never have been released and that a low price was no real substitute for quality.

Disappointed by this response, The Clash sought solace in a European tour and outside work, notably Strummer and Jones writing half of and producing all of Jones' girlfriend Ellen Foley's second album, 'The Spirit Of St. Louis'. On a less serious note Topper Headon also appeared in full evening dress playing tympani in 'The 1812 Overture' with a classical orchestra in London's Albert Hall.

Come Summer of 1981 and The Clash headed back to America (where 'Sandinista!' had also received a lukewarm response). A well publicised contretemps involving angry scenes over fire limits at a New York gig — the affair was played out over a full week — then served to reawaken public interest in The Clash and 'Sandinista!' finally crept up and into the American Top 40 albums chart. It was not a little ironical that The Clash's empty leather jacketed bravado should provide such ideal consumer fodder among those who wanted a New Wave but couldn't take the real thing in a country The Clash themselves once professed to despise.

But undoubtedly the major event in those twelve lacklustre months was The Clash's managerial reunion with the formative influence of Bernie Rhodes — though whether they are still together as you read this is another matter altogether. Perhaps he will put some real spark into The Clash, for in a year when their self-created image and the music they actually put out were at such complete odds, never has their narcissistic dependence on the power of the camera stood so clearly revealed.

THE JAM

The Jam confirmed their position as one of Britain's most creative and ambitious groups in 1981 while at the same time managing to keep the rat race of the music business firmly at arm's length and conduct their life at their own pace and in their own down-to-earth fashion.

The final months of 1980 found The Jam touring Britain and Europe before retiring to complete work on their fifth album 'Sound Affects' which was released in November 1979. As usual with Weller's individual and aggressive talent it was well received by press and public alike, while the band's adventurous singles continued to make spectacularly high chart entries.

Following the release of the album, the band then went back on the road in Europe, followed by dates in Japan, Scandinavia and Canada. The response to their very British sound improved in Europe though the reaction in America must once again count as disappointing if not altogether surprising, in view of The Jam's adamant refusal to compromise their music to suit American radio. Response, however, to live dates in the more receptive regions of New York and Boston was encouraging.

The band's concern for their fans and giving value for money meant that a second single was not pulled from 'Sound Affects' but demand for their music was such that a European import single of 'That's Entertainment' was imported in sufficiently large quantities for it to reach the British Top 20. The band, powerless to stop it, could only sit and fume.

Meanwhile Paul Weller's enthusiasm for other media, notably the printed word continued. After a brief closure, his publishing company, RIOT STORIES, made a comeback with the fanzine format, enabling him to publish a couple of anthologies of young writers at lower cost. The only other outside project involving The Jam — Bruce Foxton's managerial involvement with The Vapors — ended around the beginning of the year due to lack of time available for proper involvement.

Further recording and touring commitments seem likely to keep The Jam busy until early 1982. When asked if there were any particular highlights for him over the past twelve months, Paul Weller replied that there weren't any. Unlike most people, however, he wasn't complaining. "I've enjoyed it all," he said.

GARY NUMAN

When you proclaim that "This Is The Year Of Gary Numan", as this book did last year, the underlying assumption is that Gary Numan is at least going to be around for a while. 1981 however saw Gary Numan retiring — from live gigs at any rate — and thus doing the best possible for his reputation short of actually dying: leaving the public to want more while his stock was high.

'Telekon', Numan's fourth album, was released in September 1980 to a barrage of disdainful critical sniffing — not that that affected its sales, or the hit singles taken from it. Numan's real crime in the eyes of the critics was not so much to do with the music as with the myth. Numan saw the music business much too clearly for everybody's comfort and worse still, he was painfully honest about it. He simply did not say the right things.

Numan never made any great claims. Instead he always gave credit for his sources (the dreadfully unhip Ultravox) and was always quite candid about his limitations, saying his talent was simply as an arranger of noises. He was also well aware of the ephemeral nature of much of his appeal and now, having become a pop star so easily, he was bored and wanted to quit while he was ahead. Heresy!

But quit he did. After having taken his spectacular road show on a tour of Britain and America (where the lack of a hit single like 'Cars' meant that 'Telekon' did less well than 'Pleasure Principle') he bade farewell to live performances — which he had never liked — at London's Wembley Arena in April. Two live albums featuring material from the previous two years were then released separately and together as a box set. That month the box set ('Living Ornaments '79 and '80') was at number one in the British album charts while the individual albums occupied the number eight and twelve positions at the same time.

Gary Numan will continue to make albums, though his contract allows him to deliver them when he likes. For the future however he is more interested in video — video cassettes were released of his Wembley farewell and the new album — and in flying his small plane on a three week trip round the world.

It's doubtful whether the critics matter much to Gary Numan any more but now that all the fuss has died down I don't think a reassessment of his music can be very far off.

BLONDIE

members indulged in solo projects. Debbie Harry toyed with celluloid as well as vinyl, appearing in adverts for Gloria Vanderbilt jeans alongside her serious role as a New Jersey housewife in the film 'Union City' for which she received encouraging reviews. Even before the latter's release, however, Harry had announced plans to appear in another film called 'American Rhapsody' where she was to play an American pop star (an inspired piece of casting) with whom a Russian pianist falls in love. On the recording front, she also spent much of the first half of 1981 cutting her solo album with the CHIC ORGANISATION'S team of Edwards and Rogers.

Chris Stein meanwhile, apart from his much delayed book of photographs, designed a Robert Fripp album sleeve, produced a second album for violinist Walter Steding and worked with Iggy Pop on the soundtrack for the film 'Drats'.

Of the others, Jimmy Destri was involved with production work, notably a New York compilation album '2 X 5' and ATCO signing Joey Wilson; Clem Burke was managing and producing New York teen band The Colors and preparing his drum tutor book; and Nigel Harrison was renewing his acquaintance with former Silverhead colleague Michael Des Barres by co-writing and playing on an album, and by playing in an occasional band called Chequered Past.

As a unit Blondie are committed to at least one more album. After that it's anybody's guess though it must be doubtful if anybody really cares anymore.

"I say that to entertain people is enough; Chris (Stein) thinks we should be doing something more." Thus did Debbie Harry neatly sum up the choices facing Blondie as they pondered how best to follow up the phenomenal success they had achieved to date. In the event it was hard to tell who won.

The last weeks of 1980 saw the band recording the 'Autoamerican' album under the guidance of producer Mike Chapman. A deliberate attempt to diversify, the album received a panning from the critics though it also proved to be their most successful commercially so far — especially in America — and also spawned several hit singles. Including as it did stabs at everything from reggae to rapping to a song from the musical 'Camelot', it also marked the completion of Blondie's transition from tough New York street kids to all-purpose emasculated American radio fodder.

It wasn't long after the start of 1981 that the group put its collective future on hold while its various

THE POLICE

September 1980 saw a typically tight close to a high speed and event-packed twelve months for The Police. At 4 am they finished recording their third album in a studio in Holland and the same afternoon they started their European tour in Belgium.

The album, 'Zenyatta Mondatta', received a lukewarm welcome from the critics but that didn't stop it going triple platinum in Britain as well as providing an important breakthrough in America which had hitherto remained largely indifferent to The Police. The album also provided its quota of hit singles, though once again the Americans proved hard to charm.

Three charity concerts in Britain at Christmas were followed by a wise break from what threatened to become a serious case of media overexposure for the band in Britain as they continued their far flung touring — Europe, South America, North America, Japan, New Zealand and Australia.

Spring 1981 saw Stewart Copeland and Andy Summers taking a well earned rest while Sting opted for a change — he renewed his career in front of the cameras by playing the part of the Angel of Love in a psychological thriller for television called 'Artemis '81'. Otherwise individual projects were few in number though Sting did record Dylan's 'I Shall Be Released' for the theme tune of the American TV show 'Parole' while in New York in January and his lyrics to 'Message In A Bottle' were published with his approval as illustrated by two young English fans Sharon Burn and Rossetta Woolf through VIRGIN BOOKS.

Following a further break from the public eye to write and rehearse, The Police then disappeared to Montserrat to record their fourth album. All things considered, I see no reason why The Police's considerable personal charisma, writing talent and capacity for sheer hard work should not continue their deserved success through the next twelve months.

MADNESS

To those who expected Madness to fade with the passing of the 2 TONE boom, their subsequent career must have been a real revelation. They may have been sloppy as hell as a live band but in the studio producers Langer and Winstanley waved their magic wands and Madness, with their wonderful visual sense, captured imaginations and hearts galore with their intuitive blend of catchy songs, nutty humour and all-purpose teen appeal.

Both in Britain and elsewhere, Madness proved they could outlast any passing fashion with a superb run of worthy hit singles penned by assorted band members and helped on their way by a series of inspired videos from the collective wit and wisdom of the band themselves and STIFF RECORDS boss Dave Robinson. One single, 'Baggy Trousers', was in the British charts for nearly four months.

Nor has their success been confined to the singles chart. Madness have had at least one LP in the British chart since October 30 1979 — a remarkable feat. In fact, Madness have consistently outsold their benefactors The Specials everywhere but America where their relationship with SIRE RECORDS has been something of a disaster area.

The past twelve months of Madness have also been notable for the marriages of Woody (to Jane Mo-dette) and Mike Barson (to his girlfriend Sandra), the band's pioneering of matinee concerts for younger fans excluded from licensed premises, tours of Australia (where they nearly lost Lee to a giant wave on Bondi Beach), Japan and America, plus six weeks out in the Spring to make their first feature film, 'Take It Or Leave It', scripted and directed by Dave Robinson with the nutty boys playing themselves and covering their history from 1976 to 1979.

The only real question for the next twelve months is simply how long can Madness keep up such a remarkable quality at such a remarkable pace?

TOM PETTY

Tom Petty's heartfelt wish for 1982? "For once in my life I'd like to make a record without a legal battle."

Just when it looked as if things were finally working out for Petty and his band after the quantum jump breakthrough of the 'Damn The Torpedoes' album, another confrontation with MCA — owners of Petty's BACKSTREET label contrived to spoil matters yet again. This time the row was about a proposed $1 price increase proposed by MCA which would take the price within two cents of the $10 mark, with Petty threatening not to finish work on the album if this went ahead.

While Petty's management were complaining about the damage this increase would cause to Petty's reputation as a "rank and file" rock star, Petty himself was plain enough, accusing MCA of greed and saying that they didn't "need another tower".

Eventually Petty — who provided MCA with around 25% of their profits last year — won and MCA backed down. "It's a great example of what can be done" said Petty as the new album went out at the old price. 'Hard Promises' turned out to be a conscious attempt to sound rougher than previously, with more emphasis on the songs than worrying about the sound. It sold well but didn't reach the same heights as its predecessor, though the single 'The Waiting' did capture the Number one spot. British response was very low key, not helped by Petty's continued absence.

Otherwise it was a fairly quiet year for Petty — old troubles with tendons and tonsils apart — as he continued touring in his undemonstrative fashion round America, confirming his reputation as the creditable, non-loudmouth, non-neurotic normal American boy. Reluctant to analyse his intuitively honest music — "It ain't rock'n'roll once it's an English class" — Petty is still down to earth enough to avoid the Hollywood star ghetto and to be concerned that his fans get value for money. Few would deny him his wish for 1982.

FILMS

AMERICAN POP
Ralph Bakshi
If you're looking for a movie that will really set your teeth on edge, look no further. This contains some of the most pretentious and annoying moments in animated film history, and it would be preferable to sit through six thousand Woody Woodpecker cartoons than see it again. The characters are thoroughly unlovable, except as very young children, and they drag you through the gutters of alcoholism and drug addiction for two of the longest hours known to man.

ARCHIE POOL/BABYLON

BRINSLEY FORDE/BABYLON

BABYLON
Franco Rosso
Part backed by the National Film Finance Corporation and the Chrysalis group, and part subtitled to make it intelligible to the outsider, this combines old-style battle-of-the-sound-systems excitement and new-style alienated-and-harassed-black-youth political emphasis. Memorable score, impressive photography, creditable performances, but can stray into caricature to make a point.

DANCE CRAZE

DANCE CRAZE
Joe Massot
Two-Toners past and present on stage: The Specials, Bad Manners, The Selecter, The Bodysnatchers, Madness and — a cut above the others — The Beat. Goes on a bit.

DEAD ON ARRIVAL
Lech Kowalski
Fragmented Sex Pistols documentary concentrating mostly on their first and last US tour in January 1978, but also including an extraordinary interview with Sid Vicious and Nancy Spungen. The question really is who cares anymore.

THE DECLINE OF WESTERN CIVILISATION
Penelope Spheeris
A celluloid representation of West Coast punks, still living out some preposterous NATIONAL ENQUIRER idea of the way they ought to behave. Depressing in the extreme.

DIVINE MADNESS
Michael Ritchie
Shot over four days of Bette Midler concerts at the Pasadena Civic Auditorium, this elaborate deification is built on the customary mixture of sly expertise and knowing vulgarity which her audience relishes. Midler herself — like a cross-current of Barbra Streisand and some fun-town brothel madam — is unyieldingly on-the-ball.

THE IDOLMAKER
Taylor Hackford
Based on the career of Bob Marcucci, who pulled the strings for Fabian and Frankie Avalon and gave them to the world without serious retribution. A revealing and entertaining glimpse of the process behind the invention of a pop star (and the concomitant hysteria), but doesn't really go the whole way.

THE JAZZ SINGER
Richard Fleischer
Transparently a "vehicle" for the introduction of Neil Diamond to cinema audiences, this lavish reconstruction of what was once Al Jolson's finest moment is big on production values, negligible on characterisation beyond the cardboard. Laurence Olivier, who is rapidly lapsing into caricature, gives one of his Jewish impersonations.

McVICAR
Tom Clegg
Roger Daltrey, looking increasingly like a scaled-down Action Man, plays the superstar of British criminals in this questionable adaptation of his autobiography. Could easily have been intended for television, and indeed probably was.

MORE AMERICAN GRAFITTI
B.W.L. Norton
More Sixties nostalgia, lacking any of its predecessor's charm, all split-screen and parallel-narratives. Passable enough, but lacking any real conviction and reeking of opportunism.

DOLLY PARTON/NINE TO FIVE

NINE TO FIVE
Colin Higgins
Lightweight but amusing tale of office mutiny, in which a tyrannical boss finds himself suspended from his bedroom ceiling while the aggrieved trio of secretaries who put him there improvise their victory. Fonda, Tomlin and Parton's pot party is the best scene in the film.

DEBBIE HARRY/UNION CITY

REGGAE SUNSPLASH II
Stefan Paul
Bob Marley, Peter Tosh, Third World and Burning Spear filmed during the festival of the same name at Montego Bay. Superficial, tiresome and not even particularly well filmed, it is the ultimate European trendy's view of reggae.

ROCK SHOW
director not credited
Wings filmed on stage in Seattle in 1976. Hardly of great significance at the time, it now seems utterly inconsequential.

BOB MARLEY/REGGAE SUNSPLASH

THIS IS ELVIS
**Malcolm Leo
and Andrew Solt**
Fulfilling the aspirations suggested by its title, this is the model film biography, featuring an abundance of often rare documentary material, some recreated scenes and, above all, a real sense of the individual. Surprisingly candid too, when one considers there was co-operation from the Presley estate.

TIMES SQUARE
Alan Moyle
Punk and New York, as viewed by the Robert Stigwood Organisation. Possibly one of the worst films ever made, it even succeeds in wasting a moderately good soundtrack.

UNION CITY
Mark Reichert
Creditable debuts for Reichert and Debbie Harry, effectively underplaying a bored, unfaithful accountant's wife in 1953 New Jersey. Music by Chris Stein and a brief appearance from Pat Benatar.

URGH! A MUSIC WAR
Derek Burbridge
Modest, effective introduction to many of today's more interesting (and exportable) groups. Well filmed, but only as enjoyable as the band performing at the time.

XANADU
Robert Greenwald
A laughable load of old cobblers in roller-disco clothes, with Olivia Newton-John, a doddering Gene Kelly and a thousand nonentities.

BOOKS

THE ARRIVAL OF B.B. KING
(Doubleday)
Charles Sawyer
The now customary examination of the mechanics-behind-the-myth.

CHASE THE FADE
(Blandford)
Anne Nightingale
The recollections of a Radio One disc-jockey, including the Isle of Wight Festival, Keith Moon's familiar atrocities and The Police in unfamiliar locations. Cheerful, engaging, but pointlessly and disproportionately expensive.

THE CLASH, BEFORE AND AFTER
(Eel Pie)
Pennie Smith
All photos — and very good ones at that — of a group which, for all its inflated double and triple albums and barricades-storming aspirations, really does nothing better than get its picture taken.

DAVID BOWIE BLACK BOOK
DAVID BOWIE IN HIS OWN WORDS
JOHN LENNON IN HIS OWN WORDS
(Quick Fox/Omnibus)
PINK FLOYD, AN ILLUSTRATED DISCOGRAPHY
ROLLING STONES, AN ILLUSTRATED DISCOGRAPHY
THE TWO-TONE BOOK FOR RUDE BOYS
THE JAM
THE RAMONES
THE PRETENDERS
THE CLASH
TALKING HEADS
(Omnibus)
Miles

Eleven new instalments from the world leader in part-affectionate, part-opportunistic quickies. The first, without pretending to be either profound or analytical, is an ideal Bowie compendium and has the additional advantage of *looking* really impressive. The second and third are the expected amalgam of elementary wisdom and the wholesale daftness, agreeably presented. Four and five are exhaustive chronicles of every bleep and fart, including bootlegged ones, by the groups in question. The remainder are routine beginners' guides, straight from the filing cabinet, thin, messy but well documented. The Talking Heads one is no bigger than the others but seems so.

DAVID BOWIE, AN ILLUSTRATED DISCOGRAPHY
(Omnibus)
Stuart Hoggard
The recordings employed as a backdrop for the story everybody seems to want to tell. Concise and informed, it acts as the completists' counterpart of Miles's 'Black Book'.

A DAY IN THE LIFE
(Quick Fox/Omnibus)
Tom Schulteiss
The chronological minutiae of The Beatles. More than you would want to know presented in a manner which might make you want to know less.

DEEP BLUES
(Viking)
Robert Palmer
A history of the blues, normally to be avoided for the same reasons as books about Morris-dancing (tedium incarnate for the outsider), but in this case livened somewhat by an appealing emphasis on the people who made it happen.

ELECTRIC LIGHT ORCHESTRA
(Mushroom)
Bev Bevan
ELO drummer tells story of world's most faceless group, reinforced by plenty of photos, which make them only marginally less so.

ENCYCLOPEDIA METALLICA
(Bobcat)
Brian Harrigan and Malcolm Dome
The story of Heavy Metal assembled by two of its most assiduous enthusiasts. Really little more than a heavily illustrated extended article, the live photographs providing a risible catalogue of poses. Even *reading* this sort of stuff deafens you.

ENCYCLOPEDIA OF BRITISH BEAT GROUPS OF THE SIXTIES
(Omnibus)
Colin Cross with Paul Kendall and Mick Farren
Mandatory reading for those interested in the likes of Andromeda, The Beatstalkers, The Cherokees, The Doughnut Ring, Eyes Of Blue, Ferris Wheel, The Giant Sun Trolley, Harmony Grass and The In Crowd, or for those wondering who they were. A bit like a stamp collector's manual, but interesting browsing fodder for fact fetishists.

FREE SPIRIT
(Mushroom)
Angie Bowie
For all its brazen sensationalism, bad poetry and prose of purest Mirror-ese, a thoroughly readable and extremely well presented account of fame by proxy.

GARY NUMAN BY COMPUTER
ADAM AND THE ANTS
(Omnibus)
Fred and Judy Vermorel
In accordance with its title, Numan's book looks and reads like an especially pretentious computer manual. Adam, meanwhile, likes sex and skiffle. He also likes African tribal music, erotic art, Bauhaus, Futurism, Dadaism, Nietzsche and "the kids". He doesn't like Malcolm McLaren, British films or old punks.

THE GIMMIX BOOK OF RECORDS
(Virgin Books)
Frank Goldmann and Klaus Hiltscher
Twelve inches square and full of colour reproductions of rare, illustrated, oddly-sleeved or funny-smelling records. Its sizeable errata slip rather deflates the intended air of authority, and there are too many exclamation marks for comfort (or indeed irony) in the captions. Engaging enough otherwise.

HAVING THEIR PICTURE TAKEN: THE BOOMTOWN RATS
(Star)
Peter Stone
Lots of photos. Negligible text. Pointless.

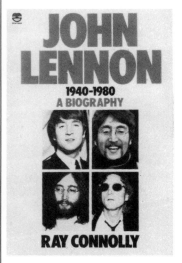

JOHN LENNON, A BIOGRAPHY
(Fontana)
Ray Connolly
The familiar mixture, written stylishly and with some authority. A sound, well-assembled summary.

SHARON BURN/STING/ROSSETTA WOOLF

JAH MUSIC
(Heinemann)
Sebastian Clarke
Solid, substantial study of reggae, outlining its evolution in historical as well as musical terms. Occasionally betrays its origins as an "education" book but is mostly educational in the best sense.

KATE BUSH
(Proteus)
Paul Kerton
There is no chance that anyone will write an interesting biography of Kate Bush until she has something to say for herself. She still doesn't and this litany of clichés confirms that nobody is going to say it for her. Impressive pictures though, and well reproduced.

THE LENNON TAPES
(BBC)
Andy Peebles
Peebles became a minor celebrity out of this exchange, recorded shortly before Lennon's death in December and milked in various ways after the event. Interesting enough, but nothing that isn't expressed more candidly in the PLAYBOY interview.

MESSAGE IN A BOTTLE
(Virgin Books)
Sting, Rossetta Woolf and Sharon Burn
Sting's lyrics to the song presented in bottle shape and, unsurprisingly, dominated by its colourful illustrations. Laughably flimsy, it manages to include four pages which feature no more than a word each. One of them is "an".

MOON THE LOON
(Star)
Dougal Butler with Chris Trengrove and Peter Lawrence
Former Who roadie and Moon minder spills the beans and reinforces the myth. A sorry (but funny) tale of drunkenness and debauchery related in the appropriate vernacular. Full of bacon assegais, beaver pies, berks, bints, crumpet, moolah and woofers.

THE NEW MUSIC
(Harmony/Bay Books)
Glenn Baker and Stuart Coupe
Attractive enough in appearance, and useful enough in its sheer undiscriminating range (despite omissions), this is the ultimate press release book. Anything, it would seem, is the New Music.

THE ROCK MUSIC SOURCE BOOK
(Doubleday/Anchor)
Bob Macken, Peter Fornatale and Bill Ayres
Subtitled "a thematic guide to the popular music of our time" and prefaced by a hilariously solemn introductory section, positively suffocating with caring-aware-rock-fan clichés, this massive book of subject-divided lists somehow omits the subject chronicled so obsessively by hippy groups for the past fifteen years — *rock and roll itself man!* A commendable book in many respects — and an invaluable one for disc-jockeys and journalists with short memories — it seems to have nothing at all to do with the present. Towards the end, the authors choose your record collection for you.

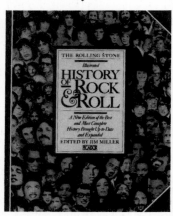

THE ROLLING STONE ILLUSTRATED HISTORY OF ROCK AND ROLL 1950-1980
(Random House/Pan)
edited by Jim Miller
The Victor Mature of rock books, all size and oiled biceps. Jumbo illustrated 30-year survey in the form of articles whose sum total tries to tell the tale. Doesn't, but makes it enjoyable for those in possession of very large desks.

SHOUT!
(Simon & Schuster/Elm Tree)
Philip Norman
Far from being impaired by the absence of The Beatles' own reminiscences, this exhaustive (and exhausting) Fabs biography benefits instead from the concomitant objectivity. Always literate and informative, occasionally revealing, it is, one hopes, the last word on a subject pleading for clemency and a long holiday.

THE ROLLING STONES IN THEIR OWN WORDS
(Quick Fox/Omnibus)
David Dalton
What you'd expect.

STRAWBERRY FIELDS FOREVER
(Bantam/Corgi)
Vic Garbarini and Others
Supposedly written and published in the fortnight after Lennon's death, this contains his interview with NEWSWEEK. Competence personified but lacking any qualities of consequence.

STYLE WARS
(Sidgwick & Jackson)
Peter York
Not much to do with *rock and roll* as such — except at the point where it overlaps with the way its followers view themselves — but without question the most tendentious, perceptive, funny and readable book of the lot.

SUN RECORDS
(Omnibus)
Colin Escott and Martin Hawkins
The record label chronicled. No detail is left unturned for those who want to know.

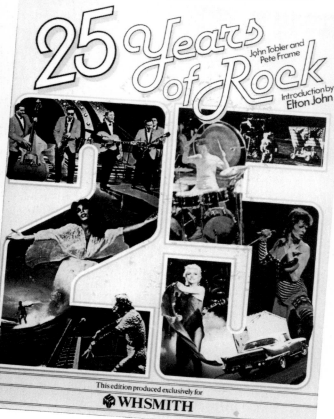

WOODY GUTHRIE, A LIFE
(Knopf/Faber)
Joe Klein
A biography of Guthrie, a treatise on folk music and a socio-political examination of what they both meant to American culture. As weighty as this suggests.

VISIONS OF ROCK
(Proteus)
Mal Burns
Clearly intended as a belated sequel to 'Rock Dreams', with the same mixture of gaudy illustration and pretentious text. Probably the most dated and redundant book of the year.

25 YEARS OF ROCK
(Hamlyn)
John Tobler and Pete Frame
The book of the BBC radio series. Good looking, comprehensively illustrated but ultimately insubstantial, it never really gets beyond the needs of the novice at whom, presumably, it is aimed. Both Tobler and Frame — who has disowned it since some "creative" editing took place — are capable of being witty as well as encyclopaedic. This permits them to be neither.

YOUR CHEATIN' HEART
(Simon & Schuster)
Chet Flippo
Biography of Hank Williams emphasising his considerable liabilities as well as obvious assets. In the style of Jerry Hopkins's Elvis Presley biographies, with similar candour and regard for detail.

BEST & WORST

A section in which our contributors, camouflaged by anonymity, are encouraged to make
all kinds of opinionated and boorish judgments about album covers, people they think are going
to be successful, people they'd rather just went away and what counted most for them during the year.
Some are included as a result of unanimous voting; others are just petty prejudices.

◆

ALBUM COVERS
OF THE YEAR

— SELECTED/REJECTED —

JOHN LENNON/YOKO ONO
DOUBLE FANTASY (GEFFEN)
Design:
CHRISTOPHER WHORF/ART HOTEL
Photography:
KISHIN SHINOYAMA
Art Direction:
JOHN LENNON/YOKO ONO

DAVID BOWIE
SCARY MONSTERS AND SUPER-CREEPS (RCA)
Design/Illustration:
EDWARD BELL

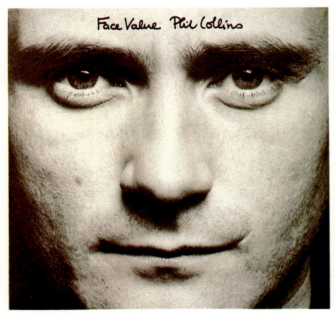

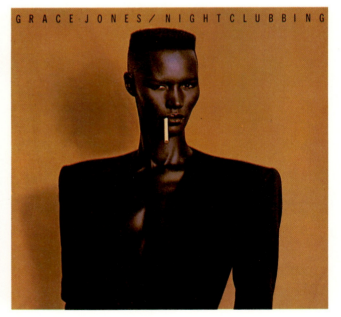

GENE CHANDLER
JUST BE TRUE (CHARLY)
Design:
HAMISH

PHIL COLLINS
FACE VALUE (VIRGIN)
Design:
PHIL COLLINS
Photography:
TREVOR KEY

SLOW CHILDREN
SLOW CHILDREN (ENSIGN)
Design:
PAL SHAZER/COOKE KEY
Photography:
BRIAN COOKE

GRACE JONES
NIGHTCLUBBING (ISLAND)
Design/Illustration:
JEAN PAUL GOUDE

SELECTED

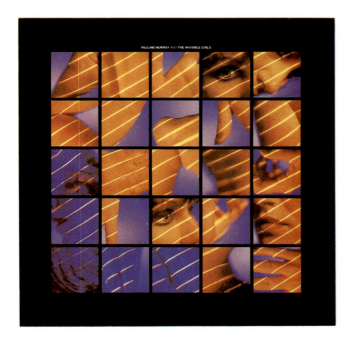

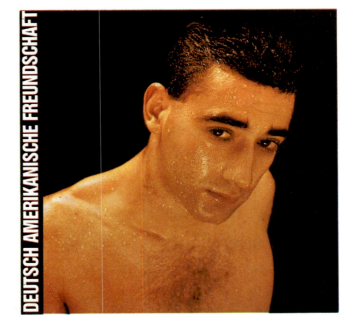

PAULINE MURRAY AND THE INVISIBLE GIRLS
PAULINE MURRAY AND THE INVISIBLE GIRLS (ILLUSIVE)
Design:
PETER SAVILLE
Photography:
TREVOR KEY

JOHN CALE
HONI SOIT (A&M)
Concept:
ANDY WARHOL
Design:
JOHN VOGEL
Photography:
FRED LOREY

ECHO AND THE BUNNEYMEN
HEAVEN UP HERE (KOROVA)
Design:
MARTYN ATKINS
Photography:
BRIAN GRIFFIN

DEUTSCH AMERIKANISCHE FREUNDSCHAFT
ALLES IST GUT (VIRGIN)
Concept:
GABI
Photography:
SHEILA ROCK

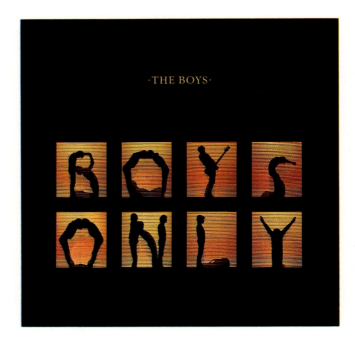

ORIGINAL MIRRORS
HEART-TWANGO & RAW-BEAT (MERCURY)
Design:
PETER SAVILLE

KID CREOLE AND THE COCONUTS
FRESH FRUIT IN FOREIGN PLACES (ZE RECORDS)
Design:
TONY WRIGHT

THE BOYS
BOYS ONLY (SAFARI)
Design:
JOHN GORDON
Photography:
GEOFF HOWES

THE UNDERTONES
POSITIVE TOUCH (EMI)
Design:
BUSH HOLLYHEAD

SELECTED

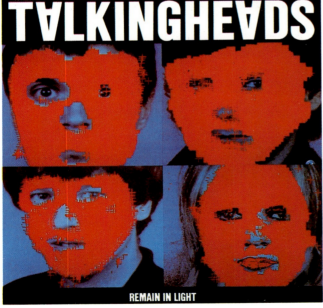

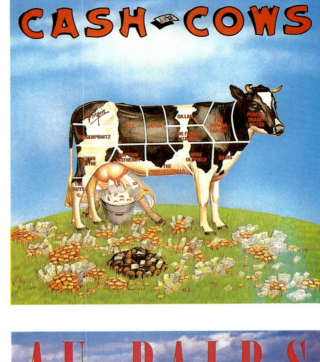

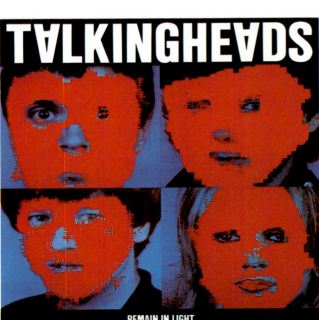

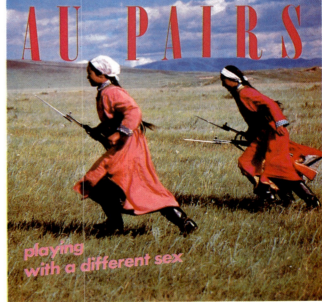

JOE JACKSON BAND
BEAT CRAZY (A&M)
Illustration:
WILLIE SMAX

TALKING HEADS
REMAIN IN LIGHT (SIRE RECORDS)
Design:
M & CO., NEW YORK
Computer Images:
HCL, JPT, DDD, WALTER, GP, PAUL, C/T

VARIOUS ARTISTS
CASH COWS (VIRGIN)
Design/Illustration:
THE SMALL BACK ROOM

AU PAIRS
PLAYING WITH A DIFFERENT SEX (HUMAN RECORDS)
Design:
MARTIN/ROCKING RUSSIAN
Photography:
EVE ARNOLD

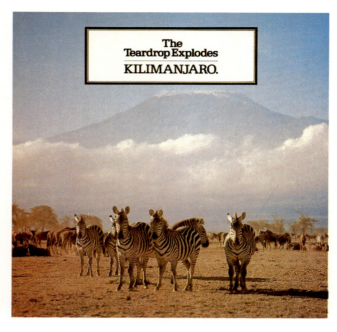

THE WHO
FACE DANCES (POLYDOR)
Design:
PETER BLAKE
Graphics:
RICHARD EVANS
Portraits painted by:
BILL JACKLIN/TOM PHILLIPS
COLIN SELF OF NORWICH
RICHARD HAMILTON
R.B. KITAJ/MIKE ANDREWS
ALLEN JONES/DAVID INSHAW
JOE TILSON/DAVID HOCKNEY
CLIVE BARKER
HOWARD HODGKIN

PATRICK CAULFIELD
PETER BLAKE/DAVID TINDLE
PATRICK PROCKTOR

**MAX ROACH FEATURING
ANTHONY BRAXTON**
ONE IN TWO-TWO IN ONE
(HAT HUT RECORDS)
Design:
ROBINE CLIGNETT
Illustration:
KLAUS BAUMGARTNER

THE TEARDROP EXPLODES
KILIMANJARO (MERCURY)
Design:
MARTYN ATKINS
Photography:
ARDEA LONDON

XTC
BLACK SEA (VIRGIN)
Concept:
ANDY PARTRIDGE
Photography:
CHRIS DENNEY
Backdrop:
KEN WHITE

REJECTED

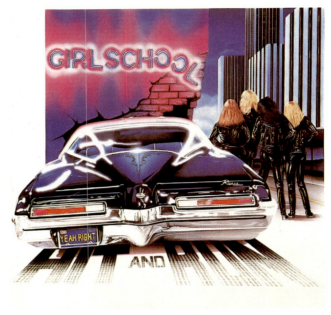

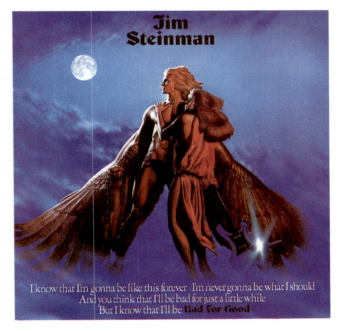

THE TEARDROP EXPLODES
KILIMANJARO (MERCURY)
Design:
ROCKING RUSSIAN
Photography:
BRIAN GRIFFIN

GILLAN
FUTURE SHOCK (VIRGIN)
Painting:
ALAN DANIELS

GIRLSCHOOL
HIT AND RUN (BRONZE)
Design/Illustration:
ALAN DANIELS

JIM STEINMAN
BAD GOR GOOD (EPIC)
Concept:
JIM STEINMAN
Design:
JOHN BERG
Illustration:
RICHARD CORBEN

REJECTED

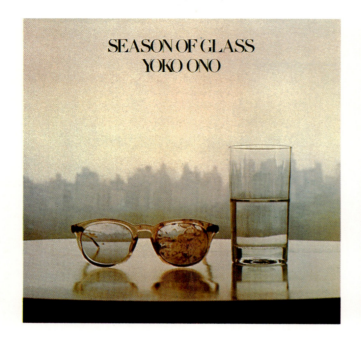

YOKO ONO
SEASON OF GLASS (GEFFEN)
Design:
YOKO ONO
Photography:
YOKO ONO
Artwork:
CHRISTOPHER WHORF/ART HOTEL

THE MOODY BLUES
LONG DISTANCE VOYAGER (THRESHOLD RECORDS)
Design:
CREAM
Painting:
COURTESY OF ARTS UNION, GLASGOW

TOYAH
ANTHEM (SAFARI)
Concept:
TOYAH
Illustration:
STEVE WESTON
Design:
JOHN GORDON

RAINBOW
DIFFICULT TO CURE (POLYDOR)
Design:
HIPGNOSIS
Photography:
HIPGNOSIS/MAXON

REJECTED

JUDIE TZUKE
I AM THE PHOENIX (ROCKET)
Design/Illustration:
KEITH McEWAN

BARBRA STREISAND
GUILTY (CBS)
Visual Coordination:
TONY LANE
Photography:
MARIO CASILLI

HAZEL O'CONNOR
SONS AND LOVERS (ALBION)
Design/Illustration:
EDWARD BELL

VISAGE
VISAGE (POLYDOR)
Design:
VISAGE
Illustration:
IAN GILLIES
Typography:
KATE WILSON

REJECTED

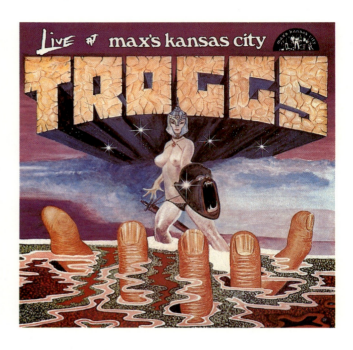

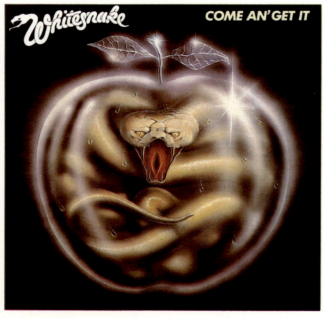

THE ROLLING STONES
SUCKING IN THE SEVENTIES (ROLLING STONES RECORDS)
Design:
JOHN PASHE

WHITESNAKE
COME AN' GET IT (LIBERTY)
Design/Illustration:
MALCOLM HORTON

TROGGS
LIVE AT MAX'S KANSAS CITY (MAX'S KANSAS CITY)
Design/Illustration:
GERALD FIFER

LANDSCAPE
FROM THE TEA-ROOMS OF MARS...
TO THE HELL OF URANUS (RCA)
Graphics:
JOHN WARWICKER-LE BRETON
Photography:
RAY MASSEY
Tea Cup and Saucer:
CAROL McNICOLL

REJECTED

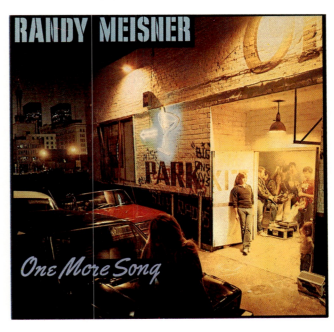

IRON MAIDEN
KILLERS (EMI)
Illustration:
DEREK RIGGS

FATS WALLER
AT THE ORGAN (ACADEMY SOUND AND VISION)
Design:
A THOMSON/CHESS CREATIVE SERVICES

RANDY MEISNER
ONE MORE SONG (EPIC)
Design:
KOSH
Photography:
AARON RAPOPORT

THE BEAT
WHA'PPEN? (GO FEET RECORDS)
Design/Illustration:
HUNT EMERSON

REJECTED

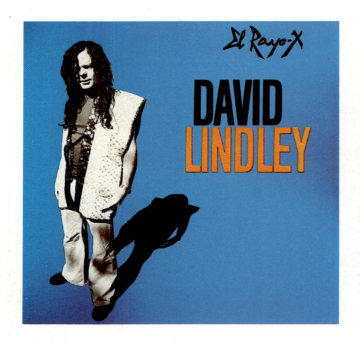

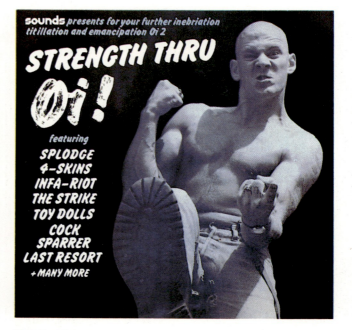

DAVID LINDLEY
EX RAYO-X (ASYLUM)
Design:
JIMMY WACHTEL/DAWN PATROL
Photography:
KAZ SAKAMOTO
Typography:
GLORIA VON JANSKY

KIM CARNES
MISTAKEN IDENTITY (EMI AMERICA)
Design:
BILL BURKS
Photography:
DAVID ALEXANDER

TENPOLE TUDOR
EDDIE OLD BOB DICK AND GARY (STIFF)
Design/Illustration:
ED TUDOR

VARIOUS ARTISTS
STRENGTH THRU OI! (DECCA/SKIN)
Concept:
GARY BUSHELL
Photography:
MARTIN DEAN

THANKS...
— FUTURE FORECASTS —

OK JIVE

ALTERNATIVE TV REFORMED

KID CREOLE & THE COCONUTS

WAH!

THE CRAMPS

SQUEEZE

JACKIE LEVEN/DOLL BY DOLL

PRINCE

JAPAN

KIM WILDE

WAY OF THE WEST

SIMPLE MINDS

ECHO & THE BUNNYMEN

AZTEC CAMERA

THE BELLE STARS

LINDSAY COOPER

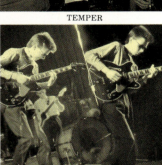

TEMPER

FREEEZ

DEPARTMENT S

BUMBLE & THE BEES

JOSEF K

RICHARD MAZDA

KIRSTY MacCOLL

RICHARD STRANGE

ORANGE JUICE

...BUT NO THANKS

— PAST AGONIES —

GARY NUMAN

STEVE STRANGE

TOYAH

CHICK COREA

KELLY MARIE

HEAVY METAL

THE EAGLES

HAZEL O'CONNOR

LOGOS WITH BACKWARD LETTERS

NUCLEAR WEAPONS

KEITH JARRETT

B.A. ROBERTSON

REVIVALS IN GENERAL

THE OLD GREY WHISTLE TEST

SPANDAU BALLET

THE WAY IT WAS

— RANDOM MEMORIES OF A YEAR —

BRUCE SPRINGSTEEN ON STAGE

MADNESS' VIDEOS IN GENERAL

JOHN LENNON'S ASSASSINATION

ADAM AND THE ANTS
AT THE RITZ IN NEW YORK
(WHERE MOST OF THE ROCK PRESS
COULDN'T GET IN TO REVIEW THEM)

BOWIE'S 'ASHES TO ASHES' VIDEO

SEBASTIAN COE

RONALD REAGAN'S NEAR MISS

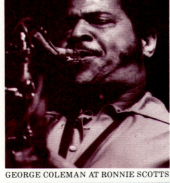

GEORGE COLEMAN AT RONNIE SCOTTS

OZZY OSBOURNE
AND THE DECAPITATED DOVE

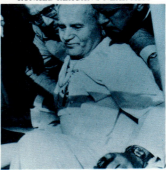

THE POPE'S NEAR MISS

THE CND REVIVAL

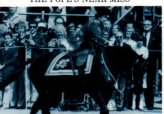

THE QUEEN'S NEAR MISS

THE ROYAL WEDDING

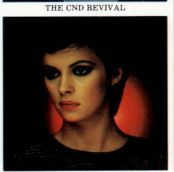

THE RISE OF SHEENA EASTON

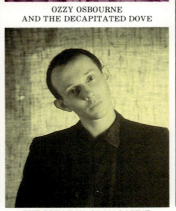

THE BREAK-UP OF MAGAZINE

BOB MARLEY'S FUNERAL

TRANS-OCEANIC CROSS-FERTILISATION

How the Copeland brothers cocked a snook at the tyrants of disc

Small is beautiful, but big is...BIG. As manager of The Police, Miles Axe Copeland 111 is just BIG. On the other hand through a hyperkinetic confusion of energy, imagination and luck he could still turn out to be the most significant entrepreneur of the new wave in Britain and, especially, in America. He's outlasted McLaren, outshone Rhodes and outreached Rivera.

Which seemed less than likely back in March, 1977, as he reassembled the fragments of his broken BTM empire into the rickety shape of FAULTY PRODUCTS. Even the logo was printed upside down to tell the world what to expect.

Out went his "progressive" stable of Wishbone Ash, Renaissance, Climax Blues Band and Curved Air and in came the first singles from Sham 69, Chelsea, Squeeze and brother Stewart's little band The Police (their would-be punk effort 'Fallout'). Out went grandiose budgets for recording and self-indulgence and in came raw punk very cheap. The FAULTY umbrella covered Miles' labels, ILLEGAL, STEP FORWARD and DEPTFORD FUN CITY plus distribution of dozens of other tiny independents.

On the new scale of values the initial releases sold brilliantly — maybe 10,000 copies each. Against an outlay of a few hundred pounds this solution wasn't only danceable, it was profitable, it was practical. Fuelled by loathing of the older bands' excesses which had so nearly finished him, Miles took inspiration from what was happening all around him.

Mark Perry editing *Sniffin' Glue* on the floor of his office, a new band every night, a deluge of home-made demos. Acumen and gut-feeling co-mingled. At thirty-two, Miles

MILES COPELAND

discovered youth culture — he admits to being an accountancy rocker before — and he had a dream of a FAULTY future.

Voice rising like a passionate chainsaw he declaimed: "Right now we have a job to do. We have to take this generation and make it fulfil itself." This was before he switched to contact lenses and the evangelical gleam of his spectacles when he said such things was fearsome to behold.

FAULTY rode the punk rollercoaster with panache that year, but the first step beyond purely parochial excitement was early in '78 when Miles' agent brother Ian returned to their American homeland they'd

rarely seen because of their father's work as a senior CIA officer around the Middle East.

Ian got a job with the PARAGON agency, a southern boogie offshoot of CAPRICORN RECORDS in Macon, Georgia. There was no punk nowhere outside New York. Patti Smith, The Ramones, Talking Heads, Television and that was it. British front-runners like The Pistols, Clash and Stranglers had gone over, treated America as the enemy and been greeted with matching hostility. The prospects were numbing — but the Copelands were all adrenalin and, given a free hand, Ian set about reviving the torpid American club circuit.

Translating the FAULTY tactic into American terms, the brothers tackled it from the basement up. Ian fixed the gigs and Miles volunteered Squeeze, who he managed, as guinea pigs.

Fly over by Laker. Hire a van and a back line. Drive it yourself. Hump it yourself. Stay in cheap hotels in double rooms. Stun the promoter by taking the 200 dollars he'd be paying a local band. Everywhere you go spot the hippest kid on the street and ask what's the best radio station and record shop. Go and chat them up. Kick ass. And break even!

Because of fair pay and savings allowed by in-house PAs it could be done, when in the UK it would have been impossible. A&M did back Squeeze with $8,000, but in the autumn The Police, without support or safety net, blazed the trail for the independents. Barnstorming from Poughkeepsie to Willimantic, Swissvale and Centerville they played twenty-three gigs in twenty-seven days and grossed $7,142. "The Copeland Tour" had begun. For the first time British bands could travel America irrespective of whether they had a record deal.

Soon Freddie Laker's planes were cluttered with guitar cases. Bands made out. Some even struck it rich. Unfashionable 999 brought home $25,000 from two jaunts. Ultravox, in a trough after their original ISLAND contract had lapsed, not only made $11,000 on the tour but attracted the attention of CHRYSALIS (USA), which duly led to 'Vienna' and Number One.

However, Miles' overall strategy was "cross-fertilisation" rather than invasion. Traversing the Atlantic like a computer table-tennis blip his next move was to stir up indie-level American bands to come to Europe. It seemed reasonable, but this is where the wings started to wiggle.

Ghoulabilly artists The Cramps, who had a couple of own-lable singles out, signed to ILLEGAL and came over to promote their 'Gravest Hits' debut release in summer '79.

Although they went down fine with audiences their presence revealed a huge gulf between Miles's Manhattan and Ladbroke Grove activities. A former FAULTY employee (a composite figure, hereinafter "FFE") says: "I'd never heard of The Cramps until Miles flew in from Washington, threw a few snaps and a date sheet down and told us to get on with it, then looked at his watch and flew off again. This was a fortnight before the band were due in and we didn't even have a demo to listen to.

"The trouble is working for Miles there's a complete lack of connection between one room and another, let alone one continent and another."

Worse was to follow in the uncompromising shape of Root Boy Slim, a gross error by Miles in many senses. The band were abysmal live. On a very long tour guesting with Ian Dury they were booed off most nights. Their ILLEGAL album, which was actually quite entertaining, sold less than 1,500 copies and they were a very large band to feed and water.

FFE was in anguish: "We felt threatened by this American influx which had no relevance to our lives. We could work the English bands on a really tight budget. But start to fly people over, put them up in hotels and you were bleeding the company dry." For their part the Americans didn't seem willing to rough it in the way FAULTY'S British exports would.

Apart from the arithmetic these episodes hardly expressed respect from Miles for the commitment and creative skills of his staff. My impression is that temporarily he had lost his soul to sheer velocity. With The Police's 'Message In A Bottle' and 'Reggatta De Blanc' simultaneous UK Number Ones broad strokes of the brush were the thing.

By a complete accident he and Ian both went "independent" in the US at the same time in late summer '79, as record label and

agency. For Ian it happened suddenly because the fall of CAPRICORN RECORDS brought down PARAGON. Just married, a baby on the way and three bands on the road, he moved rather fast. PARAGON closed on a Friday and the following Monday he was installed with a desk and a phone in New York — the FBI (Frontier Booking International) was born and the "Copeland Tour" continued its growth without pause for breath (though sustained briefly by The Police leaving the $13,000 from one of their post-'Roxanne' tours with Ian to tide him over).

Meanwhile, Miles was ready to launch the similarly punful IRS (International Record Syndicate). He'd struck a unique deal with A&M. He would deliver most of the FAULTY/FBI roster of British

new wave acts while A&M would pay for pressing and distribution and donate office space in their Los Angeles HQ for IRS to handle their own cheap production, marketing and publicity. But there would be no advances and in return A&M would claim no artistic control and give a high royalty on any sales achieved.

The "major" had bought low-risk access to unknown possibilities. Coupled with FBI, Miles had an unprecedented vehicle to present British bands on American streets. "Because it's such a big country you need a major record company behind you," he argued to those who doubted whether IRS merited its "indie" badge.

It was quite a set-up. The potential was proved immediately when Buzzcocks

and Stranglers LPs sold about 50,000 each. But IRS certainly wasn't any magic trick and before long some of the people involved began to feel that the Copeland record labels were stagnating.

It didn't take Philip Marlowe to spot the main cause of the gripes. The Police explosion was engrossing more and more of Miles's time on both sides of the Atlantic, and, indeed, in Hong Kong, Bombay and Cairo. A more graphic conflict with "the independent ethic" could hardly have arisen.

FFE says that on the occasions when Miles did drop by at FAULTY there would be a roomful of bands and managers "awaiting an audience" with him. And, while they resented seeing so little of him, the staff often

THE CRAMPS

wished he hadn't shown up at all: "It was 'What's he doing here? Come to foul us up again?'. You would be working on a fairly complex project and he'd say 'Drop this rubbish! Root Boy Slim's coming to town'.

"You know, working for Miles you have to be psychic. If you haven't done it before he's told you to do it he has no respect for you whatsoever."

The Fall, the most fiercely idealistic of groups, were among those who couldn't take him any more. Their manager, Kay Carroll, says it was an American tour in the winter of '79 that did it. For three weeks they suffered transport cock-ups and offhand treatment from IRS. When they got home they told Miles they were through.

In retrospect though Kay

concedes that the Copelands arranged the trip at short notice because she threatened to leave STEP FORWARD if they didn't. Then she did when they did. Such band-v.-biz wrangles are rarely one-sided even when Miles is doing his most convincing pantomime-ogre routine.

By contrast XTC guitarist Dave Gregory rhapsodises about the service they received from FBI (they weren't with IRS) on their path-finding tour in early '80: "Ian Copeland is full of enthusiasm. Not like an agent at all. He went to every gig he could get to and he still does.

"We played assorted toilets, washrooms and broom cupboards and drove 13,000 miles in a tiny van. I think the fact that we took on a ridiculous number of dates

and didn't cancel one did us a lot of good in FBI's eyes. We went out with the killer instinct — and we came back killed." But they also scored the support spot on The Police's breakthrough 'Zenyatta' tour and had a US Top 50 album themselves with 'Black Seas' by the end of the year.

Overall the agency's circuit carried on working well enough considering it was in a state of constant experiment and exploration. Its scope stretched from those "toilets" to what Ian is pleased to call "big rooms like Madison Square Garden", and from New York to Los Angeles. After less than two years life FBI was voted one of the top five agencies in the States by the show biz weekly Variety which Ian fondly viewed as a stiff one right up the establishment.

But IRS's role remained worthy and challenging rather than sensational, despite their gravitation from a shed on the A&M lot to a suite of offices. Ultra-straight Miles' proclivity for musicians of a weirdness beyond the ambit of public taste was interfering with his A&R judgement — the androgynous Jim Skafish was destined to follow Root Boy and earlier Copeland protegés W/Jayne County and Cherry Vanilla into obscurity.

If these matters were put to Miles he was wont to point out that at least IRS was surviving in the States while VIRGIN and STIFF beat a retreat and SIRE was absorbed by the WEA conglomerate: "We're the only game in town!"

However, FAULTY PRODUCTS did seem to be going down

bolts — pressing, promotion, marketing and distribution — while FAULTY/IRL provided information, liason and policy.

But what did it all mean? "More investment" by A&M was announced. Miles said: "They're putting up the heavy dollars you need to take an act from 50,000 record sales up to a million." Even if those dollars weren't strictly in the form of advances many thought back to Miles' credo on founding IRS. "We want total freedom. The minute we take an advance they're going to have the right to say 'We're not releasing this. It isn't commercial enough and we won't get our money back'."

FFE was sore distressed at the prospect of FAULTY becoming an A&M "satellite". "If you are committed to independents you can't work

a second away from 1975, the dying days of BTM and the dinosaurs.

As usual for Copeland-watchers, ambiguities abound. Although The Cramps were transferred from ILLEGAL to IRS the FAULTY labels were left intact and did have the occasional record out in '81. In the States IRS were opening up new possibilities by initiating their own releases, entirely independent of the A&M machine, such as The Dead Kennedys LP (distribution is by FAULTY USA!).

Add it up and the long-range possibility which could make sense of it all is that Miles is hoping IRS will eventually mutate into a big-league independent just as A&M or CHRYSALIS did in the past.

Perhaps this would be the

Copeland? Well....

Tannett, who admittedly has been promoted by Miles to "general dogsbody" from basement lance-corporal, says his boss is "a gentleman" and "a mate" and "the last of the old English eccentrics — even though he's an American".

Okay. But even FFE, whose various selves have all been fired by Miles and have no prospect of re-engagement, enthuses: "He's great. I genuinely like him. I've seen him on the verge of cracking up with fatigue, talking gobbledegook into a phone — though he came back bouncing after a night's sleep. I've seen him wrecked on half a glass of wine, which is all it takes, slapping people on the back and nearly breaking ribs — did you know he used to be a karate instructor to the Lebanese army?

"I think I respect him partly because I've seen those weaknesses in the human machine, the chinks in the brick wall."

Regrettably for those who relish a good cliché Miles just isn't the standard managerial monster. More a quirkish Cleopatra of infinite variety. The most surprising testimony is from Kay Carroll who went back to Miles in August, '81, to arrange release of an early Fall compilation album: "It may sound crazy but I love the guy no matter how often I've called him. He taught me a lot — through trial and error I mean, not by lecturing. When we moved to ROUGH TRADE they were keen to help, but it takes the joy out of learning in a sense because they tell you how to do everything.

"Best of luck to him. I hope he owns the world one day."

With Miles' political upbringing and the occasional whisper of distant presidential aspirations that may not be quite as extravagant as it sounds. Still, for the moment he would probably settle for owning a successful independent record company...and you'd buy shares wouldn't you?

Listen to the man: "We don't take risks at all! I'm the safest guy in the business because my budgets relate to sales! The major record companies think I'm nuts, but *they* are the highest-risk operations around! All this weird stuff — it's the safest of the lot!" PHIL SUTCLIFFE

THE GO-GO'S

the pan and it looked as though Miles was fixing the roof while the foundations cracked. There were precious few releases on any of his UK labels in 1980. The Cramps were the only going concern really — pretty lame when the comparable ROUGH TRADE organisation, with their shop only a few hundred yards away, was prospering so vigorously.

Yet, as FFE says: "If Miles hadn't put thousands of his own income from The Police into FAULTY we would have been finished. It was his money. He could have just said 'Screw it!'"

Clearly Miles was hanging on with a purpose and as soon as The Police began their sabbatical in February, '81, it happened. He launched IRS in the UK (as "IRL") with A&M handling all the nuts and

with multi-nationals because they always gain the upper hand." His fears veil some of the issues though. The "alternative" record companies are not "revolutionary", but smaller capitalist enterprises. IRS itself is already an independent multinational *like* A&M.

What's more, both sides aver that IRS has final say-so on every creative decision — a shaky notion in many instances which may prove realistic because of Miles' Police power if nothing else.

Yet FFE's worries take on substance again when you consider that IRS's first Top 100 album in the States was the Go-Go's produced by the very pricey Richard Gottehrer. Unless some extraordinary deal was struck this doesn't sound more than

logical conclusion to the Copeland caper: a compromise between his gung-ho visionary streak and his voracious ambition.

Whatever, his secure pride in The Police adventure and the pause for thought it allowed him in '81 have permitted a glimpse of a milder Miles. He even *looks* better. He's started having smart haircuts and abandoned the rancid cowboy boots FFE saw him wearing for three years until "he sincerely believed he was rich".

Not that the chainsaw has been silenced. His self-esteem is more vibrant than ever — as FAULTY/IRL's Steve Tannett says "Miles truly thinks the future of American music lies at his door." But the remarkable fact seems to be that this eminence has made him almost lovable. Cuddly

STADIUM ROCK

Stadium rock is a phenomenon that belongs almost exclusively to the youth of America. The music is more than loud, it is earth shattering. The credo is have a good time, get drunk, get stoned, forget school and your parents. Stadium rock is a violent romance, and only the strong survive. Bands that fall into this category have a harder time getting good press than Barry Manilow, they spend so much time on the road that reality becomes fantasy, and keeping relationships going with wives and girlfriends is next to impossible.

At this point in the history of rock and roll, there are very few groups that can realise a profit by touring. Most of the money is made through the sales of records and by performances on television. But REO Speedwagon, Journey and Styx are still selling out concerts all over the nation, without the benefit of support by the press or radio. These are the strong. The last heroes.

REO Speedwagon has managed to withstand the agonies and the ecstasies of the road for more than ten years. Bludgeoned by critics at every turn, they have always sold to SRO standards, and this year they finally made it to the top of the US charts with the single 'Keep On Loving You' and the album 'Hi Infidelity'. The curious thing is, almost no one, not even their fans, can name everyone in the group. Rock writers have long deplored the facelessness of REO, but it doesn't seem to have bothered the millions of teenagers who flock to see them perform.

Kevin Cronin, REO's lead singer, guitarist and composer, has always gone out of his way to provide the press with great stories. "This hotel is right on a canal," Cronin once cackled to CIRCUS writer Philip Bashe, "so if they don't come up and fix the TV set, they'll never find it!" The rest of the band,

REO SPEEDWAGON
RIGHT: STYX

Bruce Hall — bass, Neal Doughty — keyboards, Alan Gratzer — drums and Gary Richrath — lead guitar, vocals and composition, fall right in with Kevin's crusade to destroy the hotels of America and keep the band in the news.

On the road, REO could strike terror even into the heart of 'Psycho' motel manager Norman Bates. They've been banned by almost every motel in the country at one time or another, and Kevin writes sweet notes of apology to the managers to coax them into lifting the bans. Last year, REO threw a toga party in the hall of one hotel and then wrote a letter claiming the sheets were so clean they just couldn't help themselves. They were allowed to return this spring, but the in-house cable TV included a showing of 'Apocalypse Now' in the schedule, and as soon as the movie was over the boys were down in the lobby, staging their own version complete with water bombs. When the smoke cleared, the manager was counting his blessings that there was no fountain in the lobby — REO might have tried to surf in it!

Even the incredible sales record of 'Hi Infidelity' hasn't brought REO all the respect they deserve. When they went to pick up their gold record for the LP, they discovered that the disc was inscribed 'Red Speedwagon'.

You just can't win sometimes.

Rock journalist Ed Naha once wrote, "Like their watery namesake, Styx delivers goods that are strictly dead on arrival." But Styx has been knocking out hits since the 1975 release of 'Lady', so someone must be listening. With their present tour in support of 'Paradise Theater', Styx has been knocking out audiences everywhere, even while critics are still throwing stones at every opportunity. "I think people are tired of seeing some guys in blue jeans jam for an hour," guitarist JY Young explains. "They want to see a show."

It's a show they get, after hours of waiting on line. The 'Paradise' tour opens with nothing on stage but a player piano reproducing hits from the 1920s and a little old man sweeping his way from stage left to stage right. The concept stretches through the show, just as it does on the album, and the audience is given the sense that they are watching history in the making — no small feat for a concert that lasts less than two hours. Band members Dennis DeYoung — vocals, keyboards, Chuck Panozzo — drums, John Panozzo — bass, Tommy Shaw — guitars, vocals, teen dream and JY give their fans what they come for, and then some. Why should it matter to anyone that the critics can't tell them apart?

Journey's identity crisis goes beyond personnel. Their latest hit single, 'The Party's Over' from the album 'Captured' lost a few sales because everyone was asking for a song called 'Hopelessly In Love', the hook line from the song. Singer-songwriter Steve Perry felt the obvious title was the line the song fades on, and the band that trains for platinum albums the way athletes train to win gold medals at the Olympics was momentarily set back. Oh but Journey fans are clever. And loyal.

Journey has just gone through yet another

reconstruction in its line-up, to add to the confusion. Founding member and keyboardist Greg Rolie recently made his final bow, after seven years on the road with Journey, preceded by eight years with Santana, for a long-deserved rest from touring and a possible reunion with Carlos Santana and former Santana drummer Michael Shrieve. His replacement is former Babys keyboardist Jonathan Cain, and Journey is hoping that this will mean another new direction for their music. Guitarist Neal Schon, bassist Ross Valory and drummer Steve Smith are looking for a return to hard rock. Whatever happens, Journey intends to take their audience with them. Steve Perry insists, "They say hard rock can't have class, but we educate our audience to see that they can appreciate good musicianship and still have a good time."

I remember seeing Stephen Stills in concert in Paris when I was 13. My friends and I were seated so high above the stage that we could have been on the next block for all we knew. We weren't there to see the show so much as to have a good time, and we were too young to hang out in bars. We did have a good time, we could say we had seen Stills at a high point in his career (if there was such a thing) and we had been out for an evening without our parents tagging along.

When I went to see Eric Clapton at the Yale Bowl, my boyfriend's mother hired a cop to take us there and back, and we held a watermelon filled with LSD on our knees all the way to the concert. It was pouring down rain. Clapton had a tent over his head and he had the audacity to sing 'Let It Rain' while we got drenched. I had a miserable time and swore I'd stay off acid for the rest of my life. I was never a candidate for stadium rock fever, but I do understand why others might feel its attraction. And I have a theory as to why it frightens some critics so much they feel they have to shrug it off as useless.

Writers, critics, journalists are not, as a rule, high school students. They are not trying

ERIC CLAPTON

to escape from anything to music, most of the time they are trying to escape *from* music. In particular, they are trying to escape from loud music played by people whose names they cannot remember. Their rock and roll heroes had names and personalities. Everyone knew that Paul was the cute Beatle, that Mick was his Satanic Majesty, that Jim Morrison was the Lizard King. Their idols had a more tangible charisma. How do you write about music when it's just music?

What is really frightening, though, is that rock publications are dying a slow death. Since there are so few personalities, and no one has discovered a way to write about music of this genre and make it interesting, stadium rock may be turning these critics into the new dinosaur. The River Styx is waiting...
DREW MOSELEY

JOURNEY

THE BUSINESS YEAR

U.S. SUMMER 1980: They don't make record companies like they used to, or maybe the problem is that those baby boom teenagers who made rock and roll soar as a business by buying records are now record company executives. Sales are down, jobs are few and everyone is trying to figure out what the trend for the Eighties is going to be. Gone are the days when an artist could get a recording deal just by standing out on a street corner with a guitar in his hand. A&R representatives live under the shadow of an axe. Those who once loved the glitter of cocaine are now searching for the oblivion of heroin.

The catchword for the coming decade may well be "safe". In the last year, no record company has managed to break a new act on its debut album. No new American act has emerged from the ashes of the Seventies to take its place among the established sellers like Billy Joel, Bruce Springsteen and Fleetwood Mac. Radio stations will only give airplay to bands that have already proved they have mass-market appeal, and without airplay a band has little or no chance of getting onto the charts.

Summer 1980 also signalled the beginning of the end for the much loved television programme, 'Saturday Night Live'. One of the very few programmes that offered up and coming bands a chance to give a live, two song concert nationwide that would be viewed by millions bit the dust, with the departure of Gilda Radner, Bill Murray and producer Lorne Michaels. New producer Jean Doumanian could not hope to follow in their footsteps.

WINTER 1980—81: The Sam Goody trial continues in earnest. Accused of pirating tapes and preventing artists from collecting royalties, the Sam Goody chain of record stores faced witnesses for the prosecution that included a gum-chewing Billy Joel, who claimed that his fans were getting a lower quality recording for the same amount of money and that it reflected on his integrity as an artist to allow the pirating to continue. However, Joel could not distinguish between the pirated tapes and his own COLUMBIA-pressed record. Is it live or is it Memorex? Sam Goody was forced to pay damages and the case faded into the back pages.

Meanwhile, the death of John Lennon has forced many heretofore accessible rockers to run for cover. Dark rumours raged about the life insurance policy David Geffen had taken out on his star artist. 'Starting Over', the first single from the 'Double Fantasy' album had been doing only lukewarm business before Lennon's untimely demise, but with his death the album reached new heights in sales. Yoko Ono was finally forgiven. Fighting back tears, record companies and book publishers had a field day packaging John Lennon souvenirs.

One engineer from the Hit Factory, the studio John and Yoko had used to record their album, told me that he had been awakened in the middle of the night when John was shot and told to report in for work immediately. They were to finish mastering the tracks that had not been used on the album. Fortunately, someone had an attack of good taste and this follow-up LP remains unreleased.

About this time, another controversy arose in the pages of America's trade papers. Chris Blackwell, head of ISLAND RECORDS, had announced his intention of releasing pre-recorded tapes by some of the artists on his label featuring the album on one side and a blank on the other, thus allowing the listeners to record whatever they wanted on the B side.

Following on the heels of the Sam Goody fiasco, other record companies exhibited a bit of anxiety over the idea of allowing record buyers to create their own pirate tapes. The anxiety bordered on hysteria when it was pointed out that anyone could walk into a store and buy their own completely blank cassette for an average of three dollars, a fact which record companies have been hoping will "go away" for years.

Chris Blackwell pointed out that most people who record albums onto blank cassettes have already bought the album and are only recording it in order to make the music more portable. However no other record company seems to be following his example.

Rock publications are dying a slow death. ROLLING STONE, once the vanguard of rock

A&R REPRESENTATIVES LIVE UNDER THE SHADOW OF AN AXE. THOSE WHO ONCE LOVED THE GLITTER OF COCAINE ARE NOW SEARCHING FOR THE OBLIVION OF HEROIN.

music, now features movie personalities like Goldie Hawn and Mary Tyler Moore on the cover, not to mention politicians of Teddy Kennedy's ilk. The articles are geared towards politics rather than music, although they still feature "Random Notes" and record reviews. CIRCUS appears to be transforming itself into a heavy metal rag and the main articles are now about Judas Priest and AC/DC. I'm told that heavy metal is the safest thing to write about right now, because it is one of the few musical forms that has not changed its audience over the years. It appeals directly to the fourteen year old American male mentality. The adolescent boys in this country choose their heroes from among those bands that best express their anger and frustration through the biggest and loudest amplifiers available on the market today. Heavy metal may never die, but what's happening to rock and roll? I can still remember the good old days when heavy metal was a four letter word around the CIRCUS offices. NEW YORK ROCKER, when you can find it, is still acclaiming new wave music and trying to hype new wave fashions. MUSICIAN AND GUITAR PLAYER cater to the more technical side of music. If you're looking for a good article about a new band, you have to go to CREEM, and even then you have to figure out what is sarcasm and what is true.

SPRING 1981: I arrived at the offices of one of New York's major record companies to conduct an interview with a heavily promoted new artist upon the release of his second album. Imagine my surprise when I noticed that the receptionist was selling pocket books from behind her desk while she was supposed to be announcing visitors and answering phones. Nobody else seemed to find it extraordinary. After all, it wasn't affecting her work for the record company... Many of the small independent labels have given up the ghost — they simply cannot afford even the minimum of staffing.

RSO, on the other hand, is not a label to beat around the bush. On Friday, March 31, the entire staff at RSO with the exception of three or four key appointments, were fired

IMAGINE MY SURPRISE WHEN I NOTICED THAT THE RECEPTIONIST WAS SELLING POCKET BOOKS FROM BEHIND HER DESK WHILE SHE WAS SUPPOSED TO BE ANNOUNCING VISITORS AND ANSWERING PHONES. NOBODY ELSE SEEMED TO FIND IT EXTRAORDINARY.

with two hours notice. By the end of the afternoon, only Al Coury, Bob Edson and Ronnie Lippin remained, along with some of the people in accounting.

The staff were not caught completely unaware. There had been rumours that RSO would close shop as early as October of 1980. But no one was prepared for the quick shut-down that did occur. Many cite the lawsuit brought against Robert Stigwood by his biggest act (and closest friends), the Bee Gees, as an integral reason for RSO's demise. Although the suit was settled in a friendly manner, it did shake Stigwood up, and it forced him to take a long look at how much he really wanted to be in the music business. RSO did not manage to break any acts in the years 1979

and 1980, and even the acquisition of Mike Chapman's DREAMLAND label didn't help — it only added one more weight to the feet of the drowning RSO. The failure of 'Times Square' as both a movie and an LP was the last straw. RSO changed its deal with POLYGRAM, who had been serving merely as distributors, and they are now working together on rebuilding Stigwood's fallen empire. Both companies are putting on an optimistic front.

Appearances notwithstanding, some good has come out of this year in music. Because sales are down so low, record companies and promoters have been forced to take a second look at what is happening within this industry, and solutions are being sought. COLUMBIA RECORDS has sunk a lot of its money into a new video scheme, entitled COLUMBIA VIDEO ENTERPRISES or CVE for short. CVE is a division of the records group and its purpose is to incite interest in bands before they enter the market with a new album or a tour. After completing a video shoot, they will license the shows to cable and network television as well as marketing the tapes on the home video front. As Jock McClean, an executive in CVE explained, "This helps Columbia Records in any number of ways. I came over here from the artist development area because I think that the inherent cost of touring is going to make people do these videos in order to hit the tertiary markets. The mileage between gigs and the number of halls where you can really realise a profit is dwindling, and more and more artists are starting on the West Coast and scooting along the bottom of the country, maybe sneaking into Florida and the East Coast and completely

neglecting the Mid-West because it's just too hard to make money there. This is a way to penetrate the Mid-West via video. And it's not a pre-concocted promotional video which costs about half as much as the tape we can do that is also for sale."

To this end, CVE has purchased space in COLUMBIA's new record plant, located in Carlton, Georgia. They plan to produce not only video tapes, but video discs in the RCA format. Once the bugs in producing laser discs have been worked out, they may also license that format.

MANY ROCK STARS TODAY ARE MORE MARKETING EXPERTS THAN MUSICIANS, AND THEIR EXPERTISE IS BEING PUT TO THE TEST BY THE RECESSION.

There are also plans to launch a new channel on cable TV which will present music 24 hours a day. The channel is a joint venture between WARNER COMMUNICATIONS and AMERICAN EXPRESS, and it will give a simultaneous broadcast from coast to coast via satellite, so that viewers in LA and viewers in New York will be seeing the same thing at the same time. The show will be presented on a free-access cable, which means that if you are already hooked up to a certain configuration of cable, the show will come to you at no charge. Instead, there will be

six minutes of commercials every hour. It is hoped that the show will run along much the same lines as AOR radio.

No matter how publicity conscious the move, it was also nice to read that artist Tom Petty wasn't taking the price hikes lying down. He waged a one-man war against his record company, MCA, this spring in order to stop them from releasing his new album, 'Hard Promises' at the absurd list-price of $9.98. He won and the LP was released at the list-price of $8.98.

There was a time when rock music was a symbol of change and revolution, and if it resembled anyone, it resembled James Dean, Janis Joplin, Jimi Hendrix and Jim Morrison. Musicians were supposed to be so close to the edge of destruction that it was a miracle that they could come back and tell the tale. Their dedication to going as far as possible won them the undying admiration of hundreds of millions and, right or wrong, they were willing to become whatever was demanded of them.

It's hard to say what became of that idealism. Whether it was swept away with the realisation that you could really get hurt if you went out on that limb, or with the discovery that you could really make a lot of money if you stopped viewing music in terms of emotion and started trying to figure out what you could do that would sell. Many rock stars today are more marketing experts than musicians, and their expertise is being put to the test by the recession. Or maybe America just got bored with rock and roll drama. Whatever the reason, America is desperately in need of something to believe in, and unless the industry finds a way to give it, we'll have to find it in some other form. DREW MOSELEY

U.K. The drama had all taken place the previous year, when the two erstwhile giants of the UK record industry, EMI and DECCA, had both capitulated to trading conditions and surrendered their

independence. There was, this year, little drama of that nature. There was just an overall awareness of biting austerity, as companies were forced to adjust, in many cases to newly straightened circumstances, and to carry on as best they could in the teeth of the recession. It was not easy.

In such conditions, the

threat of redundancy hung over many, and few companies managed to avoid staff cuts entirely. RCA sacked a number of their London staff in October 1980, and in June 1981 were forced to far more stringent measures, when they closed down entirely their Washington (Tyne and Wear) pressing plant, with the loss

of 270 jobs. The factory, opened in 1970, had never proved a successful investment and, as the new managing director Don Ellis pointed out, all companies had to recognise that there was excess pressing capacity in the UK. "CBS and EMI between them can handle the entire industry's needs — and I can acquire outside pressing at a lower price than in my own company taking into account overheads and operating costs."

It was therefore no surprise that other plant was lost. DECCA's pressing plant at New Malden had closed in July 1980, and twelve months later PYE too closed its Mitcham factory, putting 100 workers on the dole. Now reorganised as PRT, PYE like EMI and DECCA, had once been a cornerstone of the UK record industry (albeit a smaller one), but it had been stuttering along for years, and the breakdown of its projected sale to RCA in September 1980 had meant that the company could not even look forward to a decent burial. After the failure of

IT WAS NOT A GOOD PERIOD FOR WEA. THEIR OVERALL SALES FIGURES DROPPED, THEY WERE IMPLICATED IN CHART HYPING SCANDALS ON TWO SEPARATE OCCASIONS, AND THEY LOST THEIR MANAGING DIRECTOR.

that sale, Louis Benjamin, chairman for 21 years, stepped down, at which time optimistic noises were made about continuing PRT as a record company, but continued lack of success explained both why it was finally put up for sale the following spring, and why it then failed to attract any buyers. The closure of the Mitcham plant signalled the beginning of the disintegration of the outfit by its parent company, Lord Grade's Associated Communications Corporation.

More jobs were lost elsewhere. The continuing reorganisation at EMI, following the THORN takeover, meant that a further 300 staff

jobs were lost in August 1980. Jobs were also lost at WEA, and in September Don Arden slashed the number on the payroll of his JET company.

PHONOGRAM was one of the organisations with something to celebrate, since they established themselves more securely in the UK market, and also managed to divest EMI of virtually their entire A&R team. In the first quarter of 1981 the new POLYGRAM conglomerate (which now had three strings to its bow in the UK: PHONOGRAM, POLYDOR and DECCA) won the distinction for the first time of achieving a greater market share than any other corporation in sales of both singles and albums. Even so, the first POLYGRAM conference at which all three concerns were represented took place in Bournemouth against a background of sales force redundancies.

It was a good year for CBS, who at one point in November held the top three places in the albums chart, thanks to Abba, Barbra Streisand and Adam and The Ants; and also for CHRYSALIS, who continued to make astute signings, like Spandau Ballet, no matter how fierce the competition. In the market survey for 1980, though, it was EMI who maintained their traditional lead in both singles and albums.

However, it was certainly not a good period for WEA. Their overall sales figures dropped, they were implicated in chart hyping scandals on two separate occasions, and they lost their managing director.

In fact, chart hyping, the scourge of the industry in recent years, once again figured prominently in the news. On August 8 1980 there was a BBC-2 'Newsnight' report on illegal chart fixing practices, which was rapidly followed by a major 'World In Action' investigation from Granada TV just a fortnight later. This report named names: WEA were the company involved, and The Pretenders one of the acts to have benefited (not, it should be stressed, that the group themselves would have known anything of this).

There had been a chart hyping scandal only two years earlier — A&M suffered on that occasion — but clearly that scare had resulted in no widespread

outbreak of honesty, the industry as a whole having quickly resumed traditional malpractices.

The BPI therefore set up its own committee of enquiry to examine the latest allegations. Its report at the end of October was considered disgraceful by many in the industry. On the one hand, it admitted that there had been a widespread infringement of its own Code of Conduct on this matter; on the other, it concluded that "it is not possible to state firmly that it has been a corporate policy of some companies to manipulate the charts, and it is therefore difficult to recommend that any one company should be expelled from the BPI".

In other words, the companies that had been examining their own behaviour had concluded that their conduct was not what it should have been, but that nevertheless they were going to take no punitive action against themselves. The whitewash caused considerable outrage, and one company, RIVA RECORDS, resigned from the BPI in protest.

By the time the report was published, though, WEA had already lost its managing director, since John Fruin had left the company in early October (with everyone concerned emphasising that this had absolutely nothing to do with chart-fixing allegations). Fruin thus automatically lost his position as chairman of the BPI, and he was succeeded by Chris Wright of CHRYSALIS. He immediately made clear his determination to outlaw chart-rigging. "It does not benefit anyone," he said, "if the chart is seen to be an inaccurate representation, with adverse publicity over allegations of people using 'dubious' methods to influence it — above and beyond certain accepted reasonable marketing practices." (Of course, it is the fine distinction between reasonable and unreasonable marketing practices that had long been the kernel of the problem.)

Wright, however, made good his promise to see that more effective action was taken. By the end of January the number of chart return shops scrutinised for the weekly survey was increased to 750, and all the BPI

member companies were circularised with a new Code of Conduct (although this only gave guidelines to which they all should have been adhering anyway).

The problem still wouldn't go away, though. It erupted again the following April, when an internal investigation jointly pursued by the BPI and the British Market Research Bureau (BMRB) uncovered damning evidence of further manipulations of the chart, once again perpetrated on behalf of WEA, by an independent sales rep. "The evidence was so conclusive,"

THE RECORD COMPANIES, HOWEVER, COULD REASONABLY CLAIM THAT NOT ALL THEIR DIFFICULTIES HAD BEEN SELF-INFLICTED ONES. LIKE ALL OTHER BUSINESSES THEY WERE CONDEMNED TO OPERATE IN THE PERSISTENTLY UNFAVOURABLE CLIMATE OF RECESSION.

a BPI statement disclosed, "that the investigators' findings were completely accepted by WEA. WEA does not consider that the person involved was acting under instructions from the company, but it has agreed to pay the costs of the investigation of £10,000 in the interests of eliminating further malpractice."

It is perhaps a symptom of the fresher atmosphere introduced by Chris Wright that such action was dealt with so promptly, so decisively and so publicly. In the meantime, WEA undoubtedly suffered, and its market share began to show a marked decline.

The record companies, however, could reasonably claim that not all their difficulties had been self-inflicted ones. Like all other businesses they were condemned to operate in the persistently unfavourable climate of recession. For example, the continuing strength of the pound meant that it was still more economic for wholesalers to purchase their records abroad than in the UK. No one suggested the re-application of Resale Price Maintenance, but it is clear that many retailers were able to survive entirely through undercutting their competitors by selling cheaper, imported albums. The industry did what little it could to stem the flow: the Mechanical Copyright Protection Society (MCPS) managed to obtain an import ban on copies of Stevie Wonder's 'Hotter Than July', when EMI Holland jumped the gun and issued it prematurely, and the following year CHRYSALIS obtained an injunction to prevent Blondie's 'Autoamerican' being imported from Canada.

Counterfeiting and piracy remained problems that were just as intractable. One problem with counterfeiting was the high quality of many forgeries, which were thus almost impossible to distinguish from the real thing. CHRYSALIS tried to play a part in this direction, too, by including a US-developed anti-counterfeiting device on Pat Benatar's 'Crimes Of Passion', in a determined attempt to root out such crimes of premeditation. Meanwhile, the IFPI conference in Copenhagen in June 1980 reported growing successes in its fight against piracy, particularly in South-East Asia.

The home-taping issue continued to smoulder throughout the year, although the long-anticipated publication of the Department of Trade and Industry's Green Paper on the subject remained long-anticipated. Industry pressure in favour of a levy nevertheless accumulated steadily. Support came from such august bodies as the Consumers' Association and Lord Goodman; Austria became the first country to impose a blank tape levy.

To step up the pressure in the UK, the MCPS abolished its licences (£1.50p. plus VAT), a moving-the-goalposts tactic designed to put all home-tapers, however well-intentioned, outside the law.

However even while the BPI continued to amass data purporting to prove that home taping was damaging the record industry, the UK market for blank tapes was in a hazardous position, and in March both THORN/EMI and RACAL (DECCA) pulled irrevocably out of the market for manufacturing blank audio tapes, saying that the world cassette market had contracted. The entire field was thus left to the (mainly Japanese) importers, and THORN closed its tape factory

HOME TAPING WAS CLEARLY A PROBLEM WHICH THE INDUSTRY VASTLY OVERSTATED, NO DOUBT IN AN EFFORT TO DISGUISE ITS OWN MANAGEMENT FAILINGS OF A DECADE.

at Hayes with the loss of 270 jobs. (Union leaders argued unsuccessfully that the factory should be kept on, and production switched to video tapes; THORN management rejected this line of argument, and in June announced they would be opening a new video disc factory in Swindon.)

Home-taping was clearly a problem which the industry vastly over-stated, no doubt in an effort to disguise its own management failings of a decade, but during the year there were indications that a sense of proportion was being restored to the debate. In February, ISLAND RECORDS started marketing cassettes in a "One Plus One" campaign: one side featured a current recording, and the other was blank. For this tacit inducement to home-taping, ISLAND was blacklisted by the BPI. Company boss Chris Blackwell defended his actions: "Twenty years after the invention of the cassette is not the time to start complaining." He pointed out that the industry had never understood how to market cassettes, which had always been inferior products to albums. "The industry is encouraging home taping by over-pricing cassettes."

Chris Wright also suggested that the problem was being tackled in the wrong way. He agreed that cassettes had always been marketed badly. "As record companies, we're still too busy thinking 12″ records instead of thinking in other areas. I used to think that blank taping was the major problem, and the recession the minor problem, yet in countries with booming economies sales are enormous."

Perhaps the central problem is that the record industry had never previously needed to sell itself. From its birth, it grew incrementally, and in the post-war years it simply boomed — all without anyone ever needing to suggest to the public that purchasing records could be good for you.

In the less buoyant atmosphere of the early Eighties, the industry belatedly appreciated the need for self-advertisement. The BPI engaged the well-known advertising company Saatchi & Saatchi (if they can sell Margaret Thatcher, they can sell anything) in order to develop an all-industry campaign to promote the concept of buying records. (A similar approach, launched with the slogan Give The Gift Of Music was already underway in the US.) An initial market survey undertaken by the company revealed just how fruitful such a campaign might be. "The market for recorded music is stagnating not just because of the recession, but because large numbers of would-be buyers are not being given enough information about albums, or even incentive to buy them", MUSIC AND VIDEO WEEK reported.

This was one sensible move undertaken by the industry to redress its problems. Another was the formation of a BPI technical committee which suggested that records and tapes should be manufactured to some kind of BSI-style specifications. This would immensely benefit the industry, since the majority of the record-buying public appreciates that quality control on pressings tends to be non-existent; as hi-fi equipment becomes ever more impeccable, so the poor quality of most popular records becomes ever more apparent.

All the major companies abolished Recommended Retail Price, which had originally been an attempt to preserve some kind of price orthodoxy after the abolition of Resale Price Maintenance. The companies now recognised RRP's obsolescence, since the cut-price record business had affected all retailers in the last few years. This, indeed, could also have been an explanation of declining record sales, since it placed a premium on back catalogue items. It was therefore no surprise that two companies with extensive and prestigious back-catalogues, WEA and CBS, should both introduce a mid-price series for many of these recordings. Most other companies took steps along similar lines; one result of this was that for the first time ever both Beatles and Rolling Stones original recordings were available at less than full price.

Meanwhile, the decision to scrap RRP angered the Mechanical Rights Society (MRS); since royalties were always paid as a percentage of the official retail price, how were they now to be assessed? This was another dispute between record industry bodies that simmered throughout the year.

Altogether it was a time for facing up to the harsh realities of the present and squaring up to the fantastic possibilities of the future. A compact disc digital audio system was unveiled at Salzburg, but the real developments were expected in quite new areas. The development of the market in both video cassettes and video discs was eagerly awaited by industry figures. THORN/EMI anticipated vast profits, declaring that video was one of the few marketing areas ignoring the recession.
BOB WOFFINDEN

THE INDEPENDENTS

Mention the word "independent" in the British music industry, and your listener will adopt a more reverential expression, stand a little straighter, and murmur something about independent companies being the backbone of British music, the foundation of the business. But behind that benevolent smile there often lurks a jackal's mind: how can I take this mug for a ride, and where's my cut? The indie scene has proved itself to be a fertile source of talent, but that strength is also its weakness, because it cannot always hold onto what it found.

There was a time when being independent really did mean being out in a wilderness, frustrated at every turn, whether it was trying to get records played on the radio or meeting stony defences from retailers who refused to stock records which were not being played on the radio. But STIFF broke down the doors at Radio One, launching Elvis Costello in the face of derision and apathy and following through with Ian Dury, while ROUGH TRADE invented a whole new method of distributing records to back-street record-cum-head-shops whose managers never listened to the radio except maybe to John Peel last thing at night. For a while, it seemed that a record on an independent label was virtually guaranteed to sell out its original pressing of a thousand copies, especially if John Peel played it a couple of times.

Those heady days have passed, and there are cupboards across the country from Lincolnshire to Lancashire to Lanarkshire stacked with desolate boxes of singles that nobody wanted because John Peel didn't like the things enough to play them even once. He hangs his head in guilt and shame, but what can he do: there is not time in his programme to fit in every one of the records released each week, although there was a period when it seemed as if that was his intention and when his show

was hard work to listen to because the standard was inevitably uneven.

Valiant researchers attempt to keep on top of the chaos by logging every release: ZIG ZAG, the longest-enduring and most professional fanzine in the country, has published a couple of catalogues of small labels, inspiring a more polished version from the trade magazine RECORD BUSINESS, and an ambitious book-format compendium in America called VOLUME which has a cross-index of artists and even attempts to provide personnel of the groups involved.

But while the cottage-industry side of the indie scene encourages (and to some extent thrives upon) the fanatical "completism" of collectors, the real dynamic comes from those records which somehow surface at the top of the pyramid. There is an identifiable route which the more ambitious labels on the indie scene hope to follow: the first step, for the majority, is a play or two on John Peel's Radio One show, with some back-up from the Rock shows which most of the commercial radio stations put on during weekday evenings (although most of these favour the more mainstream rock supplied by major labels).

Step two is a place in the indie chart logged every week by RECORD BUSINESS from its sample of 50 shops around the country which specialise in indie label releases; the sole qualification is that the records are not supplied by any of the major distributors, which rules out any label with affiliations to CBS, EMI, POLYGRAM or WEA, (and thus eliminates such pioneer British independents as VIRGIN, ISLAND, CHRYSALIS, STIFF, and even 2-TONE). Most records which do appear on the indie chart will have had substantial help from ROUGH TRADE, although the London-based collective does its best to encourage labels to supply their releases direct to equivalent "one-stops" around the country like FAST PRODUCTS (Edinburgh), PROBE (Liverpool), SERVICE (Manchester), RED RHINO (York), INFERNO

(Birmingham), REVOLVER (Bristol), FRESH and LIGHTNING (both London); with the exception of FAST and FRESH, these distributors are all based at record shops, with a delivery van which supplies to neighbouring shops and enables them to achieve a turnover which qualifies them for a distributor discount from the indie labels.

For ROUGH TRADE, the important function of this distribution network is to enable an independent label to sell enough copies of its releases to cover all the costs of recording and manufacturing, with hopefully enough left over to pay for phone bills and some of the other costs incurred in running a label. Sometimes, to help a label survive, ROUGH TRADE will take on some of the

The paranoia for the indie label is that the radio stations may lose their nerve and stop playing a record which shows no sign of becoming a hit.

initiation costs and help to promote records and bands through their own radio promotion department and band agency. POSTCARD RECORDS of Glasgow have been lucky recipients of ROUGH TRADE'S benevolent assistance during the past year, and have enjoyed a succession of indie hits with Orange Juice, Josef K, and Aztec Camera.

But for many labels and bands, success on the indie scene is not an end in itself, merely a stage in the ultimate game of "getting a deal". For most such labels, ROUGH TRADE is just a useful platform, kind enough to distribute a few hundred records early on, but not worth sticking with when the pace hots up. If they time

their move right, the labels can reach step three: the pop charts.

One of the hidden benefits of being an indie label is that radio stations actually like to play records which are not controlled by the PPL, a body which represents the larger companies and on their behalf charges a levy for every broadcast of their records; as it is cheaper to play the non-PPL indie releases, which are also outside a "needle-time" restriction imposed by the PPL on behalf of the Musicians Union, both Radio One and the commercial stations are happy to find indie releases whose sound is compatible with what they already play from the major labels.

The paranoia for the indie label is that the radio stations may lose their nerve and stop playing a record which shows no sign of becoming a hit; most radio stations will stick by their guns for at least four weeks, but after that they may begin to ask questions: can you guys really deliver a hit? Not surprisingly, several indie labels lose their nerve and jump-ship to a major distributor; this year we have seen, among others, Susan Fassbender ('Twilight Cafe')move from CRIMINAL to CBS, Jane Kennaway ('I.O.U') go from HOLLYWOOD to DERAM, Dave Stewart and Colin Blunstone ('What Becomes of the Broken Hearted') take their BROKEN label to STIFF, and Department S ('Is Vic There?') shift their DEMON record to RCA — each artist sticking with the indie scene for a little longer than the one before. Less conspicuous, but probably more common, is the artist who moves to a major after making his or her mark on the indie scene, the most notable examples this year being Adam and The Ants, scoring bullseyes every time on CBS after missing the board with DO IT, and The Teardrop Explodes, whose 'Treason (It's Just a Story)'was an indie hit for ZOO RECORDS of Liverpool in June 1980 but got hardly any airplay; the band signed for PHONOGRAM, had a couple more hits, and then enjoyed the satisfaction of seeing 'Treason'make it almost exactly a year later as a *bona fide* pop hit.

If this year's report on the indie scene had nothing more to add to the above, it would have to conclude that prospects were dim; but for every indie-originated hit which needed assistance from a major distributor, this year there have been several which stayed entirely within the indie system, distributed by SPARTAN, PINNACLE, or STAGE ONE.

The Professional Indies
Getting a record into the national chart is a special craft, and it is central to the British music industry as reflected and stimulated by the weekly BBC-TV Show 'Top of the Pops'. Occasionally, a record charges into the chart on its own steam, most often a novelty record, occasionally a cult record by an artist whose following is so strong that even the notoriously insensitive retail trade responds to demand and finds out the source of the record. In the period covered by last year's 'Yearbook' there were two such indie hits, both distributed by SPARTAN of Wembley — 'Daytrip To Bangor' by Fiddler's Dram (DINGLE'S RECORDS) and the cult record 'Food For Thought/King' by UB40 (GRADUATE RECORDS). These hits attracted indie labels to SPARTAN by the dozen, but the business at large was still sceptical: could SPARTAN *nurture* a record through those awkward early weeks of patchy airplay, motivating retailers to stock a record by a new artist on an unknown label without the kind of back-up that majors were able to put behind their hopefuls; "back-up" is used here as a euphemism for giving away so many records, it was hard to make sense of the major companies' policies, which often seemed to set more store by achieving a chart position than on actually showing a profit at the end of the day. Among all kinds of funny business from rival major labels, UB40 made number two on the album charts by the simple method of releasing the kind of record that the people who had been buying their singles hoped they would make.

What SPARTAN learned from working with UB40 and GRADUATE RECORDS (which included making use of the invaluable independent radio-and-TV promotion man Neil Ferris), they were able to put to good effect on behalf of some of the other labels they distributed; among those who enjoyed substantial hits were ALBION (with 'D-Days' by Hazel O'Connor), DINGLE'S (another novelty hit, this time 'Capstick's Dream' by Tony Capstick), SAFARI (several singles and a couple of albums by Toyah), DO IT (the back catalogue of Adam and The Ants, including the singles 'Zerox' and 'Car Trouble' and the album 'Dirk Wears White Sox', all of which enjoyed a new lease of life in the wake of Adam's success on CBS) and DEP

A MONG ALL KINDS OF FUNNY BUSINESS FROM RIVAL MAJOR LABELS, UB40 MADE NUMBER TWO ON THE ALBUM CHARTS BY THE SIMPLE METHOD OF RELEASING THE KIND OF RECORD THAT THE PEOPLE WHO HAD BEEN BUYING THEIR SINGLES HOPED THEY WOULD MAKE.

INTERNATIONAL, the label formed by UB40 after they left GRADUATE RECORDS.

For most of the period covered here, SPARTAN's main rival as a distributor, with national distribution and a team of salesmen, has been PINNACLE, primarily a distributor of replacement parts for hi-fi equipment but increasingly a record distributor of stature. An early coup for PINNACLE was the defection of FACTORY RECORDS from SPARTAN, which landed PINNACLE with a national hit in 'Love Will Tear Us Apart' by Joy Division, jointly distributed with ROUGH TRADE. Mournful, melodic, and given extra emotional weight by the suicide of the group's lead singer Ian Curtis just before the record was released, 'Love Will Tear Us Apart' was perhaps *the* classic independent single; it certainly had an extraordinary influence on the sound and approach of records released on the indie scene in the rest of the year, but it was not at all typical of the kind of record PINNACLE had most success with. Apart from 'Ceremony' by New Order (the name that the surviving members of Joy Division adopted), the PINNACLE hits were mostly in the traditional commercial pop vein, notably 'Only Crying' by Keith Marshall (on ARRIVAL RECORDS of Harpenden) and 'Rabbit Rabbit' by Chas and Dave (on their own ROCKNEY label). Out in a category of its own was 'Too Drunk To Fuck' by the Dead Kennedys on CHERRY RED RECORDS. Having been the first label distributed by SPARTAN, CHERRY RED preferred the arrangement at PINNACLE which allowed its labels more freedom to sell records direct to one-stops themselves, stimulating the early interest which is always harder for a large operation to initiate.

The third independent distributor with ambitions to cover the whole of Britain is STAGE ONE, based in Haslemere, Surrey, and formerly an exporter/importer. STAGE ONE established itself on the domestic scene through a deal with NEMS which gave STAGE ONE exclusive UK rights to distribute an extensive back catalogue of Black Sabbath material, resulting in a bizarre indie LP chart for a week or two when it seemed that heavy metal had wiped out the new wave; ORIGINAL RECORDS followed with 'The Hitch-Hiker's Guide To The Galaxy', a cult BBC Radio series which was transferred to TV; HUMAN RECORDS, set up by Bonaparte shops signed The Au Pairs, whose single 'It's Obvious' and album 'Playing With A Different Sex' topped the indie charts and came close to the "real thing" as compiled by the British Market Research Bureau for the BBC; SECRET RECORDS, allied to NEMS, put The Exploited in the top twenty albums nationwide under the slogan "Punks Not Dead". ARMAGEDDON, previously with SPARTAN, joined STAGE ONE in the hope of better service for an eclectic roster including Blurt, The Soft Boys, and some weird Americans; and HAPPY BIRTHDAY RECORDS bought Girls At Our Best, previously with ROUGH TRADE.

Most of the people who managed the labels mentioned here were in some way already experienced in the record business, and hoped to be able on the one hand to work more closely and efficiently with their artists in their capacity as an A&R department, and on the other hand to respond more directly to reactions in the outside world — press, radio, shops, customers. Having seen the process badly mangled in major labels, they hoped to do it better; but essentially, they were doing the same things, and for many of the same reasons, as people in bigger companies. In almost another world, some other people ran indie labels in less conventional ways.

The Indie Spirit
The sharpest contrast to any of the Indie Professionals is offered by CRASS, who are more than a band and a label, and may even be a way of life. Their records are emotional and ideological tirades, sounding like the kind of thing Johnny Rotten might have made if he were not so much an artist but more of a politician. For this sceptic, the packaging is more attractive than the actual music on the record, presenting witty collages as the centre of poster-sized fold-up sleeves which often print the entire lyrics of all the songs, thereby offering the message separately from the music.

CRASS confound the normal economics of the retail business by insisting on selling their records to the public at the price which would normally be the price that the dealer buys his copies at, but somehow, with the invaluable assistance of ROUGH TRADE, CRASS have sold over 50,000 copies of the single 'Bloody Revolutions', and most of their records are permanently somewhere in the indie charts throughout the year. Despite having apparently no profit margin in their records, CRASS have financed a successful 24-track studio from their earnings, and it must give them amused satisfaction when major labels join their list of clients.

Where CRASS are somewhere "beyond reach" for anybody conditioned by the mores of the record business, ROUGH TRADE itself is more fascinating because so much of what the co-operative does is the perfect embodiment of what the record business should be, but elsewhere never attains.

Formed in 1977 by Geoff Travis and Richard Scott, ROUGH TRADE was first a shop, then a mail order outlet, and only became a distributor because some of its mail order clients started ordering in such bulk, it became clear that these customers were themselves shops or mini-distributors of some sort. And so ROUGH TRADE has continued to evolve, organically and almost always by responding to pressure rather than imposing it.

From distributing records that bands and small labels had already made, it was a short step to releasing tapes from bands who could not afford the pressing costs, and then even paying for people to go into the studio. ROUGH TRADE's reputation is that it does not sign its artists to long contracts, but shares the profit on each release for as long as the artist feels like staying. A few bands have moved on, lured sometimes by promises that another company would sell more copies than the apparently uncommercial ROUGH TRADE could muster, but among those who have stayed, The Fall and Scritti Politti may yet turn out to be major artists with world-wide sales to match such stature.

Among the labels with whom ROUGH TRADE enjoys a close relationship, the most interesting are probably MUTE, FACTORY, ERIC'S and INEVITABLE of Liverpool, and POSTCARD (already mentioned earlier). MUTE is the flight of imagination of Daniel Miller, whose first record as the Normal (T.V.O.D/Warm Leatherette) was a brave stab in the dark by a musical illiterate with a synthesiser; records by the Silicone Teens (Daniel again, in pop disguise) and Fad Gadget furthered the same concept, but more recently Depeche Mode gave the label an unexpected sophistication and a foot in the door of the pop charts.

FACTORY is probably the most perverse of all the substantial indie labels, hiding its artists behind sleeve designs of impenetrable pretentiousness, delaying releases for months, making its British pressings go out of stock while allowing imports in from Belgium or the United States to cultivate that precious sense of being rare but not quite unobtainable.

ERIC'S and INEVITABLE are sister, or brother, or feuding labels with not-quite-clear distinctions, notable primarily for Wah! (previously Wah! Heat), whose 'Seven Minutes to Midnight' seemed poised to sell more than it finally achieved; from the same stable a character called Holly ('Hobo Joe') and an outfit called Dead or Alive ('Number 11') both delivered a similar abundance of self-important passion which affected this listener more than most, to judge from the lack of evident sales logged in the indie charts. Theatre of Hate, released on an entirely unconnected London-based label which changed its name in mid-season from SS to BURNING ROME, did the same kind of thing but sold a lot more records.

As space runs out, the structure of this piece must yield to allow random mention of: FRESH RECORDS, who operate a label and distribution service from an office in London's Edgware Road, working valiantly on behalf of their own favourites and one of the least fashionable but still popular bands, Wasted Youth, whose 'Jealousy' on BRIDGE HOUSE RECORDS was on the lower reaches of the indie chart for months; FETISH RECORDS, whose claim to fame was Clock DVA, a menacing presence from Sheffield; and, always important, FAST PRODUCTS, the umbrella name for the distribution firm and family of labels supervised by Bob Last in Edinburgh: Last played a major role in the early indie days by launching The Human League, Mekons, Gang of Four, Joy Division and others on compilation records and one-off singles, and he recently introduced The Fire Engines on POP AURAL or some such subsidiary, first on an album 'Lubricate Your Living Room', in which they played a one-riff idea for longer than was reasonable, and then on a single called 'Candy Skin' which justice could have declared a natural pop hit.

As we go into next season, hope is delicately poised: will enough bands stay in the indie circuit, to sell enough records, to keep afloat enough distributors, to allow enough labels to retain their independence, for long enough to enable the indie scene become a permanent alternative to the major companies? CHARLIE GILLETT

EUROPE

Merely by calling it European, one suggests that European music somehow differs from its British, American Canadian or Australian counterparts. It also implies some dubious anthropology; tacitly stating that half a dozen or so wildly different, often mutually antagonistic, cultures can be thrown together under the convenient flag, "European" — almost as though the word itself is self-explanatory. While the confines of this fictious genre wil serve to frame much good music, it is also an unpleasant side-effect of tourism. Coach parties "do" the capital rollercoaster of Paris-Amsterdam-Brussels-Berlin et al. Rock fans "do" European music. Students of irony will not fail to chuckle at the fact that their greatest applause is usually reserved for that European music which most affirms Anglo-American verities.

Without being wilfully controversial, it would seem reasonable to argue that European rock is only worth listening to if it sings of itself, rather than of mid-Atlantic boogie-isms which are, frankly, alien to Europe. Certainly there is and always will be a large audience for American, blues-derived rock'n'roll. But for "Europeans" to emulate that style — as they have done in their wretched dozens — is only slightly less pathetic than starting your own cargo cult. There are few sights more saddening, as many European musicians have observed, than a German or French band forced to sing in English with an American twang because their audience has no trust in its own culture.

If European musicians are to bother at all, their music must be a polite but firm rejection of British and American precedents. Europe has more than its fair share of Genesis, Zep and Stones clones. They meet the required standards of being able to entertain, but are too lazy/scared to flout the rules of an externally imposed market. That market demands that they sing in the international language of English, and that their music marry into the family of American, or British, rock and roll.

What psychological damage that market inflicts on the European musician can only be guessed at. But ultimately there is something suspicious and unpleasant about a band rejecting their own culture in favour of entertaining well-heeled tourists.

It should be said that neither this nor the statements of European musicians are nationalistic calls-to-arms. As Kraftwerk's Ralph Hutter says, "We are not interested in flags or passports." But the European musician has to find him or herself, his or her own culture, for the music to ring true.

Nowhere is this idea intensified more than in Germany. Many German artists and musicians feel that the grand sweep of

German culture (good or ill though its logical extensions may have been) came to an abrupt halt during World War Two. Pre-war Fascism, wartime conflagration and the post-war Allied sector-snatching binge reduced the German psyche to rubble. In a state akin to anomy, Germany had to struggle to find, again, its own identity. Out of this chaos, it is said, were born the likes of Fassbinder, Grass and Stockhausen. Stockhausen especially, adopted and latterly despised for making a "Teutonic" racket, has acted as a guiding beacon and, in certain cases, a patron for young German musicians.

Yet it has taken the mainstream far, far longer to start rummaging in its own backyard. Only a few years ago it was still rare to find a young German who was aware of the "avant-garde" bands active for over a decade in that country. Glib it may sound, but the Americanisation of post-war Germany left a deep imprint. The imported culture begat swing begat r'n'b begat rock; all disseminating their language, symbols and images like the chewing gum Ralph Hutter remembers seeing the invading Americans distribute on the streets after VE Day. When describing this, and the continuing presence of foreign forces on German soil, his words sound like old, barely-healed wounds.

The first wave of specifically German bands can be traced to 1969, which saw the debut album from Can, the transition of Tangerine Dream from a rock group into a "free music" group, and the arrival of Amon Duul. At that time a rock group called The Organisation was also watching with interest the Fluxus "happenings" in Dusseldorf and Cologne; a year or two later they would change their name to Kraftwerk.

Apart from Amon Duul 11 (Amon Duul 1 disappeared beneath the metaphorical rubble of a Berlin hippie commune) — who were themselves semaphoring wildly at counterparts in San Francisco and London's Middle Earth club — these bands had little or no interest in the bricks and mortar of four-square rock'n'roll.

Can took outrageous liberties with free music, jazz, ethnic musics and the ideas taught to some of them by Berio and Stockhausen; ditching rock'n'roll, Tangerine Dream started borrowing freely from Xenakis and Ligeti; and by the time their debut album arrived, Kraftwerk were dealing in the sort of violent concrete/electronic music still unsurpassed today by even the confrontationist assaults of Faust or Throbbing Gristle.

The next shock-wave to pass through Germany came over a decade later, with the debut 'Produkt' album of Deutsche Amerikanische

CERTAINLY THERE IS AND ALWAYS WILL BE A LARGE AUDIENCE FOR AMERICAN, BLUES-DERIVED ROCK 'N' ROLL. BUT FOR 'EUROPEANS' TO EMULATE THAT STYLE — AS THEY HAVE DONE IN THEIR WRETCHED DOZENS — IS ONLY SLIGHTLY LESS PATHETIC THAN STARTING YOUR OWN CARGO CULT.

Freundschaft, itself a vanguard for the next wave of young German innovators like Der Plan, S.Y.P.H. and Pyrolator. Prior to this second eruption, a slew of second-string German bands had flourished briefly. There were rock-folkies like Novalis, art rockers like Grobschnitt and Jane, and the theatrical oddities like Guru Guru — intially an avant-garde band but they quickly turned into Germany's answer (as they claim themselves) to The Tubes.

Commendations must, of course, go to the likes of Cluster, Neu, Popul Vuh, Uli Trepte and La Dusseldorf (who resurfaced this year with 'Individuellos'), but even this loose ambient/systems groove has led many of them into the realms of coffee table music.

The archetypal German label from this period is BRAIN, in its formative years responsible for interesting, if hardly ground-breaking, albums from Harmonia (alias Cluster), Schulze and others. For a while it also played host to Amon Duul 11 — perhaps tellingly, at the nadir of their career. Nowadays, perhaps under orders from its parent, the enormous METRONOME GMBH, it can offer you simulacra of any Anglo-American style you care to name. Anyone's Daughter are a poor man's Genesis; Midnight Sun take the stage in billows of black silk and are surrounded by lighted black candles when they version Hendrix's 'Machine Gun'; The Scorpions went overboard on US boogie, and gave the world Michael Schenker, Guru Guru have become bosom-buddies of The Tubes, and the list goes on to include nondescript HM and rock'n'roll bands like Accept and Message (featuring — roll up! — a midget on a kid's tricycle).

Due to the obsessive monomania and desperate elitism of the majority of "Eurorock" fans, these and many other no-hopers have been able to haul themselves onto the European bandwagon merely by giving themselves wacky names (most showing an endearingly naive grasp of English) or chucking the odd oscillator twirl into some very average rock'n'roll.

In the spectrum of innovation, Germany only becomes interesting when you reach and pass the level of the acts on IC RECORDS (Poul Vuh, Richard Wahnfried, Baffo Banfi), and SKY (Cluster, Roedelius, Schickert et al), but even many of these are sinking slowly into the mire of their own cuteness. From there on up it can only get better, with the aforementioned young bands and the stalwarts who are still moving on from that first wave of the late Sixties. Thanks to bands like DAF and Der Plan, young Germans are now (finally) recognising and supporting their own rock culture. It would have been unheard of a few years ago, but recent German tours by DAF quickly sold out, forcing promoters to organise return gigs. Perhaps sensing this thaw, Faust — the band you thought or hoped you'd seen the last of — have resurfaced, and are at present hawking 'Faust 5', an album of musique concrete, around the companies.

Although France has an equally strong rock scene, its innovators complain of a similar lack of exposure. The likes of Jean Michel Jarre are, naturally, household names in France and abroad, and the more mainstream bands like Telex and Telephone (no relation) have gained the patronage of British record labels. But there are many progressive French bands recording and playing to an indifferent home and foreign audience.

The most obvious and abiding example of this is Magma. It's been a few years since their last studio work, 'Attahk', but RCA-FRANCE has just released their 'Retrospective Volume Three' — although no-one can actually remember seeing volumes one or two. Due more to Christian Vander's deranged, megalomanic vision than the support of fans or record companies, Magma have soldiered on through the last decade, their thunderous update of Carl Orff gaining a legendary status of suitably Wagnerian proportions. Earlier this year Vander resurrected the live Magma for a fortnight's residence in a small Montparnasse theatre (this, a contact alleges, to finance Vander's obsession with fast, expensive cars!) British pilgrims to Vander's Nuremberg were, they say, so awestruck they lost the gift of speech for a few days afterwards.

Students who find they can stomach Magma's onslaught should now move on to Etron Fou Leloublan (in their own translation, Mad Shit White Wolf). This elusive trio have just released 'Live In New York', which for the uninitiated might be the safest route into their work. Their studio albums ('Batelages' and 'Les Trois Perdignants...') consist of relentless concussive Beefheartisms and positively homicidal assaults on rhythmic time, but live they temper this with humorous free improvisations. If medical supervision cannot be arranged, you should at least have a glass of sal volatile handy when listening to their albums.

Oddly, the dour Teutonic classicism typified by Magma has had considerable effect on French rock, although it has exerted no visible influence on German groups. Bands like Art Zoyd ('Generation Sans Futur' is their most recent), Vortex, Weidorje and Belgian neighbours, Univers Zero all, to differing degrees, inhabit the gap between Van Der Graaf Generator and Schoenberg. But that should be taken as anything but a put-down; compared to British "Crossover" (sic) bands, the neo-classicism of Art Zoyd and Univers Zero offers the *highest* common denominator between rock and classical. Weidorje, possibly the most jazz-tinged of the bunch, go squalling right off the Richter scale, driven by Magman Bernard Paganotti's volcanic bass.

At the lighter end of the spectrum, the recent re-release of ZNR's 'Barricade 3' is well worth investigating, even for those who bought the original. Due to corner-cutting in the production stages of its first DIY release, the hand-glueing of the labels left liberal quantities of glue smeared across the vinyl, drastically reducing sound quality. The British RECOMMENDED label re-pressed it with a classical pressing factory. Dedicated to Beefheart (what is it between the French and senor Vliet?), it's an album of short, squiggly filigree cameos for keyboards, guitar and guest woodwind/brass, sounding not unlike a collaboration between Chopin and Eno. Beefheart also cops a dedication on 'Musique Pour Garcons Et Filles', the 10 inch "algle" (somewhere between an album and a single) from Video Adventures, who mix a silly pop sensibility with the seriousness of the abovementioned heavies.

After that, unless you really want to make a case for Little Bob Storey representing the pinnacle of French music, you're left with the likes of Szajner, Pinhas and the slightly incestuous Pinhas dining club (Messrs Gauthier, Auger, Grunblatt, Paganotti and others) who, apart from roaming around fashionable Paris like a existentialist version of Sinatra's Rat Pack, appear on

each others' albums in all possible permutations.

Down in the Lowlands, things are still rather quiet. Out of respect we should draw discreet veils over Focus' disastrous collaboration with Chris Farlowe and the tandem descent of van Leer and Akkerman into syrupy orchestral mood music. Amsterdam and its neighbouring cities do, of course, play genial host to a great deal of imported music, but natives and visitors alike

DUE MORE TO CHRISTIAN VANDER'S DERANGED, MEGALOMANIC VISION THAN THE SUPPORT OF FANS OR RECORD COMPANIES, MAGMA HAVE SOLDIERED ON THROUGH THE LAST DECADE, THEIR THUNDEROUS UPDATE OF CARL ORFF GAINING A LEGENDARY STATUS OF SUITABLY WAGNERIAN PROPORTIONS.

say that the cosmopolitan liberalism of Amsterdam disappears into thin air when you drive into the countryside. Excepting perhaps Brussels, Belgium starts from a position of in-bread conservatism and gets worse. Bands like Univers Zero offer the suggestion that there is a general intolerance of young progressive music, brought about by the realisation that the liberalism

which came so cheaply in the Sixties has become too costly in these decades of decline. This would seem to find support in the spectre of street violence recently seen on the streets of Switzerland, Germany and, most recently, in Holland and Britain. If they were still alive, the Baader-Meinhof might even be prompted into saying "We told you so", considering their avowed aims of using terrorism as a means of forcing the cosy burghers into showing their "True" reactionary colours. In the case of Holland and Belgium some would say that both countries are built on a conservatism, underpinned by church and state, which extends to their attitude towards music and the arts in general. Certainly, for the right price you can buy cocaine and any form of sex in certain parts of Amsterdam, but it is also obvious from a casual glance how unstable are the foundations of that Open City.

While the tolerant atmosphere remains, Amsterdam is second only to New York in the diversity of music it offers. It's also much prettier. Its rock clubs have an insatiable appetite for imported music, from skinhead punks to the most obscure post-Joy Division combo. Their audiences are either highly eclectic, or are getting something terribly wrong, in the way they show equally high enthusiasm for Fifties rock'n'roll one minute, and PiL/DAF the next.

Apart from little-known homebred talents like Minnypops (and, a few years ago, a bevy of second-generation punks hurling expletives around in a bemusing fashion), Amsterdam has become the second home of many avant-garde jazzers and such oddities as Red Balune, a splinter from the Henry Cow camp. Confusingly, Red Balune now travel under the name of Contakt Mikrofoon Orkester. An unpredictable flux of experimentalists, led by saxophonist Geoff Leigh, their latest offering is 'Do The Residue', available in Europe and America via RECOMMENDED RECORDS.

Mention must also be made of the Willem Breuker Kollektif, the thinking person's Carla Bley. Like Bley, Breuker's vaguely left-

wing big band mixes modern big band arrangements with rock riffing, topping the result with liberal helpings of theatre and comedy (which sometimes involves assaulting members of the audience with a rubber chicken). In among the hilarity, though, there's some excellent "jazz-rock" (misnomer) going on.

The ascendance of Univers Zero to a point where their name inspires the sort of reverence usually reserved for Magma, has shed light on other bands working in a similar, darkly classical vein. Univers Zero themselves are in a state of chaos at present, and a splinter group, Present, have just released their own debut album 'Triskaidekaphobie'. What is said to be the final, and definitive, Univers Zero album (after their last, excellent, 'Heresie') is now at the mixing and cutting stage, although it has yet to be titled.

While Marc Hollander's Aksak Maboul have been silent since 'Onze Danses', Hollander has formed his own label, CRAM DISCS, and is promising more vinyl outings in the near future. The latest to join the fold are Julverne, whose 'Julverne A Neuf' presents a gentle, chamber-ish contrast to the sometimes morbid Univers Zero.

A few years ago, when the likes of Tasavallan Presidentii and Wigwam were receding into memory, Samla Mammas Manna were seen as Scandinavia's sole contribution to "European" music. Based in the Swedish university town of Uppsala, they took indigenous folk themes and (it must be said) received rock ideas and put them together in a lively, if at times poppy, manner. The live Samlas are far removed from those early records, mixing that style with heady, inspired improvisations with the fire of a band like This Heat. These dual personalities finally met in 1979, on the double album 'Schlagerns Mystik', which gives two sides to each aspect of the band, and is an important purchase for anyone wishing to investigate their work. Their next album 'Familes Prickor', is due soon, and they are promising/threatening a completely new departure.

You may get the sneaking suspicion that Pynchon's Zone is somehow involved in all this when you hear that the band whose name translates roughly as The Reptile Asylum are strongly influenced by...Captain Beefheart, but rest assured that they do far more than lay their own palimpsest over the good Captain's music. And it's with a sigh of relief that I write that those two terrible words have never been invoked when describing Archimedes Badkor, whose debut album, 'Tre', veers in from the realms of free jazz and does some very upsetting things to the old jazz-rock warhorse.

In the world of jazz Scandinavia has provided Europe with many of its top composers and musicians, like Jan Garbarek, Palle Mikkelborg, Terje Rypdal and others. One album which definitely deserves inclusion here is 'Cloud Line Blue', a duet from vocalist Karin Krog and saxophonist John Surman. Surman's sax stands alongside Gato Barbieri in the world eminence stakes, and his use of electronics, alongside Krog's sweet range, make 'Cloud Line Blue' an album to shame the efforts of many synth-doodlers mentioned herein.

The Iron Curtain does, nowadays, allow Western rock musicians in, from Elton John to Tangerine Dream and beyond. The problem, of course, is that it will let neither its musicians or music *out*, although the likes of Ligeti and Penderecki are said to commute both ways, on paper and in person.

In Russia and the Soviet satellites, popular music is organised on an ascending scale of ability and cultural suitability. Musicians are auditioned by party officials, who then decide what (if any) level of the musical hierarchy a band or musician may work on and those levels involve differing pay-structures. If, for reasons of instrumental ability, ideology or the use of "bourgeois" musical styles, they fail the audition, they do not receive the all-important permit. Without that permit, they are effectively forbidden to play.

Much to the chagrin of the authorities, that has not put a stop to it. Officially it doesn't exist — a few years ago I was politely escorted out of the London Czechoslovak Embassy when the Cultural Attache took a dislike to the way my questions were

going. He "knew" what I was going on about but, to all intents and purposes, this underground music just didn't exist. But a few brave individuals have proved this to be wrong and, in one case, made an underground Czech band a rallying-point for human rights campaigners.

For many years now, Czech bands like Plastic People Of The Universe and the now-defunct SP 307 have been organising "secret" gigs in rural areas — all too frequently violently broken

IN RUSSIA AND THE SOVIET SATELLITES, POPULAR MUSIC IS ORGANISED ON AN ASCENDING SCALE OF ABILITY AND CULTURAL SUITABILITY. MUSICIANS ARE AUDITIONED BY PARTY OFFICIALS, WHO THEN DECIDE WHAT (IF ANY) LEVEL OF THE MUSICAL HIERARCHY A BAND OR MUSICIAN MAY WORK ON.

up by the secret police — and circulating *samizdat* recordings. Many of their members are Charter 77 signatories, and suffer the same harassment, fake trials and imprisonment as other dissidents. Just how petty and, beneath it all, scared the authorities can act when confronted with this music can be seen in the novella 'The Bass Saxophone', by exiled Czech writer Josef Skvorecky, who now lives in Canada.

So far, two Plastic People albums have been smuggled,

hair-raisingly, out of Czechoslovakia; 'Egon Bondy's Lonely Hearts Club Banned' and 'Passion Play'. The first arrived in Britain at the height of punk, and 'Passion Play' appeared early last year. 'Banned' is a musical setting of the poems of dissident writer Egon Bondy and, while showing roots in the West Coast (due, quite probably, to the lack of newer influences) connects in a very strange way with the passionate extremists who grew out of punk. Both are available from indie distributors and human rights groups in Europe and America. Hearteningly, some equally brave and daring individuals are also smuggling copies *back* into Czechoslovakia and elsewhere for discreet distribution.

For more detailed information on Iron Curtain rock I'd refer you to the series of articles written last year by NME writer Chris Bohn. A few white lies enabled Bohn to tour the Soviet satellites — although events in Gdansk precluded his entering Poland — and return with news of the underground musicians, *samizdat* publications and the black market in Western records.

Slipping down towards warmer climes, at present Switzerland's biggest export is Yello, the lunatic electronic trio dealt with elsewhere here, and a few minor league punks like Lilliput.

Italy's biggest contribution to European rock (barring PFM or Banco — two different types of ELP pasta with a watery Bolognese sauce) are Stormy Six. When last seen live they were, in fact, a seven-piece, but we can quickly dispense with that peculiarity and move on to their sultry, swinging amalgam of Italian folk music, modern jazz and progressive rock. They are highly politicised, but both on record and in their theatrical live performances, they jettison grim dialectic for passionate, gritty metaphor and verity. It took them quite a while to transfer this onto vinyl, but both 'L'Apprendista' and their most recent, 'Machina Maccaronica' are sterling examples of their gorgeous, warm music. In terms of "crossover", they are to the usual clumsy mis-marriage of styles what Nino Rota is to Rodgers and Hammerstein.

It's a dreadful cue, but in a similar vein Rota's soundtracks, especially to the likes of Fellini's '8½' and 'Juliet Of The Spirits', are also worth a listen.

Although they're actually German, the improbably titled Sogenanates Linksradikales Blasorkester (The So-Called Left-Wing Wind Orchestra) have taken up temporary residence in Italy and have released an eponymous debut album. It is, quite literally, a massive wind orchestra, numbering among its ranks members of France's Urban Sax. Hearing records by either of these groups is an event, not only for the fact of amassing so many players in one studio but for the stunning architecture of their sound.

If any tag can be hung around the necks of European musicians, it's that they are unquestionably more adventurous than their British or American counterparts. In these diverse attempts at establishing their own music, they have consciously left themselves open to any influence that may happen by, inane or sublime, traditional or modern, cerebral or physical. Importantly, when approaching these various strands of music, they exhibit none of the rabid anti-intellectual feelings which make British and American fans despise "Art" music and demand instead something lound, allegro and preferably in four/four. Nor do they fall foul of the opposite; elevating the cerebral at the considerable expense of the physical. To do this they have had to sever their umbilical ties with good ol' rock and roll and go off in search of newer, fresher ground rules, or tread gingerly into the area of improvisation, where the only ground rule is that there aren't any. To them and thousands of their fans, Anglo-American rock has become the nightmarish, archetypal party bore; repeating himself and repeating himself until the listeners' eyes glaze over and they begin to twitch involuntarily. Without the risks and chances taken by European musicians, I and thousands of others would be under heavy, permanent sedation by now. When the FM/AOR palsy begins to take hold, you now know what to do. JOHN GILL

I'M NOT GOING OUT WITH YOU

DRESSED LIKE THAT

A pictorial survey of today's young concertgoer.
Photographed by Virginia Turbett and Jill Furmanovsky

QUOTES OF THE YEAR

"I was outraged when Reagan was shot. I voted for the man and I really believe that he's going straight to the heart of a lot of our problems. He's a good man, a strong man, and he's got a good reputation."
Tommy Shaw, Styx

"I had this feeling, this vision and feeling. There was a presence in the room that couldn't have been anybody but Jesus."
Bob Dylan

"**W**E USE SYNTHESISERS BECAUSE THEY'RE SIMPLE. ONCE YOU GET A GRIP ON THEM YOU CAN DO PRETTY MUCH ANYTHING YOU WANT. WE CAN'T PLAY ANY OTHER INSTRUMENTS."
PHILIP OAKEY/THE HUMAN LEAGUE

"We don't want to be labelled as a bozo's band. We are not bozos."
Paul Cook, The Professionals

"It wasn't called heavy metal when I invented it."
Dave Davies, The Kinks

"Seriously, my only ambition in the world is to go to Egypt, stand on top of the central pyramid, and piss all over it."
Ozzy Osbourne, Blizzard of Ozz

"I just don't feel easy when I see a policeman anymore. When it's publicly stated that policemen aren't racist it's so ludicrous I don't even bother to laugh.'
David Grant, Linx

"We want to record something in Clapham Common tube station...it's got a really strange echo."
Dom, Furious Pig

"One of Ritchie Blackmore's favourite tricks was setting up new roadies with transvestites - some of them look so much like women that the only way you can find out for sure is by feeling the bulge in their knickers."
Graham Bonnet

"**I** ALWAYS LIVE AS IF I'M IN A FILM. I WANT TO BE GREAT MORE THAN I WANT TO BE FAMOUS."
JULIAN COPE
THE TEARDROP EXPLODES

"I've only ever written three types of songs: I write songs about walking, about beaches, and...I can't remember the third thing."
David Thomas, Pere Ubu

"You can't really understand the lyrics unless you're out of your brain on something and you build pictures in your mind. That's the way that Jon used to work."
Alan White, Yes

"**O**NE BLOKE RECENTLY SAID TO ME, 'COR, MATE, YOU'RE NOT ON STAGE NOW' — SO I TURNED ROUND AND SAID TO HIM 'MY DEAR, I'M ON STAGE 24 HOURS A DAY'... AND I AM."
STEVE STRANGE/VISAGE

"I'm hoping I can live to be 60 years old and be called Billy De Ville and have a pencil moustache and a canary yellow suit and sit at a piano and just play great, great stuff."
Willy De Ville

"I feel cushioned off, too comfortable. Things used to be hard. The heartaches then used to be how we'd afford the groceries. What I really need now is a whole new reason for struggling."
Stewart Copeland, The Police

"There's a whole generation of kids out there who hopefully are wise enough not to miss out on us."
Roger Daltrey, The Who

"I was banned from most folk clubs. I mean, it's difficult for a serious traditional singer to follow some screeching lunatic who has just crawled around the stage, ripped his shirt off, burst into tears and terrorised the front rows of the audience."
John Otway

"Japanese girls don't say 'Do you want to fuck?' They're much more discreet about it, fluttering their eyelids and that sort of thing. Not like some of the old boilers you get to meet on the road."
Graham Bonnet

"I've had my allotment of liquor — and probably 20 other people's."
Grace Slick

"I do all my songs in one take, two takes at the most...after that I get tired of 'em. A song's just like a woman."
Jerry Lee Lewis

"WE WANT TO BE THE BAND TO DANCE TO WHEN THE BOMB DROPS."
SIMON LE BON/DURAN DURAN

"WE TRY TO WRITE SEVEN SONGS A WEEK. THAT IS THE GOAL, ANYWAY. WE HAVEN'T MET IT RECENTLY."
CHRIS DIFFORD/SQUEEZE

"Our producer, Shadow Morton, just disappeared. He left a note at the studio reception desk saying 'Gone out for a blood transfusion'. That was the last we saw of him."
Holly, of The Italians

"TONY WILSON OF FACTORY RECORDS SAID TO US 'GIVE UP YOUR DAY JOBS AND GO OUT THERE AND MAKE HIT SINGLES' WE DIDN'T BELIEVE HIM AT THE TIME."
ANDY McCLUSKEY
ORCHESTRAL MANOEUVRES
IN THE DARK

"This country is no better off than it was 25 years ago. No President ever did anything about freeing up the black man. Go all the way back as far as you want...ain't no-one ever free the black people yet."
James Brown

"We did a gig at the Marquee once, the loudest we've ever done. I got home and put on 'Blow By Blow' by Jeff Beck and I couldn't hear the guitar playing at all. All the top end was completely gone off my ears."
Eddie Clarke, Motorhead

"On the last American tour we spent a quarter of a million dollars on a laser system that we never even used — it wasn't good enough."
Gene Simmons, Kiss

"The reason I haven't given any interviews in recent years is simply because I've become very private. Also, to be honest, I really don't think I've got that much to say."
David Bowie

"Futurist music isn't even worth thinking about. It's like having diarrhoea on a hot day."
Ozzy Osbourne, Blizzard of Ozz

"I'm back. I've been working my bollocks off for a year now."
Gary Glitter

"WE HAVE A TOTAL OF TWO FRIENDS IN NEW YORK."
LUX INTERIOR/THE CRAMPS

"I like to ridicule myself. I don't take it too seriously. I wouldn't wear those clothes if I was serious. The one thing that keeps me going is that I like to laugh at myself."
Freddie Mercury, Queen

"We used to rehearse in the cellar below Earl's place. It was so wet down there we had to stand on bricks. When they flushed the loo upstairs, turds floated past our feet."
Robin Campbell, UB 40

"Ever since I kicked heroin and cleaned up, I've been bombarded with requests to make statements or to give lectures to people. I've even been asked to address judges! What would I say in front of 800 judges? The chance I've been waiting for...'FUCK YOU'."
Keith Richards, The Rolling Stones

"We sacked our producer half an hour into the first day. He said something like 'I want to go for a nice poppy drum sound' — so we had a little conference and told him to get out of the studio as quickly as possible. He'd just flown in from the States, specially to produce us."
Captain Sensible, The Damned

"We've got nothing in common with other musical groups."
Kevin Rowland, Dexy's Midnight Runners

"THERE'S A HAIRSPRAY CALLED 'FINAL NET' WE USED IN NEW YORK. CAN'T GET IT HERE. ENGLISH HAIRSPRAY IS TRASH."
BRIAN SETZER/STRAY CATS

I

"DON'T HAVE A SINGLE ORIGINAL THOUGHT — I'M THE PRODUCT OF WHAT'S BEEN LAID ON ME. ALL MY IDEAS ARE JUST REHASHES."
ADAM ANT

"The bottom's been kicked out of the rock'n'roll industry. I'm going to fall in line and make some MOR records."
Mike Chapman, producer

"The music press really seemed to hate us and I never quite understood why. We were used as a yardstick for what was bad. As the slagging built up, we got used to it and developed skins like rhinoceroses."
Tony James, Generation X

"I'll be remembered by some for my songs, by others because I make a good cup of tea."
Pete Shelley, Buzzcocks

"I think I'm an embarrassment to CBS. They don't know why I'm still around. Everybody else is 20 years younger than me."
Leonard Cohen

B

"ASICALLY I'VE ALWAYS FELT THAT I WAS A WOMAN WITH A MAN'S BRAIN, A MAN TRAPPED INSIDE A WOMAN'S BODY. I ALWAYS HAD THE INITIATIVE OF A MAN BUT WAS ALWAYS TREATED LIKE SOME IDIOTIC CREATURE, SOME LITTLE BUZZY BEAUTY."
DEBBIE HARRY/BLONDIE

"**I**'M GOING TO BE ONE OF THE SURVIVORS IN THE NEW ERA BECAUSE I KNOW WHERE TO BE AND WHAT TO DO."
MARVIN GAYE

"I shot a cat once for shitting on my car. I had to shoot it seven times...the bastard wouldn't die, it haunted me. It was wild, living in my garage, and it kept having kittens and shitting everywhere. I said to my old lady 'It's either me or the cat'. I shot it in the eye first, with a .22 bullet. Next morning it came crawling back to eat our food, and it shat on the car again...so I loaded up and shot it straight through the neck. Three days later, it hobbled back and shat on the bonnet — with one eye all white and glazed, like something out of that film 'Zombies'. So I shot it again. A couple of weeks later I came back from Australia and there was this cat back...it had so much lead in it I could have sold it for scrap metal. I took a double barrelled shotgun and blew it clean over the fence. God's honest truth — three days later it was back again, so it had to be the water treatment. That finally finished it off."
Ozzy Osbourne,
Blizzard of Ozz

"**W**E SHOULD HOLD A JUMBLE SALE OF OUR OLD CLOTHES AND INVITE DURAN DURAN AND CLASSIX NOUVEAUX."
MARTIN KEMP/SPANDAU BALLET

"Los Angeles is like one of those machines that treat flour. When the wheat comes in, it's full of interesting ingredients — but it goes through this machine and what you get out at the end is perfect white crap."
Eno

"A lot of kids ask what they should do with their lives, as if I should know. They regard me as some sort of God, but I'm just a scruffy cunt from Anglesey."
Lemmy, Motorhead

"I don't want to be a has-been musician at the age of 29."
Paul Research, The Scars
(He should be so lucky —
he'll probably be a never-was
musician at the age of 22.)

"There are those people, actors and rock'n'roll singers, who actually believe they have to live up to some kind of image — like being great fucks or something. I actually don't think like that...not now, at least."
Mick Jagger,
The Rolling Stones

"Some people think of us as a bunch of Maoists."
John King, Gang of Four

"He doesn't allow nobody to drink on his job; if he catch somebody drinking on his job, they gone. No drugs, no nothing on his job. This man will fire anybody he catch with narcotics. He come around and smell some reefer in this room and everybody in this room is fired. Everybody."
His personal manager Henry
Stallings on James Brown

— 193 —

"Maybe my next song will be about death and destruction in the third world."
Sheena Easton

"I want to be an actor. There's no thinking involved in acting and you don't have to write anything down."
Randy Newman

"People always think I'm on speed all the time. It's not true — I never take drugs. This is just exactly the way I am."
Jimmy Pursey

Y"OU WRITE YOUR NAME ON INFINITY OR YOU BLOW IT. I'M WRITING MY NAME ON INFINITY. I'VE DECIDED. AND HE KNOWS."
HAZEL O'CONNOR

"English fans don't wait for a computer to tell them what to buy. In America, it's all statistics. If Americans like something, it's probably crap."
Stewart Copeland, The Police

"Are women my age supposed to sing rock'n'roll?"
Grace Slick

"I have boundless agony, I have boundless anguish. I have enough anguish, anxiety and despair to fuel at least another 10 to 15 years of a career."
Leonard Cohen

"The promoter suddenly appeared, nearly in tears, shouting 'For fuck's sake get off the stage. You've ruined our reputation, we're totally discredited'."
Cabaret Voltaire, (on their first gig)

"At school I was a clean cut kid with top grades, but I always felt more comfortable with the kids that smoked joints in the back room."
Pat Benatar

"Like it or not, I am not going to go away."
John Hiatt

"If I made a serious attempt at singing, I'd probably fail miserably."
Brian Johnson, AC/DC

"I take some things for granted now. I walk off stage and I scream if there's not a towel there. I wouldn't have done that four years ago...but we didn't pay a guy to handle our towels four years ago.'
Bun E. Carlos, Cheap Trick

"I like a bit of Beethoven."
Siouxsie of The Banshees

"We got home safe in the knowledge that we've deafened a few."
Phil Taylor, Motorhead

"If the system can't handle four guys who play instruments, then that system is well fucked up."
Jean Jacques Burnel, The Stranglers

"I wouldn't mind playing keyboards in Kim Wilde's backing group for a couple of months."
Howard Devoto, (on his leaving Magazine)

" 'Ace of Spades' is the only album we've done that we play at home."
Lemmy, Motorhead

"I haven't had a week off in the last two years; I've been living out of a suitcase like some sort of tramp."
Jerry Dammers, The Specials

"In the bible, they blew the horns and the walls of the city crumbled. Well, punk rock was like that."
Joe Strummer, The Clash

"I like writing about tits. I like writing about fannies."
Ian Gillan

"There's nothing on the radio worth listening to anymore, so I don't bother."
Ric Ocasek, The Cars

"It came to the point where I'd rather have killed myself than get a job. I told social security to give the jobs to those that want them, that I'd rather stay at home listening to music. I brewed home-made lager so I wouldn't have to spend a lot of money drinking — which is a good hint for all you out of work people."
Robert Smith, The Cure

"If they (the police) hadn't come smashing through my front door, no-one would have known what example I was setting. They made it public, not me."
Keith Richard, The Rolling Stones

"One time, this geezer came up all distressed and said 'Hey man, I've been trying black magic and it doesn't work, what do you advise?' So I said 'try milk tray'."
Ozzy Osbourne, Blizzard of Ozz

"I don't see any connection between our band and America. It's like trying to convert an Eskimo to Christianity when you don't know the language."
Eddie Tudor, Ten Pole Tudor

"I'm not a thick turd."
Bob Geldof, The Boomtown Rats

"I'm sure it takes a long time to sink in, but there's no dog shit on 'Sandinista'."
Joe Strummer, The Clash

"When it comes to the end of a tour, I've always got something wrong with me. At the moment I feel about 107...bits of me are dropping off."
Jake Burns, Stiff Little Fingers

"My great dream would be to sit in the seats and watch us perform."
Marlon Jackson, The Jacksons

"There's nothing romantic, nothing grand, nothing heroic, nothing brave, nothing like that about drinking. It's a real coward's death."
Warren Zevon

"**I**'M TIRED OF RE-FORMED BANDS. IN THE END IT BECOMES FAIRLY PATHETIC; A BUNCH OF OVERWEIGHT MUSICIANS IN FRONT OF AN AUDIENCE WHO'VE ALL GROWN OLDER."
STEVE WINWOOD

"There isn't much difference between rock'n'roll and teaching...you're entertaining delinquents."
Sting, The Police

"In 1969, Kim Fowley called me up one day and asked very simply 'Are you prepared to wear black leather and chains, fuck a lot of teenage girls, and get rich?' I said yes."
Warren Zevon

"I can remember when we used to change our phone numbers just because we thought it was cool."
Kevin Cronin, REO Speedwagon

"It's a depressing, crappy time to live in."
Paul Weller, The Jam

"Somebody's vomiting, you step in dogshit, you sit in a dressing room with three inches of water on the floor. That's what makes it so exciting, but that's why people flip out."
Debbie Harry, Blondie

"The English press is so hyperbolic and over-indulgent that you can't even deal with it anymore. The only interesting thing is that we've been able to garner their hatred for a good year and a half now, which is more than I can say for most bands."
Jerry Casale, Devo

"Everyone in PiL is equal; we have equal say, equal merits, we each have our part to play. Hopefully, we're not just crawling up our own arseholes."
John Lydon, PiL

"We've still got all the old freaks on our side."
Doug Sahm, Sir Douglas Quintet

"What's Venezuela going to be like? Is it going to be full of Aztecs or what?"
Terry Chambers, XTC

"I'm not the ultimate stud, but I'm pretty good at it. I've had a lot of practice. I mean, I'll have anybody's old lady - I'm not proud."
Lemmy, Motorhead

"**I** USED TO READ MY MOTHER'S PORNO BOOKS WHEN I WAS NINE, AND I GUESS THEY INTERESTED ME MORE THAN THE HARDY BOYS."
PRINCE

"Mick (Jagger) is one of the sexiest men in the world and the best lover I've ever had."
Jerry Hall

"It's that Mrs Thatcher I blame. Really, she is terrible, she is really bad. She's an evil woman. She does her hair every week, goes to a hair salon, and there's all that make-up and clothes she gets. She doesn't give a damn about what is happening to this country. It's terrible. Iron Lady, my foot! She's not the Iron Lady, she's just a bloody bitch."
Annabella, Bow Wow Wow

"I'm not a very sociable person. I seem to get trapped in semi-conversations with people jabbering at me incessantly, and I'm too polite to say 'Fuck Off'. The truth is that most of the things people say to me, I don't want to know. I wish they'd shut up and leave me alone."
Eno

"Elton John said in a paper 'Be careful, Ian. Don't become the Roy Hudd of rock'n'roll music.' That really smacked me in the chops. I don't want to be that."
Ian Dury

"Most of the music papers were very slow to pick up on it (The New Romantics). In 20 years time, critics will probably write great nostalgic dewy-eyed retrospectives on how good it was in these London clubs and how these innovators were doing this, that and the other."
Gary Kemp, Spandau Ballet

"Very few people are saying 'Fuck the market, I think *this* is great and I'm good at doing it'. Most people are too busy constructing stuff which is suitable for FM radio — and that's why there are so many dull groups, dull people, dull records, dull disc jockeys, dull everything."
Nick Lowe

"I can't stand being in a room full of people who have taken drugs."
Eno

"The fucking place should be wiped off the face of the earth."
David Bowie, (on Los Angeles)

"I LISTEN TO THE RADIO ALL THE TIME, MAN, AND I DON'T HEAR NOTHING BUT SHIT."
JOE "KING" CARRASCO

"When I was a kid I put a lot of my energy into things like shoplifting. I got in a lot of trouble. I used to bite people."
Ellen Foley

"The reason there's so much smog in LA is so God can't see what they're doing down there."
Glen Campbell

"What time is it? They keep telling me the big bucks are coming in any minute. Debbie got more money from the jeans deal than both of us have from our record sales."
Chris Stein, Blondie

"I'm not interested in what Mrs Thatcher's doing with the fucking Blue Streak missile or whatever.
Lemmy, Motorhead

"I'd just like to say we've had a wonderful time here in Caracas; we've stayed at your Hilton, we've been to your bars, we've drunk your wine, and we've nobbed your tarts."
Jools Holland (at Millionaires gig in Venezuela)

"We always have really sweet letters from fans. We've only had one dirty letter."
Kelly Johnson, Girlschool

"A few years ago, Paul (McCartney) turned up at the door and I said 'Look, do you mind ringing first — I've had a hard day with the baby. I'm worn out and you're walking in with a damned guitar'."
John Lennon

"I'd never really wanted to become a solo singer, but suddenly I had no choice."
Jon Anderson

"We insist that what we're doing is a totally new contemporary art form whose time has now come."
John Lurie, The Lounge Lizards

"It was really strange in Berlin...you could feel the evil, you could feel it from the war. It had a cold atmosphere. It was quite a lot like Manchester."
Bernard Albrecht, New Order

"The Police are a pop band, certainly not a rock band. We are making music for window cleaners to whistle."
Sting, The Police

"What I'm watching, along with everybody else, is the way the first bunch of Sixties musicians move into senility."
Peter Gabriel

"The people that know me know I'm not an ogre."
Ritchie Blackmore, Rainbow

"**I**'M EASY TO TAKE THE PISS OUT OF BECAUSE I'M SIX FOOT TWO AND GOING BALD."
JOE JACKSON

"We're neither today's hot news nor a band that can be written off. I believe that we're at a very invigorating time in the life of Jethro Tull."
Ian Anderson

"There are just so many average girl singers around now — I don't want to be lumped in with that lot. I think they're all third-rate artists capitalising on the work people like me have done in the last three or four years."
Pauline Murray

"Johnny Rotten was always difficult. He probably spoke about three words to Steve Jones in the entire two years."
Malcolm McLaren

"I've only just recovered from the last recording sessions. Beat my own record — nine days on a stretch. Once you get in the studio, it doesn't really matter; it's timeless, like hibernation. When one tape-op drops, you wake up another."
Keith Richards, The Rolling Stones

"**P**IL HAVE PISS-ARSED AROUND FOR FAR TOO LONG. IT'S MORE THAN FUCKING HIGH TIME THINGS GOT SERIOUS."
JOHN LYDON/PUBLIC IMAGE LTD

"I'd say that more than 50% of the stuff written about me is bullshit. I don't know how people can sleep at night making a living out of slandering folks like that."
Greg Allman

"Always stay one step ahead of your hangover."
Lee Brilleaux, Dr Feelgood

"Living on the brink of disaster at all times is what rock'n'roll's all about."
Kevin Cronin, REO Speedwagon

"My real name is Preliminary Drawing — but most people find that a bit of a mouthful."
Sketch, Linx

"My ultimate adventure was taking psychedelic drugs in the Seventies."
Todd Rundgren

"Our fans have this intense loyalty. They want to be part of it. They want a t-shirt that says 'I like AC/DC and I'll fight anybody who says different.'"
Brian Johnson, AC/DC

"It's a bloody good way to make a living — going all over the world with your mates."
Nick Lowe

"In his Independence Day show, Sammy Hagar comes out and says 'Alright, now I'm gonna get rid of the man we all want to kill' and unveils a huge picture of Ayatollah Khomeini. He mimes like he's shooting him and the picture blows up — and the crowd goes nuts with joy. If that doesn't prove that heavy metal and fascism have become one and the same, I don't know what does."
Jello Biafra, The Dead Kennedys

WHY SHOULDN'T I SHOW MY TITS OFF? I'VE GOT A 38-24-34 FIGURE."

WENDY O WILLIAMS
THE PLASMATICS

"When I left England, I still couldn't go on the street...it took me two years to unwind. I would be walking around tense like, waiting for somebody to say something or jump on me. I can go right out this door now and go in a restaurant. You want to know how great that is?"
John Lennon

"I'VE GOT A VERY BIG FEAR OF BEING A HAS-BEEN."

GARY NUMAN

"Originally the album was going to be called 'You Can't Keep A Good Dog Off Your Leg' and we had a picture of about 20 chicks literally climbing up my leg."
Ted Nugent

"I just love drinking and getting drunk. I'll drink any thing. The Dean Martin of heavy metal, I am. I'm not as mad as everyone makes out — I'm worse."
Ozzy Osbourne, Blizzard of Ozz

"You've got to be an idiot to be in a rock group."
Nick Lowe

"The double bass rips my fingers, so I have to tape them up when I play, but it's much better than a bass guitar. It's like dancing with a real fat woman."
Lee Rocker, The Stray Cats

"I remember going to gigs in 1977 and being branded as an outcast because I wasn't wearing the right sort of bondage trousers."
Steve Strange, Visage

"Sex is still an influence, still a motivation. I find sex a very enjoyable and positive thing. It's the great equaliser, in all its forms."
Adam Ant

"We've never been able to be cool. God, we've tried. I'm afraid we'll always be uncool."
Jimmy Lea, Slade

"I've signed kids' arms on one tour and next time they've come along with it tattooed in."
Lemmy, Motorhead

"I love all the merchandising, in fact I'm crazy about it. I want a Kiss car — and that's being worked on at the moment by Chrysler in the States. I want Kiss World, a travelling amusement park — and that's also being planned."
Gene Simmons, Kiss

"I'm fed up with defending Virgin."
Mike Oldfield

"I'm fed up with reading all these fucking music papers."
Pete Frame

HOW CHARTS ARE COMPILED

Back in my long lost youth, I remember listening diligently every Sunday afternoon whilst at school to Radio London (the pirate station) as it broadcast its weekly Top 40. I wrote every position down in my red Silvine exercise book — the one with the Arithmetical tables on the back — for many months without fail. It never occured to me how the chart was put together, and to be honest I was never really that interested. I suspect the vast majority of avid 'Top Of The Pops' viewers have the same feelings today. Although to most people the chart broadcast by the BBC is completely irrelevant, it is — to the record industry — one of the most important aspects of the whole business. It causes more frustration, annoyance, and accusation than anything, and — but more of that later.

The history of the charts goes back almost 20 years when on November 14th, 1952 the consumer paper the NEW MUSICAL EXPRESS published the first ever list of best selling records. In those days it was a Top 12 (although in fact 15 records were included because of tied positions). Other papers followed suit, but it wasn't until 1964 with the advent of BBC TVs 'Top Of The Pops' that a chart reached such a wide audience. This chart was compiled on a points basis from an aggregation of the NME, MELODY MAKER, DISC and RECORD MIRROR. (In some ways a combined chart would be the most satisfactory solution to today's problems.)

This system continued until early 1969 when the record industry through its organising body, the British Phonographic Industry, engaged the BMRB (British Market Research Bureau) to compile a weekly singles and albums sales chart. Since then the BBC has had sole broadcasting rights to the charts, and MUSIC WEEK the sole publishing rights. In the dozen or so years that the BMRB has been faithfully carrying out this task, efforts have been strenuously made to ensure that fair play is done. In early 1978, an alternative trade paper, RECORD BUSINESS, was first published using methods adopted by the American trade weekly RECORD WORLD. This comprised an in house research team which was responsible for compiling a variety of charts. At this point MUSIC WEEK was publishing a Top 60 singles chart — the BBC has never added to its Top 40 format. RECORD BUSINESS, however, introduced a Top 100 singles chart, based on a sales only Top 30, with the rest of the 100 mixing sales with airplay.

The two systems of compiling the charts are widely different. The BMRB has a panel of approximately 750 shops, recently upped from 450, who tick off sales of records in a diary from Monday morning to Saturday. These diaries are then delivered to the BMRB who throughout Monday feed the sales into a computer. Of those 750 shops, a cross section is chosen for the actual compilation — this is done to prevent record companies knowing which shop's sales are used which weeks. Each shop is carefully selected based on region and type, otherwise you could have a situation where one week a chart is rock influenced and the next disco. Having processed all the relevant information, the chart is checked first thing on Tuesday morning for any discrepancies, before all is revealed on an expectant record industry and the BBC who then broadcast it at midday on Radio 1. The chart is first published in MUSIC WEEK the following day.

RECORD BUSINESS have a full time research team who in addition to compiling weekly singles and album charts, devote a fair amount of time to the collation of new release and airplay information and Disco and Independent charts. The singles chart is based on a phone out system, where the panel of shops is called once a week on either Wednesday or Thursday to give their weekly sales. The shops will have already received a list of singles which they log sales against. The sales taken over the telephone are then fed into a computer, which can sort those sales into regional or type breakdowns. Similar systems are used by both BMRB and RECORD BUSINESS for the compilation of their album charts.

The main failings of the respective charts are that, in the case of RECORD BUSINESS, it is financially prohibitive to sample a panel as large as BMRB's — RB in fact has in excess of 250 shops. The idea of mixing sales with airplay below the Top 30 is a good one, in that sales at that end of the chart are so inconsequential and airplay is so significant. The problem therefore becomes slightly chicken and egg, because if a radio station is broadcasting a chart based on what is being played, it becomes self-perpetuating. The problems with the BMRB chart are more due to the significance of the chart than anything else — if RECORD BUSINESS was contracted to do BMRB's job it would probably be faced with those problems just as much.

Getting a record into the chart is of paramount importance to a company, and therefore most lengths will be gone to to see that this is done — and however much is done to stamp out illegal practices, there seems little way of resolving the problem, despite many attempts over the last decade. But the real question to be asked is does the industry really want to correct the position? The BPI does after all represent the record industry, and is it in anyone's interest to investigate too deeply into dirty tricks?

In certain instances "hyping" seems a legitimate practice. There undoubtedly are some acts who need some initial marketing push before they start selling in large quantities; and obviously a new act can be broken in similar fashion. Therefore in formulating a "hype-proof" chart, such practices would become impossible. There are, without doubt, ways in which a chart could accurately reflect what is selling nationwide, without any chance of interference; and with further advances in technological know-how, the day when that chart could be implemented is not far off. But is this what the industry will want?

What of course is possible is that the Independent Television Network will screen an alternative to 'Top Of The Pops' using a different chart. With two charts equally important in terms of media reach, any major discrepancy will be noted immediately, and could anyone afford the expenditure involved in "hyping" both charts?

I think that things will remain the same, every now and then a TV programme will do an exposé on the subject, and after the fuss has died down everything will continue as if nothing had happened. Oh for a return to the days when the chart didn't mean so much, and "hyping" was when a radio producer was taken off to Majorca for a holiday.

DAFYDD REES

I can remember sitting in a record executive's office two years ago, admiring the mosaic of gold and platinum records on his wall, while he explained to me that all radio programming was done by a group of men in California whose names had never been revealed to the rest of the industry. All his story lacked were the white costumes and peaked hoods these men would wear to their meetings. These imaginary demi-gods could be blamed for every debut album that wound up in the bargain bins due to lack of airplay and chart action. Wouldn't it be nice for the record companies if they really existed?

It is interesting to note that while the trade papers and radio do have such enormous control in the selling of music, most people in the industry have no idea how the charts are formulated or how a record gets put on the air. They regard it as one of the mysteries of life, an enigma. The edicts sent down from Mount Olympus are to be accepted, not scrutinised.

Therefore, I assumed that this article was going to give me some trouble. I was surprised that the trade papers were so generous with their time that the men who actually put the charts together every week could sit down and patiently describe to me every detail that goes into this supposedly nefarious business. Radio stations all over America returned my calls. The whole system is so simple and so open, I can't believe I actually bought the men-in-a-smoke-filled-room story.

The chain of command begins with airplay. In order for an album or record to begin an ascent on the charts, it must first get past the ears of programme directors and, in some cases, DJs, all over the country. Record companies do have some measure of influence here, as it is up to them to make sure that the programme directors are aware of the new record and its airplay possibilities. To this end, record companies chose what tracks will be sent out as singles, or they mail the entire album and leave it up to the programme directors to decide which tracks will instigate the most listener interest. The flaw in the latter method is that, if the album offers too many potential single tracks, it will wind up so divided that it will be impossible to chart.

Promotional tricks are also useful at this stage. If the artist makes the time to visit various radio stations across the country and talk with the staff, goodwill is established and the chances are that the DJs will work harder on selling the single. This sounds somewhat cold, and obviously many artists have established relationships within the radio station circuit and just visit for fun. Nevertheless, this is a viable means of getting your album on the air. While visiting the station, taking part in an interview is helpful, as is playing live from the booth. Or you can try the Grace Slick interview technique, which is to send out a separate album that contains the artist's voice answering questions, accompanied by a list of suggested questions. In this way, the jockey can ask a question and cue the record to the appropriate response. These are just a few ideas, but you can see the picture.

The bigger stations are more likely to play it safe than the smaller stations, who reach only one or two towns. It is not unusual for a large station to hold back until they see the results that a tertiary station is getting on a single by a new artist. The smaller stations tend to depend more on their intuition. The programme directors will hold a meeting with the jockeys and talk about which tracks they feel have hit potential, and they will tally requests from listeners when the singles they decide to go with start out on the air. They will then indicate to the trade papers which singles they would describe as Prime movers (increased airplay) Top adds (new singles with airplay priority) and Breakouts (hits) and the trades translate these into charting factors.

Most trade papers employ an average of seven and a half people whose sole priority is to tabulate airplay and sales for the charts. This job entails phoning hundreds of radio stations and retailers all over the US and graphing the results of those calls. The method is clear and simple. All the single records charted below 50 are based on airplay. Radio stations are given a certain number of points by the trade papers and these points reflect the number of listeners that station reaches per week. The reason that airplay is so crucial to the singles chart is that singles sales are not great enough to allow for a chart based solely on sales. As you move up the singles chart, sales come more into play, and by the time you reach the top few tracks, sales alone play a part.

Bullets are an indication of significant upward activity in a record on both the album chart and the singles chart. Significant upward activity is measured by how many points a single or an album moves each week, and fewer points are needed as you move closer to number one. For example, if your album moves ten points from 100 to 90 in one week, that may not win you a bullet. But if you move six points, from eight to two, a bullet is indicated.

Where the album chart is concerned, sales play a far more important role. There could be an artist whose LP gets airplay on every single station in the US, but if he hasn't sold more than ten albums, chances are he won't make it onto the album chart. Some of the trades get what they call a "feel" from the retailers they call. This means they will ask which the top selling albums are, and then they will ask what albums the retailers think will increase in sales in the next few weeks. The reason for this being that the retailers may have run out of an album during the week, which would prevent that record from giving any indication of sales increase, but they may have had requests for that album. RECORD WORLD bases its album charts on numbers — ie. they find out exactly how many copies of each album the retailers have sold that particular week, but they also take the "feel" into account.

The exception to the rules described above is the country singles chart. For the most part, that chart is based solely on airplay since sales of country singles are negligible at this point in time. The country album chart, however, adheres to the methods mentioned.

There are the occasional dark horses on the charts. If one group has a new album out that is doing exceptionally well, it is possible that some of that group's old catalogue will appear on the chart for a brief visit. John Lennon's death, for example, resulted in a phenomenal amount of action for all of his solo albums and a number of Beatle LPs. These sales figures have a way of dropping off without warning, and those albums can go from being 20 on the chart back to oblivion. For the most part, however, albums that have been near to the top do a slow fade from the chart.

So much for mystery. To those of you who were counting on the hooded gang of ten to get you through the coming year, we tender our apologies. They just don't exist. They never did.

DREW MOSELEY

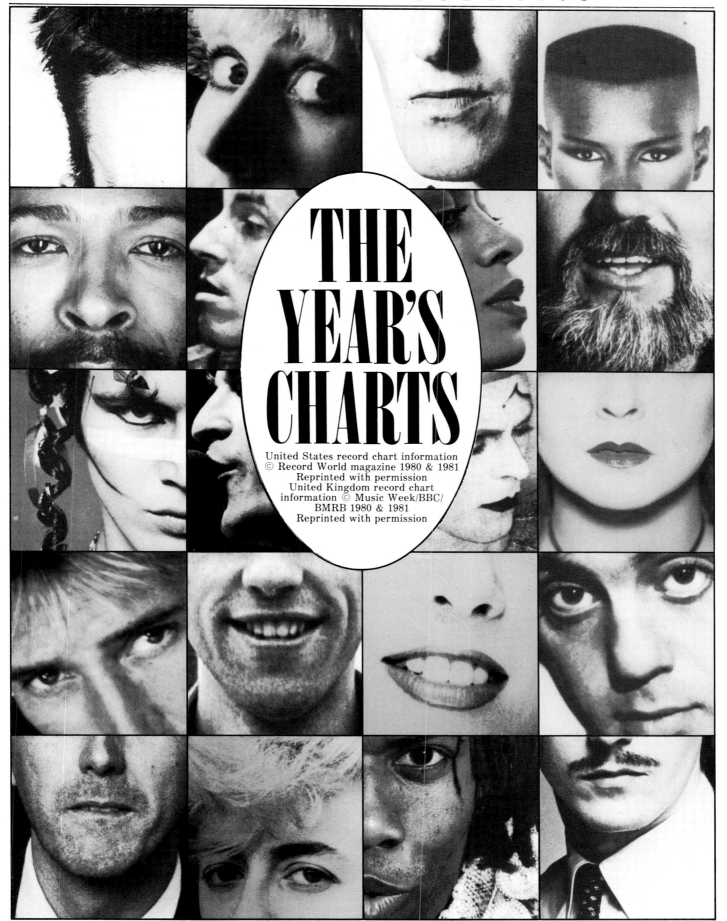

THE YEAR'S CHARTS

United States record chart information
© Record World magazine 1980 & 1981
Reprinted with permission
United Kingdom record chart
information © Music Week/BBC/
BMRB 1980 & 1981
Reprinted with permission

US SINGLES

1. **STILL ROCK AND ROLL TO ME**
   Billy Joel-Columbia
2. **MAGIC**
   Olivia Newton-John-MCA
3. **FUNKYTOWN**
   Lipps, Inc.-Casablanca
4. **CUPID/LOVED YOU LONG**
   The Spinners-Atlantic
5. **SHINING STAR**
   The Manhattans-Columbia
6. **TAKE YOUR TIME**
   S.O.S. Band-Tabu
7. **COMING UP**
   Paul McCartney-Columbia
8. **THE ROSE**
   Bette Midler-Atlantic
9. **MISUNDERSTANDING**
   Genesis-Atlantic
10. **LOVE THE WORLD AWAY**
    Kenny Rogers-United Artists
11. **LITTLE JEANNIE**
    Elton John-MCA
12. **MORE LOVE**
    Kim Carnes-EMI-America
13. **TIRED OF TOEIN' THE LINE**
    Rocky Burnette-EMI-America
14. **IN AMERICA**
    Charlie Daniels Band-Epic
15. **EMOTIONAL RESCUE**
    The Rolling Stones-Rolling Stones
16. **SAILING**
    Christopher Cross-Warner Bros
17. **EMPIRE STRIKES BACK**
    MECO/RSO
18. **LET MY LOVE OPEN THE DOOR**
    Pete Townshend-Atco
19. **TAKE A LITTLE RHYTHM**
    Ali Thomson-A&M
20. **STEAL AWAY**
    Robbie Dupree-Elektra

US ALBUMS

1. **GLASS HOUSES**
   Billy Joel-Columbia
2. **EMOTIONAL RESCUE**
   The Rolling Stones-Rolling Stones
3. **URBAN COWBOY**
   Various Artists-Full Moon-Asylum
4. **HOLD OUT**
   Jackson Browne-Asylum
5. **AGAINST THE WIND**
   Bob Seger-Capitol
6. **BLUES BROTHERS**
   (Original Soundtrack)-Atlantic
7. **THE GAME**
   Queen-Elektra
8. **DIANA**
   Diana Ross-Motown
9. **HEROES**
   The Commodores-Motown
10. **S.O.S.**
    S.O.S. Band-Tabu
11. **OFF THE WALL**
    Michael Jackson-Epic
12. **STAR WARS/EMPIRE STRIKES**
    (Original Soundtrack)-RSO
13. **CHRISTOPHER CROSS**
    Christopher Cross-Warner Bros
14. **McCARTNEY II**
    Paul McCartney-Columbia
15. **EMPTY GLASS**
    Pete Townshend-Atco
16. **FAME**
    (Original Soundtrack)-RSO
17. **ONE FOR THE ROAD**
    Kinks-Arista
18. **MICKEY MOUSE DISCO**
    Disneyland-Vista
19. **JUST ONE NIGHT**
    Eric Clapton-RSO
20. **THE ROSE**
    (Original Soundtrack)-Atlantic

UK SINGLES

1. **USE IT UP**
   Odyssey-RCA
2. **MORE THAN I CAN SAY**
   Leo Sayer-Chrysalis
3. **UPSIDE DOWN**
   Diana Ross-Motown
4. **XANADU**
   Olivia Newton-John/ELO-Jet
5. **BABOOSHKA**
   Kate Bush-EMI
6. **COULD YOU BE LOVED**
   Bob Marley & The Wailers-Island
7. **THERE THERE MY DEAR**
   Dexy's Midnight Runners-Parlophone
8. **JUMP TO THE BEAT**
   Stacy Lattisaw-Atlantic
9. **WINNER TAKES IT ALL**
   Abba-Epic
10. **CUPID**
    Detroit Spinners-Atlantic
11. **WEDNESDAY WEEK**
    Undertones-Sire
12. **EMOTIONAL RESCUE**
    Rolling Stones-Rolling Stones
13. **LET'S HANG ON**
    Darts-Magnet
14. **MY WAY OF THINKING**
    UB40-Graduate
15. **LIP UP FATTY**
    Bad Manners-Magnet
16. **LOVE WILL TEAR US APART**
    Joy Division-Factory
17. **A LOVERS HOLIDAY**
    Change-WEA
18. **OOPS UPSIDE YOUR HEAD**
    Gap Band-Mercury
19. **THEME FROM THE INVADERS**
    Yellow Magic Orchestra-A&M
20. **9 TO 5**
    Sheena Easton-EMI

UK ALBUMS

1. **DEEPEST PURPLE**
   Deep Purple-Harvest
2. **XANADU**
   Soundtrack-Jet
3. **EMOTIONAL RESCUE**
   Rolling Stones-Rolling Stones
4. **FLESH AND BLOOD**
   Roxy Music-Polydor
5. **THE GAME**
   Queen-EMI
6. **CLOSER**
   Joy Division-Factory
7. **GIVE ME THE NIGHT**
   George Benson-Warner Bros
8. **THE YOUNG SOUL REBELS**
   Dexy's Midnight Runners-Parlophone
9. **OFF THE WALL**
   Michael Jackson-Epic
10. **UPRISING**
    Bob Marley-Island
11. **SKY**
    Sky-Ariola
12. **ME MYSELF I**
    Joan Armatrading-A&M
13. **McCARTNEY 11**
    Paul McCartney-Parlophone
14. **VIENNA**
    Ultravox-Chrysalis
15. **PETER GABRIEL**
    Peter Gabriel-Charisma
16. **ANOTHER STRING OF HITS**
    Shadows-EMI
17. **CROCODILES**
    Echo & The Bunnymen-Korova
18. **MANILOW MAGIC**
    Barry Manilow-Arista
19. **MAGIC REGGAE**
    Various-K-Tel
20. **ALL FOR YOU**
    Johnny Mathis-CBS

US SINGLES

1. **MAGIC**
   Olivia Newton-John-MCA
2. **STILL ROCK AND ROLL TO ME**
   Billy Joel-Columbia
3. **FUNKYTOWN**
   Lipps, Inc.-Casablanca
4. **SHINING STAR**
   The Manhattans-Columbia
5. **TAKE YOUR TIME**
   S.O.S. Band-Tabu
6. **CUPID/LOVED YOU LONG**
   The Spinners-Atlantic
7. **COMING UP**
   Paul McCartney-Columbia
8. **LOVE THE WORLD AWAY**
   Kenny Rogers-United Artists
9. **MISUNDERSTANDING**
   Genesis-Atlantic
10. **SAILING**
    Christopher Cross-Warner Bros
11. **MORE LOVE**
    Kim Carnes-EMI-America
12. **LITTLE JEANNIE**
    Elton John-MCA
13. **EMOTIONAL RESCUE**
    The Rolling Stones-Rolling Stones
14. **TIRED OF TOEIN' THE LINE**
    Rocky Burnette-EMI-America
15. **IN AMERICA**
    Charlie Daniels Band-Epic
16. **LET MY LOVE OPEN THE DOOR**
    Pete Townshend-Atco
17. **EMPIRE STRIKES BACK**
    MECO-RSO
18. **JOJO**
    Boz Scaggs-Columbia
19. **TAKE A LITTLE RHYTHM**
    Ali Thomson-A&M
20. **STAND BY ME**
    Mickey Gilley-Full Moon-Asylum

US ALBUMS

1. **EMOTIONAL RESCUE**
   The Rolling Stones-Rolling Stones
2. **GLASS HOUSES**
   Billy Joel-Columbia
3. **URBAN COWBOY**
   Various Artists-Full Moon-Asylum
4. **HOLD OUT**
   Jackson Browne-Asylum
5. **AGAINST THE WIND**
   Bob Seger-Capitol
6. **BLUES BROTHERS**
   (Original Soundtrack)-Atlantic
7. **THE GAME**
   Queen-Elektra
8. **DIANA**
   Diana Ross-Motown
9. **CHRISTOPHER CROSS**
   Christopher Cross-Warner Bros
10. **HEROES**
    The Commodores-Motown
11. **STAR WARS/EMPIRE STRIKES**
    (Original Soundtrack-RSO)
12. **OFF THE WALL**
    Michael Jackson-Epic
13. **S.O.S.**
    S.O.S. Band-Tabu
14. **FAME**
    (Original Soundtrack)-RSO
15. **McCARTNEY II**
    Paul McCartney-Columbia
16. **MICKEY MOUSE DISCO**
    Disneyland-Vista
17. **ONE FOR THE ROAD**
    Kinks-Arista
18. **EMPTY GLASS**
    Pete Townshend-Atco
19. **THE ROSE**
    (Original Soundtrack)-Atlantic
20. **ANYTIME ANYPLACE**
    Rossington Collins Band-MCA

UK SINGLES

1. **WINNER TAKES IT ALL**
   Abba-Epic
2. **UPSIDE DOWN**
   Diana Ross-Motown
3. **USE IT UP WEAR IT OUT**
   Odyssey-RCA
4. **MORE THAN I CAN SAY**
   Leo Sayer-Chrysalis
5. **9 TO 5**
   Sheena Easton-EMI
6. **BABOOSHKA**
   Kate Bush-EMI
7. **OOPS UPSIDE YOUR HEAD**
   Gap Band-Mercury
8. **COULD YOU BE LOVED**
   Bob Marley & The Wailers-Island
9. **OH YEAH**
   Roxy Music-Polydor
10. **GIVE ME THE NIGHT**
    George Benson-Warner Bros.
11. **THERE THERE MY DEAR**
    Dexy's Midnight Runners-Parlophone
12. **WEDNESDAY WEEK**
    Undertones-Sire
13. **XANADU**
    Olivia Newton-John/ELO-Jet
14. **MARIANA**
    Gibson Brothers-Island
15. **LIP UP FATTY**
    Bad Manners-Magnet
16. **FUNKIN' FOR JAMAICA**
    Tom Browne-Arista
17. **JUMP TO THE BEAT**
    Stacy Lattisaw-Atlantic
18. **LET'S HANG ON**
    Darts-Magnet
19. **EMOTIONAL RESCUE**
    Rolling Stones-Rolling Stones
20. **CUPID**
    Detroit Spinners-Atlantic

UK ALBUMS

1. **BACK IN BLACK**
   AC/DC-Atlantic
2. **DEEPEST PURPLE**
   Deep Purple-Harvest
3. **XANADU**
   Soundtrack-Jet
4. **FLESH AND BLOOD**
   Roxy Music-Polydor
5. **EMOTIONAL RESCUE**
   Rolling Stones-Rolling Stones
6. **THE YOUNG SOUL REBELS**
   Dexy's Midnight Runners-Parlophone
7. **GIVE ME THE NIGHT**
   George Benson-Warner Bros
8. **CLOSER**
   Joy Division-Factory
9. **OFF THE WALL**
   Michael Jackson-Epic
10. **SKY 2**
    Sky-Ariola
11. **THE GAME**
    Queen-EMI
12. **UPRISING**
    Bob Marley-Island
13. **McCARTNEY II**
    Paul McCartney-Parlophone
14. **DIANA**
    Diana Ross-Motown
15. **LIVE 1979**
    Hawkwind-Bronze
16. **REGGATTA DE BLANC**
    The Police-A&M
17. **ANOTHER STRING OF HITS**
    Shadows-EMI
18. **MAGIC REGGAE**
    Various-K-Tel
19. **MANILOW MAGIC**
    Barry Manilow-Arista
20. **VIENNA**
    Ultravox-Chrysalis

US SINGLES	US ALBUMS	UK SINGLES	UK ALBUMS
1 **MAGIC** *Olivia Newton-John*	1 **URBAN COWBOY** *Various Artists-Full Moon-Asylum*	1 **WINNER TAKES IT ALL** *Abba-Epic*	1 **BACK IN BLACK** *AC/DC-Atlantic*
2 **STILL ROCK AND ROLL TO ME** *Billy Joel-Colombia*	2 **GLASS HOUSES** *Billy Joel-Columbia*	2 **UPSIDE DOWN** *Diana Ross-Tamla Motown*	2 **FLESH AND BLOOD** *Roxy Music-Polydor*
3 **TAKE YOUR TIME** *S.O.S. Band-Tabu*	3 **EMOTIONAL RESCUE** *The Rolling Stones-Rolling Stones*	3 **9 TO 5** *Sheena Easton-EMI*	3 **GLORY ROAD** *Gillan-Virgin*
4 **SHINING STAR** *The Manhattans-Columbia*	4 **HOLD OUT** *Jackson Browne-Asylum*	4 **ASHES TO ASHES** *David Bowie-RCA*	4 **DEEPEST PURPLE** *Deep Purple-Harvest*
5 **FUNKYTOWN** *Lipps, Inc.-Casablanca*	5 **AGAINST THE WIND** *Bob Seger-Capitol*	5 **OH YEAH** *Roxy Music-Polydor*	5 **GIVE ME THE NIGHT** *George Benson-Warner Bros*
6 **SAILING** *Christopher Cross-Warner Bros*	6 **THE GAME** *Queen-Elektra*	6 **OOPS UPSIDE YOUR HEAD** *Gap Band-Mercury*	6 **OFF THE WALL** *Michael Jackson-Epic*
7 **EMOTIONAL RESCUE** *The Rolling Stones-Rolling Stones*	7 **DIANA** *Diana Ross-Motown*	7 **GIVE ME THE NIGHT** *George Benson-Warner Bros*	7 **XANADU** *Original Soundtrack-Jet*
8 **LOVE THE WORLD AWAY** *Kenny Rogers-United Artists*	8 **BLUES BROTHERS** **(Original Soundtrack)-Atlantic**	8 **MORE THAN I CAN SAY** *Leo Sayer-Chrysalis*	8 **YOUNG SOUL REBELS** *Dexy's Midnight Runners-Parlophone*
9 **ALL OUT OF LOVE** *Air Supply-Arista*	9 **CHRISTOPHER CROSS** *Christopher Cross-Warner Bros*	9 **USE IT UP AND WEAR IT OUT** *Odyssey-RCA*	9 **KALEIDOSCOPE** *Siouxsie and The Banshees-Polydor*
10 **EMPIRE STRIKES BACK** *MECO-RSO*	10 **HEROES** *The Commodores-Motown*	10 **FUNKIN' FOR JAMAICA** *Tom Browne-Arista*	10 **SKY 2** *Sky-Ariola*
11 **MORE LOVE** *Kim Carnes-EMI-America*	11 **GIVE ME THE NIGHT** *George Benson-Qwest-WB*	11 **MARIANA** *Gibson Brothers-Island*	11 **EMOTIONAL RESCUE** *The Rolling Stones-Rolling Stones*
12 **STAND BY ME** *Mickey Gilley-Full Moon-Asylum*	12 **FAME** *(Original Soundtrack)-RSO*	12 **BABOOSHKA** *Kate Bush-EMI*	12 **DIANA** *Diana Ross-Tamla Motown*
13 **CUPID/LOVED YOU LONG** *The Spinners-Atlantic*	13 **S.O.S.** *S.O.S. Band-Tabu*	13 **TOM HARK** *Piranhas-Sire/Hansa*	13 **UPRISING** *Bob Marley and The Wailers-Island*
14 **LET MY LOVE OPEN THE DOOR** *Pete Townshend-Atco*	14 **OFF THE WALL** *Michael Jackson-Epic*	14 **COULD YOU BE LOVED** *Bob Marley and The Wailers*	14 **THE GAME** *Queen-EMI*
15 **GIVE ME THE NIGHT** *George Benson-Qwest-WB*	15 **STAR WARS/EMPIRE STRIKES** *(Original Soundtrack)-RSO*	15 **LIP UP FATTY** *Bad Manners-Magnet*	15 **McCARTNEY II** *Paul McCartney-Parlophone*
16 **INTO THE NIGHT** *Benny Mordones-Polydor*	16 **FULL MOON** *Charlie Daniels Band-Epic*	16 **FEELS LIKE I'M IN LOVE** *Kelly Marie-Calibre*	16 **MANILOW MAGIC** *Barry Manilow-Arista*
17 **FAME** *Irene Cara-RSO*	17 **EMPTY GLASS** *Pete Townshend-Atco*	17 **ARE YOU GETTING ENOUGH** *Hot Chocolate-RAK*	17 **CLOSER** *Joy Division-Factory*
18 **JOJO** *Boz Scaggs-Columbia*	18 **ANYTIME ANYPLACE** *Rossington Collins Band-MCA*	18 **ALL OVER THE WORLD** *Electric Light Orchestra-Jet*	18 **LIVE 1979** *Hawkwind-Bronze*
19 **TAKE A LITTLE RHYTHM** *Ali Thomson-A&M*	19 **MICKEY MOUSE DISCO** *Disneyland-Vista*	19 **THERE THERE MY DEAR** *Dexy's Midnight Runners-Parlophone*	19 **ME MYSELF I** *Joan Armatrading-A&M*
20 **LATE IN THE EVENING** *Paul Simon-Warner Bros*	20 **ONE FOR THE ROAD** *Kinks-Arista*	20 **XANADU** *Olivia Newton-John/ELO-Jet*	20 **REGGATTA DE BLANC** *The Police-A&M*

US SINGLES	US ALBUMS	UK SINGLES	UK ALBUMS
1 **MAGIC** *Olivia Newton-John-MCA*	1 **URBAN COWBOY** *Various Artists-Full Moon-Asylum*	1 **ASHES TO ASHES** *David Bowie-RCA*	1 **FLESH AND BLOOD** *Roxy Music-Polydor*
2 **SAILING** *Christopher Cross-Warner Bros*	2 **GLASS HOUSES** *Billy Joel-Columbia*	2 **WINNER TAKES IT ALL** *Abba-Epic*	2 **BACK IN BLACK** *AC/DC-Atlantic*
3 **TAKE YOUR TIME** *S.O.S. Band-Tabu*	3 **EMOTIONAL RESCUE** *The Rolling Stones-Rolling Stones*	3 **START** *Jam-Polydor*	3 **GLORY ROAD** *Gillan-Virgin*
4 **ALL OUT OF LOVE** *Air Supply-Arista*	4 **HOLD OUT** *Jackson Browne-Asylum*	4 **9 TO 5** *Sheena Easton-EMI*	4 **GIVE ME THE NIGHT** *George Benson-Warner Bros*
5 **EMOTIONAL RESCUE** **The Rolling Stones-Rolling Stones**	5 **THE GAME** *Queen-Elektra*	5 **UPSIDE DOWN** *Diana Ross-Tamla Motown*	5 **KALEIDOSCOPE** *Siouxsie and The Banshees-Polydor*
6 **STILL ROCK AND ROLL TO ME** *Billy Joel-Columbia*	6 **DIANA** *Diana Ross-Motown*	6 **OH YEAH** *Roxy Music-Polydor*	6 **DEEPEST PURPLE** *Deep Purple-Harvest*
7 **SHINING STAR** *The Manhattans-Columbia*	7 **GIVE ME THE NIGHT** *George Benson-Qwest-WB*	7 **OOPS UPSIDE YOUR HEAD** *Gap Band-Mercury*	7 **XANADU** *Original Soundtrack-Jet*
8 **FAME** *Irene Cara-RSO*	8 **CHRISTOPHER CROSS** *Christopher Cross-Warner Bros*	8 **FEELS LIKE I'M IN LOVE** *Kelly Marie-Calibre*	8 **YOUNG SOUL REBELS** *Dexy's Midnight Runners-Parlophone*
9 **EMPIRE STRIKES BACK** *MECO-RSO*	9 **AGAINST THE WIND** *Bob Seger-Capitol*	9 **TOM HARK** *Piranhas-Sire/Hansa*	9 **OFF THE WALL** *Michael Jackson-Epic*
10 **MORE LOVE** *Kim Carnes-EMI-America*	10 **BLUES BROTHERS** *(Original Soundtrack)-Atlantic*	10 **GIVE ME THE NIGHT** *George Benson-Warner Bros*	10 **SKY 2** *Sky-Ariola*
11 **GIVE ME THE NIGHT** *George Benson-Qwest-WB*	11 **FAME** *(Original Soundtrack)-RSO*	11 **ALL OVER THE WORLD** *Electric Light Orchestra-Jet*	11 **UPRISING** *Bob Marley and The Wailers-Island*
12 **STAND BY ME** *Mickey Gilley-Full Moon-Asylum*	12 **FULL MOON** *Charlie Daniels Band-Epic*	12 **FUNKIN' FOR JAMAICA** *Tom Browne-Arista*	12 **EMOTIONAL RESCUE** *The Rolling Stones-Rolling Stones*
13 **INTO THE NIGHT** *Benny Mardones-Polydor*	13 **HEROES** *The Commodores-Motown*	13 **SUNSHINE OF YOUR SMILE** *Mike Berry-Polydor*	13 **MANILOW MAGIC** *Barry Manilow-Arista*
14 **LET MY LOVE OPEN THE DOOR** *Pete Townshend-Atco*	14 **S.O.S.** *S.O.S. Band-Tabu*	14 **MORE THAN I CAN SAY** *Leo Sayer-Chrysalis*	14 **DIANA** *Diana Ross-Tamla Motown*
15 **UPSIDE DOWN** *Diana Ross-Motown*	15 **XANADU** *(Original Soundtrack)-MCA*	15 **MARIANA** *Gibson Brothers-Island*	15 **CLOSER** *Joy Division-Factory*
16 **FUNKYTOWN** *Lipps, Inc.-Casablanca*	16 **OFF THE WALL** *Michael Jackson-Epic*	16 **THERE THERE MY DEAR** *Dexy's Midnight Runners-Parlophone*	16 **ME MYSELF I** *Joan Armatrading-A&M*
17 **LATE IN THE EVENING** *Paul Simon-Warner Bros*	17 **ANYTIME ANYPLACE** *Rossington Collins Band-MCA*	17 **PRIVATE LIFE** *Grace Jones-Island*	17 **McCARTNEY II** *Paul McCartney-Parlophone*
18 **LOVE THE WORLD AWAY** *Kenny Rogers-United Artists*	18 **TP** *Teddy Pendergrass-Phila. Intl.*	18 **USE IT UP AND WEAR IT OUT** *Odyssey-RCA*	18 **THE GAME** *Queen-EMI*
19 **BOULEVARD** *Jackson Browne-Asylum*	19 **STAR WARS/EMPIRE STRIKES** *(Original Sountrack)-RSO*	19 **LIP UP FATTY** *Bad Manners-Magnet*	19 **BREAKING GLASS** *Hazel O'Connor-A&M*
20 **CUPID/LOVED YOU LONG** *The Spinners-Atlantic*	20 **ONE FOR THE ROAD** *Kinks/Arista*	20 **DREAMIN'** *Cliff Richard-EMI*	20 **VIENNA** *Ultravox-Chrysalis*

US SINGLES

#	Title	Artist-Label
1	SAILING	Christopher Cross-Warner Bros
2	ALL OUT OF LOVE	Air Supply-Arista
3	MAGIC	Olivia Newton-John-MCA
4	TAKE YOUR TIME	S.O.S. Band-Tabu
5	EMOTIONAL RESCUE	The Rolling Stones-Rolling Stones
6	FAME	Irene Cara-RSO
7	UPSIDE DOWN	Diana Ross-Motown
8	STILL ROCK AND ROLL TO ME	Billy Joel-Columbia
9	INTO THE NIGHT	Benny Mardones-Polydor
10	GIVE ME THE NIGHT	George Benson-Qwest/WB
11	SHINING STAR	The Manhattans-Columbia
12	LOOKIN' FOR LOVE	Johnny Lee-Full Moon-Asylum
13	LET MY LOVE OPEN THE DOOR	Pete Townshend-Atco
14	LATE IN THE EVENING	Paul Simon-Warner Bros
15	EMPIRE STRIKES BACK	MECO-RSO
16	DRIVIN' MY LIFE AWAY	Eddie Rabbitt-Elektra
17	ONE IN A MILLION YOU	Larry Graham-Warner Bros
18	BOULEVARD	Jackson Browne-Asylum
19	HOT ROD HEARTS	Robbie Dupree-Elektra
20	YOU'RE THE ONLY WOMAN	Ambrosia-Warner Bros

US ALBUMS

#	Title	Artist-Label
1	URBAN COWBOY	Various Artists-Full Moon-Asylum
2	GLASS HOUSES	Billy Joel-Columbia
3	EMOTIONAL RESCUE	The Rolling Stones-Rolling Stones
4	HOLD OUT	Jackson Browne-Asylum
5	THE GAME	Queen-Elektra
6	DIANA	Diana Ross-Motown
7	GIVE ME THE NIGHT	George Benson-Qwest-WB
8	CHRISTOPHER CROSS	Christopher Cross-Warner Bros
9	AGAINST THE WIND	Bob Seger-Capitol
10	FULL MOON	Charlie Daniels Band-Epic
11	FAME	(Original Soundtrack)-RSO
12	XANADU	(Original Soundtrack)-MCA
13	TP	Teddy Pendergrass-Phila. Intl.
14	BLUES BROTHERS	(Original Soundtrack)-Atlantic
15	BACK IN BLACK	AC/DC-Atlantic
16	ANYTIME ANYPLACE	Rossington Collins Band-MCA
17	S.O.S.	S.O.S. Band-Tabu
18	HEROES	The Commodores-Motown
19	OFF THE WALL	Michael Jackson-Epic
20	CRIMES OF PASSION	Pat Benatar-Chrysalis

UK SINGLES

#	Title	Artist-Label
1	ASHES TO ASHES	David Bowie-RCA
2	START	Jam-Polydor
3	9 TO 5	Sheena Easton-EMI
4	WINNER TAKES IT ALL	Abba-Epic
5	FEELS LIKE I'M IN LOVE	Kelly Marie-Calibre
6	TOM HARK	Piranhas-Sire/Hansa
7	UPSIDE DOWN	Diana Ross-Tamla Motown
8	I DIE YOU DIE	Gary Numan-Beggars Banquet
9	OOPS UPSIDE YOUR HEAD	Gap Band-Mercury
10	SUNSHINE OF YOUR SMILE	Mike Berry-Polydor
11	OH YEAH	Roxy Music-Polydor
12	GIVE ME THE NIGHT	George Benson-Warner Bros
13	EIGHTH DAY	Hazel O'Connor-A&M
14	DREAMIN'	Cliff Richard-EMI
15	ALL OVER THE WORLD	Electric Light Orchestra-Jet
16	FUNKIN' FOR JAMAICA	Tom Browne-Arista
17	CAN'T STOP THE MUSIC	Village People-Mercury
18	MODERN GIRL	Sheena Easton-EMI
19	BANK ROBBER	Clash-CBS
20	IT'S STILL ROCK & ROLL TO ME	Billy Joel-CBS

UK ALBUMS

#	Title	Artist-Label
1	FLESH AND BLOOD	Roxy Music-Polydor
2	DRAMA	Yes-Atlantic
3	BACK IN BLACK	AC/DC-Atlantic
4	GIVE ME THE NIGHT	George Benson-Warner Bros
5	XANADU	Original Soundtrack-Jet
6	GLORY ROAD	Gillan-Virgin
7	KALEIDOSCOPE	Siouxsie and The Banshees-Polydor
8	ME MYSELF I	Joan Armatrading-A&M
9	DEEPEST PURPLE	Deep Purple-Harvest
10	OFF THE WALL	Michael Jackson-Epic
11	SKY 2	Sky-Ariola
12	BREAKING GLASS	Hazel O'Connor-A&M
13	I JUST CAN'T STOP IT	The Beat-Beat
14	DIANA	Diana Ross-Tamla Motown
15	LIVING IN A FANTASY	Leo Sayer-Chrysalis
16	UPRISING	Bob Marley and The Wailers-Island
17	EMOTIONAL RESCUE	The Rolling Stones-Rolling Stones
18	YOUNG SOUL REBELS	Dexy's Midnight Runners-Parlophone
19	MANILOW MAGIC	Barry Manilow-Arista
20	BAT OUT OF HELL	Meat Loaf-Epic

US SINGLES

#	Title	Artist-Label
1	ALL OUT OF LOVE	Air Supply-Arista
2	UPSIDE DOWN	Diana Ross-Motown
3	FAME	Irene Cara-RSO
4	SAILING	Christopher Cross-Warner Bros
5	TAKE YOUR TIME	S.O.S. Band-Tabu
6	MAGIC	Olivia Newton-John-MCA
7	EMOTIONAL RESCUE	The Rolling Stones-Rolling Stones
8	GIVE ME THE NIGHT	George Benson-Qwest
9	INTO THE NIGHT	Benny Mardones-Polydor
10	LOOKIN' FOR LOVE	Johnny Lee-Full Moon-Asylum
11	LATE IN THE EVENING	Paul Simon-Warner Bros
12	STILL ROCK AND ROLL TO ME	Billy Joel-Columbia
13	DRIVIN' MY LIFE AWAY	Eddie Rabbitt-Elektra
14	HOT ROD HEARTS	Robbie Dupree-Elektra
15	SHINING STAR	The Manhattans-Columbia
16	ONE IN A MILLION YOU	Larry Graham-Warner Bros
17	LET MY LOVE OPEN THE DOOR	Pete Townshend-Atco
18	YOU'RE THE ONLY WOMAN	Ambrosia-Warner Bros
19	ALL OVER THE WORLD	ELO-MCA
20	DON'T ASK ME WHY	Billy Joel-Columbia

US ALBUMS

#	Title	Artist-Label
1	URBAN COWBOY	Various Artists-Full Moon-Asylum
2	GLASS HOUSES	Billy Joel-Columbia
3	EMOTIONAL RESCUE	The Rolling Stones-Rolling Stones
4	HOLD OUT	Jackson Browne-Asylum
5	THE GAME	Queen-Elektra
6	DIANA	Diana Ross-Motown
7	GIVE ME THE NIGHT	George Benson-Qwest-WB
8	CHRISTOPHER CROSS	Christopher Cross-Warner Bros
9	XANADU	(Original Soundtrack)-MCA
10	FULL MOON	Charlie Daniels Band-Epic
11	FAME	(Original Soundtrack)-RSO
12	TP	Teddy Pendergrass-Phila. Intl.
13	AGAINST THE WIND	Bob Seger-Capitol
14	BACK IN BLACK	AC/DC-Atlantic
15	CRIMES OF PASSION	Pat Benatar-Chrysalis
16	ANYTIME ANYPLACE	Rossington Collins Band-MCA
17	PANORAMA	Cars-Elektra
18	S.O.S.	S.O.S. Band-Tabu
19	BLUES BROTHERS	(Original Soundtrack)-Atlantic
20	ONE TRICK PONY	Paul Simon-Warner Bros

UK SINGLES

#	Title	Artist-Label
1	START	Jam-Polydor
2	ASHES TO ASHES	David Bowie-RCA
3	FEELS LIKE I'M IN LOVE	Kelly Marie-Calibre
4	9 TO 5	Sheena Easton-EMI
5	EIGHTH DAY	Hazel O'Connor-A&M
6	I DIE YOU DIE	Gary Numan-Beggars Banquet
7	TOM HARK	Piranhas-Sire/Hansa
8	WINNER TAKES IT ALL	Abba-Epic
9	SUNSHINE OF YOUR SMILE	Mike Berry-Polydor
10	DREAMIN'	Cliff Richard-EMI
11	CAN'T STOP THE MUSIC	Village People-Mercury
12	BANK ROBBER	Clash-CBS
13	MODERN GIRL	Sheena Easton-EMI
14	UPSIDE DOWN	Diana Ross-Tamla Motown
15	OOPS UPSIDE YOUR HEAD	Gap Band-Mercury
16	GIVE ME THE NIGHT	George Benson-Warner Bros
17	IT'S ONLY LOVE	Elvis Presley-RCA
18	ALL OVER THE WORLD	Electric Light Orchestra-Jet
19	OH YEAH	Roxy Music-Polydor
20	IT'S STILL ROCK & ROLL TO ME	Billy Joel-CBS

UK ALBUMS

#	Title	Artist-Label
1	FLESH AND BLOOD	Roxy Music-Polydor
2	DRAMA	Yes-Atlantic
3	GIVE ME THE NIGHT	George Benson-Warner Bros
4	BACK IN BLACK	AC/DC-Atlantic
5	BREAKING GLASS	Hazel O'Connor-A&M
6	XANADU	Original Soundtrack-Jet
7	GLORY ROAD	Gillan-Virgin
8	I JUST CAN'T STOP IT	The Beat-Beat
9	CAN'T STOP THE MUSIC	Soundtrack-Mercury
10	SKY 2	Sky-Ariola
11	I AM A WOMAN	Various-Polystar
12	OFF THE WALL	Michael Jackson-Epic
13	DIANA	Diana Ross-Tamla Motown
14	DEEPEST PURPLE	Deep Purple-Harvest
15	ME MYSELF I	Joan Armatrading-A&M
16	KALEIDOSCOPE	Siouxsie and The Banshees-Polydor
17	SIGNING OFF	UB 40-Graduate
18	WILD CAT	Tygers of Pan Tang-MCA
19	MICHAEL SCHENKER GROUP	Michael Schenker Group-Chrysalis
20	GLASS HOUSES	Billy Joel-CBS

US SINGLES	US ALBUMS	UK SINGLES	UK ALBUMS
1 ALL OUT OF LOVE *Air Supply-Arista*	1 GLASS HOUSES *Billy Joel-Columbia*	1 FEELS LIKE I'M IN LOVE *Kelly Marie-Calibre*	1 TELEKON *Gary Numan-Beggars Banquet*
2 UPSIDE DOWN *Diana Ross-Motown*	2 URBAN COWBOY *Various Artists-Full Moon-Asylum*	2 START *Jam-Polydor*	2 SIGNING OFF *UB 40-Graduate*
3 FAME *Irene Cara-RSO*	3 THE GAME *Queen-Elektra*	3 ASHES TO ASHES *David Bowie-RCA*	3 FLESH AND BLOOD *Roxy Music-Polydor*
4 SAILING *Christopher Cross-Warner Bros*	4 EMOTIONAL RESCUE *The Rolling Stones-Rolling Stones*	4 ONE DAY I'LL FLY AWAY *Randy Crawford-Warner Bros*	4 I'M NO HERO *Cliff Richard-EMI*
5 TAKE YOUR TIME *S.O.S. Band-Tabu*	5 XANADU *(Original Soundtrack)-MCA*	5 EIGHTH DAY *Hazel O'Connor-A&M*	5 MANILOW MAGIC *Barry Manilow-Arista*
6 GIVE ME THE NIGHT *George Benson-Qwest/WB*	6 HOLD OUT *Jackson Browne-Asylum*	6 9 TO 5 *Sheena Easton-EMI*	6 GIVE ME THE NIGHT *George Benson-Warner Bros*
7 MAGIC *Olivia Newton-John-MCA*	7 GIVE ME THE NIGHT *George Benson-Qwest-WB*	7 IT'S ONLY LOVE *Elvis Presley-RCA*	7 DRAMA *Yes-Atlantic*
8 LOOKIN' FOR LOVE *Johnny Lee-Full Moon-Asylum*	8 CHRISTOPHER CROSS *Christopher Cross-Warner Bros*	8 DREAMIN' *Cliff Richard-EMI*	8 MICHAEL SCHENKER GROUP *Michael Schenker Group-Chrysalis*
9 EMOTIONAL RESCUE *The Rolling Stones-Rolling Stones*	9 DIANA *Diana Ross-Motown*	9 TOM HARK *Piranhas-Sire/Hansa*	9 BACK IN BLACK *AC/DC-Atlantic*
10 LATE IN THE EVENING *Paul Simon-Warner Bros*	10 FULL MOON *Charlie Daniels Band-Epic*	10 MODERN GIRL *Sheena Easton-EMI*	10 I JUST CAN'T STOP IT *The Beat-Beat*
11 DRIVIN' MY LIFE AWAY *Eddie Rabbitt-Elektra*	11 TP *Teddy Pendergrass-Phila. Intl.*	11 SUNSHINE OF YOUR SMILE *Mike Berry-Polydor*	11 BREAKING GLASS *Hazel O'Connor-A&M*
12 HOT ROD HEARTS *Robbie Dupree-Elektra*	12 AGAINST THE WIND *Bob Seger-Capitol*	12 I DIE YOU DIE *Gary Numan-Beggars Banquet*	12 ME MYSELF I *Joan Armatrading-A&M*
13 INTO THE NIGHT *Benny Mardones-Polydor*	13 BACK IN BLACK *AC/DC-Atlantic*	13 BANK ROBBER *Clash-CBS*	13 XANADU *Original Soundtrack-Jet*
14 ALL OVER THE WORLD *ELO-MCA*	14 CRIMES OF PASSION *Pat Benatar-Chrysalis*	14 CAN'T STOP THE MUSIC *Village People-Mercury*	14 OFF THE WALL *Michael Jackson-Epic*
15 STILL ROCK AND ROLL TO ME *Billy Joel-Columbia*	15 PANORAMA *Cars-Elektra*	15 IT'S STILL ROCK & ROLL TO ME *Billy Joel-CBS*	15 GLORY ROAD *Gillan-Virgin*
16 ONE IN A MILLION YOU *Larry Graham-Warner Bros*	16 ANYTIME ANYPLACE *Rossington Collins Band-MCA*	16 WINNER TAKES IT ALL *Abba-Epic*	16 CAN'T STOP THE MUSIC *Soundtrack-Mercury*
17 YOU'RE THE ONLY WOMAN *Ambrosia-Warner Bros*	17 FAME *(Original Soundtrack)-RSO*	17 PARANOID *Black Sabbath-Nems*	17 ONE TRICK PONY *Paul Simon-Warner Bros*
18 DON'T ASK ME WHY *Billy Joel-Columbia*	18 HONEYSUCKLE ROSE *Willie Nelson and Family-Columbia*	18 BITES THE DUST *Queen-EMI*	18 WILD PLANET *B 52's-Island*
19 BITES THE DUST *Queen-Elektra*	19 ONE-TRICK PONY *Paul Simon-Warner Bros*	19 OOPS UPSIDE YOUR HEAD *Gap Band-Mercury*	19 DEEPEST PURPLE *Deep Purple-Harvest*
20 THEME FROM CADDYSHACK *Kenny Loggins-Columbia*	20 HEROES *The Commodores-Motown*	20 A WALK IN THE PARK *Nick Straker Band-CBS*	20 I AM A WOMAN *Various-Polystar*

US SINGLES	US ALBUMS	UK SINGLES	UK ALBUMS
1 UPSIDE DOWN *Diana Ross-Motown*	1 URBAN COWBOY *Various Artists-Full Moon-Asylum*	1 FEELS LIKE I'M IN LOVE *Kelly Marie-Calibre*	1 NEVER FOREVER *Kate Bush-EMI*
2 ALL OUT OF LOVE *Air Supply-Arista*	2 XANADU *(Original Soundtrack)-MCA*	2 ONE DAY I'LL FLY AWAY *Randy Crawford-Warner Bros*	2 SIGNING OFF *UB 40-Graduate*
3 FAME *Irene Cara-RSO*	3 THE GAME *Queen-Elektra*	3 IT'S ONLY LOVE *Elvis Presley-RCA*	3 TELEKON *Gary Numan-Beggars Banquet*
4 LOOKIN' FOR LOVE *Johnny Lee-Full Moon-Asylum*	4 GLASS HOUSES *Billy Joel-Columbia*	4 MASTER BLASTER (JAMMIN') *Stevie Wonder-Tamla Motown*	4 MANILOW MAGIC *Barry Manilow-Arista*
5 BITES THE DUST *Queen-Elektra*	5 EMOTIONAL RESCUE *The Rolling Stones-Rolling Stones*	5 START *Jam-Polydor*	5 I'M NO HERO *Cliff Richard-EMI*
6 GIVE ME THE NIGHT *George Benson-Qwest/WB*	6 HOLD OUT *Jackson Browne-Asylum*	6 EIGHTH DAY *Hazel O'Connor-A&M*	6 FLESH AND BLOOD *Roxy Music-Polydor*
7 DRIVIN' MY LIFE AWAY *Eddie Rabbitt-Elektra*	7 HONEYSUCKLE ROSE *Willie Nelson and Family-Columbia*	7 ASHES TO ASHES *David Bowie-RCA*	7 BLIZZARD OF OZZ *Ozzy Osbourne's Blizzard Of Ozz-Jet*
8 MAGIC *Olivia Newton-John-MCA*	8 CHRISTOPHER CROSS *Christopher Cross-Warner Bros*	8 MODERN GIRL *Sheena Easton-EMI*	8 GIVE ME THE NIGHT *George Benson-Warner Bros*
9 HOT ROD HEARTS *Robbie Dupree-Elektra*	9 PANORAMA *Cars-Elektra*	9 DREAMIN' *Cliff Richard-EMI*	9 HANX *Stiff Little Fingers-Chrysalis*
10 LATE IN THE EVENING *Paul Simon-Warner Bros*	10 CRIMES OF PASSION *Pat Benatar-Chrysalis*	10 BITES THE DUST *Queen-EMI*	10 NOW WE MAY BEGIN *Randy Crawford-Warner Bros*
11 ALL OVER THE WORLD *ELO-MCA*	11 TP *Teddy Pendergrass-Phila. Intl.*	11 9 TO 5 *Sheena Easton-EMI*	11 BACK IN BLACK *AC/DC-Atlantic*
12 SAILING *Christopher Cross-Warner Bros*	12 AGAINST THE WIND *Bob Seger-Capitol*	12 SUNSHINE OF YOUR SMILE *Mike Berry-Polydor*	12 DRAMA *Yes-Atlantic*
13 EMOTIONAL RESCUE *The Rolling Stones-Rolling Stones*	13 BACK IN BLACK *AC/DC-Atlantic*	13 CAN'T STOP THE MUSIC *Village People-Mercury*	13 MICHAEL SCHENKER GROUP *Michael Schenker Group-Chrysalis*
14 THEME FROM CADDYSHACK *Kenny Loggins-Columbia*	14 GIVE ME THE NIGHT *George Benson-Qwest-WB*	14 PARANOID *Black Sabbath-Nems*	14 SKY 2 *Sky-Ariola*
15 TAKE YOUR TIME *S.O.S. Band-Tabu*	15 DIANA *Diana Ross-Motown*	15 IT'S STILL ROCK & ROLL TO ME *Billy Joel-CBS*	15 I JUST CAN'T STOP IT *The Beat-Beat*
16 XANADU *Olivia Newton-ELO-MCA*	16 FULL MOON *Charlie Daniels Band-Epic*	16 BANK ROBBER *Clash-CBS*	16 BLACK SEA *XTC-Virgin*
17 DON'T ASK ME WHY *Billy Joel-Columbia*	17 ANYTIME ANYPLACE *Rossington Collins Band-MCA*	17 TOM HARK *Piranhas-Sire/Hansa*	17 CHANGE OF ADDRESS *Shadows-Polydor*
18 INTO THE NIGHT *Benny Mardones-Polydor*	18 ONE-TRICK PONY *Paul Simon-Warner Bros*	18 I DIE YOU DIE *Gary Numan-Beggars Banquet*	18 BREAKING GLASS *Hazel O'Connor-A&M*
19 YOU'LL ACCOMPANY ME *Bob Seger-Capitol*	19 FAME *(Original Soundtrack)-RSO*	19 MARIE MARIE *Shakin' Stevens-Epic*	19 DIANA *Diana Ross-Tamla Motown*
20 HE'S SO SHY *Pointer Sisters-Planet*	20 DRAMA *YES-Atlantic*	20 A WALK IN THE PARK *Nick Straker Band-CBS*	20 ME MYSELF I *Joan Armatrading-A&M*

US SINGLES	US ALBUMS	UK SINGLES	UK ALBUMS
1 **UPSIDE DOWN** *Diana Ross-Motown*	1 **XANADU** *(Original Soundtrack)-MCA*	1 **DON'T STAND SO CLOSE TO ME** *The Police-A&M*	1 **SCARY MONSTERS** *David Bowie-RCA*
2 **BITES THE DUST** *Queen-Elektra*	2 **THE GAME** *Queen-Elektra*	2 **ONE DAY I'LL FLY AWAY** *Randy Crawford-Warner Bros*	2 **NEVER FOREVER** *Kate Bush-EMI*
3 **ALL OUT OF LOVE** *Air Supply-Arista*	3 **URBAN COWBOY** *Various Artists-Full Moon-Asylum*	3 **MASTER BLASTER (JAMMIN')** *Stevie Wonder-Tamla Motown*	3 **SIGNING OFF** *UB 40-Graduate*
4 **LOOKIN' FOR LOVE** *Johnny Lee-Full Moon-Asylum*	4 **GLASS HOUSES** *Billy Joel-Columbia*	4 **FEELS LIKE I'M IN LOVE** *Kelly Marie-Calibre*	4 **MOUNTING EXCITEMENT** *Various-K-Tel*
5 **DRIVIN' MY LIFE AWAY** *Eddie Rabbitt-Elektra*	5 **EMOTIONAL RESCUE** *The Rolling Stones-Rolling Stones*	5 **BAGGY TROUSERS** *Madness-Stiff*	5 **TELEKON** *Gary Numan-Beggars Banquet*
6 **GIVE ME THE NIGHT** *George Benson-Qwest-WB*	6 **DIANA** *Diana Ross-Motown*	6 **IT'S ONLY LOVE** *Elvis Presley-RCA*	6 **MANILOW MAGIC** *Barry Manilow-Arista*
7 **HOT ROD HEARTS** *Robbie Dupree-Elektra*	7 **HONEYSUCKLE ROSE** *Willie Nelson and Family-Columbia*	7 **BITES THE DUST** *Queen-EMI*	7 **BEST OF DON McLEAN** *Don McLean-United Artists*
8 **ALL OVER THE WORLD** *ELO-MCA*	8 **CHRISTOPHER CROSS** *Christopher Cross-Warner Bros*	8 **D.I.S.C.O.** *Ottowan-Carrere*	8 **CRASH COURSE** *UK Subs-Gem*
9 **LATE IN THE EVENING** *Paul Simon-Warner Bros*	9 **PANORAMA** *Cars-Elektra*	9 **MODERN GIRL** *Sheena Easton-EMI*	9 **THE ABSOLUTE GAME** *Skids-Virgin*
10 **THEME FROM CADDYSHACK** *Kenny Loggins-Columbia*	10 **CRIMES OF PASSION** *Pat Benatar-Chrysalis*	10 **EIGHTH DAY** *Hazel O'Connor-A&M*	10 **I'M NO HERO** *Cliff Richard-EMI*
11 **FAME** *Irene Cara-RSO*	11 **HOLD OUT** *Jackson Browne-Asylum*	11 **START** *Jam-Polydor*	11 **FLESH AND BLOOD** *Roxy Music-Polydor*
12 **MAGIC** *Olivia Newton-John-MCA*	12 **GIVE ME THE NIGHT** *George Benson-Qwest-WB*	12 **DREAMIN'** *Cliff Richard-EMI*	12 **HANX** *Stiff Little Fingers-Chrysalis*
13 **XANADU** *Olivia Newton-John-ELO-MCA*	13 **BACK IN BLACK** *AC/DC-Atlantic*	13 **MY OLD PIANO** *Diana Ross-Tamla Motown*	13 **BLIZZARD OF OZZ** *Ozzy Osbourne's Blizzard of Ozz-Jet*
14 **WOMAN IN LOVE** *Barbra Streisand-Columbia*	14 **TP** *Teddy Pendergrass-Phila. Intl.*	14 **IT'S STILL ROCK & ROLL TO ME** *Billy Joel-CBS*	14 **NOW WE MAY BEGIN** *Randy Crawford-Warner Bros*
15 **REAL LOVE** *Doobie Brothers-Warner Bros*	15 **AGAINST THE WIND** *Bob Seger-Capitol*	15 **ASHES TO ASHES** *David Bowie-RCA*	15 **SKY 2** *Sky-Ariola*
16 **SAILING** *Christopher Cross-Warner Bros*	16 **FULL MOON** *Charlie Daniels Band-Epic*	16 **I OWE YOU ONE** *Shalamar-Solar*	16 **I AM A WOMAN** *Various-Polystar*
17 **DON'T ASK ME WHY** *Billy Joel-Columbia*	17 **ONE-TRICK PONY** *Paul Simon-Warner Bros*	17 **9 TO 5** *Sheena Easton-EMI*	17 **GIVE ME THE NIGHT** *George Benson-Warner Bros*
18 **HE'S SO SHY** *Pointer Sisters-Planet*	18 **FAME** *(Original Soundtrack)-RSO*	18 **SUNSHINE OF YOUR SMILE** *Mike Berry-Polydor*	18 **I JUST CAN'T STOP IT** *The Beat-Beat*
19 **YOU'LL ACCOMPANY ME** *Bob Seger-Capitol*	19 **CHIPMUNK PUNK** *Chipmunks-Excelsior*	19 **PARANOID** *Black Sabbath-Nems*	19 **BLACK SEA** *XTC-Virgin*
20 **EMOTIONAL RESCUE** *The Rolling Stones-Rolling Stones*	20 **DRAMA** *Yes-Atlantic*	20 **A WALK IN THE PARK** *Nick Straker Band-CBS*	20 **GOLD** *Three Degrees-Ariola*

US SINGLES	US ALBUMS	UK SINGLES	UK ALBUMS
1 **BITES THE DUST** *Queen-Elektra*	1 **THE GAME** *Queen-Elektra*	1 **DON'T STAND SO CLOSE TO ME** *The Police-A&M*	1 **SCARY MONSTERS** *David Bowie-RCA*
2 **UPSIDE DOWN** *Diana Ross-Motown*	2 **XANADU** *(Original Soundtrack)-MCA*	2 **MASTER BLASTER (JAMMIN')** *Stevie Wonder-Tamla Motown*	2 **MOUNTING EXCITEMENT** *Various-K-Tel*
3 **WOMAN IN LOVE** *Barbra Streisand-Columbia*	3 **URBAN COWBOY** *Various Artists-Full Moon-Asylum*	3 **D.I.S.C.O.** *Ottowan-Carrere*	3 **NEVER FOREVER** *Kate Bush-EMI*
4 **LOOKIN' FOR LOVE** *Johnny Lee-Full Moon-Asylum*	4 **DIANA** *Diana Ross-Motown*	4 **BAGGY TROUSERS** *Madness-Stiff*	4 **BEST OF DON McLEAN** *Don McLean-United Artists*
5 **DRIVIN' MY LIFE AWAY** *Eddie Rabbitt-Elektra*	5 **HOLD OUT** *Jackson Browne-Asylum*	5 **ONE DAY I'LL FLY AWAY** *Randy Crawford-Warner Bros*	5 **SIGNING OFF** *UB 40-Graduate*
6 **ALL OUT OF LOVE** *Air Supply-Arista*	6 **GIVE ME THE NIGHT** *George Benson-Qwest-WB*	6 **MY OLD PIANO** *Diana Ross-Tamla Motown*	6 **MORE SPECIALS** *Specials-Chrysalis*
7 **HOT ROD HEARTS** *Robbie Dupree-Elektra*	7 **HONEYSUCKLE ROSE** *Willie Nelson and Family-Columbia*	7 **FEELS LIKE I'M IN LOVE** *Kelly Marie-Calibre*	7 **ABSOLUTELY** *Madness-Stiff*
8 **ALL OVER THE WORLD** *ELO-MCA*	8 **GLASS HOUSES** *Billy Joel-Columbia*	8 **BITES THE DUST** *Queen-EMI*	8 **BREAKING GLASS** *Hazel O'Connor-A&M*
9 **LATE IN THE EVENING** *Paul Simon-Warner Bros*	9 **PANORAMA** *Cars-Elektra*	9 **IT'S ONLY LOVE** *Elvis Presley-RCA*	9 **MANILOW MAGIC** *Barry Manilow-Arista*
10 **THEME FROM CADDYSHACK** *Kenny Loggins-Columbia*	10 **CRIMES OF PASSION** *Pat Benatar-Chrysalis*	10 **AMIGO** *Black Slate-Ensign*	10 **PARIS** *Supertramp-A&M*
11 **XANADU** *Olivia Newton-John-ELO-MCA*	11 **EMOTIONAL RESCUE** *The Rolling Stones-Rolling Stones*	11 **SEARCHING** *Change-WEA*	11 **THE ABSOLUTE GAME** *Skids-Virgin*
12 **GIVE ME THE NIGHT** *George Benson-Qwest/WB*	12 **CHRISTOPHER CROSS** *Christopher Cross-Warner Bros*	12 **I GOT YOU** *Split Enz-A&M*	12 **TELEKON** *Gary Numan-Beggars Banquet*
13 **FAME** *Irene Cara-RSO*	13 **BACK IN BLACK** *AC/DC-Atlantic*	13 **I OWE YOU ONE** *Shalamar-Solar*	13 **NOW WE MAY BEGIN** *Randy Crawford-Warner Bros*
14 **REAL LOVE** *Doobie Brothers-Warner Bros*	14 **ONE-TRICK PONY** *Paul Simon-Warner Bros*	14 **EIGHTH DAY** *Hazel O'Connor-A&M*	14 **FLESH AND BLOOD** *Roxy Music-Polydor*
15 **HE'S SO SHY** *Pointer Sisters-Planet*	15 **FAME** *(Original Soundtrack)-RSO*	15 **MODERN GIRL** *Sheena Easton-EMI*	15 **CRASH COURSE** *UK Subs-Gem*
16 **SAILING** *Christopher Cross-Warner Bros*	16 **TP** *Teddy Pendergrass-Phila. Intl.*	16 **IT'S STILL ROCK & ROLL TO ME** *Billy Joel-CBS*	16 **GIVE ME THE NIGHT** *George Benson-Warner Bros*
17 **JESSE** *Carly Simon-Warner Bros*	17 **AGAINST THE WIND** *Bob Seger-Capitol*	17 **THREE LITTLE BIRDS** *Bob Marley and The Wailers-Island*	17 **SKY 2** *Sky-Ariola*
18 **LOOK WHAT YOU'VE DONE** *Boz Scaggs-Columbia*	18 **CHIPMUNK PUNK** *Chipmunks-Excelsior*	18 **KILLER ON THE LOOSE** *Thin Lizzy-Vertigo*	18 **I'M NO HERO** *Cliff Richard-EMI*
19 **YOU'LL ACCOMPANY ME** *Bob Seger-Capitol*	19 **WILD PLANET** *B-52s-Warner Bros*	19 **PARANOID** *Black Sabbath-Nems*	19 **BLIZZARD OF OZZ** *Ozzy Osbourne's Blizzard of Ozz-Jet*
20 **MAGIC** *Olivia Newton-John-MCA*	20 **BEATIN' THE ODDS** *Molly Hatchet-Epic*	20 **IF YOU'RE LOOKIN' FOR A WAY** *Odyssey-RCA*	20 **THE GAME** *Queen-EMI*

WEEK ENDING OCTOBER 11 1980

US SINGLES

1. **BITES THE DUST**
   Queen-Elektra
2. **UPSIDE DOWN**
   Diana Ross-Motown
3. **WOMAN IN LOVE**
   Barbra Streisand-Columbia
4. **LOOKIN' FOR LOVE**
   Johnny Lee-Full Moon-Asylum
5. **DRIVIN' MY LIFE AWAY**
   Eddie Rabbitt-Elektra
6. **ALL OUT OF LOVE**
   Air Supply-Arista
7. **XANADU**
   Olivia Newton-John-ELO-MCA
8. **ALL OVER THE WORLD**
   ELO-MCA
9. **HE'S SO SHY**
   Pointer Sisters-Planet
10. **THEME FROM CADDYSHACK**
    Kenny Loggins-Columbia
11. **REAL LOVE**
    Doobie Brothers-Warner Bros
12. **HOT ROD HEARTS**
    Robbie Dupree-Elektra
13. **JESSE**
    Carly Simon-Warner Bros
14. **LOOK WHAT YOU'VE DONE**
    Boz Scaggs-Columbia
15. **GIVE ME THE NIGHT**
    George Benson-Qwest-WB
16. **LATE IN THE EVENING**
    Paul Simon-Warner Bros
17. **FAME**
    Irene Cara-RSO
18. **SAILING**
    Christopher Cross-Warner Bros
19. **THE WANDERER**
    Donna Summer-Geffen
20. **YOU'LL ACCOMPANY ME**
    Bob Seger-Capitol

US ALBUMS

1. **THE GAME**
   Queen-Elektra
2. **XANADU**
   (Original Soundtrack)-MCA
3. **URBAN COWBOY**
   Various Artists-Full Moon-Asylum
4. **DIANA**
   Diana Ross-Motown
5. **HOLD OUT**
   Jackson Browne-Asylum
6. **GIVE ME THE NIGHT**
   George Benson-Qwest-WB
7. **GUILTY**
   Barbra Streisand-Columbia
8. **HONEYSUCKLE ROSE**
   Willie Nelson and Family-Columbia
9. **GLASS HOUSES**
   Billy Joel-Columbia
10. **CRIMES OF PASSION**
    Pat Benatar-Chrysalis
11. **ONE STEP CLOSER**
    Doobie Brothers-Warner Bros
12. **BACK IN BLACK**
    AC/DC-Atlantic
13. **PANORAMA**
    Cars-Elektra
14. **ONE-TRICK PONY**
    Paul Simon-Warner Bros
15. **FAME**
    (Original Soundtrack)-RSO
16. **CHRISTOPHER CROSS**
    Christopher Cross-Warner Bros
17. **EMOTIONAL RESCUE**
    The Rolling Stones-Rolling Stones
18. **TP**
    Teddy Pendergrass-Phila. Intl.
19. **WILD PLANET**
    B-52s-Warner Bros
20. **BEATIN' THE ODDS**
    Molly Hatchet-Epic

UK SINGLES

1. **DON'T STAND SO CLOSE TO ME**
   The Police-A&M
2. **D.I.S.C.O.**
   Ottawan-Carrere
3. **BAGGY TROUSERS**
   Madness-Stiff
4. **MASTER BLASTER (JAMMIN')**
   Stevie Wonder-Tamla Motown
5. **MY OLD PIANO**
   Diana Ross-Tamla Motown
6. **STEREOTYPE**
   Specials-2 Tone
7. **IF YOU'RE LOOKIN' FOR A WAY**
   Odyssey-RCA
8. **ONE DAY I'LL FLY AWAY**
   Randy Crawford-Warner Bros
9. **AMIGO**
   Black Slate-Ensign
10. **KILLER ON THE LOOSE**
    Thin Lizzy-Vertigo
11. **AND THE BIRDS WERE SINGING**
    Sweet People-Polydor
12. **FEELS LIKE I'M IN LOVE**
    Kelly Marie-Calibre
13. **SEARCHING**
    Change-WEA
14. **TROUBLE**
    Gillan-Virgin
15. **WHEN YOU ASK ABOUT LOVE**
    Matchbox-Magnet
16. **BITES THE DUST**
    Queen-EMI
17. **THREE LITTLE BIRDS**
    Bob Marley and The Wailers-Island
18. **I GOT YOU**
    Split Enz-A&M
19. **CASANOVA**
    Coffee-De Lite
20. **IT'S ONLY LOVE**
    Elvis Presley-RCA

UK ALBUMS

1. **ZENYATTA MONDATTA**
   The Police-A&M
2. **ABSOLUTELY**
   Madness-Stiff
3. **SCARY MONSTERS**
   David Bowie-RCA
4. **MOUNTING EXCITEMENT**
   Various-K-Tel
5. **MORE SPECIALS**
   Specials-Chrysalis
6. **NEVER FOREVER**
   Kate Bush-EMI
7. **PARIS**
   Supertramp-A&M
8. **BEST OF DON McLEAN**
   Don McLean-United Artists
9. **BREAKING GLASS**
   Hazel O'Connor-A&M
10. **SIGNING OFF**
    UB 40-Graduate
11. **MANILOW MAGIC**
    Barry Manilow-Arista
12. **GUILTY**
    Barbra Streisand-CBS
13. **I AM A WOMAN**
    Various-Polystar
14. **GIVE ME THE NIGHT**
    George Benson-Warner Bros
15. **NOW WE MAY BEGIN**
    Randy Crawford-Warner Bros
16. **A TOUCH OF LOVE**
    Gladys Knight and The Pips-K-Tel
17. **FLESH AND BLOOD**
    Roxy Music-Polydor
18. **GOLD**
    Three Degrees-K-Tel
19. **TELEKON**
    Gary Numan-Beggars Banquet
20. **I'M NO HERO**
    Cliff Richard-EMI

WEEK ENDING OCTOBER 18 1980

US SINGLES

1. **BITES THE DUST**
   Queen-Elektra
2. **WOMAN IN LOVE**
   Barbra Streisand-Columbia
3. **UPSIDE DOWN**
   Diana Ross-Motown
4. **XANADU**
   Olivia Newton-John-ELO-MCA
5. **HE'S SO SHY**
   Pointer Sisters-Planet
6. **ALL OUT OF LOVE**
   Air Supply-Arista
7. **JESSE**
   Carly Simon-Warner Bros
8. **DRIVIN' MY LIFE AWAY**
   Eddie Rabbitt-Elektra
9. **REAL LOVE**
   Doobie Brothers-Warner Bros
10. **THEME FROM CADDYSHACK**
    Kenny Loggins-Columbia
11. **LOOKIN' FOR LOVE**
    Johnny Lee-Full Moon-Asylum
12. **THE WANDERER**
    Donna Summer-Geffen
13. **LOOK WHAT YOU'VE DONE**
    Boz Scaggs-Columbia
14. **ALL OVER THE WORLD**
    ELO-MCA
15. *NEVER KNEW LOVE LIKE THIS*
    Stephanie Mills-20th Century Fox
16. **DREAMING**
    Cliff Richard-EMI-America
17. **LADY**
    Kenny Rogers-Liberty
18. **HOT ROD HEARTS**
    Robbie Dupree-Elektra
19. **GIVE ME THE NIGHT**
    George Benson-Qwest-WB
20. **LATE IN THE EVENING**
    Paul Simon-Warner Bros

US ALBUMS

1. **GUILTY**
   Barbra Streisand-Columbia
2. **THE GAME**
   Queen-Elektra
3. **ONE STEP CLOSER**
   Doobie Brothers-Warner Bros
4. **DIANA**
   Diana Ross-Motown
5. **XANADU**
   (Original Soundtrack)-MCA
6. **URBAN COWBOY**
   Various Artists-Full Moon-Asylum
7. **CRIMES OF PASSION**
   Pat Benatar-Chrysalis
8. **PANORAMA**
   Cars-Elektra
9. **BACK IN BLACK**
   AC/DC-Atlantic
10. **GIVE ME THE NIGHT**
    George Benson-Qwest-WB
11. **HOLD OUT**
    Jackson Browne-Asylum
12. **HONEYSUCKLE ROSE**
    Willie Nelson and Family-Columbia
13. **GLASS HOUSES**
    Billy Joel-Columbia
14. **ONE-TRICK PONY**
    Paul Simon-Warner Bros
15. **CHRISTOPHER CROSS**
    Christopher Cross-Warner Bros
16. **EMOTIONAL RESCUE**
    The Rolling Stones-Rolling Stones
17. **TP**
    Teddy Pendergrass/Phila. Intl.
18. **GREATEST HITS**
    Kenny Rogers-Liberty
19. **TRIUMPH**
    The Jacksons-Epic
20. **KENNY LOGGINS ALIVE**
    Kenny Loggins-Columbia

UK SINGLES

1. **DON'T STAND SO CLOSE TO ME**
   The Police-A&M
2. **D.I.S.C.O.**
   Ottawan-Carrere
3. **BAGGY TROUSERS**
   Madness-Stiff
4. **AND THE BIRDS WERE SINGING**
   Sweet People-Polydor
5. **WHAT YOU'RE PROPOSING**
   Status Quo-Vertigo
6. **MASTER BLASTER (JAMMIN')**
   Stevie Wonder-Tamla Motown
7. **IF YOU'RE LOOKIN' FOR A WAY**
   Odyssey-RCA
8. **MY OLD PIANO**
   Diana Ross-TamlaMotown
9. **WOMAN IN LOVE**
   Barbra Streisand-CBS
10. **WHEN YOU ASK ABOUT LOVE**
    Matchbox-Magnet
11. **AMIGO**
    Black Slate-Ensign
12. **KILLER ON THE LOOSE**
    Thin Lizzy-Vertigo
13. **CASANOVA**
    Coffee-Mercury
14. **PULL MYSELF TOGETHER**
    Nolans-Epic
15. **YOU'RE LYING**
    Linx-Chrysalis
16. **SEARCHING**
    Change-WEA
17. **THREE LITTLE BIRDS**
    Bob Marley and The Wailers-Island
18. **ENOLA GAY**
    Orchestral Manoeuvres-DinDisc
19. **ONE DAY I'LL FLY AWAY**
    Randy Crawford-Warner Bros
20. **TROUBLE**
    Gillan-Virgin

UK ALBUMS

1. **ZENYATTA MONDATTA**
   The Police-A&M
2. **GUILTY**
   Barbra Streisand-CBS
3. **ABSOLUTELY**
   Madness-Stiff
4. **MOUNTING EXCITEMENT**
   Various-K Tel
5. **NEVER FOREVER**
   Kate Bush-EMI
6. **SCARY MONSTERS**
   David Bowie-RCA
7. **CHINATOWN**
   Thin Lizzy-Vertigo
8. **BEST OF DON McLEAN**
   Don McLean-United Artists
9. **MORE SPECIALS**
   Specials-Chrysalis
10. **MANILOW MAGIC**
    Barry Manilow-Arista
11. **BREAKING GLASS**
    Hazel O'Connor-A&M
12. **PARIS**
    Supertramp-A&M
13. **TRIUMPH**
    Jacksons-Epic
14. **THE LOVE ALBUM**
    Various-K Tel
15. **I AM A WOMAN**
    Various-Polystar
16. **SIGNING OFF**
    UB40-Graduate
17. **MONSTERS OF ROCK**
    Various-Polydor
18. **FLESH AND BLOOD**
    Roxy Music-Polydor
19. **GOLD**
    Three Degrees-Ariola
20. **GIVE ME THE NIGHT**
    George Benson-Warner Bros

US SINGLES	US ALBUMS	UK SINGLES	UK ALBUMS
1 **BITES THE DUST** *Queen-Elektra*	1 **GUILTY** *Barbra Streisand-Columbia*	1 **WOMAN IN LOVE** *Barbara Streisand-CBS*	1 **ZENYATTA MONDATTA** *The Police-A&M*
2 **WOMAN IN LOVE** *Barbra Streisand-Columbia*	2 **THE GAME** *Queen-Elektra*	2 **D.I.S.C.O.** *Ottawan-Carrere*	2 **THE RIVER** *Bruce Springsteen-CBS*
3 **UPSIDE DOWN** *Diana Ross-Motown*	3 **ONE STEP CLOSER** *Doobie Brothers-Warner Bros*	3 **DON'T STAND SO CLOSE TO ME** *The Police-A&M*	3 **GUILTY** *Barbra Streisand-CBS*
4 **XANADU** *Olivia Newton-John-ELO-MCA*	4 **GREATEST HITS** *Kenny Rogers-Liberty*	4 **WHAT YOU'RE PROPOSING** *Status Quo-Vertigo*	4 **JUST SUPPOSIN'** *Status Quo-Vertigo*
5 **HE'S SO SHY** *Pointer Sisters-Planet*	5 **XANADU** *Original Soundtrack-MCA*	5 **BAGGY TROUSERS** *Madness-Stiff*	5 **ABSOLUTELY** *Madness-Stiff*
6 **THE WANDERER** *Donna Summer-Geffen*	6 **DIANA** *Diana Ross-Motown*	6 **WHEN YOU ASK ABOUT LOVE** *Matchbox-Magnet*	6 **THE LOVE ALBUM** *Various-K Tel*
7 **JESSE** *Carly Simon-Warner Bros*	7 **CRIMES OF PASSION** *Pat Benatar-Chrysalis*	7 **IF YOU'RE LOOKIN' FOR A WAY** *Odyssey-RCA*	7 **NEVER FOREVER** *Kate Bush-EMI*
8 **LADY** *Kenny Rogers-Liberty*	8 **PANORAMA** *Cars-Elektra*	8 **AND THE BIRDS WERE SINGING** *Sweet People-Polydor*	8 **CHINATOWN** *Thin Lizzy-Vertigo*
9 **REAL LOVE** *Doobie Brothers-Warner Bros*	9 **BACK IN BLACK** *AC/DC-Atlantic*	9 **PULL MYSELF TOGETHER** *Nolans-EMI*	9 **MANILOW MAGIC** *Barry Manilow-Arista*
10 **ALL OUT OF LOVE** *Air Supply-Arista*	10 **URBAN COWBOY** *Original Soundtrack-Full Moon-Asylum*	10 **LOVE X LOVE** *George Benson-Warner Bros*	10 **SCARY MONSTERS** *David Bowie-RCA*
11 **DRIVIN' MY LIFE AWAY** *Eddie Rabbitt-Elektra*	11 **GIVE ME THE NIGHT** *George Benson-Qwest-WB*	11 **MY OLD PIANO** *Diana Ross-Tamla Motown*	11 **PARIS** *Supertramp-A&M*
12 **NEVER KNEW LOVE LIKE THIS** *Stephanie Mills-20th Century Fox*	12 **TRIUMPH** *The Jacksons-Epic*	12 **ENOLA GAY** *Orchestral Manoeuvres-DinDisc*	12 **I AM A WOMAN** *Various-Polystar*
13 **DREAMING** *Cliff Richard-EMI-America*	13 **HOLD OUT** *Jackson Browne-Asylum*	13 **CASANOVA** *Coffee-De-Lite*	13 **MOUNTING EXCITEMENT** *Various-K Tel*
14 **THEME FROM CADDYSHACK** *Kenny Loggins-Columbia*	14 **HONEYSUCKLE ROSE** *Willie Nelson and Family-Columbia*	14 **MASTER BLASTER (JAMMIN')** *Stevie Wonder-Tamla Motown*	14 **CONTRACTURAL OBLIGATION** *Monty Python-Charisma*
15 **LOOK WHAT YOU'VE DONE** *Boz Scaggs-Columbia*	15 **TP** *Teddy Pendergrass-Phila.Intl.*	15 **SPECIAL BREW** *Bad Manners-Magnet*	15 **BEST OF DON McLEAN** *Don McLean-United Artists*
16 **LOOKIN' FOR LOVE** *Johnny Lee-Full Moon-Asylum*	16 **KENNY LOGGINS ALIVE** *Kenny Loggins-Columbia*	16 **AMIGO** *Black Slate-Ensign*	16 **MONSTERS OF ROCK** *Various-Polydor*
17 **ALL OVER THE WORLD** *ELO-MCA*	17 **PARIS** *Supertramp-A&M*	17 **YOU'RE LYING** *Linx-Chrysalis*	17 **TRIUMPH** *Jacksons-Epic*
18 **HOT ROD HEARTS** *Robbie Dupree-Elektra*	18 **GLASS HOUSES** *Billy Joel-Columbia*	18 **KILLER ON THE LOOSE** *Thin Lizzy-Vertigo*	18 **GIVE ME THE NIGHT** *George Benson-Warner Bros*
19 **ON THE ROAD AGAIN** *Willie Nelson-Columbia*	19 **ONE-TRICK PONY** *Paul Simon-Warner Bros*	19 **DOG EAT DOG** *Adam and The Ants-CBS*	19 **BREAKING GLASS** *Hazel O'Connor-A&M*
20 **DREAMER** *Supertramp-A&M*	20 **EMOTIONAL RESCUE** *The Rolling Stones-Rolling Stones*	20 **ALL OUT OF LOVE** *Air Supply-Arista*	20 **GOLD** *Three Degrees-K Tel*

US SINGLES	US ALBUMS	UK SINGLES	UK ALBUMS
1 **BITES THE DUST** *Queen-Elektra*	1 **GUILTY** *Barbra Streisand-Columbia*	1 **WOMAN IN LOVE** *Barbra Streisand-CBS*	1 **ZENYATTA MONDATTA** *The Police-A&M*
2 **WOMAN IN LOVE** *Barbra Streisand*	2 **THE RIVER** *Bruce Springsteen-Columbia*	2 **WHAT YOU'RE PROPOSING** *Status Quo-Vertigo*	2 **GUILTY** *Barbra Streisand-CBS*
3 **LADY** *Kenny Rogers-Liberty*	3 **ONE STEP CLOSER** *Doobie Brothers-Warner Bros*	3 **D.I.S.C.O.** *Ottawan-Carrere*	3 **THE RIVER** *Bruce Springsteen-CBS*
4 **UPSIDE DOWN** *Diana Ross-Motown*	4 **GREATEST HITS** *Kenny Rogers*	4 **WHEN YOU ASK ABOUT LOVE** *Matchbox-Magnet*	4 **JUST SUPPOSIN'** *Status Quo-Vertigo*
5 **THE WANDERER** *Donna Summer-Geffen*	5 **THE GAME** *Queen-Elektra*	5 **SPECIAL BREW** *Bad Manners-Magnet*	5 **MANILOW MAGIC** *Barry Manilow-Arista*
6 **HE'S SO SHY** *Pointer Sisters-Planet*	6 **BACK IN BLACK** *AC/DC-Atlantic*	6 **LOOKIN' FOR A WAY OUT** *Odyssey-RCA*	6 **ORGANISATION** *Orchestral Manoeuvres-Din Disc*
7 **JESSE** *Carly Simon-Warner Bros*	7 **CRIMES OF PASSION** *Pat Benatar-Chrysalis*	7 **BAGGY TROUSERS** *Madness-Stiff*	7 **THE LOVE ALBUM** *Various-K Tel*
8 **XANADU** *Olivia Newton-John/ELO-MCA*	8 **XANADU** *Original Soundtrack-Full Moon-Asylum*	8 **ENOLA GAY** *Orchestral Manoeuvres-DinDisc*	8 **ABSOLUTELY** *Madness-Stiff*
9 **REAL LOVE** *Doobie Brothers-Warner Bros*	9 **DIANA** *Diana Ross-Motown*	9 **PULL MYSELF TOGETHER** *Nolans-Epic*	9 **NEVER FOREVER** *Kate Bush-EMI*
10 **NEVER KNEW LOVE LIKE THIS** *Stephanie Mills-20th Century Fox*	10 **TRIUMPH** *The Jacksons-Epic*	10 **DON'T STAND SO CLOSE TO ME** *The Police-A&M*	10 **FACES** *Earth, Wind and Fire-CBS*
11 **DREAMING** *Cliff Richard-EMI-America*	11 **GIVE ME THE NIGHT** *George Benson-Qwest-WB*	11 **ALL OUT OF LOVE** *Air Supply-Arista*	11 **MAKIN' MOVIES** *Dire Straits-Vertigo*
12 **DRIVIN' MY LIFE AWAY** *Eddie Rabbitt-Elektra*	12 **PANORAMA** *Cars-Elektra*	12 **LOVE X LOVE** *George Benson-Warner Bros*	12 **SCARY MONSTERS** *David Bowie-RCA*
13 **ALL OUT OF LOVE** *Air Supply*	13 **PARIS** *Supertramp-A&M*	13 **DOG EAT DOG** *Adam and The Ants-CBS*	13 **CONTRACTURAL OBLIGATION** *Monty Python-Charisma*
14 **THEME FROM CADDYSHACK** *Kenny Loggins-Columbia*	14 **HOLD OUT** *Jackson Browne-Asylum*	14 **AND THE BIRDS WERE SINGING** *Sweet People-Polydor*	14 **GIVE ME THE NIGHT** *George Benson-Warner Bros*
15 **LOOK WHAT YOU'VE DONE** *Boz Scaggs-Columbia*	15 **URBAN COWBOY** *Original Soundtrack-Full Moon-Asylum*	15 **CASANOVA** *Coffee-De-Lite*	15 **TRIUMPH** *Jacksons-Epic*
16 **LOOKIN' FOR LOVE** *Johnny Lee-Full Moon-Asylum*	16 **KENNY LOGGINS ALIVE** *Kenny Loggins-Columbia*	16 **ARMY DREAMERS** *Kate Bush-EMI*	16 **I AM A WOMAN** *Various-Polystar*
17 **LOST THAT LOVIN' FEELING** *Daryl Hall and John Oates-RCA*	17 **TEDDY PENDERGRASS** *Teddy Pendergrass-Phila Intl.*	17 **ONE MAN WOMAN** *Sheena Easton-EMI*	17 **REGATTA DE BLANC** *The Police-A&M*
18 **ON THE ROAD AGAIN** *Willie Nelson-Columbia*	18 **GLASS HOUSES** *Billy Joel-Columbia*	18 **YOU'RE LYING** *Linx-Chrysalis*	18 **GOLD** *Three Degrees-K Tel*
19 **DREAMER** *Supertramp-A&M*	19 **HONEYSUCKLE ROSE** *Willie Nelson and Family-Columbia*	19 **WHAT'S IN A KISS** *Gilbert O'Sullivan-CBS*	19 **BEST OF DON McLEAN** *Don McLean-United Artists*
20 **I'M COMING OUT** *Diana Ross-Motown*	20 **EMOTIONAL RESCUE** *The Rolling Stones-Rolling Stones*	20 **FASHION** *David Bowie-RCA*	20 **MY GENERATION** *The Who-Virgin*

US SINGLES

1. **WOMAN IN LOVE**
   Barbra Streisand
2. **BITES THE DUST**
   Queen-Elektra
3. **LADY**
   Kenny Rogers-Liberty
4. **THE WANDERER**
   Donna Summer-Geffen
5. **UPSIDE DOWN**
   Diana Ross-Motown
6. **HE'S SO SHY**
   Pointer Sisters-Planet
7. **JESSE**
   Carly Simon-Warner Bros
8. **NEVER KNEW LOVE LIKE THIS**
   Stephanie Mills-20th Century Fox
9. **DREAMING**
   Cliff Richard-EMI-America
10. **LOST THAT LOVIN' FEELING**
    Daryl Hall and John Oates-RCA
11. **XANADU**
    Olivia Newton-John/ELO-MCA
12. **LOVELY ONE**
    The Jacksons-Epic
13. **ALL OUT OF LOVE**
    Air Supply-Arista
14. **I'M COMING OUT**
    Diana Ross-Motown
15. **REAL LOVE**
    Doobie Brothers-Warner Bros
16. **DRIVIN' MY LIFE AWAY**
    Eddie Rabbitt-Elektra
17. **ON THE ROAD AGAIN**
    Willie Nelson-Columbia
18. **THEME FROM CADDYSHACK**
    Kenny Loggins-Columbia
19. **DREAMER**
    Supertramp-A&M
20. **MORE THAN I CAN SAY**
    Leo Sayer-Warner Bros

US ALBUMS

1. **GREATEST HITS**
   Kenny Rogers-Liberty
2. **THE RIVER**
   Bruce Springsteen-Columbia
3. **GUILTY**
   Barbra Streisand-Columbia
4. **THE GAME**
   Queen-Elektra
5. **ONE STEP CLOSER**
   Doobie Brothers-Warner Bros
6. **BACK IN BLACK**
   AC/DC-Atlantic
7. **CRIMES OF PASSION**
   Pat Benatar-Chrysalis
8. **XANADU**
   Original Soundtrack-MCA
9. **HOTTER THAN JULY**
   Stevie Wonder-Motown
10. **TRIUMPH**
    The Jacksons-Epic
11. **DIANA**
    Diana Ross-Motown
12. **PARIS**
    Supertramp-A&M
13. **THE WANDERER**
    Donna Summer-Geffen
14. **URBAN COWBOY**
    Original Soundtrack-Full Moon-Asylum
15. **GIVE ME THE NIGHT**
    George Benson-Qwest-WB
16. **KENNY LOGGINS ALIVE**
    Kenny Loggins-Columbia
17. **HOLD OUT**
    Jackson Browne-Asylum
18. **GLASS HOUSES**
    Billy Joel-Columbia
19. **PANORAMA**
    Cars-Elektra
20. **HONEYSUCKLE ROSE**
    Willie Nelson and Family-Columbia

UK SINGLES

1. **WOMAN IN LOVE**
   Barbra Streisand-CBS
2. **WHAT YOU'RE PROPOSING**
   Status Quo-Vertigo
3. **SPECIAL BREW**
   Bad Manners-Magnet
4. **DOG EAT DOG**
   Adam and The Ants-CBS
5. **THE TIDE IS HIGH**
   Blondie-Chrysalis
6. **WHEN YOU ASK ABOUT LOVE**
   Matchbox-Magnet
7. **LOOKIN' FOR A WAY OUT**
   Odyssey-RCA
8. **FASHION**
   David Bowie-RCA
9. **ENOLA GAY**
   Orchestral Manoeuvres-DinDisc
10. **D.I.S.C.O.**
    Ottawan-Carrere
11. **PULL MYSELF TOGETHER**
    Nolans-Epic
12. **ALL OUT OF LOVE**
    Air Supply-Arista
13. **BAGGY TROUSERS**
    Madness-Stiff
14. **ONE MAN WOMAN**
    Sheena Easton-EMI
15. **SUDDENLY**
    Olivia N-J/Cliff Richard-Jet
16. **DONT STAND SO CLOSE TO ME**
    The Police-A&M
17. **ARMY DREAMERS**
    Kate Bush-EMI
18. **NEVER KNEW LOVE LIKE THIS**
    Stephanie Mills-20th Century
19. **I COULD BE SO GOOD FOR YOU**
    Dennis Waterman-EMI
20. **LOVE X LOVE**
    George Benson-Warner Bros

UK ALBUMS

1. **GUILTY**
   Barbra Streisand-CBS
2. **HOTTER THAN JULY**
   Stevie Wonder-Tamla Motown
3. **ZENYATTA MONDATTA**
   The Police-A&M
4. **ACE OF SPADES**
   Motorhead-Bronze
5. **THE HEART OF THE CITY**
   Whitesnake-United Artists
6. **ORGANISATION**
   Orchestral Manoeuvres-DinDisc
7. **JUST SUPPOSIN'**
   Status Quo-Vertigo
8. **THE RIVER**
   Bruce Springsteen-CBS
9. **GOLD**
   Three Degrees-K Tel
10. **NEVER FOREVER**
    Kate Bush-EMI
11. **MANILOW MAGIC**
    Barry Manilow-Arista
12. **ABSOLUTELY**
    Madness-Stiff
13. **THE LOVE ALBUM**
    Various-K Tel
14. **SCARY MONSTERS**
    David Bowie-RCA
15. **MAKING MOVIES**
    Dire Straits-Vertigo
16. **MAKING WAVES**
    Nolans-Epic
17. **FACES**
    Earth, Wind and Fire-CBS
18. **BREAKING GLASS**
    Hazel O'Connor-A&M
19. **NOT THE 9 O'CLOCK NEWS**
    Various-BBC
20. **LITTLE MISS DYNAMITE**
    Brenda Lee-Warwick

US SINGLES

1. **BITES THE DUST**
   Queen-Elektra
2. **LADY**
   Kenny Rogers-Liberty
3. **WOMAN IN LOVE**
   Barbra Streisand-Columbia
4. **THE WANDERER**
   Donna Summer-Geffen
5. **HE'S SO SHY**
   Pointer Sisters-Planet
6. **JESSE**
   Carly Simon-Warner Bros
7. **DREAMING**
   Cliff Richard-EMI-America
8. **NEVER KNEW LOVE LIKE THIS**
   Stephanie Mills-20th Century Fox
9. **LOVELY ONE**
   The Jacksons-Epic
10. **LOST THAT LOVIN' FEELING**
    Daryl Hall and John Oates-RCA
11. **I'M COMING OUT**
    Diana Ross-Motown
12. **MORE THAN I CAN SAY**
    Leo Sayer-Warner Bros
13. **UPSIDE DOWN**
    Diana Ross-Motown
14. **NEVER BE THE SAME**
    Christopher Cross-Warner Bros
15. **HIT ME WITH YOUR BEST SHOT**
    Pat Benatar-Chrysalis
16. **ON THE ROAD AGAIN**
    Willie Nelson-Columbia
17. **XANADU**
    Olivia Newton-John/ELO-MCA
18. **ALL OUT OF LOVE**
    Air Supply-Arista
19. **DREAMER**
    Supertramp-A&M
20. **WHIP IT**
    Devo-Warner Bros

US ALBUMS

1. **GREATEST HITS**
   Kenny Rogers-Liberty
2. **THE RIVER**
   Bruce Springsteen-Columbia
3. **GUILTY**
   Barbra Streisand-Columbia
4. **THE GAME**
   Queen-Elektra
5. **HOTTER THAN JULY**
   Stevie Wonder-Motown
6. **BACK IN BLACK**
   AC/DC-Atlantic
7. **CRIMES OF PASSION**
   Pat Benatar
8. **ONE STEP CLOSER**
   Doobie Brothers-Warner Bros
9. **TRIUMPH**
   The Jacksons-Epic
10. **DIANA**
    Diana Ross-Motown
11. **THE WANDERER**
    Donna Summer-Geffen
12. **PARIS**
    Supertramp-A&M
13. **XANADU**
    Original Soundtrack-MCA
14. **GIVE ME THE NIGHT**
    George Benson-Qwest-WB
15. **KENNY LOGGINS ALIVE**
    Kenny Loggins-Columbia
16. **TP**
    Teddy Pendergrass-Phila.Intl.
17. **ANNE MURRAY'S GREATEST**
    Anne Murray-Capitol
18. **URBAN COWBOY**
    Original Soundtrack-Full Moon-Asylum
19. **HOLD OUT**
    Jackson Browne-Asylum
20. **CHRISTOPHER CROSS**
    Christopher Cross-Warner Bros

UK SINGLES

1. **THE TIDE IS HIGH**
   Blondie-Chrysalis
2. **WOMAN IN LOVE**
   Barbra Streisand-CBS
3. **SPECIAL BREW**
   Bad Manners-Magnet
4. **I COULD BE SO GOOD FOR YOU**
   Dennis Waterman-EMI
5. **WHAT YOU'RE PROPOSING**
   Status Quo-Vertigo
6. **FASHION**
   David Bowie-RCA
7. **DOG EAT DOG**
   Adam and The Ants-CBS
8. **ENOLA GAY**
   Orchestral Manoeuvres-DinDisc
9. **NEVER KNEW LOVE LIKE THIS**
   Stephanie Mills-20th Century
10. **LOOKIN' FOR A WAY OUT**
    Odyssey-RCA
11. **WHEN YOU ASK ABOUT LOVE**
    Matchbox-Magnet
12. **SAME OLD SCENE**
    Roxy Music-Polydor
13. **SUPER TROUPER**
    Abba-Epic
14. **EARTH DIES SCREAMING**
    UB 40-Graduate
15. **ACE OF SPADES**
    Motorhead-Bronze
16. **PULL MYSELF TOGETHER**
    Nolans-Epic
17. **SUDDENLY**
    Olivia N-J/Cliff Richard-Jet
18. **ONE MAN WOMAN**
    Sheena Easton-EMI
19. **ALL OUT OF LOVE**
    Air Supply-Arista
20. **STARTING OVER**
    John Lennon-Geffen

UK ALBUMS

1. **GUILTY**
   Babara Streisand-CBS
2. **ZENYATTA MONDATTA**
   The Police-A&M
3. **HOTTER THAN JULY**
   Stevie Wonder-Tamla Motown
4. **KINGS OF THE WILD FRONTIER**
   Adam and The Ants-CBS
5. **ACE OF SPADES**
   Motorhead-Bronze
6. **THE HEART OF THE CITY**
   Whitesnake-United Artists
7. **ORGANISATION**
   Orchestral Manoeuvres-DinDisc
8. **NOT THE 9 O'CLOCK NEWS**
   Various-BBC
9. **GOLD**
   Three Degrees-K Tel
10. **MANILOW MAGIC**
    Barry Manilow-Arista
11. **COUNTRY LEGENDS**
    Various-Ronco
12. **MAKING WAVES**
    Nolans-Epic
13. **THE RIVER**
    Bruce Springsteen-CBS
14. **JUST SUPPOSIN'**
    Status Quo-Vertigo
15. **LITTLE MISS DYNAMITE**
    Brenda Lee-Warwick
16. **THE LOVE ALBUM**
    Various-K Tel
17. **SCARY MONSTERS**
    David Bowie-RCA
18. **STRONG ARM OF THE LAW**
    Saxon-Carrere
19. **NEVER FOREVER**
    Kate Bush-EMI
20. **ABSOLUTELY**
    Madness-Stiff

US SINGLES	US ALBUMS	UK SINGLES	UK ALBUMS
1 **LADY** *Kenny Rogers-Liberty*	1 **GREATEST HITS** *Kenny Rogers-Liberty*	1 **THE TIDE IS HIGH** *Blondie-Chrysalis*	1 **SUPER TROUPER** *Abba-Epic*
2 **BITES THE DUST** *Queen-Elektra*	2 **GUILTY** *Barbra Streisand-Columbia*	2 **SUPER TROUPER** *Abba-Epic*	2 **GUILTY** *Barbra Streisand-CBS*
3 **WOMAN IN LOVE** *Barbra Streisand-Columbia*	3 **HOTTER THAN JULY** *Stevie Wonder-Motown*	3 **WOMAN IN LOVE** *Barbra Streisand-CBS*	3 **KINGS OF THE WILD FRONTIER** *Adam and The Ants-CBS*
4 **THE WANDERER** *Donna Summer-Geffen*	4 **THE GAME** *Queen-Elektra*	4 **I COULD BE SO GOOD FOR YOU** *Dennis Waterman-EMI*	4 **ZENYATTA MONDATTA** *The Police-A&M*
5 **HE'S SO SHY** *Pointer Sisters*	5 **THE RIVER** *Bruce Springsteen-Columbia*	5 **FASHION** *David Bowie-RCA*	5 **NOT THE 9 O'CLOCK NEWS** *Various-BBC*
6 **MORE THAN I CAN SAY** *Leo Sayer-Warner Bros*	6 **BACK IN BLACK** *AC/DC-Atlantic*	6 **NEVER KNEW LOVE LIKE THIS** *Stephanie Mills-20th Century*	6 **HOTTER THAN JULY** *Stevie Wonder-Tamla Motown*
7 **DREAMING** *Cliff Richard-EMI-America*	7 **CRIMES OF PASSION** *Pat Benatar-Columbia*	7 **SPECIAL BREW** *Bad Manners-Magnet*	7 **FOOLISH BEHAVIOUR** *Rod Stewart-Riva*
8 **JESSE** *Carly Simon-Warner Bros*	8 **ONE STEP CLOSER** *Doobie Brothers-Warner Bros*	8 **DOG EAT DOG** *Adam and The Ants-CBS*	8 **MANILOW MAGIC** *Barry Manilow-Arista*
9 **LOVELY ONE** *The Jacksons-Epic*	9 **TRIUMPH** *The Jacksons-Epic*	9 **ENOLA GAY** *Orchestral Manoeuvres-DinDisc*	9 **ACE OF SPADES** *Motorhead-Bronze*
10 **I'M COMING OUT** *Diana Ross-Motown*	10 **THE WANDERER** *Donna Summer-Geffen*	10 **WHAT YOU'RE PROPOSING** *Status Quo-Vertigo*	10 **COUNTRY LEGENDS** *Various-Ronco*
11 **NEVER BE THE SAME** *Christopher Cross-Warner Bros*	11 **DIANA** *Diana Ross-Motown*	11 **EARTH DIES SCREAMING** *UB 40-Graduate*	11 **STRONG ARM OF THE LAW** *Saxon-Carrere*
12 **NEVER KNEW LOVE LIKE THIS** *Stephanie Mills-20th Century Fox*	12 **XANADU** *Original Soundtrack-MCA*	12 **CELEBRATION** *Kool and The Gang-De Lite*	12 **MAKING WAVES** *Nolans-Epic*
13 **HIT ME WITH YOUR BEST SHOT** *Pat Benatar-Chrysalis*	13 **ANNE MURRAY'S GREATEST** *Anne Murray-Capitol*	13 **STARTING OVER** *John Lennon-Geffen*	13 **RADIO ACTIVE** *Various-Ronco*
14 **LOVE ON THE ROCKS** *Neil Diamond-Capitol*	14 **KENNY LOGGINS ALIVE** *Kenny Loggins-Columbia*	14 **SAME OLD SCENE** *Roxy Music-Polydor*	14 **ORGANISATION** *Orchestral Manoeuvres-DinDisc*
15 **LOST THAT LOVIN' FEELING** *Daryl Hall and John Oates-RCA*	15 **PARIS** *Supertramp-A&M*	15 **ACE OF SPADES** *Motorhead-Bronze*	15 **LITTLE MISS DYNAMITE** *Brenda Lee-Warwick*
16 **MASTER BLASTER (JAMMIN')** *Stevie Wonder-Motown*	16 **TP** *Teddy Pendergrass-Phila. Intl.*	16 **LOOKING FOR A WAY OUT** *Odyssey-RCA*	16 **SCARY MONSTERS** *David Bowie-RCA*
17 **(JUST LIKE) STARTING OVER** *John Lennon-Geffen*	17 **FACES** *Earth, Wind & Fire-ARC-Columbia*	17 **WHEN YOU ASK ABOUT LOVE** *Matchbox-Magnet*	17 **THE HEART OF THE CITY** *Whitesnake-United Artists*
18 **ON THE ROAD AGAIN** *Willie Nelson-Columbia*	18 **CHRISTOPHER CROSS** *Christopher Cross-Warner Bros*	18 **I'M COMING OUT** *Diana Ross-Tamla Motown*	18 **ABSOLUTELY** *Madness-Stiff*
19 **WHIP IT** *Devo-Warner Bros*	19 **ZENYATTA MONDATTA** *The Police-A&M*	19 **TO CUT A LONG STORY SHORT** *Spandau Ballet-Chrysalis*	19 **THE RIVER** *Bruce Springsteen-CBS*
20 **UPSIDE DOWN** *Diana Ross-Motown*	20 **GLASS HOUSES** *Billy Joel-Columbia*	20 **SUDDENLY** *Olivia N.J./Cliff Richard-Jet*	20 **GOLD** *Three Degrees-K-Tel*

WEEK ENDING NOVEMBER 29 1980

US SINGLES	US ALBUMS	UK SINGLES	UK ALBUMS
1 **LADY** *Kenny Rogers-Liberty*	1 **GREATEST HITS** *Kenny Rogers-Liberty*	1 **SUPER TROUPER** *Abba-Epic*	1 **SUPER TROUPER** *Abba-Epic*
2 **BITES THE DUST** *Queen-Elektra*	2 **GUILTY** *Barbra Streisand-Columbia*	2 **THE TIDE IS HIGH** *Blondie-Chrysalis*	2 **GUILTY** *Barbra Streisand-CBS*
3 **MORE THAN I CAN SAY** *Leo Sayer-Warner Bros*	3 **HOTTER THAN JULY** *Stevie Wonder-Motown*	3 **SO GOOD FOR YOU** *Dennis Waterman-EMI*	3 **AUTOAMERICAN** *Blondie-Chrysalis*
4 **WOMAN IN LOVE** *Barbra Streisand-Columbia*	4 **THE GAME** *Queen-Elektra*	4 **NEVER KNEW LOVE LIKE THIS** *Stephanie Mills-20th Century*	4 **FOOLISH BEHAVIOUR** *Rod Stewart-Riva*
5 **THE WANDERER** *Donna Summer-Geffen*	5 **THE RIVER** *Bruce Springsteen-Columbia*	5 **FASHION** *David Bowie-RSA*	5 **NOT THE 9 O'CLOCK NEWS** *Various-BBC*
6 **HE'S SO SHY** *Pointer Sisters-Planet*	6 **BACK IN BLACK** *AC/DC-Atlantic*	6 **WOMAN IN LOVE** *Barbra Streisand-CBS*	6 **ZENYATTA MONDATTA** *The Police-A&M*
7 **HIT ME WITH YOUR BEST SHOT** *Pat Benatar-Chrysalis*	7 **CRIMES OF PASSION** *Pat Benatar-Chrysalis*	7 **CELEBRATION** *Kool and The Gang-De Lite*	7 **CHART EXPLOSION** *Various-K-Tel*
8 **JESSE** *Carly Simon-Warner Bros*	8 **ONE STEP CLOSER** *Doobie Brothers-Warner Bros*	8 **STARTING OVER** *John Lennon-Geffen*	8 **KINGS OF THE WILD FRONTIER** *Adam and The Ants-CBS*
9 **I'M COMING OUT** *Diana Ross-Motown*	9 **THE WANDERER** *Donna Summer-Geffen*	9 **BANANA REPUBLIC** *Boomtown Rats-Ensign*	9 **COUNTRY LEGENDS** *Various-Ronco*
10 **NEVER BE THE SAME** *Christopher Cross-Warner Bros*	10 **TRIUMPH** *The Jacksons-Epic*	10 **EARTH DIES SCREAMING** *UB40-Graduate*	10 **MANILOW MAGIC** *Barry Manilow-Arista*
11 **NEVER KNEW LOVE LIKE THIS** *Stephanie Mills-20th Century Fox*	11 **ANNE MURRAY'S GREATEST** *Anne Murray-Capitol*	11 **TO CUT A LONG STORY SHORT** *Spandau Ballet-Chrysalis*	11 **MAKING WAVES** *Nolans-Epic*
12 **LOVE ON THE ROCKS** *Neil Diamond-Capitol*	12 **LIVE** *The Eagles-Asylum*	12 **EMBARRASSMENT** *Madness-Stiff*	12 **HOTTER THAN JULY** *Stevie Wonder-Tamla Motown*
13 **(JUST LIKE) STARTING OVER** *John Lennon-Geffen*	13 **XANADU** *Original Soundtrack-MCA*	13 **ENOLA GAY** *Orchestral Manoeuvres-DinDisc*	13 **INSPIRATION** *Elvis Presley-K-Tel*
14 **LOST THAT LOVIN' FEELING** *Daryl Hall and John Oates-RCA*	14 **ZENYATTA MONDATTA** *The Police-A&M*	14 **SPECIAL BREW** *Bad Manners-Magnet*	14 **DOUBLE FANTASY** *John Lennon/Yoko Ono-Geffen*
15 **MASTER BLASTER (JAMMIN')** *Stevie Wonder-Motown*	15 **TP** *Teddy Pendergrass-Phila. Intl.*	15 **DO YOU FEEL MY LOVE** *Eddy Grant-Ensign*	15 **ACE OF SPADES** *Motorhead-Bronze*
16 **GUILTY** *Barbra Streisand-Columbia*	16 **FACES** *Earth, Wind & Fire-ARC-Columbia*	16 **SAME OLD SCENE** *Roxy Music-Polydor*	16 **RADIO ACTIVE** *Various-K-Tel*
17 **DREAMING** *Cliff Richard-EMI-America*	17 **CHRISTOPHER CROSS** *Christopher Cross-Warner Bros.*	17 **PASSION** *Rod Stewart-Riva*	17 **THE LOVE ALBUM** *Various-K-Tel*
18 **WHIP IT** *Devo-Warner Bros*	18 **DIANA** *Diana Ross-Motown*	18 **I'M COMING OUT** *Diana Ross-Tamla Motown*	18 **JAZZ SINGER** *Neil Diamond-Capitol*
19 **HUNGRY HEART** *Bruce Springsteen-Columbia*	19 **THE JAZZ SINGER** *Neil Diamond-Capitol*	19 **DOG EAT DOG** *Adam and The Ants-CBS*	19 **AXE ATTACK** *Various-K-Tel*
20 **LOVELY ONE** *The Jacksons-Epic*	20 **GREATEST HITS — VOLUME II** *Linda Ronstadt-Asylum*	20 **I LIKE WHAT YOU'RE DOING** *Young and Co.-Excelibur*	20 **ABSOLUTELY** *Madness-Stiff*

US SINGLES

1. **LADY**
   Kenny Rogers-Liberty
2. **BITES THE DUST**
   Queen-Elektra
3. **MORE THAN I CAN SAY**
   Leo Sayer-Warner Bros.
4. **WOMAN IN LOVE**
   Barbra Streisand-Columbia
5. **THE WANDERER**
   Donna Summer-Geffen
6. **HE'S SO SHY**
   Pointer Sisters-Planet
7. **HIT ME WITH YOUR BEST SHOT**
   Pat Benatar-Chrysalis
8. **LOVE ON THE ROCKS**
   Neil Diamond-Capitol
9. **(JUST LIKE) STARTING OVER**
   John Lennon-Geffen
10. **DUKES OF HAZZARD THEME**
    Waylon Jennings-RCA
11. **NEVER KNEW LOVE LIKE THIS**
    Stephanie Mills-20th Century Fox
12. **HUNGRY HEART**
    Bruce Springsteen-Columbia
13. **GUILTY**
    Barbra Streisand-Columbia
14. **NEVER BE THE SAME**
    Christopher Cross-Warner Bros
15. **I'M COMING OUT**
    Diana Ross-Motown
16. **LOST THAT LOVIN' FEELING**
    Daryl Hall and John Oates-RCA
17. **WHIP IT**
    Devo-Warner Bros
18. **EVERY WOMAN IN THE WORLD**
    Air Supply-Arista
19. **I BELIEVE IN YOU**
    Don Williams-MCA
20. **DREAMING**
    Cliff Richard-EMI-America

US ALBUMS

1. **GREATEST HITS**
   Kenny Rogers-Liberty
2. **GUILTY**
   Barbra Streisand-Columbia
3. **HOTTER THAN JULY**
   Stevie Wonder-Motown
4. **THE GAME**
   Queen-Elektra
5. **BACK IN BLACK**
   AC/DC-Atlantic
6. **CRIMES OF PASSION**
   Pat Benatar-Chrysalis
7. **THE RIVER**
   Bruce Springsteen-Columbia
8. **THE JAZZ SINGER**
   Neil Diamond-Capitol
9. **THE WANDERER**
   Donna Summer-Geffen
10. **LIVE**
    The Eagles-Asylum
11. **ANNE MURRAY'S GREATEST**
    Anne Murray-Capitol
12. **TRIUMPH**
    The Jacksons-Epic
13. **ZENYATTA MONDATTA**
    The Police-A&M
14. **FACES**
    Earth, Wind & Fire-ARC-Columbia
15. **TP**
    Teddy Pendergrass-Phila. Intl.
16. **ONE STEP CLOSER**
    Doobie Brothers-Warner Bros
17. **CHRISTOPHER CROSS**
    Christopher Cross-Warner Bros
18. **XANADU**
    Original Soundtrack-MCA
19. **DOUBLE FANTASY**
    John Lennon/Yoko Ono-Geffen
20. **GREATEST HITS - VOLUME II**
    Linda Ronstadt-Asylum

UK SINGLES

1. **SUPER TROUPER**
   Abba-Epic
2. **THE TIDE IS HIGH**
   Blondie-Chrysalis
3. **BANANA REPUBLIC**
   Boomtown Rats-Ensign
4. **EMBARRASSMENT**
   Madness-Stiff
5. **TO CUT A LONG STORY SHORT**
   Spandau Ballet/Chrysalis
6. **I COULD BE SO GOOD FOR YOU**
   Dennis Waterman-EMI
7. **NEVER KNEW LOVE LIKE THIS**
   Stephanie Mills-20th Century
8. **CELEBRATION**
   Kool and The Gang-De-Lite
9. **DO YOU FEEL MY LOVE**
   Eddy Grant-Ensign
10. **STARTING OVER**
    John Lennon-Geffen
11. **EARTH DIES SCREAMING**
    UB 40-Graduate
12. **FASHION**
    David Bowie-RCA
13. **I'M COMING OUT**
    Diana Ross-Tamla Motown
14. **WOMAN IN LOVE**
    Barbra Streisand-CBS
15. **STOP THE CAVALRY**
    Jona Lewie-Stiff
16. **NO ONE QUITE LIKE GRANDMA**
    St. Winifred's School Choir-MFP
17. **ROCK 'N' ROLL POLLUTION**
    AC/DC-Atlantic
18. **ACE OF SPADES**
    Motorhead-Bronze
19. **PASSION**
    Rod Stewart-Riva
20. **I LIKE WHAT YOU'RE DOING**
    Young and Co.-Excalibur

UK ALBUMS

1. **SUPER TROUPER**
   Abba-Epic
2. **SOUND AFFECTS**
   Jam-Polydor
3. **GUILTY**
   Barbra Streisand-CBS
4. **AUTOAMERICAN**
   Blondie-Chrysalis
5. **DR. HOOK'S GREATEST HITS**
   Dr. Hook-Capitol
6. **CHART EXPLOSION**
   Various-K-Tel
7. **NOT THE 9 O'CLOCK NEWS**
   Various-BBC
8. **INSPIRATION**
   Elvis Presley-K-Tel
9. **FOOLISH BEHAVIOUR**
   Rod Stewart-Riva
10. **ZENYATTA MONDATTA**
    The Police-A&M
11. **MANILOW MAGIC**
    Barry Manilow-Arista
12. **BARRY**
    Barry Manilow-Arista
13. **KINGS OF THE WILD FRONTIER**
    Adam and The Ants-CBS
14. **SINGS 20 NO. 1 HITS**
    Brotherhood of Man-Warwick
15. **JAZZ SINGER**
    Neil Diamond-Capitol
16. **COUNTRY LEGENDS**
    Various-Ronco
17. **ABSOLUTELY**
    Madness-Stiff
18. **HOTTER THAN JULY**
    Stevie Wonder-Tamla Motown
19. **AXE ATTACK**
    Various-K-Tel
20. **THE LOVE ALBUM**
    Various-K-Tel

US SINGLES

1. **LADY**
   Kenny Rogers-Liberty
2. **BITES THE DUST**
   Queen-Elektra
3. **MORE THAN I CAN SAY**
   Leo Sayer-Warner Bros
4. **LOVE ON THE ROCKS**
   Neil Diamond-Capitol
5. **THE WANDERER**
   Donna Summer-Geffen
6. **(JUST LIKE) STARTING OVER**
   John Lennon-Geffen
7. **HIT ME WITH YOUR BEST SHOT**
   Pat Benatar-Chrysalis
8. **DUKES OF HAZZARD**
   Waylon Jennings-RCA
9. **GUILTY**
   Barbra Streisand-Columbia
10. **HUNGRY HEART**
    Bruce Springsteen-Columbia
11. **HE'S SO SHY**
    Pointer Sisters-Planet
12. **WOMAN IN LOVE**
    Barbra Streisand-Columbia
13. **EVERY WOMAN IN THE WORLD**
    Air Supply-Arista
14. **NEVER KNEW LOVE LIKE THIS**
    Stephanie Mills-20th Century Fox
15. **NEVER BE THE SAME**
    Christopher Cross-Warner Bros
16. **LOST THAT LOVIN' FEELING**
    Daryl Hall and John Oates-RCA
17. **I BELIEVE IN YOU**
    Don Williams-MCA
18. **I'M COMING OUT**
    Diana Ross-Motown
19. **WHIP IT**
    Devo-Warner Bros
20. **THE TIDE IS HIGH**
    Blondie-Chrysalis

US ALBUMS

1. **GREATEST HITS**
   Kenny Rogers-Liberty
2. **GUILTY**
   Barbra Streisand-Columbia
3. **HOTTER THAN JULY**
   Stevie Wonder-Motown
4. **THE GAME**
   Queen-Elektra
5. **BACK IN BLACK**
   AC/DC-Atlantic
6. **CRIMES OF PASSION**
   Pat Benatar-Chrysalis
7. **THE RIVER**
   Bruce Springsteen-Columbia
8. **THE JAZZ SINGER**
   Neil Diamond-Capitol
9. **LIVE**
   The Eagles-Asylum
10. **ZENYATTA MONDATTA**
    The Police-A&M
11. **TRIUMPH**
    The Jacksons-Epic
12. **FACES**
    Earth, Wind & Fire-ARC-Columbia
13. **ANNE MURRAY'S GREATEST**
    Anne Murray-Capitol
14. **DOUBLE FANTASY**
    John Lennon/Yoko Ono-Geffen
15. **THE WANDERER**
    Donna Summer-Geffen
16. **GREATEST HITS/LIVE**
    Heart-Epic
17. **GAUCHO**
    Steely Dan-MCA
18. **ONE STEP CLOSER**
    Doobie Brothers-Warner Bros
19. **FOOLISH BEHAVIOUR**
    Rod Stewart-Warner Bros
20. **DIANA**
    Diana Ross-Motown

UK SINGLES

1. **SUPER TROUPER**
   Abba-Epic
2. **NO ONE QUITE LIKE GRANDMA**
   St. Winifred's School Choir-MFP
3. **STOP THE CAVALRY**
   Jona Lewie-Stiff
4. **EMBARRASSMENT**
   Madness-Stiff
5. **BANANA REPUBLIC**
   Boomtown Rats-Ensign
6. **TO CUT A LONG STORY SHORT**
   Spandau Ballet-Chrysalis
7. **THE TIDE IS HIGH**
   Blondie-Chrysalis
8. **DO YOU FEEL MY LOVE**
   Eddy Grant-Ensign
9. **DE DO DO DO DE DA DA DA**
   The Police-A&M
10. **RUNAWAY BOYS**
    Stray Cats-Arista
11. **CELEBRATION**
    Kool and The Gang-De Lite
12. **LADY**
    Kenny Rogers-United Artists
13. **NEVER KNEW LOVE LIKE THIS**
    Stephanie Mills-20th Century
14. **I COULD BE SO GOOD FOR YOU**
    Dennis Waterman-EMI
15. **ROCK 'N' ROLL POLLUTION**
    AC/DC-Atlantic
16. **ANTMUSIC**
    Adam and The Ants-CBS
17. **LIES**
    Status Quo-Vertigo
18. **EARTH DIES SCREAMING**
    UB 40-Graduate
19. **I'M COMING OUT**
    Diana Ross-Tamla Motown
20. **FLASH**
    Queen-EMI

UK ALBUMS

1. **SUPER TROUPER**
   Abba-Epic
2. **DR. HOOK'S GREATEST HITS**
   Dr. Hook-Capitol
3. **GUILTY**
   Barbra Streisand-CBS
4. **SOUND AFFECTS**
   Jam-Polydor
5. **MANILOW MAGIC**
   Barry Manilow-Arista
6. **INSPIRATION**
   Elvis Presley-K-Tel
7. **AUTOAMERICAN**
   Blondie-Chrysalis
8. **NOT THE 9 O'CLOCK NEWS**
   Various-BBC
9. **ZENYATTA MONDATTA**
   The Police-A&M
10. **CHART EXPLOSION**
    Various-K-Tel
11. **BARRY**
    Barry Manilow-Arista
12. **CLASSICS FOR DREAMING**
    James Last-Polydor
13. **FOOLISH BEHAVIOUR**
    Rod Stewart-Riva
14. **JAZZ SINGER**
    Neil Diamond-Capitol
15. **AXE ATTACK**
    Various-K-Tel
16. **ABSOLUTELY**
    Madness-Stiff
17. **KINGS OF THE WILD FRONTIER**
    Adam and The Ants-CBS
18. **SINGS 20 NO. 1 HITS**
    Brotherhood of Man-Warwick
19. **COUNTRY LEGENDS**
    Various-Ronco
20. **20 GREATS OF KEN DODD**
    Ken Dodd-Warwick

US SINGLES	US ALBUMS	UK SINGLES	UK ALBUMS
1 LADY *Kenny Rogers-Liberty*	1 GREATEST HITS *Kenny Rogers-Liberty*	1 STARTING OVER *John Lennon-Geffen*	1 SUPER TROUPER *Abba-Epic*
2 BITES THE DUST *Queen-Elektra*	2 GUILTY *Barbra Streisand-Columbia*	2 NO ONE QUITE LIKE GRANDMA *St. Winifred's School Choir-MFP*	2 DOUBLE FANTASY *John Lennon-Geffen*
3 MORE THAN I CAN SAY *Leo Sayer-Warner Bros*	3 HOTTER THAN JULY *Stevie Wonder-Motown*	3 STOP THE CAVALRY *Jona Lewie-Stiff*	3 DR. HOOK'S GREATEST HITS *Dr. Hook-Capitol*
4 LOVE ON THE ROCKS *Neil Diamond-Capitol*	4 THE GAME *Queen-Elektra*	4 SUPER TROUPER *Abba-Epic*	4 GUILTY *Barbra Streisand-CBS*
5 (JUST LIKE) STARTING OVER *John Lennon-Geffen*	5 BACK IN BLACK *AC/DC-Atlantic*	5 DE DO DO DO DE DA DA DA *The Police-A&M*	5 MANILOW MAGIC *Barry Manilow-Arista*
6 GUILTY *Barbra Streisand-Barry Gibb-Columbia*	6 CRIMES OF PASSION *Pat Benatar-Chrysalis*	6 EMBARRASSMENT *Madness-Stiff*	6 NOT THE 9 O'CLOCK NEWS *Various-BBC*
7 DUKES OF HAZZARD THEME *Waylon Jennings-RCA*	7 THE RIVER *Bruce Springsteen-Columbia*	7 BANANA REPUBLIC *Boomtown Rats-Ensign*	7 ZENYATTA MONDATTA *The Police-A&M*
8 HIT ME WITH YOUR BEST SHOT *Pat Benatar-Chrysalis*	8 THE JAZZ SINGER *Neil Diamond-Capitol*	8 TO CUT A LONG STORY SHORT *Spandau Ballet-Chrysalis*	8 BARRY *Barry Manilow-Arista*
9 EVERY WOMAN IN THE WORLD *Air Supply-Arista*	9 LIVE *The Eagles-Asylum*	9 RUNAWAY BOYS *Stray Cats-Arista*	9 CHART EXPLOSION *Various-K-Tel*
10 HUNGRY HEART *Bruce Springsteen-Columbia*	10 ZENYATTA MONDATTA *The Police-A&M*	10 ANTMUSIC *Adam and The Ants-CBS*	10 20 GREATS OF KEN DODD *Ken Dodd-Warwick*
11 THE WANDERER *Donna Summer-Geffen*	11 DOUBLE FANTASY *John Lennon-Yoko Ono-Geffen*	11 DO YOU FEEL MY LOVE *Eddy Grant-Ensign*	11 INSPIRATION *Elvis Presley-K-Tel*
12 WOMAN IN LOVE *Barbra Streisand-Columbia*	12 FACES *Earth, Wind & Fire-ARC-Columbia*	12 FLASH *Queen-EMI*	12 CLASSICS FOR DREAMING *James Last-Polydor*
13 I BELIEVE IN YOU *Don Williams-MCA*	13 TRIUMPH *The Jacksons-Epic*	13 LADY *Kenny Rogers-United Artists*	13 AUTOAMERICAN *Blondie-Chrysalis*
14 I MADE IT THROUGH THE RAIN *Barry Manilow-Arista*	14 GAUCHO *Steely Dan-MCA*	14 THE TIDE IS HIGH *Blondie-Chrysalis*	14 ABSOLUTELY *Madness-Stiff*
15 NEVER BE THE SAME *Christopher Cross-Warner Bros*	15 GREATEST HITS/LIVE *Heart-Epic*	15 LIES/DON'T DRIVE MY CAR *Status Quo-Vertigo*	15 JAZZ SINGER *Neil Diamond-Capitol*
16 NEVER KNEW LOVE LIKE THIS *Stephanie Mills-20th Century Fox*	16 ANNE MURRAY'S GREATEST *Anne Murray-Capitol*	16 CELEBRATION *Kool and The Gang-De-Lite*	16 SOUND AFFECTS *Jam-Polydor*
17 LOST THAT LOVIN' FEELING *Daryl Hall and John Oates-RCA*	17 BARRY *Barry Manilow-Arista*	17 ROCK 'N' ROLL POLLUTION *AC/DC-Atlantic*	17 FLASH GORDON *Queen-EMI*
18 THE TIDE IS HIGH *Blondie-Chrysalis*	18 FOOLISH BEHAVIOUR *Rod Stewart-Warner Bros*	18 RABBIT *Chas and Dave-Rockney*	18 FOOLISH BEHAVIOUR *Rod Stewart-Riva*
19 DE DO DO DO, DE DA DA DA *The Police-A&M*	19 DIANA *Diana Ross-Motown*	19 LOVE ON THE ROCKS *Neil Diamond-Capitol*	19 SANDINISTA *Clash-CBS*
20 TELL IT LIKE IT IS *Heart-Epic*	20 AUTOAMERICAN *Blondie-Chrysalis*	20 NEVER KNEW LOVE LIKE THIS *Stephanie Mills-20th Century*	20 SINGS 20 NO.1 HITS *Brotherhood of Man-Warwick*

US SINGLES	US ALBUMS	UK SINGLES	UK ALBUMS
1 (JUST LIKE) STARTING OVER *John Lennon-Geffen*	1 GREATEST HITS *Kenny Rogers-Liberty*	1 NO ONE QUITE LIKE GRANDMA *St. Winifred's School Choir-MFP*	1 SUPER TROUPER *Abba-Epic*
2 BITES THE DUST *Queen-Elektra*	2 DOUBLE FANTASY *John Lennon/Yoko Ono-Geffen*	2 STARTING OVER *John Lennon-Geffen*	2 DOUBLE FANTASY *John Lennon/Yoko Ono-Geffen*
3 LOVE ON THE ROCKS *Neil Diamond-Capitol*	3 GUILTY *Barbra Streisand-Columbia*	3 STOP THE CAVALRY *Jona Lewie-Stiff*	3 DR. HOOK'S GREATEST HITS *Dr. Hook-Capitol*
4 LADY *Kenny Rogers-Liberty*	4 THE GAME *Queen-Elektra*	4 HAPPY CHRISTMAS *John Lennon-Apple*	4 MANILOW MAGIC *Barry Manilow-Arista*
5 MORE THAN I CAN SAY *Leo Sayer-Warner Bros*	5 BACK IN BLACK *AC/DC-Atlantic*	5 SUPER TROUPER *Abba-Epic*	5 ZENYATTA MONDATTA *The Police-A&M*
6 GUILTY *Barbra Streisand-Columbia*	6 CRIMES OF PASSION *Pat Benatar-Chrysalis*	6 DE DO DO DO DE DA DA DA *The Police-A&M*	6 GUILTY *Barbra Streisand-CBS*
7 DUKES OF HAZZARD *Waylon Jennings-RCA*	7 HOTTER THAN JULY *Stevie Wonder-Motown*	7 ANTMUSIC *Adam and The Ants-CBS*	7 NOT THE 9 O'CLOCK NEWS *Various-BBC*
8 EVERY WOMAN IN THE WORLD *Air Supply-Arista*	8 THE RIVER *Bruce Springsteen-Columbia*	8 EMBARRASSMENT *Madness-Stiff*	8 20 GREATS OF KEN DODD *Ken Dodd-Warwick*
9 HIT ME WITH YOUR BEST SHOT *Pat Benatar-Chrysalis*	9 LIVE *The Eagles-Asylum*	9 IMAGINE *John Lennon-Parlophone*	9 BARRY *Barry Manilow-Arista*
10 HUNGRY HEART *Bruce Springsteen-Columbia*	10 THE JAZZ SINGER *Neil Diamond-Capitol*	10 RUNAWAY BOYS *Stray Cats-Arista*	10 INSPIRATION *Elvis Presley-K-Tel*
11 I MADE IT THROUGH THE RAIN *Barry Manilow-Arista*	11 BARRY *Barry Manilow-Arista*	11 BANANA REPUBLIC *Boomtown Rats-Ensign*	11 CLASSICS FOR DREAMING *James Last-Polydor*
12 I BELIEVE IN YOU *Don Williams-MCA*	12 ANNE MURRAY'S GREATEST *Anne Murray-Capitol*	12 LIES/DON'T DRIVE MY CAR *Status Quo-Vertigo*	12 AUTOAMERICAN *Blondie-Chrysalis*
13 THE WANDERER *Donna Summer-Geffen*	13 GAUCHO *Steely Dan-Gaucho*	13 RABBIT *Chas and Dave-Rockney*	13 ABSOLUTELY *Madness-Stiff*
14 THE TIDE IS HIGH *Blondie-Chrysalis*	14 GREATEST HITS/LIVE *Heart-Epic*	14 LADY *Kenny Rogers-United Artists*	14 CHART EXPLOSION *Various-K-Tel*
15 PASSION *Rod Stewart-Warner Bros*	15 ZENYATTA MONDATTA *The Police-A&M*	15 FLASH *Queen-EMI*	15 KINGS OF THE WILD FRONTIER *Adam and The Ants-CBS*
16 TELL IT LIKE IT IS *Heart-Epic*	16 FOOLISH BEHAVIOUR *Rod Stewart-Warner Bros*	16 TO CUT A LONG STORY SHORT *Spandau Ballet-Chrysalis*	16 JAZZ SINGER *Neil Diamond-Capitol*
17 LOST THAT LOVIN' FEELING *Daryl Hall and John Oates-RCA*	17 AUTOAMERICAN *Blondie-Chrysalis*	17 NEVER MIND THE PRESENTS *Barron Knights-Epic*	17 FOOLISH BEHAVIOUR *Rod Stewart-Riva*
18 DE DO DO DO, DE DA DA DA *The Police-A&M*	18 TRIUMPH *The Jacksons-Epic*	18 LOVE ON THE ROCKS *Neil Diamond-Capitol*	18 AXE ATTACK *Various-K-Tel*
19 CELEBRATION *Kool and The Gang-De-Lite*	19 GLASS HOUSES *Billy Joel-Columbia*	19 OVER THE RAINBOW *Matchbox-Magnet*	19 SINGS 20 NO. 1 HITS *Brotherhood Of Man-Warwick*
20 SUDDENLY *Olivia Newton-John/Cliff Richard-MCA*	20 XANADU *Original Soundtrack-MCA*	20 THE TIDE IS HIGH *Blondie-Chrysalis*	20 FLASH GORDON *Queen-EMI*

US SINGLES	US ALBUMS	UK SINGLES	UK ALBUMS
1 (JUST LIKE) STARTING OVER *John Lennon-Geffen*	1 GREATEST HITS *Kenny Rogers-Liberty*	1 IMAGINE *John Lennon-Parlophone*	1 SUPER TROUPER *Abba-Epic*
2 BITES THE DUST *Queen-Elektra*	2 DOUBLE FANTASY *John Lennon/Yoko Ono-Geffen*	2 HAPPY CHRISTMAS *John Lennon-Apple*	2 DOUBLE FANTASY *John Lennon/Yoko Ono-Geffen*
3 LOVE ON THE ROCKS *Neil Diamond-Capitol*	3 GUILTY *Barbra Streisand-Columbia*	3 STOP THE CAVALRY *Jona Lewie-Stiff*	3 GUILTY *Barbra Streisand-CBS*
4 LADY *Kenny Rogers-Liberty*	4 THE GAME *Queen-Elektra*	4 ANTMUSIC *Adam and The Ants-CBS*	4 DR. HOOK'S GREATEST HITS *Dr. Hook-Capitol*
5 MORE THAN I CAN SAY *Leo Sayer-Warner Bros*	5 BACK IN BLACK *AC/DC-Atlantic*	5 STARTING OVER *John Lennon-Geffen*	5 MANILOW MAGIC *Barry Manilow-Arista*
6 GUILTY *Barbra Streisand-Barry Gibb-Columbia*	6 CRIMES OF PASSION *Pat Benatar-Chrysalis*	6 NO ONE QUITE LIKE GRANDMA *St. Winifred's School Choir-MFP*	6 ZENYATTA MONDATTA *The Police-A&M*
7 DUKES OF HAZZARD THEME *Waylon Jennings-RCA*	7 HOTTER THAN JULY *Stevie Wonder-Motown*	7 DE DO DO DO DE DA DA DA *The Police-A&M*	7 NOT THE 9 O'CLOCK NEWS *Various-BBC*
8 EVERY WOMAN IN THE WORLD *Air Supply-Arista*	8 THE RIVER *Bruce Springsteen-Columbia*	8 SUPER TROUPER *Abba-Epic*	8 20 GREATS OF KEN DODD *Ken Dodd-Warwick*
9 HIT ME WITH YOUR BEST SHOT *Pat Benatar-Chrysalis*	9 LIVE *The Eagles-Asylum*	9 EMBARRASSMENT *Madness-Stiff*	9 KINGS OF THE WILD FRONTIER *Adam and The Ants-CBS*
10 HUNGRY HEART *Bruce Springsteen-Columbia*	10 THE JAZZ SINGER *Neil Diamond-Capitol*	10 FLASH *Queen-EMI*	10 BARRY *Barry Manilow-Arista*
11 I MADE IT THROUGH THE RAIN *Barry Manilow-Arista*	11 BARRY *Barry Manilow-Arista*	11 RABBIT *Chas and Dave-Rockney*	11 ABSOLUTELY *Madness-Stiff*
12 I BELIEVE IN YOU *Don Williams-MCA*	12 ANNE MURRAY'S GREATEST *Anne Murray-Capitol*	12 RUNAWAYS BOYS *Stray Cats-Arista*	12 FLASH GORDON *Queen-EMI*
13 THE WANDERER *Donna Summer-Geffen*	13 GAUCHO *Steely Dan-Gaucho*	13 BANANA REPUBLIC *Boomtown Rats-Ensign*	13 THE VERY BEST OF BOWIE *David Bowie-K-Tel*
14 THE TIDE IS HIGH *Blondie-Chrysalis*	14 GREATEST HITS/LIVE *Heart-Epic*	14 LIES/DON'T DRIVE MY CAR *Status Quo-Vertigo*	14 AUTOAMERICAN *Blondie-Chrysalis*
15 PASSION *Rod Stewart-Warner Bros*	15 ZENYATTA MONDATTA *The Police-A&M*	15 DO NOTHING/MAGGIES FARM *Specials-2Tone*	15 CHART EXPLOSION *Various-K-Tel*
16 TELL IT LIKE IT IS *Heart-Epic*	16 FOOLISH BEHAVIOUR *Rod Stewart-Warner Bros*	16 TO CUT A LONG STORY SHORT *Spandau Ballet-Chrysalis*	16 INSPIRATION *Elvis Presley-K-Tel*
17 LOST THAT LOVIN' FEELING *Daryl Hall and John Oates-RCA*	17 AUTOAMERICAN *Blondie-Chrysalis*	17 LOVE ON THE ROCKS *Neil Diamond-Capitol*	17 SOUND AFFECTS *Jam-Polydor*
18 DE DO DO DO, DE DA DA DA *The Police-A&M*	18 TRIUMPH *The Jacksons-Epic*	18 OVER THE RAINBOW *Matchbox-Magnet*	18 FOOLISH BEHAVIOUR *Rod Stewart-Riva*
19 CELEBRATION *Kool and The Gang-De-Lite*	19 GLASS HOUSES *Billy Joel-Columbia*	19 LADY *Kenny Rogers-United Artists*	19 HOTTER THAN JULY *Stevie Wonder-Tamla Motown*
20 SUDDENLY *Olivia Newton-John-Cliff Richard-MCA*	20 XANADU *Original Soundtrack-MCA*	20 TOO NICE TO TALK TO *The Beat-Go Feet*	20 MAKING WAVES *Nolans-Epic*

US SINGLES	US ALBUMS	UK SINGLES	UK ALBUMS
1 (JUST LIKE) STARTING OVER *John Lennon-Geffen*	1 GREATEST HITS *Kenny Rogers-Liberty*	1 IMAGINE *John Lennon-Parlophone*	1 SUPER TROUPER *Abba-Epic*
2 BITES THE DUST *Queen-Elektra*	2 DOUBLE FANTASY *John Lennon/Yoko Ono-Geffen*	2 ANTMUSIC *Adam and The Ants-CBS*	2 DOUBLE FANTASY *John Lennon-Geffen*
3 LOVE ON THE ROCKS *Neil Diamond-Capitol*	3 GUILTY *Barbra Streisand-Columbia*	3 HAPPY CHRISTMAS *John Lennon-Apple*	3 KINGS OF THE WILD FRONTIER *Adam and The Ants-CBS*
4 EVERY WOMAN IN THE WORLD *Air Supply-Arista*	4 BACK IN BLACK *AC/DC-Atlantic*	4 DO NOTHING/MAGGIES FARM *Specials-2Tone*	4 DR. HOOK'S GREATEST HITS *Dr. Hook-Capitol*
5 MORE THAN I CAN SAY *Leo Sayer-Warner Bros*	5 CRIMES OF PASSION *Pat Benatar-Chrysalis*	5 STARTING OVER *John Lennon-Geffen*	5 BEST OF DAVID BOWIE *David Bowie-K-Tel*
6 GUILTY *Barbra Streisand-Barry Gibb-Columbia*	6 THE JAZZ SINGER *Neil Diamond-Capitol*	6 STOP THE CAVALRY *Jona Lewie-Stiff*	6 GUILTY *Barbra Streisand-CBS*
7 THE TIDE IS HIGH *Blondie-Chrysalis*	7 THE GAME *Queen-Elektra*	7 TOO NICE TO TALK TO *The Beat-Go Feet*	7 NOT THE 9 O'CLOCK NEWS *Various-BBC*
8 LADY *Kenny Rogers-Liberty*	8 HOTTER THAN JULY *Stevie Wonder-Motown*	8 RABBIT *Chas and Dave-Rockney*	8 ZENYATTA MONDATTA *The Police-A&M*
9 HIT ME WITH YOUR BEST SHOT *Pat Benatar-Chrysalis*	9 THE RIVER *Bruce Springsteen-Columbia*	9 DE DO DO DO DE DA DA DA *The Police-A&M*	9 MANILOW MAGIC *Barry Manilow-Arista*
10 PASSION *Rod Stewart-Warner Bros*	10 LIVE *The Eagles-Asylum*	10 FLASH *Queen-EMI*	10 FLASH GORDON *Queen-EMI*
11 I MADE IT THROUGH THE RAIN *Barry Manilow-Arista*	11 BARRY *Barry Manilow-Arista*	11 LIES/DON'T DRIVE MY CAR *Status Quo-Vertigo*	11 ABSOLUTELY *Madness-Stiff*
12 I BELIEVE IN YOU *Don Williams-MCA*	12 ANNE MURRAY'S GREATEST *Anne Murray-Capitol*	12 WHO'S GONNA ROCK YOU *Nolans-Epic*	12 MAKING WAVES *Nolans-Epic*
13 HUNGRY HEART *Bruce Springsteen-Columbia*	13 GAUCHO *Steely Dan-MCA*	13 EMBARRASSMENT *Madness-Stiff*	13 HOTTER THAN JULY *Stevie Wonder-Tamla Motown*
14 DUKES OF HAZZARD THEME *Waylon Jennings-RCA*	14 GREATEST HITS/LIVE *Heart-Epic*	14 I AM THE BEAT *The Look-MCA*	14 SCARY MONSTERS *David Bowie-RCA*
15 CELEBRATION *Kool and the Gang-De-Lite*	15 ZENYATTA MONDATTA *The Police-A&M*	15 OVER THE RAINBOW *Matchbox-Magnet*	15 IMAGINE *John Lennon-Parlophone*
16 TELL IT LIKE IT IS *Heart-Epic*	16 FOOLISH BEHAVIOUR *Rod Steward-Warner Bros*	16 RUNAWAY BOYS *Stray Cats-Arista*	16 JAZZ SINGER *Neil Diamond-Capitol*
17 I LOVE A RAINY NIGHT *Eddie Rabbitt-Elektra*	17 AUTOAMERICAN *Blondie-Chrysalis*	17 I AIN'T GONNA STAND FOR IT *Stevie Wonder-Tamla Motown*	17 AUTOAMERICAN *Blondie-Chrysalis*
18 HEY NINETEEN *Steely Dan-MCA*	18 CHRISTOPHER CROSS *Christopher Cross-Warner Bros*	18 RUNAROUND SUE *Racey-RAK*	18 BARRY *Barry Manilow-Arista*
19 SUDDENLY *Olivia Newton-John-Cliff Richard-MCA*	19 GLASS HOUSES *Billy Joel-Columbia*	19 DON'T STOP THE MUSIC *Yarborough and Peoples-Mercury*	19 SIGNING OFF *UB 40-Graduate*
20 IT'S MY TURN *Diana Ross-Motown*	20 ONE STEP CLOSER *Doobie Brothers-Warner Bros*	20 THIS WRECKAGE *Gary Numan-Beggars Banquet*	20 SHAVED FISH *John Lennon/Plastic Ono Band-Parlophone*

US SINGLES	US ALBUMS	UK SINGLES	UK ALBUMS
1 (JUST LIKE) STARTING OVER *John Lennon-Geffen*	**1 GREATEST HITS** *Kenny Rogers-Liberty*	**1 IMAGINE** *John Lennon-Parlophone*	**1 KINGS OF THE WILD FRONTIER** *Adam and The Ants-CBS*
2 THE TIDE IS HIGH *Blondie-Chrysalis*	**2 DOUBLE FANTASY** *John Lennon-Yoko Ono-Geffen*	**2 ANTMUSIC** *Adam and The Ants*	**2 DOUBLE FANTASY** *John Lennon/Yoko Ono-Geffen*
3 EVERY WOMAN IN THE WORLD *Air Supply-Arista*	**3 GUILTY** *Barbra Streisand-Columbia*	**3 WOMAN** *John Lennon-Geffen*	**3 BEST OF DAVID BOWIE** *David Bowie-K-Tel*
4 BITES THE DUST *Queen-Elektra*	**4 THE JAZZ SINGER** *Neil Diamond-Capitol*	**4 IN THE AIR TONIGHT** *Phil Collins-Virgin*	**4 DR. HOOK'S GREATEST HITS** *Dr. Hook-Capitol*
5 HIT ME WITH YOUR BEST SHOT *Pat Benatar-Chrysalis*	**5 CRIMES OF PASSION** *Pat Benatar-Chrysalis*	**5 DO NOTHING/MAGGIES FARM** *Specials-2Tone*	**5 SUPER TROUPER** *Abba-Epic*
6 PASSION *Rod Stewart-Warner Bros*	**6 BACK IN BLACK** *AC/DC-Atlantic*	**6 I AM THE BEAT** *The Look-MCA*	**6 GUILTY** *Barbra Streisand-CBS*
7 MORE THAN I CAN SAY *Leo Sayer-Warner Bros*	**7 HOTTER THAN JULY** *Stevie Wonder-Motown*	**7 TOO NICE TO TALK TO** *The Beat-Go Feet*	**7 IMAGINE** *John Lennon-Parlophone*
8 GUILTY *Barbra Streisand-Barry Gibb-Columbia*	**8 THE GAME** *Queen-Elektra*	**8 DON'T STOP THE MUSIC** *Yarborough and Peoples-Mercury*	**8 MANILOW MAGIC** *Barry Manilow-Arista*
9 CELEBRATION *Kool and the Gang-De-Lite*	**9 GAUCHO** *Steely Dan-MCA*	**9 HAPPY CHRISTMAS** *John Lennon-Apple*	**9 MONDO BONGO** *Boomtown Rats-Mercury*
10 I MADE IT THROUGH THE RAIN *Barry Manilow-Arista*	**10 LIVE** *The Eagles-Asylum*	**10 FLASH** *Queen-EMI*	**10 PARADISE THEATER** *Styx-A&M*
11 LADY *Kenny Rogers-Liberty*	**11 THE RIVER** *Bruce Springsteen-Columbia*	**11 YOUNG PARISIANS** *Adam and The Ants-Decca*	**11 SHAVED FISH** *John Lennon/Plastic Ono Band-Parlophone*
12 LOVE ON THE ROCKS *Neil Diamond-Capitol*	**12 ZENYATTA MONDATTA** *The Police-A&M*	**12 I AIN'T GONNA STAND FOR IT** *Stevie Wonder-Tamla Motown*	**12 ZENYATTA MONDATTA** *The Police-A&M*
13 I LOVE A RAINY NIGHT *Eddie Rabbitt-Elektra*	**13 GREATEST HITS-LIVE** *Heart-Epic*	**13 RUNAROUND SUE** *Racey-RAK*	**13 ARC OF A DIVER** *Steve Winwood-Island*
14 HUNGRY HEART *Bruce Springsteen-Columbia*	**14 AUTOAMERICAN** *Blondie-Chrysalis*	**14 RAPTURE** *Blondie-Chrysalis*	**14 FLASH GORDON** *Queen-EMI*
15 HEY NINETEEN *Steely Dan-MCA*	**15 BARRY** *Barry Manilow-Arista*	**15 STARTING OVER** *John Lennon-Geffen*	**15 NOT THE 9 O'CLOCK NEWS** *Various-BBC*
16 I BELIEVE IN YOU *Don Williams-MCA*	**16 FOOLISH BEHAVIOUR** *Rod Stewart-Warner Bros*	**16 VIENNA** *Ultravox-Chrysalis*	**16 HOTTER THAN JULY** *Stevie Wonder-Tamla Motown*
17 KEEP ON LOVING YOU *REO Speedwagon-Epic*	**17 ANNE MURRAY'S GREAT HITS** *Anne Murray-Capitol*	**17 WHO'S GONNA ROCK YOU** *Nolans-Epic*	**17 MAKING MOVIES** *Dire Straits-Vertigo*
18 GIVING IT UP FOR YOUR LOVE *Delbert McClinton-Capitol-MSS*	**18 CHRISTOPHER CROSS** *Christopher Cross-Warner Bros*	**18 RABBIT** *Chas and Dave-Rockney*	**18 ABSOLUTELY** *Madness-Stiff*
19 TELL IT LIKE IT IS *Heart-Epic*	**19 HI INFIDELITY** *REO Speedwagon-Epic*	**19 STOP THE CAVALRY** *Jona Lewie-Stiff*	**19 WILD WILLING AND INNOCENT** *UFO-Chrysalis*
20 SUDDENLY *Olivia Newton-John-Cliff Richard-MCA*	**20 GLASS HOUSES** *Billy Joel-Columbia*	**20 SCARY MONSTERS** *David Bowie-RCA*	**20 SIGNING OFF** *UB 40-Graduate*

US SINGLES	US ALBUMS	UK SINGLES	UK ALBUMS
1 THE TIDE IS HIGH *Blondie-Chrysalis*	**1 GREATEST HITS** *Kenny Rogers-Liberty*	**1 IMAGINE** *John Lennon-Parlophone*	**1 KINGS OF THE WILD FRONTIER** *Adam and The Ants-CBS*
2 (JUST LIKE) STARTING OVER *John Lennon-Geffen*	**2 DOUBLE FANTASY** *John Lennon-Yoko Ono-Geffen*	**2 WOMAN** *John Lennon-Geffen*	**2 DOUBLE FANTASY** *John Lennon/Yoko Ono-Geffen*
3 EVERY WOMAN IN THE WORLD *Air Supply-Arista*	**3 GUILTY** *Barbra Streisand-Columbia*	**3 IN THE AIR TONIGHT** *Phil Collins-Virgin*	**3 BEST OF DAVID BOWIE** *David Bowie-RCA*
4 CELEBRATION *Kool and the Gang-De-Lite*	**4 THE JAZZ SINGER** *Neil Diamond-Capitol*	**4 ANTMUSIC** *Adam and The Ants-CBS*	**4 MANILOW MAGIC** *Barry Manilow-Arista*
5 HIT ME WITH YOUR BEST SHOT *Pat Benatar-Chrysalis*	**5 CRIMES OF PASSION** *Pat Benatar-Chrysalis*	**5 RAPTURE** *Blondie-Chrysalis*	**5 BARRY** *Barry Manilow-Arista*
6 PASSION *Rod Stewart-Warner Bros*	**6 BACK IN BLACK** *AC/DC-Atlantic*	**6 VIENNA** *Ultravox-RCA*	**6 IMAGINE** *John Lennon-Parlophone*
7 I LOVE A RAINY NIGHT *Eddie Rabbitt-Elektra*	**7 HOTTER THAN JULY** *Stevie Wonder-Motown*	**7 DON'T STOP THE MUSIC** *Yarborough and Peoples-Mercury*	**7 GUILTY** *Barbra Streisand-CBS*
8 BITES THE DUST *Queen-Elektra*	**8 ZENYATTA MONDATTA** *The Police-A&M*	**8 I AM THE BEAT** *The Look-MCA*	**8 DR. HOOK'S GREATEST HITS** *Dr. Hook-Capitol*
9 KEEP ON LOVING YOU *REO Speedwagon-Epic*	**9 GAUCHO** *Steely Dan-MCA*	**9 YOUNG PARISIANS** *Adam and The Ants-Decca*	**9 TRUST** *Elvis Costello-F-Beat*
10 9 TO 5 *Dolly Parton-RCA*	**10 AUTOAMERICAN** *Blondie-Chrysalis*	**10 I AIN'T GONNA STAND FOR IT** *Stevie Wonder-Tamla Motown*	**10 SUPER TROUPER** *Abba-Epic*
11 I MADE IT THROUGH THE RAIN *Barry Manilow-Arista*	**11 LIVE** *The Eagles-Asylum*	**11 DO NOTHING** *Specials-2Tone*	**11 MONDO BONGO** *Boomtown Rats-Ensign*
12 HEY NINETEEN *Steely Dan-MCA*	**12 HI INFIDELITY** *REO Speedwagon-Epic*	**12 FADE TO GREY** *Visage-Polydor*	**12 PARADISE THEATER** *Styx-A&M*
13 MORE THAN I CAN SAY *Leo Sayer-Warner Bros*	**13 THE RIVER** *Bruce Springsteen-Columbia*	**13 TOO NICE TO TALK TO** *The Beat-Go Feet*	**13 MAKING MOVIES** *Dire Straits-Vertigo*
14 LOVE ON THE ROCKS *Neil Diamond-Capitol*	**14 FOOLISH BEHAVIOUR** *Rod Stewart-Warner Bros*	**14 FLASH** *Queen-EMI*	**14 SHAVED FISH** *John Lennon/Plastic Ono Band-Parlophone*
15 HUNGRY HEART *Bruce Springsteen-Columbia*	**15 THE GAME** *Queen-Elektra*	**15 RUNAROUND SUE** *Racey-Rak*	**15 NOT THE 9 O'CLOCK NEWS** *Various-BBC*
16 GIVING IT UP FOR YOUR LOVE *Delbert McClinton-Capitol-MSS*	**16 GREATEST HITS-LIVE** *Heart-Epic*	**16 ROMEO AND JULIET** *Dire Straits-Vertigo*	**16 ABSOLUTELY** *Madness-Stiff*
17 LADY *Kenny Rogers-Liberty*	**17 PARADISE THEATER** *Styx-A&M*	**17 A LITTLE IN LOVE** *Cliff Richard-EMI*	**17 HOTTER THAN JULY** *Stevie Wonder-Tamla Motown*
18 SAME OLD LANG SYNE *Dan Fogelberg-Full Moon-Epic*	**18 CELEBRATE** *Kool and the Gang-De-Lite*	**18 RETURN OF THE LOS PALMAS 7** *Madness-Stiff*	**18 VIENNA** *Ultravox-Chrysalis*
19 GUILTY *Barbra Streisand-Barry Gibb-Columbia*	**19 CHRISTOPHER CROSS** *Christopher Cross-Warner Bros*	**19 GANGSTERS OF THE GROOVE** *Heatwave-GTO*	**19 SIGNING OFF** *UB 40-Graduate*
20 DE DO DO DO, DE DA DA DA *The Police-A&M*	**20 BARRY** *Barry Manilow-Arista*	**20 SCARY MONSTERS** *David Bowie-RCA*	**20 ARC OF A DIVER** *Steve Winwood-Island*

WEEK ENDING FEBRUARY 7 1981

US SINGLES	US ALBUMS	UK SINGLES	UK ALBUMS
1 THE TIDE IS HIGH *Blondie-Chrysalis*	1 GREATEST HITS *Kenny Rogers-Liberty*	1 WOMAN *John Lennon-Geffen*	1 DOUBLE FANTASY *John Lennon/Yoko Ono-Geffen*
2 (JUST LIKE) STARTING OVER *John Lennon-Geffen*	2 DOUBLE FANTASY *John Lennon-Yoko Ono-Geffen*	2 IN THE AIR TONIGHT *Phil Collins-Virgin*	2 KINGS OF THE WILD FRONTIER *Adam and The Ants-CBS*
3 9 TO 5 *Dolly Parton-RCA*	3 THE JAZZ SINGER *Neil Diamond-Capitol*	3 VIENNA *Ultravox-Chrysalis*	3 VERY BEST OF DAVID BOWIE *David Bowie-K-Tel*
4 CELEBRATION *Kool and the Gang-De-Lite*	4 GUILTY *Barbra Streisand-Columbia*	4 IMAGINE *John Lennon-Parlophone*	4 MANILOW MAGIC *Barry Manilow-Arista*
5 I LOVE A RAINY NIGHT *Eddie Rabbitt-Elektra*	5 CRIMES OF PASSION *Pat Benatar-Chrysalis*	5 RAPTURE *Blondie-Chrysalis*	5 IMAGINE *John Lennon-Parlophone*
6 PASSION *Rod Stewart-Warner Bros*	6 BACK IN BLACK *AC/DC-Atlantic*	6 ANTMUSIC *Adam and The Ants-CBS*	6 MONDO BONGO *Boomtown Rats-Mercury*
7 KEEP ON LOVING YOU *REO Speedwagon-Epic*	7 HOTTER THAN JULY *Stevie Wonder-Motown*	7 DON'T STOP THE MUSIC *Yarborough and Peoples-Mercury*	7 MAKING MOVIES *Dire Straits-Vertigo*
8 EVERY WOMAN IN THE WORLD *Air Supply-Arista*	8 ZEYATTA MONDATTA *The Police-A&M*	8 FADE TO GREY *Visage-Polydor*	8 PARADISE THEATER *Styx-A&M*
9 HIT ME WITH YOUR BEST SHOT *Pat Benatar-Chrysalis*	9 GAUCHO *Steely Dan-MCA*	9 YOUNG PARISIANS *Adam and The Ants-Decca*	9 BARRY *Barry Manilow-Arista*
10 HEY NINETEEN *Steely Dan-MCA*	10 AUTOAMERICAN *Blondie-Chrysalis*	10 I AM THE BEAT *The Look-MCA*	10 DR. HOOK'S GREATEST HITS *Dr. Hook-Capitol*
11 BITES THE DUST *Queen-Elektra*	11 HI INFIDELITY *REO Speedwagon-Epic*	11 ROMEO AND JULIET *Dire Straits-Vertigo*	11 VIENNA *Ultravox-Chrysalis*
12 MORE THAN I CAN SAY *Leo Sayer-Warner Bros*	12 PARADISE THEATER *Styx-A&M*	12 I SURRENDER *Rainbow-Polydor*	12 GUILTY *Barbra Streisand-CBS*
13 SAME OLD LANG SYNE *Dan Fogelberg-Full Moon-Epic*	13 LIVE *The Eagles-Asylum*	13 I AIN'T GONNA STAND FOR IT *Stevie Wonder-Tamla Motown*	13 SUPER TROUPER *Abba-Epic*
14 GIVING IT UP FOR YOUR LOVE *Delbert McClinton-Capitol-MSS*	14 FOOLISH BEHAVIOUR *Rod Stewart-Warner Bros*	14 RETURN OF THE LOS PALMAS 7 *Madness-Stiff*	14 SHAVED FISH *John Lennon/Plastic Ono Band-Parlophone*
15 LOVE ON THE ROCKS *Neil Diamond-Capitol*	15 THE GAME *Queen-Elektra*	15 A LITTLE IN LOVE *Cliff Richard-EMI*	15 JAZZ SINGER *Neil Diamond-Capitol*
16 I MADE IT THROUGH THE RAIN *Barry Manilow-Arista*	16 CELEBRATE *Kool and the Gang-De-Lite*	16 IT'S MY TURN *Diana Ross-Tamla Motown*	16 TRUST *Elvis Costello and The Attractions-F Beat*
17 LADY *Kenny Rogers-Liberty*	17 THE RIVER *Bruce Springsteen-Columbia*	17 THE FREEZE *Spandau Ballet-Chrysalis*	17 ABSOLUTELY *Madness-Stiff*
18 GUILTY *Barbra Streisand-Barry Gibb-Columbia*	18 GREATEST HITS-LIVE *Heart-Epic*	18 DO NOTHING/MAGGIE'S FARM *Specials-2Tone*	18 HOTTER THAN JULY *Stevie Wonder-Tamla Motown*
19 WOMAN *John Lennon-Geffen*	19 TURN OF A FRIENDLY CARD *Alan Parsons Project-Arista*	19 OLDEST SWINGER IN TOWN *Fred Wedlock-Rocket*	19 SIGNING OFF *UB 40-Graduate*
20 MISS SUN *Boz Scaggs-Columbia*	20 BARRY *Barry Manilow-Arista*	20 GANGSTERS OF THE GROOVE *Heatwave-GTO*	20 VISAGE *Visage-Polydor*

WEEK ENDING FEBRUARY 14 1981

US SINGLES	US ALBUMS	UK SINGLES	UK ALBUMS
1 CELEBRATION *Kool and the Gang-De-Lite*	1 DOUBLE FANTASY *John Lennon-Yoko Ono-Geffen*	1 WOMAN *John Lennon-Geffen*	1 DOUBLE FANTASY *John Lennon/Yoko Ono-Geffen*
2 9 TO 5 *Dolly Parton-RCA*	2 GREATEST HITS *Kenny Rogers-Liberty*	2 VIENNA *Ultravox-Chrysalis*	2 KINGS OF THE WILD FRONTIER *Adam and The Ants-CBS*
3 I LOVE A RAINY NIGHT *Eddie Rabbitt-Elektra*	3 THE JAZZ SINGER *Neil Diamond-Capitol*	3 SHADDAP YOU FACE *Joe Dolce-Epic*	3 VERY BEST OF DAVID BOWIE *David Bowie-K Tel*
4 THE TIDE IS HIGH *Blondie-Chrysalis*	4 PARADISE THEATER *Styx-A&M*	4 IN THE AIR TONIGHT *Phil Collins-Virgin*	4 MAKING MOVIES *Dire Straits-Vertigo*
5 KEEP ON LOVING YOU *REO Speedwagon-Epic*	5 CRIMES OF PASSION *Pat Benatar-Chrysalis*	5 I SURRENDER *Rainbow-Polydor*	5 VIENNA *Ultravox-Chrysalis*
6 PASSION *Rod Stewart-Warner Bros*	6 GUILTY *Barbra Streisand-Columbia*	6 IMAGINE *John Lennon-Parlophone*	6 MANILOW MAGIC *Barry Manilow-Arista*
7 (JUST LIKE) STARTING OVER *John Lennon-Geffen*	7 BACK IN BLACK *AC/DC-Atlantic*	7 OLDEST SWINGER IN TOWN *Fred Wedlock-Rocket*	7 DANCE CRAZE *Soundtrack-2 Tone*
8 EVERY WOMAN IN THE WORLD *Air Supply-Arista*	8 HI INFIDELITY *REO Speedwagon-Epic*	8 RAPTURE *Blondie-Chrysalis*	8 GUILTY *Barbra Streisand-CBS*
9 HIT ME WITH YOUR BEST SHOT *Pat Benatar-Chrysalis*	9 HOTTER THAN JULY *Stevie Wonder-Motown*	9 ANTMUSIC *Adam and The Ants-CBS*	9 IMAGINE *John Lennon-Parlophone*
10 HEY NINETEEN *Steely Dan-MCA*	10 GAUCHO *Steely Dan-MCA*	10 RETURN OF THE LOS PALMAS 7 *Madness-Stiff*	10 JAZZ SINGER *Neil Diamond-Capitol*
11 SAME OLD LANG SYNE *Dan Fogelberg-Full Moon-Epic*	11 AUTOAMERICAN *Blondie-Chrysalis*	11 DON'T STOP THE MUSIC *Yarborough and Peoples-Mercury*	11 MONDO BONGO *Boomtown Rats-Mercury*
12 THE BEST OF TIMES *Styx-A&M*	12 ZENYATTA MONDATTA *The Police-A&M*	12 ROMEO AND JULIET *Dire Straits-Vertigo*	12 SHAVED FISH *John Lennon/Plastic Ono Band-Parlophone*
13 GIVING IT UP FOR YOUR LOVE *Delbert McClinton-Capitol-MSS*	13 CELEBRATE *Kool and the Gang-De-Lite*	13 FADE TO GREY *Visage-Polydor*	13 BARRY *Barry Manilow-Arista*
14 WOMAN *John Lennon-Geffen*	14 FOOLISH BEHAVIOUR *Rod Stewart-Warner Bros*	14 ROCK THIS TOWN *Stray Cats-Arista*	14 VISAGE *Visage-Polydor*
15 A LITTLE IN LOVE *Cliff Richard-EMI-America*	15 THE RIVER *Bruce Springsteen-Columbia*	15 YOUNG PARISIANS *Adam and The Ants-Decca*	15 ARC OF A DIVER *Steve Winwood-Island*
16 GAMES PEOPLE PLAY *Alan Parsons Project-Arista*	16 TURN OF A FRIENDLY CARD *Alan Parsons Project-Arista*	16 A LITTLE IN LOVE *Cliff Richard-EMI*	16 DR HOOK'S GREATEST HITS *Dr Hook-Capitol*
17 BITES THE DUST *Queen-Elektra*	17 LIVE *The Eagles-Asylum*	17 BRING THE HOUSE DOWN *Slade-Cheapskate*	17 TAKE MY TIME *Sheena Easton-EMI*
18 MISS SUN *Boz Scaggs-Columbia*	18 THE GAME *Queen-Elektra*	18 THE FREEZE *Spandau Ballet-Chrysalis*	18 PARADISE THEATER *Styx-A&M*
19 HEARTBREAK HOTEL *The Jacksons-Epic*	19 GREATEST HITS-LIVE *Heart-Epic*	19 SERGEANT ROCK *XTC-Virgin*	19 TRUST *Elvis Costello and The Attractions-F Beat*
20 I AIN'T GONNA STAND FOR IT *Stevie Wonder-Motown*	20 TRIUMPH *The Jacksons-Epic*	20 I AM THE BEAT *The Look-MCA*	20 ABSOLUTELY *Madness-Stiff*

US SINGLES

1. **9 TO 5**
   Dolly Parton-RCA
2. **CELEBRATION**
   Kool and the Gang-De-Lite
3. **I LOVE A RAINY NIGHT**
   Eddie Rabbitt-Elektra
4. **KEEP ON LOVING YOU**
   REO Speedwagon-Epic
5. **THE TIDE IS HIGH**
   Blondie-Chrysalis
6. **WOMAN**
   John Lennon-Geffen
7. **THE BEST OF TIMES**
   Styx-A&M
8. **PASSION**
   Rod Stewart-Warner Bros
9. **SAME OLD LANG SYNE**
   Dan Fogelberg-Full Moon-Epic
10. **(JUST LIKE) STARTING OVER**
    John Lennon-Geffen
11. **EVERY WOMAN IN THE WORLD**
    Air Supply-Arista
12. **A LITTLE IN LOVE**
    Cliff Richard-EMI-America
13. **GIVING IT UP FOR YOUR LOVE**
    Delbert McClinton-Capitol-MSS
14. **GAMES PEOPLE PLAY**
    Alan Parsons Project-Arista
15. **CRYING**
    Don McLean-Millennium
16. **HELLO AGAIN**
    Neil Diamond-Capitol
17. **TREAT ME RIGHT**
    Pat Benatar-Chrysalis
18. **I AIN'T GONNA STAND FOR IT**
    Stevie Wonder-Motown
19. **HEARTBREAK HOTEL**
    The Jacksons-Epic
20. **HIT ME WITH YOUR BEST SHOT**
    Pat Benatar-Chrysalis

US ALBUMS

1. **DOUBLE FANTASY**
   John Lennon-Yoko Ono-Geffen
2. **GREATEST HITS**
   Kenny Rogers-Liberty
3. **THE JAZZ SINGER**
   Neil Diamond-Capitol
4. **PARADISE THEATER**
   Styx-A&M
5. **CRIMES OF PASSION**
   Pat Benatar-Chrysalis
6. **HI INFIDELITY**
   REO Speedwagon-Epic
7. **GUILTY**
   Barbra Streisand-Columbia
8. **BACK IN BLACK**
   AC/DC-Atlantic
9. **HOTTER THAN JULY**
   Stevie Wonder-Motown
10. **AUTOAMERICAN**
    Blondie-Chrysalis
11. **GAUCHO**
    Steely Dan-MCA
12. **ZENYATTA MONDATTA**
    The Police-A&M
13. **CELEBRATE**
    Kool and the Gang-De-Lite
14. **FOOLISH BEHAVIOUR**
    Rod Stewart-Warner Bros
15. **TURN OF A FRIENDLY CARD**
    Alan Parsons Project-Arista
16. **THE RIVER**
    Bruce Springsteen-Columbia
17. **THE GAME**
    Queen-Elektra
18. **LIVE**
    The Eagles-Asylum
19. **GAP BAND III**
    The Gap Band-Mercury
20. **THE TWO OF US**
    Yarbrough and Peoples-Mercury

UK SINGLES

1. **SHADDAP YOU FACE**
   Joe Dolce-Epic
2. **VIENNA**
   Ultravox-Chrysalis
3. **WOMAN**
   John Lennon-Geffen
4. **I SURRENDER**
   Rainbow-Polydor
5. **IN THE AIR TONIGHT**
   Phil Collins-Virgin
6. **OLDEST SWINGER IN TOWN**
   Fred Wedlock-Rocket
7. **RETURN OF THE LOS PALMAS 7**
   Madness-Stiff
8. **ROMEO AND JULIET**
   Dire Straits-Vertigo
9. **ROCK THIS TOWN**
   Stray Cats-Arista
10. **BRING THE HOUSE DOWN**
    Slade-Cheapskate
11. **MESSAGE OF LOVE**
    Pretenders-Real
12. **FADE TO GREY**
    Visage-Polydor
13. **RAPTURE**
    Blondie-Chrysalis
14. **DO THE HUCKLEBUCK**
    Coast to Coast-Polydor
15. **VALENTINE'S MASSACRE EP**
    Motorhead/Girlschool-Bronze
16. **SERGEANT ROCK**
    XTC-Virgin
17. **IMAGINE**
    John Lennon-Parlophone
18. **ANTMUSIC**
    Adam and The Ants-CBS
19. **DON'T STOP THE MUSIC**
    Yarbrough and Peoples-Mercury
20. **A LITTLE IN LOVE**
    Cliff Richard-EMI

UK ALBUMS

1. **FACE VALUE**
   Phil Collins-Virgin
2. **DOUBLE FANTASY**
   John Lennon/Yoko Ono-Geffen
3. **MOVING PICTURES**
   Rush-Mercury
4. **DIFFICULT TO CURE**
   Rainbow-Polydor
5. **VIENNA**
   Ultravox-Chrysalis
6. **KINGS OF THE WILD FRONTIER**
   Adam and The Ants-CBS
7. **DANCE CRAZE**
   Soundtrack-2 Tone
8. **THEMENINBLACK**
   Stranglers-Liberty
9. **MANILOW MAGIC**
   Barry Manilow-Arista
10. **MAKING MOVIES**
    Dire Straits-Vertigo
11. **JAZZ SINGER**
    Neil Diamond-Capitol
12. **BEST OF DAVID BOWIE**
    David Bowie-K-Tel
13. **SHAVED FISH**
    John Lennon/Plastic Ono Band-Parlophone
14. **BARRY**
    Bary Manilow-Arista
15. **GUILTY**
    Barbra Streisand-CBS
16. **IMAGINE**
    John Lennon-Parlophone
17. **ARC OF A DIVER**
    Steve Winwood-Island
18. **DIMINISHED RESPONSIBILITY**
    UK Subs-Gem
19. **VISAGE**
    Visage-Polydor
20. **HIT MACHINE**
    Various-K-Tel

US SINGLES

1. **9 TO 5**
   Dolly Parton-RCA
2. **CELEBRATION**
   Kool and the Gang-De-Lite
3. **I LOVE A RAINY NIGHT**
   Eddie Rabbitt-Elektra
4. **KEEP ON LOVING YOU**
   REO Speedwagon-Epic
5. **WOMAN**
   John Lennon-Geffen
6. **THE TIDE IS HIGH**
   Blondie-Chrysalis
7. **THE BEST OF TIMES**
   Styx-A&M
8. **HELLO AGAIN**
   Neil Diamond-Capitol
9. **SAME OLD LANG SYNE**
   Dan Fogelberg-Full Moon-Epic
10. **RAPTURE**
    Blondie-Chrysalis
11. **A LITTLE IN LOVE**
    Cliff Richard-EMI-America
12. **CRYING**
    Don McLean-Millennium
13. **GAMES PEOPLE PLAY**
    Alan Parsons Project-Arista
14. **PASSION**
    Rod Stewart-Warner Bros
15. **TREAT ME RIGHT**
    Pat Benatar-Chrysalis
16. **(JUST LIKE) STARTING OVER**
    John Lennon-Geffen
17. **GIVING IT UP FOR YOUR LOVE**
    Delbert McClinton-Capitol-MSS
18. **HIT ME WITH YOUR BEST SHOT**
    Pat Benatar-Chrysalis
19. **WHAT KIND OF FOOL**
    Barbra Streisand-Barry Gibb-Columbia
20. **WINNER TAKES IT ALL**
    Abba-Atlantic

US ALBUMS

1. **HI INFIDELITY**
   REO Speedwagon-Epic
2. **DOUBLE FANTASY**
   John Lennon-Yoko Ono-Geffen
3. **THE JAZZ SINGER**
   Neil Diamond-Capitol
4. **PARADISE THEATER**
   Styx-A&M
5. **GREATEST HITS**
   Kenny Rogers-Liberty
6. **CRIMES OF PASSION**
   Pat Benatar-Chrysalis
7. **GUILTY**
   Barbra Streisand-Columbia
8. **BACK IN BLACK**
   AC/DC-Atlantic
9. **AUTOAMERICAN**
   Blondie-Chrysalis
10. **GAUCHO**
    Steely Dan-MCA
11. **ZENYATTA MONDATTA**
    The Police-A&M
12. **CELEBRATE**
    Kool and the Gang-De-Lite
13. **HOTTER THAN JULY**
    Stevie Wonder-Motown
14. **TURN OF A FRIENDLY CARD**
    Alan Parsons Project-Arista
15. **FOOLISH BEHAVIOUR**
    Rod Stewart-Warner Bros
16. **CAPTURED**
    Journey-Columbia
17. **GAP BAND III**
    The Gap Band-Mercury
18. **THE TWO OF US**
    Yarbrough and Peoples-Mercury
19. **THE RIVER**
    Bruce Springsteen-Columbia
20. **9 TO 5 AND ODD JOBS**
    Dolly Parton-RCA

UK SINGLES

1. **SHADDAP YOU FACE**
   Joe Dolce-Epic
2. **VIENNA**
   Ultravox-Chrysalis
3. **I SURRENDER**
   Rainbow-Polydor
4. **WOMAN**
   John Lennon-Geffen
5. **VALENTINE'S MASSACRE EP**
   Motorhead/Girlschool-Bronze
6. **JEALOUS GUY**
   Roxy Music-E.G.
7. **RETURN OF THE LOS PALMAS 7**
   Madness-Stiff
8. **DO THE HUCKLEBUCK**
   Coast To Coast-Polydor
9. **SOUTHERN FREEEZ**
   Freeez-Beggars Banquet
10. **OLDEST SWINGER IN TOWN**
    Fred Wedlock-Rocket
11. **ROCK THIS TOWN**
    Stray Cats-Arista
12. **IN THE AIR TONIGHT**
    Phil Collins-Virgin
13. **BRING THE HOUSE DOWN**
    Slade-Cheapskate
14. **ROMEO AND JULIET**
    Dire Straits-Vertigo
15. **MESSAGE OF LOVE**
    Pretenders-Real
16. **FADE TO GREY**
    Visage-Polydor
17. **KINGS OF THE WILD FRONTIER**
    Adam and The Ants-CBS
18. **SERGEANT ROCK**
    XTC-Virgin
19. **SOMETHING 'BOUT YOU BABY**
    Status Quo-Vertigo
20. **ANTMUSIC**
    Adam and The Ants-CBS

UK ALBUMS

1. **FACE VALUE**
   Phil Collins-Virgin
2. **DOUBLE FANTASY**
   John Lennon/Yoko Ono-Geffen
3. **DIFFICULT TO CURE**
   Rainbow-Polydor
4. **VIENNA**
   Ultravox-Chrysalis
5. **MOVING PICTURES**
   Rush-Mercury
6. **JAZZ SINGER**
   Neil Diamond-Capitol
7. **KINGS OF THE WILD FRONTIER**
   Adam and The Ants-CBS
8. **DANCE CRAZE**
   Soundtrack-2 Tone
9. **STRAY CATS**
   Stray Cats-Arista
10. **MAKING MOVIES**
    Dire Straits-Vertigo
11. **MANILOW MAGIC**
    Barry Manilow-Arista
12. **KILLERS**
    Iron Maiden-EMI
13. **BEST OF DAVID BOWIE**
    David Bowie-K-Tel
14. **THEMENINBLACK**
    Stranglers-Liberty
15. **GUILTY**
    Barbra Streisand-CBS
16. **VISAGE**
    Visage-Polydor
17. **SOUTHERN FREEEZ**
    Freeez-Beggars Banquet
18. **IMAGINE**
    John Lennon-Parlophone
19. **HIT MACHINE**
    Various-K-Tel
20. **ABSOLUTELY**
    Madness-Stiff

US SINGLES	US ALBUMS	UK SINGLES	UK ALBUMS
1 **9 TO 5** *Dolly Parton-RCA*	1 **HI INFIDELITY** *Reo Speedwagon-Epic*	1 **SHADDAP YOU FACE** *Joe Dolce-Epic*	1 **FACE VALUE** *Phil Collins-Virgin*
2 **KEEP ON LOVING YOU** *Reo Speedwagon-Epic*	2 **PARADISE THEATER** *Styx-A&M*	2 **VIENNA** *Ultravox-Chrysalis*	2 **KINGS OF THE WILD FRONTIER** *Adam and The Ants-CBS*
3 **I LOVE A RAINY NIGHT** *Eddie Rabbitt-Elektra*	3 **DOUBLE FANTASY** *John Lennon-Yoko Ono-Geffen*	3 **JEALOUS GUY** *Roxy Music-E.G.*	3 **VIENNA** *Ultravox-Chrysalis*
4 **WOMAN** *John Lennon-Geffen*	4 **THE JAZZ SINGER** *Neil Diamond-Capitol*	4 **I SURRENDER** *Rainbow-Polydor*	4 **JAZZ SINGER** *Neil Diamond-Capitol*
5 **CELEBRATION** *Kool and The Gang-De Lite*	5 **GREATEST HITS** *Kenny Rogers-Liberty*	5 **VALENTINE'S MASSACRE EP** *Motorhead/Girlschool*	5 **DANCE CRAZE** *Soundtrack-2 Tone*
6 **THE BEST OF TIMES** *Styx-A&M*	6 **CRIMES OF PASSION** *Pat Benatar-Chrysalis*	6 **KINGS OF THE WILD FRONTIER** *Adam and the Ants-CBS*	6 **DOUBLE FANTASY** *John Lennon/Yoko Ono-Geffen*
7 **RAPTURE** *Blondie-Chrysalis*	7 **GUILTY** *Barbra Streisand-Columbia*	7 **DO THE HUCKLEBUCK** *Coast To Coast-Polydor*	7 **DIFFICULT TO CURE** *Rainbow-Polydor*
8 **HELLO AGAIN** *Neil Diamond-Capitol*	8 **BACK IN BLACK** *AC/DC-Atlantic*	8 **SOUTHERN FREEEZ** *Freeez-Beggars Banquet*	8 **STRAY CATS** *Stray Cats-Arista*
9 **THE TIDE IS HIGH** *Blondie-Chrysalis*	9 **AUTOAMERICAN** *Blondie-Chrysalis*	9 **SOMETHING 'BOUT YOU BABY** *Status Quo-Vertigo*	9 **MOVING PICTURES** *Rush-Mercury*
10 **CRYING** *Don McLean-Millennium*	10 **ZENYATTA MONDATTA** *The Police-A&M*	10 **RETURN OF THE LOS PALMAS 7** *Madness-Stiff*	10 **MAKING MOVIES** *Dire Straits-Vertigo*
11 **A LITTLE IN LOVE** *Cliff Richard-EMI-America*	11 **CELEBRATE** *Kool and The Gang-De-Lite*	11 **WOMAN** *John Lennon-Geffen*	11 **MANILOW MAGIC** *Barry Manilow-Arista*
12 **SAME OLD LANG SYNE** *Dan Fogelberg-Full Moon-Epic*	12 **GAUCHO** *Steely Dan-MCA*	12 **ROCK THIS TOWN** *Stray Cats-Arista*	12 **GUILTY** *Barbara Streisand-CBS*
13 **GAMES PEOPLE PLAY** *Alan Parsons Project-Arista*	13 **CAPTURED** *Journey-Columbia*	13 **OLDEST SWINGER IN TOWN** *Fred Wedlock-Rocket*	13 **ABSOLUTELY** *Madness-Stiff*
14 **TREAT ME RIGHT** *Pat Benatar-Chrysalis*	14 **HOTTER THAN JULY** *Stevie Wonder-Motown*	14 **ONCE IN A LIFETIME** *Talking Heads-Sire*	14 **POINT OF ENTRY** *Judas Preist-CBS*
15 **WHAT KIND OF FOOL** *Barbra Streisand-Columbia*	15 **GAP BAND 111** *The Gap Band-Mercury*	15 **HELP ME OUT** *Beggar & Co-Ensign*	15 **KILLERS** *Iron Maiden-EMI*
16 **KISS ON MY LIST** *Daryl Hall and John Oates-RCA*	16 **9 TO 5 AND ODD JOBS** *Dolly Parton-RCA*	16 **FOUR FROM TOYAH** *Toyah-Safari*	16 **DIRK WEARS WHITE SOCKS** *Adam and The Ants-Do It*
17 **WINNER TAKES IT ALL** *Abba-Atlantic*	17 **THE TWO OF US** *Yarbrough and Peoples-Mercury*	17 **ROMEO AND JULIET** *Dire Straits-Vertigo*	17 **HIT MACHINE** *Various-K-Tel*
18 **HIT ME WITH YOUR BEST SHOT** *Pat Benatar-Chrysalis*	18 **TURN OF A FRIENDLY CARD** *Alan Parsons Project-Arista*	18 **KIDS IN AMERICA** *Kim Wilde-RAK*	18 **ANOTHER TICKET** *Eric Clapton-RSO*
19 **SMOKY MOUNTAIN RAIN** *Ronnie Milsap-RCA*	19 **THE RIVER** *Bruce Springsteen-Columbia*	19 **MESSAGE OF LOVE** *Pretenders-Real*	19 **SOUTHERN FREEEZ** *Freeez-Beggars Banquet*
20 **PASSION** *Rod Stewart-Warner Bros*	20 **HORIZON** *Eddie Rabbitt-Elektra*	20 **BRING THE HOUSE DOWN** *Slade-Cheapskate*	20 **ARC OF A DIVER** *Steve Winwood-Island*

US SINGLES	US ALBUMS	UK SINGLES	UK ALBUMS
1 **9 TO 5** *Dolly Parton-RCA*	1 **HI INFIDELITY** *Reo Speedwagon-Epic*	1 **JEALOUS GUY** *Roxy Music-E.G*	1 **KINGS OF THE WILD FRONTIER** *Adam and The Ants-CBS*
2 **KEEP ON LOVING YOU** *Reo Speedwagon-Epic*	2 **PARADISE THEATER** *Styx-A&M*	2 **KINGS OF THE WILD FRONTIER** *Adam and The Ants-CBS*	2 **FACE VALUE** *Phil Collins-Virgin*
3 **WOMAN** *John Lennon-Geffen*	3 **DOUBLE FANTASY** *John Lennon/Yoko Ono-Geffen*	3 **SHADDAP YOU FACE** *Joe Dolce-Epic*	3 **VIENNA** *Ultravox-Chrysalis*
4 **CELEBRATION** *Kool and The Gang-De-Lite*	4 **THE JAZZ SINGER** *Neil Diamond/Capitol*	4 **VIENNA** *Ultravox-Chrysalis*	4 **JAZZ SINGER** *Neil Diamond-Capitol*
5 **I LOVE A RAINY NIGHT** *Eddie Rabbitt-Elektra*	5 **GREATEST HITS** *Kenny Rogers-Liberty*	5 **DO THE HUCKLEBUCK** *Coast To Coast-Polydor*	5 **DOUBLE FANTASY** *John Lennon/Yoko Ono-Geffen*
6 **THE BEST OF TIMES** *Styx-A&M*	6 **CRIMES OF PASSION** *Pat Benatar-Chrysalis*	6 **KIDS IN AMERICA** *Kim Wilde-RAK*	6 **STRAY CATS** *Stray Cats-Arista*
7 **RAPTURE** *Blondie-Chrysalis*	7 **GUILTY** *Barbra Streisand-Columbia*	7 **THIS OLE HOUSE** *Shakin' Stevens-Epic*	7 **JOURNEY TO GLORY** *Spandau Ballet-Chrysalis*
8 **HELLO AGAIN** *Neil Diamond-Capitol*	8 **BACK IN BLACK** *AC/DC-Atlantic*	8 **SOUTHERN FREEEZ** *Freeez-Beggars Banquet*	8 **DIFFICULT TO CURE** *Rainbow-Polydor*
9 **THE TIDE IS HIGH** *Blondie-Chrysalis*	9 **AUTOAMERICAN** *Blondie-Chrysalis*	9 **SOMETHING 'BOUT YOU BABY** *Status Quo-Vertigo*	9 **DANCE CRAZE** *Soundtrack-2 Tone*
10 **CRYING** *Don McLean-Millennium*	10 **ZENYATTA MONDATTA** *The Police-A&M*	10 **VALENTINE'S MASSACRE EP** *Motorhead/Girlschool-Bronze*	10 **MAKING MOVIES** *Dire Straits-Vertigo*
11 **A LITTLE IN LOVE** *Cliff Richard-EMI-America*	11 **CELEBRATE** *Kool and The Gang-De-Lite*	11 **FOUR FROM TOYAH** *Toyah-Safari*	11 **VERY BEST OF...** *Rita Coolidge-A&M*
12 **KISS ON MY LIST** *Daryl Hall and John Oates-RCA*	12 **CAPTURED** *Journey-Columbia*	12 **I SURRENDER** *Rainbow-Polydor*	12 **MOVING PICTURES** *Rush-Mercury*
13 **WHAT KIND OF FOOL** *Barbra Streisand/Barry Gibb-Columbia*	13 **GAUCHO** *Steely Dan-MCA*	13 **REWARD** *Teardrop Explodes-Mercury*	13 **MANILOW MAGIC** *Barry Manilow-Arista*
14 **TREAT ME RIGHT** *Pat Benatar-Chrysalis*	14 **MOVING PICTURES** *Rush-Mercury*	14 **ONCE IN A LIFETIME** *Talking Heads-Sire*	14 **POINT OF ENTRY** *Judas Priest-CBS*
15 **GAMES PEOPLE PLAY** *Alan Parsons Project-Arista*	15 **GAP BAND 111** *Gap Band-Mercury*	15 **HELP ME OUT** *Beggar & Co-Ensign*	15 **ABSOLUTELY** *Madness-Stiff*
16 **WINNER TAKES IT ALL** *Abba-Atlantic*	16 **9 TO 5 AND ODD JOBS** *Dolly Parton-RCA*	16 **YOU BETTER YOU BET** *The Who-Polydor*	16 **GUILTY** *Barbra Streisand-CBS*
17 **SAME OLD LANG SYNE** *Dan Fogelberg-Full Moon-Epic*	17 **HOTTER THAN JULY** *Stevie Wonder-Motown*	17 **STAR** *Kiki Dee-Ariola*	17 **SOUTHERN FREEEZ** *Freeez-Beggars Banquet*
18 **SMOKY MOUNTAIN RAIN** *Ronnie Milsap-RCA*	18 **THE TWO OF US** *Yarbrough and Peoples-Mercury*	18 **RETURN OF THE LOS PALMAS 7** *Madness-Stiff*	18 **ANOTHER TICKET** *Eric Clapton-RSO*
19 **HIT ME WITH YOUR BEST SHOT** *Pat Benatar-Chrysalis*	19 **TURN OF A FRIENDLY CARD** *Alan Parsons Project-Arista*	19 **ROCK THIS TOWN** *Stray Cats-Arista*	19 **KILLERS** *Iron Maiden-EMI*
20 **DON'T STOP THE MUSIC** *Yarbrough and Peoples-Mercury*	20 **HORIZON** *Eddie Rabbitt-Elektra*	20 **I MISSED AGAIN** *Phil Collins-Virgin*	20 **CHRISTOPHER CROSS** *Christopher Cross-Warner Bros*

US SINGLES	US ALBUMS	UK SINGLES	UK ALBUMS
1 KEEP ON LOVING YOU *Reo Speedwagon-Epic*	1 HI INFIDELITY *Reo Speedwagon-Epic*	1 JEALOUS GUY *Roxy Music-E.G.*	1 KINGS OF THE WILD FRONTIER *Adam and The Ants-CBS*
2 9 TO 5 *Dolly Parton-RCA*	2 PARADISE THEATER *Styx-A&M*	2 THIS OLE HOUSE *Shakin' Stevens-Epic*	2 FACE VALUE *Phil Collins*
3 WOMAN *John Lennon-Geffen*	3 DOUBLE FANTASY *John Lennon/Yoko Ono-Geffen*	3 KIDS IN AMERICA *Kim Wilde-RAK*	3 JAZZ SINGER *Neil Diamond-Capitol*
4 CELEBRATION *Kool and The Gang-De-Lite*	4 THE JAZZ SINGER *Neil Diamond-Capitol*	4 KINGS OF THE WILD FRONTIER *Adam and The Ants-CBS*	4 VIENNA *Ultravox-Chrysalis*
5 RAPTURE *Blondie-Chrysalis*	5 GREATEST HITS *Kenny Rogers-Liberty*	5 DO THE HUCKLEBUCK *Coast To Coast-Polydor*	5 JOURNEY TO GLORY *Spandau Ballet-Chrysalis*
6 THE BEST OF TIMES *Styx-A&M*	6 CRIMES OF PASSION *Pat Benatar-Chrysalis*	6 REWARD *Teardrop Explodes-Mercury*	6 VERY BEST OF... *Rita Coolidge-A&M*
7 I LOVE A RAINY NIGHT *Eddie Rabbitt-Elektra*	7 GUILTY *Barbra Streisand-Columbia*	7 VIENNA *Ultravox-Chrysalis*	7 DOUBLE FANTASY *John Lennon/Yoko Ono-Geffen*
8 HELLO AGAIN *Neil Diamond-Capitol*	8 BACK IN BLACK *AC/DC-Atlantic*	8 FOUR FROM TOYAH *Toyah-Safari*	8 DANCE CRAZE *Soundtrack-2 Tone*
9 CRYING *Don McLean-Millennium*	9 AUTOAMERICAN *Blondie-Chrysalis*	9 YOU BETTER YOU BET *The Who-Polydor*	9 DIFFICULT TO CURE *Rainbow-Polydor*
10 THE TIDE IS HIGH *Blondie-Chrysalis*	10 ZENYATTA MONDATTA *The Police-A&M*	10 SHADDAP YOU FACE *Joe Dolce-Epic*	10 STRAY CATS *Stray Cats-Arista*
11 KISS ON MY LIST *Daryl Hall and John Oates-RCA*	11 CAPTURED *Journey-Columbia*	11 SOUTHERN FREEEZ *Freeez-Beggars Banquet*	11 MAKING MOVIES *Dire Straits-Vertigo*
12 WHAT KIND OF FOOL *Barbra Streisand/Barry Gibb-Columbia*	12 MOVING PICTURES *Rush-Mercury*	12 SOMETHING 'BOUT YOU BABY *Status Quo-Vertigo*	12 GUILTY *Barbra Streisand-CBS*
13 TREAT ME RIGHT *Pat Benatar-Chrysalis*	13 GAUCHO *Steely Dan-MCA*	13 STAR *Kiki Dee-Ariola*	13 MOVING PICUTRES *Rush-Mercury*
14 A LITTLE IN LOVE *Cliff Richard-EMI-America*	14 CELEBRATE *Kool and The Gang-De-Lite*	14 I MISSED AGAIN *Phil Collins-Virgin*	14 MANILOW MAGIC *Barry Manilow-Arista*
15 WINNER TAKES IT ALL *Abba-Atlantic*	15 GAP BAND 111 *The Gap Band-Mercury*	15 VALENTINE'S MASSACRE EP *Motorhead/Girlschoool-Bronze*	15 HOTTER THAN JULY *Stevie Wonder-Tamla Motown*
16 SMOKY MOUNTAIN RAIN *Ronnie Milsap-RCA*	16 ARC OF A DIVER *Steve Winwood-Island*	16 ONCE IN A LIFETIME *Talking Heads-Sire*	16 DIRK WEARS WHITE SOX *Adam and The Ants-Do It*
17 JUST THE TWO OF US *Grover Washington, Jr.-Elektra*	17 CHRISTOPHER CROSS *Christopher Cross-Warner Bros.*	17 JONES VS JONES *Kool and The Gang-De-Lite*	17 SOUTHERN FREEEZ *Freeez-Beggars Banquet*
18 MORNING TRAIN (9 TO 5) *Sheena Easton-EMI-America*	18 HOTTER THAN JULY *Stevie Wonder-Motown*	18 LATELY *Stevie Wonder-Tamla Motown*	18 ABSOLUTELY *Madness-Stiff*
19 DON'T STOP THE MUSIC *Yarbrough and Peoples-Mercury*	19 THE TWO OF US *Yarbrough and Peoples-Mercury*	19 HELP ME OUT *Beggar & Co-Ensign*	19 CHRISTOPHER CROSS *Christopher Cross-Warner Bros*
20 HEARTS ON FIRE *Randy Meisner-Epic*	20 9 TO 5 AND ODD JOBS *Dolly Parton-RCA*	20 PLANET EARTH *Duran Duran-EMI*	20 KILLERS *Iron Maiden-EMI*

US SINGLES	US ALBUMS	UK SINGLES	UK ALBUMS
1 9 TO 5 *Dolly Parton-RCA*	1 HI INFIDELITY *Reo Speedwagon-Epic*	1 THIS OLE HOUSE *Shakin' Stevens-Epic*	1 KINGS OF THE WILD FRONTIER *Adam and The Ants-CBS*
2 WOMAN *John Lennon-Geffen*	2 PARADISE THEATER *Styx-A&M*	2 KIDS IN AMERICA *Kim Wilde-RAK*	2 NEVER TOO LATE *Status Quo-Vertigo*
3 RAPTURE *Blondie-Chrysalis*	3 THE JAZZ SINGER *Neil Diamond-Capitol*	3 JEALOUS GUY *Roxy Music-E.G.*	3 FACE DANCES *The Who-Polydor*
4 CELEBRATION *Kool and The Gang-De-Lite*	4 GREATEST HITS *Kenny Rogers-Liberty*	4 FOUR FROM TOYAH *Toyah-Safari*	4 FACE VALUE *Phil Collins-Virgin*
5 KEEP ON LOVING YOU *Reo Speedwagon-Epic*	5 DOUBLE FANTASY *John Lennon/Yoko Ono-Geffen*	5 KINGS OF THE WILD FRONTIER *Adam and The Ants-CBS*	5 JAZZ SINGER *Neil Diamond-Capitol*
6 THE BEST OF TIMES *Styx-A&M*	6 CRIMES OF PASSION *Pat Benatar-Chrysalis*	6 LATELY *Stevie Wonder-Tamla Motown*	6 SKY 3 *Sky-Ariola*
7 KISS ON MY LIST *Daryl Hall and John Oates-RCA*	7 GUILTY *Barbra Streisand-Columbia*	7 DO THE HUCKLEBUCK *Coast To Coast-Polydor*	7 VERY BEST OF... *Rita Coolidge-A&M*
8 I LOVE A RAINY NIGHT *Eddie Rabbitt-Elektra*	8 BACK IN BLACK *AC/DC-Atlantic*	8 REWARD *Teardrop Explodes-Mercury*	8 VIENNA *Ultravox-Chrysalis*
9 CRYING *Don McLean-Millennium*	9 AUTOAMERICAN *Blondie-Chrysalis*	9 YOU BETTER YOU BET *The Who-Polydor*	9 HOTTER THAN JULY *Stevie Wonder-Tamla Motown*
10 JUST THE TWO OF US *Grover Washington Jr.-Elektra*	10 ZENYATTA MONDATTA *The Police-A&M*	10 CAPSTICK COMES COME *Tony Capstick-Dingles*	10 DOUBLE FANTASY *John Lennon/Yoko Ono-Geffen*
11 MORNING TRAIN (9 TO 5) *Sheena Easton-EMI-America*	11 CAPTURED *Journey-Columbia*	11 EINSTEIN A GO-GO *Landscape-RCA*	11 JOURNEY TO GLORY *Spandau Ballet-Chrysalis*
12 WHAT KIND OF FOOL *Barbra Streisand/Barry Gibb-Columbia*	12 MOVING PICTURES *Rush-Mercury*	12 PLANET EARTH *Duran Duran-EMI*	12 MAKING MOVIES *Dire Straits-Vertigo*
13 THE TIDE IS HIGH *Blondie-Chrysalis*	13 ARC OF A DIVER *Steve Winwood-Island*	13 INTUITION *Linx-Chrysalis*	13 MANILOW MAGIC *Barry Manilow-Arista*
14 HELLO AGAIN *Neil Diamond-Capitol*	14 THE TWO OF US *Yarbrough and Peoples-Mercury*	14 MIND OF A TOY *Visage-Polydor*	14 STRAY CATS *Stray Cats-Arista*
15 TREAT ME RIGHT *Pat Benatar-Chrysalis*	15 CHRISTOPHER CROSS *Christopher Cross-Warner Bros*	15 STAR *Kiki Dee-Ariola*	15 VISAGE *Visage-Polydor*
16 WINNER TAKES IT ALL *Abba-Atlantic*	16 CELEBRATE *Kool and The Gang-De-Lite*	16 VIENNA *Ultravox-Chrysalis*	16 DANCE CRAZE *Soundtrack-2 Tone*
17 DON'T STOP THE MUSIC *Yarbrough and Peoples-Mercury*	17 GAP BAND 111 *The Gap Band-Mercury*	17 I MISSED AGAIN *Phil Collins-Virgin*	17 DIFFICULT TO CURE *Rainbow-Polydor*
18 SOMEBODY KNOCKIN' *Terri Gibbs-MCA*	18 GAUCHO *Steely Dan-MCA*	18 JONES VS JONES *Kool and The Gang-De-Lite*	18 20 GOLDEN GREATS *Al Jolson-MCA*
19 DON'T STAND SO CLOSE TO ME *The Police-A&M*	19 HOTTER THAN JULY *Stevie Wonder-Motown*	19 THE BROKEN HEARTED *Dave Stewart/Colin Blunstone-Stiff*	19 FLESH AND BLOOD *Roxy Music-Polydor*
20 WHILE YOU SEE A CHANCE *Steve Winwood-Island*	20 HORIZON *Eddie Rabbitt-Elektra*	20 IT'S A LOVE THING *Whispers-Solar*	20 GUILTY *Barbra Streisand-CBS*

WEEK ENDING APRIL 4 1981

US SINGLES	US ALBUMS	UK SINGLES	UK ALBUMS
1 RAPTURE *Blondie-Chrysalis*	1 HI INFIDELITY *Reo Speedwagon-Epic*	1 THIS OLE HOUSE *Shakin' Stevens-Epic*	1 KINGS OF THE WILD FRONTIER *Adam and The Ants-CBS*
2 WOMAN *John Lennon-Geffen*	2 PARADISE THEATER *Styx-A&M*	2 KIDS IN AMERICA *Kim Wilde-RAK*	2 FACE DANCES *The Who-Polydor*
3 9 TO 5 *Dolly Parton-RCA*	3 THE JAZZ SINGER *Neil Diamond-Capitol*	3 CAPSTICK COMES HOME *Tony Capstick-Dingles*	3 SKY *Sky-Ariola*
4 CELEBRATION *Kool and The Gang-De-Lite*	4 GREATEST HITS *Kenny Rogers-Liberty*	4 LATELY *Stevie Wonder-Tamla Motown*	4 JAZZ SINGER *Neil Diamond-Capitol*
5 KISS ON MY LIST *Daryl Hall and John Oates-RCA*	5 DOUBLE FANTASY *John Lennon/Yoko Ono-Geffen*	5 MAKING YOUR MIND UP *Bucks Fizz-RCA*	5 FACE VALUE *Phil Collins-Virgin*
6 KEEP ON LOVING YOU *Reo Speedwagon-Epic*	6 CRIMES OF PASSION *Pat Benatar-Chrysalis*	6 FOUR FROM TOYAH *Toyah-Safari*	6 NEVER TOO LATE *Status Quo-Vertigo*
7 THE BEST OF TIMES *Styx-A&M*	7 MOVING PICTURES *Rush-Mercury*	7 JEALOUS GUY *Roxy Music-E.G.*	7 HOTTER THAN JULY *Stevie Wonder-Tamla Motown*
8 MORNING TRAIN (9 TO 5) *Sheena Easton-EMI-America*	8 GUILTY *Barbra Streisand-Columbia*	8 EINSTEIN A GO-GO *Landscape-RCA*	8 VIENNA *Ultravox-Chrysalis*
9 JUST THE TWO OF US *Grover Washington Jr.-Elektra*	9 BACK IN BLACK *AC/DC-Atlantic*	9 DO THE HUCKLEBUCK *Coast to Coast-Polydor*	9 DOUBLE FANTASY *John Lennon/Yoko Ono-Geffen*
10 CRYING *Don McLean-Millennium*	10 ARC OF A DIVER *Steve Winwood-Island*	10 INTUITION *Linx-Chrysalis*	10 MANILOW MAGIC *Barry Manilow-Arista*
11 I LOVE A RAINY NIGHT *Eddie Rabbitt-Elektra*	11 AUTOAMERICAN *Blondie-Chrysalis*	11 IT'S A LOVE THING *Whispers-Solar*	11 VERY BEST OF... *Rita Coolidge-A&M*
12 WHAT KIND OF FOOL *Barbra Streisand/Barry Gibb-Columbia*	12 ZENYATTA MONDATTA *The Police-A&M*	12 D-DAYS *Hazel O'Connor-Albion*	12 MAKING MOVIES *Dire Straits-Vertigo*
13 ANGEL OF THE MORNING *Juice Newton-Capitol*	13 CAPTURED *Journey-Columbia*	13 MIND OF A TOY *Visage-Polydor*	13 VISAGE *Visage-Polydor*
14 SOMEBODY'S KNOCKIN' *Terri Gibbs-MCA*	14 THE TWO OF US *Yarbrough and Peoples-Mercury*	14 YOU BETTER YOU BET *The Who-Polydor*	14 GUILTY *Barbra Streisand-CBS*
15 DON'T STAND SO CLOSE TO ME *The Police-A&M*	15 CHRISTOPHER CROSS *Christopher Cross-Warner Bros*	15 REWARD *Teardrop Explodes-Mercury*	15 JOURNEY TO GLORY *Spandau Ballet-Chrysalis*
16 WHILE YOU SEE A CHANCE *Steve Winwood-Island*	16 FACE DANCES *The Who-Warner Bros*	16 PLANET EARTH *Duran Duran-EMI*	16 BARRY *Barry Manilow-Arista*
17 DON'T STOP THE MUSIC *Yarbrough and Peoples-Mercury*	17 WINELIGHT *Grover Washington Jr.-Elektra*	17 THE BROKEN HEARTED *Dave Stewart/Colin Blunstone-Stiff*	17 INTUITION *Linx-Chrysalis*
18 HELLO AGAIN *Neil Diamond-Capitol*	18 ANOTHER TICKET *Eric Clapton-RSO*	18 KINGS OF THE WILD FRONTIER *Adam and The Ants-CBS*	18 ROGER WHITTAKER ALBUM *Roger Whittaker-K-Tel*
19 I CAN'T STAND IT *Eric Clapton and His Band-RSO*	19 DAD LOVES HIS WORK *James Taylor-Columbia*	19 STAR *Kiki Dee-Ariola*	19 DIFFICULT TO CURE *Rainbow-Polydor*
20 HER TOWN TOO *James Taylor/J.D.Souther-Columbia*	20 GAP BAND 111 *The Gap Band-Mercury*	20 JONES VS JONES *Kool and The Gang-De-Lite*	20 STRAY CATS *Stray Cats-Arista*

WEEK ENDING APRIL 11 1981

US SINGLES	US ALBUMS	UK SINGLES	UK ALBUMS
1 RAPTURE *Blondie-Chrysalis*	1 HI INFIDELITY *Reo Speedwagon-Epic*	1 THIS OLE HOUSE *Shakin' Stevens-Epic*	1 KINGS OF THE WILD FRONTIER *Adam and The Ants-CBS*
2 WOMAN *John Lennon-Geffen*	2 PARADISE THEATER *Styx-A&M*	2 MAKING YOUR MIND UP *Bucks Fizz-RCA*	2 FACE DANCES *The Who-Polydor*
3 KISS ON MY LIST *Daryl Hall and John Oates-RCA*	3 THE JAZZ SINGER *Neil Diamond-Capitol*	3 LATELY *Stevie Wonder-Tamla Motown*	3 HOTTER THAN JULY *Stevie Wonder-Tamla Motown*
4 MORNING TRAIN (9 TO 5) *Sheena Easton-EMI-America*	4 GREATEST HITS *Kenny Rogers-Liberty*	4 KIDS IN AMERICA *Kim Wilde-RAK*	4 JAZZ SINGER *Neil Diamond-Capitol*
5 9 TO 5 *Dolly Parton-RCA*	5 DOUBLE FANTASY *John Lennon/Yoko Ono-Geffen*	5 EINSTEIN A GO-GO *Landscape-RCA*	5 SKY 3 *Sky-Ariola*
6 KEEP ON LOVING YOU *Reo Speedwagon-Epic*	6 FACE DANCES *The Who-Warner Bros*	6 CAPSTICK COMES HOME *Tony Capstick-Dingles*	6 NEVER TOO LATE *Status Quo-Vertigo*
7 CELEBRATION *Kool and The Gang-De-Lite*	7 MOVING PICTURES *Rush-Mercury*	7 INTUITION *Linx-Chrysalis*	7 FACE VALUE *Phil Collins-Virgin*
8 JUST THE TWO OF US *Grover Washington Jr.-Elektra*	8 CRIMES OF PASSION *Pat Benatar-Chrysalis*	8 FOUR FROM TOYAH *Toyah-Safari*	8 THIS OLE HOUSE *Shakin' Stevens-Epic*
9 ANGEL OF THE MORNING *Juice Newton-Capitol*	9 ARC OF A DIVER *Steve Winwood-Island*	9 IT'S A LOVE THING *Whispers-Solar*	9 MAKING MOVIES *Dire Straits-Vertigo*
10 THE BEST OF TIMES *Styx-A&M*	10 GUILTY *Barbra Streisand-Columbia*	10 D-DAYS *Hazel O'Connor-Albion*	10 MANILOW MAGIC *Barry Manilow-Arista*
11 WHILE YOU SEE A CHANCE *Steve Winwood-Island*	11 AUTOAMERICAN *Blondie-Chrysalis*	11 CAN YOU FEEL IT *Jacksons-Epic*	11 DOUBLE FANTASY *John Lennon/Yoko Ono-Geffen*
12 SOMEBODY'S KNOCKIN' *Terri Gibbs-MCA*	12 ZENYATTA MONDATTA *The Police-A&M*	12 NIGHT GAMES *Graham Bonnet-Vertigo*	12 INTUITION *Linx-Chrysalis*
13 DON'T STAND SO CLOSE TO ME *The Police-A&M*	13 WINELIGHT *Grover Washington Jr.-Elektra*	13 THE BROKEN HEARTED *Dave Stewart/Colin Blunstone-Stiff*	13 VERY BEST OF... *Rita Coolidge-A&M*
14 I LOVE A RAINY NIGHT *Eddie Rabbitt-Elektra*	14 BACK IN BLACK *AC/DC-Atlantic*	14 GOOD THING GOING *Sugar Minott-RCA*	14 VIENNA *Ultravox-Chrysalis*
15 BEING WITH YOU *Smokey Robinson-Motown*	15 ANOTHER TICKET *Eric Clapton-RSO*	15 ATTENTION TO ME *Nolans-Epic*	15 JOURNEY TO GLORY *Spandau Ballet-Chrysalis*
16 I CAN'T STAND IT *Eric Clapton and His Band-RSO*	16 DAD LOVES HIS WORK *James Taylor-Columbia*	16 MIND OF A TOY *Visage-Polydor*	16 VISAGE *Visage-Polydor*
17 HER TOWN TOO *James Taylor/J.D.Souther-Columbia*	17 CAPTURED *Journey-Columbia*	17 DO THE HUCKLEBUCK *Coast To Coast-Polydor*	17 BARRY *Barry Manilow-Arista*
18 CRYING *Don McLean-Millennium*	18 SUCKING IN THE SEVENTIES *The Rolling Stones-Rolling Stones*	18 JEALOUS GUY *Roxy Music-E.G.*	18 CHRISTOPHER CROSS *Christopher Cross-Warner Bros*
19 DON'T STOP THE MUSIC *Yarbrough and Peoples-Mercury*	19 OVER THE RAINBOW *Willie Nelson-Columbia*	19 CHI MAI THEME TUNE *Ennio Morricone-BBC*	19 ROLL ON *Various-Polystar*
20 JUST BETWEEN YOU AND ME *April Wine-Capitol*	20 THE TWO OF US *Yarbrough and Peoples-Mercury*	20 JUST A FEELING *Bad Manners-Magnet*	20 FROM THE TEAROOMS *Landscape-RCA*

US SINGLES

1. **KISS ON MY LIST**
   Daryl Hall and John Oates-RCA
2. **MORNING TRAIN (9 TO 5)**
   Sheena Easton-EMI America
3. **RAPTURE**
   Blondie-Chrysalis
4. **ANGEL OF THE MORNING**
   Juice Newton-Capitol
5. **9 TO 5**
   Dolly Parton-RCA
6. **JUST THE TWO OF US**
   Grover Washington Jr.-Elektra
7. **KEEP ON LOVING YOU**
   Reo Speedwagon-Epic
8. **BEING WITH YOU**
   Smokey Robinson-Motown
9. **WHILE YOU SEE A CHANCE**
   Steve Winwood-Island
10. **WOMAN**
    John Lennon-Geffen
11. **SOMEBODY'S KNOCKIN'**
    Terri Gibbs-MCA
12. **DON'T STAND SO CLOSE TO ME**
    The Police-A&M
13. **HER TOWN TOO**
    James Taylor/J.D.Souther-Columbia
14. **I CAN'T STAND IT**
    Eric Clapton and His Band-RSO
15. **THE BEST OF TIMES**
    Styx-A&M
16. **CELEBRATION**
    Kool and The Gang-De-Lite
17. **TAKE IT ON THE RUN**
    Reo Speedwagon-Epic
18. **JUST BETWEEN YOU AND ME**
    April Wine-Capitol
19. **CRYING**
    Don McLean-Millennium
20. **YOU BETTER YOU BET**
    The Who-Warner Bros

US ALBUMS

1. **HI INFIDELITY**
   Reo Speedwagon-Epic
2. **PARADISE THEATER**
   Styx-A&M
3. **FACE DANCES**
   The Who-Warner Bros
4. **GREATEST HITS**
   Kenny Rogers-Liberty
5. **MOVING PICTURES**
   Rush-Mercury
6. **DOUBLE FANTASY**
   John Lennon/Yoko Ono-Geffen
7. **THE JAZZ SINGER**
   Neil Diamond-Capitol
8. **ARC OF A DIVER**
   Steve Winwood-Island
9. **CRIMES OF PASSION**
   Pat Benatar-Chrysalis
10. **WINELIGHT**
    Grover Washington Jr.-Elektra
11. **GUILTY**
    Barbra Streisand-Columbia
12. **AUTOAMERICAN**
    Blondie-Chrysalis
13. **ZENYATTA MONDATTA**
    The Police-A&M
14. **ANOTHER TICKET**
    Eric Clapton-RSO
15. **DAD LOVES HIS WORK**
    James Taylor-Columbia
16. **BACK IN BLACK**
    AC/DC-Atlantic
17. **SUCKING IN THE SEVENTIES**
    The Rolling Stones-Rolling Stones
18. **CAPTURED**
    Journey-Columbia
19. **OVER THE RAINBOW**
    Willie Nelson-Columbia
20. **GAP BAND 111**
    The Gap Band-Mercury

UK SINGLES

1. **MAKING YOUR MIND UP**
   Bucks Fizz-RCA
2. **THIS OLE HOUSE**
   Shakin' Stevens-Epic
3. **LATELY**
   Stevie Wonder-Tamla Motown
4. **CHI MAI THEME TUNE**
   Ennio Morricone-BBC
5. **EINSTEIN A GO-GO**
   Landscape-RCA
6. **NIGHT GAMES**
   Graham Bonnet-Vertigo
7. **GOOD THING GOING**
   Sugar Minott-RCA
8. **CAN YOU FEEL IT**
   Jacksons-Epic
9. **IT'S A LOVE THING**
   Whispers-Solar
10. **INTUITION**
    Linx-Chrysalis
11. **KIDS IN AMERICA**
    Kim Wilde-RAK
12. **D-DAYS**
    Hazel O'Connor-Albion
13. **THE BROKEN HEARTED**
    Dave Stewart/Colin Blunstone-Stiff
14. **ATTENTION TO ME**
    Nolans-Epic
15. **JUST A FEELING**
    Bad Manners-Magnet
16. **FOUR FROM TOYAH**
    Toyah-Safari
17. **CAPSTICK COMES HOME**
    Capstick/Frickley Colliery Band-Dingles
18. **MUSCLE BOUND/GLOW**
    Spandau Ballet-Chrysalis
19. **AND THE BANDS PLAYED ON**
    Saxon-Carrere
20. **NEW ORLEANS**
    Gillan-Virgin

UK ALBUMS

1. **KINGS OF THE WILD FRONTIER**
   Adam and The Ants-CBS
2. **COME AND GET IT**
   Whitesnake-Liberty
3. **HOTTER THAN JULY**
   Stevie Wonder-Tamla Motown
4. **THIS OLE HOUSE**
   Shakin' Stevens-Epic
5. **SKY 3**
   Sky-Ariola
6. **JAZZ SINGER**
   Neil Diamond-Capitol
7. **MAKING MOVIES**
   Dire Straits-Vertigo
8. **INTUITION**
   Linx-Chrysalis
9. **FACE VALUE**
   Phil Collins-Virgin
10. **MANILOW MAGIC**
    Barry Manilow-Arista
11. **FACE DANCES**
    The Who-Polydor
12. **FLOWERS OF ROMANCE**
    Public Image Ltd.-Virgin
13. **NEVER TOO LATE**
    Status Quo-Vertigo
14. **JOURNEY TO GLORY**
    Spandau Ballet-Chrysalis
15. **DOUBLE FANTASY**
    John Lennon/Yoko Ono-Geffen
16. **FROM THE TEAROOMS**
    Landscape-RCA
17. **ADVENTURES OF THIN LIZZY**
    Thin Lizzy-Vertigo
18. **FUN IN SPACE**
    Roger Taylor-EMI
19. **VIENNA**
    Ultravox-Chrysalis
20. **BARRY**
    Barry Manilow-Arista

US SINGLES

1. **MORNING TRAIN (9 TO 5)**
   Sheena Easton-EMI-America
2. **KISS ON MY LIST**
   Daryl Hall and John Oates-RCA
3. **ANGEL OF THE MORNING**
   Juice Newton-Capitol
4. **RAPTURE**
   Blondie-Chrysalis
5. **JUST THE TWO OF US**
   Grover Washington Jr.-Elektra
6. **BEING WITH YOU**
   Smokey Robinson-Motown
7. **9 TO 5**
   Dolly Parton-RCA
8. **KEEP ON LOVING YOU**
   Reo Speedwagon-Epic
9. **WHILE YOU SEE A CHANCE**
   Steve Winwood-Island
10. **SOMEBODY'S KNOCKIN'**
    Terri Gibbs-MCA
11. **HER TOWN TOO**
    James Taylor/J.D.Souther-Columbia
12. **TAKE IT ON THE RUN**
    Reo Speedwagon-Epic
13. **I CAN'T STAND IT**
    Eric Clapton and His Band-RSO
14. **DON'T STAND SO CLOSE TO ME**
    The Police-A&M
15. **WOMAN**
    John Lennon-Geffen
16. **JUST BETWEEN YOU AND ME**
    April Wine-Capitol
17. **TOO MUCH TIME ON MY HANDS**
    Styx-A&M
18. **YOU BETTER YOU BET**
    The Who-Warner Bros
19. **WATCHING THE WHEELS**
    John Lennon-Geffen
20. **CELEBRATION**
    Kool and The Gang-De-Lite

US ALBUMS

1. **HI INFIDELITY**
   Reo Speedwagon-Epic
2. **PARADISE THEATER**
   Styx-A&M
3. **FACE DANCES**
   The Who-Warner Bros
4. **MOVING PICTURES**
   Rush-Mercury
5. **GREATEST HITS**
   Kenny Rogers-Liberty
6. **ARC OF A DIVER**
   Steve Winwood-Island
7. **THE JAZZ SINGER**
   Neil Diamond-Capitol
8. **WINELIGHT**
   Grover Washington Jr.-Elektra
9. **DOUBLE FANTASY**
   John Lennon/Yoko Ono-Geffen
10. **CRIMES OF PASSION**
    Pat Benatar-Chrysalis
11. **ANOTHER TICKET**
    Eric Clapton-RSO
12. **DIRTY DEEDS DIRT CHEAP**
    AC/DC-Atlantic
13. **ZENYATTA MONDATTA**
    The Police-A&M
14. **DAD LOVES HIS WORK**
    James Taylor-Columbia
15. **GUILTY**
    Barbra Streisand-Columbia
16. **AUTOAMERICAN**
    Blondie-Chrysalis
17. **SUCKING IN THE SEVENTIES**
    The Rolling Stones-Rolling Stones
18. **BACK IN BLACK**
    AC/DC-Atlantic
19. **GAP BAND 111**
    The Gap Band-Mercury
20. **BEING WITH YOU**
    Smokey Robinson-Motown

UK SINGLES

1. **MAKING YOUR MIND UP**
   Bucks Fizz-RCA
2. **CHI MAI THEME TUNE**
   Ennio Morricone-BBC
3. **THIS OLE HOUSE**
   Shakin' Stevens-Epic
4. **GOOD THING GOING**
   Sugar Minott-RCA
5. **LATELY**
   Stevie Wonder-Tamla Motown
6. **EINSTEIN A GO-GO**
   Landscape-RCA
7. **CAN YOU FEEL IT**
   Jacksons-Epic
8. **NIGHT GAMES**
   Graham Bonnet-Vertigo
9. **IT'S A LOVE THING**
   Whispers-Solar
10. **ATTENTION TO ME**
    Nolans-Epic
11. **INTUITION**
    Linx-Chrysalis
12. **AND THE BANDS PLAYED ON**
    Saxon-Carrere
13. **JUST A FEELING**
    Bad Manners-Magnet
14. **KIDS IN AMERICA**
    Kim Wilde-RAK
15. **MUSCLE BOUND/GLOW**
    Spandau Ballet-Chrysalis
16. **D-DAYS**
    Hazel O'Connor-Albion
17. **STARS ON 45**
    Star Sound-CBS
18. **NEW ORLEANS**
    Gillan-Virgin
19. **THE BROKEN HEARTED**
    Dave Stewart/Colin Blunstone-Stiff
20. **GREY DAYS**
    Madness-Stiff

UK ALBUMS

1. **KINGS OF THE WILD FRONTIER**
   Adam and The Ants-CBS
2. **FUTURE SHOCK**
   Gillan-Virgin
3. **HOTTER THAN JULY**
   Stevie Wonder-Tamla Motown
4. **COME AND GET IT**
   Whitesnake-Liberty
5. **HIT 'N' RUN**
   Girlschool-Bronze
6. **THIS OLE HOUSE**
   Shakin' Stevens-Epic
7. **MAKING MOVIES**
   Dire Straits-Vertigo
8. **JAZZ SINGER**
   Neil Diamond-Capitol
9. **MANILOW MAGIC**
   Barry Manilow-Arista
10. **FACE VALUE**
    Phil Collins-Virgin
11. **FLOWERS OF ROMANCE**
    Public Image Ltd.-Virgin
12. **JOURNEY TO GLORY**
    Spandau Ballet-Chrysalis
13. **SKY 3**
    Sky-Ariola
14. **FAITH**
    The Cure-Fiction
15. **INTUITION**
    Linx-Chrysalis
16. **FROM THE TEAROOMS**
    Landscape-RCA
17. **DOUBLE FANTASY**
    John Lennon/Yoko Ono-Geffen
18. **GO FOR IT**
    Stiff Little Fingers-Chrysalis
19. **BARRY**
    Barry Manilow-Arista
20. **ADVENTURES OF THIN LIZZY**
    Thin Lizzy-Vertigo

US SINGLES

1. **MORNING TRAIN (9 TO 5)**
   Sheena Easton-EMI-America
2. **ANGEL OF THE MORNING**
   Juice Newton-Capitol
3. **KISS ON MY LIST**
   Daryl Hall and John Oates-RCA
4. **BEING WITH YOU**
   Smokey Robinson-Motown
5. **JUST THE TWO OF US**
   Grover Washington Jr.-Elektra
6. **RAPTURE**
   Blondie-Chrysalis
7. **TAKE IT ON THE RUN**
   Reo Speedwagon-Epic
8. **KEEP ON LOVING YOU**
   Reo Speedwagon-Epic
9. **WHILE YOU SEE A CHANCE**
   Steve Winwood-Island
10. **SOMEBODY'S KNOCKIN'**
    Terri Gibbs-MCA
11. **HER TOWN TOO**
    James Taylor/J.D.Souther-Columbia
12. **TOO MUCH TIME ON MY HANDS**
    Styx-A&M
13. **I CAN'T STAND IT**
    Eric Clapton and his Band-RSO
14. **WATCHING THE WHEELS**
    John Lennon-Geffen
15. **9 TO 5**
    Dolly Parton-RCA
16. **JUST BETWEEN YOU AND ME**
    April Wine-Capitol
17. **YOU BETTER YOU BET**
    The Who-Warner Bros
18. **LIVING INSIDE MYSELF**
    Gino Vannelli-Arista
19. **HOW 'BOUT US**
    Champaign-Columbia
20. **BETTE DAVIS EYES**
    Kim Carnes-EMI-America

US ALBUMS

1. **HI INFIDELITY**
   Reo Speedwagon-Epic
2. **PARADISE THEATER**
   Styx-A&M
3. **FACE DANCES**
   The Who-Warner Bros
4. **MOVING PICTURES**
   Rush-Mercury
5. **ARC OF A DIVER**
   Steve Winwood-Island
6. **DIRTY DEEDS DIRT CHEAP**
   AC/DC-Atlantic
7. **WINELIGHT**
   Grover Washington Jr.-Elektra
8. **GREATEST HITS**
   Kenny Rogers-Liberty
9. **THE JAZZ SINGER**
   Neil Diamond-Capitol
10. **ANOTHER TICKET**
    Eric Clapton-RSO
11. **DOUBLE FANTASY**
    John Lennon/Yoko Ono-Geffen
12. **CRIMES OF PASSION**
    Pat Benatar-Chrysalis
13. **ZENYATTA MONDATTA**
    The Police-A&M
14. **DAD LOVES HIS WORK**
    James Taylor-Columbia
15. **GUILTY**
    Barbra Streisand-Columbia
16. **AUTOAMERICAN**
    Blondie-Chrysalis
17. **BEING WITH YOU**
    Smokey Robinson-Motown
18. **BACK IN BLACK**
    AC/DC-Atlantic
19. **THE DUDE**
    Quincy Jones-A&M
20. **GAP BAND 111**
    The Gap Band-Mercury

UK SINGLES

1. **MAKING YOUR MIND UP**
   Bucks Fizz-RCA
2. **CHI MAI THEME TUNE**
   Ennio Morricone-BBC
3. **STARS ON 45**
   Star Sound-CBS
4. **GOOD THING GOING**
   Sugar Minott-RCA
5. **GREY DAY**
   Madness-Stiff
6. **CAN YOU FEEL IT**
   Jacksons-Epic
7. **THIS OLE HOUSE**
   Shakin' Stevens-Epic
8. **NIGHT GAMES**
   Graham Bonnet-Vertigo
9. **EINSTEIN A GO-GO**
   Landscape-RCA
10. **LATELY**
    Stevie Wonder-Tamla-Motown
11. **IT'S A LOVE THING**
    Whispers-Solar
12. **ATTENTION TO ME**
    Nolans-Epic
13. **MUSCLE BOUND/GLOW**
    Spandau Ballet/Chrysalis
14. **ONLY CRYING**
    Keith Marshall-Arrival
15. **AND THE BANDS PLAYED ON**
    Saxon-Carrere
16. **JUST A FEELING**
    Bad Manners-Magnet
17. **NEW ORLEANS**
    Gillan-Virgin
18. **CAN'T GET ENOUGH OF YOU**
    Eddy Grant-Ice/Ensign
19. **INTUITION**
    Linx-Chrysalis
20. **D-DAYS**
    Hazel O'Connor-Albion

UK ALBUMS

1. **KINGS OF THE WILD FRONTIER**
   Adam and The Ants-CBS
2. **FUTURE SHOCK**
   Gillan-Virgin
3. **CHART BLASTERS '81**
   Various-K-Tel
4. **LIVING ORNAMENTS 1979-80**
   Gary Numan-Beggars Banquet
5. **COME AND GET IT**
   Whitesnake-Liberty
6. **HOTTER THAN JULY**
   Stevie Wonder-Tamla Motown
7. **HIT 'N' RUN**
   Girlschool-Bronze
8. **MAKING MOVIES**
   Dire Straits-Vertigo
9. **JAZZ SINGER**
   Neil Diamond-Capitol
10. **THIS OLE HOUSE**
    Shakin' Stevens-Epic
11. **JOURNEY TO GLORY**
    Spandau Ballet-Chrysalis
12. **FACE VALUE**
    Phil Collins-Virgin
13. **SKY 3**
    Sky-Ariola
14. **GO FOR IT**
    Stiff Little Fingers-Chrysalis
15. **CHRISTOPHER CROSS**
    Christopher Cross-Warner Bros.
16. **VIENNA**
    Ultravox-Chrysalis
17. **DOUBLE FANTASY**
    John Lennon/Yoko Ono-Geffen
18. **FAITH**
    The Cure-Fiction
19. **MANILOW MAGIC**
    Barry Manilow-Arista
20. **INTUITION**
    Linx-Chrysalis

US SINGLES

1. **MORNING TRAIN (9 TO 5)**
   Sheena Easton-EMI-America
2. **ANGEL OF THE MORNING**
   Juice Newton-Capitol
3. **BEING WITH YOU**
   Smokey Robinson-Motown
4. **TAKE IT ON THE RUN**
   Reo Speedwagon-Epic
5. **JUST THE TWO OF US**
   Grover Washington Jr.-Elektra
6. **KISS ON MY LIST**
   Daryl Hall and John Oates-RCA
7. **BETTE DAVIS EYES**
   Kim Carnes-EMI-America
8. **RAPTURE**
   Blondie-Chrysalis
9. **TOO MUCH TIME ON MY HANDS**
   Styx-A&M
10. **SOMEBODY'S KNOCKIN'**
    Terri Gibbs-MCA
11. **WATCHING THE WHEELS**
    John Lennon-Geffen
12. **KEEP ON LOVING YOU**
    Reo Speedwagon-Epic
13. **LIVING INSIDE MYSELF**
    Gino Vannelli-Arista
14. **YOU BETTER YOU BET**
    The Who-Warner Bros
15. **SUKIYAKI**
    Taste of Honey-Capitol
16. **JUST BETWEEN YOU AND ME**
    April Wine-Capitol
17. **HOW 'BOUT US**
    Champaign-Columbia
18. **A WOMAN NEEDS LOVE**
    Ray Parker, Jr/Raydio-Arista
19. **SWEETHEART**
    Franke and The Knockouts-Millennium
20. **WHILE YOU SEE A CHANCE**
    Steve Winwood-Island

US ALBUMS

1. **HI INFIDELITY**
   Reo Speedwagon-Epic
2. **PARADISE THEATER**
   Styx-A&M
3. **FACE DANCES**
   The Who-Warner Bros
4. **DIRTY DEEDS DIRT CHEAP**
   AC/DC-Atlantic
5. **ARC OF A DIVER**
   Steve Winwood-Island
6. **MOVING PICTURES**
   Rush-Mercury
7. **WINELIGHT**
   Grover Washington Jr.-Elektra
8. **GREATEST HITS**
   Kenny Rogers-Liberty
9. **THE JAZZ SINGER**
   Neil Diamond-Capitol
10. **ANOTHER TICKET**
    Eric Clapton-RSO
11. **DOUBLE FANTASY**
    John Lennon/Yoko Ono-Geffen
12. **BACK IN BLACK**
    AC/DC-Atlantic
13. **CRIMES OF PASSION**
    Pat Benatar-Chrysalis
14. **ZENYATTA MONDATTA**
    The Police-A&M
15. **BEING WITH YOU**
    Smokey Robinson-Motown
16. **GUILTY**
    Barbra Streisand-Columbia
17. **DAD LOVES HIS WORK**
    James Taylor-Columbia
18. **THE DUDE**
    Quincy Jones-A&M
19. **GAP BAND 111**
    The Gap Band-Mercury
20. **LOVERBOY**
    Loverboy-Columbia

UK SINGLES

1. **STAND AND DELIVER**
   Adam and The Ants-CBS
2. **STARS ON 45**
   Star Sound-CBS
3. **CHI MAI THEME TUNE**
   Ennio Morricone-BBC
4. **MAKING YOUR MIND UP**
   Bucks Fizz-RCA
5. **YOU DRIVE ME CRAZY**
   Shakin' Stevens-Epic
6. **GREY DAY**
   Madness-Stiff
7. **GOOD THING GOING**
   Sugar Minott-RCA
8. **CAN YOU FEEL IT**
   Jacksons-Epic
9. **ATTENTION TO ME**
   Nolans-Epic
10. **MUSCLE BOUND/GLOW**
    Spandau Ballet-Chrysalis
11. **NIGHT GAMES**
    Graham Bonnet-Vertigo
12. **ONLY CRYING**
    Keith Marshall-Arrival
13. **CAN'T GET ENOUGH OF YOU**
    Eddy Grant-Ice/Ensign
14. **IT'S A LOVE THING**
    Whispers-Solar
15. **BERMUDA TRIANGLE**
    Barry Manilow-Arista
16. **AND THE BANDS PLAYED ON**
    Saxon-Carrere
17. **DON'T BREAK MY HEART AGAIN**
    Whitesnake-Liberty
18. **JUST A FEELING**
    Bad Manners-Magnet
19. **THIS OLE HOUSE**
    Shakin' Stevens-Epic
20. **EINSTEIN A GO-GO**
    Landscape-RCA

UK ALBUMS

1. **KINGS OF THE WILD FRONTIER**
   Adam and The Ants-CBS
2. **LIVING ORNAMENTS 1979-80**
   Gary Numan-Beggars Banquet
3. **CHART BLASTERS '81**
   Various-K-Tel
4. **THIS OLE HOUSE**
   Shakin' Stevens-Epic
5. **FUTURE SHOCK**
   Gillan-Virgin
6. **HOTTER THAN JULY**
   Stevie Wonder-Tamla Motown
7. **COME AND GET IT**
   Whitesnake-Liberty
8. **ROLL ON**
   Various-Polystar
9. **JAZZ SINGER**
   Neil Diamond-Capitol
10. **JOURNEY TO GLORY**
    Spandau Ballet-Chrysalis
11. **MAKING MOVIES**
    Dire Straits-Vertigo
12. **HIT 'N' RUN**
    Girlschool-Bronze
13. **MANILOW MAGIC**
    Barry Manilow-Arista
14. **CHRISTOPHER CROSS**
    Christopher Cross-Warner Bros.
15. **GO FOR IT**
    Stiff Little Fingers-Chrysalis
16. **CHARIOTS OF FIRE**
    Vangelis-Polydor
17. **SKY 3**
    Sky-Ariola
18. **FACE VALUE**
    Phil Collins-Virgin
19. **FAITH**
    The Cure-Fiction
20. **DOUBLE FANTASY**
    John Lennon/Yoko Ono-Geffen

US SINGLES	US ALBUMS	UK SINGLES	UK ALBUMS
1 **ANGEL OF THE MORNING** *Juice Newton-Capitol*	1 **HI INFIDELITY** *Reo Speedwagon-Epic*	1 **STAND AND DELIVER** *Adam and The Ants-CBS*	1 **KINGS OF THE WILD FRONTIER** *Adam and The Ants-CBS*
2 **MORNING TRAIN (9 TO 5)** *Sheena Easton-EMI-America*	2 **PARADISE THEATER** *Styx-A&M*	2 **YOU DRIVE ME CRAZY** *Shakin' Stevens-Epic*	2 **THIS OLE HOUSE** *Shakin' Stevens-Epic*
3 **BEING WITH YOU** *Smokey Robinson-Motown*	3 **FACE DANCES** *The Who-Warner Bros*	3 **STARS ON 45** *Star Sound-CBS*	3 **ROLL ON** *Various-Polystar*
4 **TAKE IT ON THE RUN** *Reo Speedwagon-Epic*	4 **DIRTY DEEDS DIRT CHEAP** *AC/DC-Atlantic*	4 **GREY DAY** *Madness-Stiff*	4 **HOTTER THAN JULY** *Stevie Wonder-Tamla Motown*
5 **BETTE DAVIS EYES** *Kim Carnes-EMI-America*	5 **ARC OF A DIVER** *Steve Winwood-Island*	5 **CHI MAI THEME TUNE** *Ennio Morricone-BBC*	5 **WHA'PPEN** *The Beat-Go-Feet*
6 **KISS ON MY LIST** *Daryl Hall and John Oates-RCA*	6 **GREATEST HITS** *Kenny Rogers-Liberty*	6 **MAKING YOUR MIND UP** *Bucks Fizz-RCA*	6 **FUTURE SHOCK** *Gillan-Virgin*
7 **TOO MUCH TIME ON MY HANDS** *Styx-A&M*	7 **WINELIGHT** *Grover Washington Jr.-Elektra*	7 **KEEP ON LOVING YOU** *REO Speedwagon-Epic*	7 **BAD FOR GOOD** *Jim Steinman-Epic*
8 **JUST THE TWO OF US** *Grover Washington-Jr.-Elektra*	8 **MOVING PICTURES** *Rush-Mercury*	8 **OSSIE'S DREAM** *Spurs FA Squad/Chas & Dave-Shelf*	8 **CHART BLASTERS '81** *Various-K-Tel*
9 **SUKIYAKI** *Taste of Honey-Capitol*	9 **THE JAZZ SINGER** *Neil Diamond-Capitol*	9 **CHEQUERED LOVE** *Kim Wilde-RAK*	9 **JAZZ SINGER** *Neil Diamond-Capitol*
10 **WATCHING THE WHEELS** *John Lennon-Geffen*	10 **BEING WITH YOU** *Smokey Robinson-Motown*	10 **SWORDS OF A THOUSAND MEN** *Tenpole Tudor-Stiff*	10 **CHARIOTS OF FIRE** *Vangelis-Polydor*
11 **LIVING INSIDE MYSELF** *Gino Vannelli-Arista*	11 **BACK IN BLACK** *AC/DC-Atlantic*	11 **CAN YOU FEEL IT** *Jacksons-Epic*	11 **COME AND GET IT** *Whitesnake-Liberty*
12 **YOU BETTER YOU BET** *The Who-Warner Bros*	12 **DOUBLE FANTASY** *John Lennon/Yoko Ono-Geffen*	12 **ATTENTION TO ME** *Nolans-Epic*	12 **JOURNEY TO GLORY** *Spandau Ballet-Chrysalis*
13 **RAPTURE** *Blondie-Chrysalis*	13 **WHAT CHA' GONNA DO FOR ME** *Chaka Khan-Warner Bros*	13 **GOOD THING GOING** *Sugar Minott-RCA*	13 **MAKING MOVIES** *Dire Straits-Vertigo*
14 **STARS ON 45** *Stars On-Radio*	14 **CRIMES OF PASSION** *Pat Benatar-Chrysalis*	14 **STRAY CAT STRUT** *Stray Cats-Arista*	14 **LIVING ORNAMENTS 1979-80** *Gary Numan-Beggars Banquet*
15 **A WOMAN NEEDS LOVE** *Ray Parker Jr./Raydio-Arista*	15 **LOVERBOY** *Loverboy-Columbia*	15 **MUSCLE BOUND/GLOW** *Spandau Ballet-Chrysalis*	15 **HI INFIDELITY** *REO Speedwagon-Epic*
16 **HOW 'BOUT US** *Champaign-Columbia*	16 **THE DUDE** *Quincy Jones-A&M*	16 **AI NO CORRIDA** *Quincy Jones-A&M*	16 **SKY 3** *Sky-Ariola*
17 **SOMEBODY'S KNOCKIN'** *Terri Gibbs-MCA*	17 **EXTENDED PLAY** *The Pretenders-Sire*	17 **ONLY CRYING** *Keith Marshall-Arrival*	17 **POSITIVE TOUCH** *The Undertones-Ardeck*
18 **SWEETHEART** *Franke and The Knockouts-Millennium*	18 **DAD LOVES HIS WORK** *James Taylor-Columbia*	18 **CAN'T GET ENOUGH OF YOU** *Eddy Grant-Ice/Ensign*	18 **MANILOW MAGIC** *Barry Manilow-Arista*
19 **KEEP ON LOVING YOU** *Reo Speedwagon-Epic*	19 **GUILTY** *Barbra Streisand-Columbia*	19 **BERMUDA TRIANGLE** *Barry Manilow-Arista*	19 **THE DUDE** *Quincy Jones-A&M*
20 **JUST BETWEEN YOU AND ME** *April Wine-Capitol*	20 **A WOMAN NEEDS LOVE** *Ray Parker Jr./Raydio-Arista*	20 **BETTE DAVIS EYES** *Kim Carnes-EMI-America*	20 **STARS ON 45** *Star Sound-CBS*

US SINGLES	US ALBUMS	UK SINGLES	UK ALBUMS
1 **BEING WITH YOU** *Smokey Robinson-Motown*	1 **HI INFIDELITY** *REO Speedwagon-Epic*	1 **STAND AND DELIVER** *Adam and The Ants-CBS*	1 **STARS ON 45** *Star Sound-CBS*
2 **BETTE DAVIS EYES** *Kim Carnes-EMI-America*	2 **PARADISE THEATER** *Styx-A&M*	2 **YOU DRIVE ME CRAZY** *Shakin' Stevens-Epic*	2 **KINGS OF THE WILD FRONTIER** *Adam and The Ants-CBS*
3 **TAKE IT ON THE RUN** *REO Speedwagon-Epic*	3 **DIRTY DEEDS DIRT CHEAP** *AC/DC-Atlantic*	3 **STARS ON 45** *Star Sound-CBS*	3 **WHA'PPEN** *The Beat-Go-Feet*
4 **MORNING TRAIN (9 TO 5)** *Sheena Easton-EMI-America*	4 **GREATEST HITS** *Kenny Rogers-Liberty*	4 **CHEQUERED LOVE** *Kim Wilde-RAK*	4 **THIS OLE HOUSE** *Shakin' Stevens-Epic*
5 **ANGEL OF THE MORNING** *Juice Newton-Capitol*	5 **ARC OF A DIVER** *Steve Winwood-Island*	5 **OSSIE'S DREAM** *Spurs FA Cup Final Squad-Shelf*	5 **HOTTER THAN JULY** *Stevie Wonder-Motown*
6 **STARS ON 45** *Stars On-Radio*	6 **FACE DANCES** *The Who-Warner Bros*	6 **SWORDS OF A THOUSAND MEN** *Tenpole Tudor-Stiff*	6 **ADVENTURES OF THIN LIZZY** *Thin Lizzy-Vertigo*
7 **TOO MUCH TIME ON MY HANDS** *Styx-A&M*	7 **WINELIGHT** *Grover Washington Jr.-Elektra*	7 **KEEP ON LOVING YOU** *Reo Speedwagon-Epic*	7 **QUIT DREAMING** *Bill Nelson-Mercury*
8 **SUKIYAKI** *Taste of Honey-Capitol*	8 **MOVING PICTURES** *Rush-Mercury*	8 **GREY DAY** *Madness-Stiff*	8 **ROLL ON** *Various-Polystar*
9 **WATCHING THE WHEELS** *John Lennon-Geffen*	9 **BEING WITH YOU** *Smokey Robinson-Motown*	9 **CHI MAI THEME TUNE** *Ennio Morricone-BBC*	9 **CHARIOTS OF FIRE** *Vangelis-Polydor*
10 **LIVING INSIDE MYSELF** *Gino Vannelli-Arista*	10 **BACK IN BLACK** *AC/DC-Atlantic*	10 **BETTE DAVIS EYES** *Kim Carnes-EMI-America*	10 **HI INFIDELITY** *Reo Speedwagon-Epic*
11 **KISS ON MY LIST** *Daryl Hall and John Oates-RCA*	11 **THE JAZZ SINGER** *Neil Diamond-Capitol*	11 **STRAY CAT STRUT** *Stray Cats-Arista*	11 **BAD FOR GOOD** *Jim Steinman-Epic*
12 **YOU BETTER YOU BET** *The Who-Warner Bros*	12 **WHAT CHA' GONNA DO FOR ME** *Chaka Kahn-Warner Bros*	12 **WHEN HE SHINES** *Sheena Easton-EMI*	12 **MAKING MOVIES** *Dire Straits-Vertigo*
13 **A WOMAN NEEDS LOVE** *Ray Parker Jr.-Raydio-Arista*	13 **DOUBLE FANTASY** *John Lennon-Yoko Ono-Geffen*	13 **I WANT TO BE FREE** *Toyah-Safari*	13 **JAZZ SINGER** *Neil Diamond-Capitol East*
14 **JUST THE TWO OF US** *Grover Washington Jr.-Elektra*	14 **THE DUDE** *Quincy Jones-A&M*	14 **AI NO CORRIDA** *Quincy Jones-A&M*	14 **DISCO DAZE AND DISCO NITES** *Various-Ronco*
15 **HOW 'BOUT US** *Champaign-Columbia*	15 **LOVERBOY** *Loverboy-Columbia*	15 **THE SOUND OF THE CROWD** *Human League-Virgin*	15 **COMPUTER WORLD** *Kraftwerk-EMI*
16 **SWEETHEART** *Franke and The Knockouts-Millennium*	16 **EXTENDED PLAY** *The Pretenders-Sire*	16 **MAKING YOUR MIND UP** *Bucks Fizz-RCA*	16 **LONG DISTANCE VOYAGER** *Moody Blues-Threshold*
17 **SOMEBODY'S KNOCKIN'** *Terri Gibbs-MCA*	17 **CRIMES OF PASSION** *Pat Benatar-Chrysalis*	17 **ONLY CRYING** *Keith Marshall-Arrival*	17 **STRAY CATS** *Stray Cats-Arista*
18 **RAPTURE** *Blondie-Chrysalis*	18 **A WOMAN NEEDS LOVE** *Ray Parker Jr.-Raydio-Arista*	18 **TREASON (IT'S JUST A STORY)** *Teardrop Explodes-Mercury*	18 **I AM THE PHOENIX** *Judie Tzuke-Rocket*
19 **I LOVE YOU** *Climax Blues Band-Warner Bros*	19 **ZEBOP!** *Santana-Columbia*	19 **KILLERS LIVE EP** *Thin Lizzy-Vertigo*	19 **COME AND GET IT** *Whitesnake-Liberty*
20 **KEEP ON LOVING YOU** *REO Speedwagon-Epic*	20 **MISTAKEN IDENTITY** *Kim Carnes-EMI-America*	20 **ATTENTION TO ME** *The Nolans-Epic*	20 **PUNK'S NOT DEAD** *Exploited-Secret*

US SINGLES	US ALBUMS	UK SINGLES	UK ALBUMS
1 BETTE DAVIS EYES *Kim Carnes-EMI-America*	1 HI INFIDELITY *REO Speedwagon-Epic*	1 STAND AND DELIVER *Adam and The Ants-CBS*	1 STARS ON 45 *Star Sound-CBS*
2 BEING WITH YOU *Smokey Robinson-Motown*	2 PARADISE THEATER *Styx-A&M*	2 YOU DRIVE ME CRAZY *Shakin' Stevens-Epic*	2 KINGS OF THE WILD FRONTIER *Adam and The Ants-CBS*
3 TAKE IT ON THE RUN *REO Speedwagon-Epic*	3 DIRTY DEEDS DIRT CHEAP *AC/DC-Atlantic*	3 STARS ON 45 *Star Sound-CBS*	3 ANTHEM *Toyah-Safari*
4 MORNING TRAIN (9 TO 5) *Sheena Easton-EMI-America*	4 GREATEST HITS *Kenny Rogers-Liberty*	4 CHEQUERED LOVE *Kim Wilde-RAK*	4 THIS OLE HOUSE *Shakin' Stevens-Epic*
5 STARS ON 45 *Stars On-Radio*	5 ARC OF A DIVER *Steve Winwood-Island*	5 OSSIE'S DREAM *Spurs FA Cup Final Squad-Shelf*	5 WHA'PPEN *The Beat-Go-Feet*
6 ANGEL OF THE MORNING *Juice Newton-Capitol*	6 MOVING PICTURES *Rush-Mercury*	6 SWORDS OF A THOUSAND MEN *Tenpole Tudor-Stiff*	6 DISCO DAZE AND DISCO NITES *Various-Ronco*
7 A WOMAN NEEDS LOVE *Ray Parker Jr.-Raydio-Arista*	7 WINELIGHT *Grover Washington Jr.-Elektra*	7 BEING WITH YOU *Smokey Robinson-Motown*	7 LONG DISTANCE VOYAGER *Moody Blues-Threshold*
8 SUKIYAKI *Taste of Honey-Capitol*	8 FACE DANCES *The Who-Warner Bros*	8 KEEP ON LOVING YOU *Reo Speedwagon-Epic*	8 BAD FOR GOOD *Jim Steinman-Epic*
9 WATCHING THE WHEELS *John Lennon-Geffen*	9 BEING WITH YOU *Smokey Robinson-Motown*	9 I WANT TO BE FREE *Toyah-Safari*	9 HI INFIDELITY *Reo Speedwagon-Epic*
10 LIVING INSIDE MYSELF *Gino Vannelli-Arista*	10 BACK IN BLACK *AC/DC-Atlantic*	10 BETTE DAVIS EYES *Kim Carnes-EMI-America*	10 HOTTER THAN JULY *Stevie Wonder-Motown*
11 TOO MUCH TIME ON MY HANDS *Styx-A&M*	11 WHAT CHA' GONNA DO FOR ME *Chaka Khan-Warner Bros*	11 HOW 'BOUT US *Champaign-CBS*	11 ADVENTURES OF THIN LIZZY *Thin Lizzy-Vertigo*
12 KISS ON MY LIST *Daryl Hall and John Oates-RCA*	12 THE JAZZ SINGER *Neil Diamond-Capitol*	12 THE SOUND OF THE CROWD *Human League-Virgin*	12 CHARIOTS OF FIRE *Vangelis-Polydor*
13 YOU BETTER YOU BET *The Who-Warner Bros*	13 THE DUDE *Quincy Jones-A&M*	13 ALL THOSE YEARS AGO *George Harrison-Dark Horse*	13 SECRET COMBINATION *Randy Crawford-Warner Bros*
14 HOW 'BOUT US *Champaign-Columbia*	14 DOUBLE FANTASY *John Lennon-Yoko Ono-Geffen*	14 STRAY CAT STRUT *Stray Cats-Arista*	14 MAKING MOVIES *Dire Straits-Vertigo*
15 SWEETHEART *Franke and The Knockouts-Millennium*	15 MISTAKEN IDENTITY *Kim Carnes-EMI-America*	15 GREY DAY *Madness-Stiff*	15 QUIT DREAMING *Bill Nelson-Mercury*
16 JUST THE TWO OF US *Grover Washington Jr.-Elektra*	16 EXTENDED PLAY *The Pretenders-Sire*	16 DON'T SLOW DOWN *UB40-DEP International*	16 JAZZ SINGER *Neil Diamond-Capitol East*
17 I LOVE YOU *Climax Blues Band-Warner Bros*	17 A WOMAN NEEDS LOVE *Ray Parker Jr.-Raydio-Arista*	17 AIN'T NO STOPPING *Enigma-Creole*	17 I AM THE PHOENIX *Judie Tzuke-Rocket*
18 AMERICA *Neil Diamond-Capitol*	18 CHRISTOPHER CROSS *Christopher Cross-Warner Bros*	18 IT'S GOING TO HAPPEN *The Undertones-Ardeck*	18 ROLL ON *Various-Polystar*
19 SOMEBODY'S KNOCKIN' *Terri Gibbs-MCA*	19 ZEBOP! *Santana-Columbia*	19 WHEN HE SHINES *Sheena Easton-EMI*	19 THEMES *Various-K-Tel*
20 ALL THOSE YEARS AGO *George Harrison-Dark Horse*	20 HARD PROMISES *Tom Petty and The Heartbreakers-MCA*	20 CHI MAI THEME TUNE *Ennio Morricone-BBC*	20 EAST SIDE STORY *Squeeze-A&M*

US SINGLES	US ALBUMS	UK SINGLES	UK ALBUMS
1 BETTE DAVIS EYES *Kim Carnes-EMI-America*	1 HI INFIDELITY *REO Speedwagon-Epic*	1 STAND AND DELIVER *Adam and The Ants-CBS*	1 STARS ON 45 *Star Sound-CBS*
2 STARS ON 45 *Stars On-Radio*	2 PARADISE THEATER *Styx-A&M*	2 YOU DRIVE ME CRAZY *Shakin' Stevens-Epic*	2 ANTHEM *Toyah-Safari*
3 TAKE IT ON THE RUN *REO Speedwagon-Epic*	3 DIRTY DEEDS DIRT CHEAP *AC/DC-Atlantic*	3 BEING WITH YOU *Smokey Robinson-Motown*	3 KINGS OF THE WILD FRONTIER *Adam and The Ants-CBS*
4 MORNING TRAIN (9 TO 5) *Sheena Easton-EMI-America*	4 FAIR WARNING *Van Halen-Warner Bros*	4 FUNERAL PYRE *The Jam-Polydor*	4 DISCO DAZE AND DISCO NITES *Various-Ronco*
5 A WOMAN NEEDS LOVE *Ray Parker Jr.-Raydio-Arista*	5 GREATEST HITS *Kenny Rogers-Liberty*	5 CHEQUERED LOVE *Kim Wilde-RAK*	5 THIS OLE HOUSE *Shakin' Stevens-Epic*
6 ANGEL OF THE MORNING *Juice Newton-Capitol*	6 MOVING PICTURES *Rush-Mercury*	6 HOW 'BOUT US *Champagne-CBS*	6 THEMES *Various-K-Tel*
7 BEING WITH YOU *Smokey Robinson-Motown*	7 HARD PROMISES *Tom Petty and The Heartbreakers-MCA*	7 STARS ON 45 *Star Sound-CBS*	7 CHARIOTS OF FIRE *Vangelis-Polydor*
8 SUKIYAKI *Taste of Honey-Capitol*	8 MISTAKEN IDENTITY *Kim Carnes-EMI-America*	8 I WANT TO BE FREE *Toyah-Safari*	8 WHA'PPEN *The Beat-Go-Feet*
9 WATCHING THE WHEELS *John Lennon-Geffen*	9 ARC OF A DIVER *Steve Winwood-Island*	9 SWORDS OF A THOUSAND MEN *Tenpole Tudor-Stiff*	9 LONG DISTANCE VOYAGER *The Moody Blues-Threshold*
10 LIVING INSIDE MYSELF *Gino Vannelli-Arista*	10 WHAT CHA' GONNA DO FOR ME *Chaka Khan-Warner Bros*	10 WILL YOU *Hazel O'Connor-A&M*	10 HEAVEN UP HERE *Echo and The Bunnymen-Korova*
11 ALL THOSE YEARS AGO *George Harrison-Dark Horse*	11 WINELIGHT *Grover Washington Jr.-Elektra*	11 BETTE DAVIS EYES *Kim Carnes-EMI-America*	11 PRESENT ARMS *UB40-DEP Int*
12 TOO MUCH TIME ON MY HANDS *Styx-A&M*	12 FACE DANCES *The Who-Warner Bros*	12 ONE DAY IN YOUR LIFE *Michael Jackson-Motown*	12 THE FOX *Elton John-Rocket*
13 AMERICA *Neil Diamond-Capitol*	13 THE DUDE *Quincy Jones-A&M*	13 MORE THAN IN LOVE *Kate Robbins-RCA*	13 HI INFIDELITY *Reo Speedwagon-Epic*
14 I LOVE YOU *Climax Blues Band-Warner Bros*	14 CHRISTOPHER CROSS *Christopher Cross-Warner Bros*	14 KEEP ON LOVING YOU *Reo Speedwagon-Epic*	14 BAD FOR GOOD *Jim Steinman-Epic*
15 SWEETHEART *Franke and The Knockouts-Millennium*	15 DOUBLE FANTASY *John Lennon-Yoko Ono-Geffen*	15 ALL THOSE YEARS AGO *George Harrison-Dark Horse*	15 MAGNETIC FIELDS *Jean Michel Jarre-Polydor*
16 KISS ON MY LIST *Daryl Hall and John Oates-RCA*	16 A WOMAN NEEDS LOVE *Ray Parker Jr.-Raydio-Arista*	16 AIN'T NO STOPPING *Enigma-Creole*	16 HOTTER THAN JULY *Stevie Wonder-Motown*
17 HOW 'BOUT US *Champaign-Columbia*	17 BACK IN BLACK *AC/DC-Atlantic*	17 OSSIE'S DREAM *Spurs FA Cup Final Squad-Shelf*	17 JAZZ SINGER *Neil Diamond-Capitol East*
18 THE ONE THAT YOU LOVE *Air Supply-Arista*	18 THE JAZZ SINGER *Neil Diamond-Capitol*	18 THE SOUND OF THE CROWD *Human League-Virgin*	18 ADVENTURES OF THIN LIZZY *Thin Lizzy-Vertigo*
19 WHAT ARE WE DOIN' IN LOVE *Dottie West-Liberty*	19 ZEBOP! *Santana-Columbia*	19 CHARIOTS OF FIRE *Vangelis-Polydor*	19 MAKING MOVIES *Dire Straits-Vertigo*
20 JESSIE'S GIRL *Rick Springfield-RCA*	20 BEING WITH YOU *Smokey Robinson-Motown*	20 STRAY CAT STRUT *Stray Cats-Arista*	20 QUIT DREAMING *Bill Nelson-Mercury*

US SINGLES	US ALBUMS	UK SINGLES	UK ALBUMS
1 **STARS ON 45** *Stars On-Radio*	1 **HI INFIDELITY** *REO Speedwagon-Epic*	1 **BEING WITH YOU** *Smokey Robinson-Motown*	1 **STARS ON 45** *Star Sound-CBS*
2 **BETTE DAVIS EYES** *Kim Carnes-EMI-America*	2 **PARADISE THEATER** *Styx-A&M*	2 **MORE THAN IN LOVE** *Kate Robbins-RCA*	2 **PRESENT ARMS** *UB40-DEP Int*
3 **ALL THOSE YEARS AGO** *George Harrison-Dark Horse*	3 **DIRTY DEEDS DIRT CHEAP** *AC/DC-Atlantic*	3 **ONE DAY IN YOUR LIFE** *Michael Jackson-Motown*	3 **DISCO DAZE AND DISCO NITES** *Various-Ronco*
4 **A WOMAN NEEDS LOVE** *Ray Parker Jr.-Raydio-Arista*	4 **FAIR WARNING** *Van Halen-Warner Bros*	4 **FUNERAL PYRE** *The Jam-Polydor*	4 **ANTHEM** *Toyah-Safari*
5 **TAKE IT ON THE RUN** *REO Speedwagon-Epic*	5 **MISTAKEN IDENTITY** *Kim Carnes-EMI-America*	5 **STAND AND DELIVER** *Adam and The Ants-CBS*	5 **CHARIOTS OF FIRE** *Vangelis-Polydor*
6 **ANGEL OF THE MORNING** *Juice Newton-Capitol*	6 **HARD PROMISES** *Tom Petty and The Heartbreakers-MCA*	6 **HOW 'BOUT US** *Champaign-CBS*	6 **THEMES** *Various-K-Tel*
7 **MORNING TRAIN (9 TO 5)** *Sheena Easton-EMI-America*	7 **GREATEST HITS** *Kenny Rogers-Liberty*	7 **YOU DRIVE ME CRAZY** *Shakin' Stevens-Epic*	7 **MAGNETIC FIELDS** *Jean Michael Jarre-Polydor*
8 **SUKIYAKI** *Taste of Honey-Capitol*	8 **MOVING PICTURES** *Rush-Mercury*	8 **GOING BACK TO OUR ROOTS** *Odyssey-RCA*	8 **KINGS OF THE WILD FRONTIER** *Adam and The Ants-CBS*
9 **AMERICA** *Neil Diamond-Capitol*	9 **ARC OF A DIVER** *Steve Winwood-Island*	9 **WILL YOU** *Hazel O'Connor-A&M*	9 **THIS OLE HOUSE** *Shakin' Stevens-Epic*
10 **BEING WITH YOU** *Smokey Robinson-Motown*	10 **WHAT CHA' GONNA DO FOR ME** *Chaka Khan-Warner Bros*	10 **I WANT TO BE FREE** *Toyah-Safari*	10 **FACE VALUE** *Phil Collins-Virgin*
11 **THE ONE THAT YOU LOVE** *Air Supply-Arista*	11 **WINELIGHT** *Grover Washington Jr.-Elektra*	11 **AIN'T NO STOPPING** *Enigma-Creole*	11 **LONG DISTANCE VOYAGER** *The Moody Blues-Threshold*
12 **I LOVE YOU** *Climax Blues Band-Warner Bros*	12 **STREET SONGS** *Rick James-Gordy*	12 **CHARIOTS OF FIRE** *Vangelis-Polydor*	12 **HI INFIDELITY** *Reo Speedwagon-Epic*
13 **TOO MUCH TIME ON MY HANDS** *Styx-A&M*	13 **CHRISTOPHER CROSS** *Christopher Cross-Warner Bros*	13 **STARS ON 45** *Star Sound-CBS*	13 **SOMEWHERE IN ENGLAND** *George Harrison-Dark Horse*
14 **WATCHING THE WHEELS** *John Lennon-Geffen*	14 **THE DUDE** *Quincy Jones-A&M*	14 **BETTE DAVIS EYES** *Kim Carnes-EMI-America*	14 **HEAVEN UP HERE** *Echo and The Bunnymen-Korova*
15 **JESSIE'S GIRL** *Rick Springfield-RCA*	15 **A WOMAN NEEDS LOVE** *Ray Parker Jr.-Raydio-Arista*	15 **ALL THOSE YEARS AGO** *George Harrison-Dark Horse*	15 **WHA'PPEN** *The Beat-Go-Feet*
16 **THIS LITTLE GIRL** *Gary US Bonds-EMI-America*	16 **STARS ON LONG PLAY** *Stars On-Radio*	16 **SWORDS OF A THOUSAND MEN** *Tenpole Tudor-Stiff*	16 **SECRET COMBINATION** *Randy Crawford-Warner Bros*
17 **LIVING INSIDE MYSELF** *Gino Vannelli-Arista*	17 **ZEBOP!** *Santana-Columbia*	17 **ALL STOOD STILL** *Ultravox-Chrysalis*	17 **BAD FOR GOOD** *Jim Steinman-Epic*
18 **YOU MAKE MY DREAMS** *Daryl Hall and John Oates-RCA*	18 **THE JAZZ SINGER** *Neil Diamond-Capitol*	18 **CHEQUERED LOVE** *Kim Wilde-RAK*	18 **THE FOX** *Elton John-Rocket*
19 **WHAT ARE WE DOIN' IN LOVE** *Dottie West-Liberty*	19 **FACE DANCES** *The Who-Warner Bros*	19 **DON'T SLOW DOWN** *UB40-DEP Int*	19 **HOTTER THAN JULY** *Stevie Wonder-Motown*
20 **SWEETHEART** *Franke and The Knockouts-Millennium*	20 **FACE VALUE** *Phil Collins-Atlantic*	20 **KEEP ON LOVING YOU** *Reo Speedwagon-Epic*	20 **MAKING MOVIES** *Dire Straits-Vertigo*

US SINGLES	US ALBUMS	UK SINGLES	UK ALBUMS
1 **BETTE DAVIS EYES** *Kim Carnes-EMI-America*	1 **HI INFIDELITY** *REO Speedwagon-Epic*	1 **BEING WITH YOU** *Smokey Robinson-Motown*	1 **STARS ON 45** *Star Sound-CBS*
2 **STARS ON 45** *Stars On-Radio*	2 **PARADISE THEATER** *Styx-A&M*	2 **ONE DAY IN YOUR LIFE** *Michael Jackson-Motown*	2 **DISCO DAZE AND DISCO NITES** *Various-Ronco*
3 **ALL THOSE YEARS AGO** *George Harrison-Dark Horse*	3 **DIRTY DEEDS DIRT CHEAP** *AC/DC-Atlantic*	3 **MORE THAN IN LOVE** *Kate Robbins-RCA*	3 **PRESENT ARMS** *UB40-DEP Int.*
4 **A WOMAN NEEDS LOVE** *Ray Parker Jr.-Raydio-Arista*	4 **FAIR WARNING** *Van Halen-Warner Bros*	4 **TEDDY BEAR** *Red Sovine-Starday*	4 **ANTHEM** *Toyah-Safari*
5 **THE ONE THAT YOU LOVE** *Air Supply-Arista*	5 **MISTAKEN IDENTITY** *Kim Carnes-EMI-America*	5 **HOW 'BOUT US** *Champaign-CBS*	5 **KINGS OF THE WILD FRONTIER** *Adam and The Ants-CBS*
6 **TAKE IT ON THE RUN** *REO Speedwagon-Epic*	6 **HARD PROMISES** *Tom Petty and The Heartbreakers-MCA*	6 **GOING BACK TO OUR ROOTS** *Odyssey-RCA*	6 **MAGNETIC FIELDS** *Jean Michael Jarre-Polydor*
7 **MORNING TRAIN (9 TO 5)** *Sheena Easton-EMI-America*	7 **MOVING PICTURES** *Rush-Mercury*	7 **STAND AND DELIVER** *Adam and The Ants-CBS*	7 **THIS OLE HOUSE** *Shakin' Stevens-Epic*
8 **SUKIYAKI** *Taste of Honey-Capitol*	8 **GREATEST HITS** *Kenny Rogers-Liberty*	8 **WILL YOU** *Hazel O'Connor-A&M*	8 **THEMES** *Various-K-Tel*
9 **AMERICA** *Neil Diamond-Capitol*	9 **ZEBOP!** *Santana-Columbia*	9 **ALL STOOD STILL** *Ultravox-Chrysalis*	9 **CHARIOTS OF FIRE** *Vangelis-Polydor*
10 **I LOVE YOU** *Climax Blues Band-Warner Bros*	10 **STREET SONGS** *Rick James-Gordy*	2 **YOU DRIVE ME CRAZY** *Shakin' Stevens-Epic*	10 **FACE VALUE** *Phil Collins-Virgin*
11 **ANGEL OF THE MORNING** *Juice Newton-Capitol*	11 **ARC OF A DIVER** *Steve Winwood-Island*	11 **I WANT TO BE FREE** *Toyah-Safari*	11 **LONG DISTANCE VOYAGER** *The Moody Blues-Threshold*
12 **JESSIE'S GIRL** *Rick Springfield-RCA*	12 **STARS ON LONG PLAY** *Stars On-Radio*	12 **FUNERAL PYRE** *Jam-Polydor*	12 **HI INFIDELITY** *Reo Speedwagon-Epic*
13 **ELVIRA** *Oak Ridge Boys-MCA*	13 **CHRISTOPHER CROSS** *Christopher Cross-Warner Bros*	13 **AIN'T NO STOPPING** *Enigma-Creole*	13 **VIENNA** *Ultravox-Chrysalis*
14 **YOU MAKE MY DREAMS** *Daryl Hall and John Oates-RCA*	14 **LONG DISTANCE VOYAGER** *Moody Blues-Threshold*	14 **CHARIOTS OF FIRE** *Vangelis-Polydor*	14 **SOMEWHERE IN ENGLAND** *George Harrison-Dark Horse*
15 **THIS LITTLE GIRL** *Gary US Bonds-EMI-America*	15 **WINELIGHT** *Grover Washington Jr.-Elektra*	15 **MEMORY** *Elaine Paige-Polydor*	15 **SECRET COMBINATION** *Randy Crawford-Warner Bros*
16 **TOO MUCH TIME ON MY HANDS** *Styx-A&M*	16 **THE DUDE** *Quincy Jones-A&M*	16 **SWORDS OF A THOUSAND MEN** *Tenpole Tudor-Stiff*	16 **THE RIVER** *Bruce Springsteen-CBS*
17 **WATCHING THE WHEELS** *John Lennon-Geffen*	17 **A WOMAN NEEDS LOVE** *Ray Parker Jr.-Raydio-Arista*	17 **PIECE OF THE ACTION** *Bucks Fizz-RCA*	17 **MAKING MOVIES** *Dire Straits-Vertigo*
18 **BEING WITH YOU** *Smokey Robinson-Motown*	18 **THE JAZZ SINGER** *Neil Diamond-Capitol*	18 **DON'T SLOW DOWN** *UB40-DEP International*	18 **HOTTER THAN JULY** *Stevie Wonder-Motown*
19 **THE WAITING** *Tom Petty and The Heartbreakers-MCA*	19 **BACK IN BLACK** *AC/DC-Atlantic*	19 **BODY TALK** *Imagination-R&B*	19 **EAST SIDE STORY** *Squeeze-A&M*
20 **WINNING** *Santana-Columbia*	20 **FACE VALUE** *Phil Collins-Atlantic*	20 **ALL THOSE YEARS AGO** *George Harrison-Dark Horse*	20 **BAT OUT OF HELL** *Meat Loaf-Epic/Cleveland*

US SINGLES

1. **ALL THOSE YEARS AGO**
   George Harrison-Dark Horse
2. **THE ONE THAT YOU LOVE**
   Air Supply-Arista
3. **AMERICA**
   Neil Diamond-Capitol
4. **I DON'T NEED YOU**
   Kenny Rogers-Liberty
5. **BOY FROM NEW YORK CITY**
   Manhattan Transfer-Atlantic
6. **AMERICAN HERO**
   Joey Scarbury-Elektra
7. **BETTE DAVIS EYES**
   Kim Carnes-EMI-America
8. **WHAT ARE WE DOIN' IN LOVE**
   Dottie West-Liberty
9. **STARS ON 45**
   Stars On-Radio
10. **ELVIRA**
    Oak Ridge Boys-MCA
11. **FOOL IN LOVE WITH YOU**
    Jim Photoglo-20th Century Fox
12. **IS IT YOU?**
    Lee Ritenour-Elektra
13. **MODERN GIRL**
    Sheena Easton-EMI-America
14. **SEVEN YEAR ACHE**
    Rosanne Cash-Columbia
15. **RIGHT HERE IN MY HEART**
    Pure Prairie League-Casablanca
16. **PROMISES**
    Barbra Streisand-Columbia
17. **A WOMAN NEEDS LOVE**
    Ray Parker Jr.-Raydio-Arista
18. **STRONGER THAN BEFORE**
    Carole Bayer Sager-Boardwalk
19. **SAY WHAT**
    Jesse Winchester-Bearsville
20. **HEARTS**
    Marty Balin-EMI-America

US ALBUMS

1. **HI INFIDELITY**
   REO Speedwagon-Epic
2. **PARADISE THEATER**
   Styx-A&M
3. **MISTAKEN IDENTITY**
   Kim Carnes-EMI-America
4. **DIRTY DEEDS DIRT CHEAP**
   AC/DC-Atlantic
5. **FAIR WARNING**
   Van Halen-Warner Bros
6. **HARD PROMISES**
   Tom Petty and The Heartbreakers-MCA
7. **STREET SONGS**
   Rick James-Gordy
8. **GREATEST HITS**
   Kenny Rogers-Liberty
9. **ZEBOP!**
   Santana-Columbia
10. **STARS ON LONG PLAY**
    Stars On-Radio
11. **LONG DISTANCE VOYAGER**
    Moody Blues-Threshold
12. **SOMEWHERE IN ENGLAND**
    George Harrison-Dark Horse
13. **MOVING PICTURES**
    Rush-Mercury
14. **THE ONE THAT YOU LOVE**
    Air Supply-Arista
15. **CHRISTOPHER CROSS**
    Christopher Cross-Warner Bros
16. **ARC OF A DIVER**
    Steve Winwood-Island
17. **FACE VALUE**
    Phil Collins-Atlantic
18. **BACK IN BLACK**
    AC/DC-Atlantic
19. **THE FOX**
    Elton John-Geffen
20. **FANCY FREE**
    Oak Ridge Boys-MCA

UK SINGLES

1. **ONE DAY IN YOUR LIFE**
   Michael Jackson-Motown
2. **BEING WITH YOU**
   Smokey Robinson-Motown
3. **MORE THAN IN LOVE**
   Kate Robbins and Beyond-RCA
4. **TEDDY BEAR**
   Red Sovine-Starday
5. **GOING BACK TO OUR ROOTS**
   Odyssey-RCA
6. **GHOST TOWN**
   The Specials-2-Tone
7. **HOW 'BOUT US**
   Champaign-CBS
8. **ALL STOOD STILL**
   Ultravox-Chrysalis
9. **MEMORY**
   Elaine Page-Polydor
10. **WILL YOU**
    Hazel O'Connor-A&M
11. **BODY TALK**
    Imagination-R&B
12. **PIECE OF THE ACTION**
    Bucks Fizz-RCA
13. **STAND AND DELIVER**
    Adam and The Ants-CBS
14. **I WANT TO BE FREE**
    Toyah-Safari
15. **TAKE IT TO THE TOP**
    Kool and The Gang-DeLite
16. **YOU DRIVE ME CRAZY**
    Shakin' Stevens-Epic
17. **IF LEAVING ME IS EASY**
    Phil Collins-Virgin
18. **CAN CAN**
    Bad Manners-Magnet
19. **AIN'T NO STOPPING**
    Enigma-Creole
20. **NO WOMAN NO CRY**
    Bob Marley and The Wailers-Island

UK ALBUMS

1. **NO SLEEP TIL HAMMERSMITH**
   Motorhead-Bronze
2. **STARS ON 45**
   Star Sound-CBS
3. **DISCO DAZE AND DISCO NITES**
   Various-Ronco
4. **PRESENT ARMS**
   UB40-DEP Int.
5. **ANTHEM**
   Toyah-Safari
6. **THEMES**
   Various-K-Tel
7. **JU JU**
   Siouxsie and The Banshees-Polydor
8. **KINGS OF THE WILD FRONTIER**
   Adam and The Ants-CBS
9. **DURAN DURAN**
   Duran Duran-EMI
10. **FACE VALUE**
    Phil Collins-Virgin
11. **MAGNETIC FIELDS**
    Jean Michel Jarre-Polydor
12. **HI INFIDELITY**
    Reo Speedwagon-Epic
13. **CHARIOTS OF FIRE**
    Vangelis-Polydor
14. **SECRET COMBINATION**
    Randy Crawford-Warner Bros
15. **VIENNA**
    Ultravox-Chrysalis
16. **THIS OLE HOUSE**
    Shakin' Stevens-Epic
17. **BEING WITH YOU**
    Smokey Robinson-Motown
18. **BAD FOR GOOD**
    Jim Steinman-Epic
19. **HOTTER THAN JULY**
    Stevie Wonder-Motown
20. **LONG DISTANCE VOYAGER**
    The Moody Blues-Threshold

US SINGLES

1. **ALL THOSE YEARS AGO**
   George Harrison-Dark Horse
2. **THE ONE THAT YOU LOVE**
   Air Supply-Arista
3. **I DON'T NEED YOU**
   Kenny Rogers-Liberty
4. **AMERICAN HERO**
   Joey Scarbury-Elektra
5. **BOY FROM NEW YORK CITY**
   Manhattan Transfer-Atlantic
6. **AMERICA**
   Neil Diamond-Capitol
7. **BETTE DAVIS EYES**
   Kim Carnes-EMI-America
8. **ELVIRA**
   Oak Ridge Boys-MCA
9. **MODERN GIRL**
   Sheena Easton-EMI-America
10. **IS IT YOU?**
    Lee Ritenour-Elektra
11. **FOOL IN LOVE WITH YOU**
    Jim Photoglo-20th Century Fox
12. **PROMISES**
    Barbra Streisand-Columbia
13. **STARS ON 45**
    Stars On-Radio
14. **SEVEN YEAR ACHE**
    Rosanne Cash-Columbia
15. **RIGHT HERE IN MY HEART**
    Pure Prairie League-Casablanca
16. **STRONGER THAN BEFORE**
    Carole Bayer Sager-Boardwalk
17. **HEARTS**
    Marty Balin-EMI-America
18. **QUEEN OF HEARTS**
    Juice Newton-Capitol
19. **WHAT ARE WE DOIN' IN LOVE**
    Dottie West-Liberty
20. **SLOW HAND**
    Pointer Sisters-Planet

US ALBUMS

1. **HI INFIDELITY**
   Reo Speedwagon-Epic
2. **MISTAKEN IDENTITY**
   Kim Carnes-EMI-America
3. **PARADISE THEATER**
   Styx-A&M
4. **DIRTY DEEDS DIRT CHEAP**
   AC/DC-Atlantic
5. **LONG DISTANCE VOYAGER**
   Moody Blues-Threshold
6. **FAIR WARNING**
   Van Halen-Warner Bros
7. **STREET SONGS**
   Rick James-Gordy
8. **HARD PROMISES**
   Tom Petty and The Heartbreakers-MCA
9. **MOVING PICTURES**
   Rush-Mercury
10. **STARS ON LONG PLAY**
    Stars On-Radio
11. **SOMEWHERE IN ENGLAND**
    George Harrison-Dark Horse
12. **ZEBOP!**
    Santana-Columbia
13. **THE ONE THAT YOU LOVE**
    Air Supply-Arista
14. **GREATEST HITS**
    Kenny Rogers-Liberty
15. **FACE VALUE**
    Phil Collins-Atlantic
16. **CHRISTOPHER CROSS**
    Christopher Cross-Warner Bros
17. **FANCY FREE**
    Oak Ridge Boys-MCA
18. **LOVERBOY**
    Loverboy-Columbia
19. **THE FOX**
    Elton John-Geffen
20. **WILD-EYED SOUTHERN BOYS**
    38 Special-A&M

UK SINGLES

1. **ONE DAY IN YOUR LIFE**
   Michael Jackson-Motown
2. **GHOST TOWN**
   The Specials-2-Tone
3. **CAN CAN**
   Bad Manners-Magnet
4. **GOING BACK TO OUR ROOTS**
   Odyssey-RCA
5. **BEING WITH YOU**
   Smokey Robinson-Motown
6. **MEMORY**
   Elaine Page-Polydor
7. **BODY TALK**
   Imagination-R&B
8. **MORE THAN IN LOVE**
   Kate Robbins and Beyond-RCA
9. **TEDDY BEAR**
   Red Sovine-Starday
10. **HOW 'BOUT US**
    Champaign-CBS
11. **ALL STOOD STILL**
    Ultravox-Chrysalis
12. **NO WOMAN NO CRY**
    Bob Marley and The Wailers-Island
13. **PIECE OF THE ACTION**
    Bucks Fizz-RCA
14. **WORDY RAPPINGHOOD**
    Tom Tom Club-Island
15. **STARS ON 45 (VOL 11)**
    Star Sound-CBS
16. **RAZZAMATAZZ**
    Quincy Jones/Patti Austin-A&M
17. **YOU MIGHT NEED SOMEBODY**
    Randy Crawford-Warner Bros
18. **TAKE IT TO THE TOP**
    Kool and The Gang-De Lite
19. **WILL YOU**
    Hazel O'Connor-A&M
20. **WIKKA WRAP**
    Evasions-Groove

UK ALBUMS

1. **DISCO DAZE AND DISCO NITES**
   Various-Ronco
2. **STARS ON 45**
   Star Sound-CBS
3. **NO SLEEP TIL HAMMERSMITH**
   Motorhead-Bronze
4. **LOVE SONGS**
   Cliff Richard-EMI
5. **ANTHEM**
   Toyah-Safari
6. **SECRET COMBINATION**
   Randy Crawford-Warner Bros
7. **PRESENT ARMS**
   UB40-DEP. Int.
8. **KINGS OF THE WILD FRONTIER**
   Adam and The Ants-CBS
9. **JU JU**
   Siouxsie and The Banshees-Polydor
10. **FACE VALUE**
    Phil Collins-Virgin
11. **MAGNETIC FIELDS**
    Jean Michel Jarre-Polydor
12. **CHARIOTS OF FIRE**
    Vangelis-Polydor
13. **DURAN DURAN**
    Duran Duran-EMI
14. **THEMES**
    Various-K-Tel
15. **BAD FOR GOOD**
    Jim Steinman-Epic/Cleveland
16. **HI INFIDELITY**
    Reo Speedwagon-Epic
17. **VIENNA**
    Ultravox-Chrysalis
18. **THIS OLE HOUSE**
    Shakin' Stevens-Epic
19. **MADE IN AMERICA**
    Carpenters-A&M
20. **THE RIVER**
    Bruce Springsteen-CBS

US SINGLES	US ALBUMS	UK SINGLES	UK ALBUMS
1 **THE ONE THAT YOU LOVE** *Air Supply-Arista*	1 **MISTAKEN IDENTITY** *Kim Carnes-EMI-America*	1 **GHOST TOWN** *The Specials-2-Tone*	1 **LOVE SONGS** *Cliff Richard-EMI*
2 **BETTE DAVIS EYES** *Kim Carnes-EMI-America*	2 **HI INFIDELITY** *Reo Speedwagon-Epic*	2 **ONE DAY IN YOUR LIFE** *Michael Jackson-Motown*	2 **DISCO DAZE AND DISCO NITES** *Various-Ronco*
3 **ALL THOSE YEARS AGO** *George Harrison-Dark Horse*	3 **PARADISE THEATER** *Styx-A&M*	3 **CAN CAN** *Bad Manners-Magnet*	3 **NO SLEEP TIL HAMMERSMITH** *Motorhead-Bronze*
4 **ELVIRA** *Oak Ridge Boys-MCA*	4 **LONG DISTANCE VOYAGER** *Moody Blues-Threshold*	4 **STARS ON 45(VOL. 2)** *Star Sound-CBS*	4 **STARS ON 45** *Star Sound-CBS*
5 **JESSIE'S GIRL** *Rick Springfield-RCA*	5 **DIRTY DEEDS DIRT CHEAP** *AC/DC-Atlantic*	5 **GOING BACK TO OUR ROOTS** *Odyssey-RCA*	5 **PRESENT ARMS** *UB40-DEP.Int.*
6 **GREATEST AMERICAN HERO** *Joey Scarbury-Elektra*	6 **STREET SONGS** *Rick James-Gordy*	6 **BODY TALK** *Imagination-R&B*	6 **SECRET COMBINATION** *Randy Crawford-Warner Bros*
7 **YOU MAKE MY DREAMS** *Daryl Hall and John Oates-RCA*	7 **MOVING PICTURES** *Rush-Mercury*	7 **MEMORY** *Elaine Page-Polydor*	7 **ANTHEM** *Toyah-Safari*
8 **STARS ON 45** *Stars On-Radio*	8 **HARD PROMISES** *Tom Petty and The Heartbreakers-MCA*	8 **BEING WITH YOU** *Smokey Robinson-Motown*	8 **FACE VALUE** *Phil Collins-Virgin*
9 **I DON'T NEED YOU** *Kenny Rogers-Liberty*	9 **FAIR WARNING** *Van Halen-Warner Bros*	9 **NO WOMAN NO CRY** *Bob Marley & The Wailers-Island*	9 **KINGS OF THE WILD FRONTIER** *Adam and The Ants-CBS*
10 **A WOMAN NEEDS LOVE** *Ray Parker Jr. & Raydio-Arista*	10 **STARS ON LONG PLAY** *Stars On-Radio*	10 **WORDY RAPPINGHOOD** *Tom Tom Club-Island*	10 **KIM WILDE** *Kim Wilde-RAK*
11 **I LOVE YOU** *Climax Blues Band-Warner Bros*	11 **SOMEWHERE IN ENGLAND** *George Harrison-Dark Horse*	11 **RAZZAMATAZZ** *Quincy Jones/Patti Austin-A&M*	11 **DURAN DURAN** *Duran Duran-EMI*
12 **BOY FROM NEW YORK CITY** *Manhattan Transfer-Atlantic*	12 **THE ONE THAT YOU LOVE** *Air Supply-Arista*	12 **YOU MIGHT NEED SOMEBODY** *Randy Crawford-Warner Bros*	12 **MADE IN AMERICA** *Carpenters-A&M*
13 **SLOW HAND** *Pointer Sisters-Planet*	13 **ZEBOP!** *Santana-Columbia*	13 **DANCING ON THE FLOOR** *Third World-CBS*	13 **HI INFIDELITY** *Reo Speedwagon-Epic*
14 **WINNING** *Santana-Columbia*	14 **FACE VALUE** *Phil Collins-Atlantic*	14 **MOTORHEAD (LIVE)** *Motorhead-Bronze*	14 **MAGNETIC FIELDS** *Jean Michel Jarre-Polydor*
15 **MODERN GIRL** *Sheena Easton-EMI-America*	15 **GREATEST HITS** *Kenny Rogers-Liberty*	15 **PIECE OF THE ACTION** *Bucks Fizz-RCA*	15 **JU JU** *Siouxsie and The Banshees-Polydor*
16 **THIS LITTLE GIRL** *Gary US Bonds-EMI-America*	16 **FANCY FREE** *Oak Ridge Boys-MCA*	16 **THERE'S A GUY** *Kirsty MacColl-Polydor*	16 **VIENNA** *Ultravox-Chrysalis*
17 **SUKIYAKI** *Taste of Honey-Capitol*	17 **CHRISTOPHER CROSS** *Christopher Cross-Warner Bros*	17 **MORE THAN IN LOVE** *Kate Robbins and Beyond-RCA*	17 **CHARIOTS OF FIRE** *Vangelis-Polydor*
18 **HEARTS** *Marty Balin-EMI-America*	18 **LOVERBOY** *Loverboy-Columbia*	18 **HOW 'BOUT US** *Champaign-CBS*	18 **HOTTER THAN JULY** *Stevie Wonder-Motown*
19 **MORNING TRAIN (9 TO 5)** *Sheena Easton-EMI-America*	19 **WILD-EYED SOUTHERN BOYS** *38 Special-A&M*	19 **TEDDY BEAR** *Red Sovine-Starday*	19 **BAD FOR GOOD** *Jim Steinman-Epic/Cleveland*
20 **GEMINI DREAM** *Moody Blues-Threshold*	20 **BLIZZARD OF OZZ** *Ozzy Osbourne-Jet*	20 **ALL STOOD STILL** *Ultravox-Chrysalis*	20 **BEST OF MICHAEL JACKSON** *Michael Jackson-Motown*

US SINGLES	US ALBUMS	UK SINGLES	UK ALBUMS
1 **GREATEST AMERICAN HERO** *Joey Scarbury-Elektra*	1 **HI INFIDELITY** *Reo Speedwagon-Epic*	1 **GHOST TOWN** *The Specials-2-Tone*	1 **LOVE SONGS** *Cliff Richard-EMI*
2 **THE ONE THAT YOU LOVE** *Air Supply-Arista*	2 **LONG DISTANCE VOYAGER** *Moody Blues-Threshold*	2 **STARS ON 45 (VOL. 2)** *Star Sound-CBS*	2 **SECRET COMBINATION** *Randy Crawford-Warner Bros*
3 **ELVIRA** *Oak Ridge Boys-MCA*	3 **MISTAKEN IDENTITY** *Kim Carnes-EMI America*	3 **CAN CAN** *Bad Manners-Magnet*	3 **KIM WILDE** *Kim Wilde-RAK*
4 **BETTE DAVIS EYES** *Kim Carnes-EMI America*	4 **PARADISE THEATER** *Styx-A&M*	4 **BODY TALK** *Imagination-R&B*	4 **STARS ON 45** *Star Sound-CBS*
5 **JESSIE'S GIRL** *Rick Springfield-RCA*	5 **STREET SONGS** *Rick James-Gordy*	5 **ONE DAY IN YOUR LIFE** *Michael Jackson-Motown*	5 **NO SLEEP TIL HAMMERSMITH** *Motorhead-Bronze*
6 **I DON'T NEED YOU** *Kenny Rogers-Liberty*	6 **DIRTY DEEDS DIRT CHEAP** *AC/DC-Atlantic*	6 **MOTORHEAD (LIVE)** *Motorhead-Bronze*	6 **DISCO DAZE AND DISCO NITES** *Various-Ronco*
7 **STARS ON 45** *Stars On-Radio*	7 **MOVING PICTURES** *Rush-Mercury*	7 **WORDY RAPPINGHOOD** *Tom Tom Club-Island*	7 **KINGS OF THE WILD FRONTIER** *Adam and The Ants-CBS*
8 **YOU MAKE MY DREAMS** *Daryl Hall and John Oates-RCA*	8 **HARD PROMISES** *Tom Petty and The Heartbreakers-MCA*	8 **NO WOMAN NO CRY** *Bob Marley and The Wailers-Island*	8 **ANTHEM** *Toyah-Safari*
9 **ALL THOSE YEARS AGO** *George Harrison-Dark Horse*	9 **SHARE YOUR LOVE** *Kenny Rogers-Liberty*	9 **GOING BACK TO OUR ROOTS** *Odyssey-RCA*	9 **PRESENT ARMS** *UB40-DEP. Int.*
10 **BOY FROM NEW YORK CITY** *Manhattan Transfer-Atlantic*	10 **FANCY FREE** *Oak Ridge Boys-MCA*	10 **MEMORY** *Elaine Page-Polydor*	10 **DURAN DURAN** *Duran Duran-EMI*
11 **SLOW HAND** *Pointer Sisters-Planet*	11 **THE ONE THAT YOU LOVE** *Air Supply-Arista*	11 **YOU MIGHT NEED SOMEBODY** *Randy Crawford-Warner Bros*	11 **HI INFIDELITY** *Reo Speedwagon-Epic*
12 **A WOMAN NEEDS LOVE** *Ray Parker Jr and Raydio-Arista*	12 **ZEBOP!** *Santana-Columbia*	12 **DANCING ON THE FLOOR** *Third World-CBS*	12 **FACE VALUE** *Phil Collins-Virgin*
13 **MODERN GIRL** *Sheena Easton-EMI America*	13 **FAIR WARNING** *Van Halen-Warner Bros*	13 **RAZZAMATAZZ** *Quincy Jones/Patti Austin-A&M*	13 **BAD FOR GOOD** *Jim Steinman-Epic/Cleveland*
14 **WINNING** *Santana-Columbia*	14 **FACE VALUE** *Phil Collins-Atlantic*	14 **THERE'S A GUY** *Kirsty MacColl-Polydor*	14 **BEST OF MICHAEL JACKSON** *Michael Jackson-Motown*
15 **THIS LITTLE GIRL** *Gary US Bonds-EMI America*	15 **STARS ON LONG PLAY** *Stars On-Radio*	15 **SAT IN YOUR LAP** *Kate Bush-EMI*	15 **JUMPIN' JIVE** *Joe Jackson-A&M*
16 **HEARTS** *Marty Balin-EMI America*	16 **GREATEST HITS** *Kenny Rogers-Liberty*	16 **PIECE OF THE ACTION** *Bucks Fizz-RCA*	16 **HOTTER THAN JULY** *Stevie Wonder-Motown*
17 **TIME** *Alan Parsons Project-Arista*	17 **SOMEWHERE IN ENGLAND** *George Harrison-Dark Horse*	17 **LAY ALL YOUR LOVE ON ME** *Abba-Epic*	17 **THE FRIENDS OF MR. CAIRO** *Jon/Vangelis-Polydor*
18 **GEMINI DREAM** *Moody Blues-Threshold*	18 **BLIZZARD OF OZZ** *Ozzy Osbourne-Jet*	18 **CHANT NO. 1** *Spandau Ballet-Reformation/Chrysalis*	18 **VIENNA** *Ultravox-Chrysalis*
19 **QUEEN OF HEARTS** *Juice Newton-Capitol*	19 **WILD EYED SOUTHERN BOYS** *38 Special-A&M*	19 **NEW LIFE** *Depeche Mode-Mute*	19 **CHARIOTS OF FIRE** *Vangelis-Polydor*
20 **SUKIYAKI** *Taste of Honey-Capitol*	20 **DON'T SAY NO** *Billy Squier-Capitol*	20 **CAN'T HAPPEN HERE** *Rainbow-Polydor*	20 **MAGNETIC FIELDS** *Jean Michel Jarre-Polydor*

US SINGLES	US ALBUMS	UK SINGLES	UK ALBUMS
1 **I DON'T NEED YOU** *Kenny Rogers-Liberty*	1 **LONG DISTANCE VOYAGER** *The Moody Blues-Threshold*	1 **GHOST TOWN** *The Specials-2-Tone*	1 **LOVE SONGS** *Cliff Richard-EMI*
2 **GREATEST AMERICAN HERO** *Joey Scarbury-Elektra*	2 **HI INFIDELITY** *Reo Speedwagon-Epic*	2 **STARS ON 45 (VOL 11)** *Star Sound-CBS*	2 **SECRET COMBINATION** *Randy Crawford-Warner Bros*
3 **THE ONE THAT YOU LOVE** *Air Supply-Arista*	3 **SHARE YOUR LOVE** *Kenny Rogers-Liberty*	3 **CAN CAN** *Bad Manners-Magnet*	3 **STARS ON 45** *Star Sound-CBS*
4 **BOY FROM NEW YORK CITY** *Manhattan Transfer-Atlantic*	4 **MISTAKEN IDENTITY** *Kim Carnes-EMI-America*	4 **CHANT NO. 1** *Spandau Ballet-Reformation/Chrysalis*	4 **NO SLEEP TIL HAMMERSMITH** *Motorhead-Bronze*
5 **QUEEN OF HEARTS** *Juice Newton-Capitol*	5 **STREET SONGS** *Rick James-Gordy*	5 **BODY TALK** *Imagination-R&B*	5 **KIM WILDE** *Kim Wilde-RAK*
6 **MODERN GIRL** *Sheena Easton-EMI-America*	6 **PARADISE THEATER** *Styx-A&M*	6 **MOTORHEAD (LIVE)** *Motorhead-Bronze*	6 **KINGS OF THE WILD FRONTIER** *Adam and The Ants-CBS*
7 **HEARTS** *Marty Balin-EMI-America*	7 **DIRTY DEEDS DIRT CHEAP** *AC/DC-Atlantic*	7 **LAY ALL YOUR LOVE ON ME** *Abba-Epic*	7 **DURAN DURAN** *Duran Duran-EMI*
8 **WHEN WE'RE DANCING** *The Carpenters-A&M*	8 **HARD PROMISES** *Tom Petty and The Heartbreakers-MCA*	8 **WORDY RAPPINGHOOD** *Tom Tom Club-Island*	8 **ANTHEM** *Toyah-Safari*
9 **NO GETTIN' OVER ME** *Ronnie Milsap-RCA*	9 **FANCY FREE** *Oak Ridge Boys-MCA*	9 **HAPPY BIRTHDAY** *Stevie Wonder-Motown*	9 **DISCO DAZE AND DISCO NITES** *Various-Ronco*
10 **ELVIRA** *Oak Ridge Boys-MCA*	10 **THE ONE THAT YOU LOVE** *Air Supply-Arista*	10 **DANCING ON THE FLOOR** *Third World-CBS*	10 **BAD FOR GOOD** *Jim Steinman-Epic/Cleveland*
11 **ALL THOSE YEARS AGO** *George Harrison-Dark Horse*	11 **MOVING PICTURES** *Rush-Mercury*	11 **SAT IN YOUR LAP** *Kate Bush-EMI*	11 **HOTTER THAN JULY** *Stevie Wonder-Motown*
12 **ENDLESS LOVE** *Diana Ross & Lionel Richie-Motown*	12 **STARS ON LONG PLAY** *Stars On-Radio*	12 **NO WOMAN NO CRY** *Bob Marley and The Wailers-Island*	12 **HI INFIDELITY** *Reo Speedwagon-Epic*
13 **SLOW HAND** *The Pointer Sisters-Planet*	13 **ZEBOP!** *Santana-Columbia*	13 **ONE DAY IN YOUR LIFE** *Michael Jackson-Motown*	13 **BEST OF MICHAEL JACKSON** *Michael Jackson-Motown*
14 **AMERICA** *Neil Diamond-Capitol*	14 **FAIR WARNING** *Van Halen-Warner Bros*	14 **YOU MIGHT NEED SOMEBODY** *Randy Crawford-Warner Bros*	14 **JUMPIN' JIVE** *Joe Jackson-A&M*
15 **TIME** *Alan Parsons Project-Arista*	15 **BLIZZARD OF OZZ** *Ozzy Osbourne-Jet*	15 **NEW LIFE** *Depeche Mode-Mute*	15 **BAT OUT OF HELL** *Meat Loaf-Epic/Cleveland*
16 **IS IT YOU?** *Lee Ritenour-Elektra*	16 **DON'T SAY NO** *Billy Squier-Capitol*	16 **FOR YOUR EYES ONLY** *Sheena Easton-EMI*	16 **PRESENT ARMS** *UB40-DEP. Int.*
17 **IT'S NOW OR NEVER** *John Schneider-Scotti Bros*	17 **FACE VALUE** *Phil Collins-Atlantic*	17 **GOING BACK TO OUR ROOTS** *Odyssey-RCA*	17 **FACE VALUE** *Phil Collins-Virgin*
18 **STRONGER THAN BEFORE** *Carole Bayer Sager-Boardwalk*	18 **GREATEST HITS** *Kenny Rogers-Liberty*	18 **NEVER SURRENDER** *Saxon-Carrere*	18 **CHARIOTS OF FIRE** *Vangelis-Polydor*
19 **SWEET BABY** *Stanley Clarke/George Duke-Epic*	19 **WORKING CLASS DOG** *Rick Springfield-RCA*	19 **MEMORY** *Elaine Page-Polydor*	19 **MAGNETIC FIELDS** *Jean Michel Jarre-Polydor*
20 **PROMISES** *Barbra Streisand-Columbia*	20 **IT MUST BE MAGIC** *Teena Marie-Gordy*	20 **WALK RIGHT NOW** *Jacksons-Epic*	20 **THE RIVER** *Bruce Springsteen-CBS*

US SINGLES	US ALBUMS	UK SINGLES	UK ALBUMS
1 **JESSIE'S GIRL** *Rick Springfield-RCA*	1 **HI INFIDELITY** *Reo Speedwagon-Epic*	1 **GREEN DOOR** *Shakin' Stevens-Epic*	1 **LOVE SONGS** *Cliff Richard-EMI*
2 **GREATEST AMERICAN HERO** *Joey Scarbury-Elektra*	2 **LONG DISTANCE VOYAGER** *The Moody Blues-Threshold*	2 **GHOST TOWN** *The Specials-2-Tone*	2 **SECRET COMBINATION** *Randy Crawford-Warner Bros*
3 **THE ONE THAT YOU LOVE** *Air Supply-Arista*	3 **SHARE YOUR LOVE** *Kenny Rogers-Liberty*	3 **CHANT NO. 1** *Spandau Ballet-Reformation/Chrysalis*	3 **STARS ON 45** *Star Sound-CBS*
4 **ELVIRA** *Oak Ridge Boys-MCA*	4 **PRECIOUS TIME** *Pat Benatar-Chrysalis*	4 **HAPPY BIRTHDAY** *Stevie Wonder-Motown*	4 **KIM WILDE** *Kim Wilde-RAK*
5 **I DON'T NEED YOU** *Kenny Rogers-Liberty*	5 **STREET SONGS** *Rick James-Gordy*	5 **STARS ON 45 (VOL 11)** *Star Sound-CBS*	5 **NO SLEEP TIL HAMMERSMITH** *Motorhead-Bronze*
6 **SLOW HAND** *The Pointer Sisters-Planet*	6 **4** *Foreigner-Atlantic*	6 **CAN CAN** *Bad Manners-Magnet*	6 **CATS** *Various-Polydor*
7 **QUEEN OF HEARTS** *Juice Newton-Capitol*	7 **MISTAKEN IDENTITY** *Kim Carnes-EMI-America*	7 **HOOKED ON CLASSICS** *Louis Clarke/RPO-RCA*	7 **HI INFIDELITY** *Reo Speedwagon-Epic*
8 **BETTE DAVIS EYES** *Kim Carnes-EMI-America*	8 **HARD PROMISES** *Tom Petty and The Heartbreakers-MCA*	8 **BODY TALK** *Imagination-R&B*	8 **HOTTER THAN JULY** *Stevie Wonder-Motown*
9 **BOY FROM NEW YORK CITY** *Manhattan Transfer-Atlantic*	9 **FANCY FREE** *Oak Ridge Boys-MCA*	9 **LAY ALL YOUR LOVE ON ME** *Abba-Epic*	9 **KINGS OF THE WILD FRONTIER** *Adam and The Ants-CBS*
10 **HEARTS** *Marty Balin-EMI-America*	10 **THE ONE THAT YOU LOVE** *Air Supply-Arista*	10 **DANCING ON THE FLOOR** *Third World-CBS*	10 **DURAN DURAN** *Duran Duran-EMI*
11 **STARS ON 45** *Stars On-Radio*	11 **DIRTY DEEDS DIRT CHEAP** *AC/DC-Atlantic*	11 **FOR YOUR EYES ONLY** *Sheena Easton-EMI*	11 **BEST OF MICHAEL JACKSON** *Michael Jackson-Motown*
12 **YOU MAKE MY DREAMS** *Daryl Hall and John Oates-RCA*	12 **STARS ON LONG PLAY** *Stars On-Radio*	12 **NEW LIFE** *Depeche Mode-Mute*	12 **BAT OUT OF HELL** *Meat Loaf-Epic/Cleveland*
13 **TIME** *Alan Parsons Project-Arista*	13 **MOVING PICTURES** *Rush-Mercury*	13 **SAT IN YOUR LAP** *Kate Bush-EMI*	13 **BAD FOR GOOD** *Jim Steinman-Epic/Cleveland*
14 **GEMINI DREAM** *Moody Blues-Threshold*	14 **DON'T SAY NO** *Billy Squier-Capitol*	14 **BACK TO THE SIXTIES** *Tight Fit-Jive*	14 **PRESENT ARMS** *UB40-DEP. Int.*
15 **ENDLESS LOVE** *Diana Ross & Lionel Richie-Motown*	15 **BLIZZARD OF OZZ** *Ozzy Osbourne-Jet*	15 **WALK RIGHT NOW** *The Jacksons-Epic*	15 **ANTHEM** *Toyah-Safari*
16 **DOUBLE DUTCH BUS** *Frankie Smith-WMOT*	16 **PARADISE THEATER** *Styx-A&M*	16 **WORDY RAPPINGHOOD** *Tom Tom Club-Island*	16 **DISCO DAZE AND DISCO NITES** *Various-Ronco*
17 **LADY (YOU BRING ME UP)** *Commodores-Motown*	17 **WORKING CLASS DOG** *Rick Springfield-RCA*	17 **YOU MIGHT NEED SOMEBODY** *Randy Crawford-Warner Bros*	17 **FACE VALUE** *Phil Collins-Virgin*
18 **(THERE'S) NO GETTIN' OVER ME** *Ronnie Milsap-RCA*	18 **ZEBOP!** *Santana-Columbia*	18 **NO WOMAN NO CRY** *Bob Marley and The Wailers-Island*	18 **JUMPIN' JIVE** *Joe Jackson-A&M*
19 **SWEET BABY** *Stanley Clarke and George Duke-Epic*	19 **FACE VALUE** *Phil Collins-Atlantic*	19 **MOTORHEAD (LIVE)** *Motorhead-Bronze*	19 **CHARIOTS OF FIRE** *Vangelis-Polydor*
20 **IN THE AIR TONIGHT** *Phil Collins-Atlantic*	20 **IT MUST BE MAGIC** *Teena Marie-Gordy*	20 **NEVER SURRENDER** *Saxon-Carrere*	20 **THE RIVER** *Bruce Springsteen-CBS*

ROCK REFERENCE
VENUES/US

ATLANTA

Agora Ballroom
(404) 881 1301
665 Peachtree, Atlanta, Georgia.
Atlanta's main showcase club for name and up-and-coming talent. Directly across the street from The Fox.

The Fox
(404) 881 1977
660 Peachtree, Atlanta, Georgia.
A very large and very attractive old movie palace with excellent acoustics. Major rock names.

The Omni
(404) 681 2100
100 Techwood Drive NW, Atlanta, Georgia.
Major rock acts play this 17,000 capacity hall within a vast shop/restaurant/hotel complex.

688
(404) 874 7500
688 Spring Street, Atlanta, Georgia.
British and American new wave rock bands, occasional reggae.

AUSTIN

Alamo Lounge
(512) 472 0033
400 West 6th Street, Austin, Texas.
Small club featuring solos and duos — like local favourites Butch Hancock and Jimmie Dale Gilmore.

Austin Opera House
(512) 443 7037
200 Academy, Austin, Texas.
Willie Nelson-owned theatre that features national and well-known Texan names.

The Back Room
(512) 441 4677
2015 East Riverside Drive, Austin, Texas.
Small club, popular for unannounced and impromptu jam sessions.

Club Foot
(512) 472 4345
110 East 4th Street, Austin, Texas.
British and American name new wave bands, plus some of the most popular local bands like the extraordinary Uranium Savages.

Continental
(512) 442 9904
1315 South Congress, Austin, Texas.
Local rock and blues bands.

Duke Royal's Coach Inn
(512) 472 0321
Club featuring new wave rock at weekends.

Hondo's Saloon
(512) 477 9114
2915 Guadalupe, Austin, Texas.
Good place to see local country and rock bands.

Municipal Auditorium
(512) 476 5461
South 1st Street and Riverside, Austin, Texas.
Major touring rock acts. 6,000 capacity.

Paramount Theater
(512) 472 5411
713 Congress, Austin, Texas.
1,300 seat theatre for national name rock acts.

Raul's
(512) 477 1431
2610 Guadalupe, Austin, Texas.
Austin's first new wave rock club, located on "the drag".

Rockin' M Club
State Highway 183 between Lockhart and Austin, Texas.
Country dance hall with Musica Nortena (Tex-Mex) dance every Sunday night. Flaco Jiminez frequently.

Silver Dollar
(512) 837 1824
9323 Burnet road, Austin, Texas
Mainstream Nashville acts frequently featured at this traditional country dance hall.

Soap Creek Saloon
(512) 835 0509
11306 North Lamar Boulevard, Austin, Texas.
Austin's leading "progressive country" club with local favourites like Western Swing band, Alvin Crow and the Pleasant Valley Boys.

Steamboat Springs 1874
(512) 478 2912
403 East 6th Street, Austin, Texas.
Popular local bands.

UT Special Events Center
(512) 471 7744
University of Texas, Austin, Texas.
1700 capacity. Major rock acts like Bruce Springsteen and successful local boy Christopher Cross.

BOSTON

Berklee Performance Center
(617) 266 7455
1140 Boylston Street, Boston, Massachusetts.
Eclectic range of name acts — from Spyro Gyra to George Thorogood and the Destroyers.

Boston Garden Arena
(617) 227 3204
Causeway Street, Boston, Massachusetts.
Vast arena for major names — Doobie Brothers, Styx, etc.

Cantone's
(617) 338 7677
69 Broad Street, Boston, Massachusetts.
Modern rock bands nightly.

The Channel
(617) 451 1905
25 Necco Street, Boston, Massachusetts.
Claims to be "Boston's largest concert and dance club". Showcases name and up-and-coming acts.

Inn Square Men's Bar
(617) 491 9672
1350 Cambridge Street, Cambridge, Massachusetts.
Women welcome too — eclectic range of music.

Jonathan Swift's
(617) 661 9887
30 Boylston Street, Harvard Square, Cambridge, Massachusetts.
Popular showcase club that features an eclectic range of name guest artists — blues, folk.

Lulu White's
(617) 423 3652
3 Appleton Street, Boston, Massachusetts.
Jazz club - name acts.

The Metro
(617) 15 Lansdowne, Boston, Massachusetts.
New wave rock club.

Modern Theater
(617) 426 8445
523 Washington Street, Boston, Massachusetts.

Orpheum Theater
(617) 482 0651
Hamilton Place, Boston, Massachusetts.
Big rock names.

Oxford Ale House
(617) 876 5353
36 Church Street, Cambridge, Massachusetts.
Local rock bands.

Paradise
(617) 254 2052
967 Commonwealth Avenue, Boston, Massachusetts.
Showcase theatre with top-notch talent. Usually two shows a night.

Passim
(617) 492 7679
47 Palmer Street, Boston, Massachusetts.
Good folk club.

Pooh's
(617) 262 6911
464 Commonwealth Avenue,
Boston, Massachusetts.
Popular jazz club with good
atmosphere.

The Rat
(617) 247 7713
528 Commonwealth Avenue,
Boston, Massachusetts.
Boston's first new wave rock club
still features.

Sandy's Jazz Revival
(617) 922 7515
54 Cabot Street, Beverly,
Massachusetts.
Blues and jazz name talent in
club that's minutes away from
Boston on Route 128N.

Speakeasy
(617) 354 2525
24 Norfolk Street, Cambridge,
Massachusetts.
Blues and jazz nightly, many well
known names perform here.

Sword In The Stone
(617) 523 9168
13 Charles Street, Boston,
Massachusetts.
Long established folk club.

Symphony Hall
(617) 266 1492
301 Massachusetts Avenue,
Boston, Massachusetts.
Soft rock and pop names featured
here.

Uncle Sam's
(617) 925 5300
296 Nantasket Avenue, Hull,
Massachusetts.
Name talent featured in one of
the biggest clubs in the north
east.

Underground
1110 Commonwealth Avenue,
Allston, Massachusetts.
New wave rock club.

1369 Club
(617) 491 9625
1369 Cambridge Street,
Cambridge, Massachusetts.
Local jazz musicians every night.

CHICAGO

Aragon Ballroom
(312) 561 9500
1106 West Lawrence Avenue,
Chicago, Illinois.
Capacity 5,500. Atmospheric rock
'n' roll venue in once glorious
ballroom.

Auditorium Theater
(312) 922 2110
70 East Congress Parkway,
Chicago, Illinois.
4,000 seater hall with better
sound than many of the city's
larger theatres.

Biddy Mulligan's
(312) 761 6532
7644 North Sheridan, Chicago,
Illinois.
Top notch names in blues,
rockabilly and rhythm and blues.

B.L.U.E.S.
(312) 528 1021
2519 North Halsted, Chicago,
Illinois.
Small club that features fine
blues every night of the week.
Blues is alive and well in Chicago,
and this is one of the best of the
thirty or more venues in the city
that features the music.

Charlotte's Web
(815) 965 8933
728 First Avenue, Rockford,
Illinois.
Worth the long drive from
Chicago for a favourite act, as the
club is housed in such a pleasant
and comfortable room. Local folk,
rock and blues, interesting
newcomers and occasional
national acts.

The Checkerboard Lounge
(312) 373 5948
423 East 43rd Street, Chicago,
Illinois.
Historic blues club in Chicago's
south-side, with a warm, friendly
atmosphere inside the club;
though East 43rd can be very
dangerous for those unfamiliar
with the city.

Chicago Stadium
(312) 733 5300
1800 West Madison, Chicago,
Illinois.
20,000 capacity stadium for major
touring rock acts.

Clearwater Saloon
(312) 935 6545
3447 North Lincoln, Chicago,
Illinois.
Good for local blue grass and
country talent.

Earl Of Old Town
(312) 642 5206
1615 North Wells, Chicago,
Illinois.
A Chicago folk landmark where
Steve Goodman and Bonnie Koloc
made their names. Booking policy
rather erratic these days but
there are still occasional great
nights that evoke the old days.

Gaspar's
(312) 871 6680
3159 North Southport, Chicago,
Illinois.
Eclectic mix of local rock, folk
and jazz acts in comfortable and
unpretentious surroundings.

Holsteins!
(312) 327 3331
2464 North Lincoln, Chicago,
Illinois.
Excellent folk club run by long-
respected Chicago folkies Fred,
Ed and Allen Holstein.

International Amphitheater
(312) 927 5580
4300 South Halsted Street,
Chicago, Illinois.
12,000 capacity.

Nashville North
(312) 595 0170
101 East Irving Park Road,
Bensenville, Illinois.
Authentic hard-core country
honky-tonk with occasional
visiting names from Tennessee.

Park West
(312) 929 5959
322 West Armitage, Chicago,
Illinois.
Expensive showcase club with
fine sight lines and frequent top-
notch guests — national rock,
soul and jazz talent.

STEVE WINWOOD

Redford's
(312) 549 1250
2548 North Halsted, Chicago,
Illinois.
Good local jazz musicians
featured in comfortable club.

Rick's Café American
(312) 943 9200
Holiday Inn Lakeshore, East
Ontario Street at North
Lakeshore Drive, Chicago,
Illinois.
Top name jazz artists on the set
of Humphrey Bogart's
'Casablanca'!

Riviera Theater
(312) 561 5049
4746 North Ravine Avenue,
Chicago, Illinois.

Tut's
(312) 477 3365
959 West Belmont, Chicago,
Illinois.
New wave rock club housed on
the sight of the famed Quiet
Knight. Best of new wave British
and American bands featured.
Headliners rarely start playing
until after midnight.

Waves
(312) 935 2299
3730 North Clark, Chicago,
Illinois.
Small, crowded club featuring
local modern rock bands.

**Wild Hare and Singing Armadillo
Frog Sanctuary**
(312) 327 0800
3530 North Clark, Chicago,
Illinois.
Can anyone find a more unusual
club name than this? The centre
of Chicago's growing reggae
scene.

Wise Fools Pub
(312) 929 1510
2270 North Lincoln, Chicago,
Illinois.
Mainly blues, but some jazz and
modern country.

CINCINNATI

Bogart's
(513) 281 8400
2621 Vine Street, Cincinnati,
Ohio.
Popular showcase club for
national artists, cult favourites
and promising newcomers.
Capacity 550.

Cincinnati Music Hall
(513) 621 1919
1243 Elm Street, Cincinnati, Ohio.
3,600 seat theatre.

Cincinnati Riverfront Coliseum
(513) 241 1818
100 Broadway, Cincinnati, Ohio

CLEVELAND

Agora Ballroom
(216) 696 8833
1730 E. 24th Street,
Cleveland, Ohio.
The original club in the Agora
chain which someone unkindly
dubbed "the McDonald's of rock".
National and local acts.

Akron-Agora
(716) 929 7123
4193 Akron-Cleveland Road,
Akron, Ohio.
National and local acts.

The Bank
(716) 762 8237
South Main Street, Akron, Ohio.
The best club in the area for new
wave rock.

Euclid Tavern
(216) 229 7788
11629 Euclid Avenue, Cleveland,
Ohio.
Club near the university
featuring new wave rock, reggae
and occasional blues.

Flipside
(216) 291 4272
3935 Mayfield, Cleveland
Heights, Ohio.
An electic mixture of folk, rock,
blues and country acts.

The Grange
(216) 321 5551
1920 South Taylor Road,
Cleveland Heights, Ohio.
Long established folk club. Small
and intimate.

Hennessy's
(216) 521 2636
11729 Detroit Avenue, Lakewood,
Cleveland, Ohio.
Long established showcase
venues features some of the most
popular Ohio based bands.

The Mistake
(216) 696 8333
1730 East 24th Street, Cleveland,
Ohio.
Showcases new local bands.

Palace Theater
Playhouse Square, East 14th and
Euclid, Cleveland, Ohio.
Twenties movie palace renovated
for MOR and rock acts.

Peabody's Café
(216) 321 4073
2140 South Taylor Road,
Cleveland Heights, Ohio.
Jazz club that features occasional
big names.

Richfield Coliseum
(216) 659 9100
2923 Streetsboro Road, Richfield,
Ohio.
20,000 capacity stadium for major
rock acts.

Tommy's River Nightclub
(216) 331 2943
19015 Lake Road, Cleveland,
Ohio.
Rivals Peabody's for the name
jazz and blues acts it brings in.
Also country and rock bands.

Urban Cowboy Saloon
54 State Street, Painesville, Ohio.
Former movie theatre, then an
Agora club, now a country music
saloon. Major country names.

DALLAS

Agora
(214) 696 3724
6532 East Northwest Highway at
Abrams, Dallas, Texas.
Formerly The Palladium,
showcases top names and up-and-
coming local talent.

Belle Star
(214) 750 4787
7724 North Central Expressway,
Dallas, Texas.
Country music club.

Bijou
(214) 691 0648
500 Medallion Center, Dallas,
Texas.

Billy Bob's Texas
920 North Main (the Stockyards),
Fort Worth, Texas.
Vast country music stadium —
major acts

Dallas Convention Center Arena
(214) 658 7000
650 South Griffin, Dallas, Texas.
Major rock concerts.

Grapevine Opry
(817) 481 3505
Grapevine Opry House, 302 Main,
Grapevine, Texas.
Chisai Childs and other country
stars every Saturday night.

Hot Klub
(214) 526 9432
4350 Maple Avenue, Dallas,
Texas.
New wave rock centre.

Longhorn Ballroom
(214) 428 3128
216 Corinth at Industrial, Dallas,
Texas
Historic country music dance hall.

Moody Coliseum
(214) 692 2864
Southwest Methodist University,
Dallas, Texas.
Major rock bands.

Nick's Uptown
(214) 827 4802
3606 Greenville Avenue, Dallas,
Texas.
Showcase club.

Reunion Arena
(214) 651 1020
1507 Pacific Avenue, Dallas,
Texas.

**Sneaky Pete's Rock 'n' Roll
Heaven**
(214) 369 1874
714 Medallion Center, Dallas,
Texas.
Local rock bands.

St. Christopher's
(214) 361 7517
6848 Greenville Avenue, Dallas,
Texas.
Local rock and blues bands.

**Tarrant County Convention
Center**
(817) 332 9222
1111 Houston Street, Fort Worth,
Texas.
Major rock acts.

Whiskey River
(214) 369 9221
5421 Greenville Avenue, Dallas,
Texas.
Progressive Texas country and
rock acts. Down home
atmosphere.

Will Rogers Memorial Center
(817) 335 0734
3301 West Lancaster, Fort
Worth, Texas.
10,000 capacity.

Zero's
(817) 535 9512
2637 East Lancaster, Fort Worth,
Texas.
New wave bands featured.

DENVER

The Blue Note
(303) 443 0523
1116 Pearl Street, Boulder,
Colorado.
Local and national talent —
country music to rock.

Café Nepenthes
(303) 534 5423
1416 Market Street, Denver,
Colorado.
Local folk, blues and jazz talent.

Four Seasons Nightclub
(303) 366 9111
14451 East Colfax Avenue,
Denver, Colorado.
Country music.

Macky Auditorium
(303) 492 6309
University of Colorado, Boulder,
Colorado.
Major rock concerts.

McNichols Sports Arena
(303) 778 0700
1635 Clay, Denver, Colorado.
19,000 capacity arena for heavy
metal and rock bands.

The Rainbow Music Hall
(303) 753 1800
Evans and Monaco, Denver,
Colorado.
Showcase venue with varied fare
— from Cliff Richard to U2.

Red Rocks Amphitheater
(303) 575 2637
Morrison Street, Denver,
Colorado.
One of the most attractive
concert sites in the USA. Open
air — summer only.
9,000 capacity.

DETROIT

Clutch Cargoes
(313) 965 2060
44 West Elizabeth, Detroit,
Michigan.
New wave rock acts.

Cobo Arena
(313) 962 1800
301 Civic Center Drive, Detroit,
Michigan.
12,000 capacity arena for major
rock acts and the alleged "best
rock 'n' roll audience in the
world".

db's Club
(313) 593 1234
Hyatt Regency Hotel, Dearborn,
Detroit, Michigan.
New wave rock showcase, plus
occasional blues and jazz.

Soup Kitchen
(313) 259 1374
Top notch blues talent regularly.

HARTFORD

Bushnell Memorial Hall
527 Capitol Avenue, Hartford,
Connecticut.

Great American Music Hall
(203) 562 7220
130 Walley Street, New Haven,
Connecticut.

Hartford Civic Center
(203) 566 6588
1 Civic Plaza, Hartford,
Connecticut.
16,000 capacity.

Toad's
(203) 777 7431
300 York Street, New Haven,
Connecticut.
Showcase venue, including new
wave rock acts.

HOUSTON

Anderson Fair
(713) 528 8576
2007 Grant (behind Texas Art
Suppliers), Houston, Texas.
Houston's leading folk venue in
the heart of the Montrose area.

Agora Ballroom
(713) 960 1318
5134 Richmond, Houston, Texas.
Showcase venue with name acts
during the week and local top 40
bands at the weekend.

Astrodome
(713) 748 4500
Kirby Drive, Houston, Texas.
Vast sports stadium features
occasional big name rock
concerts.

Bavarian Gardens
(713) 861 6300
3926 Feagan, Houston, Texas.
Authentic German-American beer
hall with genuine oompah music
for polka dancing.

Birdwatchers
(713) 527 0595
907 Westheimer, Houston, Texas.
Jazz club.

Coliseum
(713) 222 3267
1810 Bagley, Houston, Texas.
11,500 capacity. Major rock
concerts.

Fool's Gold
(713) 497 2501
12845 Westheimer, Houston,
Texas.
Sophisticated honky tonk with
chandeliers and plush carpets.

Gilley's Club
(713) 941 7990
4500 Spencer Highway, Pasedena,
Texas.
Twenty miles from downtown
Houston, the vast country music
club owned by Mickey Gilley
which was the real star of the
film 'Urban cowboy'.

The Island
(713) 520 9040
4700 Main, Houston, Texas.
Suitably tacky venue for new
wave rock.

Johnny Lee's
(713) 479 9185
7325 Spencer Highway, Houston,
Texas.
Formerly the Nesadel, now a
country venue named after the
singer who used to lead Mickey
Gilley's band.

Moe and Joe's Honky Tonk
(713) 443 1832
3040 FM 1960, Houston, Texas.
Country music club owned by
stars Moe Bandy and Joe
Stampley. The "bucking
armadillo" rivals Gilley's
mechanical bulls.

Miller Outdoor Theater
(713) 222 3576
Hermann Park, Houston, Texas.
Outdoor summer venue for free
festivals including prestigious
Juneteenth Blues Festival in mid-
June.

Mum's Jazzplace
(713) 659 1004
Ambassador Hotel, 2016 Main,
Houston, Texas.
Name jazz and blues acts.

Rockefeller's
(713) 864 6242
3620 Washington, Houston,
Texas.
Showcase venue in a converted
bank.

Steamboat Springs
(713) 629 6650
4919 West Alabama, Houston,
Texas.
Folk and rock.

The Summit
(713) 627 9470
10 Greeway Plaza, Houston,
Texas.
17,500 capacity.

Whiskey River
(713) 777 5225
8670 South Gessner at SW
Freeway, Houston, Texas.
Country bands nightly.

Winchester Club
(713) 667 7994
5714 Bissonnet, Houston, Texas.
Authentic honky tonk with
country music nightly. Further
proof that Houston is the leading
city in the US for live country
shows.

KANSAS CITY

Kemper Arena
(816) 421 6460
1800 Genesee Street, Kansas
City, Missouri.
17,000 capacity hall for major
acts — Clapton, Styx, etc.

Memorial Hall
(816) 371 7555
600 North Seventh Street,
Kansas City, Missouri.
Major rock concerts.

Parody Hall
(816) 531 5031
811 West 39th Street, Kansas
City, Missouri.
Home base for the Kansas City
Blues Society. Name blues talent.

Plaza East
47th Street, Kansas City,
Missouri.
New wave rocks acts.

Uptown Theater
(816) 756 3370
3700 Broadway, Kansas City,
Missouri.
Showcase venue with national
names.

LOS ANGELES

The Country Club
(213) 881 9800
18415 Sherman Way,
Reseda California.
Converted supermarket.
Capacity: 1000

The Golden Bear
(714) 536 3192
306 Pacific Coast Highway,
Huntington Beach, California.
Good place to play before or after
playing L.A.
Capacity: 350

Madam Wong's West
(213) 642 5346
949 Sun Mun Way, Los Angeles,
California.
Capacity: N/A

The Palomino
(213) 765 9256
6907 Lankersham Boulevard, Los
Angeles, California.
Country-rock to Elvis Costello.
Capacity: 400

DAVID SANCIOUS

Perkins' Palace
(213) 796 0657
129 N. Raymond, Pasadena,
California.
New and wonderful.
Capacity: 1800

The Roxy
(213) 878 2222
9009 Sunset Boulevard, Los
Angeles, California.
Star-studded audience.
Everybody's home away from
home.
Capacity: 500

The Starwood
(213) 656 2200
8151 Santa Monica Boulevard,
Los Angeles, California.
Heavy metal Van Halen clones
play here.
Capacity: 600

The Whiskey
(213) 652 4202
8901 Sunset Boulevard, Los
Angeles, California.
If they're not at the Roxy,
they're here. And vice versa.
Capacity: 400

The Woodstock Club
(714) 761 9840
Anaheim, California.
The place to be if you're stuck in
Anaheim.
Capacity: N/A

MEMPHIS

Blues Alley
(901) 523 7144
60 South Front Street, Memphis,
Tennessee.
Blues club in a converted cotton
house in downtown Memphis,
near to Beale Street. Big Sam
and the Blues Alley Allstars are
regulars.

Cactus Jack's
(901) 398 6221
White Haven Plaza, Memphis,
Tennessee.
Occasional name country
performers at club one block
south of Graceland, off Elvis
Presley Boulevard.

Mid-South Coliseum
(901) 274 3982
Mid-South Fairgrounds,
Memphis, Tennessee.
12,000 capacity for major rock
and soul acts.

Orpheum Theater
Beale Street and Main, Memphis,
Tennessee.
Vaudeville theatre on historic
Beale Street (most of which has
now been demolished) and being
restored to its original splendour.
Big name soul/jazz-funk artists at
weekends.

P.O.E.T.S. Music Hall
1819 Madison, Memphis,
Tennessee.
New wave bands at this
renovated movie theatre in the
mid-town strip.

Trader Dick's
2012 Madison, Memphis,
Tennessee.
Local rock bands.

MIAMI

Agora Ballroom
(305) 454 0001
100 Ansin Boulevard, Hollywood,
Florida.
Showcase venue for up-and-
coming acts.

Hollywood Sportatorium
(305) 625 2900
16661 Hollywood Boulevard,
Hollywood, Florida.
Major rock acts in the
Springsteen, Dylan league.

Maurice Grisman Cultural Center
(305) 374 2444
174 East Flagler Street, Miami, Florida.
There is very little in the way of live rock music in either Miami or Miami Beach, except for occasional concerts here. Rock fans usually have to head north to Broward County, or the university town of Fort Lauderdale for live shows.

Mr. Pips
(305) 561 0331
3485 North Federal Highway, Fort Lauderdale, Florida.
Showcase venue for established and up-and-coming rock acts.

Sunrise Musical Theater
(305) 741 7300
5555 North West 95th Avenue, Sunrise, Florida.
4,000 seat auditorium features national rock, soul and country talent.

NASHVILLE

Exit In
(615) 327 2784
2208 Elliston Place, Nashville, Tennessee.
Showcase club for country, rock and jazz. Closed at press time — hopefully reopened by now.

Grand Ole Opry
(615) 889 3060
2800 Opryland Drive, Nashville, Tennessee.
A country music tradition, the Grand Ole Opry has had several different homes in over fifty years. The latest is a purpuse built theatre in the middle of a theme park. The famous radio show is broadcast live from here every Saturday night.

J Austin's
(615) 383 7322
4104 Hillsboro Road, Nashville, Tennessee.
Small club which books some of the best "new country" artists.

Nashville Municipal Auditorium
(615) 259 5367
417 Fourth Avenue, Nashville, Tennessee.
9,000 capacity for major rock acts.

Wind In The Willows
(615) 320 9154
2205 State Street, Nashville, Tennessee.
Bluegrass nightly.

NEW ORLEANS

Jed's
(504) 861 2585
8301 Oak, New Orleans, Louisiana.
Varied Musical fare including new wave rock.

Jimmy's
(504) 866 9549
8200 Willow Street, New Orleans, Louisiana.
Popular local bands like The Neville Brothers and The Meters.

Kingfish
(504) 343 0148
Perkins Road, Southdowns Shopping Center, Baton Rouge, Louisiana.
Showcase club with name and local talent.

Louisiana Super Dome
(504) 587 3663
1500 Coydras, New Orleans, Louisiana.
Vast stadium for major rock acts.

Municipal Auditorium
(504) 586 4314
1201 St. Peter's Street, New Orleans, Louisiana.
8,000 capacity arena for big name rock acts.

Ole Man River's
(504) 435 4000
2125 Highway 90 West, New Orleans, Louisiana.
Showcase venue for name acts and local bands — jazz, rock and country.

Preservation Hall
(504) 523 8939
726 St. Peter's Street, New Orleans, Louisiana.
Traditional New Orleans jazz every night.

Tipitina's
(504) 899 9114
501 Napoleon, New Orleans, Louisiana.
Named after a song by Professor Longhair, this is the best place in town to find some of the most revered names in New Orleans rhythm and blues.

NEW YORK

Bond's
(212) 944 5880
1526 Broadway, New York.
Capacity: 2000

Bottom Line
(212) 228 6300
15 W. 4th Street, New York.
Record companies use this club to showcase new acts.
Capacity: 400

MEAT LOAF

Camouflage
(212) 631 7656
38-17 Bell Blvd., Bayside, New York.
Capacity: 500

CBGB's
(212) 473 9671
315 Bowery Street, New York.
Die-hard punk paradise.
Capacity: 350

Club 57
(212) 475 9671
17 Irving Plaza, New York.
New Jersey bar band hang-out
Capacity: 600

Cody's
(212) 620 0377
579 6th Avenue, New York.
Country rock at its biggest.
Capacity: 380

Ear Inn
(212) 226 9060
326 Spring Street, New York.
Jazz orientated.
Capacity: N/A

The 80's
(212) 348 4991
231 E. 86th Street, New York.
Capacity: N/A

The Electric Room
(212) 989 7457
100 5th Avenue, New York.
Nostalgia rock.
Capacity: 2000

Emerald City
(609) 488 0222
Cherry Hill, New Jersey.
Suburban punk.
Capacity: N/A

Great Gildersleeves
(212) 533 3940
331 Bowery, New York.
Loud new wave acts.
Capacity: 500

Home
(212) 876 0744
1748 Second Avenue, New York.
Good atmosphere.
Capacity: 70

JP's
(212) 288 1022
1471 First Avenue, New York.
Singer-songwriter heaven.
Capacity: 200

Kenny's Castaways
(212) 473 9870
157 Bleecker Street, New York.
Willie Nile and Steve Forbert began here.
Capacity: 180

Left Bank
(914) 699 6619
20 E. 1st Street, Mt. Vernon, New York.
Capacity: 800

Lone Star Café
(212) 242 1664
61 Fifth Avenue, New York.
Established acts only
Capacity: 400

Malibu
(516) 889 1122
Lido Blvd, Lido Beach
Long Island, New York.
Everybody's favourite place to play.
Capacity: 1300

Max's Kansas City
(212) 777 7870
213 Park Avenue South, New York.
Two floors, with live music upstairs.
Capacity: 500

Maxwell's
(210) 656 9632
1039 Washington Street
Hoboken, New Jersey.
Capacity: 200

Mudd Club
(212) 227 7777
77 White Street, New York.
Yes, they're still open.
Capacity: 400

Ones
(212) 925 0011
111 Hudson Street, New York.
Capacity: 500

The Other End
(212) 673 7030
149 Bleeker Street, New York.
Record company showcase.
Lousy guacamole.
Capacity: 200

Peppermint Lounge
(212) 719 3176
128 W. 45th Street, New York.
Making a return engagement.
Capacity: 1000

Possible 20
(212) 558 1100
253 W. 55th Street, New York.
Session musicians hang out here.
Best music around.
Capacity: 200

Privates
(212) 744 1973
150 E. 85th Street, New York.
Three floors, including a game room.
Capacity: 1000 +

The Ritz
(212) 228 8888
119 E. 11th Street, New York.
The Studio 54 of New Wave/Rock.
Capacity: N/A

Rock Away
(212) 474 5984
113-20 Beach Drive,
Rockaway Beach, New York.
This ain't no party, but this ain't no foolin' around, either.
Capacity: N/A

The Savoy
(212) 921 9490
141 W. 44th Street, New York.
Seated concerts.
Capacity: 955

Snafu
(212) 691 3535
676 Sixth Avenue, New York.
From poetry to plays to rock.
Capacity: 100

Tramps
(212) 777 5077
125 E. 15th Street, New York.
Capacity: 250

Trax
(212) 799 1448
100 W. 72nd Street, New York.
Showcase for record companies.
Also features a rock photo gallery.
Capacity: 280

UK Club
(212) 473 9647
106 Third Avenue, New York.
What happened to British civility?
Capacity: N/A

The Village Gate
(212) 475 5120
Bleeker and Thompson Streets, New York.
Two theatres with a capacity of 425 each.

Zappa's
(212) 339 9275
3521 Quentin Road, Brooklyn, New York.
Not to be confused with Frank.
Capacity: N/A

Zzyzx
(212) 431 7327
64 N. Moore Street, New York.
Capacity: N/A

PHILADELPHIA

Academy of Music
(215) 893 1935
Broad and Locust Streets, Philadelphia, Pennsylvania.
Name jazz and rock acts.

Bijou Café
1409 Lombard Street, Philadelphia, Pennsylvania.
Popular local bands and occasional national names.

Emerald City
Route 70, Cherry Hill, New Jersey.
1,600 capacity. Showcase with many new wave rock bands.

The Ripley Music Hall
(215) 923 1860
608 South Street, Philadelphia, Pennsylvania.
Small showcase club featuring a wide range of name talent — from James Brown to Steve Forbert.

Tower Theater
(215) 352 0313
South 69 Boulevard and Ludlow Street, Upper Darby, Pennsylvania.
3,000 capacity for major rock names.

Valley Forge Music Fair
(215) 644 5000
Devon, Pennsylvania.
Long established showcase theatre — major rock, soul and country acts.

PHOENIX

Boojum Tree
(602) 248 0222
Second Avenue and Osborn, in the Doubletree Inn, Phoenix, Arizona.
Jazz club.

Dooley's
(602) 968 2446
1216 E. Apache, Phoenix, Arizona.
Showcase venue — national names.

Veteran's Memorial Coliseum
(602) 252 6771
1826 West McDowell, Phoenix, Arizona.
13,000 capacity for rock concerts.

Whiskey River
825 North Scottsdale Road, Phoenix, Arizona.
One of the many local clubs featuring country music.

PROVIDENCE

Center Stage
(401) 438 6903
2224 Pawtucket, Providence, Rhode Island.
Showcase club, frequent new wave rock.

Ocean State Performing Arts Center
(401) 421 2997
220 Weybasset Street, Providence, Rhode Island.

Providence Civic Center
(401) 331 0700
1 LaSalle Square, Providence, Rhode Island.
Large rock concerts.

ST. LOUIS

BB's Jazz, Blues and Soups Inc
700 South Broadway, St. Louis, Missouri.
Blues and jazz acts.

Checkerdome
(314) 644 0900
5700 Oakland Avenue, St. Louis, Missouri.
Major rock acts in auditorium that seats 20,000.

Fourth and Pine
(314) 241 2184
401 Pine Street, St. Louis, Missouri.
Nightspot in downtown St. Louis that regularly showcases up-and-coming acts promoting their new albums.

SAN ANTONIO

Convention Center Arena
(512) 225 6351
East Market and South Alamo Street, San Antonio, Texas.
San Antonio is probably the "heavy metal capital" of America and this 16,000 auditorium is an essential stop on tours by name British or American bands, who can be assured of a full house and a raptuous reception.

Cotton-Eyed Joe
(512) 340 8787
3625 West Avenue, San Antonio, Texas.
Mainstream country and occasional progressive Texas bands in the "outlaw" mould.

Jimmy's Mexican Restaurant and Party House.
(512) 826 7485
4400 Rittiman Road, San Antonio, Texas.
One of San Antonio's many clubs that features the conjunto music of the large Spanish-American population. Jimmy's is a recommended north-side venue, and regularly features accordionist Santiago Jiminez Snr., one of the acknowledged fathers of the music.

Skip Willy's
(512) 824 0696
1502 Bitters Road, San Antonio, Texas.
Showcase venue for name acts and cult favourites.

SAN FRANCISCO

Alpen Glow
(415) 276 2310
18564 Mission Boulevard, Hayward, California.
The best of the local rock bands.

Berkeley Square
(415) 849 3374
1333 University Avenue, Berkley, California.
Showcase club with visiting rock acts and the best local bands.

The Boarding House
(415) 441 4334
901 Columbus at Lombard, San Francisco, California.
Respected SF club now at a new location. Local bands plus country/folk orientated rock names — Jesse Winchester, Rick Danko, etc.

California Hall
625 Polk Street at Turk, San Francisco, California.
Showcast theatre for up-and-coming name talent.

The Cellar
(415) 964 0220
4926 El Camino, Los Altos, California.
Popular club with good atmosphere, well-suited to the folkish, countryish bands featured.

MICHAEL JACKSON

Country Palace
(415) 827 2294
1500 Monument Boulevard, Concord, California.
National country music names.

Eli's Mile High club
(415) 655 6661
3629 Grove Street, Oakland, California.
Excellent blues club — the best in the area.

Freight and Salvage
(415) 548 1761
1827 San Pablo Avenue, Berkeley, California.
Modern folk, bluegrass and country. Name acts that you would associate with the Arhoolie or Flying Fish record labels.

Great American Music Hall
(415) 885 0750
859 O'Farrell, San Francisco, California.
Soft rock, bluegrass and ethnic music.

Inn Of The Beginning
(707) 795 9955
Downtown Cotati, California.
Eclectic range of good music from bluegrass to zydeco.

Jazz Palace
(415) 434 0530
638 Broadway, San Francisco, California.
Major jazz names frequently.

Keystone Berkeley
(415) 841 9903
2119 University Avenue, Berkeley, California.
Owned by the same people as The Stone and Keystone Palo Alto — they frequently book the same acts into all their clubs.
Name and up-and-coming rock.

Keystone Korner
(415) 781 0697
750 Vellejo Street, San Francisco, California.
Respected jazz club with name acts.

Keystone Palo Alto
(415) 324 1402
260 California, Palo Alto, California.

Larry Blake's
(415) 848 0886
2367 Telegraph, Berkeley, California.
Jazz, folk and occasional rock.

The Last Day Saloon
(415) 387 6343
406 Clement Street, San Francisco, California.
Local blues, country, bluegrass and folk.

Mabuhay Gardens
(415) 956 3315
443 Broadway, San Francisco, California.
Also know as the Fab Mab — the original SF new wave rock club, still brings in hot new bands from Britain and New York, plus the best from the active local scene.

Mr. Majors
(415) 569 6000
8021 MacArthur Boulevard, Oakland, California.
Name jazz and blues acts.

Oakland Coliseum
(415) 569 2121
Nimitz Freeway and Hegenberger Road, Oakland, California.
The Stadium holds 60,000, the Arena 14,200. Where famed promotor Bill Graham puts on concerts featuring the biggest names in rock music.

The Old Waldorf
(415) 397 3884
44 Battery Street, San Francisco, California.
Bill Graham-owned showcase club that regularly features some of the most interesting up-and-coming and name rock bands and singers.

Palms
(415) 673 7771
1406 Polk, San Francisco, California.
Enterprising booking policy attracts some of the most interesting local singers and bands.

Paramount Theater
(415) 893 2300
2025 Broadway, Oakland, California.

San Francisco Civic Auditorium
(415) 558 5065
99 Grove Street, San Francisco, California.

The Stone
(415) 391 8282
412 Broadway, San Francisco, California.
Showcase venue — strong on new wave rock and the best of the area's up-and-coming bands.

Venetian Room
(415) 772 5163
The Fairmont Hotel, California and Mason, San Francisco, California.
Classy joint that features big name acts, many "golden oldies". Dress code.

Zellerbach Auditorium
(415) 642 9988
University College, Berkeley, California.

TUCSON

Dooley's
(602) 624 8588
745 East University Boulevard, Tucson, Arizona.
Rock showcase club.

Night Train
(602) 792 0088
424 North Fourth Avenue, Tucson, Arizona.
Local rock bands.

Tucson Community Center
(602) 965 4266
260 South Church Avenue, Tucson, Arizona.
10,000 capacity, major rock acts.

TULSA

Cain's Ballroom
(918) 582 2078
423 North Main Street, Tulsa, Oklahoma.
Historic country dance hall where Bob Wills — the king of western swing — used to perform in the Thirties. Today features national and local country and rock acts.

Cedar Creek Saloon
(918) 932 9157
South Lewis, Tulsa, Oklahoma.
Popular club for country and bluegrass fans.

Mabee Center
(918) 492 7545
8100 South Lewis, Tulsa, Oklahoma.
11,000 capacity hall.

WASHINGTON

The Bajou
(202) 333 2897
3131 K Street NW, Washington, DC.
Showcase club for national rock acts promoting new albums, plus local bands like The Nighthawks, who draw big crowds.

Beneath It All
3259 M Street NW, Washington, DC.
Local rock bands in club next to the Crazy Horse in Georgetown.

Blues Alley
(202) 337 4141
1073 (rear of) Wisconsin Avenue NW, Washington, DC.
The very best names in jazz. Three shows nightly.

Capitol Center
(301) 350 3400
1 Harry S. Truman Drive, Landover, Maryland.
19,000 capacity. Where the big rock names play.

Cellar Door
(202) 338 3300
34th and M Streets NW, Washington, DC.
Popular showcase club in the Georgetown area of the city. Hosts name jazz, folk and country orientated performers.

D A R Constitution Hall
(202) 628 4780
1776 D Street NW, Washington, DC.

d.c. space
(202) 347 4960
Seventh and East NM, Washington, DC.
New wave, reggae, experimental and jazz. Frequent well-known names.

Desperado's
(202) 338 5200
34th and M Streets NM, Washington, DC.
Across the street from the Cellar Door. Less well-known but equally eclectic range of good music.

DiGennaro's
(301) 953 3444
Corner of 197 and Contree Road, Laurel, Maryland.
Washington is acknowledged as the centre of the bluegrass world and this is one of the best area clubs. Occasional local rock here.

Ontario Theater
(202) 462 7118
1700 Columbia Road NW, Washington, DC.
Name rock acts.

Psyche Delly
(301) 654 6611
4846 Cordell Avenue, Bethesda, Maryland.
Popular rock club with local favourites and visiting names.

MARVIN GAYE

Takoma Tap Room
(301) 589 1600
8210 Piney Branch Road, Silver Spring, Maryland.
Bluegrass, country rock and folk.

Warner Theater
(202) 347 7801
513 13th Street NW, Washington, DC.
2,000 capacity theatre.

9.30 Club
(202) 393 0930
930 F Street NW, Washington, DC.
Leading new wave venue with national and local acts.

THE PLASMATICS

VENUES/UK

ABERDEEN

The Capitol
(0224) 23141
431 Union Street, Aberdeen
Capacity: 2010

Ruffles
(0224) 29092
13 Diamond Street, Aberdeen
Capacity: 1000

Aberdeen University
(0224) 572751
Students Union, Broad Street,
Aberdeen
Capacity: 1000

ABERYSTWYTH

Aberystwyth University
(0970) 4242
Students Union, Laura Place,
Aberystwyth
Capacity: 1250

AYLESBURY

Civic Centre
(0296) 5900
Civic Centre, Aylesbury
Capacity: 700

Friars
(0296) 84568
Maxwell Hall, Market Square,
Aylesbury
Capacity: 1250

AYR

Pavilion
(0292) 65489
Esplanade, Pavilion Road, Ayr
Capacity: 1000

BARNSTAPLE

Chequers
(0271) 2717
The Strand, Barnstaple
Capacity: 550

BARROW-IN-FURNESS

(0229) 25795
28 Duke Street,
Barrow-in-Furness
Capacity: 1000

BASILDON

Towngate Theatre
(0268) 22881
Towngate, Basildon, Essex
Capacity: N/A

BATH

Moles Club
(0225) 333423
14 George Street, Bath
Capacity: 130

Pavilion
(0225) 25628
North Parade, Bath
Capacity: 900

Tiffanys
(0225) 65342
Kingsmead Square, Saw Close,
Bath
Capacity: 700

University
(0225) 63228
Claverton Road, Bath
Capacity: 600

BEXHILL

De La Warr Pavilion
(0424) 212022
The Marine, Bexhill-on-Sea
Capacity: 1120

BIRMINGHAM

Digbeth Civic Hall
(021) 235 2434
Milk Street Entrance, Digbeth
Capacity: 950

National Exhibition Centre
(021) 780 2516
Birmingham B40 1NT
Capacity: 11,000

Night Out
(021) 622 2283
Horsefair, Birmingham
Capacity: 1273

Odeon
(021) 643 6101
New Street, Birmingham
Capacity: 2579

Romeo & Juliet's
(021) 643 6696
Smallbrook Ringway,
Birmingham
Capacity: 1330

Top Rank
(021) 236 3226
Dale End, Birmingham
Capacity: 2000

Town Hall
(021) 235 3942
Victoria Square, Birmingham
Capacity: 1543

University
(021) 472 1841
Edgbaston Park Road,
Birmingham
Capacity: 1000

BLACKBURN

King George's Hall
(0254) 58424
Northgate, Blackburn
Capacity: 1800

BLACKPOOL

Norbreck Castle
(0253) 52341
Queens Promenade, Blackpool
Capacity: 600

The Opera House
(0253) 25252
Church Street, Blackpool
Capacity: 3176

Tiffanys
(0253) 21572
Central Drive, Blackpool
Capacity: 2800

BOGNOR

Riverside Ballroom
(0243) 865823
Shripney Road, Bognor Regis
Capacity: 1200

BOURNEMOUTH

Pavilion Theatre
(0202) 28404
Westover Road, Bournemouth
Capacity: 1518

Town Hall
(0202) 22066
St. Stevens Street, Bournemouth
Capacity: 1000

Winter Gardens
(0202) 27338
Exeter Road, Bournemouth
Capacity: 2600

BRACKNELL

Sports Centre
(0344) 54203
Bagshot Road, Bracknell
Capacity: 2000

BRADFORD

St. Georges Hall
(0274) 32515
Hall Ings, Bradford
Capacity: 1911

BRIDLINGTON

The Spa Royal Hall
(0262) 78255
The Spa, Bridlington
Capacity: 2000 — 3000

BRIGHTON

Centre
(0273) 203131
Kings Road, Brighton
Capacity: 5000

Dome
(0273) 682046
29 New Road, Brighton
Capacity: 2100

Jenkinsons
(0273) 25897
Kings West (Seafront), Brighton
Capacity: 900

Top Rank
(0273) 25895
Kings West, West Street,
Brighton
Capacity: 2000

BRISTOL

Colston Hall
(0272) 293891
Colston Street, Bristol
Capacity: 1886

Granary
(0272) 28272
32 Welsh Back, Bristol
Capacity: 500

Locarno
(0272) 26193
Bristol New Centre,
Frogmore Street, Bristol
Capacity: 2000

Polytechnic
(0272) 656261
Students Union, Coldharbour
Lane, Frenchay, Bristol
Capacity: 450

Trinity Hall
(0272) 551544
Trinity Road, St, Philips,
Bristol
Capacity: 400

University
(0272) 35035
Ansom Room, Queens Road,
Clifton, Bristol
Capacity: 920

BURTON

76 Club
(0283) 61037
76 High Street, Burton-on-Trent
Capacity: 300

CAERPHILLY

The Recreation Centre
(0222) 869845
Virginia Park, Caerphilly
Capacity: 1000

CANTERBURY

Odeon
(0227) 62480
The Friars, Canterbury
Capacity: 1068

University
(0227) 65224
Elliot Masters House, Students
Union, Kent University,
Canterbury
Capacity: N/A

CARDIFF

Sophia Gardens
(0222) 27657
Sophia Gardens, Cardiff
Capacity: 2050

Top Rank
(0222) 26687
43 Queen Street, Cardiff
Capacity: 1950

CHELMSFORD

Chancellor Hall
(0245) 65848
Market Road, Chelmsford
Capacity: 650

The Odeon
(0245) 53677
Baddow Road, Chelmsford
Capacity: 1436

CHESTER

Deeside Leisure Centre
(0244) 817000
Queensferry, Deeside, Clywd
3 Halls. Capacities:
6000/2400/1000

CHESTERFIELD

Fusion
(0246) 32594
Holywell Street, Chesterfield
Capacity: 550

CLEETHORPES

Peppers
(0472) 67128
Grant Street, Cleethorpes
Capacity: 764

JUDIE TZUKE

Winter Gardens
(0472) 62925
Kingsway, Cleethorpes
Capacity: 1150

COLCHESTER

Essex University
(0206) 863211
Wivenhoe Park, Colchester
Capacity: 900

COVENTRY

Lanchester Polytechnic
(0203) 21167
Students Union, Priory Street,
Coventry
Capacity: 1600

Theatre
(0203) 56121
Hales Street, Coventry

Tiffanys
(0203) 24570
Smithford Way, Coventry
Capacity: 770

University
(0203) 217406
Students Union, University of
Warwick, Coventry
Capacity: 1500

CRAWLEY

Leisure Centre
(0293) 37431
Haslett Avenue, Crawley
Capacity: 1838

CROMER

West Runton Pavilion
(026 375) 203
West Runton, Norfolk
Capacity: 1200

CROYDON

Fairfield Hall
(01) 681 0821
Park Lane, Croydon, Surrey
Capacity: 1800

DERBY

Assembly Rooms
(0332) 3111
Market Place, Derby
Capacity: 1500

Ajanta Club
(0332) 32906
Sacheveral Street, Derby
Capacity: 700

DONCASTER

The Gaumont
(0302) 4626
Hallgate, Doncaster DN1 3NL
Capacity: 1003

Rotters Club
(0302) 27448
Silver Street, Doncaster
Capacity: 1800

DUDLEY

JB's
(0384) 53597
King Street, Dudley
Capacity: 500

DUMFRIES

Stagecoach
(0387) 75493
Collin, Dumfries
Capacity: 300

DUNDEE

Barracuda
(0382) 27373
Marketgait, Dundee
Capacity: 700

Caird Hall
(0382) 22200
City Square, Dundee
Capacity: 2680

Marryatt Hall
(0382) 22200
City Square, Dundee
Capacity: 400

University
(0382) 21841
Students Union, Airlie Place,
Dundee
Capacity: 650

DUNSTABLE

Civic Hall
(0582) 603166
Vernon Place, Queensway,
Dunstable
Capacity: 1000

DURHAM

University
(0385) 68430
Students Union, Durelm House,
New Elvet, Durham
Capacity: 850

EDINBURGH

Astoria
(031) 661 1662
Abbey Mount, Edinburgh
Capacity: N/A

Clouds
(031) 229 5753
3 West Tolcross, Edinburgh
Capacity: N/A

Nite Club
(031) 557 2590
The Playhouse, 20 Greenside
Place, Leith Walk, Edinburgh
Capacity: 420

Odeon
(031) 667 3805
7 Clerk Street, Edinburgh
Capacity: 1894

Playhouse Theatre
(031) 557 2590
18-22 Greenside Place, Edinburgh
Capacity: 3030

Tiffanys
(031) 556 6292
St. Stephen Street, Edinburgh
Capacity: 800

Usher Hall
(031) 228 6611
Lothian Road, Edinburgh
Capacity: 1900

Valentinos
(031) 229 5151
3a East Fountain Bridge
Edinburgh
Capacity: N/A

EXETER

Routes
(0392) 58615
13 Okehampton Street, Exeter
Capacity: 780

Tiffanys
(0392) 55679
The Quay, Exeter
Capacity: 1200

University
(0392) 75023
Great Hall, Stocker Road, Exeter
Capacity: 1800

GLASGOW

Apollo Theatre
(041) 332 9221
Renfield Street, Glasgow
Capacity: 3181

Strathclyde University
(041) 552 1895
90 John Street, Glasgow
Capacity: 1000

Tiffanys
(041) 332 0992
Sauchiehall Street, Glasgow
Capacity: 1500

GLOUCESTER

Leisure Centre
(0452) 36788
Station Road, Gloucester
Capacity: 2100

GRANGEMOUTH

Town Hall
(032 44) 5133
Boness Road, Grangemouth
Capacity: 550

GRAVESEND

Woodville Halls
(0474) 4244
Civic Centre, Windmill Street,
Gravesend
Capacity: 1000

GREAT YARMOUTH

Tiffanys
(0493) 57018
Marine Parade, Great Yarmouth
Capacity: 1500

GRIMSBY

Central Halls
(0472) 55796
Duncombe Street, Grimsby
Capacity: 740

GUILDFORD

Civic Hall
(0483) 67314
London Road, Guildford
Capacity: 1200

HANLEY

The Odeon
(0782) 25805
Piccadilly, Hanley,
Stoke-on-Trent
Capacity: 1337

Victoria Hall
(0782) 24641
Albion Square, Hanley,
Stoke-on-Trent
Capacity: 1580

HASTINGS

The Pier Pavilion
(0424) 422566
The Pier Hastings
Capacity: 1600

White Rock Pavilion
(0424) 421840
White Rock, Hastings
Capacity: 1250

HEMEL HEMPSTEAD

Pavilion
(0442) 64451
The Marlowes, Hemel Hempstead
Capacity: 1041

HIGH WYCOMBE

Nags Head
(0494) 21758
63 London Road, High Wycombe,
Bucks
Capacity: 350

Town Hall
(0494) 26100
Queen Victoria Road, High
Wycombe, Bucks
Capacity: 714

HUDDERSFIELD

Coach House
(0484) 20930
Kings Street, Huddersfield
Capacity: 300

Polytechnic
(0484) 38156
Great Hall, Queensgate,
Huddersfield
Capacity: 800

HULL

City Hall
(0482) 26525
Victoria Square, Hull
Capacity: 1805

New Theatre
(0482) 20463
Kingston Square, Hull
Capacity: 1179

Tiffanys
(0482) 28250
Ferensway, Hull
Capacity: N/A

University
(0482) 445361
Students Union, Cottingham
Road, Hull
Capacity: 900

Wellington Club
(0482) 23262
105 Beverly Road, Hull
Capacity: N/A

ILFORD

Tiffanys
(01) 478 3128
The High Road, Ilford, Essex
Capacity: 1200

IPSWICH

Corn Exchange
(0473) 55851
King Street, Ipswich
Capacity: 893
Gaumont
(0473) 53641
Majors Corner, 8 St. Helens
Street, Ipswich
Capacity: 1666

KEELE

University
(0782) 625411
Keele, Staffs
Capacity: 770

LANCASTER

University
(0524) 63352
Great Hall, Bailirigg, Lancaster
Capacity: 1600

LEEDS

Fan Club
(0532) 663252
Brannigans, Call Lane, Leeds
Capacity: 450

Fforde Green Hotel
(0532) 490984
Roundhay Road, Harehills, Leeds
Capacity: 350

Grand Theatre
(0532) 456014
46 Briggate Street, Leeds
Capacity: 1554

Polytechnic
(0532) 30171
Assembly Hall, Calverley Street,
Leeds
Capacity: 600

Queens Hall
(0532) 31961
Sovereign Street, Leeds
Capacity: 4000

University
(0532) 39071
Refectory, PO Box 157, Leeds
Capacity: 1500

The Warehouse
(0532) 468287
19-20 Sommers Lane, Leeds
Capacity: 450

LEICESTER

De Montfort Hall
(0533) 276326
University Road, Leicester
Capacity: 2556

University
(0533) 553760
Queens Hall, Percy Lee Building,
University Road, Leicester
Capacity: 1630

LINCOLN

Drill Hall
(0522) 24393
Broadgate, Lincoln
Capacity: 1200

LIVERPOOL

Empire Theatre
(051) 709 1555
Lime Street, Liverpool
Capacity: 2550

Royal Court Theatre
(051) 708 7411
Roe Street, Liverpool
Capacity: 1500

University
2 Bedford Street North,
Liverpool
Capacity: 1500

LONDON

CONCERT HALLS THEATRES AND CINEMAS

Apollo Theatre, Victoria
(01) 828 6491
Wilton Road, London SW1
Large theatrical auditorium. Only
occasional rock gigs between
musicals and pantomimes.

Dominion Theatre
(01) 580 9562
Tottenham Court Road,
London
Occasional gigs — usually a
cinema, in shadow of Centrepoint.

Drury Lane Theatre
(01) 836 3687
Catherine Street, London WC2
Traditional theatre auditorium.
Gigs rare between runs.

Gaumont State
(01) 624 8081
High Road, Kilburn,
London NW6
Large cinema — only occasional
gigs.

Hammersmith Odeon
(01) 748 4081
Queen Caroline Street, London W6
The prestige gig. Best for bands
with ardent followings to create
atmosphere in the spaciousness.
Sadly the kill-joy security staff
are allergic to dancers.

London Palladium
(01) 437 7373
8 Argyll Street, London W1
Only for the Eltons and Cliffs.

Rainbow Theatre 1 & 2
(01) 272 5169
232 Seven Sisters Road, Finsbury
Park, London N4
Mock Moroccan decor —
crumbling grandeur. The most
"rock and roll" of the theatre
venues.
Rainbow 2: New venture
attempts club atmosphere in the
one-time foyer.

Royal Albert Hall
(01) 589 3203
Kensington Gore, London SW7
Only for the polite acts who don't
offend walking decibel meters.

Royal Festival Hall
(01) 928 3191
Belvedere Road, London SE1
Rarely used except for what used
to be called "soft rock" acts.

Queen Elizabeth Hall
(01) 928 3191
Belvedere Road, London SE1
Ditto but smaller.

THE NOLANS

Theatre Royal
(01) 534 0310
Gerry Raffles Square,
Angel Lane, London E15
Community orientated theatre.
Gigs on rare occasions.

LONDON

ROCK PUBS

The Bridge House
(01) 476 2889
Barking Road,
Canning Town, London E16
Home of "Oi". Spirit of Punk
lives on with heavier, Skinhead
trappings.

Golden Lion
(01) 385 3942
490 Fulham Road, London SW6
Pub gig with some scoops eg.
early Stray Cats gig.

Green Man
(01) 534 1637
196 Stratford High Street,
London E15
Recently opened — only East
End pub venue beside Bridge
House.

Greyhound
(01) 385 0526
175 Fulham Palace Road,
London W6
Above average pub gig.

Half Moon
(01) 737 4580
Half Moon Lane,
Herne Hill, London SE25
Comfortable pub gig.

Hope and Anchor
(01) 359 4510
207 Upper Street, London N1
"Grope And Wanker" — ultimate
sweaty cellar. However
cornerstone of the pub circuit.

Old Queens Head
(01) 274 3829
133 Stockwell Road,
London SW9
Promoted by the discriminating
Charlie Gillett.

The Pits
(01) 889 9615
Green Man,
383 Euston Road, London NW1
New pub cellar. Surprisingly
comfortable and intimate.

Windsor Castle
(01) 286 8403
309 Harrow Road, London W9
Regular pub gig.

LONDON

CLUBS, BALLROOMS AND MISCELLANEOUS VENUES

Acklam Hall
(01) 960 4590
Acklam Road, Portobello Road,
London W10
Community Hall under motorway
flyover. A bit "Clockwork
Orange".

Africa Centre
(01) 836 1973
38 King Street, London WC2
Recently more adventurous
promotions by "Jamming"
fanzine.

Chat's Palace
(01) 986 6714
42-44 Brooksby's Walk,
London E9
Another community style venue.

Dingwalls
(01) 267 4967
Camden Lock, Chalk Farm Road,
London NW1
Long running late night rock
club. Awkward layout is only
detrimental aspect. Video facility
compensates.

Earls Court Exhibition Centre
(01) 580 3692
Warwick Road,
London SW5
Aircraft hanger for superstars
with ego or stature to match. Buy
a poster to remind yourself what
the speck on stage looks like.

Embassy Club
(01) 499 5974
7 Old Bond Street,
London W1
The cocktail set roughing it with
Rock and Roll.

Empire Ballroom
(01) 437 1446
Leicester Square,
London WC2
A large tourist orientated disco.
Gigs very rare.

Hammersmith Palais
(01) 748 2812
242 Shepherds Bush Road,
London W6
Large dance hall — good
atmosphere. Useful alternative to
Odeon around the corner.

Heaven
(01) 839 3862
The Arches, Charing Cross,
London WC2
Atmospheric, cavern-like gig.
Occasional mixed audience rock
gigs in a venue that's usually a
gay disco.

Institute of Contemporary Arts
(01) 930 3647
ICA, The Mall, London SW1
Uncharacteristically clean
surroundings. Noble championing
of unknown, interesting bands in
occasional "rock weeks".

Jacksons Rock Club
(01) 340 5226
Jacksons Lane Community
Centre, 271 Archway Road,
London N6
Only occasional promotions.

**London Musicians Collective
(LMC)**
(01) 722 0456
42 Gloucester Avenue,
London NW1
Avante-gardists.

The Lyceum
(01) 836 3715
Wellington Street,
Strand, London WC2
Key dance hall style venue with
Sunday night packages of current
media faves, including some "up
and comings".

The Marquee
(01) 437 6603
90 Wardour Street, London W1
Most widely known club.
Audience usually a mix of curious
tourists and the bands' hardcore
following.

The Moonlight Club
(01) 624 7611
100 West End Lane, West
Hampstead, London NW6
Reasonable pub gig with some
adventurous bookings.

Riverside Studios
(01) 748 3354
Crisp Road, London W6
Only occasional "artsy" gigs.

Rock Garden
(01) 240 3916
King Street, Covent Garden,
London WC2
Bands nightly under late night
hamburger and coleslaw joint.
Reasonably decorated cellar.

Royal Nitespot
(01) 886 8141
Winchmore Hill Road,
Southgate, London N14
Large disco — home of soul and
funk movement. Only occasional
bands.

The Starlight Rooms
(01) 624 7611
Railway Hotel,
100 West End Lane,
London NW6
Above Moonlight — with more
cabaret feel.

Sundown
(01) 734 6963
157 Charing Cross Road,
London WC2
Useful sized venue for middle
league bands. Should be used
more often.

Tramshed
(01) 855 3371
51 Woolwich New Road,
London SE18
Big community theatre — tiered
seating.

The Tabernacle
Powis Square,
London W11
Community centre — Left field
or reggae bands on occasional
basis.

Upstairs at Ronnie's
(01) 439 0747
47 Frith Street, London W1
Obscure bands.

The Venue
(01) 834 5500
160 Victoria Street, London SW1
Bands in middle of evening. Disco
'til late. Dance floor with disco
rig, tables for food and drink.
Works best with bands with
ardent followings or who can
work a reticent audience.

Wembley Arena
(01) 902 1234
Empire Way, Wembley,
Middlesex
Famous football stadium. Rarely
used — with good reason.

YMCA
(01) 636 7289
112 Great Russell Street,
London W1
Comfortable gig. Useful size —
below centrally located hotel.

100 Club
(01) 636 0933
100 Oxford Street, London W1
Jazz and Blues club —
occasionally booking rock or
reggae. Venue for early Pistol
gigs.

101 Club
(01) 223 8309
101 St. John's Hill, SW10
Have championed up and coming
bands by issuing compilation LPs
of bands who have played there.

LONDON

UNIVERSITIES AND COLLEGES

City of London Polytechnic
(01) 247 1441
Fairholt House,
102-105 Whitechapel Street,
London E1

London School of Economics
(01) 405 8593
Houghton Street,
London WC2

Queen Mary College
(01) 980 1240
Mile End Road
London E1

**School of Oriental and African
Studies**
(01) 580 0916
Malet Street,
London WC1

University of London Union
(01) 348 2041
Malet Street,
London WC1

Southbank Polytechnic
(01) 261 1525
Rotary Street,
London SE1

LOUGHBOROUGH

University
(0509) 66600
Students Union Building, Ashby
Road, Loughborough
Capacity: 1100

LOWESTOFT

The Talk of the East
(0502) 4793
The South Pier, Lowestoft
Capacity: 800

MAIDSTONE

Greenways
(0732) 84455
London Road, West Malling,
Maidstone

MALVERN

Winter Gardens
(06845) 66266
Grange Road, Malvern
Capacity: 1000

MANCHESTER

Apollo Theatre
(061) 273 3533
Ardwick Green, Manchester
Capacity: 2645

Free Trade Hall
(061) 834 3697
Peter Street, Manchester
Capacity: 2529

The Golden Garter
(061) 437 7614
Rowlandsway, Wythenshawe,
Manchester
Capacity: 1400

Polytechnic
(061) 273 1162
Cavendish House, Cavendish
Street, All Saints, Oxford Road,
Manchester
Capacity: 650

Russell Club
(061) 226 6821/6366
Royce Road, Hulme, Manchester
Capacity: 1470

University
(061) 273 5111
Oxford Road, Charlton-upon-
Medlock, Manchester
Capacity: 1200

MARGATE

Winter Gardens
(8043) 22795
Fort Crescent, Margate
Capacity: 1500

MIDDLESBOROUGH

Rock Garden
(0642) 241995
208 Newport Road,
Middlesbrough, Cleveland
Capacity: 450

Town Hall
(0642) 245432
Albert Road, Middlesbrough,
Cleveland
Capacity: 1247

NEWCASTLE-UPON-TYNE

City Hall
(0632) 20007
Northumberland Street,
Newcastle
Capacity: 2168

Mayfair Ballroom
(0632) 23109
Newgate Street, Newcastle
Capacity: 2100

Polytechnic
(0632) 28761
Students Union, Education
Precinct, 2 Sandyford Road,
Newcastle
Capacity: 1500

The Theatre Royal
(0632) 22061
Grey Street, Newcastle
Capacity: 1379

University
(0632) 28402
King's Walk, Newcastle
Capacity: 1400

NEWPORT (GWENT)

The Stowaway
(0633) 50978
40 Stow Hill, Newport
Capacity: 600

NEWPORT (SALOP)

The Village
(0952) 811949
The Square, Newport
Capacity: 400

NEWTON ABBOTT

Seale Hayne Agricultural College
(0626) 60557
Newton Abbott
Capacity: 550

NORTHAMPTON

Cricket Club
(0604) 32697
Wantage Road, Northampton
Capacity: 1000

NORWICH

Cromwells
(0603) 612909
Edward Street, Norwich
Capacity: 1500

University of East Anglia
(0603) 56161
The Plain, Norwich
Capacity: 920

NOTTINGHAM

Boat Club
(0602) 869032
Trentside, Trent Bridge,
Nottingham
Capacity: 500

Palais
(0602) 51075
Lower Parliament Street,
Nottingham
Capacity: 2000

Rock City
(0602) 412544
Talbot Street, Nottingham
Capacity: 1700

University
(0602) 55912
Portland Building, University
Park, Nottingham
Capacity: 800

NUNEATON

77 Club
(0682) 386323
Queens Road, Nuneaton
Capacity: N/A

OXFORD

New Theatre
(0865) 43041
George Street, Oxford
Capacity: 1697

Polytechnic
(0865) 61998
Gypsy Lane, Headington, Oxford
Capacity: 1000

PAIGNTON

The Festival Theatre
(0803) 558641
Paignton
Capacity: 1494

PAISLEY

Bungalow Bar
(041) 889 6667
9 Renfrew Road, Paisley
Capacity: N/A

PENZANCE

Demelza's
(0736) 2475
Penzance
Capacity: 600

PLYMOUTH

Fiesta
(0752) 25721
Mayflower Street, Plymouth
Capacity: 1100

POOLE

Arts Centre
(020 13) 70521
England Road, Poole, Dorset
Capacity: 1500

PORTSMOUTH

Guildhall
(0705) 834773
Guildhall Square, Portsmouth,
Capacity: 2017

The Locarno
(0705) 25491
Arundel Street, Portsmouth
Capacity: 2400

PORT TALBOT

Troubadour
(063 96) 77968
Abervan Shopping Precinct, Port
Talbot
Capacity: 600

PRESTON

Guildhall
(0772) 21921
Lancaster Road, Preston, Lancs.
Capacity: 2146

READING

Hexagon Theatre
(0734) 55911
PO Box 600, Civic Centre,
Reading
Capacity: 1200

Target
(0734) 585887
Butto Centre, Reading
Capacity: 250

Top Rank
(0734) 51464
Station Hill, Reading
Capacity: 2000

University
(0734) 64396
Upper Redlands Road, Reading
Capacity: 800

REDCAR

Coatham Bowl
(02872) 2013
Majuba Road, Redcar
Capacity: 900

RETFORD

Porterhouse
(0777) 704981
20 Carolgate, Retford, Notts.
Capacity: 600

SALFORD

The Wilows Leisure Centre
(061) 736 8541
Willows Road, Salford
Capacity: 900

SALISBURY

The City Hall
(0722) 27676
Fisherton Street, Salisbury
Capacity: 1120

SCARBOROUGH

Penthouse
(0723) 63204
35 St. Nicholas Street,
Scarborough
Capacity: 308

SHEFFIELD

City Hall
(0742) 734550
Barker's Pool, Sheffield
Capacity: 2292

The Crucible Theatre
(0742) 760621
55 Norfolk Street, Sheffield
Capacity: 1013

Limit Club
(0742) 730940
70-82 West Street, Sheffield
Capacity: 300

Polytechnic
(0742) 738934
The Phoenix Building,
Pond Street, Sheffield
Capacity: 1200

Top Rank
(0742) 21927
Arundel Gate, Sheffield
Capacity: 2500

SHREWSBURY

Tiffanys
(0743) 58786
Raven Meadows, Shrewsbury
Capacity: 1200

SKEGNESS

The Festival Theatre
(0754) 4761
Tower Esplanade, Skegness
Capacity: 1500

SLOUGH

Fulcrum Theatre
(0753) 38669
Queensmere, Slough
Capacity: 1800

SOUTHAMPTON

Gaumont
(0703) 22001
Commercial Road, Southampton
Capacity: 2165

Top Rank
(0703) 26080
Bannister Road, Southampton
Capacity: 2000

SOUTHEND

Zero 6
(0702) 546344
Aviation Way, Southend
Capacity: 800

SOUTHPORT

The Floral Hall
(0704) 40404
The Promenade, Southport
Capacity: 1300

The Theatre
(0704) 40404
The Promenade, Southport
Capacity: 1651

STAFFORD

Bingley Hall
(0785) 58060
Stafford
Capacity: 7300

ST. ALBANS

City Hall
(0727) 64511
Civic Centre, St. Albans
Capacity: 1100

ST. ANDREWS

University
(0334) 770000
St. Mary's Place, St. Andrews
Capacity: 1000

ST. AUSTELL

New Cornish Riviera Lido
(0726) 81 4261
Carlyon Bay, St. Austell,
Cornwall
Capacity: 2500

STOKE

The Kings Hall
(0782) 48241
The Town Hall, Stoke-on-Trent
Capacity: N/A

North Staffs Polytechnic
(0782) 412416
College Road, Stoke
Capacity: 450

Tiffanys
(0782) 614702
Crystal Buildings, Hasell Street,
Newcastle-under-Lyme, Stoke
Capacity: 1200

SUNDERLAND

Mayfair Ballroom
(0783) 57568
Newcastle Road, Sunderland
Capacity: 2500

SWANSEA

The Brongwyn Hall
(0792) 50821
The Guildhall, Swansea
Capacity: 1352

University
(0792) 24851
College House, University
College, Singleton Park
Capacity: 800

SWINDON

Brunel Rooms
(0793) 31384
Havelock Square, Swindon
Capacity: 1000

The Oasis Leisure Centre
(0793) 33404
North Star Avenue, Swindon
Capacity: 1500

TAUNTON

Odeon
(0823) 72283
Corporation Street, Taunton
Capacity: 1272

TORQUAY

Festival Theatre
(0803) 26244
The Esplanade, Paignton
Capacity: 1494

Town Hall
(0803) 26244
Castle Circus, Torquay
Capacity: 1200

400 Ballroom
(0803) 28103
Victoria Parade, Torquay
Capacity: 550

TOTNES

Civic Hall
(0803) 864499
Market Place, High Street,
Totnes
Capacity: 400

UXBRIDGE

Brunel University
(0895) 5724
Kingston Lane, Uxbridge
Capacity: 400

WAKEFIELD

Unity Hall
(0924) 75719
Smythe Street, Wakefield
Capacity: 1000

WATFORD

Baileys
(0923) 39848
127 The Parade, Watford
Capacity: 2000

WHITEHAVEN

The Whitehouse Disco
(0946) 2215
Strand Street, Whitehaven
Capacity: 450

WOLVERHAMPTON

Civic Hall
(0902) 28482
North Street, Wolverhampton
Capacity: 1780

Lafayette Club
(0902) 26285
Thornley Street, Wolverhampton
Capacity: 1000

YORK

University
(0904) 412328
Central Hall, Heslington, York
Capacity: 1326

GARY NUMAN

RECORD COMPANIES/US

A&M Records
(212) 469 3411
146 N. LaBrea, Los Angeles,
California.
New York Offices
(212) 826 0477
595 Madison Avenue, New York.
Also ILLEGAL RECORDS, and IRS
RECORDS. Stasis in the recession.

Arista Records
(212) 489 7400
6 W. 57th Street, New York.
California Offices
(213) 553 1777
1888 Century Park East, Suite
1510, Los Angeles, California.
Barry Manilow and Air Supply
are this label's only visible means
of support.

Atlantic Records
(212) 484 6000
75 Rockefeller Plaza, New York.
California Offices
(213) 278 9230
9229 Sunset Boulevard, Los
Angeles, California.
Atlanta Offices
(404) 344 4033
250 Villanova Drive, Atlanta,
Georgia.
Also ATCO RECORDS, COTILLION
RECORDS, ROLLING STONE RECORDS,
MIDSONG RECORDS, SCOTTI BROTHERS
RECORDS, SWAN SONG RECORDS and
MODERN RECORDS.
Some of the finest publicists in
the US work for Atlantic.

Capitol Records
(213) 462 6252
1750 N. Vine Street, Hollywood,
California.
New York Offices
(212) 757 7470
1370 Avenue Of The Americas,
New York.
Nashville Offices
(615) 244 1842
38 Music Square East, Nashville,
Tennessee.
Slipshod in every sense of the
word, but they still managed to
break a new act this year.

Chrysalis Records
(213) 550 0171
9255 Sunset Boulevard, Los
Angeles, California.
New York Offices
(212) 935 8750
115 E. 57th Street, New York.
Small but mighty.

Columbia Records
(212) 975 4321
51 W. 52nd Street, New York.
California Offices
(213) 556 4700
1801 Century Park West, Los
Angeles, California.
Nashville Offices
(615) 259 4321
Also ARC RECORDS, STIFF RECORDS
and CBS RECORDS.
Best of the biggies.

ECM Records
(212) 888 1122
509 Madison Avenue, Suite 512,
New York.
Well-known jazz talents do their
best work for this small label.

Elektra Records
(213) 655 8280
962 N. LaCienaga, Los Angeles,
California.
New York Offices
(212) 355 7610
665 5th Avenue, New York.
Nashville Offices
(615) 320 7525
1201 16th Avenue South,
Nashville, Tennessee.
Also ASYLUM RECORDS, NONESUCH
RECORDS and PLANET RECORDS.
Singer-songwriter label with
emphasis on the California sound.

EMI-America Records
(213) 464 2488
6464 Sunset Boulevard,
Penthouse Suite, Los Angeles,
California.
New York Offices
(212) 757 7470
1370 Avenue Of The Americas,
New York.
EMI really works at breathing life
into old acts and breaking new
ones.

Epic Records
(212) 975 4321
51 W. 52nd Street, New York.
California Offices
(213) 556 4700
1801 Century Park West, Los
Angeles, California.
Nashville Offices
(615) 329 2134
49 Music Square West, Nashville,
Tennessee.
Also FULL MOON RECORDS,
PORTRAIT RECORDS, NEMPERER
RECORDS, STIFF RECORDS and JET
RECORDS.
Nothing recedes like success.

Fantasy Records
(415) 549 2500
10th and Parker Street, Berkeley,
California.
New York Offices
(212) 757 2134
1775 Broadway, Suite 617,
New York.
With artists like Sylvester, and
Two Tons of Fun, we have to
wonder whose fantasy this is.

Island Records
(212) 355 6500
444 Madison Avenue, New York.
Low quantity, but consistantly
high quality.

MCA Records
(213) 985 4321
100 Universal City Plaza,
Universal City, California.
New York Offices
(212) 888 9700
10 E. 53rd Street, New York.
Nashville Offices
(615) 244 8944
27 Music Square East, Nashville,
Tennessee.
Also ABC RECORDS and
BACKSTREET RECORDS.
Going down for the third time.

Mercury/Phonogram Records
(312) 645 6300
1 IBM Plaza, Chicago, Illinois.
New York Offices
(212) 399 7485
810 7th Avenue, New York.
California Offices
(213) 466 9771
6255 Sunset Boulevard, Los
Angeles, California.
Nashville Offices
(615) 244 3776
10 Music Circle South, Nashville,
Tennessee.
Memphis Offices
(901) 726 6000
2000 Madison Avenue, Memphis,
Tennessee.
Victims of the Future Shock
conglomerate sprawl syndrome.

Motown Records
(213) 468 3500
6255 Sunset Boulevard, Los
Angeles, California.
Also TAMLA RECORDS.
Stevie Wonder hangs in there.

PVC/Passport Records
(201) 753 6100
3619 Kennedy Rd, South
Plainfield, New Jersey.
Main distributor of British
imports.

Polydor Records
(212) 399 7100
810 7th Avenue, New York.
California Offices
(213) 466 9574
6255 Sunset Boulevard, Los
Angeles, California.
Guess it's hard to concentrate
when you have so many other
things to do ...

RCA Records
(212) 930 4000
1133 Avenue Of The Americas,
New York.
California Offices
(213) 468 4000
6363 Sunset Boulevard, Los
Angeles, California.
Nashville Offices
(615) 244 9880
30 Music Square West, Nashville,
Tennessee.
Also WINDSONG RECORDS.
Bring your own promotional
team.

Rounder Records
(617) 354 0700
186 Willow Avenue, Somerville,
Massachusetts.
Still waiting for Woodstock II.

Salsoul Records
(212) 889 7340
240 Madison Avenue, New York.
Trying to live up to its potential.

Sire Records
(212) 595 5000
165 W. 74th Street, New York.
Warner baby growing up fast.

United Artists Records
(213) 461 9141
6920 Sunset Boulevard, Los
Angeles, California.
New York Offices
(212) 757 7470
1370 Avenue Of The Americas,
New York.
Nashville Offices
(615) 329 9356
50 Music Square West, Nashville,
Tennessee.
Big but bewildered.

Warner Brothers Records
(213) 846 9090
3300 Warner Boulevard, Burbank,
California.
New York Offices
(212) 832 0600
3 E. 54th Street, New York.
Nashville Offices
(615) 256 4282
1706 Grand Avenue, Nashville,
Tennessee.
On a par with Columbia, but WB
is everyone's favourite.

RECORD COMPANIES/UK

A&M Records
(01) 736 3311
136-140 Kings Road, London SW6
Some US acts — Styx, Quincy Jones — contribute to annual turnover, as does founder Herb Alpert, but the most buoyant acts remain the home-produced ones: The Police, Squeeze, Joe Jackson, Joan Armatrading.

Absurd Records
(061) 445 2661
20 Cotton Lane, Withington, Manchester 20
Also RABID.
Idiosyncratic roster of local loonies.

Albion Records
(01) 734 9072
147 Oxford Street, London W1
A small, growing label, with Hazel O'Connor in the vanguard.

Ariola Records
(01) 580 5566
3 Cavendish Square, London W1
Sky remain the heavyweight act, though label newcomer Kiki Dee started promisingly, and great expectations are also held for Herman Brood.

Arista Records
(01) 580 5566
3 Cavendish Square, London W1
Also GO FEET and I SPY. UK roster tends to be small but select, with The Beat and The Stray Cats. The whole operation is buttressed by the eternally top-selling Barry Manilow.

Aura Records
(01) 486 5288
1 Kendall Place,
London W1H 3AG
No real chart success yet for this small independent, with a roster ranging from Annette Peacock to The Soft Boys and Alex Chilton.

Ballistic Records
(01) 961 3363
94 Craven Park Road,
Harlesden, London NW10
Caribbean specialists.

B&C Records
(01) 326 6651
326 Kensal Road,
London W10 5BL
Also MOONCREST, SAGA.
Little to report other than continuing sales of early Steeleye Span albums.

Barn Records
(01) 637 2111
35 Portland Place, London W1
Also CHEAPSKATE.
The now-renascent Slade remain its blue-chip property.

BBC Records
(01) 580 4468
Portland Place,
London W1A 1AA
Strong performances from the theme to 'The Life and Times Of Lloyd George' in the singles charts, and 'Not The Nine O'Clock News' in the albums charts allowed the record company to offset at least some of the corporation's mounting deficit.

Beggars Banquet Records
(01) 370 6175
8 Hogarth Road, London SW5
Also 4 A.D.
The company remained resilient, thanks to Gary Numan and Freeez.

Bronze Records
(01) 267 4499
100 Chalk Farm Road,
London NW1 8EH
While the company switched distribution from EMI to POLYDOR, Motorhead, Girlschool and Hawkwind ensured an uninterrupted supply of chart material.

Carrere Records
(01) 493 7406
20-22 Queen Street, London W1
A varied roster, with chart success from the unlikely pairing of Ottawan and Saxon.

CBS Records
(01) 734 8181
17-19 Soho Square,
London W1V 6HE
Also EMBASSY, EPIC, FULL MOON, MONUMENT, PHILADELPHIA INT., BLUE SKY, KIRSHNER, TABU, MUMS, CARIBOU, T.K., ODE, UNLIMITED GOLD, DIRECTION.
The company hardly needed its established heavies — Dylan, Springsteen, Joel — to fall back on, as 80/81 proved a rich period. At one point, the company took the top three places in the albums charts, through Abba, Barbra Streisand and Adam and The Ants, and they similarly dominated the singles through Shakin' Stevens, Joe Dolce, The Jacksons, The Nolans, Stars On 45, Abba and Adam.

Charisma Records
(01) 434 1351
90 Wardour Street, London W1
Also PRE.
The Genesis crew ensure the label's survival, but losing Phil Collins must have been a major blow.

Charly Records
(01) 741 0011
9 Beadon Road, London W6 OEA
Also AFFINITY, SUN, SMACK.
The label still scores with an excellent catalogue of mostly late-Fifties material, and still flops with contemporary acts.

Cherry Red Records
(01) 229 8854/5
53 Kensington Gardens,
London W2 4BA
The label earned notoriety and chart success, though more of the former than the latter, through The Dead Kennedys.

Chiswick Records
(01) 267 5192
3 Kentish Town Road,
London NW1
Also ACE, BIG BEAT.
Small label pioneers operating in controlled chaos, tempering fun with reality. The Damned and Sniff 'n' the Tears are principal names.

Chrysalis Records
(01) 408 2355
12 Stratford Place,
London W1N 9AF
Also 2-TONE, REFORMATION.
The independent that's done so well it begins to seem like a major. The big guns — Jethro Tull, Leo Sayer, Blondie — are regularly joined by thrusting colts — Spandau Ballet, Linx and, from the US, Pat Benatar; The Specials and Stiff Little Fingers remained chart acts, while Ultravox were established as one.

Creole Records
(01) 965 9223
91-93 High Street,
Harlesden, London NW10
Also POLO.
Success on the POLO label through Adrian Baker's Liquid Gold.

Decca Records
(01) 491 4600
50 New Bond Street,
London W1Y 9HA
Also DERAM, London, UK.
After almost a decade of spluttering failure, absorption into the POLYGRAM group brought with it a modicum of success with acts such as Splodgenessabounds and old Adam and The Ants material.

Dep International
(021) 233 1064
Office 6, 11 Albert Street,
Birmingham.
The new independent formed by UB40 after leaving GRADUATE.

Dindisc Records
(01) 221 7535
61-63 Portobello Road,
London W11 3DD
Young VIRGIN offshoot, enjoying its first major chart success with Orchestral Manoeuvres In The Dark; roster also includes Nash The Slash and Martha and the Muffins.

Dingle's Records
(01) 952 3551
322 Whitchurch Lane, Cannons Park, Edgware,
Middlesex HA8 6QX
Also MICKEYPOPS.
Lost the one-hit wonder image that had prevailed since 'Day Trip To Bangor' thanks to 'Capstick Comes Home'.

DJM Records
(01) 242 6886
James House, 5 Theobalds Road, Holborn, London WC1X 8SE
Also CHAMPAGNE, RAGE
Still offering little more than Elton John's fading glories.

Do It Records
(01) 486 3602
PO Box 403, 81 Harley House, Marylebone Road,
London NW1 5HT
Famous as the last company to have Adam and The Ants before CBS turned them into international superstars.

Double D Records
(01) 493 9701
25 Bruton Street, London, W1
Dave Dee's label.

Dread At The Controls Records
(01) 229 8235
The Basement, 32 Alexander Street, London W2
Reggae label launched by Clash and Dury cohorts and starring Mikey Dread.

Eagle Records
(01) 235 2117
186 Sloane Street, London SW1
The company that re-launched Gary Glitter.

E.G. Records
(01) 730 2162
63A Kings Road, London SE3 4NT
Also AMBIENT.
Roxy Music have always been the company mainstay, though Killing Joke made a bright debut.

EMI Records
(01) 486 4488
EMI House, 20 Manchester Square, London W1A 1ES
Also CAPITOL, HARVEST, LIBERTY, PARLOPHONE, REGAL ZONOPHONE, ARDECK.
Once upon a time 'the greatest recording organisation in the world'. No longer thriving, but also no longer traumatised, it ploughs an even furrow. Paul McCartney, Cliff Richard, Kate Bush, Sheena Easton and The Undertones provide a ready supply of chart material.

Ensign Records
(01) 723 8464
44 Seymour Place, London W1H 5WQ
The Boomtown Rats continue to be the company's major name, but chart success has also been provided by Black Slate, Beggar and Co. and Incognito.

Eric's Records
(051) 733 5854
4 Rutland Avenue, Liverpool 17
Also INEVITABLE.
Presenting some of the more interesting aspects of the burgeoning group scene in Liverpool.

Factory Records
(061) 434 3876
86 Palatine Road, Manchester 20
Presenting some of the more interesting aspects of the burgeoning group scene in Manchester; Joy Division and its successor New Order and A Certain Radio are the company flag-bearers.

Fast Product
(031) 661 5811
3-4 East Norton Place, Edinburgh.
Also POPAURAL.
Iconoclastic talent-scoop.

Faulty Products
(01) 727 0734
41b Codrington Mews, Blenheim Crescent, London W11 2EF
Also DEPTFORD FUN CITY, ILLEGAL, KRYPTONE, STEP-FORWARD.
Ramshackle premises belie intriguing catalogue which includes debut singles by The Police, Sham 69 and Squeeze.

F-Beat Records
(01) 993 4731
6 Horn Lane, Acton, London W3 9NJ
Also DEMON.
Enterprising small company founded by Radar personnel after that company's dissolution. Roster is headed by Elvis Costello and Nick Lowe.

Fetish Records
(01) 828 1978
Flat 3, 40 Denbigh Street, London SW1
Tendency towards occultist electronics.

Fiction Records
(01) 459 8681
165-7 High Road, London NW10
Founded by Chris Parry, discoverer and first producer of The Jam, with The Cure as his leading act.

Flyright Records
(0424) 214 390
20 Endwell Road, Bexhill-on-Sea, East Sussex.
Mainly US R&B reissues.

Free Reed Records
(0773) 826264
Belper, Derbyshire.
Folk specialists.

Fresh Records
(01) 258 0572
359 Edgware Road, London W2
New wave mixture, but primarily distributors.

Gem Records
(01) 485 5622
GTO City, 115-123 Bayham Street, London NW1 0AL
Present prime contenders for chart placings are UK Subs.

Graduate Records
(0384) 59048
196 Wolverhampton Street, West Midlands.
With UB40, a buoyant independent; without them, the future looks bleak.

Greensleeves Records
(01) 749 3277
44 Uxbridge Road, London W12
Sounds of the Carribean, including Dr. Alimantado and Keith Hudson.

GTO Records
(01) 439 8971
37 Soho Square, London W1V 5DG
A fading chart singles-oriented company.

Heartbeat Records
(0272) 30458
4 Melrose Place, Clifton, Bristol BS8 2NQ
Local new wavers including the Glaxo Babies.

Human Records
(01) 278 3481
284 Pentonville Road, London N1 9NR
Newly-born independent hoping for chart success from The Au Pairs and Dangerous Girls.

Ice Records
(01) 806 3252
81A Osbaldeston Road, Stamford Hill, London N16
Eddy Grant is the most successful act on this, his own label.

Industrial Records
(01) 254 9178
10 Martello Street, London E8
Home of Throbbing Gristle.

Island Records
(01) 741 1511
22 St Peters Square, London W6 9NW
Also BEARSVILLE, ZE, GROVE, HANNIBAL.
Pioneering independent which broke loose with Traffic in the second half of the Sixties. Current roster is still headed by Stevie Winwood, with Bob Marley; other artists include U2, Linton Kwesi Johnson, the B52s and Marianne Faithfull.

Jet Records
(01) 486 6040
102-104 Gloucester Place, London W1H 3PH
A new eight-album deal with ELO should sustain the label over the next few years.

Korova
(01) 637 3775
17 Berners Street, London W1
The label which brings Echo and The Bunnymen to the world.

K-Tel Records
(01) 992 8000
620 Western Avenue, London W3
The company subsistss on TV-advertised compilations.

Leader Sound
(0422) 76161
209 Rochdale Road, Greetland, Halifax, West Yorks HX4 8JE
The nation's folk heritage as collected by Bill Leader.

Lightning Records
(01) 969 7155
841 Harrow Road, London NW10 5NH
Also SCOPE, GALLERY, OLD GOLD, REVIVAL.
Primarily a distribution outfit, though Old Gold has acquired the rights to a wide range of classic UK and UK Fifties and Sixties singles.

Logo Records
(01) 734 6710
119 Wardour Street, London W1V 3TD
Its most recent chart successes — with The Tourists and Driver 67 — are fast fading into history.

Magnet Records
(01) 486 8151
Magnet House, 22 York Street, London W1H 1FD.
Darts, Matchbox, Bad Manners keep the company in the charts; Doll By Doll are a more recent acquisition.

MCA Records
(01) 439 9951
1 Great Pulteney Street, London W1R 3FW
Also ABC, INFINITY.
Tom Petty, The Crusaders and the now-departed Steely Dan wave the flag for the old guard, while the company looks to the future with Joe Ely, The Tygers Of Pan Tang and The Look.

Motown Records
(01) 493 1603
16 Curzon Street, London W1Y 7FF
Even for a company with such an illustrious pedigree, 80/81 proved a notable period, with major chart successes from Stevie Wonder, Diana Ross, Smokey Robinson, Michael Jackson and newcomer Teena Marie.

Mute Records
(01) 458 9950
16 Decoy Avenue, London NW11
Interesting independent which achieves occasional crossover with electronic pop - e.g. Depeche Mode.

New Hormones Records
(061) 236 9849
182 Oxford Street, Manchester 13
Also OBJECT.
Small local concern which carried The Buzzcocks' first recordings,and is now re-active.

Oval Records
(01) 622 0111
11 Liston Road, London SW4
A small set-up which has never
fulfilled its early promise.

Phonogram
(01) 491 4600
49 New Bond Street,
London W1Y 9HA
Also PHILIPS, VERTIGO, MERCURY,
FONTANA, BACK DOOR, DE-LITE,
CASABLANCA.
Part of a large continental
conglomerate, now more firmly
established in the UK record
market than at any time in the
past 25 years. Major acts include
Status Quo, Thin Lizzy and Dire
Straits; Graham Bonnet and The
Teardrop Explodes are beginning
to enjoy success, while there are
high hopes of The Polecats and
Sector 27.

Pickwick International
(01) 200 7000
The Hyde Industrial Estate,
The Hyde,
London NW9 6JU
No new act — just budget-priced
compilations by firmly-established
ones.

Pinnacle Records
(01) 582 7712
371-375 Kennington Lane,
London SE11 5QY
Idiosyncratic small label which
has acts of its own, and which
offers production and distribution
deals to other independents.

Polydor Records
(01) 499 8686
17-19 Stratford Place,
London W1N OBL
Like PHONOGRAM and DECCA, a
part of the POLYGRAM
conglomerate. The company can
boast megastars ranging from
James Last to The Who, and
chart appearances from The Jam,
Siouxsie and The Banshees and
Visage.

PRT Records
(01) 648 7000
132 Western Road,
Mitcham,
Surrey CR4 3UT
Also BLUEPRINT, CALIBRE,
PRECISION, PICCADILLY, PYE.
The tattered remnants of the
once-flourishing PYE company.
Only success came from CALIBRE
with Kelly Marie and the Real
Thing.

PVK Records
(0494) 36351
Unit 2, Hillbottom Road, Sands
Industrial Estate, High
Wycombe, Bucks.
Leading company names are
seasoned guitar virtuosos, Peter
Green and Gordon Giltrap.

RAK Records
(01) 586 2012
42-48 Charlbert Street,
London NW8
Singles success inevitably
sustained — this time through
Marty Wilde's daughter, Kim.

RCA Records
(01) 499 4100
1 Bedford Avenue,
London WC1B 3DT
Also GRUNT, SOLAR, 20TH CENTURY,
WINDSONG.
The company still has its
enduring stars — David Bowie,
Elvis Presley and Jim Reeves —
as well as a host of country
names, but during 1980/81 began
to enjoy contemporary success of
a varied nature with Sugar
Minott, Landscape and Buck's
Fizz. Solar also did well with
Shalamar and The Whispers.

Recommended Records
(01) 622 8834
583 Wandsworth Road,
London SW8
Restricted release sheet
distinguished by Faust.

Red Lightnin' Records
(037) 988 693
The White House, The Street,
North Lopham, Diss, Norfolk.
US R&B aficionados.

Rialto Records
(01) 584 2441
4 Yeomans Row, London SW3
The company failed to capitalise
on early success with The
Regents and The Korgis.

Riva Records
(01) 731 4131
2 New Kings Road, London SW6
Success for John Cougar in the
US suddenly meant that founder
Rod Stewart wasn't the
company's only hit artist.

Rockburgh Records
(01) 351 4333
PO Box 283, London SW6 2JU
Ian Matthews remains the
company's leading light.

Rocket Records
(01) 258 3585
104 Lancaster Gate,
London W2 3NT
Elton John's company continues
to make slow but steady
progress. Fred Wedlock's 'Oldest
Swinger In Town' became the
label's biggest non-Elton hit.

Rockney Records
(01) 794 6702
32-34 Gondar Gardens,
London NW6
The home of Chas'n'Dave.

Rolling Stones Records
(01) 352 0005
2 Munro Terrace,
London SW10 ODL
Very exclusive; only Peter Tosh
joins The Stones on the label.

Ronco Teleproducts
(01) 876 8682
111 Mortlake Road, Kew,
Richmond, Surrey.
TV advertised product.

Rough Trade Records
(01) 221 1100
202 Kensington Park Road,
London W11
A retail outlet which blossomed
into a record company and
national distributor for a wealth
of interesting independents.
Clever, caring and imbued with
an integrity rare in the record
business.

RSO Records
(01) 629 9121
67 Brook Street,
London W1
Also DREAMLAND, ILLUSIVE.
A company that had swelled
astonishingly three years earlier
now contracted just as suddenly,
with its major acts inoperative —
Eric Clapton through illness, and
The Bee Gees through multi-
million-dollar legal disputes.

Safari Records
(01) 486 6141
42 Manchester Street,
London W1M 5PE
Much success, all thanks to
Toyah.

Small Wonder Records
(01) 520 2727
162 Hoe Street,
London E17
The culprits who first unleashed
The Cockney Rejects and The
Angelic Upstarts.

Sonet Records
(01) 229 7267
121 Ledbury Road, London W11
Also KICKING MULE, SPECIALITY,
ALLIGATOR.
Rooted in folk, country and blues;
comes up with a massive pop hit
about once every five years.

Stiff Records
(01) 289 6221
9-11 Woodfield Road, London W9
Despite the departure of Ian
Dury to POLYDOR, the company
remained buoyant, with chart
success from Madness, Jona
Lewie, Tenpole Tudor and Dave
Stewart and Colin Blunstone.

Swan Song Records
(01) 351 4151
484 Kings Road, London SW10
With no new material
forthcoming from either
company-founders Led Zeppelin,
or Bad Company, the label is only
rescued from atrophy by the
regular Dave Edmunds release.

Topic Records
(01) 263 6403
50 Stroud Green Road,
London N4 3EF
Massive folk catalogue headed by
The Watersons.

Trojan Records
(01) 965 4565
104 High Street, Harlesden,
London NW10 4SL
Also ATTACK, HORSE.
Early recordings by Toots and
Bob Marley continue to sell.

Virgin Records
(01) 727 8070
2-4 Vernon Yard, Portobello
Road, London W11
Also FRONT LINE, METALBEAT, CUBA
LIBRE.
A heterogeneous roster puts
Mike Oldfield and Tangerine
Dream alongside Gillan and
Japan, as well as Phil Collins,
The Human League, Public
Image Ltd. and XTC. There are
high hopes for Simple Minds and
Holly and The Italians.

WEA Records
(01) 434 3232
20 Broadwick Street,
London W1V 2BH
Also ASYLUM, ATLANTIC, ELEKTRA,
ENIGMA, NONESUCH, POGO, REPRISE,
WARNER BROS, SIRE, REAL,
AUTOMATIC, GEFFEN, RADAR.
Like CBS, an American-owned
major. Gigantic roster and
multitude of licensed labels
ensure non-stop chart activity,
though 80/81 honours inevitably
stolen by newly-launched GEFFEN
label in general, and the late
John Lennon in particular.

Why-Fi Records
(01) 481 1722
6th Floor, Warehouse D,
Metropolitan Wharf,
Wapping Wall, London E1
Paul McNally, formerly of SIRE
debuts his own label with a
release from Sparks.

Zoo Records
(051) 227 3343
1 Chicago Buildings, Whitechapel,
Liverpool 1
Interesting independent
nurturing cream of local talent.

RADIO STATIONS/US

The following are many of the rock radio stations in America, including most major stations in the Top 50 markets (ranked by 1979 population) and the major Top 40 and Album-Oriented-Rock stations in many secondary markets, listed alphabetically by state.

ALABAMA

Birmingham
WENN-FM 107.7 Disco
WERC-AM 960 Top 40
WKXX-FM 106.9 Top 40
WSGN-AM 610 Top 40
WVOK-FM 99.5 AOR

Mobile
WABB-AM 1480 Top 40
WABB-FM 97.5 AOR
WKRG-FM 99.9 Sft Rk
WXLK-AM 1270 Top 40

Montgomery
WHHY-AM 1440 Top 40
WHHY-FM 101.9 AOR
WLSQ-AM 950 Top 40

ALASKA

Fairbanks
KFAR-AM 660 Top 40

ARIZONA

Phoenix
KBBC-FM 98.7 Sft Rk
KDKB-AM 1510 Top 40
KDKB-FM 93.3 AOR
KIOG-FM 104.7 Sft Rk
KOOL-FM 94.7 Sft Rk
KQXE-AM 1310 Top 40
KRUX-AM 1360 Top 40
KSGR-AM 1440 Oldies
KUPD-AM 1060 Top 40
KUPD-FM 97.9 Top 40

Tucson
KLPX-FM 96 TOP 40
KLPX-AM 99 Top 40
KWFM-FM 92.3 AOR

ARKANSAS

Little Rock
KAAY-AM 1090 Top 40
KLAZ-FM 98.5 Top 40
KOKY-AM 1250 Top 40

CALIFORNIA

Bakersfield
KAFY-AM 550 Top 40
KERN-AM 1410 Top 40

Fresno
KYNO-AM 1300 Top 40
KYNO-FM 96 Top 40

Los Angeles Metropolitan Area
KEZY-AM 1190 Top 40
KEZY-FM 95.5 Sft Rk
KFI-AM 640 Top 40
KGIL-AM 1260 Sft Rk
KGIL-FM 94.3 AOR
KHJ-AM 930 Top 40
KHTZ-FM 97.1 Top 40
KHS-AM 1150 Sft Rk
KHS-FM 102.7 Sft Rk
KIQQ-FM 100.3 Top 40
KLOS-FM 95.5 AOR
KMET-FM 94.7 AOR
KMPC-AM 710 Sft Rk
KNAC-FM 105.5 AOR
KNX-FM 93.1 Sft Rk
KPOL-FM 93.9 AOR
KRLA-AM 1110 Top 40
KROQ-AM 1500 AOR
KROQ-FM 106.7 AOR
KRTH-FM 101.1 Top 40
KWIZ-AM 1480 Sft Rk
KWIZ-FM 96.7 Sft Rk
KWST-FM 105.9 AOR
KWOW-AM 1600 Top 40

Sacramento
KNDE-AM 1470 Top 40
KROI-FM 96.9 AOR
KROY-AM 1240 Top 40
KSFM-FM 102.5 AOR
KZAP-FM 98.5 AOR

San Bernadino
KFXM-AM 590 Top 40
KMEN-AM 1290 Top 40
KOLA-FM 99.9 AOR

San Diego
KCBQ-AM 1170 Top 40
KFMB-AM 760 Top 40
KGB-AM 1360 Top 40
KGB-FM 101.5 AOR
KMJC-AM 910 Top 40
KPRI-FM 106.5 AOR

San Francisco
KFRC-AM 610 Top 40
KMEL-FM 106.1 AOR
KSAN-FM 94.9 AOR
KTIM-AM 1510 AOR
KTIM-FM 100.9 AOR
KYA-AM 1260 Top 40
KYA-FM 93.3 AOR

San Jose
KLIV-AM 1590 Top 40
KOME-FM 98.5 AOR
KSJO-FM 92.3 AOR

Santa Barbara
KIST-AM 1340 Sft Rk
KTMS-FM 97.5 AOR
KTYD-AM 990 AOR
KTYD-FM 99.9 AOR

Ventura
KACY-AM 1520 Top 40

COLORADO

Aspen
KSPN-FM 97.7 AOR

Colorado Springs
KKFM-FM 96.5 AOR

Denver
KBCO-FM 97.3 AOR
KAZY-FM 106.7 AOR
KBPI-FM 105.9 AOR
KIMN-AM 950 Top 40
KIMN-FM 98.5 Top 40
KOAQ-FM 103.5 Top 40
KTLK-AM 1280 Top 40
KXKX-FM 95.7 AOR

HAZEL O'CONNOR

CONNECTICUT

Hartford
WCCC-FM 106.9 AOR
WDRC-AM 1360 Top 40
WHCN-FM 105.9 AOR
WRCQ-AM 910 Oldies
WTIC-FM 96.5 Top 40

New Haven
WAVZ-
—AM 1300 Top 40
WKCI-FM 101 Top 40
WPLR-FM 99.1 AOR
WYBC-FM 94.3 AOR

DELAWARE

Wilmington
WAMS-AM 1380 Top 40

DISTRICT OF COLUMBIA (WASHINGTON)

WHFS-FM 102.3 AOR
WPGC-FM 95.5 Top 40
WRQX-FM 107.3 AOR
WWDC-FM 101.1 AOR

FLORIDA

Daytona Beach
WMFJ-AM 1450 Top 40

Ford Lauderdale Hollywood
WAXY-FM 105.9 Top 40
WHYI-FM 100.7 Top 40
WSRF-AM 1580 AOR
WSHE-FM 103.5 AOR

Gainesville
WGVL-FM 105.5 AOR

Jacksonville
WAIV-FM 96.9 AOR
WAPE-AM 690 Top 40
WIVY-FM 102.9 Top 40

Miami
WGBS-AM 710 Top 40
WINZ-FM 94.9 AOR
WMJX-FM 96.3 Top 40
WQAM-AM 560 Top 40
WWWL-FM 93.9 AOR

Orlando
WBJW-FM 105.1 Top 40
WDIZ-FM 100.3 Top 40
WLOF-AM 950 Top 40
WORJ-FM 107.7 AOR

Tallahasee
WGLF-FM 104.1 Sft Rk
WOWD-FM 103.1 AOR

Tampa-St. Petersburg
WAZE-AM 860 Oldies
WLCY-AM 1380 Top 40
WQSR-FM 102.5 AOR
WRBQ-FM 104.7 Top 40

GEORGIA

Athens
WRFC-AM 960 Top 40

Atlanta
WFOM-AM 1230 Top 40
WKLS-FM 96.1 AOR
WQXI-AM 790 Top 40
WQXI-FM 94.1 Top 40
WRAS-FM 88.5 AOR
WREK-FM 91.1 AOR
WZGC-FM 92.9 Top 40

Savannah
WSGA-AM 1400 Top 40
WSGF-FM 95 Top 40
WKDX-AM 630 Top 40

HAWAII

Honolulu
KIKI-AM 830 AOR
KIOE-AM 1080 Top 40
KKUA-AM 690 Top 40
KORL-AM 650 Top 40
KQMQ-FM 93.3 AOR

IDAHO

Boise
KFXD-AM 580 Top 40

Lewiston
KOZE-AM 1300 Top 40

Moscow
KRPL-AM 1400 Top 40
KUID-FM 91.7 AOR

ILLINOIS

Chicago Metropolitan Area
WBBM-FM 96.3 Sft Rk
WDAI-FM 94.7 AOR
WEFM-FM 99.5 Top 40
WFYR-FM 103.5 Top 40
WJKL-FM 94.3 AOR
WKQX-FM 101.1 AOR
WLS-AM 890 Top 40
WLUP-FM 97.9 AOR
WMET-FM 95.5 Top 40
WXRT-FM 93.1 AOR

Peoria/Bloomington
WIRL-AM 1290 Top 40
WWCT-FM 105.7 AOR

Rockford
WROK-AM 1440 Top 40
WYFE-FM 95.3 AOR
WZOK-FM 97.5 AOR

INDIANA

Indianapolis
WFBQ-FM 94.7 AOR
WIBC-AM 1070 Sft Rk
WIFE-AM 1310 AOR
WNAP-FM 93.1 Top 40
WNDE-AM 1260 Top 40

IOWA

Cedar Rapids
KLWW-AM 1450 Top 40
KQCR-FM 102.9 Oldies

Davenport
KSTT-AM 1170 Top 40

Des Moines
KCBC-AM 1390 AOR
KGGO-FM 94.9 Top 40
KIOA-AM 940 Top 40
KRNQ-FM 102.5 AOR

Waterloo
KWWL-AM 1330 Top 40

KANSAS

Wichita
KELO-AM 1480 Top 40
KFDI-FM 101.3 AOR
KEYN-FM 103.7 Top 40
KGCS-FM 96 Country
KWKN-AM 1480 Top 40

KENTUCKY

Lexington
WKQQ-FM   98.1   AOR
WLAP-FM   94.5   AOR
WVLK-AM   590   Top 40

Louisville
WAKY-AM   790   Top 40
WKLO-AM   1080   Top 40
WLRS-FM   102.3 AOR
WQHI-FM   95.7   AOR

LOUISIANA

Baton Rouge
WAIL-AM   1260   Sft Rk
WFMF-FM   102.5 Top 40

Lake Charles
KGRA-FM   103.7 AOR

New Orleans
WEZB-FM   97   Top 40
WNOE-AM   1060   Top 40
WNOE-FM   101.1 AOR
WQUE-FM   93.3   Top 40
WRNO-FM   99.5   AOR
WTIX-AM   690   Top 40

Shreveport
KEEL-AM   710   Top 40
KROK-FM   94.5   Rock

MAINE

Bangor
WABI-AM   910   Top 40
WGUY-AM   1250   Top 40

Lewiston
WBLM-FM   107.5 AOR

MARYLAND

Baltimore
WAYE-AM   860   AOR
WBKZ-FM   96   Sft Rk
WCAO-AM   600   Top 40
WIYY-FM   97.9   AOR
WKTK-FM   105.7 AOR
WLPL-FM   92.3   Top 40
WFBR-AM   1300   Top 40

Hagerstown
WQCM-FM   96.7   AOR

MASSACHUSETTS

Boston Metropolitan Area
WACQ-AM   1150   Top 40
WBCN-FM   104.1 AOR
WBZ-FM   106.7 Top 40
WCAS-AM   740   AOR
WCGY-FM   93.7   Top 40
WCOZ-FM   94.5   AOR
WEEI-FM   103.3 Sft Rk
WRKO-AM   680   Top 40
WVBF-FM   105.7 Top 40

Worcester
WAAF-FM   104.3 Top 40
WNCR-AM   1440   Top 40
WORC-AM   1310   Oldies
WETQ-AM   1400   Top 40

MICHIGAN

Ann Arbor
WCBN-FM   88.3   AOR
WIQB-FM   102.9 AOR

Detroit Metropolitan Area
CKLW-AM   800   Top 40
WABX-FM   99.5   AOR
WDRQ-FM   93.1   Top 40
WHND-AM   560   Oldies
WRIF-FM   101.1 AOR
WWKR-AM   1310   Top 40
WWWW-FM   106.7 AOR
WXYZ-AM   1270   Top 40

Flint
WTAC-AM   600   Top 40
WWCK-FM   105.5 AOR

Grand Rapids
WGRD-AM   1410   Top 40
WGRD-FM   97.9   Top 40
WLAV-FM   96.9   AOR
WZZR-FM   95.7   Top 40

Saginaw
WIOG-FM   106.3 AOR
WSAM-AM   1400   Top 40

MINNESOTA

Duluth
WAKX-FM   98.9   Top 40
WEBC-AM   560   Top 40

Minneapolis/St. Paul
KQRS-AM   1440   AOR
KDWB-AM   630   AOR
KDWB-FM   101.3 AOR
KSTP-AM   1500   Top 40
WCCO-FM   102.9 AOR
WMIN-AM   1010   Top 40

Rochester
KWWK-FM   96.7   AOR
KWEB-AM   1270   Top 40

St. Cloud
WJON-AM   1240   Top40

MISSISSIPPI

Jackson
WJDX-AM   620   Top 40
WZZO-FM   102.9 Top 40

Tupelo
WTUP-AM   1490   Top 40

MISSOURI

Kansas City
KBEQ-FM   104.3 Top 40
KWKI-FM   93.3   AOR
KYYS-FM   102.1 AOR
WHB-AM   710   Top 40

St. Louis
KADI-FM   96.3   AOR
KKOJ-AM   1320   Top 40
KSD-AM   550   Sft Rk
KSHE-FM   94.7   AOR
KSLQ-FM   98.1   Top 40
KXOK-AM   630   Top 40

MONTANA

Great Falls
KEIN-AM   1310   Top 40

Missoula
KDXT-FM   93.3   AOR

NEBRASKA

Lincoln
KFMQ-FM   101.9 Rock

Omaha
KGOR-FM   99.9   Top 40
KOIL-AM   1290   Top 40
KQKQ-FM   98.5   Top 40
WOW-AM   590   Rk/Tp40

NEVADA

Las Vegas
KENO-AM   1460   Top 40
KENO-FM   92.3   AOR
KLUC-FM   98.5   AOR

KIM CARNES

NEW HAMPSHIRE

Manchester
WFEA-AM 1370 Top 40

NEW JERSEY

Asbury Park
WJLK-FM 94.3 Oldies

Atlantic City
WMGM-FM 103.7 AOR

Trenton
WPRB-FM 103.3 AOR

NEW MEXICO

Albuquerque
KQEQ-AM 920 Top 40
KRKE-FM 94.l AOR
KRST-FM 92.3 AOR

NEW YORK

Albany-Troy
WFLY-FM 92.3 Top 40
WGFM-FM 99.5 Top 40
WPTR-AM 1450 Top 40
WQBK-FM 103.9 AOR
WTRY-AM 980 Top 40
WWWD-AM 1240 AOR

Buffalo
WBEN-FM 102.5 Top 40
WBUF-FM 92.9 AOR
WGRQ-FM 96.9 AOR
WKBW-AM 1520 Top 40
WNIA-AM 1230 Top 40
WYSL-AM 1400 Top 40

New York City
Metropolitan Area
WABC-AM 770 Top 40
WBAB-FM 102.2 AOR
WBLS-FM 107.5 Black
WCBS-FM 101.1 Oldies
WFMU-FM 91.l AOR
WLIR-FM 92.7 AOR
WNBC-AM 660 Top 40
WNEW-FM 102.7 AOR
WPIX-FM 101.9 AOR
WPLJ-FM 95.5 AOR
WRNW-FM 107.1 AOR
WRVR-FM 106.7 Jazz
WXLO-FM 98.7 Top 40
WYNY-FM 97.l Adlt.Rk

Rochester
WWWG-AM 1460 Top 40
WBBF-AM 950 Top 40
WCMF-FM 96.5 AOR
WHFM-FM 98.9 Top 40

Syracuse
WOLF-AM 1490 Top 40

Utica-Rome
WOUR-FM 96.9 AOR

NORTH CAROLINA

Asheville
WISE-AM 1310 Top 40

Charlotte
WAYS-AM 610 Top 40
WBT-AM 1110 Top 40
WIST-AM 1240 Oldies
WROQ-FM 95.1 AOR
WRLP-AM 1540 AOR

Greensboro
WBIG-AM 1470 Top 40
WCOG-AM 1320 Top 40
WRQK-FM 98.7 AOR

Raleigh
WKIX-AM 850 Top 40
WQDR-FM 94.7 AOR
WRAL-FM 101.5 Top 40

Winston-Salem
WAIR-AM 1340 Top 40
WKZL-FM 107.5 AOR
WRQK-FM 98.7 AOR
WTOB-AM 1380 Top 40

NORTH DAKOTA

Bismarck
KFYR-AM 550 Top 40
KFYR-FM 92.9 OldTp40

Minot
KCJB-FM 97.1 AOR
KKOA-AM 1390 Top 40

OHIO

Akron/Canton
WCUE-AM 1150 Top 40
WKDD-FM 96.5 AOR
WQIQ-AM 1060 Oldies
WINW-AM 1520 Top 40

Cincinnati
WEBN-FM 102.7 AOR
WKRQ-FM 101.9 Top 40
WMOH-AM 1450 Top 40

Cleveland
WGCL-FM 98.5 Top 40
WWWE-AM 1100 Sft Rk
WMMS-FM 100.7 AOR
WWWM-FM 105.7 AOR
WZZP-FM 106.5 Top 40

Columbus
WCOL-AM 1230 Top 40
WCOL-FM 92.3 AOR
WLVO-FM 96.3 AOR
WNCI-FM 97.9 Top 40
WRMZ-FM 99.7 AOR
WXGT-FM 92.3 Top 40

Dayton
WING-AM 1410 Top 40
WTUE-FM 104.7 AOR
WVUD-FM 99.9 AOR

Toledo
WIOT-FM 104.7 AOR
WMHE-FM 92.5 AOR
WOHO-AM 1470 Top 40

Youngston
WFMJ-AM 1390 Top 40
WHOT-AM 1330 Top 40
WHOT-FM 101.1 AOR

OKLAHOMA

Oklahoma City
KATT-FM 100.5 AOR
KGOU-FM 106.5 AOR
KOMA-AM 1520 Top 40
WKY-AM 930 Top 40

Tulsa
KAKC-AM 970 Top 40
KAKC-FM 92.9 Oldies
KELI-AM 1430 Top 40

OREGON

Eugene
KBDF-AM 1280 Top 40
KFMY-FM 97.9 AOR
KZEL-FM 96.1 AOR

Portland
KGON-FM 92.3 Top 40
KGW-AM 620 Top 40
KINK-FM 101.9 AOR
KMJK-FM 106.7 Top 40
KPAM-FM 97.1 Top 40
KVAN-AM 1480 AOR

PENNSYLVANIA

Allentown
WEEX-AM 1230 Oldies
WEZV-FM 95.l AOR
WKAP-AM 1320 Top 40
WSAN-AM 1470 AOR

Harrisburg
WKBO-AM 1230 Top 40
WRHY-FM 92.7 AOR

Philadelphia
WFIL-AM 560 Top 40
WIFI-FM 92.5 Top 40
WIOQ-FM 102.1 AOR
WMMR-FM 93.3 AOR
WYSR-FM 94.1 AOR
WZZD-AM 990 Top 40

Pittsburgh
WDVE-FM 102.5 AOR
WKTQ-AM 1320 Top 40
WPEZ-FM 94.5 Top 40
WWKS-FM 106.7 Top 40
WXKX-FM 96.1 Top 40
WYDD-FM 104.7 AOR
WWSW-AM 970 Top 40
WWSW-FM 94.5 AOR

RHODE ISLAND

Providence
WBRU-FM 95.5 AOR
WPJB-FM 105.1 Top 40
WPRO-AM 630 Top 40
WPRO-FM 92.3 Top 40

SOUTH CAROLINA

Charleston
WCSC-AM 1390 Top 40
WKTM-FM 102.5 Top 40
WQSN-AM 1450 Oldies
WTMA-AM 1250 Top 40
WWWZ-FM 93.5 AOR

OKLAHOMA

SOUTH DAKOTA

Rapid City
KKLS-AM 920 Top 40
KGGG-FM 100.8 Top 40

TENNESSEE

Memphis
WHBQ-AM 560 Top 40
WMC-FM 99.7 Top 40
WMPS-AM 680 Country
WREC-AM 600 Sft Rk
WZXR-FM 102.7 AOR

Nashville
WIZO-FM 100.1 Top 40
WBYQ-FM 92.3 Top 40
SKDF-FM 103.3 AOR
WLAC-AM 1510 Top 40
WMAK-AM 1310 Top 40
WSM-FM 95.5 Sft Rk

TEXAS

Austin
KCSW-FM 103.7 Hits
KHFI-FM 98.3 Top 40
KLBJ-FM 93.7 AOR
KNOW-AM 1490 Top 40
KOKE-FM 95.5 Country

Beaumont
KAYC-AM 1450 Top 40
KAYD-FM 97.5 Top 40
KOBS-FM 104.5 Top 40

Corpus Christi
KEYS-AM 1400 Top 40
KRYS-AM 1360 Top 40
KZFM-FM 95.5 AOR

Dallas/Fort Worth
KEGL-FM 96.9 Top 40
KFJZ-FM 97.1 Top 40
KFWD-FM 102.1 AOR
KLIF-AM 1190 Top 40
KNUS-FM 98.7 Top 40
KZEW-FM 97.9 AOR

Houston
KAUM-FM 96.5 AOR
KILT-AM 610 Top 40
KILT-FM 100.3 AOR
KLOL-FM 101.1 AOR
KRBE-FM 104.1 Top 40

Lubbock
KLBK-FM 94.5 AOR
KSEL-AM 950 Top 40

San Antonio
KISS-FM 99.5 AOR
KITE-AM 930 Top 40
KITE-FM 104.5 Top 40
KTFM-FM 102.7 AOR
KTSA-AM 550 Top 40
KZZY-FM 100.3 Top 40

UTAH

Salt Lake City
KCPX-AM 1320 Top 40
KCPX-FM 98.7 AOR
KRSP-AM 1060 Top 40
KRSP-FM 103.5 Top 40
KWHO-FM 93.3 Top 40

VERMONT

Burlington
WRUV-FM 90.1 AOR

VIRGINIA

Norfolk
WNOR-AM 1230 Top 40
WNOR-FM 98.7 AOR
WQRK-FM 104.5 Top 40

Richmond
WGOE-AM 1590 AOR
WLEE-AM 1480 Top 40
WRVQ-FM 94.5 Top 40
WRXL-FM 102.l AOR

Roanoke
WROV-AM 1240 Top 40
WSLQ-FM 99.1 Oldies

WASHINGTON

Seattle-Tacoma
KING-AM 1090 Top 40
KISW-FM 99.9 AOR
KJR-AM 950 Top 40
KLAY-FM 106.1 AOR
KRKO-AM 1380 Top 40
KTAC-AM 850 Top 40
KVI-FM 101.5 Top 40
KYYX-FM 96.5 Top 40
KZAM-AM 1540 AOR
KZAM-FM 92.5 AOR
KZOK-AM 1590 AOR
KZOK-FM 102.5 AOR

Spokane
KHQ-FM 98.1 Top 40
KJRB-AM 790 Top 40
KREM-AM 970 Top 40
KREM-FM 92.9 AOR

WEST VIRGINIA

Charleston
WVAF-FM 99.9 AOR

Wheeling
WEIF-AM 1370 Oldies
WKWK-AM 1400 Top 40
WOMP-FM 100.5 AOR

WISCONSIN

Madison
WIBA-FM 101.5 AOR
WISM-AM 1480 Top 40
WYXE-FM 92.1 Top 40

Milwaukee
WLPX-FM 97.3 AOR
WQKY-AM 920 Top 40
WQFM-FM 93.3 AOR
WZMF-FM 98.3 AOR
WZUU-AM 1290 AOR
WZUU-FM 95.7 AOR

WYOMING

Caspar
KAWY-FM 94.5 AOR

Cheyenne
KFBC-AM 1240 Top 40
KFBC-FM 97.9 Top 40

RADIO STATIONS/UK

BBC RADIO

Radios 1, 2, 3 & 4
(01) 580 4468
Broadcasting House, Portland
Place, London W1A 1AA

Radio Birmingham
(021) 472 5141
Broadcasting Centre, Pebble Mill
Road, Birmingham.

Radio Blackburn
(0254) 62411
King Street, Blackburn,
Lancs. BB2 2EA

Radio Brighton
(0273) 680188
Marlborough Place, Brighton,
Sussex. BN1 1TU

Radio Bristol
(0272) 311111
3 Tyndalls Park Road, Bristol 8.

Radio Carlisle
(0228) 31661
Hilltop Heights, London Road,
Carlisle, CA1 2NA

Radio Cleveland
(0642) 248491
91 Linthorpe Road,
Middlesbrough,
Cleveland. TS1 5DG

Radio Derby
(0332) 361111
56 St Helens Street,
Derby, DE1 3HY

Radio Humberside
(0482) 23232
63 Jameson Street,
Hull, HU1 3NU

Radio Leeds
(0532) 442131
Broadcasting House, Woodhouse
Lane, Leeds, LS2 9PN

Radio Leicester
(0533) 27113
Epic House, Charles Street,
Leicester, LE1 3SH

Radio Lincolnshire
(0522) 40011
Radion Buildings, Newport,
Lincoln, LN1 3DF

Radio London
(01) 486 7611
35A Marylebone High Street,
London W1A 4LG

Radio Manchester
(061) 228 3434
New Broadcasting House, Oxford
Road, Manchester, M60 1SJ

Radio Medway
(0634) 46284
30 High Street, Chatham,
Kent, ME4 4EZ

Radio Merseyside
(051) 236 3355
Commerce House, 13/17 Sir
Thomas Street,
Liverpool L15 5BS

Radio Newcastle
(0632) 814243
Crestine House,
Archbold Terrace,
Newcastle-upon-Tyne, NE2 1DZ

Radio Norfolk
(0603) 617411
Norfolk Tower, Surrey Street,
Norwich, NR1 3PA

Radio Nottingham
(0602) 47643
York House, Mansfield Road,
Nottingham, NG1 3JB

Radio Oxford
(0865) 53411
242/245 Banbury Road,
Oxford, OX2 7DW

Radio Scotland
(041) 339 8844
Broadcasting House, Queen
Margaret Drive,
Glasgow G12 8DG

Radio Sheffield
(0742) 686185
Ashdell Grove, 60 Westbourne
Road, Sheffield, S10 2QU

Radio Solent
(0703) 31311
South Western House, Canute
Road, Southampton, SO9 4PJ

Radio Stoke-on-Trent
(0782) 24827
Conway House, Cheapside,
Hanley, Stoke-on-Trent.

Radio Ulster
(0232) 44400
Broadcasting House, Ormeau
Avenue, Belfast BT2 8HQ

Radio Wales
(0222) 564888
Broadcasting House, Llandrisant
Road, Llandaff,Cardiff CF5 2QY

COMMERCIAL RADIO

Radio Avonside
(0272) 290651
4th Floor, Bush House, 72 Prince
Street, Bristol BS1 4NU
On air — Autumn 1981

Radio Ayrshire
(0655) 82583
Galbraith McEwan & Co., 10
Barns Street, Ayrshire.
On air — Late 1981

Beacon Radio
(0902) 757211
267 Tettenhall Road,
Wolverhampton, WV6 0DQ

BRMB Radio
(021) 359 4481
PO Box 555, Radio House, Aston
Road North, Birmingham B6 4BX

Capital Radio
(01) 388 1288
Euston Tower, Euston Road,
London NW1 3DR

CBC Radio
(0222) 384041
Radio House, West Canal Wharf,
Cardiff, CF1 5XJ

Centre Radio
(0533) 887065
59 Long Street, Wigston,
Leicester LE8 2AJ
On air - Autumn 1981

Chiltern Radio
(0582) 850544
Hicks Road, Markyate, Herts.
On air — Autumn 1981

Radio City
(051) 227 5100
8-10 Stanley Street,
Liverpool L69 1LD

THE DEAD KENNEDYS

Radio Clyde
(041) 204 2555
Ranken House, Blythwood Court,
Anderston Cross Centre,
Glasgow G2 7LB

DevonAir Radio
(0392) 30703
35/37 St David's Hill, Exeter.

Downtown Radio
(0247) 815555
Kiltonga Radio Centre,
PO Box 293, Newtonards,
Co. Down, BT23 4ES

Essex Radio
(0702) 42080
Radio House, Clifftown Road,
Southend-on-Sea,
Essex, SS1 1AW
On air — September 1981

GILLAN

Radio Forth
(031) 556 9255
Forth House, Forth Street,
Edinburgh, EH1 3LF

Radio Hallam
(0742) 71188
PO Box 194, Hartshead,
Sheffield, S1 1GP

Hereward Radio
(0733) 46225
PO Box 225, 114 Bridge Street,
Peterborough, Cambs.

London Broadcasting (LBC)
(01) 353 1010
Communications House, Gough
Square, London EC4 4IP

Radio Luxembourg
(01) 493 5961
38 Hertford Street,
London W1Y 8BA

Manx Radio
(0624) 3277
Douglas Head, Isle of Man.

Mercia Sound
(0203) 28451
Hertford Place, Coventry CV1
3TT

THE HUMAN LEAGUE

Metro Radio
(0632) 883131
Radio House, Longrigg, Swalwell,
Newcastle-Upon-Tyne, NE99 1BB

NorthSound
(0224) 52684
45 Kings Gate, Aberdeen.

Radio Orwell
(0473) 216971
Electric House, Lloyds Avenue,
Ipswich, IP1 3HZ

Pennine Radio
(0274) 31521
PO Box 235, 39 Wells Street,
Forster Square,
Bradford, BD1 5NP

Piccadilly Radio
(061) 236 9913
127 The Piazza, Piccadilly Plaza,
Manchester, M1 4AW.

Plymouth Sound
(0752) 27272
Earl's Acre, Plymouth PL3 4HX

Severn Sound
(0452) 423791
Old Talbot House, 67 Southgate
Street, Gloucester.

Swansea Sound
(0792) 893751
Victoria Road, Gowerton,
Swansea, West Glam.

Radio Tay
(0382) 29551
PO Box 123, Dundee DD1 9UF

Radio Tees
(0642) 615111
74 Dovecot Street, Stockton-on-
Tees, Cleveland TS18 1HB

Radio Trent
(0602) 581731
29/31 Castle Gate, Nottingham,
NG1 7AP

Two Counties Radio (2CR)
(0202) 294881
5/7 Southcote Road,
Bournemouth, BH1 3LR

Radio 210
(0734) 413131
Thames Valley Broadcasting, PO
Box 210, Reading, Berks, RG3
5RX

Radio Victory
(0705) 27799
PO Box 257, Portsmouth PO1
5RT

West Yorkshire Broadcasting
(0532) 444721
Tower House, Merrion Way,
Leeds LS2 8HU
On air - Summer 1981

KID CREOLE & THE COCONUTS

ROCK PUBLICATIONS/US

Ampersand
1680 Vine St., Suite 900,
Hollywood, CA 90028
A student newspaper distributed
on college campuses. A fore-
runner of the "Safety First" rock
movement. Monthly during the
school year.

The Aquarian Weekly
470 Bloomfield, Montclair, NJ
07042.
Dependent on advertising, this
paper is distributed to rock clubs
in the New York metropolitan
area.

TENPOLE TUDOR

Billboard
1515 Broadway, New York,
NY 10036
America's most respected trade
magazine. Published weekly.

BOMP!
Box 7112, Burbank, CA 91510
The voice of West coast pop
afficionados. Bimonthly.

Boulevards
1008 Sutter Street, San
Francisco, CA 94109
Superslick and trendy, this
magazine is emerging as one of
the better places to look for real
rock coverage. Monthly.

Buddy
PO Box 8366, Dallas, Texas 75205
Named after Buddy Holly, this
mag is subtitled "The Original
Texas Music Magazine". Every
state should be so lucky.
Biweekly.

Circus
419 Park Avenue South, New
York, NY 10016.
Weighed down by all of its recent
coverage of heavy metal, Circus
will jump on anyone's
bandwagon. Monthly.

Contemporary Keyboard
Frets
Guitar Player
20605 Lazaneo, Cupertino,
CA 95014
Magazines for players, by players
and with players in mind. Each
comes out monthly.

Creem
187 S. Woodward Ave.
Birmingham, Mich. 48011
Best captions in the business. But
they seem to have a strange
fixation on Bebe Buell. Monthly.

Downbeat
222 W. Adams Street, Chicago,
Illinois 60606.
All that jazz, from the experts.
Monthly.

FMI (Friday Morning
Quarterback)
Cherry Hill Plaza, 1415 E.
Marlton Pike, Cherry Hill,
NJ 08034
The most important radio tip
sheet in the entire world.
Weekly.

Goldmine
PO Box 187, Fraser, Mich.48026
Goldmine for oldies fans only.
Monthly.

Good Times
1619 E. Sunrise Blvd., Fort
Lauderdale, Fla. 33304
Regional and biweekly.

High Fidelity
The Publishing House, Great
Barrington, Mass. 01230.
Serious coverage of music and
hardware. Check the cover lines
before you buy. Monthly.

Hollywood Reporter
6715 Sunset Blvd., Hollywood,
CA. 90028
Wanna know where the money
you spent on buying records is
being spent. Check it out, daily.

Hit Parader
Charleton Publications,
Derby Ct. 06418
Latest top 40 song lyrics included
so that you can sing along.
Monthly, in supermarkets
everywhere.

International Musician
1500 Broadway, New York,
NY 10036
Broad coverage of the music
business from the artist's
standpoint. Monthly, by
subscription only.

Interview Magazine
860 Broadway, New York,
NY 10003
Andy Warhol is still trying to be
chic, but he does get a good
interview every now and then.
Check the contents page.
Monthly.

Music City News
PO Box 22975, Nashville,
Tenn. 37202
Down-home country coverage.
Monthly.

Musician/Player And Listener
1515 Broadway, New York,
NY 10036
Esoteric at times, but gaining
momentum.Monthly.

New York Rocker
166 Fifth Avenue, New York,
NY 10010
Suffering from punk post-partum.
Every six weeks or so.

Night
210 Fifth Avenue, New York,
NY 10010
Amusing last-clutch-at-glitter
kind of magazine. Monthly.

Radio And Records
1930 Century Park West, Los
Angeles, Ca. 90067
Insider's choice of trade paper.
Weekly.

Record World
1700 Broadway, New York,
NY 10019
Most human and readable of the
three major trade papers,they
also have the most accurate
charts around. The NEW YORK
TIMES and US magazine both go to
RW to find out who's on top.
Every week.

Relix
PO Box 94, Brooklyn, NY 11229
Who cares about the Grateful
Dead? If you do, this is your kind
of magazine. Bimonthly.

Rock Love
515 Hempstead Turnpike, West
Hempstead, NY 11552
Fan magazine. Bimonthly.

Rolling Stone
745 Fifth Avenue, New York,
NY 10022
Slowly but surely leaving the
music scene behind. Every third
cover story is music-oriented, but
the two between go to politics or
film. Kiss the legend good-bye.
Biweekly while it lasts.

Rolling Stone College Papers
745 Fifth Avenue, New York,
NY 10022
An "Animal House" off-shoot.
Irregular.

Slash
PO Box 48888, Los Angeles,
CA 90048
New wave underground
newspaper. Monthly.

Thunder Road
PO Box 171, Bogota,
NJ 07603
Covers Bruce Springsteen and his
pals with loving care. Quarterly.

Trouser Press
Trouser Press Collector's
Magazine
212 5th Avenue, Room 1310, New
York, NY 10010
Profiles and reviews with
intelligence and depth. Monthly.
("Collector" lists releases and
auctions and comes out
bimonthly.)

Walrus
Box 35, Narberth, PA 19072
Radio tipsheet. Biweekly.

ROCK PUBLICATIONS/UK

Black Echoes
113 High Holborn,
London WC1
Specialist paper with enthusiastic
approach. Recently changed
publisher. Weekly at 30p.

Black Music and Jazz Review
153 Praed Street, London W2
Soul, reggae, jazz and rhythm
and blues is dealt with in an
authoritative manner. Monthly at
60p.

Blues & Soul
153 Praed Street, London W2
For and by the real devotee.
Fortnightly at 60p.

Blues Unlimited
36 Belmont Park, London SE13
Encyclopaedic and definitive in
bi-monthly doses.

Buy Gone
30 Radcliffe Road, West
Bridgford, Nottingham.
Specialist rock and roll collectors
forum. Essential to avid
collectors. Monthly.

Comstock Lode
51 Bollo Lane,
Chiswick, London W4
Previously preoccupied with San
Francisco heyday. A fanzine in
the true sense of the word which
has now broadened its horizons.
Literate, accurate, dedicated.
Appears when it's ready.

Country Music People
128a Lowfield Street,
Dartford, Kent.
Exhaustive coverage of Country
and Western scene. Monthly at
60p.

Dark Star
58 Islip Manor Road, Northolt,
Middlesex.
Formerly infatuated with Sixties
Californian music. Lately a much
healthier cross-section dealt with
in a conscientious and
enthusiastic manner. Detailed
interviews. Highly informative.
Sympathetic layout. Bi-monthly
at 75p.

Disco International & Club News
410 St John Street, London EC1
Emphasis on glossy publicity and
technological reportage. Monthly
at 70p.

Disco 45
23 Claremont, Hastings,
E. Sussex.
Opportunist songbook magazine.
Pics and lyrics from current hits
with some cursory news and
reviews. Monthly at 25p.

The Face
43-47 Broadwick Street,
London W1.
Now steaming into its second
year and essential reading.
Editor Nick Logan has a sign on
his door which questions
"Masochist or Maverick?"
Following an exemplary track
record — making money for
major publishers — his own baby
has turned out a real beauty.
The emphasis is on quality visual
design and its finger is firmly on
the pulse beat of what's
happening in "music, movies and
style". It is beginning to explore
broader issues, extending its own
opportunities. The only criticism
is the tendency to fall back on
last year's rebel writers. Monthly
at 65p.

Flexipop
38 Mount Pleasant,
London WC2.
A tackier version of SMASH HITS
with a flexi-disc on the front
cover. If you're interested in the
flexi, worthwhile, if not, hardly
so. Monthly at 60p.

RICHARD STRANGE

Hot Press
New Hibernia House,
Winchester Walk, London SE1.
Rock paper of Irish origin, now
pitching for UK readers.
Beginning to find its own point of
view but will it survive in this
already crowded market?
Fortnightly at 30p.

ID
(available from Better Badges,
286 Portobello Road,
London W10.)
Fashion manual, fanzine-style, for
the eclectic show-off. Irregular
60p.

In The City
234 Camden High Street,
London NW1.
A survivor from the heyday of
the punk fanzine. Competently
pursuing a refreshing viewpoint
although it could be more
adventurous in searching out new
ground. Irregular.

**International Musician &
Recording World**
Grosvenor House, 141-143 Drury
Lane, London WC2
Packed with advertising,
technological features and
interviews with establishment
musicians. Some reviews.
Monthly at 50p.

Kerrang!
40 Long Acre, London WC2.
A collation of heavy metal tour
programme material, published
by SOUNDS. The first issue sold
out and more are planned. Well
packaged and obviously catering
for ardent market. It's a surprise
that nobody has attempted
something similar before.
Irregular — 50p.

Melody Maker
Berkshire House,
168-173 High Holborn,
London WC1.
Recently making a brave effort to
lose its dowdy reputation.
They've taken on new writers
and kept the best and most
entertaining of the old. They
even occasionally add a splash of
full colour. One suspects,
however, that IPC continue to
keep a wary eye on sales. Weekly
at 30p.

Music Week
40 Long Acre, London WC2
Staple diet is fodder for retail
and industry people. Retail and
marketing information, industry
news and gossip. A bit staid.
Most significant feature is the,
unfortunately, all-important
BMRB chart. "Video" has been
recently added to the mast-head
and coverage of this growth area
consists of regular news and
occasional supplements, creating
new pasture for the advertising
dept. as well as extending the
editorial sphere. Weekly at 90p.

New Kommotion
3 Bowrons Avenue, Wembley,
Middlesex.
Nirvana for factoid rock 'n' roll
collectors. Quarterly at 75p.

IAN DURY

NME
5-7 Carnaby Street, London W1
Can still provide the most
stimulating read when the
amateur hour semeiologists
haven't consumed too much lager.
 Good coverage of rock culture
as opposed to simply rock music.
There have been some curiously
neurotic attitudes towards
current developments in music.
Examination of the average age
of the editorial staff could reveal
some surprises to those who have
assumed that it is a mouthpiece
for vibrant, enquiring youth.
They are currently furtively
peering over their shoulders at
the rising sales figures of rival
publications and are not sure how
to react without compromising
the "party line". If they relax and
find some youthful spirit again,
the NME would once more
deserve their hard earned
reputation. Weekly at 30p.

Omaha Rainbow
10 Laeley Court, Harcourt Road,
Wallington, Surrey.
Long standing quarterly.
Preoccupied with country and
"progressive" country musicians,
particularly from Texas. For
specialists. Quarterly at 50p.

Record Business
Hyde House, 13 Langley Street,
London WC2
The other contender for trade
and retail market. A livelier
approach than MUSIC WEEK with
more detailed coverage of the
independents — which often
represents the sharp end of the
business. Their research team
compile a useful alternative chart
which is often worth comparing
against the BMRB. However,
while the BBC continues to use
the BMRB chart they must
resign themselves to playing
second fiddle. They also produce
a regular VIDEO BUSINESS
supplement magazine. Weekly at
60p.

Record Mirror
40 Long Acre, London WC2
The brightest of the newspaper
format rock publications. Enjoyed
a circulation boost a while ago
but advertising and therefore
pages are a bit thin on the
ground. They have recently
tightened up on their chart
orientated approach. Weekly at
30p.

Smash Hits
Lisa House, 52-55 Carnaby
Street, London W1
Appearing fortnightly and the
publishing success of recent
years, this youthful but
intelligent magazine is very well
put together. Its circulation
figures have overtaken the
weeklies. The formula of bright
graphics, song lyrics, informed
comments and interviews in a
"matey" style is obviously a
winner. Their problem is
sustaining the idea and coming
up with fresh angles in order to
maintain popularity. Fortnightly
at 35p.

SHEENA EASTON

Sound International
incl. **Beat Instrumental**
Link House, Dingwall
Avenue, Croydon.
Another gear and studio
orientated magazine with a
mixture of informative and
technological articles and
rock star interviews, with
more emphasis on music than
sociology. Monthly at 60p.

Sounds
40 Long Acre, London WC2
The most opportunist of the
weeklies, which seems to be
paying off as circulation is rising.
The differing factions on the staff
cover varying areas of music,
thus attracting readers from all
quarters. This creates a paper
rife with contradictions,
particularly when the endemically
sexist schoolboy sense of humour
competes with the "modernes"
viewpoint. SOUNDS can also be
decidedly irresponsible. It has
practically created the
"Oi" movement, a confused
mixture of skinhead macho strut
meets the spirit of punk. In their
defence, they do give good
coverage to young, up and
coming bands. Weekly at 30p.

JOHN COOPER CLARKE

Zigzag
118 Talbot Road,
London W11
Still going after all these years.
It seems to have lost its direction
somewhat. They have
endeavoured to branch out from
their fanzine roots to a more
generalised market. However the
territory they could have moved
into has been occupied by THE
FACE. Recently though they have
injected a lot of full colour and a
few new writers but they will
need to regain their previous
pioneering spirit in order to
maintain their reputation.
Monthly at 50p.

THE BELLE STARS

CONTRIBUTORS

MICK BROWN is a freelance writer who contributes to THE SUNDAY TIMES, THE GUARDIAN, ROLLING STONE and other publications.

AL CLARK used to write for TIME OUT, ROLLING STONE and NEW MUSICAL EXPRESS before becoming, he recalls with some amusement, "the most famous PR in rock". He is now co-editor of the magazine EVENT and author of the book *Raymond Chandler In Hollywood.*

IAN CRANNA was a contributor to NEW MUSICAL EXPRESS from his home town of Edinburgh before leading SMASH HITS to new heights during two years as editor. He is currently working as a freelance journalist before following in the footsteps of his mentor, Nick Logan, and starting his own publishing empire.

GIOVANNI DADOMO was born in London of Italian parents. He learnt the lyrics of 'Green Door' much too young. Presentable, well-hung, left-handed with own ample wardrobe. Will listen to anything and write about it for money.

ROBIN DENSELOW is the rock music correspondent on THE GUARDIAN and a producer/reporter for BBC TV Current Affairs.

MARK ELLEN — a sometime writer for NEW MUSICAL EXPRESS, NEW MUSIC NEWS, TRAX, TIME OUT and THE FACE — is assistant editor of SMASH HITS.

JOHN FORDHAM has been the editor of TIME OUT since November 1979. Originally a freelance music writer, he has contributed articles on jazz to TIME OUT, MELODY MAKER, SOUNDS, THE SUNDAY TIMES and THE GUARDIAN.

PETE FRAME lives in remotest Buckinghamshire, isolated from reality. There he continues to convince himself that the world of rock is still exciting enough to write about. He is currently bashing together a second volume of *Rock Family Trees.*

SIMON FRITH teaches sociology at Warwick University and writes for the NEW YORK ROCKER.

JOHN GILL is a regular contributor to SOUNDS and also writes for a number of British video magazines.

CHARLIE GILLETT is co-director of the independent OVAL RECORDS and OVAL MUSIC and presents a weekly show on Capital Radio, 'Undercurrents', which features new releases on British indie labels.

MARY HARRON is a freelance journalist who writes about rock music for THE GUARDIAN.

DAVID HEPWORTH is the editor of SMASH HITS magazine, appears on BBC TV's 'Old Grey Whistle Test' and contributes to BBC radio's 'Rock On' and 'Kaleidoscope'.

COLIN IRWIN has written for MELODY MAKER for the last seven years and is now its features editor.

NICK KIMBERLEY has written for TIME OUT, NEW MUSICAL EXPRESS, NEW MUSIC NEWS and ZIG ZAG. He now runs Duck Soup, a bookshop in London.

FRANCES LASS has written for TIME OUT, MELODY MAKER, THE FACE and NEW MUSIC NEWS. She is presently the music editor of EVENT.

BARRY LAZELL currently writes and researches for RECORD BUSINESS, contributes to SOUNDS and is working on a couple of books. He lives with an understanding wife and two beautiful daughters in Essex.

DREW MOSELEY is a New York based freelance writer. She is also the rock correspondent for three American magazines.

ALEXEI PANSHIN is the author of five novels, a book of short stories, and three books of criticism. He has been been published in France, Germany, Holland, Portugal, Italy, Yugoslavia, Israel and Japan. His most recent book is *Earth Magic.* He is a personal friend of Wild Dog Lewis and once met Lester Bangs.

DAFYYD REES is a former DECCA and MOTOWN Press Officer and is currently Research Director of RECORD BUSINESS. He is the compiler of the *Star File* chart books and contributor to Radio One's 'Musicology' and BBC TV's 'Pop Quiz' series.

TONY RUSSELL writes a column in JAZZ JOURNAL and edits/publishes OLD TIME MUSIC. He is also Press Officer for the folk label TOPIC.

JON SAVAGE is a freelance writer who has contributed to SOUNDS, MELODY MAKER and THE FACE.

ROSS STAPLETON is an Australian journalist who has been writing since 1970 and has contributed to NEW MUSICAL EXPRESS, SOUNDS, RECORD MIRROR, ROLLING STONE and PENTHOUSE. He is currently working for VIRGIN RECORDS.

PHIL SUTCLIFFE, the self-styled "vegetarian who brings home the bacon", is the co-author of *L'Historia Bandido*, contributes to SOUNDS, THE FACE, SMASH HITS and NEW SOUNDS, NEW STYLES and broadcasts on BBC radio's 'Rock On' and 'Kaleidoscope'.

STEVE TAYLOR is a freelance feature writer who contributes to THE OBSERVER MAGAZINE, TIME OUT, HONEY, SMASH HITS and THE FACE, of which he is associate editor. He runs a minute record label and is currently thinking of ways of getting record companies to send him to Europe as often as possible.

BOB WOFFINDEN is co-author of the best selling *NME Illustrated Encyclopedia of Rock* and author of *The Beatles Apart.* He works as a freelance journalist on NEW STATESMAN and TIME OUT.

RICHARD WOOTTON is a London-based freelance journalist who writes regularly for MELODY MAKER, TIME OUT and COUNTRY MUSIC PEOPLE, and is editor of HONKY TONKIN' — a travel guide to American music.

— *F I L E   U N D E R :   T I M E   F L I E S* —

The ROCK YEARBOOK went to press in August 1981, at which time it had its facts right. Since then several groups, including some for whom we may foolishly have forecasted success, have broken up or changed their formation. Josef K, for example, no longer exist. You'll just have to put up with it, as we have.

ACKNOWLEDGEMENTS

The ROCK YEARBOOK is the result of unyielding perseverance, escalating hysteria and a disregard for sleep bordering on downright foolishness.

Fuelled only by peanuts, bars of chocolate and inferior brands of lager, several people did more than could reasonably have been expected of them and then stayed around to do more, ruining their health and leaving their private lives in disarray. They know who they are and so should you: Catherine Cardwell, David Martin and Amynta Cardwell.

Many of the photographs in this book were supplied by London Features International. The ones that weren't came from Jill Furmanovsky, Virginia Turbett, Chantal Coves, Jak Kilby, Pennie Smith, Eric Beaumont, Jay Myrdal, Keystone Press Agency, Peter Bould, Mike Doyle, Melody Maker, Osiris Films, United Artists and 20th Century Fox. Others were sent by record companies, publishing houses and film distributors too numerous to mention. To all of them, and to the picture researchers Dee Thorne and Marie Ryan, our thanks.

And a doff of the cap to the Virgin Megastore, who allowed a team of bad-tempered quality-control inspectors to ransack their place in search of record covers.

Photoset by AGP (Typesetting) Ltd., 33 West Hill, Wandsworth, SW18.
Colour separations and reproduction by Moonlight Reproductions Limited., 14a Clerkenwell Green, London EC1 0DP.